Learning and Memory

Learning and Memory
From Brain to Behavior

SECOND EDITION

Mark A. Gluck
Rutgers University – Newark

Eduardo Mercado
University at Buffalo, The State University of New York

Catherine E. Myers
Department of Veterans Affairs, New Jersey Health Care System, and
New Jersey Medical School–University of Medicine and Dentistry

Worth Publishers ▪ New York

Senior Vice President, Editorial and Production: Catherine Woods
Publisher: Kevin Feyen
Acquisitions Editor: Daniel DeBonis
Marketing Manager: Jennifer Bilello
Marketing Assistant: Julie Tompkins
Director of Print and Digital Development: Tracey Kuehn
Developmental Editor: Moira Lerner
Associate Media and Supplements Editor: Elizabeth Block
Assistant Media and Supplements Editor: Anthony Casciano
Assistant Editor: Nadina Persaud
Associate Managing Editor: Lisa Kinne
Project Editor: Jane O'Neill
Photo Editor: Cecilia Varas
Photo Researcher: Jacquelyn S. Wong
Art Director and Cover Designer: Babs Reingold
Interior Designers: Lissi Sigillo and Kevin Kall
Illustrations: Matthew Holt, Christy Krames, Todd Buck, and Hans Neuhart
Production Manager: Sarah Segal
Supplements Production Manager: Stacey Alexander
Composition: MPS Limited
Printing and Binding: Quad/Graphics Versailles

Cover Art: © 2011 Michael Glenwood Gibbs. All rights reserved.
Chapter Opening Photos: p. xxiv: William Wegman; p. 38: age fotostock/SuperStock; p. 74: Reinhard Dirsherl/Alamy; p. 116: Tony Evans/naturepl.com; p. 166: The National Trust Photolibrary/Alamy; p. 208: © Arco Images GmbH/Alamy; p. 258: T. J. Rich/naturepl.com; p. 300: Steve Bloom Images/Alamy; p. 342: © Arco Images GmbH/Alamy; p. 384: Steve Bloom Images/Alamy; p. 426: A. Morris/VIREO; p. 458: David Bagley/Alamy.

Library of Congress Control Number: 2012941411
ISBN-13: 978-1-4292-4014-7
ISBN-10: 1-4292-4014-8

First Printing

Worth Publishers
41 Madison Avenue
New York, NY 10010
www.worthpublishers.com

ABOUT THE AUTHORS

Mark A. Gluck is Professor of Neuroscience at Rutgers University–Newark, director of the Memory Disorders Project at Rutgers–Newark, co-director of the Newark African-American Alzheimer's Awareness and Brain Health Initiative, and publisher of the public health newsletter *Memory Loss and the Brain*. His research focuses on computational and experimental studies of the neural bases of learning and memory and the consequences of memory loss due to aging, trauma, and disease. He is co-author of *Gateway to Memory: An Introduction to Neural Network Modeling of the Hippocampus and Learning* (MIT Press, 2001) and co-editor of three other books: *Neuroscience and Connectionist Theory* (Lawrence Erlbaum Associates, 1990), *Model Systems and the Neurobiology of Associative Learning: A Festschrift for Richard F. Thompson* (Lawrence Erlbaum Associates, 2001), and *Memory and Mind: A Festschrift for Gordon H. Bower* (Taylor & Francis, 2007). In 1996, he was awarded an NSF Presidential Early Career Award for Scientists and Engineers by President Bill Clinton. That same year, he received the American Psychological Association (APA) Distinguished Scientific Award for Early Career Contribution to Psychology.

Eduardo Mercado is Associate Professor of Psychology and of Evolution, Ecology, and Behavior at the University at Buffalo, The State University of New York, and principal investigator at the Temporal Dynamics of Learning Center, an NSF Science of Learning Center. His research focuses on how different brain systems interact to develop representations of experienced events and how these representations change over time. Dr. Mercado uses techniques from experimental psychology, computational neuroscience, electrical engineering, and behavioral neuroscience to explore questions about auditory learning and memory in rodents, cetaceans, and humans. In 2009, he was selected as a Fellow at the Center for Advanced Studies in the Behavioral Sciences at Stanford University and in 2011 was a visiting researcher at the Max Planck Institute for Human Development.

Catherine E. Myers is a Research Scientist with the Department of Veterans Affairs, New Jersey Health Care System, and a Professor of Neurology and Neurosciences at the New Jersey Medical School–University of Medicine and Dentistry of New Jersey. Her research includes both computational neuroscience and experimental psychology and focuses on human memory, specifically on memory impairments following damage to the hippocampus and associated brain structures. She is co-author of *Gateway to Memory: An Introduction to Neural Network Modeling of the Hippocampus and Learning* (MIT Press, 2001) and author of *Delay Learning in Artificial Neural Networks* (Chapman and Hall, 1992).

BRIEF CONTENTS

CONTENTS

Learning Module

This is the second edition of *Learning and Memory: From Brain to Behavior*, following the success of our first edition, published in 2008. The new edition continues our approach of presenting a comprehensive, accessible, and engaging introduction to the scientific study of learning and memory. The biggest change we have introduced in the second edition is the adapting of chapters into a new, modular table of contents that allows the course to be taught in any of at least four different ways: (1) Learning first, then Memory; (2) Memory first, then Learning; (3) Memory only; or (4) Learning only. This new organization, in which the book as a whole is divided into conceptual modules consisting of from two to four chapters each, extends the theme established in the first edition (and continued here) in which all the core chapters have the same three subsections: Behavioral Processes, Brain Substrates, and Clinical Perspectives. As explained in more detail below, the innovative organization of our second edition results in a highly flexible curriculum suited to the many different ways that teachers prefer to teach this material. Other notable changes since the first edition include

- *Increased use of real-world examples*, concrete applications, and clinically relevant perspectives.
- *Enhancement and integration of pedagogy* to help students assess their own progress and understanding. By integrating pedagogy into the body of each chapter, we provide students with immediate practice and feedback, help them organize and prioritize information, and generally assist them in using the book more effectively.
- *Stronger and more extensive teacher support* through supplemental materials and a complete, ready-to-use package of PowerPoint slides for each section of each chapter.
- *Expanded tutorial discussions of anatomy and biochemistry* for students with little or no biology background.
- *Even more integration of topics across chapters*, highlighting connections between themes and concepts that arise repeatedly in different parts of the book.
- *About 20% new references*, reflecting rapid recent advances in the field and emphasizing important breakthroughs in all aspects of learning and memory research since the publication of the first edition in 2008.

As detailed in the following discussions, *Learning and Memory: From Brain to Behavior*, 2nd Edition, is notable among textbooks in its field for the flexibility of its novel modular structure and for its strong neuroscience focus, integrative coverage of animal learning and human memory, engaging writing style, helpful pedagogical features incorporated throughout each chapter, extensive four-color art program, and emphasis on showing students how basic research has direct implications for everyday life and clinical practice.

Flexible Modular Table of Contents—New for 2nd Edition

There are at least four different ways in which teachers can choose to teach this material:

1. **Learning only.** Focusing on animal conditioning and behaviorist approaches; teachers may or may not include neuroscience perspectives.
2. **Memory only.** Focusing primarily on human memory and cognition; teachers include varying degrees of cognitive neuroscience perspectives.
3. **Learning, then memory.** Starting with basic learning phenomena such as habituation, sensitization, and associative conditioning—phenomena most extensively studied in animals—and progressing to the more complex facets of human memory.

Neuroscience coverage, when included, begins with the most elemental building blocks of neurons and circuits and works up to the larger anatomical perspectives required by the human memory studies.

4. **Memory, then learning.** Here, teachers start with the most engaging and familiar material on human memory, including its many failings and idiosyncrasies, topics that students usually find especially relevant and appealing. As the course progresses, teachers present material on how human memory is built up from basic processes that can be studied in greater precision in animal models. Neuroscience coverage begins with the most accessible and easily understandable big-picture view of anatomical regions and their functional relevance and then works toward presenting the greater detail and neuronal focus of studies that can be done invasively in animal preparations, especially studies of conditioning and other forms of associative learning.

Does the field really need four different types of textbooks to support the diversity of approaches to teaching this material? In the past, the answer was, unfortunately, "yes": every textbook followed one of these approaches, and instructors had to find the book whose orientation, organization, and coverage best matched their own plans for the course. However, with the introduction this year of *Learning and Memory: From Brain to Behavior*, 2nd Edition, there is now available, for the first time, a single textbook that is sufficiently modular in its overall structure and in the execution of individual chapters to accommodate all four approaches to teaching this material.

How can one textbook suit every teaching approach?

To accomplish this feat, we have divided the book into four multichapter modules:

- The **Introductory Module** is the natural starting point for all courses; teachers can assign either or both of two introductory chapters, one a conceptual and historical overview of the study of psychology and behavior, the other an introduction to the neuroscience of learning and memory.

- The heart of the book consists of two "parallel" modules, the **Learning Module** and the **Memory Module**. These can be covered singly (for those teachers who wish to teach only learning or only memory) or in either order, allowing for a learning-then-memory syllabus or a memory-then-learning syllabus. Each of these modules is a self-contained collection of chapters, neither of which assumes that the student has read the other module. The Learning Module has four chapters, covering non-associative learning (primarily habituation and sensitization); classical conditioning; instrumental conditioning; and, finally, generalization, discrimination, and similarity. The Memory Module has three chapters, covering episodic and semantic memory, skill memory, and working memory and cognitive control.

- The final module of the book, the **Integrative Topics Module**, consists of three optional stand-alone chapters (so that any subset of the three can be assigned), covering emotional learning and memory, social learning and memory, and lifespan changes in learning and memory, from prenatal development to old age.

Given the book's flexible, modifiable, and modular structure, we believe we have written the first textbook for every instructor in the fields of learning and/or memory, reflecting and respecting the heterogeneity and diversity of the many different approaches to teaching this material.

Can this book be used for a Principles of Learning and Behavior course?

Indeed it can. Although more and more colleges are offering courses that integrate animal learning and human memory and include ever-increasing amounts of neuroscience, there are still a large number of teachers who prefer to focus primarily on animal learning and conditioning, along with modest coverage of related studies of human associative learning, all presented primarily from a behavioral perspective.

For such a course, we recommend starting with Chapter 1, "The Psychology of Learning and Memory," then covering the four chapters of the Learning Module (Chapters 3 through 6), and concluding with Chapter 10, "Emotional Influences on Learning and Memory," which examines key topics in fear conditioning. Together these six chapters present a lucid, compelling, accessible, and engaging introduction to the principles of learning and behavior. We recognize, of course, that six chapters cannot provide as much detailed coverage as a single-approach textbook with 12 or more chapters on these topics. For this reason, we have included extensive additional materials on learning and behavior in the teacher's supplemental materials for the Learning Module chapters. These materials provide the additional flexibility and content to support spending two weeks, rather than one week, on each of the four Learning Module chapters. This combination of textbook and supplemental materials serves well the teacher who wishes to spend 10 or more weeks on principles of learning and behavior with a primary focus on animal learning and conditioning.

Specialized learning and behavior textbooks are often dry and unappealing to most students. By adopting our book, instructors who prefer the learning and behavior approach will be providing their students with a text that has a uniquely engaging writing style, helpful integrated pedagogy, extensive four-color art, and a strong focus on showing students how basic research has direct implications for everyday life and clinical practice.

Neuroscience Focus

Neuroscience has altered the landscape for behavioral research, shifting priorities and changing our ideas about the brain mechanisms of behavior. *Learning and Memory: From Brain to Behavior* integrates neuroscience research into each chapter, emphasizing how new findings from neuroscience have allowed psychologists to consider the functional and physiological mechanisms that underlie the behavioral processes of learning and memory. Chapter 2, "The Neuroscience of Learning and Memory," offers an accessible introduction to neuroscience for students unfamiliar with the basics of brain structure and function. Thereafter, the "Brain Substrates" section of each of the book's core chapters (3 through 12) presents the neuroscience perspectives relevant to the chapter topic, to be assigned or not as the teacher wishes (omitted by those teachers who prefer to present only a behavioral perspective).

Integrated Presentation of Learning and Memory Research across Species

The field of learning and memory has undergone enormous changes over the last decade, primarily as a result of new developments in neuroscience. As we have gained a greater understanding of the neurobiological bases of behavior, the strict conceptual boundary between the biological approach and the psychological approach to the study of learning and memory has begun to disappear. Moreover, after several decades during which learning by humans was studied and described in one field of science and learning by animals was studied in another, the discovery of basic biological mechanisms common to all species has launched a unified approach to behavioral studies. Although our book takes a modular approach to teaching this course, distinguishing the chapters that focus primarily on learning from those that focus primarily on memory, the story that emerges from covering both sets of chapters is, we believe, the strongest and most up-to-date representation of the field as a whole.

Clinical Perspectives

In addition to examining and explaining new research in learning and memory, *Learning and Memory: From Brain to Behavior*, 2nd Edition, traces how these findings have spurred the development of new diagnoses and treatments for a variety of neurological and psychiatric disorders. Recent advances in neuroscience have produced dramatic changes in clinical practices over the last decade, greatly affecting how neurologists, psychiatrists, clinical psychologists, nurses, and rehabilitation specialists diagnose and treat the clinical disorders of learning and memory. Alzheimer's disease, autism, schizophrenia, Parkinson's disease, Huntington's disease, dyslexia, ADHD, and stroke are just a few of the disorders for which new treatment options have been developed as a result of basic behavioral and cognitive neuroscience studies of learning and memory. To reflect this broader impact of the field of learning and memory, each of the core chapters (Chapters 3 through 12) includes a "Clinical Perspectives" section that shows how knowledge of behavioral processes and brain substrates is being applied to understand clinical disorders that lead to disruptions of learning and memory. These sections are one way in which the book emphasizes the influence of learning and memory research in the real world and shows how neuropsychological research informs our understanding of memory mechanisms.

Student Friendliness

- **No Prerequisites**. We understand that students may come to this course from different backgrounds, even different disciplines, so we do not assume any previous level of familiarity with basic psychology or neuroscience concepts. The first two chapters of the text offer a complete overview of the field of the psychology of learning and memory and the neuroscience foundations of behavior. Later chapters explain all new concepts clearly with emphasis on real-life examples and teaching-oriented illustrations.

- **Engaging Narrative**. Our aim has been to create a lively, clear, and example-rich narrative, a colorful conversation between authors and readers that communicates our vision of an exciting field in transition and captures the interest of students by igniting their curiosity.

- **Full-Color Art Program**. The full-color art program consists of original anatomical art, state-of-the-art brain scans, and color-coded figures to help students visualize the processes involved in learning and memory. Photos offer a link to the real world, as well as a look back in time; cartoons provide occasional comical commentary (and often additional insights) alongside the main narrative.

- **Real-World Implications**. *Learning and Memory: From Brain to Behavior* is noted for a strong focus on applications and on the relevance of learning and memory concepts to everyday life. In addition to the "Clinical Perspectives" section at the end of every core chapter, we have included throughout each chapter many concrete, real-world examples of learning and memory that help students grasp the implications of what they are studying and its relevance in their own lives.

- **Consistent Organization.** The integration of both neuroscience and relevant clinical issues throughout the text is made more accessible to the student by the book's consistent tripartite division of each chapter into the sections "Behavioral Processes," "Brain Substrates," and "Clinical Perspectives." As described above, this also allows teachers to selectively omit the discussions of brain substrates or clinical perspectives from some or all of the reading assignments if that better suits a teacher's syllabus.

Extensive Pedagogy

- **Test Your Knowledge** exercises introduced at intervals throughout each chapter give students the opportunity to check their comprehension and retention of more challenging topics immediately after having read about them. Suggested answers are provided.
- **Learning and Memory in Everyday Life** boxes in each chapter illustrate the practical implications of research, especially those that are relevant and interesting to undergraduate students.
- **Interim Summaries** follow each chapter subsection to help students review major concepts presented in the pages they have just finished reading.
- **Concept Checks** at the end of each chapter ask critical-thinking questions that require an understanding and synthesis of the key material in the chapter. These exercises ask students to apply the knowledge they've gained to a real-life situation. Suggested answers are provided at the end of the book.
- **Key Terms** with page references appear at the end of each chapter to help students review new terminology presented in the chapter. All key terms with their definitions are included in an end-of-text glossary.

Media/Supplements

Book Companion Site at www.worthpublishers.com/gluck2e

The companion site serves students as a virtual study guide, 24 hours a day, 7 days a week. The password-protected instructor's section offers a variety of assessment, presentation, and course management resources.

Book-Specific Lecture and Art PowerPoint Slides

To ease your transition to *Learning and Memory*, a prepared set of lecture and art slides, in easy-to-adopt PowerPoint format, is available to download from the instructor's side of the Book Companion Site.

Instructor's Resource Manual and Test Bank

The Instructor's Resource Manual includes extensive chapter-by-chapter suggestions for in-class presentations, projects and assignments, as well as tips for integrating multimedia into your course. It also provides more comprehensive material on animal learning for instructors who allocate more of their courses to the classic studies of animal learning. The Test Bank features approximately 100 questions per chapter as well as an assortment of short-answer and essay questions. Also included in the Test Bank are the chapter-specific Web quizzes (10–15 questions each) that appear on the Book Companion Site.

Diploma Computerized Test Bank (Available in Windows and Macintosh on one CD-ROM)

The Test Bank software allows instructors to add an unlimited number of questions, edit questions, format a test, scramble questions, and include pictures, equations, or multimedia links. With the accompanying grade book, instructors can record students' grades throughout a course, sort student records and view detailed analyses of test items, curve tests, generate reports, add weights to grades, and more.

Course Management Aids

As a service for adopters who use course management systems, the various resources for this textbook are available in the appropriate format to be downloaded into their campus CMS. The files can be customized to fit specific course needs or they can be used as is. Course outlines, prebuilt quizzes, links, and activities are included, eliminating hours of work for instructors.

Acknowledgments, to Our Colleagues

This book has benefited from the wisdom of expert reviewers and instructors from laboratories and classrooms around the country. From the earliest stages of the development process, we solicited feedback and advice from the leading voices in the field of learning and memory to ensure that the book expresses the most current and accurate understanding of the topics in each chapter. Over the course of the book's development, we have relied on these experts' criticism, corrections, encouragement, and thoughtful contributions. We thank them for lending us their insight, giving us their time, and above all for sharing in our commitment to creating a new textbook and a new curriculum that reflects a contemporary perspective on the field.

Michael Todd Allen
University of Northern Colorado

John Anderson
Carnegie Mellon University

Hal Arkes
Ohio State University

Amy Arnsten
Yale University

Ed Awh
University of Oregon

Padmini Banerjee
Delaware State University

Deanna Barch
Washington University, St. Louis

Carol Barnes
University of Arizona

Mark Basham
Metropolitan State College of Denver

Mark Baxter
Oxford University

Kevin Beck
VA New Jersey Health Care System and New Jersey Medical School

Matthew Bell
Santa Clara University

April Benasich
Rutgers University—Newark

Anjan Bhattacharyya
New Jersey City University

Evelyn Blanch-Payne
Georgia Gwinnett College

Gordon Bower
Stanford University

Jennifer Breneiser
Valdosta State University

György Buzsáki
New York University

John Byrnes
University of Massachusetts

Larry Cahill
University of California, Irvine

Robert Calin-Jageman
Dominican University

Thomas Carew
University of California, Irvine

KinHo Chan
Hartwick College

Henry Chase
Cambridge University

Jennifer Coleman
Western New Mexico University

Roshan Cools
Cambridge University

James Corter
Columbia University

Stephen Crowley
Indiana University

Clayton Curtis
New York University

Irene Daum
Ruhr University Bochum Germany

Nathaniel Daw
New York University

Mauricio Delgado
Rutgers University—Newark

Dennis Delprato
Eastern Michigan University

Mark D'Esposito
University of California, Berkeley

David Diamond
University of South Florida

Michael Domjan
University of Texas, Austin

Howard Eichenbaum
Boston University

William Estes
Indiana University

Marianne Fallon
Central Connecticut State University

Robert Ferguson
Buena Vista University

Julia Fisher
Coker College

John Forgas
University of South Wales

Aubyn Fulton
Pacific Union College

Joaquin Fuster
University of California, Los Angeles

Sherry Ginn
Wingate University

Robert Goldstone
Indiana University

John Green
University of Vermont

Robert Greene
Case Western Reserve University

Martin Guthrie
Bordeaux University

Lisa Haber-Chalom
Rutgers University—Newark

Karl Haberlandt
Trinity College

Stephen Hanson
Rutgers University—Newark

Kent Harber
Rutgers University—Newark

Michael Hasselmo
Boston University

Robert Hawkins
Columbia University

Mohammad Herzallah
Rutgers University—Newark

Kathleen Hipp
Daniel Webster University

Kurt Hoffman
Virginia Tech University

Ramona Hopkins
Brigham Young University

Merritt Hoover
*University of California—
Santa Cruz*

Steven Horowitz
Central Connecticut State University

James Hunsicker
*Southwestern Oklahoma State
University*

Sterling Johnson
University of Wisconsin

Stephen Joy
Albertus Magnus College

Lee Jussim
Rutgers University—New Brunswick

Daniel Kahneman
Princeton University

Narinder Kapur
London Memory Clinic

E. James Kehoe
University of South Wales

Szabolcs Kéri
University of Szeged, Hungary

Kristopher Kimbler
Florida Gulf Coast University

Alan Kluger
Lehman College, CUNY

Stephen Kosslyn
Harvard University

John Kruschke
Indiana University

Joseph LeDoux
New York University

Derek Lindquist
Ohio State University

Elizabeth Loftus
University of California, Irvine

Robert Lubow
Tel-Aviv University

Elliot Ludvig
University of Alberta

Gail Mauner
University at Buffalo, SUNY

James McClelland
Stanford University

James McGaugh
University of California, Irvine

Martijn Meeter
*Vrije Universiteit Amsterdam,
Netherlands*

Barbara Mellers
University of California, Berkeley

Earl Miller
Massachusetts Institute of Technology

George Miller
Princeton University

Mortimer Mishkin
National Institutes of Mental Health

John Moore
University of Massachusetts

Lynn Nadel
University of Arizona

Michelle Nicolle
*Wake Forest University School of
Medicine*

Ken Norman
Princeton University

Robert Nosofsky
Indiana University

Laura O'Sullivan
Florida Gulf Coast University

Ken Paller
Northwestern University

Mauricio Papini
Texas Christian University

Denis Paré
Rutgers University—Newark

Michael Petrides
McGill University

Elizabeth Phelps
New York University

Raymond Phinney
Wheaton College

Steven Pinker
Harvard University

Russell Poldrack
University of California, Los Angeles

Sarah Queller
Indiana University

Sheila Quinn
Salve Regina University

Garbiel Radvansky
Notre Dame

Arthur Reber
*Brooklyn College, Graduate Center
CUNY*

Lisa Rezi
University of Georgia

Trevor Robbins
University of Cambridge

Herbert Roitblat
OrcaTec

Carolyn Rovee-Collier
*Rutgers University—
New Brunswick*

Jerry Rudy
University of Colorado

Linda Rueckert
Northeastern Illinois University

Michelle Ryder
Daniel Webster University

Jeffery Sables
University of Memphis

Sharleen Sakai
Michigan State University

Richard Schiffrin
Indiana University

Ana Schwartz
University of Texas at El Paso

Richard Servatius
*VA New Jersey Health Care
System and New Jersey Medical
School*

David Shanks
University College London

Sonya Sheffert
Central Michigan University

Art Shimamura
University of California, Berkeley

Daphna Shohamy
Columbia University

Shepard Siegel
McMaster University

Edward Smith
Columbia University

Patrick Smith
Florida Southern College

Paul Smolensky
Johns Hopkins University

Larry Squire
*University of California, School of
Medicine, San Diego*

Mark Stanton
University of Delaware

Joseph Steinmetz
Indiana University

Helen Sullivan
Rider University

Lauren Taglialatela
Kennesaw State

Paula Tallal
Rutgers University—Newark

Herbert Terrace
Columbia University

Philip Tetlock
University of California, Berkeley

Frederic Theunissen
University of California, Berkeley

Richard Thompson
University of Southern California

Endel Tulving
University of Toronto

Barbara Tversky
Stanford University

Nehal Vadhan
*Columbia University Medical
School*

Anthony Wagner
Stanford University

Jonathon Wallis
University of California, Berkeley

Xiao Wang
University of South Dakota

Mary Waterstreet
Saint Ambrose University

Sheree Watson
University of Southern Mississippi

Daniel Weinberger
National Institutes of Health

Norman Weinberger
University of California, Irvine

J. W. Whitlow, Jr.
Rutgers University—Camden

James Woodson
University of Tampa

Bonnie Wright
Gardner-Webb University

Laszlo Zaborszky
Rutgers University—Newark

Susan Zelinski
Rutgers University—Newark

Thomas Zentall
University of Kentucky

Acknowledgments, to the Team at Worth Publishers

Textbooks share much in common with Hollywood movies or Broadway shows: the people you see onstage or whose names are on the marquee (or book cover) are only the tip of the proverbial iceberg. Behind them stands a much larger supporting team that is essential to putting on the show. In our case, the two people most central to this book's production and quality are **Daniel DeBonis**, our editor, who served as the effective executive producer of the entire project, managing the various people and components and keeping everyone and everything on track and oriented toward a common vision (and deadline); and **Moira Lerner,** our developmental editor, who functioned like a shadow (but mostly uncredited) fourth author, revising our drafts, identifying problematic gaps in logic and pedagogy, and generally raising the level of coherence, consistency, and communication in the book far beyond what any of the three authors would have been capable of on our own. Special thanks also goes to Marketing Manager Jennifer Bilello for her hard work promoting our book and Director of Print and Digital Development Tracey Kuehn for her help throughout the production process.

Many other people at Worth Publishers provided important contributions to various facets of the book, including Elizabeth Block, Christine Burak, Anthony Casciano, Stephanie Ellis, Kevin Feyen, Kevin Kall, Lukia Kliossis, Jane O'Neill, Nadina Persaud, Babs Reingold, Sarah Segal, Cecilia Varas, and Catherine Woods. We are grateful to each and every one of them for their outstanding attention to our book.

The Psychology of Learning and Memory

A T AGE 46, CLIVE WEARING HAD IT all. He was a well-known, highly regarded symphony conductor; he was handsome, charming, and witty; and he was deeply in love with his wife, Deborah. Then his memory was stripped from him. Clive had developed a rare condition in which the herpes simplex virus, which usually causes nothing more serious than cold sores, invaded his brain. His brain tissue swelled, crushing against the confines of his skull. Although most patients die when this happens, Clive survived, but his brain remained significantly damaged.

When Clive awoke in the hospital, he had lost most of his past. He could recognize Deborah but couldn't remember their wedding. He knew he had children but couldn't remember their names or what they looked like. He could speak and understand words, but there were huge gaps in his knowledge. On one test, when shown a picture of a scarecrow, he replied: "A worshipping point for certain cultures." Asked to name famous musicians, he could produce four names: Mozart, Beethoven, Bach, and Haydn. Conspicuously absent from this list was the sixteenth-century composer Lassus: Clive had been the world expert on this composer (Wilson & Wearing, 1995).

But Clive Wearing hadn't just lost the past: he'd also lost the present. Now he would remain conscious for only a few seconds of whatever he happened to be experiencing, and then the information would melt away without forming even a temporary memory. During his stay in the hospital, he had no idea where he was or why he was surrounded by strangers. Whenever he caught sight of Deborah—even if she'd only left the room for a few minutes—he'd run to her and kiss her joyously, as if she'd been absent for years.

Jiri Rezac, 2006

Clive Wearing with his wife, Deborah

A few minutes later, he'd catch sight of her again and stage another passionate reunion. Clive now lived "in the moment," caught in an endless loop of reawakening. His numerous journals show his desperate efforts to make sense of what he was experiencing: "7:09 A.M.: Awake. 7:34 A.M.: Actually finally awake. 7:44 A.M.: Really perfectly awake . . . 10:08 A.M.: Now I am superlatively awake. First time aware for years. 10:13 A.M.: Now I am overwhelmingly awake. . . . 10:28 A.M.: Actually I am now first time awake for years. . . ." Each time he added a new entry, he might go back and scratch out the previous line, angry that a stranger had written misleading entries in his journal.

Yet even when Clive knew nothing else, he knew that he loved his wife. Emotional memory—love—survived when almost everything else was gone. And he could still play the piano and conduct an orchestra so competently that a nonmusician wouldn't suspect anything was wrong with Clive's mind. Those specialized skill memories survived, along with more mundane skills, such as making coffee or playing card games. And although Clive was unable to consciously learn any new facts, he could acquire some new habits through repeated practice. After moving to a nursing home, he eventually learned the route from the dining hall to his room, and when prompted to put on his coat for his daily walk past the local pond, he would ask if it was time to go feed the ducks (Wilson & Wearing, 1995). Clive's memory was more like an imperfectly erased blackboard than a blank slate.

Clive Wearing's case is tragic but makes two important points. The first is the unrivaled importance of learning and memory to our lives. Most of the time, we take for granted our memories of who we are and what we know. When these are stripped away, life becomes a series of unrelated moments, isolated from past and future, like those fuzzy moments we all experience when we've just awakened and are disoriented.

The second point is that speaking of memory as if it were a single, cohesive process is misleading. In fact, there are many different kinds of memory, and as happened in Clive's case, some can be damaged while others are spared. Normally, these different kinds of memory function together seamlessly, and we aren't aware of whether a given instance of learning has been preserved as a fact, habit, skill, or emotion. But this cohesion is in many ways an illusion. By confronting the limits of this illusion, we can begin to understand how memory works, both in healthy people and in individuals whose memory has broken down. You will read more about amnesic patients like Clive Wearing in Chapter 7, "Semantic and Episodic Memory: Memory for Facts and Events."

This book is about **learning,** the process by which changes in behavior arise as a result of experience interacting with the world, and **memory,** the record of our past experiences, which are acquired through learning. The study of learning and memory began far back in human history and continues today. Some of humanity's greatest minds have struggled with the question of how we learn and remember. As you read this chapter, we hope that you will see why the questions that fascinated philosophers and psychologists of long ago are still relevant today. Some of the insights may apply to your own efforts to improve your memory at school and in other aspects of your daily life. To whet your appetite, see "Learning and Memory in Everyday Life" on page 4.

In the course of this chapter, five themes emerge that have reappeared in different guises across the centuries. These five themes are

1. How do sensations or ideas become linked in the mind?

2. How are memories built from the components of experience?

3. To what extent are behaviors and abilities determined by biological inheritance (nature) and to what extent by life experiences (nurture)?

4. In what ways are human learning and memory similar to learning and memory in other animals, and in what ways do they differ?

5. Are there universal principles of learning and memory that can be described by mathematical equations and considered fundamental laws?

1.1 From Philosophy to Psychology

Today, learning and memory researchers consider themselves scientists. They develop new theories and test those theories with carefully designed experiments, just like researchers in any other branch of science. However, this wasn't always the case. In fact, for most of human history, the study of learning and memory was a branch of *philosophy*, the abstract study of principles that govern the universe, including human conduct. Philosophers gain insight not through scientific experiments but through a process of reasoned thought and logical argument. These insights may be no less important than those gained through modern science; some are so profound that people continue talking about them centuries after they were first disseminated.

> ◤ **LEARNING AND MEMORY IN EVERYDAY LIFE**
>
> # Top Ten Tips for a Better Memory
>
> 1. *Pay attention.* Often when we "forget" something, it's not that we've somehow lost the memory of it but that we didn't learn the thing properly in the first place. If you pay full attention to what you are trying to learn, you'll be more likely to remember it later.
> 2. *Create associations.* Associate what you're trying to learn with other information you already know. For example, it will be easier to remember that Ag is the chemical symbol for silver if you know it is short for *argentum*, the Latin word for "silver." It might also help if you know that Argentina got its name from early European explorers who mistakenly thought the region was rich in silver.
> 3. *A picture is worth a thousand words.* Names and dates and such are more memorable if you can link them to an image. The effort you expend generating an image strengthens the memory. For example, in an art history course, you might have to remember that Manet specialized in painting figures and his contemporary, Monet, is famous for paintings of haystacks and water lilies. Picture the human figures lined up acrobat-style to form a letter "A" for Manet and the water lilies arranged in a daisy chain to form the letter "O" for Monet.
> 4. *Practice makes perfect.* There's a reason to drill kindergarteners on their ABCs and make third graders repeatedly recite their multiplication tables. Memories for facts are strengthened by repetition. The same principle holds for memories for skills, such as bike riding and juggling: they are improved by practice.
> 5. *Use multiple senses.* Instead of just reading information silently, read it aloud. You will encode the information aurally as well as visually. You can also try writing it out; the act of writing activates sensory systems and also forces you to think about the words you're copying.
> 6. *Reduce overload.* Use memory aids such as Post-it notes, calendars, or electronic schedulers to remember appointments, due dates, and other obligations, freeing you to focus on remembering items that must be called to mind without written aids—say, during an exam!
> 7. *Time travel.* Remembering information for facts doesn't depend on remembering the exact time and place where you acquired it. Nevertheless, if you can't remember a fact, try to remember where you first heard it. If you can remember your high school history
> teacher lecturing on Napoleon, perhaps what she said about the causes of the Napoleonic Wars will also come to mind.
> 8. *Get some sleep.* Two-thirds of Americans don't get enough sleep. Consequently, they are less able to concentrate during the day, which makes it harder for them to encode new memories and retrieve old ones (see Tip 1). Sleep is also important for helping the brain organize and store memories.
> 9. *Try a rhyme.* Do you have to remember a long string of random information? Create a poem (or better yet, a song) that includes the information. Remember the old standard " 'I' before 'E' except after 'C' or sounded as 'A,' as in 'neighbor' or 'weigh' "? This ditty uses rhythm and rhyme to make it easier to remember a rule of English spelling.
> 10. *Relax.* Sometimes trying hard to remember is less effective than turning your attention to something else; often, the missing information will pop into your awareness later. If you are stumped by a question on a test, skip that one and come back to it later, when perhaps the missing information won't be so hard to retrieve.

The Empiricism and Associationism of Aristotle

Aristotle (384–322 BC), a Greek philosopher and teacher, was one of the earliest thinkers to write about memory. Like many wealthy young men of his day, Aristotle was educated in Athens, the preeminent intellectual center of the western world at that time. There, he studied under Plato (c. 427–347 BC), perhaps the greatest of the Greek philosophers. Years later, Aristotle himself became a mentor to many students, including a young prince later known as Alexander the Great, who went on to conquer much of the world.

A keen observer of the natural world, Aristotle loved **data,** the facts and figures from which he could infer conclusions. He collected plants and animals from around the world and made careful notes about their structure and behavior. From such data, Aristotle attempted to formulate **theories,** sets of statements devised to explain a collection of facts. His data-oriented approach to understanding the world stood in marked contrast to the methods of his intellectual forebears, including Plato and Plato's teacher, Socrates, both of whom relied primarily on intuition and logic rather than natural observation.

One of Aristotle's key interests was memory. His theory about it, called **associationism,** argued that memory depends on the formation of linkages ("associations") between pairs of events, sensations, or ideas, so that recalling or experiencing one member of the pair elicits a memory or anticipation of the other. Imagine someone reading a list of words and for each word asking you to say the first word that comes to mind. If he says "hot," you might say "cold"; if he says "chair," you might say "table," and so on. The words "hot" and "cold" are linked, or associated, in most people's minds, as are "table" and "chair." How do these associations come about?

Aristotle (right) and his teacher, **Plato**

Aristotle described such linkages as reflecting three principles of association. The first principle is **contiguity,** or nearness in time and space: events experienced at the same time (temporal contiguity) or place (spatial contiguity) tend to be associated. The ideas of "chair" and "table" are linked because we often see chairs and tables together at the same time and in the same place. The second principle is *frequency*: the more often we experience events that are contiguous, the more strongly we associate them. Thus, the more often we see tables and chairs together, the stronger the table-chair link grows. Modern behavioral and neurobiological studies of the interaction between contiguity and frequency in learning will be discussed further in Chapter 4, "Classical Conditioning: Learning to Predict Important Events."

Aristotle's third principle is *similarity*: if two things are similar, the thought or sensation of one will tend to trigger a thought of the other. Chairs and tables are similar in that both are often made of wood, both are found in kitchens, and both have a function associated with eating meals. This similarity strengthens the association between them. In Chapter 6, "Generalization and Discrimination Learning," you will see why similarity has continued to be a core focus of research on learning. Together, Aristotle concluded, these three principles of association—contiguity, frequency, and similarity—are the basic ways humans organize sensations and ideas.

Aristotle's ideas, refined in the ensuing two millennia, have provided the foundation for modern theories of learning in both psychology and neuroscience. Aristotle's view was that knowledge emerges from experience. This idea identifies him with a philosophical school of thought known as **empiricism,** which holds that all the ideas we have are the result of experience. (The Greek word *empiricus* means "experience.") To Aristotle, the mind of a newborn child is like a blank slate, not yet written on.

In this regard, Aristotle differed sharply from his teacher Plato, who believed staunchly in **nativism,** which holds that the bulk of our knowledge is inborn (or native), acquired during the past lifetimes of our eternal souls. In fact, Plato's most influential book, *The Republic*, describes an idealized society in which people's innate differences in skills, abilities, and talents form the basis for their fixed roles in life: some rule while others serve. The tension between empiricism and nativism has continued through the centuries, although today it is more often called the "nature versus nurture" debate: researchers argue about whether our "nature," including genes, or our "nurture," including upbringing and environment, has the greater influence on our learning and memory abilities. Table 1.1 shows some of the major

Table 1.1

Nativism and empiricism: The role of nature and nurture in learning and memory

Nativism: Knowledge is inborn	Empiricism: Knowledge is acquired through experience
Plato (c. 427–347 BC) Most of our knowledge is inborn and acquired during past lifetimes of the soul.	**Aristotle (384–322 BC)** Memory depends on the formation of associations, for which there are three principles: contiguity, frequency, and similarity.
René Descartes (1596–1650) The mind and the body are distinct entities, governed by different laws. The body functions as a machine with innate and fixed responses to stimuli.	**John Locke (1632–1704)** A newborn's mind is a blank slate (a *tabula rasa*) that is written on by experience. Education and experience (learning) allow common people to transcend their class.
Gottfried Leibniz (1646–1716) Three quarters of human knowledge is learned, but one quarter is inborn.	**William James (1842–1910)** Habits are built up from inborn reflexes through learning; memory is built up through networks of associations.
Charles Darwin (1809–1882) Natural selection: species evolve when they posses a trait that is inheritable, varies across individuals, and increases the chances of survival and reproduction.	**Ivan Pavlov (1849–1936)** In classical (Pavlovian) conditioning, animals learn through experience to predict future events.
Francis Galton (1822–1911) Humans' natural talents are hereditary.	**Edward Thorndike (1874–1949)** The law of effect (instrumental conditioning): an animal's behaviors increase or decrease depending on the consequences that follow the response.

philosophers and scientists who have contributed to this debate over the millennia and which side of the debate they espoused; the names and ideas in the table will be revisited throughout the book.

Western philosophy and science have deep roots in the ideas and writings of the ancient Greeks, whose philosophy and science continued to flourish under the Roman Empire. By the fifth century AD, however, the empire had collapsed, and Europe plunged into the Dark Ages, overrun by successive waves of warring tribes who seemed to care little for philosophy or learning. (Meanwhile, in China, India, Persia, and the Arabian Peninsula, flourishing civilizations achieved major advances in science, mathematics, medicine, and astronomy—but that's another story.) It was not until the middle of the fifteenth century that European science flourished once again. This was the Renaissance, the era that brought forth the art of Leonardo da Vinci, the plays of William Shakespeare, and the astronomy of Nicolaus Copernicus and Galileo Galilei. This cultural and scientific revival set the stage for the emergence of new ideas about the nature of mind and memory.

I René Descartes

Musée des Augustins, Toulouse, France/The Bridgeman Art Library

Descartes and Dualism

René Descartes (1596–1650) grew up in France as the son of a provincial noble family. His family inheritance gave him the freedom to spend his life studying, thinking, and writing, most of which he did in bed (he hated to get up before noon). Although raised as a Roman Catholic and trained by the Jesuits, Descartes harbored deep doubts about the existence of everything, including

God. Despairing of being able to know anything for certain, he concluded that the only evidence that he himself even existed was his ability to think: "*Cogito ergo sum,*" or "I think, therefore I am" (Descartes, 1637).

Where does Descartes' *cogito*—the ability to think—come from? Descartes was a firm believer in **dualism,** the principle that the mind and body exist as separate entities, each with different characteristics, governed by its own laws (Descartes, 1662). The body, Descartes reasoned, functions like a self-regulating machine, much like the clockwork statues and fountains that were so fashionable during the Renaissance. A person strolling through the royal gardens of Saint-Germain-en-Laye, just outside Paris, would step on a hidden trigger, releasing water into pipes that caused a gargoyle to nod its head, a statue of the god Neptune to shake its trident, and the goddess Diana to modestly retreat. The body, Descartes reasoned, works through a similar system of hydraulics and switches. The process begins when a **stimulus,** a sensory event from the outside world, enters the system; for example, light reflected off a bird enters the eye as a visual stimulus. Like the trigger switch in the gardens, this stimulus causes fluids (Descartes called them "spirits") to flow through hollow tubes from the eyes to the brain and then to be "reflected" back as an outgoing motor **response,** the behavioral consequence of perception of the stimulus, as illustrated by Descartes' sketch in Figure 1.1 (Descartes, 1662). Such a pathway from sensory stimulus to motor response is called a **reflex arc.**

Descartes got many of the details of reflexes wrong. There are no spirits that flow through the body to produce movement hydraulically as he described. Nevertheless, Descartes was the first to show how the body might be understood through the same mechanical principles that underlie physical machinery. This mechanistic view of the processes that give rise to behavior returned in full force many centuries later in the mathematical and engineering models of the brain and behavior described in several of the chapters in this book.

In contrast to Aristotle, who was a staunch empiricist, Descartes was strongly in the nativist camp with Plato. Descartes had no interest in theories of learning. He acknowledged that people do derive some information from experience, but he believed that much of what we know is innate. The nature–nurture debate continues today to inform our efforts at understanding how and to what degree we are able to change and evolve within the span of our own lifetimes, a topic covered in Chapter 12, "Development and Aging: Learning and Memory across the Lifespan."

Figure 1.1 **Descartes' reflex** A mechanism for producing an automatic reaction in response to external events, as illustrated in Descartes' *De Homine* (1662). The diagram shows the flow of information from the outside world, through the eyes, to the brain, and then through the muscles of the arm, creating a physical response in which the arm moves to point to an object in the external world.

John Locke and His Reliance on Empiricism

By the late 1600s, England (along with the rest of Europe) had undergone the conflicts of the Reformation, a religious and political movement that weakened the political power of the Roman Catholic Church and placed new emphasis on individual rights and responsibilities. This was a period when science flourished. Famous scientists were the celebrities of their day; people attended lectures on philosophy and natural sciences the way they now go to movies and rock concerts. One especially renowned scientist, Isaac Newton, demonstrated that white light can be refracted into component colors by a

National Portrait Gallery, London

| John Locke

prism lens and then recombined by another lens to produce white light again.

Inspired by Newton's work, John Locke (1632–1704) hoped to show that the mind, too, could be broken down into elements that when combined produced the whole of consciousness. Locke, like Descartes before him, borrowed methods from the physical sciences that would help him better understand the mind and the processes of learning and memory. This practice of philosophers and psychologists of borrowing from other, more established and rigorous domains of science continues to this day, as summarized in Table 1.2.

How did Locke envision the way elementary associations might account for the more complex ideas and concepts that make up our memories and knowledge? By once again drawing inspiration from the physical sciences, this time from his former Oxford medical instructor, Robert Boyle, who 30 years before had demonstrated that chemical compounds are composed of elementary parts (what we now know to be molecules and atoms). Locke reasoned that complex ideas are similarly formed from the combination of more elementary ideas that we passively acquire through our senses (Locke, 1690). For example, simple ideas such as "red" and "sweet" are acquired automatically by our senses of sight and taste, and more complex ideas such as "cherry" are acquired by combining these simpler components.

Perhaps Locke's most lasting idea is that all knowledge is derived from experience and experience alone. Borrowing Aristotle's analogy of a tablet on which

Table 1.2

Borrowing from the physical and natural sciences to explain the mind

Who . . .	Borrowed Ideas from . . .
René Descartes	Hydraulic engineering
John Locke	Physics (Newton), chemistry (Boyle)
Hermann Ebbinghaus	Laws of perception (Fechner and Weber)
Ivan Pavlov	Telephone exchanges
Edward Thorndike	Evolution by natural selection (Darwin)
Clark Hull	Theory of relativity (Einstein)
George Miller	Information theory (Shannon)
Herbert Simon	Computer science
David Rumelhart	Neuroscience and computer science

nothing is yet written, Locke suggested that children arrive in the world as a blank slate or tablet (in Latin, a *tabula rasa*) just waiting to be written on.

Locke's view of the power of experience to shape our capabilities through a lifetime of learning had great appeal to reformers of the eighteenth century, who were challenging the aristocratic system of government, in which kings ruled by right of birth. Locke's ideas meant that a man's worth was not determined at birth. All men are born equal, he believed, with the same potential for knowledge, success, and leadership. Common people, through striving and learning, could transcend the limits and barriers of class. Therefore, Locke argued, access to a good education should be available to all children regardless of their class or family wealth (Locke, 1693). These ideas heavily influenced Thomas Jefferson as he drafted the Declaration of Independence, which in 1776 proclaimed the American colonies' independence from Great Britain and asserted that "all men are created equal," with the same innate rights to "life, liberty, and the pursuit of happiness"—words taken almost verbatim from Locke's writings.

Although Locke's writings were influential throughout European philosophical and scientific circles, he was not without his critics. One of Locke's contemporaries, German mathematician Gottfried Wilhelm Leibniz (1646–1716), conceded to Locke that three quarters of knowledge might be acquired but claimed that the other quarter is inborn and innate, including habits, predispositions, and potentials for success or failure (Leibniz, 1704). In many ways, Leibniz's more moderate position echoes that adopted by many modern researchers, who believe that human ability is not due solely to nature (nativism) or solely to nurture (empiricism) alone but is a combination of both: nature (as encoded in our genes) provides a background of native ability and predispositions that is modified by a lifetime of experience and learning (nurture).

| William James

William James and Associationism

Born to a wealthy and prominent New York family, William James (1842–1910) spent his early years traveling around the world, living in fine hotels, and meeting many of the great writers and philosophers of his time. After receiving his medical degree in 1869, James accepted a position as an instructor of physiology and anatomy at Harvard, where he offered an introductory course in **psychology,** the study of mind and behavior. It was the first course on psychology ever given at Harvard or at any college in America. He once joked that the first psychology lecture he ever heard was his own.

James's introductory psychology course soon became one of the most popular courses at Harvard, and he signed a contract with a publisher, promising to deliver within two years a book based on his acclaimed lectures. In the end, it took him 12 years to finish the book. James's two-volume *Principles of Psychology* (1890) was an immediate scientific, commercial, and popular success. Translated into many languages, it was for decades the standard psychology text around the world.

James was especially interested in how we learn new habits and acquire new memories. He enjoyed telling the story of a practical joker who, seeing a recently discharged army veteran walking down the street carrying a load of groceries, shouted, "Attention!" The former soldier instantly and instinctively brought his hands to his side and stood ramrod straight as his mutton and potatoes rolled into the gutter. The soldier's response to this command was so deeply ingrained as a reflex that, even after he had left the army, it was all but impossible to suppress. James believed that most abilities and habits were similarly formed by our experiences, especially early in life. He proposed that a central goal of psychology should be to understand the principles that govern the formation and maintenance of new skills and memories, including how and why old learning may block or facilitate the formation of new learning (James, 1890); indeed, this tension between old memories and new learning has been an ongoing focus of experimental psychology in the last century, as reviewed in many of the chapters to follow, especially Chapter 7, "Semantic and Episodic Memory: Memory for Facts and Events," and Chapter 8, "Skill Memory: Learning by Doing."

James was a strong proponent of associationism, and his theories elaborated on the work of Aristotle and Locke. The act of remembering an event, such as a dinner party, he wrote, would involve multiple connections between the components of the evening. These might include memories for the taste of the food, the feel of his stiff dinner jacket, and the smell of the perfume of the lady seated next to him (Figure 1.2). Activation of the memory for the dinner party, with all of its components, could in turn activate the memory for a second event that shared some related elements—such as a visit to a dance hall with the same lady on the next night. This second event would be composed of its own parts: the sights of the dance hall, the movements of dancing, the smell of his partner's perfume, and so on. The two events (dinner party and dancing) would be associated by a linkage between their common or related components (the sight of the lady and the smell of her perfume).

This model, or simplified description, of memory was one of James's many seminal contributions to psychology. James took his model literally, believing that the associations it described would eventually be mapped directly onto physical connections in the brain (James, 1890). With this idea, James was far

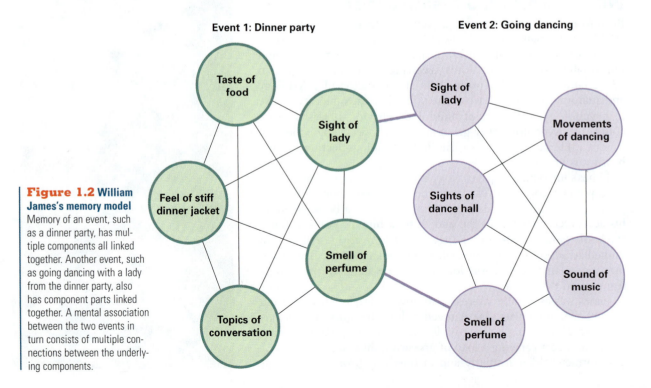

Figure 1.2 William James's memory model Memory of an event, such as a dinner party, has multiple components all linked together. Another event, such as going dancing with a lady from the dinner party, also has component parts linked together. A mental association between the two events in turn consists of multiple connections between the underlying components.

ahead of his time: linking brain processes to learned behaviors didn't attract much interest for many decades. Today, most modern theories of memory draw on James's idea of learning as a process of forming associations between the elements of an experience, as you will see in many chapters to come, including Chapter 4, "Classical Conditioning: Learning to Predict Important Events," and Chapter 7, "Semantic and Episodic Memory: Memory for Facts and Events."

Interim Summary

- Early philosophers interested in learning and memory wrestled with many key issues that are still central to modern theories.

- Aristotle was an associationist, believing that the effects of experiences can be understood as associations formed between sensations or ideas. He described three key principles of associative learning: contiguity (in space and time), frequency, and similarity. A later associationist, William James, proposed an early and influential memory model built on similar principles.

- John Locke, like Aristotle and James, was an empiricist: he believed that we are all born equal, as blank slates, to be shaped by our experiences. In contrast, René Descartes was a nativist, arguing that we are shaped primarily by our inherited nature. He argued that the body could be understood as a machine that works through mechanical (especially hydraulic) principles; as a dualist, he believed that the mind was a separate entity from the body.

- Modern researchers are less likely to be strict nativists or strict empiricists and are more likely to accept that both nature (genes) and nurture (experience) play a role in human learning and memory.

1.2 Evolution and Natural Selection

How unique are humans within the animal kingdom? Plato and other early Greek philosophers took one extreme view: they believed that humans are unique among living things because they possess an everlasting soul. Aristotle, in contrast, argued that humans exist in a continuum with other animals and that the ability to reason is their sole distinguishing feature. Renaissance philosophers tended to side with Plato, bolstered by the Church-sponsored view that mankind was created in God's image. For example, Descartes believed that humans and animals are fundamentally different, just as he believed that mind and body are separate.

But by the early 1800s, this view of humans as being fundamentally different from animals was beginning to meet serious challenge. European naturalists had begun to collect and study a wide variety of plants and animals from around the world. The geological study of rock formations that are shaped by eons of water movement, along with fossils found embedded in these rocks, suggested a world millions of years old. What naturalists and geologists saw in their studies contradicted the prevailing belief that the world was stable and unchanging. The facts they uncovered and the theories they developed upended many long-held beliefs about who we are, where we come from, and how similar we really are to other animals. These new perspectives on the relationship between animals and humans would profoundly affect all future studies of the psychology of learning and memory.

| **Charles Darwin**

Erasmus Darwin (1731–1802) was the personal doctor to King George III of England, who presided over the loss of the American colonies. A man of diverse interests, Darwin wrote books of poetry as well as books on botany and studied how the application of an electrical current to the muscle of a dead animal could cause the muscle to contract and move as if it were alive. This finding inspired his English contemporary Mary Wollstonecraft Shelley (1797–1851) in writing her classic horror story, *Frankenstein*. But Erasmus Darwin is best remembered as a vocal proponent of **evolution,** the theory that species change over time, with new traits or characteristics emerging and being passed from one generation to the next. With sufficient time, he argued, one species could evolve so far that it would come to constitute an entirely different species from its ancestor (E. Darwin, 1794). It was many years later, however, that Erasmus's grandson Charles developed a theory of how this evolutionary process might take place and in doing so made the term "evolution" synonymous with the name Darwin.

Charles Darwin and the Theory of Natural Selection

Charles Darwin (1809–1882) was Erasmus Darwin's grandson. Charles's father was a prosperous doctor, and his mother hailed from the wealthy Wedgwood family of ceramic ware fame. Expected to become a doctor like his father, Darwin began his medical studies, but he soon dropped out, nauseated by watching patients undergo surgery without anesthesia. Fortunately, his family's financial position meant that he didn't have to work for a living. Instead, what Darwin most enjoyed was to walk through the English countryside collecting and cataloging animals.

In 1831, at age 22, with no career direction other than his amateur interest in natural history, Charles Darwin accepted an offer to accompany the captain of the HMS *Beagle* on an expedition to chart the coast of South America. The *Beagle*'s voyage was scheduled to last for two years, but it stretched into five. In South America, Darwin encountered an abundance of previously unknown species, many on the Galápagos Islands, an isolated archipelago off the coast of Ecuador. Of particular interest to Darwin were the many species of birds he observed, especially the finches—of which he identified at least 14 varieties, each on a different island (Figure 1.3). On one island that had plentiful nuts and seeds, the finches had strong, thick beaks that they used to crack open nuts. On another island, with few nuts but plenty of insects, the finches had long, narrow beaks, perfect for grabbing insects from the crevices of tree bark. Each isolated island in the archipelago was populated by a different kind of finch, with a beak ideally suited to that island's distinct habitat. In his account of the trip, Darwin wrote that "one might really fancy that from an original paucity of birds in this archipelago, one species had been taken and modified for different ends" (C. Darwin,

Figure 1.3 Finches of the Galápagos Islands Note the strong, heavy beak of the bird at the upper left (good for cracking nuts) and the long, narrow beak of the bird at the lower right (good for grabbing insects from cracks in bark).

Table 1.3

Darwin's three criteria for traits to evolve through natural selection

Criterion	Giraffes	Finches
1. Inheritable trait	Neck length	Beak shape
2. Natural variability	Short to long	Thin or thick
3. Relevance to survival	Longer necks allow greater access to high branches of trees, and thus to leaves	Correct shape improves access to insects (thinner beak) or ability to crack nuts (thicker beak)

1845). Charles Darwin, like his grandfather, was convinced that life on earth was evolving and was not immutably fixed.

Darwin's most important legacy was his theory of **natural selection,** which proposed a mechanism for how evolution occurs (C. Darwin, 1859). He proposed that species evolve when they possess a trait that meets three conditions (Table 1.3). First, the trait must be inheritable, meaning it can be passed from parent to offspring. (Keep in mind that genes—the carriers of inherited traits—had not yet been discovered in Darwin's time.) Second, the trait must vary, having a range of forms among the individual members of the species. Third, the trait must make the individual more "fit," meaning that it must increase reproductive success—that is, increase the chance that the individual will survive, mate, and reproduce, passing on the trait to its offspring. This, in turn, will make the offspring more fit, increasing their chances of surviving and passing on the trait. Over time, natural selection (sometimes called "survival of the fittest") means that the trait will spread through the population. This, Darwin argued, was the underlying mechanism by which species evolve.

Darwin tinkered with his ideas for 20 years. Finally, in 1859, he published *On the Origin of Species by Means of Natural Selection, or the Preservation of Favoured Races in the Struggle for Life*, more commonly known by its abbreviated title, *The Origin of Species*. Darwin's book became a best seller, was translated into many languages, and ignited a major public controversy that resulted in thousands of reviews, articles, and satires. Why the uproar? Darwin's view of natural selection upset many people's view that there is an important distinction between "man and beast." Theologians were alarmed because the idea that humans and apes evolved from a common ancestor seemed to challenge the biblical doctrine that people were created by the hand of God, in God's own image. *The Origin of Species* is among the most controversial scientific books ever written.

What are the implications of Darwin's work for the psychology of learning and memory? Darwin argued that behavioral traits could evolve through the same process of natural selection as do physical traits (C. Darwin, 1872). Today, the study of how behavior evolves through natural selection is known as **evolutionary psychology.** The basic premise of evolutionary psychology is that learning has enormous value for survival, allowing organisms to adapt to a changing and variable world. Organisms with more capacity for learning and memory are more fit—better able to survive and more likely to breed and pass their inherited capacities on to offspring. Notice that the content of what is learned is not passed on: learned knowledge is an acquired trait, which cannot

Following publication of *The Origin of Species* in 1859, Darwin was the subject of many personal attacks, including caricatures as a half man/half ape, as in this illustration from *Hornet* magazine (March 22, 1871).

be inherited. What can be inherited is the capacity or ability for learning and memory. Further discussion of evolutionary theory, and the revolution in genetics that it spawned, will be covered in Chapter 12, "Development and Aging: Learning and Memory across the Lifespan."

Francis Galton and the Variability of Nature

Francis Galton (1822–1911) was another grandson of Erasmus Darwin. A precocious child, Galton learned to read before he was 3 years old, wrote his first letter at 4, and spoke several languages by the time he was 5. After traveling for several years through African jungles and deserts, he returned to England, fascinated by the enormous variability he had seen in human characteristics. He began to measure everyone he could, comparing mental powers, auditory acuity, physical size, even fingerprints (and, in doing so, invented the modern police method of fingerprinting).

Inspired by his cousin Charles Darwin's theory of natural selection and survival of the fittest, Galton proposed that "a man's natural abilities are derived by inheritance" (Galton, 1869, p. 1). Galton soundly rejected Locke's (and Aristotle's) view of the blank slate. It is a "fairy tale," he wrote, "that babies are all born pretty much alike" (p. 14). In no uncertain terms, Galton—who viewed himself as a genius—railed against the idea of natural equality. Was he himself, and his erudite forebears, not proof that great talent is innate and runs in families, preserved across generations?

As a by-product of his comparative studies of people's physical and mental abilities, Galton invented much of modern statistical and scientific methodology. He found that many attributes—such as height or blood pressure or scores on memory tests—show what he termed a *normal distribution*: out of a large sample of measurements, most will cluster in some middle range, with relatively few at the extreme high and low ranges (Galton, 1899). One example is shown in Figure 1.4. Data on height were collected for a national sample of American men from 1971 to 1974. For most of the men, height was between about 168 and 176 cm; relatively few had a height under 160 cm or over 190 cm. The sample approximates a normal distribution, shown in red in the figure. This is sometimes also called a *bell-shaped curve*, or simply a bell curve, because of its shape. Knowing that a variable, such as height or memory abilities, follows a normal distribution allows statisticians to make inferences about whether an individual falls within the expected "normal" range or represents an unusually high or low value.

Using his newly developed statistical techniques, Galton sought to assess the efficacy of prayer; in the process, he established many basic statistical methods still used in research today. Galton started with a **hypothesis,** a tentative explanation for an observation, phenomenon, or scientific problem that can be tested by further investigation. He hypothesized that prayer would increase the health and lifespan of the persons being prayed for (Galton, 1872). Galton then proceeded to test this hypothesis by designing a **correlational study,** seeing whether two variables (being prayed for, and health and longevity) tended to vary together: as prayer increased, did health and longevity increase too?

| Francis Galton

He considered two groups: an **experimental group,** which is a group treated in the manner dictated by the hypothesis, and a **control group,** which is not given any treatment. In Galton's study, the experimental group consisted of people who, he assumed, were the most prayed-for members of society: the ruling monarchs. The control group consisted of nonroyals, both aristocrats and common people. According to Galton's hypothesis, the highly prayed-for monarchs of English history should have lived longer and healthier lives than members of the control group. Galton calculated that the mean age of death of English sovereigns was about 64 years, whereas, on average, members of the aristocracy (other than the ruling monarchs) lived about 67 years, and common people lived even longer—70 years on average. Thus, Galton concluded, not only did prayer not increase longevity, but it seemed to have the opposite effect!

From the perspective of modern research methods, we can ask whether Galton's study was really the best way to test his hypothesis. What if royalty died young because monarchs ate and drank too much and were occasionally assassinated? The problem with Galton's correlational approach was that he was not able to control for the possibility of **confounds,** extraneous variables (such as diet and assassination) that happen to co-vary with the variable (prayer) being examined (of course, his research was also flawed in that he assumed everyone was really praying for the health of the king). Confounds can lead to erroneous assumptions about what is causing an observed result.

Following his seminal contributions to the development of experimental and statistical methods in science, Galton's later years were largely consumed with applying natural selection to the betterment of mankind. Borrowing from the Greek word for "well-born," *eugenes*, Galton introduced the term **eugenics**, a program for encouraging marriage and procreation among the healthiest, strongest, and most intelligent members of society while at the same time discouraging childbearing in the mentally or physically unfit (Galton, 1883). Galton's eugenics movement grew in popularity and respectability during the early 1900s, as people were excited by the prospect of applying Charles Darwin's ideas of natural selection to improve the human condition. Today, however, the eugenics movement is remembered mostly for the disreputable variants it spawned, such as the forced sterilization of mentally ill individuals in California in the 1920s, and for its use during World War II as a rationalization for the mass murder of Jews, Romanies, homosexuals, and other victims of the Nazis. Despite his association with eugenics, Galton's most enduring legacies are his contributions to understanding the role of inheritability in behavioral traits and the development of novel statistical and experimental methods for psychology. Further discussion of the mechanisms by which individual differences in learning and memory abilities are inherited will be discussed in Chapter 9, "Working Memory and Cognitive Control," and Chapter 12, "Development and Aging: Learning and Memory across the Lifespan."

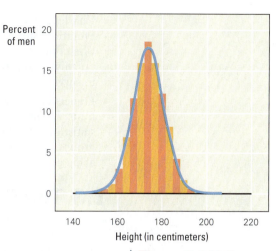

Figure 1.4 A bell curve The distribution of variables in the natural world often produces a bell-shaped curve called a normal distribution, with many values in the middle range and few extreme outliers. Here, for example, height data collected between 1971 and 1974 for 4,635 American men show that most values cluster in the middle range, around 168 to 176 cm, with relatively few extremely tall or extremely short outliers. The blue line shows the statistically expected distribution, and the height data mirror this distribution quite well. Adapted from Carl J. Schwarz.

Interim Summary

■ Erasmus Darwin and other early proponents of biological evolution believed that species evolve over time, although they did not yet know how or why evolution occurs.

- Charles Darwin's theory of natural selection proposed a mechanism for evolution: survival of the fittest. According to this theory, evolution occurs when one variation of a naturally occurring and inheritable trait gives an organism a survival advantage, making the organism more fit—more likely to survive and reproduce and pass this trait on to its offspring.
- Francis Galton was an avid proponent of the inheritability of behavioral traits. He made fundamental contributions to experimental methods and statistics, including the process of testing hypotheses by comparing two groups: an experimental group (that is subject to the variable of interest) and a control group (that is not).

1.3 The Birth of Experimental Psychology

Most of the scientists and philosophers described to this point in the chapter observed the natural world and derived general principles to explain what they saw. In the late 1800s, an important change took place, inspired by the rigorous work of Galton described earlier. Instead of merely collecting information and looking for correlations, scientists interested in psychology began to follow the lead of physical scientists such as chemists by conducting systematic **experiments,** specific tests to examine the validity of a hypothesis by actively manipulating the variables being investigated, using the approaches and methods Galton had begun to systematize. The testing of psychological theories by experimentation rather than merely by observation of natural occurrences is called **experimental psychology.**

Hermann Ebbinghaus and Human Memory Experiments

Hermann Ebbinghaus (1850–1909), a contemporary of William James, conducted the first rigorous experimental studies of human memory. After earning his PhD, Ebbinghaus lived an itinerant life, traveling, attending occasional seminars, and working for short periods as a teacher and private tutor. One day, browsing at a bookstall, he came across a book by a German physicist, Gustav Fechner (1801–1887), that described the science of human perception. Fechner showed that there are highly predictable regularities in how people perceive variations in physical stimuli, such as changes in the brightness of a light or the weight of a ball. The book showed how a simple mathematical equation could describe the relationship between the physical world and the psychological world. Captivated by these ideas, Ebbinghaus proposed that the psychology of memory could also become a rigorous natural science, defined by precise mathematical laws.

Unlike many of the scientists discussed in this chapter, Ebbinghaus was not a wealthy man. Unable to afford to pay anyone to participate in his research, he did his studies using himself as the only participant. Despite this limitation, his work laid the foundation for all future experimental studies of human memory; in fact, Ebbinghaus is often considered to be the father of modern memory research.

Ebbinghaus sought mathematical equations to explain how memories are acquired and how they fade. Early on, he realized that if he studied lists of real words, his data would be strongly affected by the fact that he was more familiar with some words than others. To avoid this problem, he used

| Hermann Ebbinghaus

Bettmann/Corbis

three-letter nonsense words, such as BAP, KEP, and DAK, which would be unfamiliar to him. Ebbinghaus's use of simple, unfamiliar nonsense words was a critical advance in the methodology for studying principles of human memory. In one of his experiments, Ebbinghaus read a list of 20 words out loud to himself, put away the list for a while, then tried to remember as many words as possible. Afterward, he checked which words he missed, reviewed the list, and tried again. He repeated this process until he could remember all 20 words from the original list. This experiment contains the four key stages of a memory experiment—learning, delay, test, relearning—that represented the basic methodology for human memory experiments for years to follow. Further examples of these kinds of studies will be discussed in Chapter 7, "Semantic and Episodic Memory: Memory for Facts and Events."

Ebbinghaus was especially interested in **forgetting,** that is, in how memory deteriorates over time. He measured forgetting by examining how long it took him to relearn a previously learned list. If it initially took him 10 minutes to learn the list and later took only 6 minutes to relearn the same list, Ebbinghaus recorded a "time savings" of 4 minutes, or 40% of the original learning time. By testing himself at various intervals after learning, Ebbinghaus was able to plot a **retention curve,** which measures how much information is retained at each point in time following learning. Figure 1.5 shows an example of this, graphing the percentage savings in time for relearning the list at various delays between the initial learning and relearning (Ebbinghaus, 1885/1913).

As you can see in Figure 1.5, there is a strong time savings (nearly 100%) if the delay between learning and relearning is short. But as the delay grows longer, to about 100 hours (approximately 4 days), the savings declines to 25%. The retention curve also illustrates that most forgetting occurs early on: if a memory can survive the first few hours after learning, there is little additional forgetting. Thus, Ebbinghaus showed a savings of 25% after 150 hours, and this dropped only to 20% after 750 hours. In other studies, Ebbinghaus showed that shorter lists were easier to remember than longer lists. He also demonstrated that increasing the amount of initial practice improved later recall.

In contrast to Galton's correlational studies of prayer, which examined the effects of prayer as it naturally occurred among members of society, Ebbinghaus designed and conducted experiments in which one variable factor, called the **independent variable,** was carefully manipulated (for example, the length of the delay between learning and relearning), and its effect on the factor under observation, the **dependent variable** (in his experiments, usually memory retention), was carefully measured. Through this design, Ebbinghaus was able to show how changes in the independent variable (e.g., delay length) determine changes in the dependent variable (e.g., memory retention).

The major limitation of Ebbinghaus's studies was that they were conducted with just one participant, Ebbinghaus himself. There are several reasons why such self-experimentation is problematic and would not meet modern scientific standards for research. First, what if Ebbinghaus's memory was different from most other people's? If so, the results of his experiments would tell us a lot about Ebbinghaus but would not be applicable to other people. For this reason, modern research on memory usually involves testing a large number of people.

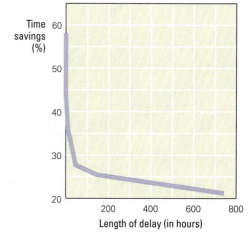

Length of delay (in hours)

Figure 1.5 Ebbinghaus's retention curve These experimental data show the percentage savings in time for relearning a list of words as a function of the delay between learning and relearning. Ebbinghaus's early study demonstrated that retention drops quickly in the first few days (up to about 100 hours for the task shown here) and then tapers off more slowly with increasing delays. Adapted from Ebbinghaus, 1885/1913.

Test Your Knowledge

Ebbinghaus and Galton's Contributions to Scientific Methodology

The impact of Galton's and Ebbinghaus's contributions to scientific methodology spread far beyond the boundaries of psychology and the study of learning and memory. Some of these contributions are described below. Fill in the blanks with the appropriate term or concept. (Answers appear in the Answers section in the back of the book.)

1. In a correlational study, Galton would distinguish between the _____, who received treatment based on the hypothesized effect of some variable, and the _____, who did not receive such treatment.

2. The ability of an experiment or study to confirm or disconfirm a hypothesis can be undermined by the presence of extraneous variables known as _____ .

3. Because Ebbinghaus was both the experimenter and subject in his experiments, his data were potentially compromised by both _____ and _____. In other words, he did not employ a _____ design.

A second problem is that, because he was the experimenter as well as the participant, Ebbinghaus knew which variables were being manipulated. If, for example, he believed that longer lists were harder to learn, then this belief might subtly influence him to take longer to learn those lists. This problem is sometimes called **subject bias.** To avoid such problems, modern studies of memory employ a **blind design,** which means that the participant does not know the hypothesis being tested or the variables being manipulated. There is also a corresponding problem of **experimenter bias,** which means that even a well-meaning experimenter might influence the outcome (for example, by implicitly encouraging the participant to respond in an expected manner). Experimenter bias can be avoided by use of a **double-blind design,** in which neither the participant nor the experimenter knows the hypothesis being tested. A common modern example of the double-blind strategy is its use to test experimental medications. Patients receive either the test drug or a **placebo** (an inactive pill that looks just like the real drug), and neither the patients nor the doctors know who is receiving which kind of pill; only the people analyzing the results (who never interact directly with the research participants) know which is which.

Despite the imperfections in his experimental designs, Ebbinghaus led the way in the use of scientific experimentation to study learning and memory. There are few studies of human memory conducted today that don't owe their methodology to the early and influential work of Hermann Ebbinghaus.

Ivan Pavlov's Conditioning Studies

While Ebbinghaus was revolutionizing the study of human memory, the Russian physiologist Ivan Pavlov (1849–1936) was developing methods for studying animal learning that are still in widespread use today. As a young man, Pavlov trained to be a Russian Orthodox priest, like his father and grandfather. In addition to his religious readings, Pavlov read Darwin's recently published *Origin of Species.* Inspired by Darwin's accomplishments,

| Ivan Pavlov

Science Photo Library

The Granger Collection, New York

(a)

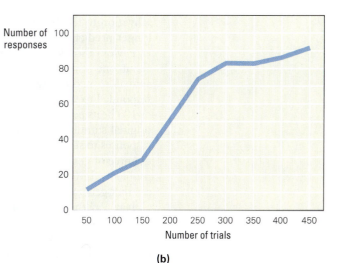

(b)

Pavlov abandoned his plan to become a priest and enrolled in the school of natural sciences at the University of St. Petersburg. For the rest of his life, Pavlov would acknowledge the enormous impact of Darwin's writings on his own career and thinking.

Although remembered today for his seminal contributions to the psychology of learning, Pavlov's 1904 Nobel Prize in Physiology or Medicine was awarded for his research on the physiology of salivation and digestion in dogs. As described in more detail in Chapter 4, "Classical Conditioning: Learning to Predict Important Events," Pavlov conducted a systematic study of the factors that influence how an animal learns. As illustrated in Figure 1.6a, he inserted surgical tubes (not shown) into the mouths of dogs to collect saliva and could then measure salivation in response to various cues. In one study, he began by training a dog to expect that the sound of a doorbell always preceded delivery of food; over many trials in which the sound of the doorbell was paired with food, the dog developed a stronger and stronger salivation response to the sound of the bell. This form of learning, in which an animal learns that one stimulus (in this case, a doorbell) predicts an upcoming important event (in this case, delivery of food), is known today as **classical conditioning** (or Pavlovian conditioning). Modern studies of classical conditioning usually report the results as a **learning curve**, like that shown in Figure 1.6b, which plots the number of training trials (the independent variable, plotted on the horizontal axis) against the animal's response (the dependent variable, plotted on the vertical axis).

Pavlov's view of how an animal learns a new behavioral response was based on an analogy to what at the time was a new technology that had recently been introduced in Russia: the telephone. As Pavlov explained it, he could call his lab from home via a *direct* private line, which was a fixed connection, much like the fixed connection between food and salivation in a dog's brain. Alternatively, he could call his lab by going through an *indirect* pathway, via a switchboard operator, creating a modifiable connection, much like the newly learned connection between the bell and the dog's salivation (Pavlov, 1927).

In other studies, Pavlov and his assistants showed that they could also *weaken* an animal's trained response to the bell. This was done by first pairing the bell with food, until the animal had learned to salivate to the bell, and then pairing the bell with the absence of food. Pavlov called this process **extinction:** the

Figure 1.6 Pavlov and learning experiments (a) Pavlov (with white beard) and his assistants in the laboratory. A restrained dog has a surgical tube (not shown here) inserted into its mouth to collect and measure salivation in response to meat placed in front of it or to a cue such as a doorbell, which predicts delivery of the food. (b) A learning curve from a modern study of classical conditioning. The curve plots the number of training trials (the independent variable) against the animal's conditioned response (the dependent variable).

salivation to the bell gradually decreased as the animal learned that the bell no longer predicted food.

Pavlov also demonstrated that an animal will transfer what it has learned about one stimulus to similar stimuli. For example, he observed that once an animal learned to respond to a metronome ticking at 90 beats per minute, it also responded to similar sounds, such as a metronome ticking at 80 beats per minute or 100 beats per minute. However, the more dissimilar the new stimulus was to the original stimulus, the less intense was the dog's salivation response. These graded responses to stimuli of varying dissimilarity to the original training stimulus are an example of **generalization,** the ability to transfer past learning to novel events and problems. In Chapter 6, "Generalization and Discrimination Learning," you will see that generalization occurs in many different forms of learning and memory.

Ivan Pavlov lived through the Russian Revolution of 1917, developing a deep animosity toward the new Communist regime (especially after it stole his Nobel Prize money). Nevertheless, when Pavlov died, in 1936, he was given an elaborate funeral with full honors as a hero of the Soviet state.

Edward Thorndike and the Law of Effect

Meanwhile, over in the United States, Edward Thorndike (1874–1949), a student of William James, was studying how animals learn the relationship or connection between a stimulus and a behavioral response that leads to a desirable outcome. Some of Thorndike's most influential studies involved how cats learn to escape from puzzle boxes—cages secured with complex locking (and unlocking) devices. Thorndike called this kind of training, in which organisms learn to make responses in order to obtain or avoid important consequences, **instrumental conditioning,** because the organism's behavior is instrumental in determining whether the consequences occur. This is in contrast, for example, to the learned response (salivation) of Pavlov's dogs, in which the dogs received their food reward regardless of whether or not they made the learned response. Instrumental conditioning, now more commonly referred to as **operant conditioning,** is the focus of Chapter 5, "Operant Conditioning: Learning the Outcome of Behaviors."

| **Edward Thorndike**

In his studies, Thorndike observed that the probability of a particular behavioral response increased or decreased depending on the consequences that followed. He called this the **law of effect** (Thorndike, 1911). If a particular response led to a desirable consequence, such as access to food, then the probability of the animal making that response in the future *increased*. On the other hand, if the response led to an undesirable consequence (say, an electric shock), then the probability of the animal making that response in the future *decreased*. Fascinated, Thorndike began to methodically investigate the factors that influence how an animal learns new behaviors to maximize its chances of obtaining desirable consequences and avoiding undesirable ones.

Like many psychologists of his era, Thorndike was strongly influenced by Charles Darwin's theory of natural selection. The basic idea of Thorndike's law of effect has much in common with Darwin's principle of survival of the fittest. In Darwin's theory of evolution, variability in traits was key: animals possessing an inherited trait that increases the likelihood of survival pass it on to future generations. Thorndike's law of effect applied the same principle to explain how behaviors evolve during an animal's lifetime. According to the law of effect, an animal has a range of behaviors: those behaviors that lead to positive consequences for the animal tend to persist; those that do not tend to die out. Starting from this basic principle, Thorndike argued that the psychology of learning should center on the search for the rules describing how, when, and to what degree connections among stimuli and responses are increased or decreased through experience (Thorndike, 1932, 1949).

In 1917, Thorndike became the first psychologist elected to the prestigious U.S. National Academy of Sciences, and in the early 1920s he was often identified as one of the most influential scientists in the United States. He died in 1949, the last of the pioneers in experimental psychology of learning and memory. Thorndike's work set the stage for the next major movement in learning research: the behaviorists of the mid-twentieth century.

Interim Summary

- With the emergence of experimental psychology in the late 1800s, the study of learning and memory, as well as other branches of psychology, began to be employ experiments designed to test specific hypotheses. Many of the central figures in this movement were strongly influenced by Charles Darwin's recent work on evolution and natural selection.

- Hermann Ebbinghaus conducted the first rigorous experimental studies of human memory. He introduced the technique of studying lists of short nonsense words and collected data on how information is retained and forgotten.

- Ivan Pavlov discovered a basic method for training animals to associate a previously neutral stimulus, such as a bell, with a naturally significant stimulus, such as food.

- Edward Thorndike showed that the probability of an animal making a behavioral response increases or decreases depending on the consequences that follow. He called this principle the law of effect. It was analogous to Darwin's idea of survival of the fittest: those responses that produce the most beneficial effects survive, while others die out.

Test Your Knowledge

Who's Who in the History of Learning and Memory?

Below is a (slightly tongue-in-cheek) review of the major researchers and ideas covered in the first three sections of this chapter. See if you can fill in the blanks with the names of the researchers. (Answers appear in the Answers section in the back of the book.)

1. Old _____ was a Greek
   Who thought about association.
   _____, the dualist, liked to speak
   Of mind-and-body separation.

2. To _____, a baby's mind was blank,
   As all empiricists have said.
   Nativists called him a crank,
   Believing knowledge is inbred.

3. _____'s models of the mind
   Had features linked together,
   Updating Greeks from ancient times
   And going them one better.

4. _____ thought all beasts
   Evolved toward perfection.
   His grandson proposed the means,
   called natural selection.

5. _____ now is known
   For championing eugenics
   But we should also note it down:
   He pioneered statistics.

6. _____ learned nonsense words;
   Dogs learned to drool for _____ .
   _____ studied food rewards
   (And coined "effect, the law of").

1.4 The Reign of Behaviorism

In the 1920s, an American approach to learning emerged that was called **behaviorism.** Building on the work of Pavlov and Thorndike, it argued that psychology should restrict itself to the study of observable behaviors (such as lever presses, salivation, and other measurable physical actions) and avoid reference to unobservable, and often ill-defined, internal mental events (such as consciousness, intent, and thought). Proponents of this approach, who were called *behaviorists*, wanted to distance themselves from philosophers and psychologists who explored the inner workings of the mind through personal introspection and anecdotal observation. Behaviorists wanted psychology to be taken seriously as a rigorous branch of natural science, no less solid than biology or chemistry.

John Watson's Behaviorism

Brash, ambitious, and self-made, John Watson (1878–1958) is considered the founder of behaviorism. He was born in Greenville, South Carolina, to a ne'er-do-well father who abandoned the family when Watson was 13 years old. Although a poor student as a child, Watson not only finished college but went on to graduate school, where he conducted research on how rats learn. In these studies, Watson placed a rat at the entrance to a maze and rewarded it with food if it found its way through the corridors to the exit.

Underwood & Underwood/Corbis

| John Watson

Initially, a "naive" (i.e., untrained) rat might spend half an hour wandering randomly through the maze until it reached the exit. After 30 training trials, however, the rat could traverse the maze in less than 10 seconds. To find out what drove the rat's performance, Watson systematically eliminated various possibilities. First, he trained rats to run through the maze under normal conditions. Then he surgically blinded the rats, or rendered them deaf, or removed their whiskers (which rats use like fingertips to feel their way). None of these treatments impaired the rats' performance. Thinking the rats might be using olfactory cues to find their way, Watson boiled the mazes to eliminate all odors. The rats still found their way through. Only when the maze was rotated or when the corridors were made shorter or longer did the rats show a significant loss in their ability to navigate the maze. From these studies, Watson argued that the rats had learned an automatic set of motor habits for moving through the maze and that these motor habits were largely independent of any external sensory cues (Watson, 1907). Such learned motor habits, or skills, are discussed further in Chapter 8, "Skill Memory: Learning by Doing."

Watson's experiments were widely admired by his scientific colleagues. Unfortunately, the reception in the popular press was not so enthusiastic. The media described Watson as a cruel torturer of animals, and he was threatened with criminal prosecution (Dewsbury, 1990). When the anti-vivisectionist (pro–animal rights) *Journal of Zoophily* reported, incorrectly, that Watson planned to do similar studies on humans, an even greater outcry ensued. Watson's department chair defended him by pointing out that the surgeries were all done under antiseptic conditions, with the animal anesthetized and with a minimum of pain.

The tension between animal rights activists and psychological researchers continues to this day. In contrast to Watson's era, when there were few constraints on animal research, studies today are strictly controlled by government agencies and professional organizations to ensure that all experimental animals are handled as humanely as possible. Before any experiment can be conducted, the researchers must seek approval from their institution's ethics board, a committee composed of scientists and lay members of the community, and describe the measures that will be taken to minimize the animals' pain or suffering. Researchers conducting studies on humans are subject to additional ethical scrutiny to ensure protection of participants' rights, privacy, and safety. Only if the ethics board approves the procedures can the research begin. In Watson's day, though, such ethical considerations were left largely to the discretion of the researcher.

According to Watson, psychology should be viewed as a "purely objective experimental branch of natural science. Its theoretical goal is the prediction and control of behavior" (Watson, 1913). Watson was a strong empiricist, sharing Locke's belief in the overwhelming influence of experience (nurture) versus heredity (nature) in determining our behaviors and capabilities. In a rousing affirmation of Aristotle's principle of the blank slate, Watson wrote: "Give me a dozen healthy infants, well-formed, and my own specified world to bring them up in, and I'll guarantee to take any one at random and train him to become any type of specialist I might select—doctor, lawyer, artist, merchant, chief, and yes even beggarman and thief, regardless of the talents, penchants, tendencies, abilities, vocations, and race of his ancestors" (Watson, 1924, p. 82). In the years following World War I, many people hoped for a new dawn of equal opportunity and freedom from class-based constraints on social progress. Watson's bold claims had a strong appeal for scientists and the wider public. By the early 1920s, behaviorism had become the predominant approach to the psychology of learning, especially in the United States.

Watson's career as an academic researcher came to a sudden end when he became involved in a relationship with his research assistant, Rosalie Rayner. Given Watson's fame as a scientist, his status as a married man, and Rayner's socially prominent family, the affair received intense media scrutiny. In the end, the scandal grew so great that Johns Hopkins University gave Watson a choice between ending his affair or resigning from his position at the university. Choosing to stay with Rayner, Watson resigned from Johns Hopkins and started a successful career in advertising, where he applied the same strict scientific principles to marketing research as to his earlier experiments. In spite of this controversy, the American Psychological Association honored him, soon before his death in 1958, with a gold medal for lifetime contributions to the field of psychology.

Clark Hull and Mathematical Models of Learning

Born on a farm near Akron, Ohio, Clark Hull (1884–1952) devoted his career to developing mathematical equations to describe the relationships among the factors that influence learning. Hull's early life was marked by life-threatening illness. He survived an attack of typhoid fever but sustained lasting brain damage, which caused memory difficulties that plagued him for the rest of his life. He also survived a bout of polio that left him paralyzed in one leg and dependent on crutches to walk.

In Hull's day, the new doctrine of behaviorism claimed that all behavior could be understood as a set of connections between stimuli and responses. When Pavlov's dogs heard the doorbell, they salivated (doorbell → salivation); when Watson's rats entered the maze, they made a series of motor-habit responses (maze entry → turn left, turn right, and so on). Such learning is often called *stimulus-response learning*, abbreviated as *S-R learning*. Of course,

Courtesy of Ernest Hilgard

Clark Hull (standing with visor) and his young graduate student **Ernest Hilgard** (seated) in a study of Pavlovian conditioning at Yale University in the 1920s. Hull trained Hilgard to blink in anticipation of a slap to the face. The slaps did not dissuade Hilgard from going on to a long and productive career in learning research.

the behaviorists acknowledged that the real world is complicated and that other factors might affect the response. For example, Pavlov's dogs might salivate to the doorbell only if they were hungry. Still, the behaviorists believed that if you could specify all the existing factors, you ought to be able to predict exactly whether and when a stimulus would provoke an animal to make a response.

Hull set himself the goal of developing a comprehensive mathematical model of animal learning that would predict exactly what an animal will learn in any given situation. Much as Einstein had recently shown that a single equation, $E = mc^2$, could explain the complex relationship between energy (E), mass (m), and the speed of light (c), Hull hoped to find a similarly powerful equation to relate all the key factors contributing to a learning experience. The variables that Hull entered into his equations included the number of learning trials, the frequency of reward, the spacing between trials, the intensity of the stimulus cues, the animal's motivation for reward, and the incentive value (desirability) of the reward (Hull, 1943). Hull conducted an intensive program of research on learning in animals and humans, seeking to test and refine his mathematical models. One measure of a model's value is its ability to serve as a basis for experimental research; in this regard, Hull's model was a great success. By the 1940s, Hull's work was cited in 70% of all scientific papers on learning published in the major journals (Spence, 1952).

Although Hull's equations were influential in their time, their specifics are no longer considered relevant today. Hull's models have been abandoned because modern psychologists have despaired of ever being able to reduce all the factors governing learning into a single equation, as Hull had hoped to do. Nevertheless, Hull's many students and followers (often called neo-Hullians) carried on toward a smaller goal: to develop mathematical equations to describe basic kinds or components of learning. (You will read in Chapter 4, "Classical Conditioning: Learning to Predict Important Events," about one of the most enduring neo-Hullian learning theories: the Rescorla-Wagner rule, which describes some of the factors governing classical conditioning, like the learning in Pavlov's dogs.) Neo-Hullian researchers showed that learning indeed follows reliable, predictable patterns and pointed the way toward an understanding of how the same basic patterns govern learning in humans as in other animals.

B. F. Skinner's Radical Behaviorism

Burrhus Frederic Skinner (1904–1990), born in rural Pennsylvania, became the most famous—and perhaps most infamous—behaviorist of the twentieth century. Although his original goal was to be a writer, Skinner instead went to graduate school in psychology. He placed himself squarely in the behaviorist camp, believing that psychologists should limit themselves to the study of observable behaviors and not try to speculate about what is going on in the mind of an animal while it learns.

In research that extended and refined the techniques Thorndike had developed to study how animals learn new responses, Skinner developed an automated learning apparatus that was widely adopted by others, who dubbed it the "Skinner box" (you'll read more about this and Skinner's other innovations in Chapter 5, "Operant Conditioning: Learning the Outcome of Behaviors"). He also made many important contributions to our understanding of how animals learn the relationship between responses and consequences. One of the most important happened by accident.

In the early 1940s, Skinner was in his laboratory on a Friday afternoon, setting up some studies in which he taught rats to perform a response in order to obtain food pellets. He realized he didn't have enough food pellets to get him through all the experiments planned for that weekend. Rather than cancel the experiments or go out and get more rat food, Skinner decided to save pellets by providing food only after the rats made two or three correct responses in a row. This led Skinner to one of his greatest discoveries: when trained with intermittent reinforcements, rats learn to respond as quickly and as frequently as when they are rewarded on every trial—in fact, sometimes even better. Skinner and his students began a massive new program of research on how learning is affected by the reliability with which an organism's responses result in consequences (such as obtaining a food pellet).

| **B. F. Skinner**

Today, B. F. Skinner's name is far better known than Watson's or Thorndike's because his influence extended beyond the laboratory. Fulfilling his early ambition of becoming a writer, Skinner wrote several popular books, including *Walden Two* (1948), which described a highly regulated utopian society in which socially desirable behaviors would be maintained through the same kind of training regimens Skinner applied to his pigeons and rats. In another best-selling book, *Beyond Freedom and Dignity* (1971), Skinner advocated an extreme form of behaviorism, often called **radical behaviorism,** in which he asserted that consciousness and free will are illusions. Humans, like all other animals, he argued, function by blindly producing pre-programmed (learned) responses to environmental stimuli. By the middle of the twentieth century, Skinner was the most famous psychologist in the world. Skinner continued promoting radical behaviorism right up until the night of his death in 1990, which he spent working on a talk for an upcoming convention. The talk was to be titled "Can Psychology Be a Science of the Mind?" (His answer, of course, was a resounding no!) But by that time, mainstream psychology had moved past the strict confines of behaviorism to focus on the very mental events that Skinner and his fellow behaviorists had fought so hard to discredit.

The Neo-Behaviorism of Edward Tolman

As a college student at the Massachusetts Institute of Technology (MIT), Edward Tolman (1886–1959) originally planned to pursue a career in chemistry. However, during his senior year he read William James's *Principles of Psychology* and was so inspired that he decided instead to pursue a graduate degree in psychology.

Tolman began building a series of rat mazes for the study of learning, much as Thorndike and Watson had done before him. In contrast to Watson, who had argued for a purely mechanical approach that described rat learning as the formation of connections between stimuli and responses, Tolman was convinced his rats were learning something more. He believed they had goals and intentions, such as the goal of finding the exit and seeking food. Rats, he argued,

| **Edward Tolman**

are intrinsically motivated to learn the general layout of mazes by forming what he called a **cognitive map,** an internal psychological representation of the spatial layout of the external world (Tolman, 1948). "Behavior reeks of purpose" was Tolman's well-known and oft-repeated maxim (Tolman, 1932).

In one series of studies, Tolman showed the value of cognitive maps for understanding how rats can apply what they have learned in novel situations. Rats, he showed, are able to find food in mazes by using alternative routes if their preferred route is blocked, as shown in Figure 1.7 (Tolman, 1948). They can also find their way to the goal if they are started from a novel position in the maze rather than the usual starting point. None of this could be explained by the learning of simple stimulus-response connections.

Tolman even showed that rats can form cognitive maps in the absence of any explicit reward (such as food). He allowed some rats to freely explore a maze (like the one in Figure 1.7), with no food in it, for several days. Later, when he placed these rats in the maze with a food reward at one point ("Goal box"), the rats learned to find the food much faster than rats not previously exposed to the maze and almost as fast as rats that had been explicitly trained to find the food in the goal box. These studies are described in more detail in Chapter 3, "Habituation, Sensitization, and Familiarization: Learning about Repeated Events" (see especially Figure 3.6). This, Tolman argued, showed that during their free exploration, the rats were learning a cognitive map that they could exploit later. He called this **latent learning,** meaning learning that takes place even when there is no specific motivation to obtain or avoid a specific consequence, such as food or shock (Tolman, 1932). Tolman argued that such latent learning is a natural part of our everyday life. The idea of latent learning challenged a strict

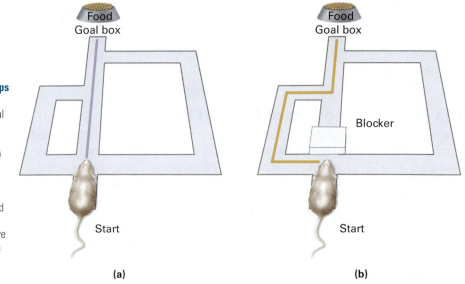

Figure 1.7 Cognitive maps in rats Tolman believed that rats form cognitive maps, internal representations of the layout of the world. (a) In one experiment, rats placed in a maze (at "Start") learned to run directly to a box ("Goal box") where food was provided; the purple line shows the rats' route. (b) If the preferred route was blocked, rats could easily find an effective alternative route (orange line); this indicates that they had information about the spatial layout of the maze.

(a)

(b)

behaviorist assumption that all learning reflects stimulus-response associations. Further discussion of the latent learning that results from exposure to places or events can be found in Chapter 3. The effects of latent learning that results from prior exposure to stimuli are discussed both in Chapter 3 and in Chapter 6, "Generalization and Discrimination Learning."

At a time when Clark Hull and other theorists were seeking to discover fundamental principles of behavior that avoided any mention of unobservable mental events, Tolman took a different approach. Emphasizing the importance of internal representations of the environment and utilizing concepts such as purpose and intent that are not directly observable, only inferred, Tolman broke away from the stricter confines of behaviorist dogma, all the while satisfying the behaviorists' high standards of experimental control and methodological rigor. For this reason, Tolman is often referred to as a *neo-behaviorist*. His influential theoretical and experimental research—though at odds with many of his behaviorist contemporaries—laid the foundation for cognitive studies of animal and human learning.

Interim Summary

- Behaviorists argue that psychologists should study only observable events and should not attempt to speculate about what's going on inside an organism. Behaviorism doesn't deny that internal mental processes exist, just that they are unnecessary and inappropriate subjects for the scientific study of behavior.

- John Watson, the father of behaviorism, proposed that psychology should be a purely experimental branch of natural science whose goal is the prediction and control of behavior in both animals and humans.

- The comprehensive mathematical theories of animal and human learning developed by Clark Hull could be rigorously tested in experimental studies.

- B. F. Skinner conducted detailed studies of the factors that control behavior while at the same time taking the behaviorists' message to the broader public through widely read and controversial books.

- Edward Tolman, a neo-behaviorist, combined the scientific rigor of the behaviorist methodology with consideration of internal mental events such as goals and cognitive maps of the environment.

1.5 The Cognitive Approach

The behaviorist approach to learning had great appeal. It was rigorous, precise, and amenable to mathematical specification. By avoiding vague and unverifiable suppositions, it offered the promise that psychology would rise in the twentieth century to the status of a serious branch of science, alongside chemistry and physics. However, by the mid-1950s, there was a growing consensus that behaviorism could not, ultimately, deliver a full account of the complexities of human behavior (and probably was insufficient to understand all of animal behavior as well). As you have just read, it failed to account for Tolman's studies of rats and their cognitive maps. It also failed to explain language, perception, reasoning, and memory, the fundamental components of higher-level human cognition.

Skinner, the radical behaviorist, had argued that language and language acquisition could be explained with behaviorist principles, as a (complex) series of stimulus-response associations (B. F. Skinner, 1957). To counter these claims, linguist Noam Chomsky wrote what may be the most influential book review ever published in the sciences: a critique of Skinner's book, demonstrating how and why behaviorist principles alone could not explain how children acquire complex aspects of language such as grammar and syntax (Chomsky, 1959). By the early 1960s, many psychologists interested in human cognition began to turn away from behaviorism, with its focus on animal research and the idea that all learning could be reduced to a series of stimulus-response associations. The stage was set for the rise of **cognitive psychology,** a new subfield of psychology that focused on human abilities such as thinking, language, and reasoning—the abilities not easily explained by a strictly behaviorist approach.

George Estes

| **W. K. Estes**

W. K. Estes and Mathematical Psychology

William K. Estes (1919-2011) had a long and productive career that encompassed the science of learning and memory from behaviorism to **cognitive science,** the interdisciplinary study of thought, reasoning, and other higher mental functions. Estes, born in 1919, began his graduate studies under the tutelage of Skinner during the early 1940s. As you will read in Chapter 4, "Classical Conditioning: Learning to Predict Important Events," Estes and Skinner developed a new method for studying classical "Pavlovian" conditioning of fear in rats. Within a few years, their method became one of the most widely used techniques for studying animal conditioning, and it is still in use today. In Chapter 10, "Emotional Influences on Learning and Memory," you will read that learning about emotions, such as fear, has become an important subfield of learning and memory research.

As soon as he completed his PhD, Estes was called into military service. He was stationed in the Philippines as the commandant of a prisoner-of-war camp—an undemanding job that gave him lots of free time to read the mathematics books his wife sent from home. When the war ended, Estes returned to the United States and to the study of psychology. Much to Skinner's dismay, Estes soon began to stray from his mentor's strict behaviorism. He began to use mathematics to describe mental events that could only be inferred indirectly from behavioral data, an approach quite unacceptable to behaviorists. Years later, in his autobiography, Skinner bemoaned the loss of Estes as a once-promising behaviorist, speculating that Estes's preoccupation with mathematical models of unobservable mental events was a war-related injury, resulting perhaps from too much time in the hot Pacific sun (Skinner, 1979).

Estes built on Hull's mathematical modeling approach to develop new methods for interpreting a wide variety of learning behaviors (Estes, 1950). Most learning theorists of that era, including Hull, assumed that learning should be viewed as the development of associations between a stimulus and a response. For example, suppose that a pigeon is trained to peck whenever it sees a yellow light, in order to obtain a bit of food. Hull assumed that this training caused the formation of a direct link between the stimulus and the response, so that later presentations of the yellow light evoked the peck-for-food response (Figure 1.8a).

Estes, however, suggested that what seems to be a single stimulus, say a yellow light, is really a collection of many different possible elements making up the yellow light, only a random subset of which are noticed (or "sampled," in Estes's terminology) on any given training trial (Figure 1.8b). Only those elements sampled on the current trial are associated with the food. On a different

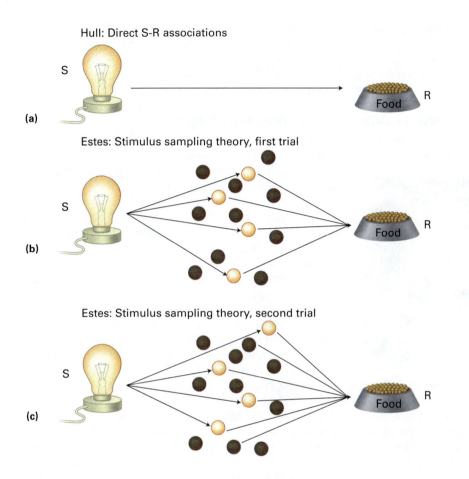

Hull: Direct S-R associations

(a)

S

Food R

Estes: Stimulus sampling theory, first trial

(b)

S

Food R

Estes: Stimulus sampling theory, second trial

(c)

S

Food R

Figure 1.8 Stimulus-response models How does a stimulus (S) become associated with a response (R)? (a) Hull assumed that a direct link was formed between a stimulus (such as a yellow light) and a learned response (such as, in pigeons, pecking for food). (b) Estes proposed an intervening stage, in which a stimulus activates a random sample of elements encoding "yellow"; the activated elements are then associated with the response. (c) On a different trial, a different random subset of elements are activated by the stimulus and associated with the response. Over time, with many such random samples, most elements that could potentially be activated by the stimulus become associated with the response. At this point, when a random sample of elements are activated by presentation of the light, most of them are already linked with the response.

trial, a different subset is sampled (Figure 1.8c), and those elements are now associated with the food. Over time, after many such random samples, most of the elements of the stimulus become associated with the correct response. At this point, any presentation of the light activates a random sample of elements, most of which are already linked with the response.

Estes called his idea *stimulus sampling theory*. A key principle is that random variation ("sampling") is essential for learning, much as it is essential for the adaptation of species in Charles Darwin's theory of evolution through natural selection (Estes, 1950). Estes's approach gave a much better account than other theories (such as Hull's) of the variability seen in both animal and human learning, and it helped to explain why even highly trained individuals don't always make the same response perfectly every time: on any given trial, it's always possible that (through sheer randomness) a subset of elements will be activated that are not yet linked to the response. In Chapter 6, "Generalization and Discrimination Learning," you will see how Estes's stimulus sampling theory also explains how animals generalize their learning from one stimulus (e.g., a yellow light) to other, physically similar stimuli (e.g., an orange light), as Pavlov had demonstrated back in the 1920s.

Estes's work marked the resurgence of mathematical methods in psychology, reviving the spirit of Hull's earlier efforts. Estes and his colleagues established a new subdiscipline of psychology, **mathematical psychology,** which uses mathematical equations to describe the laws of learning and memory. From his early work in animal conditioning, through his founding role in mathematical psychology, to his later contributions to cognitive psychology, Estes continued to be a vigorous proponent of mathematical models to inform our understanding of learning and memory. He died in 2011, following a long struggle with Parkinson's disease, a neurological disorder which destroys the brain cells required to learn new habits, and severely impairs movement (see Chapters 5 and 8).

Gordon Bower: Learning by Insight

Gordon Bower was born in 1932 in Scio, Ohio, a small town struggling to survive the Great Depression. Inspired by the movie *The Lou Gehrig Story*, Bower resolved at the age of eight to become a professional baseball player. After playing varsity baseball in college, he had two career choices: professional baseball or graduate school in psychology. Although tempted by the former, Bower figured he had a better chance of long-term success in psychology than in baseball. In graduate school at Yale, Bower got caught up in the heady excitement of mathematical psychology and the efforts of Estes and other mathematical psychologists to describe behavior through mathematical equations.

Gordon Bower (seated) and his graduate adviser **Neal Miller** conduct a rat learning experiment at Yale University in the 1950s.

The dominant psychological learning theories of the time assumed that human learning, like animal learning, proceeded gradually through incremental changes either in association strengths (the Hull approach) or in the statistical probability of a correct response (the Estes approach), both of which predicted gradual transitions in learning performance. In contrast, Bower proposed a new "one-step" model of some human learning. If you've ever solved a difficult puzzle or word game, you may have experienced an "aha" moment of insight: Initially, you don't know the answer; then, all of a sudden, you do know it. Unlike the smooth, incremental learning curves seen in classical conditioning, some learning is experienced as a transition from ignorance to knowledge in a single trial.

Although behaviorists had largely avoided talking about learning by insight, Bower thought it could be explained by a simple mathematical model (Bower, 1961; Bower & Trabasso, 1968). Suppose a person is assigned some task, such as figuring out the sequence in which to press four buttons to open a combination lock. In the beginning, he has no knowledge of the correct answer, but on each trial he will probably try out a different sequence. Odds are that it will take a few trials before he happens to try the correct order. But once he does, and he opens the lock—aha!—he knows the answer. Thereafter, he will press the correct sequence on all subsequent trials. Unlike the smooth learning curve shown in Figure 1.6b, this person's learning curve would look like the one in Figure 1.9a: a long period of 0% correct responding that transitions all at once into a period of 100% correct responding.

The problem, however, is that most psychologists report *average* learning curves for a group of people, summarizing the data from many participants in the same experiment. Bower's important insight was that if every participant solves the task in one insightful moment, the trial on which this occurs will vary from one person to another. One participant might learn on the fifth trial, another might get lucky and guess the correct answer on the first or second trial, and someone else might not guess the correct answer until the 15th trial. If a large number of participants are tested, the data will show that almost no one responds correctly on the first or second trial, a few respond correctly on the third or fourth trial, a few more respond correctly on the trials after that,

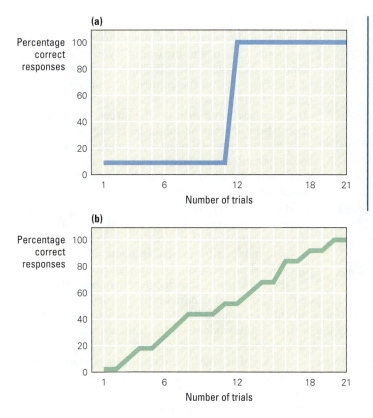

(a)

(b)

Figure 1.9 Bower's learning by insight If individuals are assigned a task and have no knowledge of the correct answer, they may start off by guessing, stumble across the correct answer, and from then on respond correctly. (a) One participant might guess incorrectly on each of the first 11 trials, making 0% correct responses, and then on trial 12 make the correct response. Thereafter, he continues to give the correct response (100% correct from trial 13 onward). Other participants might make their first correct response on a different trial, but all would show the same basic pattern of an early period of incorrect responding followed by a sharp shift to uniformly correct responding. (b) If individual performances like that in (a) are averaged across many individuals, the result may be a smooth learning curve—even though no single participant showed such incremental learning.

and so on, until, by the end of the experiment, almost everyone is giving the correct response. If we graph the percentage of subjects who give the correct response on each trial of the combination-lock task, the result will look very much like a standard learning curve that moves incrementally from 0 to 100% in the course of the experiment (Figure 1.9b), even though no *individual* participant ever showed incremental learning! By studying such phenomena, Bower showed that to understand learning, it is necessary to consider individual performance, not just averages across a large group of participants. Some other studies that show similar one-trial learning of skills are discussed in Chapter 8, "Skill Memory: Learning by Doing."

Bower's influence on the field of memory research stems not only from his own research but also from his role as a prolific educator and mentor to young psychologists, many of whom went on to play major roles in the growing field of cognitive psychology.

George Miller and Information Theory

Estes and Bower were not the only investigators becoming disillusioned with the strict confines of the behaviorist approach. Other psychologists too began to seek explanations for observations that could not be explained by the assumption of an incrementally learned association between stimulus and response. One of these was George Miller (1920–2012), another child of the Depression era, who grew up in Charleston, West Virginia.

During World War II, many of Harvard's faculty worked on problems for the military. As a graduate student at Harvard, Miller was given the task of designing a jamming signal to disrupt German radio communications. This wartime research on spoken communications led Miller to study other questions of

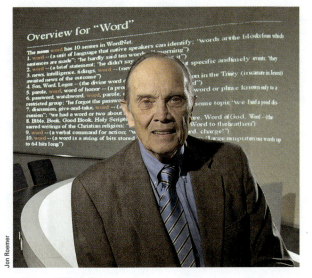

| George Miller

speech perception, such as how context affects communication. For example, if a man floundering in the sea shouts, "Help, I'm drowning!" you might understand the message easily, even if the speech is garbled or indistinct—given the context, it's obvious what the man is trying to communicate. On the other hand, if you meet the same man on the street, with no prior expectation of what he might be trying to communicate, his speech would need to be much clearer for you to understand the message: is he greeting you, asking for directions, telling you your shoelaces are untied, or soliciting money?

While puzzling over this, Miller read a paper that described *information theory*, a mathematical theory of communication that provides a precise measure of how much information is contained in a message, based not only on the message itself but also on the listener's prior knowledge (Shannon, 1948). For example, if a friend tells you that Chris, a student in his psychology class, is male, how much information is in the message? That depends on what you already know. If you already know that all the students in his class are male, then the message contains no new information. If, however, you know that the class is co-ed, information theory would say that your friend's message contains 1 *bit* of information, where a bit is a "binary digit," 1 or 0, that can represent two alternative states (such as 1 = female, 0 = male). If you ask your friend about Chris's gender, all he has to do is reply "1" (female) or "0" (male)—a message composed of a single bit of information is all the answer you need.

Miller's goal was to adapt information theory to psychology. Specifically, could information theory help us understand how people make judgments about the magnitude of various stimuli? How bright is it? How loud? How high in pitch? Miller discovered that people's capacity to make judgments concerning magnitude across a range was limited to about seven alternative values (this is why many rating scales ask you to rate your opinions on a scale of 1 to 7, such as a survey that asks you to rate your satisfaction with a new product from 1, not satisfied, to 7, totally satisfied).

At the same time, Miller was conducting a seemingly unrelated project to measure the capacity of people's short-term memory for digits: he would read aloud strings of numbers and ask people to repeat the numbers from memory. Most people, Miller found, could accurately repeat strings of up to 5 to 9 numbers, but almost no one could remember strings of 10 or more digits. The average memory capacity for numbers (sometimes called a *digit span*) seemed to be about 7 digits, plus or minus 2.

Noting that a capacity of seven appeared in both projects—magnitude rating and digit span—Miller used this seemingly superficial connection as the humorous title of a paper that summarized both projects: "The Magical Number Seven, Plus or Minus Two" (Miller, 1956). The paper became one of the most influential and oft-cited papers in cognitive psychology and spurred later research that showed similar limits on the capacity of human memory for other kinds of information: the "magic number seven" applied not just to digits but to words, pictures, and even complex ideas. Miller's central message was that the human mind is limited in capacity, that information theory provides a way to measure this capacity, and that these limits apply to a diverse range of human capabilities. Our working memory capacity and capabilities are the focus of Chapter 9, "Working Memory and Cognitive Control."

The LNR (Lindsay-Normal-Rumelhart) research group at the University of California, San Diego, in the early 1970s with **Peter Lindsay, Donald Norman,** and **David Rumelhart** in the front row (left to right) holding the flag. The group was at the forefront of research on the symbol-manipulation models of cognition, leading to their book, *Explorations in Cognition*, which applied this framework to perception, language, and memory. Later, Rumelhart grew dissatisfied with the limits of symbolic models and was instrumental in creating more brainlike parallel-distributed processing (PDP) models of cognition.

Karl Rumelhart

The Connectionist Models of David Rumelhart

David Rumelhart (1942–2011), born in rural South Dakota, was the first of his family to graduate from college. As a graduate student working under Estes, Rumelhart acquired a firm grounding in both psychology and mathematics. He began to apply the tools of mathematics to a wide range of problems in cognition and perception, hoping to improve on the cognitive models in vogue at the time. By the late 1970s, Rumelhart and his colleague James McClelland shared a growing belief that cognition was best understood as networks of connections between simple processing units that in their theory were called *nodes*. Borrowing a term from Thorndike (who had thought much the same), Rumelhart and McClelland called such networks **connectionist models** (Rumelhart & McClelland, 1986).

In connectionist models, ideas and concepts in the external world are not represented as distinct and discrete symbols but rather as patterns of activity over populations of many nodes. In a connectionist model, a golden retriever might be represented by a pattern of activation across a set of nodes (the orange circles in Figure 1.10a). A cocker spaniel might be represented by a different pattern of nodes (blue circles in Figure 1.10b). Such a representation is known as a **distributed representation,** because the information consists of the activation of many different nodes—that is, it is "distributed" across many nodes rather than represented by only one—in a process similar to what Estes had proposed in his stimulus sampling theory. In a connectionist model, the similarity of spaniels to retrievers emerges because they activate common elements—the "dog" elements coded as orange-and-blue circles in Figure 1.10c. The importance of distributed representations and shared elements is discussed in more detail in Chapter 6, "Generalization and Discrimination Learning."

Connectionist models were inspired in part by ideas about how the brain is organized (see Chapter 2, "The Neuroscience of Learning and Memory"). Part of the expectation held for connectionist models was that they would fulfill William James's hope for a psychology that links brain physiology to behavior. Connectionist models laid the groundwork for a more complete integration of neuroscience with psychology, a goal that is also a core theme of this book.

Figure 1.10 Distributed representations (a) The representation of "golden retriever" activates one subset of nodes, shown in orange. (b) "Cocker spaniel" activates a different subset, shown in blue. (c) The similarity between them—both are dogs—emerges naturally as a function of the overlap between representations, shown by the orange-and-blue nodes.

(a) "Golden retriever"

(b) "Cocker spaniel"

(c) "Dog"

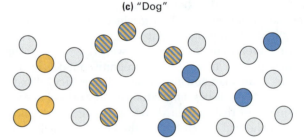

After many productive years helping psychologists understand the computational power of networks of brain connections, David Rumelhart's own brain networks began to fail him. In 1998, at the age of 56, he was diagnosed with Pick's disease, an illness (similar to Alzheimer's disease) that causes degeneration of the brain. For the last years of his life, until he died in 2011, he was no longer able to speak or recognize old friends and colleagues. Like Clive Wearing, David Rumelhart lost the vital memories that defined who he was.

Interim Summary

- W. K. Estes built on Hull's mathematical modeling approach to develop new mathematical models for interpreting a wide variety of learning behaviors.

- Gordon Bower developed a simple model of one-trial insight learning that illustrated how individual performance can look quite different from averaged group performance during learning.

- George Miller used information theory to understand memory's limits and mechanisms.

- David Rumelhart played a key role in showing how connectionist network models could link brain processes to the complexities of human memory and cognition.

> ▶ **SYNTHESIS**

At the start of this chapter summarizing the history of the psychology of learning and memory from Aristotle to David Rumelhart, we urged you to notice five themes, or basic questions, interwoven throughout.

1. *How do sensations or ideas become linked in the mind?* Aristotle identified the basic requirements for association more than 2,000 years ago: contiguity, frequency, and similarity. Pavlov showed how we can study and measure learning about associations that exist in the world. Thorndike showed how reward and punishment govern which associations we learn to make. Both Hull and Skinner built on the work of Thorndike, with Hull focusing on mathematical models to explain the factors that influence learning and Skinner expanding the experimental analyses of reward and punishment and applying his research to society. Today, most psychologists take for granted the idea that memory involves forming associations among ideas or sensations, although there are still arguments about exactly how these associations are formed and how they are used.

2. *How are memories built from the components of experience?* Early philosophers and psychologists sought to describe how elements of our experiences could be combined into the whole of consciousness (Locke) or into networks of associations that describe our memories and knowledge (James). Estes's model of memory as distributed patterns of selected elements was updated by Rumelhart and others into connectionist network models that drew inspiration from brain circuits as well as from James's early models of memory.

3. *To what extent are behaviors and abilities determined by biological inheritance (nature) and to what extent by life experiences (nurture)?* Aristotle and Locke firmly believed that we enter the world as blank slates, with our experiences the sole factor influencing our behavior and capabilities. This position, empiricism, carried over into the behaviorism of Watson and Skinner. At the other extreme, Descartes and Galton were more strongly allied with the nature (or nativist) camp and believed that we inherit our talents and abilities. Today, most researchers take the middle road: acknowledging the profound influence of genes (nature) on learning and memory, while noting that a lifetime of experience (nurture) modifies these influences.

4. *In what ways are human learning and memory similar to learning and memory in other animals, and in what ways do they differ?* Most early philosophers assumed that humans were quite distinct from and innately superior to animals, but the proponents of evolution, such as Erasmus and Charles Darwin, showed how similar we are. Behaviorists also emphasized the similarities between animal and human learning, through the study of mechanisms for associative learning that could be demonstrated in several species, including rats, pigeons, and humans. In contrast, the early cognitive psychologists chose to focus on computer-based models of language and abstract reasoning—cognitive behaviors that are not easily studied in nonhuman animals. More recent efforts to reconcile the associationist theories of animal learning and the higher capabilities of human cognition are seen in the connectionist models of Rumelhart, McClelland, and their intellectual descendants. Today, many researchers think of cognition as a continuum, with some animals (e.g., rats and pigeons) perhaps possessing only limited capability for abstract reasoning, but others (e.g., dolphins and

chimpanzees) capable of a degree of communication, reasoning, and use of symbol representation approaching that of humans.

5. *Can the psychological study of the mind meet rigorous scientific standards? If so, might there be universal principles of learning and memory that can be described by mathematical equations and considered fundamental laws?* Throughout the history of studies on learning and memory, philosophers and psychologists have borrowed methods and metaphors from physics, chemistry, and other scientific fields to enhance their understanding. Galton and Ebbinghaus were among the first to show that psychology could indeed be the subject of careful experimentation. Hull attempted to devise mathematical equations to describe learning, and the tradition was continued by Estes and others working in mathematical and cognitive approaches. In current research, most psychologists hold themselves to the same rigorous principles of experimental methodology followed by scientists in other disciplines; if psychologists want their work to be taken seriously, they have to pay close attention to experimental design and analysis.

And . . . what next? In the past few decades there has been a revolution in the field of learning and memory. As you will see in the next chapter, our growing ability to measure and manipulate brain function has fundamentally altered how we look at learning and memory. One consequence of this recent progress has been a fusion of neuroscience and psychology into the integrated study of learning and memory in animals and humans. Despite these recent changes, most current research in the field of learning and memory can be understood as building on the challenges, issues, and questions that have been evolving in philosophy and psychology over the centuries.

Key Terms

associationism, *p. 5*

behaviorism, *p. 22*

blind design, *p. 18*

classical conditioning, *p. 19*

cognitive map, *p. 26*

cognitive psychology, *p. 28*

cognitive science, *p. 28*

confound, *p. 15*

connectionist models, *p. 33*

contiguity, *p. 5*

control group, *p. 15*

correlational study, *p. 14*

data, *p. 4*

dependent variable, *p. 17*

distributed representation, *p. 33*

double-blind design, *p. 18*

dualism, *p. 7*

empiricism, *p. 5*

eugenics, *p. 15*

evolution, *p. 12*

evolutionary psychology, *p. 13*

experiment, *p. 16*

experimental group, *p. 15*

experimental psychology, *p. 16*

experimenter bias, *p. 18*

extinction, *p. 19*

forgetting, *p. 17*

generalization, *p. 20*

hypothesis, *p. 14*

independent variable, *p. 17*

instrumental conditioning, *p. 20*

latent learning, *p. 26*

law of effect, *p. 20*

learning, *p. 3*

learning curve, *p. 19*

mathematical psychology, *p. 29*

memory, *p. 3*

nativism, *p. 5*

natural selection, *p. 13*

operant conditioning, *p. 20*

placebo, *p. 18*

psychology, *p. 9*

radical behaviorism, *p. 25*

reflex arc, *p. 7*

response, *p. 7*

retention curve, *p. 17*

stimulus, *p. 7*

subject bias, *p. 18*

theory, *p. 4*

Concept Check

1. If John Watson were to conduct his studies with rats in mazes today, his methods of sensory deprivation would be reviewed by an ethics board. How might he have designed his experiments differently so as to minimize the animals' pain or suffering?

2. Several studies have shown a correlation between the serious mental illness schizophrenia and smoking: people with schizophrenia are more likely than people without schizophrenia to smoke. Does this prove that schizophrenia causes smoking? Explain your answer.

3. Several studies have shown what seems to be a genetic influence on some kinds of memory ability: parents with high memory ability are likely to have children who also have high memory ability. How would an empiricist account for such findings?

4. The 10 tips for better memory in "Learning and Memory in Everyday Life" on page 4 include several that spring directly from principles espoused by associationists (Aristotle, James, and others). Identify these tips and explain your choices.

The Neuroscience of Learning and Memory

N THE MIDST OF A NEIGHBORHOOD BASEBALL GAME, a ball hit Orlando Serrell in the head so hard that it knocked him to the ground. At the time, he was only 10 years old, and like most boys who take a hit while playing with peers, he walked it off and eventually went back to the game. This seemingly innocuous incident proved anything but typical, however. Sometime after the hit, Orlando discovered an amazing ability to remember the day of the week on which any date fell that occurred after the fateful game, as well as what the weather was like on most of those days, without making any conscious effort to memorize this information or perform calculations with dates. Orlando's case is not unique but is an instance of a rare condition called *acquired savant syndrome* (Treffert, 2009). Chapter 1 described Clive Wearing, who lost many of his memory abilities after part of his brain was destroyed. Unlike Clive, individuals with acquired savant syndrome actually gain prodigious memory capacities as the result of brain injury. The startling implication of this phenomenon is that at least some human brains (and perhaps all) appear to have a much greater capacity for storing and recalling memories than people typically exhibit. If humans have hidden learning and memory capacities, might other animals also possess capacities of which we are currently unaware? If brains have such capacities, then why can't all individuals take full advantage of them? Might it be possible to develop neural technologies that enable a person to better encode and recall specific information or to erase memories of episodes one would prefer to forget?

The story of how scientists explore such questions, and identify the biological factors that determine what

Top Five Tips for Faster Forgetting

Chapter 1 provided five tips for how you can change your behavior to improve your memory. In case you are more interested in erasing memories than retaining them (wasting time is fun!), you can also modify your brain function to improve your forgetting. Here's what you do.

1. *Don't sleep.* People who don't get enough sleep are less able to concentrate during the day, which makes it harder for them to encode new memories and retrieve old ones. Sleepy brains work worse.

2. *Stress out.* Stress generally interferes with recall. So, if you want to make retrieving information particularly troublesome, just keep fixating on trying to remember things you can't until frustration overcomes you.

3. *Overextend yourself.* The more things you try to keep in mind simultaneously, the greater the chance you'll forget a bunch of them. So put aside all your note-taking devices—your pens, pads, computers, and iPhones—if you really want to maximize your loss.

4. *Deprive your senses.* The more impoverished your sensory inputs, the less likely you will encode facts, events, and skills well enough to recall them later. Wear headphones, shades, and oven mitts. Minimize the brain activity.

5. *Be apathetic.* Nothing is more forgettable than something you couldn't care less about. Just keep chanting inside your head, "Whatever . . . Whatever . . . Whatever," and you can easily avoid the kinds of emotionally triggered brain states that make memories stick.

an individual can learn and remember, is the story of brain research. Although scientists still have a long way to go in understanding how the brain works, they are compiling fascinating information about the brain's structure and functioning and the ways it contributes to learning and memory. New imaging and sensing technologies allow researchers to observe healthy human brains as they form and retrieve memories, while new techniques for animal research allow researchers to measure and manipulate changes in the brain during learning. Insights into the neural mechanisms of learning and memory can help you to understand how your actions may impact your own attempts to learn, remember, and in some cases forget the materials you study (see "Learning and Memory in Everyday Life" above).

2.1 A Quick Tour of the Brain

Researchers in the field of **neuroscience**—the study of the brain and the rest of the nervous system—overwhelmingly believe that the brain is the seat of learning and memory. This was not always the prevailing opinion. When ancient Egyptians mummified a body, they first removed the organs they considered important, preserving them in special airtight jars—but they discarded the brain. Many centuries later, Aristotle, one of the most empirically oriented philosophers in history (as discussed in Chapter 1), argued that the brain served primarily to cool the blood. However, observations over the centuries since Aristotle's time have convinced scientists that brain activity controls behavior and, by extension, the changes in behavior associated with learning and memory.

Historically, most early studies of learning and memory focused on observable behavior rather than on the brain and how it functions. This is not because early learning and memory researchers were oblivious to the importance of the brain. Ivan Pavlov designed all of his behavioral experiments to answer questions about how the brain works. John Watson, the originator of behaviorism, started out studying how developmental changes in neural structures correlate with developmental changes in learning abilities. B. F. Skinner, introduced in Chapter 1 as the most famous behaviorist of the twentieth century, began his career as a physiologist. Why, then, did these researchers place so much emphasis on behavior?

Part of the answer is that brains are among the most complex structures in nature. Even as recently as 50 years ago, the complexity of the neural functions required for most learning tasks seemed an insurmountable barrier to the scientific analysis of their contribution to learning and behavior. As new technologies became available, however, the study of brain function became more manageable. Today, aspects of brain function that were inaccessible 50 years ago are being measured daily in laboratories and medical institutions around the world. These new technologies have dramatically increased the number and productivity of studies exploring the neural substrates of learning and memory.

The Brain and the Nervous System

The brain is just one—albeit very important—component of a collection of body organs called the **nervous system,** the organ system devoted to the distribution and processing of information. The tissues that are specialized for accomplishing these tasks include cells called **neurons,** which collect incoming information from the sensory organs of the system (information such as sight, taste, smell, touch, and sound) and from the rest of the body (information on such conditions as hunger and sleepiness), process this information, and react to it by coordinating the body's responses (such as muscle movement and activity of internal organs).

In vertebrates, the nervous system can be divided into two parts: the central nervous system and the peripheral nervous system. As its name suggests, the **central nervous system (CNS)** is where many of the events responsible for learning and memory take place: the CNS is made up of the brain and the spinal cord (Figure 2.1). The **peripheral nervous system (PNS)** consists of nerve fibers that carry information from sensory receptors (for example, visual receptors in the eye or touch receptors in the skin) into the CNS and then carry instructions from the CNS back out to the muscles and organs. Most of these fibers pass through the spinal cord, but a few—such as those from the light receptors in your eyes

Central nervous system (CNS)
Consists of the brain and the spinal cord.

Peripheral nervous system (PNS)
Consists of motor and sensory neurons that connect the brain and the spinal cord to the rest of the body.

1. Sensory organs (skin, eyes, ears, etc.)

2. Muscles

3. Body organs

Figure 2.1 Nervous system components Every vertebrate has a central nervous system (CNS) and a peripheral nervous system (PNS). The CNS consists of the brain and spinal cord. The PNS consists of motor and sensory neurons that carry information back and forth between the CNS and the rest of the body: (1) sensory receptors in the skin, eyes, ears, and so on carry sensory information to the CNS; (2) motor fibers carry motor commands from CNS to muscles; (3) PNS fibers carry commands from the CNS to regulate organs and glands.

(a)

(b)

Frontal lobe

Parietal lobe

Occipital lobe

Temporal lobe

Brainstem

Cerebellum

Cortex

© Visuals Unlimited, Ltd.

Figure 2.2 The visible surface of the human brain (a) A photograph of the human brain. (b) In each brain hemisphere, the cerebral cortex is divided into four principal areas: frontal lobe, parietal lobe, occipital lobe, and temporal lobe. Below the cortex sit the cerebellum and brainstem. The brainstem connects the brain to the spinal cord below.

and those that activate the muscles controlling eye movements—travel directly to the brain without first making connections in the spinal cord.

Although all vertebrates possess a CNS and PNS, there are big differences between the nervous systems of different species. Let's start with the vertebrate you're probably most familiar with: the human.

The Human Brain

The **cerebral cortex,** the tissue covering the top and sides of the brain in most vertebrates, is by far the largest structure of the human brain (Figure 2.2a). The word "cortex" is Latin for "bark" or "rind," reflecting that the cortex, although about the size of the front page of a newspaper if spread out flat, is only about 2 millimeters thick. To fit inside the skull, the cerebral cortex is extensively folded, much like a piece of paper crumpled into a ball. In humans, as in all vertebrates, the brain consists of two sides, or *hemispheres*, that are roughly mirror images of each other, so brain scientists talk about the cortex in the "left hemisphere" or the "right hemisphere." In each hemisphere, the cortex is divided further into the **frontal lobe** at the front of the head, the **parietal lobe** at the top of the head, the **temporal lobe** at the side of the head, and the **occipital lobe** at the back of the head (Figure 2.2b). The term *lobe* refers to the fact that these regions are anatomically distinct. The individual lobes got their somewhat odd names from the names of the skull bones that cover them. If you have trouble memorizing these four terms, remember: "*F*rontal is *F*ront, *P*arietal is at the *P*eak, *T*emporal is behind the *T*emples, and the *O*ccipital lobe is *O*ut back." Subregions within each lobe are associated with a wide variety of perceptual and cognitive processes. For example, the frontal lobes help you to plan and perform actions, the occipital lobes allow you to see and recognize the world, the parietal lobes enable you to feel the differences between silk and sandpaper, and the temporal lobes make it possible for you to hear and to remember what you've done. We will discuss the functional roles of cortical subregions in greater detail throughout this book, and knowing the names and locations of the different lobes will help you to keep track of what is happening where in the brain.

Sitting behind and slightly below the cerebral cortex is the **cerebellum** (Figure 2.2b). The cerebellum contributes to the coordination of movement and is thus especially important for learning that involves physical action. At the base of the brain is the aptly named **brainstem** (Figure 2.2b). The brainstem is a collection of structures connecting the brain to the spinal cord and playing key roles in the regulation of automatic functions, such as breathing and regulation of body temperature.

Other brain structures, buried under the cerebral cortex, are not visible in photographs such as that in Figure 2.2a. You'll learn about many of these structures later in the book; for now, we'll just introduce a few that are especially important for learning and memory (Figure 2.3).

First, near the center of the brain lies the *thalamus*, a structure that receives sensory information (sights, sounds, touch, and so forth) from the peripheral nervous system and relays this information to other parts of the brain. You can think of the thalamus as a gateway through which almost all sensory information enters the brain. Sitting near the thalamus are the *basal ganglia*, a group of structures important for planning and producing skilled movements such as throwing a football or juggling. The *hippocampus* lies a little farther away, inside the temporal lobes; it is important for learning new information about facts (say, the capital of France) or remembering autobiographical events (what you did last summer). Sitting at the tip of the hippocampus is a group of cells called the *amygdala*; this little brain region is important for adding emotional content to memories. If you remember the happiest—or saddest—day of your life, it is probably because your amygdala was particularly active at the time, adding emotional strength to those memories. Because you have two hemispheres, you actually have duplicates of each of these structures. For example, you have a left hippocampus and a right hippocampus, and a left amygdala and a right amygdala.

Scientists are only beginning to understand in any detail what these brain areas do and how they relate to learning and memory, but it is becoming increasingly clear that it's a mistake to think of the brain as a single organ, like a liver or a kidney. Instead, the brain is a society of "experts," each making its own specialized contribution to what we do and what we think.

Basal ganglia

Thalamus

Amygdala

Hippocampus

Figure 2.3 **Brain regions known to contribute to learning and memory** Lying near the center of the human brain, the basal ganglia, thalamus, hippocampus, and amygdala all contribute to learning and memory in different ways.

Comparative Neuroanatomy

In spite of the wide differences in nervous systems from species to species, much of what is known about the neural bases of learning and memory comes from studies of animals other than humans. Many aspects of a rat brain, a monkey brain, or even an insect brain are similar enough to a human brain to have made this possible. The study of similarities and differences between organisms' brains is called *comparative neuroanatomy*. Comparative neuroanatomical studies provide a foundation for understanding how brain structure and function relate to learning and memory abilities.

The brains of vertebrate species are similar in that all have a cerebral cortex, a cerebellum, and a brainstem; all vertebrate brains are also similarly organized into two hemispheres. Figure 2.4 shows the brains of some representative vertebrate species. In general, bigger animals have bigger brains. It might seem that increasing brain size should go hand in hand with increased capacity: human brains are bigger than frog brains, and humans seem to be able to learn things frogs can't. But elephant brains are larger than human brains, and elephants can't learn to read and write, build cities, or study calculus. So, just as birds with larger wings are not necessarily better at flying than smaller birds, animals with larger brains are not necessarily better learners than other animals. In general,

Fish   Frog   Bird   Human   Elephant

Figure 2.4 Comparative anatomy of the brains of several vertebrate species All vertebrate brains have two hemispheres and a recognizable cortex, cerebellum, and brainstem, but species differ in the relative volumes of these areas. In mammals (such as the human) and birds, the cortex is much larger than the cerebellum; in fish and amphibians (such as the frog), the cortex and cerebellum are closer in size.

The octopus is an invertebrate, with a brain very different from that of mammals and other vertebrates, yet the octopus is a sophisticated learner.

Mauro Fermariello/Photo Researchers

scientists don't yet fully understand the relationship between brain size and functional capacity. Recent studies of intelligence in humans suggest that differences in the size of certain subregions in the frontal and parietal lobes do predict differences in performance on intelligence tests (Jung & Haier, 2007), indicating that it is not overall brain size that counts but how different brain parts are structured (Mercado, 2008).

Aside from differences in overall brain volume, different species have different proportions of cerebral cortex. In humans, the cerebral cortex takes up a much larger percentage of total brain volume than it does in, say, frogs. Whereas the large human cortex has to be folded up to fit inside the human skull, the frog cortex can fit quite comfortably in its skull without wrinkling. The relative size of the human cortex is intriguing because the cerebral cortex is associated with functions such as language and complex thought—the very things that seem to distinguish humans from other animals. And in fact, other species with a relatively large cortex—including chimpanzees, dolphins, and, yes, elephants—are often those that we associate with greater ability for abstract thought, problem solving, and other "higher" cognitive functions.

Only vertebrates have both a CNS and a PNS. Some invertebrates—the octopus and the bee, for example—have a recognizable brain, but these brains are organized very differently from vertebrate brains. Much of the octopus "brain" is distributed in various parts of its body, particularly inside its rubbery legs. Yet the octopus is a remarkably capable learner: it can learn to find its way through a maze and to open a jar to get at the food inside. It even shows signs of social learning, that is, learning from watching another octopus's behavior.

In one study, researchers trained some octopuses to grab the white ball when presented with a choice between a white and a red one. Other, untrained octopuses were then allowed to watch the trained octopuses make their selection. Later, when the observer octopuses were offered the two balls, they promptly grabbed the white one—just as they had seen the trained octopuses doing (Fiorito, Agnisola, d'Addio, Valanzano, & Calamandrei, 1998). Such social learning was once believed to be exclusive to "higher" animals, such as humans, dolphins, and chimpanzees. But we now know that an octopus, with a decentralized brain, can do it, too.

Other invertebrates, such as worms and jellyfish, have no recognizable brains at all. These animals have neurons that are remarkably similar to vertebrate neurons, but the neurons are few in number and are not organized into a centralized structure like a brain. For example, microscopic worms known as nematodes (including the species that infects pigs and then humans who eat the pigs, causing trichinosis) have 302 individual neurons, compared with a few hundred million in the octopus and about 100 billion in the human. Nematode neurons are organized into a "nerve net" that is similar to a vertebrate PNS but with no central processing area. Yet these little organisms can learn to approach tastes or odors that predict food and to avoid tastes and odors that predict the absence of food (Rankin, 2004). Not bad for a creature without a brain.

Studies of invertebrate nervous systems have been particularly rewarding because of their very simplicity. For example, because a nematode has such a small number of neurons, scientists are able to map out the entire set of connections in its nervous system in a way not possible for a human brain or even a rat brain. Many of the important insights into human brains and human learning came from studying how invertebrates learn and remember.

Neurons

Neurons are the building blocks of the nervous system. Some act as sensory receptors (such as those in the eyes, ears, and tongue that respond to visual, auditory, and taste stimuli), and some act as "motor fibers" that carry commands from the spinal cord to the muscles. But in vertebrates, the vast majority of neurons are centralized in the brain. These neurons are capable of changing their function and modifying the way they process information. These changes, some of which we examine in Section 2.4, are the basis of learning in the brain.

The prototypical neuron has three main components: (1) **dendrites,** which are input areas that receive signals from other neurons; (2) the **cell body,** or **soma,** which integrates signals from the dendrites; and (3) one or more **axons,** which transmit information to other neurons (Figure 2.5). For the most part, information flows in one direction, from dendrites to axons.

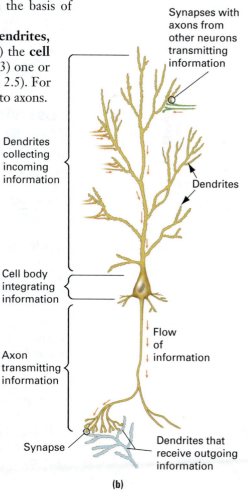

(a)

(b)

Figure 2.5 Neurons, the cells specialized to process information (a) Brain tissue, stained to make neurons evident and photographed through a powerful microscope. The pyramid-shaped cell bodies and interconnecting branches of several neurons are visible. (b) The prototypical neuron has three main components: dendrites for collecting information, a cell body (soma) that integrates information, and one or more axons that transmit information to other neurons. Information flows mainly from dendrites to axon(s).

Biophoto Associates/Photo Researchers

Dendrite
Cell body
Axon

Synapses with axons from other neurons transmitting information

Dendrites collecting incoming information

Dendrites

Cell body integrating information

Axon transmitting information

Flow of information

Synapse

Dendrites that receive outgoing information

It is convenient to talk about a "prototypical neuron," but in reality neurons, like brains, come in a wide array of shapes and sizes. For example, *pyramidal cells* are neurons with pyramid-shaped cell bodies; *stellate cells* have star-shaped cell bodies. Some neurons have a single main axon, some have two, and some have many. Neurons known as *interneurons*, which connect two or more neurons, have short axons or no axons at all. The neurons that carry signals from the spinal cord to the feet have axons that stretch a meter or more in humans. The various shapes and sizes of different kinds of neurons undoubtedly contribute to their function. But, in many cases, neuroscientists do not know the specific advantages that a particular shape or size provides.

Neurons are not the only kind of cell in the brain; they are far outnumbered by **glia,** cells that provide functional and structural support to neurons. *Astrocytes* are glia that line the outer surface of blood vessels in the brain and may help in the transfer of oxygen and nutrients from the blood to neurons. Glia called *oligodendrocytes* wrap the axons of nearby neurons in *myelin*, a fatty substance that insulates electrical signals transmitted by neurons, speeding information transmission down the axon. Glia are as important as neurons for normal brain (and overall central nervous system) function. For example, multiple sclerosis is a disease in which the myelin coating of axons degenerates; this interferes with the ability of neurons to transmit information, leading to jerky muscle movements and impaired coordination, as well as problems with vision and speech. Recent neuroscience research suggests that glia may even directly contribute to certain learning mechanisms. Even so, most neuroscientists who study the neural bases of learning and memory focus their efforts on understanding neurons: how they transmit information, and how they change to reflect learning.

Observing Learning-Related Changes in Brain Structure

In the late 1800s, Franz Joseph Gall (1758–1828), a German anatomist and physiologist, pioneered the idea that different areas of the brain are responsible for different behaviors and capabilities. In addition, he reasoned that differences in character or ability should be reflected in differences in the size of the corresponding parts of the brain: people with a special skill for learning language must have a larger-than-average part of the brain associated with speech; people prone to violence or aggressive behavior must have an overgrown "aggressiveness" area in the brain. Gall assumed that these differences in brain areas would be reflected in the shape of the skull, and he concluded that it should be possible to tell which areas of a person's brain were enlarged—and, thus, what abilities and personality traits that person would display—by examining bumps in the person's skull. Gall and his colleagues pursued a systematic study they called **phrenology,** in which they carefully measured the size and shape of many individuals' skulls and compared those measurements with the individuals' personalities and abilities (Gall & Spurzheim, 1810). The resulting maps of the skull purported to show the function of the underlying brain areas—functions such as language skill, aggressiveness, friendliness, decision making, and so on.

Phrenology captured the public imagination. The field was quickly taken over by quacks, who found various ways of making the idea pay. Victorian firms often hired phrenologists to examine job applicants, in much the same way that some companies use personality tests today. The ruling classes liked the phrenologists' idea that bumps on the skull could be used to prove the innate inferiority of criminals and other undesirables, and thus justify institutionalizing and even mistreating them.

There was another, even more serious problem than the enthusiastic overuse of phrenology. It was that phrenology's fundamental premise was wrong. Bumps on the skull do not imply bulges in the underlying brain. One of the weaknesses of Gall's work was that he had no way to examine the brain of a living person. Measuring bumps on the skull was the closest he could get. It would be nearly 200 years before technology advanced to the point where scientists could see inside the skull of a healthy, living person.

Today, several technologies are available that allow physicians to see a living person's brain without causing damage or malfunction. Collectively, these modern techniques for creating pictures of anatomical structures within the brain are called **structural neuroimaging,** brain imaging, or "brain scanning." The brain scans produced by these methods show the size and shape of brain areas and also brain **lesions,** areas of damage caused by injury or illness.

One method of structural neuroimaging, **computed tomography (CT),** produces scans created from multiple x-ray images. If you've ever passed through airport security and seen an x-ray of your luggage, you've probably noticed that, although an x-ray can show the internal contents and structure of your suitcase, everything in the image appears shadowy and flattened into two dimensions. The x-ray may show a comb and a toothbrush superimposed, but it's impossible to tell which item is on top and which is on the bottom. Similarly, when doctors x-ray the body, the resulting image can show the presence of an abnormality, such as a broken bone or a tumor, but not the depth at which it lies within the body.

CT provides a way around this problem by taking multiple x-rays at multiple angles and using a computer to integrate the various signals, thus generating images that look like "slices" or cross sections through the body. By looking at multiple slices, doctors can pinpoint the exact location of internal anatomical structures in three-dimensional space. A CT scan can show the location of an abnormality such as a tumor with much better accuracy than a single x-ray. Unfortunately, the soft tissues that make up the brain show much less clearly on CT scans than do bones and tumors. So, although the advent of CT opened new vistas in brain science, the technique is currently in waning use by brain researchers.

Today, the use of CT for structural brain imaging has largely been supplanted by **magnetic resonance imaging (MRI),** in which changes in magnetic fields generate images of internal structure. MRI employs an extremely powerful magnet, usually constructed like a giant tube. The patient lies on a pallet that slides into the tube. First, the magnet aligns the magnetic properties of a small fraction of the atoms within the patient's brain (or whatever part of the body is under study); then, radio waves are broadcast that disturb the atoms, causing them to generate tiny electrical currents. When the radio waves are stopped, the atoms return to their stable, aligned state. Different brain regions require different amounts of time to return to their stable state, depending

NAMES, NUMBERS AND LOCATION OF THE MENTAL ORGANS.

1. AMATIVENESS.—Connubial love, affection.
A. CONJUGAL LOVE.—Union for life, pairing instinct.
2. PARENTAL LOVE.—Care of offspring, and all young.
3. FRIENDSHIP.—Sociability, union of friends.
4. INHABITIVENESS.—Love of home and country
5. CONTINUITY.—Application, consecutiveness.
E. VITATIVENESS.—Clinging to life, tenacity, endurance.
6. COMBATIVENESS.—Defence, courage, criticism.
7. DESTRUCTIVENESS. — Executiveness, push, propelling power.
8. ALIMENTIVENESS.—Appetite for food, etc.
9. ACQUISITIVENESS.—Frugality, economy, to get.
10. SECRETIVENESS.—Self-control, policy, reticence.
11. CAUTIOUSNESS. — Guardedness, care-taking, safety.
12. APPROBATIVENESS.—Love of applause and display.
13. SELF-ESTEEM.—Self-respect, dignity, authority.
14. FIRMNESS.—Stability, perseverance, steadfastness.
15. CONSCIENTIOUSNESS.—Sense of right, justice.
16. HOPE.—Expectation, anticipation, perfect trust.
17. SPIRITUALITY.—Intuition, prescience, faith.
18. VENERATION.—Worship, adoration, deference.
19. BENEVOLENCE.—Sympathy, kindness, mercy.
20. CONSTRUCTIVENESS.—Ingenuity, invention, tools.
21. IDEALITY.—Taste, love of beauty, poetry and art.
B. SUBLIMITY.—Love of the grand, vast, magnificent.
22. IMITATION.—Copying, aptitude for mimicry.
23. MIRTH.—Fun, wit, ridicule, facetiousness.
24. INDIVIDUALITY.—Observation, curiosity to see.
25. FORM.—Memory of shape, looks, persons, things.
26. SIZE.—Measurement of quantity by the eye.
27. WEIGHT.—Control of motion, balancing.
28. COLOR.—Discernment, and love of colors, hues, tints.
29. ORDER.—Method, system, going by rule, arrangement.
30. CALCULATION.—Mental arithmetic, numbers.
31. LOCALITY.—Memory of place, position, travels.
32. EVENTUALITY.—Memory of facts, events, history.
33. TIME.—Telling when, time of day, dates, punctuality.
34. TUNE.—Love of music, sense of harmony, singing.
35. LANGUAGE.—Expression by words, signs or acts.
36. CAUSALITY.—Planning, thinking, philosophy
37. COMPARISON.—Analysis, inferring, illustration.
C. HUMAN NATURE.—Sagacity, perception of motives.
D. SUAVITY.—Pleasantness, blandness, politeness.

ETPN6575414 PHRENOLOGY AND PHYSIOGNOMY - The Phrenological Head, with Key. From Nelson Sizer and H.S. Drayton, Heads and Face, and How to Study Them. 1892 ©Charles Walker / Topfoto / The Image Works

© Charles Walker/Topfoto/The Image Works

Phrenology maps attributed various aspects of cognition and personality to different regions of the brain. Enlargement of a brain area was thought to represent an enhancement of the corresponding function, detectable as a bump on the skull.

In magnetic resonance imaging (MRI) of the head, the patient lies with his or her head in a tube that contains a powerful magnet and a source of radio waves. Using data obtained from this machine, a computer measures the density of atoms at various locations in the brain and constructs a high-resolution image showing the brain's interior structures.

Figure 2.6 MRI images
(a) This "slice" taken near the center of the head shows a cross section through cortex, cerebellum, brainstem, and an upper portion of spinal cord, as well as nose and mouth cavities. (b) A horizontal slice taken at the level of the eyeballs (visible at the top of the image) contains little cortex (since the slice is so low) but captures the low-hanging cerebellum.

on the density of atoms there. A computer collects all the signals emitted and, as in CT, uses them to generate images that look like slices. For example, Figure 2.6a shows a slice taken vertically through the middle of the brain, revealing a cross section of cerebral cortex, cerebellum, and brainstem, as well as some facial structures. A horizontal slice taken at the level of the eyeballs, as in Figure 2.6b, shows a different cross section.

Recently, a new type of MRI called **diffusion tensor imaging (DTI)** was developed that can measure the diffusion of water in brain tissue, permitting bundles of axons throughout the brain—the so-called white matter—to be imaged. DTI is better than conventional MRI at visualization of fiber tracts, so it's particularly useful for physicians trying to assess diffuse brain injury, as well as diseases such as multiple sclerosis that specifically target axons. Researchers also use DTI to study how different regions in the brain interact, by studying the fiber pathways between them.

Structural neuroimaging provides a way not only to directly observe physical properties of a live person's brain but also *to track changes in those properties over time*. These include changes that might occur as a function of aging, injury, or disease, as well as gross structural changes produced by learning experiences. In Chapter 7, on skill memories, we discuss recent structural neuroimaging work showing that learning to juggle leads to changes in the amount of cortical tissue. Structural images of human brains are also critical for analyzing and interpreting changes in brain *function* that occur with learning, a topic we discuss in greater detail below. It is easy to confuse structural neuroimaging, which shows what brains are physically like, with *functional neuroimaging*, which shows what brains are doing. Both types of neuroimaging can reveal changes associated with learning, and we will present examples of both throughout the following chapters. Whenever you see an image in which patches of color are superimposed on a brain, the first thing you should ask yourself is, are these colored regions showing me variations in structure, or do they represent variations in function?

Experimental studies with animals permit even more detailed measures of learning-related structural changes. Chemicals have been developed that essentially dye neurons that have recently undergone structural changes, making it possible to map out the number and distribution of neurons that have changed as a function of specific learning experiences. For these techniques, the brain tissue has to be bathed in the chemicals, and the dyed neurons are only visible

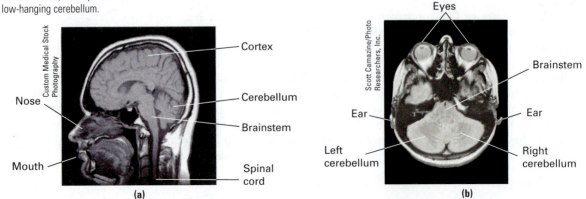

through a microscope, so the brain must be removed from the animal soon after the learning occurs. Consequently, these methods are most often employed in studies of learning that use rodents and small birds as subjects.

Interim Summary

- The brain and spinal cord make up the vertebrate central nervous system (CNS). The brain controls behavior through connections with the peripheral nervous system (PNS), which consists of sensory neurons coming from sensory receptors and motor neurons going to body muscles.
- The vertebrate brain is made up of several different regions that contribute to learning and memory, including the cerebral cortex, cerebellum, hippocampus, basal ganglia, and amygdala.
- Neurons, the building blocks of the nervous system, are capable of changing their function and modifying the way they process information.
- Modern structural brain-imaging techniques (including MRI and DTI) provide ways to measure variations in the physical structure of living brains without causing harm.

2.2 What Brains Do

Modern brain scientists assume that brains are composed of multiple systems that specialize in collecting, processing, and storing particular kinds of information. But there is no one-to-one relationship, as phrenologists supposed, in which each individual function or ability is performed in a dedicated corner of the brain. Instead, one brain area may play a role in many functions, and one function may rely on contributions from many brain areas.

What determines how brain regions contribute to learning and memory processes? Two major factors are the kinds of input a region receives and the kinds of output it produces.

Information Pathways in the Central Nervous System

Chapter 1 defined learning as a change in behavior that occurs as a result of experience. Thus, when Pavlov's dogs began to salivate after hearing a sound that predicted food, this change in behavior—salivation in response to a sound—provided evidence that the dogs learned about the relationship between the sound and the food. But even before Pavlov began using the dogs in his experiments, they would salivate in response to food. Salivation during eating is a reflexive behavior that dogs (and other mammals) develop early in life; it helps the digestive system get ready to process incoming food.

A **reflex** is an involuntary and automatic response "hardwired" into an organism; in other words, it is present in all normal members of a given species and does not have to be learned. Just like Pavlov's dogs, humans salivate when eating food. This is only one of several reflexes that humans are biologically prepared to perform: newborns suck when they encounter a nipple (sucking reflex), hold their breath when submerged underwater (the diving reflex), and grasp a finger so tightly that they can support their own weight (the palmar grasp reflex). Adults have reflexes, too, such as the knee-jerk reflex when the doctor hits your knee with a rubber mallet and an eyeblink reflex when someone blows air at your eye.

With the palmar reflex, this infant's grasp can support her full weight.

Recall from Chapter 1 that Descartes explained reflexes as hydraulic movements caused by spirits flowing from the brain into the muscles. For many years, scientists accepted this explanation, assuming that there must be some kind of fluid carrying instructions from the brain to the muscles. It wasn't until the early twentieth century that researchers discovered, first, that there is no such fluid and, second, that the brain isn't in absolute control of the muscles at all.

Instead of a hydraulic fluid, there are two distinct types of nerve fibers connecting the muscles to the spinal cord: one set carrying sensory information from the peripheral nervous system into the spinal cord, and a second set carrying motor signals back from the spinal cord to the muscles (Bell, 1811; Magendie, 1822). If a pinprick or other painful stimulus is applied to a dog's leg, the leg jerks reflexively (just as you'd pull your leg away if someone pricked you). If the sensory fibers are cut, the dog's sensation of pain disappears and the reflex fails to occur, although the dog can still move its leg normally. On the other hand, if the motor fibers are cut, the animal can still feel pain but, again, does not make reflexive leg movements. Sensory and motor fibers are separated in the spinal cord. The finding that the spinal cord has two parallel nerve pathways, one devoted to sensing and the other to responding, is called the *Bell-Magendie law of neural specialization*, after two scientists who promoted the idea. Historically, it represents the first step toward understanding the physiological mechanisms of learning.

Following up on the discovery of neural specialization, English physiologist Charles Sherrington (1857–1952) conducted many studies on dogs whose spinal cord had been surgically disconnected from their brain, so that the spinal cord no longer received any brain signals. Such surgically altered dogs show many basic reflexes, such as jerking their leg away from a painful stimulus. Because the brain could not be contributing to these reflexes, the reflexes must be generated by the spinal cord alone. In fact, we now know that sensory inputs traveling into the spinal cord can activate motor fibers traveling out of the spinal cord, without waiting for instructions from the brain. If you've ever stuck your hand into dangerously hot or cold water and jerked it away almost before realizing what you've done, or watched your knee jerk in response to the doctor's rubber mallet, then you've experienced your spinal cord responding without receiving any help from your brain.

Sherrington concluded that such simple "spinal reflexes" could be combined into complex sequences of movements and that these reflexes were the building blocks of all behavior (Sherrington, 1906). Sherrington's description of reflexes differed from that of Descartes in assuming that spinal reflexes did not depend on the brain and did not involve the pumping of spirits or fluids into the muscles. Sherrington received a Nobel Prize in 1932 for his work in this area, and he is now considered to be one of the founding fathers of neuroscience. His ideas provided the groundwork and motivation for Pavlov's early investigations of learning in dogs (Pavlov, 1927) and have continued to influence learning and memory researchers ever since.

If the spinal cord controls reflexes and complex actions can be described as combinations of these reflexes, then where does the brain come in? Sensory fibers enter the spinal cord and connect to motor fibers there, but some fibers also travel up to the brain. The brain processes these inputs and produces its own outputs, some of which may travel back down the spinal cord and out to the muscles. The parallel sensory and motor pathways traveling up and down the spinal cord, to and from the brain, are similar to the parallel sensory and motor pathways that were identified traveling into and out of the spinal cord.

Primary motor cortex (M1)

Primary somatosensory cortex (S1)

Primary auditory cortex (A1)

Primary visual cortex (V1)

Figure 2.7 **Cortical regions for processing inputs and outputs** Specific regions of cerebral cortex are specialized for processing light (primary visual cortex), sound (primary auditory cortex), and sensation produced by physical movement (primary somatosensory cortex). Other regions are specialized for generating coordinated movements (primary motor cortex).

Incoming Stimuli: Sensory Pathways into the Brain

Let's focus first on the sensory pathways that provide inputs to the brain. As noted earlier in this chapter, most sensory information enters the brain through the thalamus. The thalamus in turn distributes these inputs to cortical regions specialized for processing particular sensory stimuli, such as the primary auditory cortex (A1), for sound; the primary somatosensory cortex (S1), for sensations from skin and internal organs; and the primary visual cortex (V1), for sight. A1 is located in the temporal lobe, S1 in the parietal lobe, and V1 in the occipital lobe (Figure 2.7). Such areas are collectively called *primary sensory cortices*, as they are the first stage of cortical processing for each type of sensory information. Each primary sensory cortex can then transmit outputs to surrounding cortical regions for further processing. For example, the primary visual cortex may start the processing of stimuli from the eye by extracting simple features—say, lines and shading—from a visual scene; later stages of cortical processing elaborate by detecting motion or shape in the scene and, finally, by responding to features of individual objects and their meaning. Damage to primary sensory cortices can eliminate particular perceptual abilities. For instance, people with damage to V1 can become blind, even though their eyes are in perfect working order, and damage to A1 can cause deafness.

Outgoing Responses: Motor Control

Just as various brain regions are specialized for processing sensory inputs, other brain regions are specialized for processing the outputs that control movements. Chief of these is the primary motor cortex (M1), which generates coordinated movements. M1 is located in the frontal lobe, adjacent to S1 in the parietal lobe (Figure 2.7), and it sends output to the brainstem, which in turn sends instructions down the spinal cord to activate motor fibers that control the muscles.

M1 gets much of its input from the frontal lobes, which are responsible for making high-level plans based on the present situation, past experience, and future goals. (Should you pick up that hot coffee cup? Should you try to catch that ball with one hand or two?) Other important inputs come from the basal ganglia and cerebellum, which help to translate the high-level plans into concrete sets of movements. All these inputs help determine the outputs that M1 sends to the brainstem. Other motor areas—including the cerebellum, basal ganglia, frontal cortex, and the brainstem itself—also produce their own outputs, all of which converge on the spinal cord and travel from there to the muscles. Complex motor movements—such as picking up a hot coffee cup

Figure 2.8 How to pick up a cup of coffee (1) Visual input from V1 helps you locate the coffee cup and its handle. (2) The frontal cortex helps you plan the movement. (3) Outputs from the motor cortex (M1) travel through the brainstem and down the spinal cord to the muscles in the arm, causing you to reach out your hand. (4) The basal ganglia and cerebellum continuously monitor whether your hand is on track, making tiny adjustments to ensure that your hand reaches the correct target. (5) Sensory information travels back up the arm and spinal cord to somatosensory cortex (S1), confirming that the cup has been grasped.

without spilling the liquid or burning your hand, or picking up an egg without crushing it, or dancing without stepping on your partner's toes—require exquisitely choreographed interactions between all of these brain structures and the muscles they control.

Let's consider one of these examples in greater detail: you see a cup of coffee and pick it up (Figure 2.8). The process begins with visual input from your eyes traveling to your visual cortex (V1), which helps you find and identify the cup. Regions in your frontal lobes coordinate the necessary plans for grasping the cup, which your motor cortex (M1) then directs by means of outputs through the brainstem, down the spinal cord, and out to the muscles of the arm and fingers. As you reach for the cup, your basal ganglia and cerebellum continually track the movement, making tiny adjustments as necessary. These brain regions enable you to exert just the right amount of pressure on the cup: enough to lift it against gravity, but not so much that you yank it off the table and spill the contents. As you pick up the cup, sensory information from touch, heat, and pressure receptors in your fingers travels back up your arms, through the spinal cord, and to the somatosensory cortex (S1), providing evidence that the cup is firmly in your hand. If the handle of the cup is hotter than expected, it could produce a reflexive withdrawal of the hand. This response is the kind of spinal reflex studied by Charles Sherrington; the short path from the hand to the spinal cord and back is sometimes called a *reflex arc*.

All that input and output just to pick up a cup—before you've even taken your first sip! Infants of many vertebrate species, including humans, are born fairly clumsy and spend a large part of their infancy and childhood learning how to walk or fly or swim gracefully, reach accurately, move throat and tongue muscles to produce coherent sounds, and so on. This relatively long period spent learning coordinated motor control reflects both the complexity of the operations and the many brain structures that have to learn to interact with one another and with the outside world to perform them.

The Synapse: Where Neurons Connect

So far, we've been describing the transmission of information into and out of the brain as if signals flowed from one place to another in the nervous system like water through a pipe (similar to the way Descartes described behavior). What really happens is that neurons throughout the nervous system are continually communicating with one another in vast networks that are similar in some ways to social networking systems such as Twitter or Facebook.

Generally, neurons that communicate with each other are not actually physically connected. Rather, communicating neurons are separated by a narrow gap of about 20 nanometers (1 nanometer [nm] is one-billionth of a meter), called a **synapse,** across which the neurons pass chemical messages (Figure 2.9a). Most synapses are formed between the axon of the **presynaptic** (or sending) neuron and a dendrite of the **postsynaptic** (or receiving) neuron, but synapses can also be formed between an axon and a cell body, between an axon and another axon, and even between dendrites.

Neurons contain molecules called **neurotransmitters,** chemical substances that can cross a synapse to carry a message to a postsynaptic neuron. Neurotransmitter molecules are kept conveniently on hand at the end of the presynaptic axon, in packets known as vesicles. To send a message, one or more vesicles of the presynaptic axon burst and spill neurotransmitter molecules into the synapse (Figure 2.9b). So far, nine neurotransmitters have been the focus of most research: *glutamate, gamma-aminobutyric acid (GABA), acetylcholine, dopamine, norepinephrine, epinephrine, serotonin, histamine, and glycine.* Table 2.1 summarizes what is known of the functions of each of these neurotransmitters. In addition, there are about 100 other chemicals in the brain that can serve as neurotransmitters, and researchers are discovering new ones every year.

Once the chemical signal has been released into the synapse by the presynaptic neuron, the next step is for the postsynaptic neuron to pick it up. **Receptors** are molecules embedded in the surface of the postsynaptic neuron that are specialized to bind with and respond to particular kinds of neurotransmitters.

Figure 2.9 Information flow across a synapse (a) This photo (taken through an electron microscope) of the end of an axon of a presynaptic neuron shows the tiny gap, or synapse, between the presynaptic neuron and the dendrite of a postsynaptic neuron. Vesicles filled with neurotransmitter molecules, ready for release into the synapse, are visible as circular packets inside the presynaptic neuron. (b) Information is exchanged across a synapse when (1) the presynaptic neuron releases neurotransmitter into the synapse and (2) the neurotransmitter molecules dock at receptors on the surface of the postsynaptic neuron. This may activate the receiving neuron, passing the message along. Leftover neurotransmitter in the synapse is either (3) broken down or (4) reabsorbed into the presynaptic neuron.

Axon of presynaptic neuron

Vesicles containing neurotransmitters

Neurotransmitter molecules

Receptors

Dendrite of postsynaptic neuron

Axon

Synapse

Dendrite

(a)

(b)

Table 2.1

Nine neurotransmitters and their functions

Neurotransmitter	Function
Glutamate	Most prevalent excitatory neurotransmitter
Gamma-aminobutyric acid (GABA)	Main inhibitory neurotransmitter
Acetylcholine	Connects motor neurons and muscles Regulates attention and memory
Dopamine	Associated with voluntary movement Regulates reward-seeking behavior
Norepinephrine	Increases arousal Contributes to long-lasting memories
Epinephrine	Increases attention and concentration
Serotonin	Regulates sleep, mood, appetite, and aggression
Histamine	Regulates sleep and arousal
Glycine	Decreases neural activity

The effect of a particular neurotransmitter depends on what its corresponding postsynaptic receptors do when activated. Some receptors open a channel for the flow of electrically charged molecules into or out of the cell, thus changing the charge characteristics in a small area of the neuron. Similar electrical changes may be occurring simultaneously in other locations on the neuron as other receptors on other dendrites become active. The neuron's cell body integrates this cocktail of electrical signals; if the total electrical charge exceeds a threshold, the neuron "fires," propagating an electrical charge down its axon. This propagation is an all-or-nothing event: either the neuron fires or it doesn't; there is no in-between stage. When a neuron fires, sending an electrical charge to the end of the axon, it causes the release of neurotransmitter molecules there, passing the message along to the next postsynaptic neuron.

Some neurotransmitters—glutamate, for example—are *excitatory*, activating receptors that tend to increase the likelihood of the postsynaptic neuron firing. Other neurotransmitters—such as GABA—are *inhibitory*, activating receptors that tend to decrease the likelihood of the postsynaptic neuron firing. Usually, a given neuron produces and releases only one kind of neurotransmitter. But that neuron may be able to receive and interpret messages from many different presynaptic neurons, each releasing a different kind of neurotransmitter. As long as the postsynaptic neuron has receptors suited to a particular neurotransmitter, it will be able to receive the message.

After a neuron fires, there is a brief period, called a *refractory period*, during which it can't fire again, no matter how much input it receives. Once this refractory period has passed, the neuron is again open for business. If the neuron is still receiving a lot of input from its neighbors, it may fire again and again in rapid succession, interrupted only by the refractory period after each firing. If the excitatory inputs are less frequent or less strong or if there is a lot of inhibitory input, some time may pass before the neuron fires again.

In the meantime, neurotransmitter molecules have to be cleared out of the synapse so that the synapse can receive future messages. In some cases, this consists of breaking the neurotransmitter molecules down into their constituent parts in a process called *inactivation*. In other cases, they are reabsorbed into the presynaptic neuron and recycled for future use, a process called *reuptake*. When cleanup is complete, the synapse and receptors are ready to receive new transmissions.

Several areas in the brainstem contain neurons that send axons widely throughout the brain; when they fire, these neurons release neurotransmitters called **neuromodulators** that can affect activity in entire brain areas, rather than just at a single synapse. Neuromodulators alter, or modulate, how neurons exchange messages, although they themselves are not part of the message. For example, acetylcholine often functions as a neuromodulator, and one of its effects is to temporarily alter the number of receptors that have to be active before a postsynaptic neuron can fire. If you think of synaptic transmission as a message, then acetylcholine levels help determine whether the message is heard as a whisper or a shout. Many human diseases that affect learning and memory seem to involve a global decline in neuromodulators. Examples include Alzheimer's disease, which is associated with a reduction in acetylcholine (Francis, Palmer, Snape, & Wilcock, 1999), and Parkinson's disease, which is characterized by a reduction in dopamine (Evans & Lees, 2004).

Discovering How Different Brain Regions Function

Imagine that a Martian scientist comes to Earth and encounters an automobile, a method of transportation unknown on Mars, powered by an energy source also unknown to Martians. Since the Martian speaks no Earth languages and can't simply ask a mechanic for an explanation, how might he learn how the car works? One way would be to look under the hood and examine the many components there. But studying the car's "anatomy" would only get him so far; to really understand the car, he'd have to take it for a test drive and see how it behaves normally. Then he could try disconnecting parts, one at a time, noting the consequences in each case. If he removed the axle, he'd learn that the motor would work but couldn't transfer energy to make the wheels turn. If he removed the radiator, he'd learn that the car would run but would quickly overheat. In the end, by discovering the function of each of the components under the hood, the Martian could probably develop a pretty good idea of how the car works.

Neuroscientists trying to understand the brain have been faced with a similar challenge: that of figuring out how the brain works without help from a design manual. One of the earliest approaches they took was something like the Martian's: to examine a brain with one or more pieces removed and see how the remaining system behaved (or misbehaved). Although no one would disassemble a human the way the Martian might disassemble a car, nature has provided us with cases in which humans, through accident, injury, or disease, have suffered damage to one or more brain areas.

Neuropsychology is the branch of psychology that deals with the relation between brain function and behavior, usually by examining the functioning of patients with specific types of brain damage. These individuals volunteer their time and effort in experiments that test their learning and memory abilities, as well as other kinds of cognitive function—language, attention, intelligence, and so on. The test results can potentially be used to guide a patient's rehabilitation, but they also serve a research purpose. By recognizing patterns in the impaired and spared abilities of a group of patients who have experienced damage to a similar region of the brain, researchers hope to build a better picture of that brain region's normal function—just like the Martian trying to understand what a radiator does by watching what happens to a car that doesn't have one.

Animal researchers have conducted parallel studies by removing or deactivating specific brain regions to create animal "models" of humans with brain damage. Because human brain damage is almost always caused by accident, injury, or illness, every patient's damage—and disability—is slightly different. By contrast, in animal models, researchers can remove or disable specific brain regions with great precision, making it much easier to compare results. Instances in which the experimental results from human patients and animal models converge give the clearest picture of how the brain works normally and how it functions after damage.

Some of the most famous experimental brain lesion studies were conducted by Karl Lashley (1890–1958), an American psychologist who was looking for the location of the **engram**—the supposed physical change in the brain that forms the basis of a memory. Lashley would train a group of rats to navigate a maze, and then he'd systematically remove a different small area (covering, say, 10%) of the cortex in each rat. He reasoned that, once he'd found the lesion that erased the animal's memories of how to run through the maze, he would have located the site of the engram (Lashley, 1929).

Alas, the results were not quite so straightforward. No matter what small part of the cortex Lashley lesioned, the rats kept performing the task. Bigger lesions would cause increasingly large disruptions in performance, but no one cortical area seemed to be more important than any other. Hence, Lashley couldn't find the engram. Finally, in mock despair, he confessed that he might be forced to conclude that learning "simply is not possible" (Lashley, 1929).

Eventually, Lashley settled on a different explanation. He endorsed the **theory of equipotentiality,** which states that memories are not stored in one area of the brain; rather, the brain operates as a whole to store memories. Although Lashley is often credited with formulating this theory, it was actually first proposed in the 1800s as an alternative to phrenology (Flourens, 1824). An analogy for this idea might be a rich investor who spreads his assets over a great many investments. If any one investment fails, his net worth won't change much; if a large number of investments fail, he can still rebuild his net worth by savvy use of what's left, although it may take him some time. In effect, his wealth is a function of all of his many investments. Similarly, in the theory of equipotentiality, memories are spread over many cortical areas; damage to one or two of these areas won't completely destroy the memory, and over time the surviving cortical areas may be able to compensate for what's been lost.

Lashley's work, and his endorsement of the theory of equipotentiality, were milestones in brain science because researchers could no longer think in terms of the compartmentalized structure–function mapping that phrenologists had proposed. But, like the phrenologists before him, Lashley was only partly right. The phrenologists were in fact on the right track when they proposed that different brain areas have different specialties; the specialization just wasn't as extreme as they thought (and wasn't reflected in bumps on the skull). Lashley was also on the right track when he proposed that engrams aren't localized to tiny areas of the cortex, but we now know that the cortex isn't quite as undifferentiated as he came to believe. The truth is somewhere in the middle. Moreover, as you will discover in subsequent chapters, part of the reason Lashley's experiments did not work out the way he expected was because of his assumption that memories were mainly dependent on cerebral cortex. If Lashley had instead made his lesions beneath the cortex, he might have discovered that other brain regions (such as the hippocampus) strongly affect spatial learning (the role of the hippocampus in spatial learning is discussed in Chapters 3 and 7).

Useful as brain lesion experiments are, they are limited in what they can reveal. Suppose a researcher lesions part of a rat's cortex and then finds, as Lashley did, that the rat can still learn to run a maze. Would that prove that this cortical area is not involved in maze learning? Not necessarily; the rat may now be learning the maze in a different way. This would be analogous to your being able to find your way around a house with the lights out, even though you use visual input when it's available. Data from lesion studies are strongest when supplemented by data from other techniques that provide evidence of whether a brain region "normally" participates in a given behavior.

Test Your Knowledge

Equipotentiality versus Phrenology

What are the main differences between the explanations of brain function proposed by Joseph Gall and those ultimately proposed by Karl Lashley? What evidence supports each of these viewpoints? (Answers appear in the Answers section in the back of the book.)

Interim Summary

- Reflexes are hardwired (unlearned) responses to stimuli. Sherrington and other early neuroscientists believed that all complex learning was produced through the combination of simple spinal reflexes.

- In the brain, sensory information is initially processed in cortical regions specialized for interpreting particular sensory stimuli, such as primary auditory cortex (A1) for sounds, primary visual cortex (V1) for sights, and primary somatosensory cortex (S1) for touch stimuli.

- Primary motor cortex (M1) produces outputs that guide coordinated movements.

- Most communication between neurons takes place across tiny gaps, or synapses: the presynaptic, or sending, neuron releases a neurotransmitter into the synapse; this chemical message crosses the synapse to activate receptors on the postsynaptic, or receiving, neuron.

- Accidental brain lesions in humans have revealed much about how the brain functions. Intentional brain lesions in animal models have similarly provided insights into how different brain regions contribute to learning and memory.

2.3 Measuring and Manipulating Brain Activity

It's relatively easy to figure out the general function of brain structures such as V1, which receives visual inputs from the eyes, or M1, which sends motor outputs to the muscles. But what about the many brain areas that don't connect so obviously to external inputs and outputs? For instance, what about all the cortical areas that aren't labeled in Figure 2.7? How can we figure out what they do? Several approaches have been used, from observing blood flow in the human brain as it goes about its business, to observing and controlling neural activity in the brains of nonhumans learning tasks in laboratories.

Functional Neuroimaging and Electroencephalography

As noted above, structural neuroimaging (such as MRI) allows researchers to look at the *structure* of a living human brain, whereas **functional neuroimaging** allows them to look at the *activity*, or function, of a living brain. When a brain structure becomes active, it requires more oxygen. Within 4 to 6 seconds, blood flow (with its cargo of oxygen) increases to that region. On the other hand, when a brain structure becomes less active, it requires less oxygen, and blood flow decreases. By tracking local changes in blood flow, researchers can discover which brain regions are active or inactive.

Rather than focusing on where blood flow is heavier in the brain, neuroimaging studies typically examine how blood flow in a particular brain region *changes* depending on what the person is doing or thinking (Figure 2.10). To see such changes in blood flow, researchers may first scan the brain while the person is relaxed—not doing anything. The resulting image is called a *baseline* image. Even though the person isn't performing any task, some areas of the brain are still active (Figure 2.10b). Next, the researchers scan the brain again while the person is performing a task, such as looking at pictures or reading a story. (The pictures or words are projected on the inside ceiling of the scanner so that the person can see them while lying on his or her back.) During the task, some areas of the brain that weren't active at baseline should become more active (Figure 2.10a). Others might decrease in activity. From each point (or pixel) in the image, researchers then subtract the activity at that identical point in the baseline image. The result, called a **difference image,** shows how activity at each point in the image has increased or decreased in the task condition compared with the baseline condition (Figure 2.10c). Usually, the difference image is color coded, with white, red, or yellow indicating areas where blood flow *increased* most during the task relative to the baseline. Colors such as blue and green may indicate where blood flow *decreased* most during the task. Uncolored areas indicate regions where no significant change took place. For example, the difference image in Figure 2.10c shows the parts of the brain that become significantly more active when a person is viewing pictures than when no visual input is provided, confirming the current understanding that areas of the cerebral cortex in the occipital lobe are important for visual processing.

Figure 2.10 Creating a difference image with functional neuroimaging (a) A PET scan detecting blood flow as the brain performs a certain task (in this case, viewing pictures projected on the inside of the scanner). (b) A baseline image taken while the participant is not performing the task. (c) A point-by-point comparison of the two PET scans produces a difference image, color coded to show areas where blood flow significantly increased (or decreased) in the task condition compared with the baseline condition. The white lines are a standard drawing of the same cross section as the PET images to clarify which brain regions correspond to the colored areas.

(a) Activity during task   **(b) Activity at baseline**   **(c) Difference image**

M. E. Raichle, Mallinckrodt of Radiology, Washington University School of Medicine

Two commonly used functional neuroimaging technologies are **positron emission tomography (PET)** and **functional magnetic resonance imaging (fMRI).** PET measures brain activity by detecting radiation from the emission of subatomic particles called positrons, associated with the brain's use of glucose from the blood. fMRI makes use of the same MRI technologies employed for structural imaging described above. Researchers can take an MRI at baseline and a second one while the person is performing a task. Oxygenated blood produces slightly different signals than deoxygenated blood, so there are fluctuations in the signal received from areas of the brain that undergo a change in activity level during the task.

Difference images from PET scans and fMRI scans look very similar, with color-coded areas representing brain regions that are significantly more or less active during the task than during the baseline condition. Because both PET and fMRI measure local changes in blood composition, they can produce similar results, but the methods are sufficiently different that they can each provide unique insights into brain activity. For example, Joseph Devlin and colleagues asked a group of young men to view words while undergoing a PET scan. On each trial, the men saw a list of three words (such as "dolphin, seal, walrus") followed by a fourth word (such as "OTTER" or "BANANA") and had to judge whether the fourth word belonged to the same category as the first three. The brain activations recorded during this category-assessment task were compared with brain activations recorded during a baseline task in which the men saw three groups of letters (such as "aaaaaaaa, aaa, aaaaa") and then had to decide whether the fourth group (such as "AAAAA" or "SSSSS") was the same or different. This baseline task had many of the same features as the categorization task, but only in the categorization task did the men have to think about the *meaning* of the words. The researchers then subtracted the PET images of the baseline task from those of the categorization task to produce difference images that showed which brain areas were particularly active when the men were thinking about word meanings (Figure 2.11). Several brain areas appeared to be involved, including areas in the left frontal lobe, the left temporal lobe, and the right cerebellum (Devlin et al., 2002).

The researchers then repeated the experiment with a new group of participants but this time used fMRI to investigate brain activity. Difference images made using fMRI showed brain activation in some of the same areas as the PET study, including areas in the left frontal lobe. But there were also differences: the PET study had shown strong activation in the left temporal lobe and the right cerebellum; fMRI activation in these areas was much less evident. This study is an example in which PET picked up some areas of activation that were not detected by fMRI.

Although PET and fMRI are powerful tools for observing the brain in action, they are only indirect measures of brain activity; respectively, they measure glucose utilization and blood oxygenation in a brain region rather than directly measuring the activity of neurons. Also, because functional neuroimaging studies typically focus on differences in activity under different conditions (through difference images), they tend to emphasize associations between specific brain regions and particular functions (much like phrenology). Finally, both of these functional neuroimaging techniques are comparatively slow: fMRI allows images to be taken every few seconds, and PET images can be taken only every few minutes. Changes in the brain occur much more rapidly than that. To track changes in real time, other techniques, such as electroencephalography, are needed.

(a)

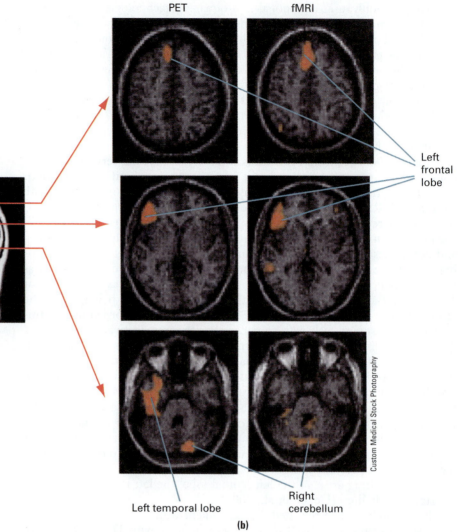

PET   fMRI

Left frontal lobe

Left temporal lobe   Right cerebellum

(b)

Custom Medical Stock Photography

Figure 2.11 PET and fMRI showing brain activation during category assessment Researchers constructed difference images of brain activation in people making category judgments compared with a baseline task that did not require category judgments. (a) Representative difference images are shown from horizontal slices at three levels in the brain. (b) PET and fMRI revealed activity in several of the same brain areas, including the left frontal lobe and the right cerebellum. But the two types of images also differed: PET revealed activity in the left temporal lobe that did not appear on fMRI, and fMRI revealed activity in the left cerebellum that was not visible on PET. Adapted from Devlin et al., 2002.

Electroencephalography (EEG) is a technique for measuring electrical activity in the brain, using the same type of recording electrodes that are used in electrocardiograms. (The Greek word *enkephalos* means "brain," and so "electro-encephalo-graphy" means drawing or graphing the electrical activity of the brain.) The electrodes simply record changes in electrical activity. When such electrodes are placed on a person's chest, they measure electrical activity resulting from heart contractions. When the electrodes are placed on the scalp, they measure the combined tiny electrical charges of large numbers of neurons in the brain, especially those near the location on the skull where the electrodes are placed. The resulting picture is called an *electroencephalogram* (also abbreviated as EEG).

Just as blood is always flowing through the brain, so electrical activity is always occurring in the brain, reflecting the firing patterns of neurons. The exact pattern of activation changes depending on what the brain is doing. For example, when a tone sounds, sensory receptors in the ear become active, and signals travel to primary auditory cortex (A1), affecting electrical activity there.

But detecting this particular electrical change in an EEG is difficult because lots of other neurons in other brain areas that are not involved in hearing may also be active—those responding to whatever visual stimuli happen to be in front of you, for instance, or those activated as you wiggle your fingers and think about what you want to have for lunch.

To detect an electrical change associated with hearing a stimulus, such as a tone, researchers typically present the same stimulus hundreds of times and then average the EEGs produced throughout those repetitions in a given individual. The principle is that activity in other brain areas will come and go, but only the neurons responding to the specific sensory stimulus will be consistently activated each time the stimulus is repeated—and so only their activity patterns will survive the averaging process. EEGs averaged across many repetitions of the same event are called **event-related potentials (ERPs).** Just as functional neuroimaging shows how the brain changes while performing a task, so ERPs can be used to show different brain states.

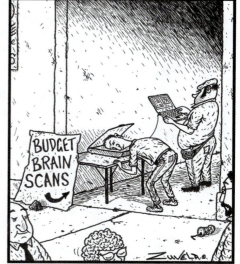

Compared with fMRI and PET, EEG recording is a simple and cheap way to monitor changes in brain activity during learning and memory tasks. It does not require a large and expensive scanner or an injection of a radioactive substance into the bloodstream. In addition, EEG can detect rapid changes in the brain with more precision than fMRI or PET. Yet what EEG gains in temporal precision it often sacrifices in spatial precision. Whereas fMRI and PET can localize activation to within a few millimeters, EEG signals show activity over a wide swath of the brain. In a promising new approach, functional neuroimaging and EEG are being used together to generate images that show precisely when and where neural activity occurs.

Recording from and Activating Neurons

In the brain, information is conveyed not only by *which* neurons fire but also by *how often* they fire. Neuroimaging and lesion studies can reveal the contributions of large areas of the brain to learning and memory, but they don't reveal much about which individual neurons are firing or how often. To gather this information, researchers have to record neural activity deep in the brain. **Neurophysiology** is the study of the activity and function of neurons.

The main technique scientists use to measure firing patterns in individual neurons is **single-cell recording** (the single cell in this case is a neuron). The microelectrodes that are used in this technique are similar in function to EEG electrodes, but they are shaped like extremely thin needles and can penetrate brain tissue with a minimum of damage. The electrode is inserted until the tip is very close to, or sometimes even inside, a target neuron.

To record neural activity from animals as they perform tasks, researchers surgically implant one or more electrodes into desired brain areas. Held in place by a "head stage" attached to the animal's head (a rat is shown here), the electrodes detect neural activity as the animal moves freely; wires transmit this information to a computer, which records and analyzes the signals.

Since neurons are so tiny, placing the recording electrode takes a lot of skill. One placement technique relies on guidance by signals transmitted from the electrode to audio speakers, so that individual spikes, or neuron firings, can be heard as clicks. When a promising pattern of clicking is heard, the researcher knows the electrode is near an interesting neuron—in much the same way beachcombers know, when their metal detector starts clicking, that some coins are buried in the sand nearby.

In some cases, researchers anesthetize an animal and surgically implant one or more recording electrodes in the brain area they wish to study. Then, when the animal wakes, the researchers can record from the neuron(s) as the animal goes about its daily business. (Most animals don't seem to be much bothered by, or even aware of, the wires connected to their heads.) Such experiments allow researchers to determine what role a given neuron might play in the animal's behavior. Alternatively, if the researcher is interested in looking more closely at how individual neurons interact, it is possible to remove pieces (or "slices") of a brain, keep the neurons alive in a bath of nutrients, and record their activity in the slices.

Single-cell recordings have provided some of the most dramatic evidence to date of how neuronal firing relates to behavior. For example, Apostolos Georgopoulos and colleagues recorded spike patterns from the motor cortex of a monkey while the monkey moved a joystick in different directions (Figure 2.12a; Georgopoulos, Taira, & Lukashin, 1993). Some neurons fired most strongly when the monkey pushed the lever in a particular direction. Figure 2.12b shows recordings from one such neuron as the monkey moved the lever toward different compass points. Each vertical line in the recording represents one spike, or neural firing event. When the monkey moved its arm toward the point labeled 6 in Figure 2.12a, the neuron initially produced several spikes, then fell silent. When the monkey moved its arm to a slightly different position, point 7, the neuron let off a more sustained burst of activity, continuing to spike for the duration of the movement. But when the monkey moved its arm directly away from its body, toward point 1, the neuron really went into action, spiking as fast and frequently as it could. By contrast, when the monkey moved its arm in the opposite direction, toward its body (point 5), the neuron fell almost silent. Thus, this neuron's behavior is correlated with arm movements, and neuroscientists would say it is specialized, or "tuned," to fire maximally during movements in a particular direction: away from the body. Georgopoulos and colleagues found that other neurons in the motor cortex were tuned to fire during movements in other directions. Given what we know about the motor cortex from functional imaging and lesion studies, it is reasonable to assume that these neurons may be playing a direct role in issuing the commands that cause the monkey's arm to move.

Figure 2.12 Recording from single neurons (a) Researchers implanted recording electrodes into the motor cortex of a monkey, which was then trained to move a joystick in different directions. (b) One recorded neuron showed spiking behavior (illustrated as vertical lines) when the monkey moved its arm. This neuron fired most when the monkey moved its arm toward position 1 and least when it moved its arm toward position 5. Thus, this neuron is tuned to fire during movements away from the monkey's body. (b) Adapted from Georgopoulos et al., 1993.

Electrode implanted in motor cortex

(a)

(b)

In addition to using recording electrodes to observe neuronal behavior, researchers can try to evoke neuronal activity by using electrodes to deliver tiny amounts of electrical stimulation. As you read above, when neurons fire, an electrical charge sweeps down the axon, triggering the release of neurotransmitter molecules into the synapse. A stimulating electrode can provide this electrical charge, causing spiking activity to happen where and when the researcher is ready to observe and record it.

Electrical stimulation of neurons was used as early as the 1800s, to prove that neuronal activity in the motor cortex produces motor behavior. Pavlov, for instance, was able to produce a wide range of movement patterns in an anesthetized dog by electrically stimulating its motor cortex (Pavlov, 1927). Similar techniques can be used in primates to map which parts of the motor cortex are responsible for generating movements in particular body parts. For example, electrical stimulation delivered to certain neurons in M1 in the right hemisphere, near the top of the brain, cause a monkey's lips to twitch. A little farther down and an arm might twitch. Still lower and movement occurs in the legs. By painstakingly testing the effects of stimulating each point in M1, scientists can draw a map—called a *homunculus* (or "little man")—on the surface of M1, showing which part of the body each region of M1 controls. The homunculus for M1 in humans (Figure 2.13a) has been worked out with the assistance of patients who were candidates for brain surgery (for example, to remove a

Figure 2.13 The homunculus corresponding to human motor cortex (a) By electrically stimulating each point of motor cortex (M1) and recording the evoked movements, researchers can map out the regions of the body controlled by each area of M1. If the homunculus so produced (here, for a male) is assembled into a model of a person (b), with the size of each body part determined by the relative amount of cortex devoted to it, the result is a figure with enlarged lips and hands—areas where human motor control is particularly precise.

Stimulating electrode

Motor cortex (M1)

The British Museum, Natural History

(a)

(b)

tumor). Before removing any brain tissue, neurosurgeons do preliminary testing, which often involves cutting away a piece of the skull to expose the brain underneath and then carefully stimulating different areas. The idea is to determine whether the brain tissue can be cut away without leaving the patient in worse shape than before. To remove a tumor, for example, it may be reasonable to risk damaging the part of M1 that controls movements in one leg, but risk to other parts—say, the areas that control the tongue and allow swallowing and speaking—may call for extra caution.

Looking at the homunculus of Figure 2.13a, you'll notice that some body areas (the lips and hands, for example) seem grossly enlarged, while others (the arms and legs) seem shrunken. In other words, the physical size of a body area doesn't directly correspond to its size in the cortical map. In fact, if the homunculus were assembled into a figurine, it would look something like Figure 2.13b. The distortions aren't random. The parts of the body that are exaggerated on the homunculus are precisely those parts in which humans have the highest degree of fine motor control: fingers that are able to type, knit, and play the piano; lips and tongue that move through the complicated contortions of speech; and facial muscles that display emotion. Other areas of the body that are physically larger, like the arms and legs, have proportionately less fine motor control, and so proportionately less area of motor cortex is devoted to them.

Neural stimulation studies in a variety of species have greatly increased our understanding of how neuronal activity is translated into behavior. The relatively new method of *transcranial magnetic stimulation* (*TMS*) allows researchers to stimulate parts of the human brain by generating strong magnetic pulses over the skull. TMS activates entire brain areas rather than individual neurons, but it has the advantage that it requires no surgery. Depending on the level of stimulation, TMS can either facilitate neural functions or disrupt them. Data from TMS studies may be most useful when combined with results from other studies of neural stimulation in animals and from functional neuroimaging in humans to help build the most complete picture possible of which parts of the brain give rise to which kinds of behavior. We describe this technique in greater detail in Chapter 8, on skill memories.

Observing the Effects of Drugs

In addition to electrical and magnetic stimulation, a third method for manipulating neural activity is the use of **drugs,** chemical substances that alter the biochemical functioning of the body. For example, memory researchers have used the drug scopolamine to temporarily impair memory abilities by disrupting the actions of acetylcholine in the brain. Researchers may not always have a clear idea of why specific drugs enhance or hinder behavior, but it is clear that drugs can change neural activity, so it is no surprise that they can alter learning and memory processes.

Drugs that work on the brain generally do so by altering synaptic transmission. The effects of the drug on behavior depend on which neurotransmitters are involved and whether their ability to carry messages across the synapse is enhanced or impaired.

Drugs can affect any of the four processes depicted in Figure 2.9b:

1. Drugs can increase or decrease the ability of the presynaptic neuron to produce or release neurotransmitter. For example, amphetamines alter the function of neurons that produce the neurotransmitter

dopamine, causing the neurons to release greater than normal quantities of dopamine. This means that postsynaptic neurons receive stronger and more frequent messages than normal. Because the dopamine system is involved in the processing of reward in the brain, the result may be feelings of pleasurable anticipation or excitement. (You will learn more about dopamine in Chapter 5, on operant conditioning.)

2. Drugs can increase or decrease the ability of postsynaptic receptors to receive the chemical message. For example, heroin and morphine are chemically very similar to a class of naturally occurring neurotransmitters called endogenous opioids. When heroin or morphine is released into the brain, molecules of the drug can activate the receptors normally activated by the endogenous opioids. In effect, the drugs "fool" the postsynaptic neuron into thinking that strong signals are being received from many presynaptic neurons. As a result, weak chemical messages that would not normally cause firing in postsynaptic neurons instead cause lots of neurons to fire. The endogenous opioids seem to be important in how the brain processes and signals pleasure, most likely explaining why drugs that mimic endogenous opioids often cause intense feelings of pleasure (also discussed further in Chapter 5).

3. and 4. Drugs can alter the mechanisms for clearing neurotransmitter molecules out of the synapse. Some antidepressant medications (including the selective serotonin reuptake inhibitors, or SSRIs) work by reducing the rate at which serotonin is cleared from synapses. Thus, each time a presynaptic neuron releases serotonin molecules into the synapse, the molecules remain in the synapse longer, increasing their chance of activating a receptor and eliciting a reaction in the postsynaptic cell.

This list is just the beginning of the ways in which drugs can affect brain function. In addition, a drug can have more than one effect, and it can affect more than one neurotransmitter system. Some of the most commonly used drugs, including alcohol and nicotine, have been intensively studied. Yet although their effects on behavior are well documented, their effects on neurons and synaptic transmission are so varied that the precise mechanisms by which these drugs affect brain activity are not yet entirely clear.

Few pharmaceutical drugs have been developed specifically to affect learning and memory abilities (see "Learning and Memory in Everyday Life" on page 66 for recent efforts in this direction). More commonly, a drug's positive or negative effects on these abilities are considered side effects. For example, some types of general anesthesia administered to ease the pain of childbirth can also inadvertently "erase" a mother's memory of her baby being born.

Interim Summary

- Functional neuroimaging methods (such as fMRI and PET) allow researchers to track brain activity indirectly by measuring increases and decreases in glucose utilization and blood oxygenation in different brain regions as the brain performs a task.
- Single-cell recordings allow researchers to monitor and record the electrical activity (or "firing") of single neurons. Researchers can also use implanted electrodes to deliver electrical charges that stimulate a neuron into activity so that the behavior it evokes can be observed.

Can a Pill Improve Your Memory?

I f you've ever studied for a difficult exam, you've probably wished for a pill that could make your brain function like a copy machine. Instead of reading, reviewing, and rehearsing, you could swallow the pill, read the material once, and have it encoded in your brain forever (or at least until the exam is over). Sounds like science fiction, right?

In fact, several companies, ranging from pharmaceutical giants to smaller biotech firms, are looking for a drug to improve memory in healthy people. Some possible candidates are currently being tested on laboratory rats, and a few are even being tested in small groups of human volunteers. It remains to be seen which, if any, of these new drugs will be safe and effective.

Until a new generation of memory-boosting drugs becomes available, researchers continue to examine existing drugs, already approved for the treatment of other illnesses, to see whether any might provide a memory boost in normal, healthy people. For example, several drugs used in treating Alzheimer's disease—including donepezil (Aricept)—increase brain levels of the neurotransmitter acetylcholine, which is abnormally low in people with Alzheimer's. These drugs can produce modest, temporary memory improvements in Alzheimer's patients, raising the possibility that they might also improve memory in healthy (or mildly impaired) adults (Whitehead et al., 2004). However, there is little evidence so far to suggest that the drugs can boost memory in otherwise healthy people (Beglinger et al., 2004).

Another approach to finding memory-enhancing drugs is based on the fact that attention and concentration can increase the storage and retention of new informa-tion. Perhaps drugs that improve attention will also improve memory. Such attention-boosting drugs include modafinil (Provigil), which is used to treat sleep disorders, and methylphenidate (Ritalin), used to treat attention deficit hyperactivity disorder (ADHD). Many college students already pop Ritalin in an effort to boost studying or exam performance. But it's not clear that boosting attention beyond normal levels is necessarily good for memory. The jury is still out on whether these drugs improve memory in healthy humans (Mehta et al., 2000; Turner et al., 2003). The bottom line is that, so far, no pill can substitute for the hard work of learning. Instead of spending money on "brain-boosting" drugs of questionable efficacy and safety, healthy people are best advised to do their learning the old-fashioned way: by devoting the necessary time to study.

▪ Drugs are chemicals that alter the biochemical functioning of the body. Drugs that affect the brain generally affect neural activity by increasing or decreasing the transfer of information between subsets of neurons.

2.4 Neural Plasticity

Learning can lead to numerous structural and functional changes in a neuron. These changes may involve alterations in the shape or size of neurons, as well as changes in supporting structures such as the blood vessels that provide oxygen and nutrients. All of these physical changes can affect how neurons communicate and how brain systems interact. Nevertheless, learning and memory researchers have focused almost exclusively on understanding the role of **synaptic plasticity,** the ability of synapses to change as a result of experience. The idea that connections between neurons change during learning was first popularized by Santiago Ramón y Cajal (1852–1934), a famous Spanish physiologist and anatomist. Specifically, Cajal theorized that learning involves strengthening or weakening connections between individual neurons (Ramón y Cajal, 1990 [1894]).

How is the brain able to weaken or strengthen the right connections? One of neuroscience's most enduring insights came from Donald Hebb, a Canadian neuroscientist who studied under Karl Lashley. Hebb's basic idea was that "neurons that fire together, wire together." In other words, if two neurons that meet at a synapse—we'll call them neuron A and neuron B—often fire at nearly the same time, then the synapse between them should be strengthened, "wiring" the two neurons together. This would increase the probability that whenever neuron A became active, it would cause neuron B to become active, too (Hebb, 1949).

According to Hebb, such changes in synaptic connections between neurons are an automatic result of the neurons' mutual activity. We now know that Hebb was on the right track. But it was several more decades before technology advanced to the point where researchers began to observe experience-related changes in neural activity.

Test Your Knowledge

Synaptic Transmission

Several complex processes that occur at the synapse allow neurons to communicate. Which if any of the statements below do not describe one of these processes? (Answers appear in the Answers section in the back of the book.)

1. Neurotransmitters are reabsorbed by the axon that released them.
2. Neurotransmitters are broken down while they remain in the synapse.
3. Neurotransmitters bind to the dendrite of the postsynaptic neuron.
4. Neurotransmitters are released from vesicles and enter the synapse.

Long-Term Potentiation and Depression

In the late 1960s, Terje Lømo was pursuing his doctoral degree in the lab of Per Andersen at the University of Oslo in Norway. Part of Lømo's research consisted of electrically stimulating the axons of presynaptic neurons that provided inputs to the hippocampus of a rabbit. He simultaneously recorded electrical activity produced by postsynaptic neurons within the hippocampus (Figure 2.14a). Normally, a certain amount of stimulation produced a certain level of response: a single weak stimulation would produce a low response in hippocampal neurons, and a strong burst of high-frequency stimulation (say, 100 stimulations in a second) would produce a more robust response. But to Lømo's surprise, the high-frequency stimulation also caused a lasting change in responding, so that hippocampal neurons would over-respond to subsequent weak stimulation (Figure 2.14b). This change could last for hours (Bliss & Gardner-Medwin, 1973; Bliss & Lømo, 1973; Lømo, 1966).

By way of analogy, imagine you have a brother who constantly torments you with his snide comments. Most of the time, you don't react. But one day he says something that's really over the top, and you respond with some strong language of your own. A few minutes later, before you've had a chance to calm down, he makes another little snide comment. Ordinarily, you might not have bothered to respond. But this time you haven't yet cooled down from the earlier explosion, so you snap back again. Your prior anger has *potentiated* your response to a weak stimulus that normally wouldn't have evoked such a strong reaction.

Potentiation of a neuron by a strong stimulus is similar (except that the "irritation" can last much longer), making the neuron more likely to respond to any subsequent stimulus. This effect, in which synaptic transmission becomes more effective as a result of recent activity, came to be called **long-term potentiation (LTP).** The reports by Lømo and his coworkers demonstrated that neurons could actually change their activity as a function of experience and that these changes could last for hours or days (Bliss & Gardner-Medwin, 1973; Bliss &

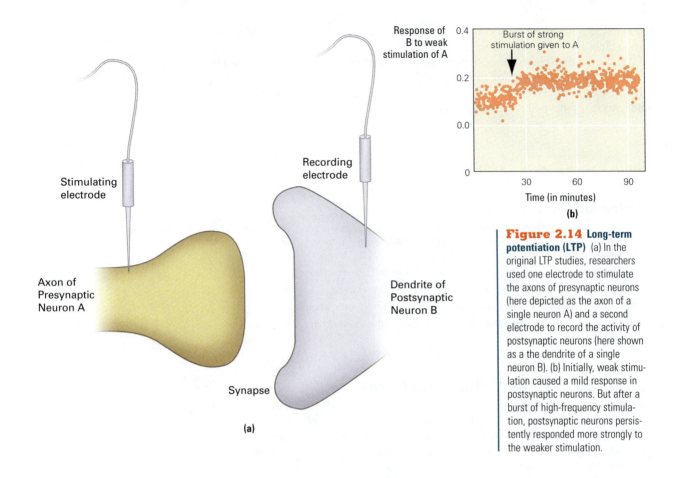

Response of B to weak stimulation of A

Burst of strong stimulation given to A

Time (in minutes)

(b)

Figure 2.14 Long-term potentiation (LTP) (a) In the original LTP studies, researchers used one electrode to stimulate the axons of presynaptic neurons (here depicted as the axon of a single neuron A) and a second electrode to record the activity of postsynaptic neurons (here shown as a the dendrite of a single neuron B). (b) Initially, weak stimulation caused a mild response in postsynaptic neurons. But after a burst of high-frequency stimulation, postsynaptic neurons persistently responded more strongly to the weaker stimulation.

Lømo, 1973). Since that time, LTP has become one of the most intensively studied phenomena in neuroscience.

Despite intensive study of LTP in the decades since it was initially reported, many questions remain about exactly what changes occur to produce it. Perhaps postsynaptic neurons change to become more responsive to subsequent inputs. This would mean that when presynaptic neurons release neurotransmitters after strong stimulation, the postsynaptic neurons will have a heightened sensitivity to that neurotransmitter, producing the enhanced response seen in Figure 2.14b.

LTP may also involve changes to presynaptic neurons. This idea is controversial, because it isn't clear exactly how signals could travel backward across the synapse. But perhaps some kind of chemical—a *retrograde messenger*—could be released by postsynaptic neurons and diffuse across the synapse, causing an increase in the amount of neurotransmitter the presynaptic neurons release in the future. These changes might occur within a few minutes and last several hours. In addition, however, most researchers currently believe there is a component of LTP that takes place over several hours and can last a lifetime. This would involve changes such as strengthening of existing synapses or even the building of new ones (Chen, Rex, Casale, Gall, & Lynch, 2007).

As excited as researchers were about the possibilities of LTP as a mechanism for learning, they were aware of a significant remaining question. LTP represents a way to strengthen neuronal connections, but this alone isn't much use. If you think of the activity patterns of a neuron as being like an audio signal, then LTP corresponds to pumping up the volume of particular input patterns. But imagine an orchestra conductor who can only make the musicians play louder. Every symphony would end in cacophony! There has to be a way to turn individual sounds down as well as up. For LTP to be effective as a way to increase the strength of useful synapses, there would also have to be a process that can decrease the strength of less useful synapses.

Soon after Lømo and others' original reports, such a process was discovered (Dunwiddie & Lynch, 1978). **Long-term depression (LTD)** occurs when synaptic transmission becomes *less* effective as a result of recent activity. One situation in which this happens is if presynaptic neurons are repeatedly active but the postsynaptic neurons do not respond. Neurons that fire together wire together, but connections between neurons that don't fire together weaken, a change that is believed to reflect a weakening in the synapse. As with the synaptic changes in LTP, researchers have various ideas about how the weakening might occur: there may be a decrease in the responsiveness of postsynaptic neurons, a decrease in neurotransmitter release by presynaptic neurons, or long-term structural changes in the neurons and synapses. As with LTP, many of the details of LTD remain to be worked out. Scientists still have a long way to go to understand synaptic plasticity and its relation to learning and memory.

Test Your Knowledge

Synaptic Plasticity

Synaptic plasticity is one of the most researched phenomena in the field of neuroscience, yet many of its features remain poorly understood. Identify which of the following statements accurately describe what is known about synaptic plasticity. (Answers appear in the Answers section in the back of the book.)

1. Synaptic change can be produced through electrical stimulation.
2. Synaptic plasticity is most easily observed by monitoring changes in the concentration of neurotransmitters.
3. Whenever firing patterns change in a neural circuit, synaptic change has occurred somewhere in the circuit.
4. Synaptic plasticity can weaken or strengthen connections between neurons.
5. Synaptic plasticity can be measured in humans with fMRI.
6. LTP is observed only in animals that have recently been learning.

Experience-Dependent Neural Growth

While conducting the research that led to the formulation of Hebb's rule, Donald Hebb studied rat behavior in his lab, and he sometimes took a few animals home for his children to play with. (Nowadays, researchers generally wouldn't be permitted to remove experimental animals from the testing facility, but in Hebb's day, the rules were less stringent.) Hebb noted that the rats raised by his children as pets performed better on laboratory tasks than rats housed in cages in the lab (Hebb, 1947).

Hebb's observation was later verified scientifically. Researchers housed one group of rats in an **enriched environment,** meaning an environment where

**(a) Standard
laboratory housing**

**(b) Enriched
laboratory environment**

**Figure 2.15 Deprived
environment vs. enriched
environment** Representations
of neurons from the cortex
of (a) a rat raised in standard
laboratory housing and (b) a rat
raised in an enriched laboratory
environment. Neurons from rats
raised in enriched environments
typically have more and longer
dendrites, and more synapses per
dendrite, than their experience-
impoverished counterparts.

there was plenty of sensory stimulation and opportunity to explore and learn. For the rats, this meant a large cage filled with toys to play with and other rats with whom to socialize. A second group of rats lived in standard laboratory housing, each rat isolated in a small chamber that contained nothing but a drinking spout and food cup. The results? The rats housed in the enriched environment showed better maze learning than the rats kept in standard laboratory housing (Rosenzweig, 1984; Renner & Rosenzweig, 1987).

These behavioral improvements appear to reflect structural changes in neurons. Rats raised in an enriched environment have cortical neurons with more and longer dendrites than their experience-impoverished counterparts (Figure 2.15). The dendrites of rats in the enriched environment also have more synapses—meaning more connections with other neurons (Globus, Rosenzweig, Bennet, & Diamond, 1973; Greenough, West, & DeVoogd, 1978). These neural changes occur quickly: as few as 60 days of housing in an enriched environment can result in a 7% to 10% increase in brain weight of young rats and a 20% increase in the number of synapses in the visual cortex. Similar changes are seen in the brains of monkeys and cats raised in enriched environments. Even the brains of fruit flies housed in large communal cages with visual and odor cues show similar changes, compared with flies housed alone in small plastic vials (Technau, 1984).

And what about humans? Recent studies have shown that preschool children placed in "high-quality" day care (with lots of toys, educational experiences, and teacher interaction) fare better in elementary school than children whose day care offers fewer opportunities for learning (Peisner-Feinberg, Burchinal, & Clifford, 2001). Just like the rats, people who have plenty of toys to play with and plenty of social interaction fare better than people who have fewer opportunities to engage their brain. Although there isn't yet definitive evidence that human brains undergo enlargement similar to that of rats after environmental enrichment, suggestive data come from a study of London taxi drivers.

London is a sprawling city with hundreds of small, crooked streets. To receive an official license, London taxi drivers must study for up to three years and pass a grueling exam that requires them, for example, to indicate the shortest path between random London addresses. This means that licensed London taxi drivers are a group of people sharing an extensive fund of spatial knowledge.

Researcher Eleanor Maguire and her colleagues compared brain volumes in a group of London taxi drivers with those of age-matched Londoners who had not studied the geography of their city so extensively (Maguire et al., 2000). The only part of the brain that differed significantly between the groups was the hippocampus: among other things, the taxi drivers had slightly larger posterior hippocampal volumes than non–taxi drivers. Further, the size of the posterior hippocampus differed even among individual taxi drivers: those who had been driving for more than a decade had a larger volume than those who had been driving for only a few years. One possible interpretation of these volume differences is that the intensive spatial learning in taxi drivers causes an increase in dendritic branching in hippocampal neurons—making those neurons take up more room, just like the rat neurons shown in Figure 2.15.

Interim Summary

- Learning requires physical changes in neurons, including changes in neurons' shape, size, and number of connections to other neurons, all of which can affect patterns of neural activity.

- The ability of synapses to change with experience is called synaptic plasticity. Strengthening or weakening the connections between neurons can influence when they fire.

- Long-term potentiation (LTP) occurs when synaptic transmission becomes more effective as a result of experience.

- An opponent process to LTP, called long-term depression (LTD), occurs when synaptic transmission becomes less effective with experience.

- Enriched environment studies show that experiences can have a profound impact on brain organization and on an individual's learning and memory abilities.

▶ SYNTHESIS

We've covered a lot of ground in this chapter. We started with the basic geography of the brain, moved on to some key principles of how the various brain regions process different kinds of information and give rise to different kinds of behavior, and ended by looking at how neurons change as a result of experience.

If you get the feeling that, for all this information, there are still a frustrating number of unresolved questions about learning and memory, you're absolutely correct. But this is also a time when technology and research are providing brain scientists with an unprecedented selection of techniques: neuroimaging and recording methods that allow visualization of brain activity, electron microscopes that make synapses and neurotransmitter-containing vesicles visible to us, and systems capable of recording single-cell activity from dozens of neurons simultaneously. These tools, now in fairly routine use, didn't even exist a few decades ago.

In the following chapters, we dig deeper into the neural substrates of learning and memory. The involvement of the hippocampus in these processes has been widely studied in humans and other animals. Consequently, this brain region is discussed in more chapters than any other part of the brain. Chapter 3 describes links between the hippocampus and spatial memories, Chapter 4 describes hippocampal contributions to eyeblink conditioning, and Chapter 7 describes the dramatic impacts of hippocampal damage on memories for facts and events. Hippocampal processing also contributes to generalization of learning (Chapter 6), emotional learning (Chapter 10), and the social transfer of information (Chapter 11). Intriguingly, the hippocampus is also one of the few regions in the mammalian brain where new neurons are born throughout adulthood, a process that may contribute to our ability to keep learning new information across a lifetime (Chapter 12).

Several regions of the cerebral cortex have also been shown to underlie various learning and memory capacities, and so discussion of cortical processing is likewise spread across multiple chapters. Changes in sensory and motor cortex associated with learning are described in Chapters 3, 6, and 8, while the roles of frontal and association cortex in memory formation and retrieval are reviewed in Chapter 7. Frontal cortex also is discussed extensively in Chapter 9, where it is related to the ability to juggle thoughts and memories and to voluntarily manipulate how memories are used.

Three other brain regions emphasized in the following discussions are the cerebellum, the basal ganglia, and the amygdala. The cerebellum has been studied extensively as a site of memory storage and processing in classical conditioning

Figure 2.16 Overview of brain regions discussed in subsequent chapters The hippocampus, cortex, cerebellum, basal ganglia, and amygdala all contribute to learning and memory in different ways. Their roles are described in further detail in the chapters indicated.

research (Chapter 4) and in relation to skill learning (Chapter 8). The basal ganglia are also implicated in skill learning, particularly when learning involves reinforcement (Chapter 5) and sensory-guided actions (Chapter 8). Finally, the amygdala is central to emotional learning, affecting how rapidly memories are formed (Chapter 10) and how long they last (Chapter 7). Figure 2.16 summarizes where each of these brain regions is discussed in the book.

We hope that the following chapters will engage all of these brain regions and more, enabling you to better encode and organize your own knowledge about learning and memory phenomena.

Key Terms

axon, *p. 45*

brainstem, *p. 42*

cell body, *p. 45*

central nervous system (CNS), *p. 41*

cerebellum, *p. 42*

cerebral cortex, *p. 42*

computed tomography (CT), *p. 47*

dendrite, *p. 45*

difference image, *p. 58*

diffusion tensor imaging (DTI), *p. 48*

drug, *p. 64*

electroencephalography (EEG), *p. 60*

engram, *p. 56*

enriched environment, *p. 69*

event-related potential (ERP), *p. 61*

frontal lobe, *p. 42*

functional magnetic resonance imaging (fMRI), *p. 59*

functional neuroimaging, *p. 58*

glia, *p. 46*

lesion, *p. 47*

long-term depression (LTD), *p. 69*

long-term potentiation (LTP), *p. 67*

magnetic resonance imaging (MRI), *p. 47*

nervous system, *p. 41*

neuromodulator, *p. 55*

neuron, *p. 41*

neurophysiology, *p. 61*

neuropsychology, *p. 55*

neuroscience, *p. 40*

neurotransmitter, *p. 53*

occipital lobe, *p. 42*

parietal lobe, *p. 42*

peripheral nervous system (PNS), *p. 41*

phrenology, *p. 46*

positron emission tomography (PET), *p. 59*

postsynaptic, *p. 53*

presynaptic, *p. 53*

receptor, *p. 53*

reflex, *p. 49*

single-cell recording, *p. 61*

soma, *p. 45*

structural neuroimaging, *p. 47*

synapse, *p. 53*

synaptic plasticity, *p. 66*

temporal lobe, *p. 42*

theory of equipotentiality, *p. 56*

Concept Check

1. In addition to learning to salivate whenever they heard a bell, some of Pavlov's dogs learned to salivate whenever Pavlov walked into the room. Why might this have occurred, and what region(s) of a dog's cortex might have changed as a result of this learning?

2. Neuroimages of different individuals performing the same task often differ greatly in the brain regions shown to be activated. Does this mean that the brains of these individuals function differently? If not, why not?

3. Drugs or genetic manipulations that block LTP in the hippocampus impair learning in some tasks but facilitate learning in other tasks. Similarly, some researchers have correlated LTP-like effects with learning in a variety of tasks, whereas others have observed learning in the absence of these LTP effects. What does this tell us about the relationship between LTP and learning?

4. Brain damage caused by carbon monoxide poisoning can result in many deficits, including color blindness, an inability to recognize objects, an inability to detect movement, and severe impairments in language and memory. How can a neuropsychologist determine what part(s) of the brain might have been damaged?

5. Lashley's findings from lesion experiments in rats suggest that the brain can function when only part of the cerebral cortex is available. Additionally, invertebrates have been learning successfully for millions of years with less than 1% of the total neurons mammals have. What does this information imply about the role of the cerebral cortex in learning and memory?

Habituation, Sensitization, and Familiarization

Learning about Repeated Events

JEFFREY'S GRANDMOTHER WAS FED UP. It was two o'clock in the morning, and once again her grandson was banging around in the basement. She couldn't remember how many times she had told him to stop making such a racket. It had taken her a couple of years to get used to the neighbor's dogs barking all night. They almost never woke her up now. But Jeffrey's noisiness was another matter altogether. Every time he started up with the sawing, banging, and yelling, it seemed worse than the last time. Eventually, she forced Jeffrey to move out of the house. If she had known what he was doing to raise such a din, it would have disturbed her a lot more.

At first Jeffrey Dahmer was annoyed at being kicked out of his grandmother's house, but he soon got used to the convenience of having his own apartment. He took to cruising around the Pink Flamingo and other bars that were popular among young gay men, his potential victims. Dahmer had learned to recognize which of the customers were most likely to take his bait and follow him home. He couldn't say what it was about them that let him know they were susceptible, but he was confident that he could discriminate the "maybes" from the "probably nots."

During this same period, reports began to appear in the news media of young men going missing from the neighborhood. But disappearances were all too common in Milwaukee; for most people this was just more of the same. When one of Dahmer's victims—a 14-year-old Laotian who spoke no English—escaped to run naked through the streets, police picked him up and returned him to Dahmer's apartment. Dahmer

Behavioral Processes
  Recognizing and Responding to Repetition
  Learning and Memory in Everyday Life: Sex on the Beach
  Perceptual Learning
  Learning and Memory in Everyday Life: Racial Bias
  Learning through Exploration

Brain Substrates
  Invertebrate Model Systems
  Perceptual Learning and Cortical Plasticity
  The Hippocampus and Spatial Recognition

Clinical Perspectives
  Rehabilitation after Stroke: Habituation Gone Awry
  Man-Machine Interfaces: Regaining Sensory Modalities through Perceptual Learning

convinced them that the boy was his lover and an adult, and that they were just having a lover's tiff. The police noticed a terrible stench in the apartment, but noxious smells weren't uncommon in that part of the city. The officers left, and the boy was not seen alive again.

It wasn't until another victim escaped and flagged down a squad car that police returned to Dahmer's apartment. This time, they noticed some photos of dismembered bodies in the bedroom. That got the officers' attention, and when they investigated further, they found a human head in the refrigerator. The public, initially blasé about the news of one more captured criminal, paid considerably more attention when they learned that Dahmer was not only killing his victims but also eating them. The Jeffrey Dahmer case quickly became the biggest news story of its day.

When an individual experiences the same event many times, the brain accumulates memories of those experiences. Sometimes the memories lead a person to ignore additional repetitions of the events. Dahmer's grandmother heard the neighbor's dogs barking many times and eventually got used to them; the Milwaukee police had experienced many smelly apartments and consequently did not investigate the source of the putrid smell in Dahmer's apartment; the public was used to news reports of disappearances and so did

Jeffrey Dahmer killed 17 people before being captured.

AP Photo/Handout

not think too much about what might be causing them. None of these occurrences elicited much of a reaction until new and more alarming aspects came to light.

Such loss of responding to repeated experiences is called *habituation*, and it's one of the most widespread forms of learning. All organisms ever tested—even those without a brain, such as protozoa—show habituation. It is just one example of how experiencing an event over and over causes learning about that event. Through habituation, a person learns to disregard an event, but in other instances, repetition can increase attention to the event. Jeffrey's grandmother became *sensitized* to the sounds she repeatedly heard coming from her basement, and ultimately they annoyed her so much that she kicked Jeffrey out. Repeated experiences can also lead to *perceptual learning*, which enabled Jeffrey Dahmer to identify suitable victims. This chapter focuses on the contrasting ways organisms respond to repeated events and looks at how memories for repeated events are acquired.

3.1 Behavioral Processes

Recall from Chapter 1 that learning is a process in which behavior changes as a result of experience. The changes in behavior caused by learning are not always immediately obvious, however. *Latent learning* is learning that takes place without any initial evidence that learning has occurred. As a student reading this chapter, you are actively attempting to understand and remember the information it contains. At the same time, you are automatically forming memories of your reading experiences. As a student reading this chapter, you are actively attempting to understand and remember the information it contains. Did that last sentence seem familiar? Although you are probably not attempting to memorize every word of every sentence in this book, it is still relatively easy for you to recognize a sentence you have just read. To an outside observer, however, you are simply a person staring at words. There is no direct evidence that you understand what the words you are looking at mean, much less that you have detected any repetition within the sentences. Your learning and recognition are effectively hidden from the world.

As a student reading this chapter, you are easily able to detect that repetition is occurring. As a student reading this chapter, you should be curious about how it is that you and other organisms do this. As a student reading this chapter, you should recognize that these are exactly the kinds of repetitions that might lead to habituation, if not for the variation in the way each repetition ends. As a student reading this chapter, you might also be aware of how this sort of persistent repetition can easily become aggravating (if so, you are beginning to understand what sensitization is like). As a student reading this chapter, you have just directly experienced some of the phenomena associated with latent learning about repeated events.

Recognizing and Responding to Repetition

Suppose a man who was born and raised in Jamaica has never seen snow. If he moves to Buffalo, New York, he will probably be excited and fascinated by his first snowfall. But a man of the same age who has grown up in Buffalo will react to the same snowfall very differently. For him, snow is recognizable, common, nothing to write home about—except, perhaps, for the inconvenience it causes on his commute to work.

Everything is novel the first time it happens to you. Even the most ordinary events only become mundane after repeated exposures. Through repetition, you may learn not to respond to a particular event, even if—like the Jamaican in the snow—you originally responded with great excitement. This kind of learning, **habituation,** is formally defined as a decrease in the strength or occurrence of a behavior after repeated exposure to the stimulus that produces the behavior. Habituation is sometimes described as the simplest or most basic kind of learning. Nevertheless, experimental studies conducted over the last 100 years have yet to reveal exactly how habituation works (Thompson, 2009). In the following sections, we describe some of what researchers have discovered about habituation and its underlying mechanisms.

The Process of Habituation

You've experienced habituation if you've ever moved to a new home. Possibly, the first night or two, you had trouble getting to sleep because of the strange noises outside your window (whether wailing police sirens or chirping crickets). But after a few nights, you probably were no longer awakened by the noises and slept until morning.

In the laboratory, researchers examine simpler examples of habituation that they can describe in terms of a single easily controlled stimulus and a single easily measurable response. One such response is the **acoustic startle reflex,** which is a defensive response to a loud, unexpected noise. When a rat in an experimental chamber is startled by a loud noise, it jumps, much as you might jump if someone sneaked up behind you and yelled in your ear. If the same noise is presented over and over again, every minute or so, the rat's startle response declines (Figure 3.1a), just as your responsiveness to noises would decrease after moving into a new home; if the process goes on long enough, the rat may cease to startle altogether. At this point, the rat's startle response has habituated to the loud noise.

Another common way to study habituation uses the **orienting response,** an organism's natural reaction to a novel stimulus or to an important event. For example, if a checkerboard pattern (or any other unfamiliar visual stimulus) is presented to an infant, the infant's orienting response is to turn her head and look at it for a few seconds before shifting her gaze elsewhere. If the checkerboard is removed for 10 seconds and then redisplayed, the infant will respond again—but for a shorter time than on the first presentation (Figure 3.1b). The duration of staring, called *fixation time,* decreases with repeated presentations of the stimulus, in a manner very much like the habituation of rats' startle response (Malcuit, Bastien, & Pomerleau, 1996).

Normally, habituation is advantageous for an organism. Through habituation to familiar stimuli, the individual avoids wasting time and energy on an elaborate response to every repeated event. But habituation carries risks. A deer that has gotten used to the sound of gunshots is a deer whose head may end up as a hunter's trophy. A poker player whose responses become habituated to the excitement of winning a small pot may start to play for larger and larger stakes, putting his finances at risk. The dangers of habituation are immortalized in the story of the boy who cried wolf. In this folk tale, the boy plays practical jokes on his neighbors, calling them to come save him from an imaginary wolf; eventually the villagers learn there is no reason to respond when he calls. Later, a real wolf attacks, but the villagers ignore the boy's cries, and no one comes to save him.

Figure 3.1 Habituation
(a) The acoustic startle response in rats declines with repeated presentation of a loud auditory stimulus. (b) The time infants spend looking at a visual stimulus declines with repeated presentation of the stimulus.

[(a) Adapted from Davis, 1980; (b) adapted from Malcuit et al., 1996.]

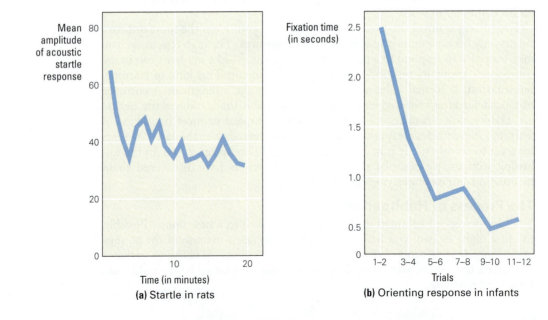

(a) Startle in rats

(b) Orienting response in infants

This might seem like a case in which the villagers just learned that the boy was unreliable. Think, however, about situations in which you have heard a fire or car alarm go off repeatedly for no apparent reason. Each time the alarm goes off, you will become more skeptical, and at the same time your orienting or startle response will likely decrease. Anytime your response decreases with repeated experiences, there is a good chance that habituation is occurring. Of course, it is also possible that you are simply falling asleep, especially if the alarm is going off at night. One way researchers are able to distinguish habituation from other causes of decreased behavioral responding to repetition is by disrupting the repetition of experienced events, as described below.

"Sometimes I get so bored with myself I can barely make it to 'doodle-do.'"

Stimulus Specificity and Dishabituation

An important feature of habituation is that habituation to one event doesn't cause habituation to every other stimulus in the same sensory modality. In other words, habituation is stimulus specific (Thompson & Spencer, 1966). After a baby's orienting response to one visual stimulus (say, a donut shape) has decreased after several repetitions, the baby will still show a strong orienting response to a new visual stimulus (say, a cross shape). This renewal of responding provides evidence of habituation to the first visual stimulus because if the baby was simply falling asleep, it should not matter what visual stimulus appears. Interestingly, a baby's fixation time when shown a "new" image depends on how similar that image is to the one that was repeatedly experienced. The more similar the image, the less the fixation time will increase. This phenomenon, called *stimulus generalization*, is observed in all forms of learning; we discuss generalization in greater detail in Chapter 6.

In some cases, presenting a novel stimulus after multiple presentations of a familiar stimulus can actually lead to recovery of the habituated response to the familiar stimulus. For example, a baby shown a donut shape many times may show little interest the twentieth time it is presented. If, however, the baby is briefly shown a live kitten after the nineteenth repetition of the donut, the baby is likely to respond to the twentieth presentation of a donut shape as if it were a novel image, showing a much longer fixation time than in the kitten-free scenario. This renewal of responding after a new stimulus has been presented is called **dishabituation.** Dishabituation often occurs when an arousing stimulus (like a kitten) is introduced into a sequence of otherwise monotonous repetitions but can also accompany less eventful changes. Simply adding motion to a familiar stimulus can lead to dishabituation, as demonstrated when adults start waving toys around in front of an infant who seems uninterested. Dishabituation provides another useful way of demonstrating that the absence of responding to a repeated stimulus is indeed the result of habituation and not some other factor like fatigue.

All organisms that show habituation also show dishabituation. In the laboratory, a male rat will mate with an unfamiliar female many times over a period of a few hours but eventually reaches a point at which the mating stops. If the now-familiar female is replaced with a new female, however, the male rat will rush to mate some more. This dishabituation of the mating response shows that habituation occurred with the first partner rather than the rat's merely running out of energy or interest in sex (Dewsbury, 1981; Fisher, 1962). The dishabituation of sexual responding is sometimes referred to as the *Coolidge effect*, after

Sex on the Beach

Advertisements for travel to exotic locales with long, sandy beaches often show happy couples falling in love all over again, rediscovering the romance that may have drained out of their everyday existence back home. Can two people really reignite their old flame simply by taking it to a new location? The answer is probably—and the reason is *dishabituation*.

It's easier to study dishabituation of sexual responding in rats than in humans. Most human research has instead focused on sexual arousal in male undergraduate volunteers during the viewing of sexually explicit photos. Such studies have shown that if the same arousing photos are presented repeatedly, human males respond less strongly, just like other animals (Koukounas & Over, 2001; Plaud, Gaither, Henderson, & Devitt, 1997).

Relatively few studies of habituation of sexual arousal have been conducted in women. One problem is that women usually do not become as aroused as their male counterparts when viewing sexually explicit photos. Obviously, it is hard for researchers to measure decreases in an arousal response if they can't reliably elicit arousal to begin with. But in studies that have managed to solve this problem, habituation to sexual arousal seems to occur to a lesser degree in female undergraduates than in male undergraduates (Laan & Everaerd, 1995; Youn, 2006).

An interesting aspect of sexual habituation is that it seems to happen without conscious awareness. For example, male students in a sexual habituation experiment often show habituation within a single session, responding less and less to the same sexually explicit photo as the session goes on—but they also show habituation across sessions, responding less and less each day of a multi-day experiment (Plaud et al., 1997). Under these circumstances, participants often report that they were aware that their arousal was decreasing within a single session, but they seemed to be unaware that their arousal also decreased across sessions. Such continuous but imperceptible decreases in arousal might be a factor in promiscuity and infidelity, which not only threaten stable relationships but may contribute to the spread of sexually transmitted diseases (Plaud et al., 1997).

How can someone in a long-term relationship deal with the scourge of sexual habituation? Prolonged abstinence could lead to *spontaneous recovery* of interest. Another option is to introduce novel stimuli to bring about dishabituation—for example, staging romantic interludes or trying a different technique. So the next time you're feeling bored with an old relationship, a trip to Tahiti might be just what the doctor ordered!

an anecdote involving President Coolidge. While touring a poultry farm, the story goes, the president and his wife were informed that a single rooster could mate dozens of times in a single day. "Ha," said Mrs. Coolidge. "Tell that to Mr. Coolidge." The president then asked the tour guide whether the rooster was always required to mate with the same female. Told that it was not, the president reportedly remarked, "Ha—tell that to Mrs. Coolidge." (See "Learning and Memory in Everyday Life" above for more on habituation and dishabituation of human sexual responses.)

Factors Influencing the Rate and Duration of Habituation

How rapidly a response habituates and how long the decrease in responding lasts depend on several factors, including how startling the stimulus is, the number of times it is experienced, and the length of time between repeated exposures. It is relatively easy to get used to the feeling of the tag in the back of your shirt—most people can learn to ignore this stimulus relatively quickly. In fact, at this point you probably would have to make an effort to notice that the tag is even there. It would probably take you longer to get used to the feeling of a spider crawling on the back of your neck—or you might never get used to that at all, even after many repeated experiences. In general, the less arousing an event is, the more rapidly a response to that event will habituate. Whenever habituation does occur, larger decreases in responding are seen after earlier repetitions than after later exposures (see Figure 3.1). In other words, the biggest changes in responding are seen when one is first becoming familiar with a stimulus. This pattern is seen for many kinds of learning and will be discussed in greater detail in Chapters 4 and 8.

Animals given sessions of multiple exposures to stimuli in which the exposures are separated by short intervals will typically show habituation after fewer exposures than animals given sessions in which the same number of exposures are spread out over time (Rankin & Broster, 1992; Thompson & Spencer, 1966): more rapid repetition of a stimulus generally leads to more rapid habituation. Exposures that are repeated closely together in time are called *massed*, whereas exposures that are spread out over time are called *spaced*. If your goal is to habituate your response to some repeated stimulus as rapidly as possible, your best bet is to find a way to make that stimulus as nonarousing as possible, to expose yourself to closely spaced repetitions of that stimulus, and to repeat the process frequently (as you do when you wear shirts with tags in the back).

The effects of habituation may last for a few minutes or several hours and under some circumstances may last a day or more. But they generally do not last forever and are especially likely to dissipate if the stimulus is absent for a while. Habituation that goes away in seconds or minutes is called *short-term habituation*; habituation that lasts longer is called *long-term habituation*. If a rat has gotten used to a loud noise and then goes through a period of an hour or so in which the noise does not occur, the rat is likely to startle anew when the noise is played again. The reappearance or increase in strength of a habituated response after a period of no stimulus presentation is called **spontaneous recovery.** The factors that determine how quickly an individual's response habituates also affect how long the effects of habituation last. Animals that experience massed exposures to a stimulus learn to ignore that stimulus faster than animals given spaced exposures, but if they are retested after a relatively long break, the animals given massed exposures are also more likely to show spontaneous recovery. When exposures are spaced in time, it takes longer for responding to habituate, but once habituation occurs, it lasts for a longer time (Gatchel, 1975; Pedreira, Romano, Tomsic, Lozada, & Maldonado, 1998).

This finding makes intuitive sense, because animals that have gotten used to the intermittent occurrence of a stimulus should find the recurrence of the stimulus after a long interval to be familiar. As a student reading this chapter, you are easily able to detect that repetition is occurring, even when that repetition occurs after moderately long intervals. If your repeated experiences are spread out over time, the likelihood is greater that you will continue to recognize repeating events farther into the future. So, if you want habituation to last for as long as possible, your best bet is to repeatedly expose yourself to the relevant stimulus after longer and longer stretches of time.

Although spontaneous recovery might seem to suggest that habituation is a temporary effect, habituation effects accumulate over time. So, if an infant is shown a donut shape 20 times during a single session, its orienting response to that image will likely habituate. If a day or two later the infant is shown the donut shape again, spontaneous recovery will probably have occurred, and the infant's fixation time will be as long as if the image were completely novel. However, this time it may only take eight trials before the infant's orienting response becomes habituated: the effects of repeated experiences have been potentiated by the prior repetitions. This shows that the effects of earlier repeated experiences have not simply faded away. Furthermore, the mechanisms underlying habituation continue to change with repeated exposures, even when behavioral responses are no longer changing. For instance, a rat exposed to a loud sound many times might stop showing any indication that it even hears the sound—its response has decreased to the point at which there no longer is a response. Nevertheless, if the sound continues to be repeated many times after this point, the amount of time required before spontaneous recovery occurs will increase. In this case, the learning associated with repeated exposures is latent, because there are no observable changes in the rat's behavior associated with the increased number of repetitions. The additional effects of repeated exposures after behavioral responding to a stimulus has ceased are only evident when subsequent tests show delayed spontaneous recovery (Thompson & Spencer, 1966).

The Process of Sensitization

Several times a year, news reports appear of a celebrity attacking a member of the paparazzi. The actor Sean Penn was charged with attempted murder after he grabbed a photographer by the ankles and held him over a ninth-floor balcony. Rapper Kanye West was arrested for attacking a reporter at Los Angeles International Airport and destroying his camera. Given that celebrities have lots of photos taken of them by lots of people on a daily basis, you might expect that they would eventually become used to all the attention and take no notice of photographers. What causes some celebrities to become so aggressive when confronted with paparazzi? Is it just a case of bad tempers?

One possible explanation is that celebrities have had negative experiences involving photographers in the past that are affecting their responses to new interactions with random members of the paparazzi. **Sensitization** is a phenomenon in which experiences with an arousing stimulus lead to stronger responses to a later stimulus. In some cases, a single, very intense stimulus can produce sensitization, whereas in others, repeated exposures are required. In some ways, sensitization seems to be almost the opposite of habituation. Whereas in habituation repeated experiences can attenuate a rat's acoustic startle reflex, in sensitization repeated experiences can heighten it. As described above, when rats are subjected to a loud noise over and over again, their startle response often habituates (Figure 3.2, green line). But if some of these rats are given an electric shock (Figure 3.2, red line) and then the loud noise is played again, their startle response will be much greater than that of the rats who did not receive a shock (Davis, 1989). In other words, the strong electric shock sensitizes the rats, increasing their startle response to a subsequent loud noise stimulus. Such sensitization is usually short-lived, however. It may persist for 10 or 15 minutes after the shock, but beyond that, the startle response drops back to normal levels. You may notice that the effect of shock in this experiment is very similar to dishabituation. In fact, some researchers have argued that dishabituation is the result of introducing a sensitizing stimulus (Thompson & Spencer, 1966).

Humans too show sensitization of startle reflexes. This is most easily revealed using the **skin conductance response (SCR)**, also known as the galvanic skin response (GSR). The SCR is a change in the skin's electrical conductivity associated with emotions such as anxiety, fear, or surprise. Fluctuations in electrical conductance can be recorded by electrodes similar to those used for an electroencephalogram (EEG; see Chapter 2 for details). Lie detector tests usually measure a person's SCR, because the emotions evoked by attempts at deception can alter the SCR. (Unfortunately, other emotions—such as nervousness or excitement—can also alter the SCR, which is why lie detector tests are not perfectly reliable indicators of truthfulness.)

Exposure to an unexpected loud noise (say, an explosion or a yell) causes a pronounced startle response in humans,

Figure 3.2 Sensitization of the rat acoustic startle reflex When a startle-provoking noise is presented repeatedly over a 20-minute period, rats' startle reflex habituates (green line). If a foot shock is then administered to a subset of the rats (at minute 21—red line), the amplitude of their startle reflex to a subsequent noise (at minute 22) is then greater than in the unshocked rats. (Adapted from Davis, 1989.)

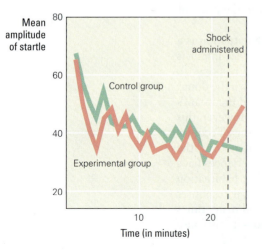

accompanied by a sharp SCR. A neutral musical tone may cause a mild startle response, which produces a small SCR. If the loud noise is played before presentation of the tone, the participant's SCRs to the tone are stronger than they would be without the loud noise (Lang, Davis, & Ohman, 2000). The loud noise sensitizes the person's startle response to the tone, just as electric shock sensitizes the startle response in rats.

Like habituation, sensitization is seen in a wide range of species, including bullfrogs, sea slugs, and humans (Bee, 2001; Eisenstein, Eisenstein, & Bonheim, 1991; Marcus, Nolen, Rankin, & Carew, 1988). Also like habituation, sensitization can rapidly dissipate in some situations and can lead to longer-lasting learning in others (Borszcz, Cranney, & Leaton, 1989; Davis, 1972, 1980). However, fewer exposures are typically necessary to produce sensitization than to produce habituation, and whereas habituation is stimulus specific, sensitization is not. For example, an animal's startle response may habituate to one loud tone that is repeated over and over; but if a different loud noise is presented, the startle response reappears in full force—habituation doesn't transfer to the new sound. By contrast, exposure to a sensitizing stimulus (such as an electric shock) can amplify the startle response to any stimulus that comes later: tone, loud noise, butterfly, or anything else. Similarly, a celebrity who catches a photographer peering into her house might be responding not just to that particular photographer but, as an aftereffect, to other even more annoying photographers that she has previously encountered. Interpreted this way, disproportionate attacks on random photographers are as much the fault of the overeager paparazzi as they are the fault of the "hot-tempered" celebrities.

Interestingly, whether or not a sequence of repeated events leads to habituation or sensitization does not depend only on what those events are or how they are distributed in time. A series of events that might normally lead to habituation can in a sick animal lead to sensitization (Domjan, 1977). In other words, the state of the observer can play a large role in what he or she learns about repeated events. So, a celebrity who repeatedly encounters paparazzi while being sleep deprived, hung over, or ill may be more likely to become sensitized to annoying intrusions of privacy and therefore more likely to strike back.

Dual Process Theory

If repeated events can potentially lead to either habituation or sensitization, how can anyone predict what an organism will learn from repeated exposures? Novel stimuli are often arousing, but what is it that determines whether an event will generate increasing arousal with repetition as opposed to becoming boring? One popular theory, called **dual process theory,** suggests that, in fact, repeated events *always lead to the processes underlying both sensitization and habituation* (Groves & Thompson, 1970; Thompson, 2009). Here's how it works. Imagine that a stimulus S is presented, evoking some chain of neural responses that eventually leads to activation of a motor response R and also activates a *state system* that signals detection of a stimulus (Figure 3.3). Habituation after repeated exposures to the stimulus (let's say 10 repetitions) can then be modeled as a weakening of the connection between S and R (Figure 3.3b), combined with mild arousal of the state system. The weaker connection decreases the likelihood of activity within motor neurons, making the response to S weaker or less likely to occur. If the stimulus is not very arousing, then the weakened connection essentially determines responding.

In dual process theory, both sensitization and habituation processes occur in response to every stimulus presentation, and it is the summed combination of these two independent processes that determines the strength of responding

Figure 3.3 The dual process theory of habituation Dual process theory suggests that both habituation and sensitization processes occur in parallel during every presentation of a stimulus and that the final response after repeated presentations results from the combination of both processes. (a) Initially, a stimulus such as S activates sensory neurons that lead to a motor response R and activates a separate state system signaling detection of the stimulus. (b) In habituation, repeated presentations of S can weaken the connections between neurons (smaller arrow), thus reducing the strength of R or the likelihood that S leads to R. (c) In sensitization, exposure to an arousing stimulus increases the likelihood that subsequent presentations of S lead to R.

[(a) Adapted from Groves and Thompson, 1970.]

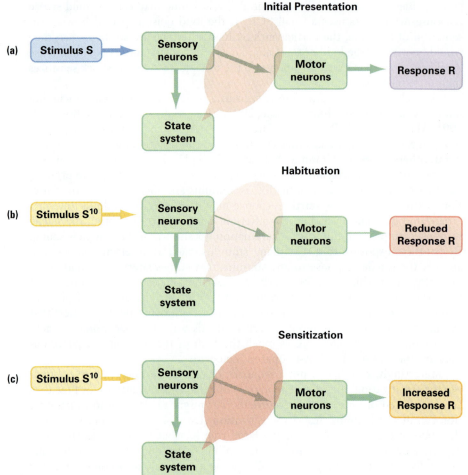

(Groves & Thompson, 1970). The actual outcome—the strength of the response to S on a given presentation—depends on such factors as how often S has been repeated and how intense and recent was the sensitizing event. It can also depend on whether other stimuli have activated the state system. For stimuli that lead to little arousal, decreases in connection strengths associated with processes of habituation will be the main determinants of how an organism's responses change over time, leading to the behavioral phenomenon that researchers call habituation. When stimuli are highly arousing, global effects of sensitization will be more evident in responses, leading to the behavioral phenomenon known as sensitization. In dual process theory, both sensitization and habituation processes change over time such that the largest effects of repetition always occur in early exposures.

The role of arousal in learning about repeated events is most evident in the habituation and sensitization of emotional responses (as discussed in "Learning and Memory in Everyday Life" on page 80). Studies of emotional responses to extreme events (say a roller-coaster ride) suggest that there are multiple phases of emotional responding—an initial phase that is scary followed by a rebound effect of exhilaration. After repeated experiences, the initial fear responses may become weaker, whereas the rebound responses grow stronger (such that what was once scary can become fun). One model of this process, called *opponent process theory*, explains this effect as a way that organisms maintain emotional stability. Opponent process theory is similar to dual process theory in that it assumes that an experienced event leads to two independent processes—in this case, two emotional processes, one that is pleasurable and one that is less pleasant. The overall emotion that one experiences in response to an event is the combined result of these two independent processes. Repeated experiences have different effects on the initial reaction versus the "rebound" reaction, such that over time the initial response habituates faster than its counterpart. Thus, your first time bungee jumping may not be nearly as much fun as your fifth time. Both dual process theory and opponent process theory suggest that the outcomes of repeated experiences are not as simple as they might at first appear. A "simple" decrease or increase in responding to an increasingly familiar event may reflect multiple learning processes occurring in parallel. Additionally, repeated experiences can change not only how an individual reflexively responds to familiar events but also how the person perceives and interprets those events, as described in the following section.

Test Your Knowledge

Maximizing Habituation

In some cases, such as in romantic relationships, it makes sense to try and minimize habituation. In contrast, if you discover that the shirt you are wearing is itchy, you'd be better off if you could maximize habituation and avoid sensitization. So what can you do (aside from changing your shirt)? Try to come up with at least three strategies that could help you to minimize your scratching. (Answers appear in the Answers section in the back of the book.)

Perceptual Learning

Habituation and sensitization are forms of learning in which repeated exposure to stimuli can lead to an increase or decrease in responding to those stimuli. But repeated exposure doesn't just change how a human or other animal responds to stimuli. Sometimes, it can change how those stimuli are perceived. **Perceptual learning** is learning in which repeated experiences with a set of stimuli makes those stimuli easier to distinguish. Let's consider a couple of examples.

Commercial poultry farmers like to sort male from female chicks as soon after hatching as possible to save the cost of feeding male chicks (males don't lay eggs, and they produce lower-quality meat than females). By the time a chick is 5 or 6 weeks old, its sex is clearly revealed by its feather patterns. But highly trained individuals, called chicken sexers, can distinguish whether a day-old chick is male or female just by glancing at the chick's rear end. Accomplished chicken sexers can make this distinction with high accuracy at a viewing rate of one chick per half second, even though the male and female chicks look identical to the untrained eye (Biederman & Shiffrar, 1987). Some chicken sexers can't even verbalize the subtle cues they use to make the distinction; they have seen so many examples of male and female chicks that they "just know which is which." Medical diagnosticians have similar sensitivities to subtle differences in symptoms. All rashes may look alike to an inexperienced medical student, but an experienced dermatologist can glance at a rash and tell immediately, and with high accuracy, whether a patient has contact dermatitis, ringworm, or some other condition.

Through extensive experience, gem assessors become attuned to subtle visual differences in stones.

Although you might not personally be an expert at distinguishing chicken genitals or rashes, you probably have become a connoisseur in other areas. Perhaps you can easily distinguish Coke from Pepsi or McDonald's french fries from those of any other fast-food restaurant. Maybe for you, the sound of a Fender electric guitar is very different from the sound of a Gibson. Whatever your specialty, you likely developed your capacities to detect subtle differences through repeated exposures to those stimuli. This is the essence of perceptual learning.

Mere Exposure Learning

Chicken sexers don't learn their trade by accident. They gain expertise through extensive, deliberate practice (such skill learning is discussed more extensively in Chapter 8). Sometimes, however, perceptual learning does happen through mere exposure to stimuli, without any conscious effort by the individual, a situation similar to what occurs during both habituation and sensitization. For example, Eleanor Gibson and colleagues exposed one group of rats to large triangular and circular shapes mounted on the walls of their home cages for about a month (E. Gibson & Walk, 1956). The researchers then trained this group and a control group of rats to approach one of the shapes but not the other. Rats familiar with the shapes learned to discriminate between them faster than rats that had never seen the shapes before. During the initial exposure phase, nothing was done to teach the rats in the experimental group about the shapes, and the shapes were irrelevant to the rats' daily activities. Nevertheless, experience viewing the shapes facilitated later learning about them. Because the perceptual learning in such experiments happens without explicit training, it is sometimes called **mere exposure learning.** This learning process is a type of latent learning (which we discussed at the chapter's beginning), because before the rats begin training with the shapes, there is no behavioral evidence that they learned anything about the shapes that were present in their home cages. This initial learning only became evident when rats were explicitly trained to respond in different ways to the two different shapes.

People show mere exposure learning too. In one study, volunteer participants learned to discriminate between complex line drawings—the scribbles seen in Figure 3.4. First, each participant was asked to look briefly at a card containing a target scribble. Then the participant was shown a series of individual cards that each contained a scribble and was told that some of the cards contained the same scribble seen on the first card. As each card was presented, the participant was asked to tell the experimenter whether it matched the target scribble. The experimenter gave no feedback—no indication of whether a participant's answer was correct or not—but at the end of the process, the same steps (beginning with the scrutiny of the target card) were repeated all over again, and then a third time. Initially, participants were pretty accurate at identifying repetitions of the target scribble, as well as correctly rejecting as unfamiliar the novel scribbles that were very unlike the target ("dissimilar scribbles"). Early in the experiment, however, participants would also incorrectly "recognize" many scribbles that were similar to the target scribble. But with more and more exposure to scribbles, the participants began to distinguish the target scribble from very

Keith Goldstein/Getty Images

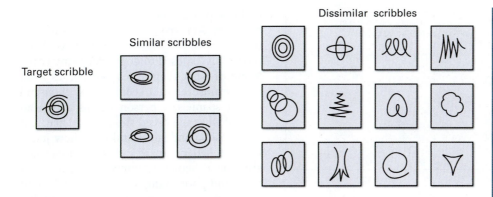

Figure 3.4 Mere exposure learning in humans A person repeatedly views a particular scribble (target), then tries to identify cards with the same scribble when they are mixed into a deck of cards with other scribbles varying in similarity to the target scribble. The ability to identify the target scribble gradually improves, even without feedback about performance.
(Adapted from J. J. Gibson and Gibson, 1955.)

similar but novel stimuli (J. J. Gibson & Gibson, 1955). This is an example of perceptual learning through mere exposure to scribbles.

Your ability to distinguish among individuals may have developed similarly. In general, you will be better at distinguishing individuals belonging to racial groups that you have frequently encountered throughout your life than individuals of racial groups you don't interact with much (for further discussion of this topic see "Learning and Memory in Everyday Life" on page 89).

Discrimination Training

Of course, as noted above, not all perceptual learning happens through mere exposure. Chicken sexers don't just wander randomly through a poultry factory until they can spot males and females, and medical diagnosticians don't just happen across their knowledge; they spend years studying and interning. Part of this training—for both doctors and chicken sexers—consists of studying examples, trying to distinguish between them, and receiving feedback about accuracy. Training with feedback can greatly facilitate perceptual learning. The availability of feedback distinguishes this type of perceptual learning from mere exposure learning.

Training an individual to respond differently to different stimuli is often referred to as **discrimination training.** During discrimination training, feedback can be provided by pairing different stimuli with different outcomes (as in classical conditioning, discussed in Chapter 4), by rewarding or punishing an individual's responses to stimuli (as in operant conditioning; see Chapter 5), or by demonstrating desired performance (as in social learning, described in Chapter 11). Perceptual learning during discrimination training is not latent, because the improvements in acuity are behaviorally evident and are noticed as part of the learning process. Because perceptual learning during discrimination training occurs in parallel with other learning phenomena, however, it is often difficult to say with certainty which behavioral changes are the result of perceptual learning versus other learning mechanisms (Hall, 1991). Nevertheless, this form of perceptual learning is often the focus of neuroscience studies, because it leads to the largest changes in perceptual sensitivities (as well as the largest changes in brain structure and function, a topic we return to in the Brain Substrates section later in this chapter).

When you look at a dog, you probably notice many different things about it. It's big, it's cute, it has two eyes, there is drool coming out of its mouth. What you might not be able to appreciate is the dog's apparent pedigree, how its tail posture compares with that of other dogs of the same breed, the ratio of its leg length to head length, its dental structure, or its monetary value. If you happen

Figure 3.5 Learning specificity in humans People are first trained to distinguish highly similar visual patterns. Next, they are trained on a task that is identical except that the original images are rotated from vertical to horizontal (a 90-degree rotation). At the start of this "new" task, their performance is the same as if they had never seen the images before—people show no benefits from their prior perceptual learning.

(Adapted from Fiorentini and Berardi, 1981.)

to be a professional judge for dog shows, however, you may notice these features at first glance. Dog-show judges have been repeatedly exposed to dogs over many years. Some of what they've learned comes from mere exposure: after seeing a few thousand cocker spaniels, a person begins to get an idea of what the breed should look like. But any sensible and successful dog-show judge hasn't relied on mere exposure alone: he's also made active attempts to learn about good and poor examples of the breed. Both processes—mere exposure learning and discrimination training—make an experienced dog-show judge better than other people at discriminating between individual dogs of the same breed.

Experts at any kind of perceptual discrimination, including dog-show judges, learn in part by practicing with many examples and receiving feedback about the accuracy of their judgments. But what happens if the dog-show judge is asked to judge the prize pigs at the county fair? Is he likely to prove as eagle-eyed an expert on pigs as he is on dogs? The answer is generally no. In most cases, perceptual learning shows a high degree of **learning specificity**, which means that learning about one group of stimuli doesn't transfer automatically to other stimuli. Like habituation, perceptual learning is stimulus specific.

For example, people can be trained to distinguish a complex visual image from the same image that is slightly tilted—less than one degree (Fiorentini & Berardi, 1981). Imagine trying to distinguish one photo of a pile of ice cubes from a second photo of that same pile made a minute later. After a minute, the positions of the ice cubes will have shifted slightly from melting, but this difference would be extremely difficult to detect. With practice, participants gradually improve on such fine visual discrimination tasks, until they choose correctly about 90% of the time (Figure 3.5). Surprisingly, if the same people are now tested on their ability to detect these same differences for images tilted at a 90-degree angle (the images are turned on their side), the earlier learning doesn't automatically transfer to the new task. In fact, people's performance discriminating the rotated images is no better than if they had been shown entirely new images. In other words, the earlier perceptual learning had high specificity and did not transfer, even to the same images at different orientations.

Models of Perceptual Learning

Habituation, sensitization, and perceptual learning might seem at first glance to be very different kinds of learning. Nevertheless, several prominent theories suggest that these seemingly different behavioral phenomena all depend on similar (or identical) learning mechanisms. For example, the *dual process theory* of habituation, introduced earlier in the chapter, explains perceptual learning as resulting from a combination of habituation and sensitization processes (Hall, 2009). Consider again the experiment on mere exposure learning in which rats lived in a cage with triangles and circles on the walls (E. Gibson & Walk, 1956). The triangles and circles shared some features: both shapes were constructed of the same material, both were located on the walls (but never, for example, on the floor of the cage), and so on. They also differed in some

> ► **LEARNING AND MEMORY IN EVERYDAY LIFE**

Racial Bias

People typically judge the faces of people from another racial group to be more similar to one another than are the faces of unfamiliar people from their own race (Malpass & Kravitz, 1969). This bias is called the "other-race effect." Current psychological theories suggest that the other-race effect results from a person's having more experience with faces from certain racial groups than from others. Consistent with this idea, non-Caucasian children who are adopted by Caucasian families show better discrimination of Caucasian faces than of faces from members of their own racial group (Meissner & Brigham, 2001).

You may like to think that you treat all strangers equally, without taking appearance or speech patterns into account. But laboratory experiments suggest that this is unlikely. Despite people's stated ideals, they also often show racial biases in situations other than the distinguishing of faces. For example, people often show evidence of unconscious negative associations when answering questions about racial groups other than their own (Greenwald, McGhee, & Schwartz, 1998). These biases are not predictable from their self-reports. You can try some of these unconscious racial bias experiments yourself online at https://implicit.harvard.edu/implicit/ if you are curious to see how you fare. Recent research suggests that people's insensitivity to facial differences among members of other races can actually contribute to unconscious racial biases (Lebrecht, Pierce, Tarr, & Tanaka, 2009). The explanation offered for this is that the less able a person is to reliably differentiate individuals of a certain racial classification, the more likely it is that they will unconsciously apply generic racial stereotypes to all individuals of that group.

If the ability to distinguish faces is a consequence of the frequency with which different types of faces are encountered, then the other-race effect is essentially a side effect of visual perceptual learning. In that case, you might expect that if you trained an individual to distinguish faces of racial groups they are not familiar with, you might be able to reduce that person's other-race effect. Furthermore, if the other-race effect contributes to unconscious racial biases, such training might reduce those biases, as well. This prediction has recently been confirmed in laboratory experiments. Caucasian participants who were extensively trained to distinguish between faces of African American individuals showed both a reduction in the other-race effect and a reduction in unconscious racial biases (Lebrecht et al., 2009). Apparently, learning to recognize individuals of other racial groups can reduce overgeneralization of racial stereotypes, even when that learning involves no social interactions that might counteract the stereotypes.

---

features: for example, the triangles had straight sides and the circles had round sides. According to dual process theory, when the rat viewed a triangle on the wall, its responses habituated to all of the features it experienced. Similarly, its responses also habituated to all visual aspects of the circle on the wall. Notice that the shared features of the shapes were experienced every time the rat viewed either shape but that distinguishing features were experienced only when the rat viewed a certain shape. Since the shared features were repeatedly experienced twice as often, the effects on responding of viewing the shared features should have been greater—there should be twice as much habituation of responses to the shared features. The end result would be that distinctive features (such as straight versus round edges) would be more likely to provoke orienting responses than shared features. In other words, for rats that lived with the shapes, the features that distinguished the two shapes became more noticeable than the shared features. Thus, rats that lived with the shapes would be expected to learn to distinguish the shapes faster than rats that had never seen them before, because the experienced rats should pay less attention to the shared features of the shapes.

Other theoretical explanations of perceptual learning suggest that habituation depends on perceptual learning, rather than the other way around. For example, the **comparator model** of habituation proposes that the changes in responses to repeated events are a consequence of the gradual construction of neural representations of stimuli and the contexts in which they occur

(Sokolov, 1963; Wagner, 1979). In the comparator model, each presentation of a stimulus results in a pattern of neural activity in the brain—a neural representation of that stimulus. The idea is that each time the brain detects a stimulus, it forms a representation of that stimulus and compares that representation with memories of previously experienced stimuli. If there is no match, then a response (such as an orienting response) is triggered, provoking the organism to further examine the stimulus. If there is a partial match, then the existing representation is modified to include additional details. On the other hand, if there is a good match, then the orienting response is suppressed and no changes are made in the representation of the stimulus. Responding to familiar stimuli naturally decreases, or habituates, because those stimuli are increasingly well represented. The more times a stimulus is repeated, the more familiar the representation becomes and the less need there is for an orienting response.

A third explanation of perceptual learning is proposed by **differentiation theory,** which suggests that representations of stimuli initially are formed rapidly and vaguely but become more precise over time by incorporating further details as the stimulus is repeated (E. Gibson, 1991). Differentiation theory assumes that the brain is limited in how much information it can collect in a single exposure to a novel stimulus. A stimulus may have many features, but the brain's perceptual representations can only capture information about a subset of those features at each encounter. Repeated exposures give the brain the opportunity to collect more information about a stimulus, and the neural representations become more refined as the amount of information stored about the stimulus increases. More complete representations allow more accurate discriminatory judgments between, as well as more accurate recognition of, stimuli. For example, the very first time you see a drawing of a complex carbohydrate molecule in chemistry class, you might only be able to recall that it has a bunch of lines and letters; the next time, you might notice that some of the lines and letters are arranged in hexagonal shapes; the next time after that, you might notice relationships in the way the hydrogen and oxygen atoms are linked; and so on. By the time you complete your graduate degree in organic chemistry, you'll be so familiar with the fine details that you can easily distinguish one complex carbohydrate from another at a glance by zeroing in on the regions of the molecule that help you make that distinction. Differentiation theory is similar in many respects to comparator models of habituation—the main difference is that it does not make any specific claims about how changes in perception affect behavioral responses and so does not provide any account of habituation.

Each of these models—dual process theory, the comparator model, and differentiation theory—makes different predictions about the relationship between habituation, sensitization, and perceptual learning. Numerous experiments have been conducted in an attempt to determine which does the best job of explaining the available data (Hall, 1991; Thompson, 2009), but there is still no consensus winner. In fact, each might explain different aspects of how organisms learn from repeated events. For example, dual process theory is well suited to explaining short-term habituation and sensitization effects, whereas comparator models are better able to account for long-term habituation and perceptual learning resulting from discrimination training (Thompson, 2009). Later in the chapter, you will see that brain studies are shedding some light on the processes underlying habituation, sensitization, and perceptual learning, which may help us to better evaluate the strengths and weaknesses of these different models.

Test Your Knowledge

Perceptual Learning versus Habituation

Both habituation and perceptual learning can result from repeated exposures to stimuli. Although the experiences that lead to these phenomena can be similar, the kinds of responses that provide evidence of these two forms of learning are notably different. For each of the following photographs, identify what kind or kinds of learning might have contributed to the scene depicted. (Answers appear in the Answers section in the back of the book.)

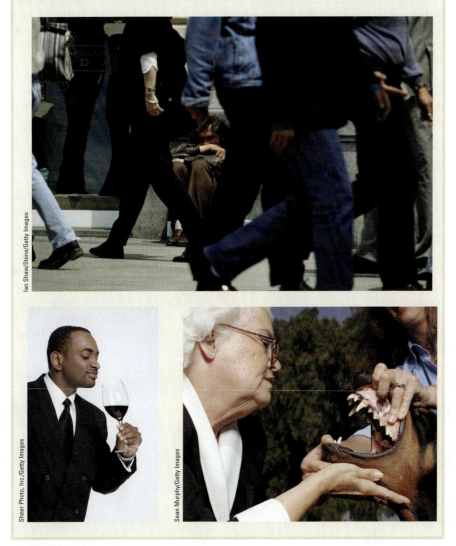

Learning through Exploration

Habituation, sensitization, and perceptual learning are forms of learning that do not necessarily require large expenditures of effort. Think, for example, of how much a couch potato can learn without ever needing to get up from his couch. He can quickly detect which commercials he's seen a thousand times and distinguish the television characters he likes from those he despises. Similarly, many of the laboratory experiments described above require little effort on the part of the learners involved. Neither rats nor babies need to do much of anything to habituate their responses to a tone.

In many situations, however—particularly in discrimination training—individuals may be far more active, exerting control over the kinds of stimuli they repeatedly experience. Animals rarely just sit around waiting for something to happen. Instead, they spend much of their time traveling, searching, and exploring the world around them and thus play a decisive role in determining the kinds of stimuli they are repeatedly exposed to, as well as the frequency of exposure. And even the most extreme couch potatoes usually have a remote control device nearby so that they can scan for what they want to watch next. In short, humans' and other animals' actions are a major factor in determining the events they experience repeatedly. This in turn affects what the individuals learn about, what they remember, and how long the memories last.

Somewhat ironically, relatively few researchers are actively exploring the role that active exploring plays in learning about repeated events, but one area where this issue *has* been considered in some detail is in studies of how individuals find their way around.

Spatial Learning

Spatial learning—the acquisition of information about one's surroundings—can be accomplished in different ways. In one of the earliest laboratory studies of exploratory spatial learning, Edward Tolman, working with C. H. Honzik, placed rats in a complex maze (Figure 3.6a) and trained them to make their way to a particular location in it—the food box—to be rewarded with a bit of food (Tolman & Honzik, 1930). These trained rats learned to run to the food box with fewer and fewer errors (wrong turns) as the days went by (Figure 3.6b). Rats in a second group were simply placed in the maze for the first 10 days of the study and allowed to explore. If they happened into the food box, they received no food but were removed from the maze. On the eleventh day, these rats started getting food every time they entered the food box. As Figure 3.6b shows, these exploration-first rats also learned to run to the food box to get

Figure 3.6 Learning by exploration in rats (a) Tolman placed rats in the start box of a complex maze. (b) Rats rewarded with food every time they reached the food box learned gradually to run to the food box. Other rats (the exposure-first rats) were simply placed in the maze and allowed to explore, with no food reward. On the 11th day, these rats began receiving rewards and immediately learned to run to the box for food. (Adapted from Tolman and Honzik, 1930.)

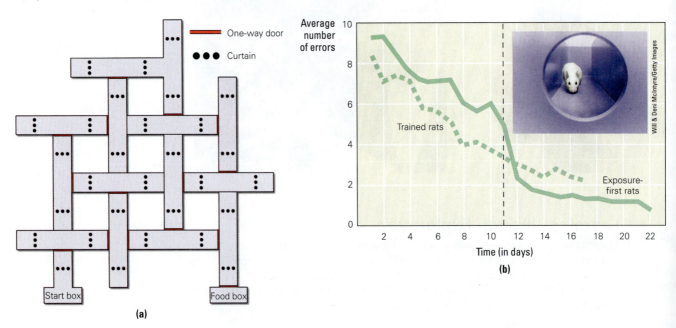

(a)

(b)

their food—and they learned this task so well that their performance quickly surpassed that of the rats who'd been training on the task all along! Tolman and Honzik concluded that both groups of rats had learned about the location of the food box. One group had learned how to get to the food box through explicit training, and the other group learned what the maze was like by exploring it. This is yet another example of latent learning, because until food was placed in the food box, there was little evidence that the explorer rats knew how to get there quickly.

What were the rats learning? Perhaps they were learning a sequence of turns that they could perform to get to certain spots: turn right from the start box, then left, and so on. Such learning does occur, but it isn't enough to account for everything the rats did in the maze, because a rat could be placed in a new start position and still find its way to the goal. Rats also appear to use visual cues to determine their location in such mazes. For example, a rat in a laboratory maze may use the sight of a window or a wall decoration visible over the edges of the maze to orient itself. As long as these cues are in sight, the rat may learn to navigate from any starting point in the maze, although if the cues are then moved around, the rat may get temporarily confused (we describe such an experiment later in the chapter). In fact, rats can learn many things while exploring a maze; as a result, spatial tasks have played a major role in studies of many different kinds of learning and memory, including studies of operant conditioning (Chapter 5), memories for events (Chapter 7), skill memories (Chapter 8), and working memory (Chapter 9). Exploration is important in all of these tasks, because a rat that refuses to explore a maze will learn very little about its spatial organization.

Animals in the wild also sometimes navigate based on visual cues they have learned through exploration. In a classic study, Niko Tinbergen studied wasps' ability to locate their home nest. Certain species of wasps and bees engage in orientation flights before leaving their hives or burrows to look for food; during these orientation flights, they circle their home base. In one study, Tinbergen and William Kruyt laid a circle of pinecones around a wasp burrow while the wasps were inside (Tinbergen & Kruyt, 1972). The experimenters left the pinecone circle intact for several orientation flights—long enough for the wasps to get used to these landmarks (Figure 3.7a). Then, while a wasp was away on a foraging trip, the experimenters moved the circle of pinecones away from the burrow (Figure 3.7b). When the wasp returned, it repeatedly searched for its burrow within the ring of pinecones.

Tinbergen and Kruyt concluded that when wasps leave home to forage, they use the orientation flight to collect visual information about landmarks that will later help them locate the burrow. If these landmarks are repositioned while the wasp is away, the wasp will search for the burrow based on the landmarks, revealing that it has learned about the spatial relationship between the burrow and surrounding landmarks. Just like Tolman's rats, the wasps learn about the spatial properties of their environments through exploration. Much of this learning is latent and does not become evident until a subsequent test challenges the animal to reveal what it has learned. As illustrated in Figure 3.7, wasps often make several passes over the nest before departing. After multiple trips, a wasp will have repeatedly experienced the visual cues surrounding its nest. Such repeated events could lead to habituation, sensitization, perceptual learning, or other forms of learning. In this sort of naturalistic experiment, there is no way to know exactly what a wasp is learning from these repeated events. The following section describes more controlled studies that are helping researchers get a better handle on what is learned about repeated events during exploration.

Figure 3.7 Use of land-marks by wasps (a) Tinbergen and Kruyt placed pinecones around a wasps' burrow (an underground nest) to provide visual information about the burrow's location. When leaving home, wasps take orientation flights, during which they seem to note local landmarks (such as the pinecones) that will help them return. (b) When the circle of pinecones was moved to flat ground near the nest, the returning wasps searched for the burrow inside the circle of pinecones.
(Adapted from Tinbergen and Kruyt, 1972.)

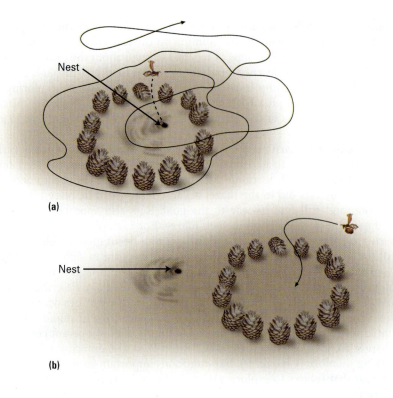

Novel Object Recognition

Earlier we noted that when a novel stimulus appears after repeated presentations of a familiar stimulus, babies show a strong orienting response to the new stimulus (because habituation is stimulus-specific). A similar phenomenon can be seen in exploratory behavior. In the **novel object recognition** task, people, monkeys, or rodents are first acclimated to the *context* of the experiment (the room or box where the tests will be given) by being allowed to freely explore it. Next, two identical objects or pictures are briefly presented within the experimental setting. After a variable delay, one of these stimuli is presented again, but this time paired with a new object or picture. Generally, individuals will spend about twice as much time examining the novel object as they will inspecting the familiar one. From this difference, researchers can infer that the individual recognizes the previously experienced object as one it has investigated before—that is, the repeated stimulus is perceived as familiar. Not all animals are so eager to investigate novel objects, however. Some actively avoid them, a phenomenon known as *neophobia*. For example, when dolphin trainers want to teach a dolphin to use an object, they often spend several sessions rewarding the dolphin for simply not bolting when the new object is brought near them (many dolphins are neophobic). In this case, the dolphin's fear response provides evidence that it does not recognize an object.

Psychologists have used variants of the novel object recognition task to determine what kinds of information individuals remember about objects and places they have inspected in the past, such as an object's position, observable properties, and the circumstances under which it was observed. This task is also useful for investigating the resilience of memories formed through observations or exploration. The perception of *familiarity* is a fundamental component of recognition memory. William James (1890) described memory in general as *"the knowledge of an event, or fact,* of which meantime we have not been think-ing, *with the additional consciousness that we have thought or experienced it before"* [italicized as in James, 1890]. **Familiarity** can be defined as the perception of similarity that occurs when an event is repeated—it is, in James's words, a "sense of sameness." Although it is difficult to know what this feeling of sameness is like for a rat or monkey, we can conclude from tasks such as the novel object recognition task that rats and monkeys discriminate different levels of familiar-ity, just as they distinguish different intensities of sound or shades of gray. In the past decade, memory researchers have intensively investigated how individuals judge familiarity, how this capacity relates to other memory abilities, and what brain mechanisms contribute to familiarity judgments (Eichenbaum, Yonelinas, & Ranganath, 2007). Consequently, a learning phenomenon that scientists once used mainly to distinguish habituation from fatigue has transformed into a cor-nerstone of modern memory research.

Priming

Prior exposure to a stimulus can lead to a sense of familiarity the next time that stimulus is observed. Even when it does not lead to a sense of familiarity, it can affect the individual's response to the stimulus (or related stimuli) the next time the stimulus is observed; this latter effect is called **priming.** For example, prim-ing in humans is often studied using a **word-stem completion task,** in which a person is given a list of word stems (MOT__, SUP__, and such) and asked to fill in the blank with the first word that comes to mind. People generally fill in the blanks to form common English words (MOTEL or MOTOR, SUPPOSE or SUPPER). But if the people were previously exposed to a list of words con-taining those stems (MOTH, SUPREME, and so on), then they are much more likely to fill in the blanks to form words that were present in that list, even if they don't consciously remember having previously seen the words on the list (Graf, Squire, & Mandler, 1984). When they complete the word stem with a previously experienced word, they do not recognize the word as one they recently saw, and yet the prior experience clearly affects their word choice. Such effects are con-sistent with the findings from sexual habituation studies described previously in "Learning and Memory in Everyday Life" on page 80 that prior exposure can affect a person's behavior and perception even if the person is not conscious of the previous exposure or its effects or both.

Nonhuman animals show priming, too. For example, blue jays like to eat moths, and moths have evolved coloration patterns that help them blend into the background where they alight. Therefore, blue jays have to be very good at detecting subtle differences in visual patterns that distinguish a tasty meal from a patch of tree bark. Researchers studied this detection ability by training blue jays to look at pictures on a screen (Figure 3.8a) and

Figure 3.8 Priming in blue jays (a) Virtual moths on a gray background are more detectable than the same moths on speckled backgrounds. Higher numbers indi-cate more cryptic backgrounds. (b) Blue jays learn to peck on screens when they detect a virtual moth and to peck on a green key when they detect no moths. (c) When a moth is similar to a recently detected moth, blue jays are better able to detect the moth, suggest-ing that prior exposure facilitates recognition. In other words, prim-ing has occurred.

(Adapted from Bond and Kamil, 1999.)

High contrast

Low contrast

(a)

(b)

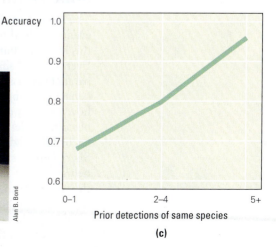

Accuracy

1.0

0.9

0.8

0.7

0.6

0–1   2–4   5+

Prior detections of same species

(c)

to peck at the screen to signal "there's a moth here" or at a key to signal "no moth" (Figure 3.8b). The birds did very well, but they were quicker and more accurate at detecting a particular species of moth if they had recently detected other members of that species, as shown in Figure 3.8c (Bond & Kamil, 1999). In other words, recent observations of one kind of moth *primed* the jays' abilities to recognize similar moths later.

Interim Summary

- Habituation is learning that leads to a decrease in the strength or frequency of a behavior after repeated exposure to the stimulus that produces the behavior. A response that has habituated can be renewed (dishabituated) by a novel stimulus.

- In sensitization, exposure to an arousing stimulus causes a heightened response to any stimuli that follow.

- Dual process theory proposes that changes in behavioral responses after repeated exposures to a stimulus reflect the combined effects of habituation and sensitization processes.

- Perceptual learning occurs when repeated experiences with a set of stimuli improve the organism's ability to distinguish those stimuli.

- In mere exposure learning (a kind of latent learning), simply being exposed to stimuli results in perceptual learning.

- Perceptual learning can also occur when an organism learns to distinguish stimuli by repeatedly practicing at making fine distinctions.

- Comparator models and differentiation theory suggest that habituation depends on perceptual learning. Differentiation theory explains perceptual learning as resulting from new details being added to existing stimulus representations.

- Spatial learning often involves latent learning about features of the environment (including encountered objects) through exploration.

- Priming is a phenomenon in which prior exposure to a stimulus, even without awareness of the exposure, affects the organism's response to that stimulus later.

3.2 Brain Substrates

The discussion above considered several ways in which experiences with repeated events can lead to learning. In some cases, gradual changes in behavior revealed this learning, but in others the learning was latent until the right test was given. Even in the "simple" case of habituation, learning seems to involve multiple parallel processes that can sometimes operate without any associated changes in behavior. Using only behavioral evidence, it is extremely difficult to understand how and what organisms learn from repeated events. Because researchers recognized this dilemma early on, there is a long history of neurophysiological studies of habituation (Thompson, 2009), starting in the early 1900s with Charles Sherrington's studies of the spinal reflex (discussed in Chapter 2). More recently, neuroimaging and electrophysiological studies have begun to shed new light on the processes underlying perceptual learning and object recognition. The ability to observe how brain function and structure changes as an individual learns about repeated events has provided many new clues about the nature of these phenomena, as the following discussions will illustrate.

Dogs and cats are natural antagonists, as any dog or cat owner knows. Some of the earliest brain studies on habituation, using dogs and cats as subjects, seemed to bear out the view that these animals are fundamentally antithetical. Ivan Pavlov, for example, found that when a dog's cortex was removed, the dog no longer showed habituation to auditory stimuli: the dog would instead continue to show orienting responses to the sounds, even after many exposures (Pavlov, 1927). Such findings led researchers to suggest that the cortex was critical for habituation and that it actively suppressed reflexive orienting responses to stimuli perceived as familiar (Sokolov, 1963). The data from cats, however, seemed completely contradictory. Cats that had their brain disconnected from their spinal cord, called *spinal cats*, still showed habituation to tactile stimulation (Thompson & Spencer, 1966). This seemed to prove that the spinal cord by itself contained all the neural machinery necessary for habituation; the cortex—and indeed the rest of the brain—wasn't needed. The cat data were consistent with the finding that many other organisms known to habituate, including roaches, protozoa, and numerous other invertebrates, don't have any cortex.

How to reconcile the dog data and the cat data? For one thing, the animals in these early studies were learning about different kinds of stimuli. Whether cortical processing is involved in habituation likely depends on the kinds of stimuli that are being repeated, where they are normally processed, and where memories of the stimuli are formed. One way to avoid these complications is to study habituation not with mammals, such as cats and dogs, but with smaller-brained animals such as everyone's favorite—the sea slug.

Invertebrate Model Systems

Much work on the neural substrates of habituation has been conducted on a group of marine invertebrates called ***Aplysia,*** the sea slugs (or sea hares), such as the species *Aplysia californica* shown in Figure 3.9. Like many marine animals, *Aplysia* breathes through gills, which extend upward from between the two wings of the mantle, the animal's outer covering. A structure called the siphon works like a tube to blow aerated water over the gills to assist respiration. The gills are delicate and easily damaged. When danger threatens, the sea hare tends to retract them under the safety of the mantle. This is called a gill-withdrawal reflex.

One advantage of studying learning in *Aplysia* is that they have a relatively simple nervous system—only about 20,000 neurons, compared with the tens of billions in a cat or human. Plus, some of the neurons are very big. A few are

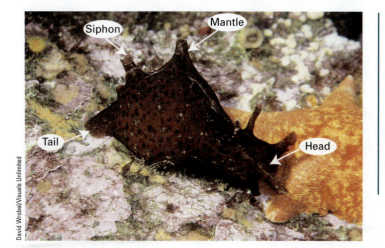

David Wrobel/Visuals Unlimited

Figure 3.9 *Aplysia californica*, **the sea hare** This marine invertebrate, a shell-less mollusk, has a relatively simple nervous system, useful for studying the neural bases of learning. If the siphon is touched lightly, both siphon and gill are protectively withdrawn (the gill-withdrawal reflex). With repeated light touches, the gill-withdrawal reflex habituates. In this photo, the gill is underneath the mantle.
(Adapted from Squire and Kandel, 2000.)

Figure 3.10 Neural circuits in *Aplysia* gill-withdrawal reflex (a) Sensory neurons S, T, and U respond to a touch on the siphon, tail, and upper mantle, respectively. These neurons converge on motor neurons such as M, which contract the gill muscles. (b) When sensory neuron S fires, it releases the neurotransmitter glutamate into the synapse between S and M. The glutamate molecules (shown in yellow) may dock at receptors on neuron M. If enough receptors are activated, neuron M will fire, retracting the gill. (c) If neuron S is activated repeatedly, it gradually releases less glutamate each time, decreasing the response of M. This synaptic depression underlies habituation of the gill-withdrawal response in sea hares.

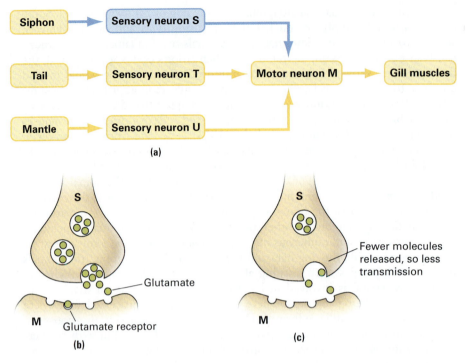

large enough to be seen with the naked eye. Best of all, the pattern of neurons in *Aplysia* seems to be "hardwired," meaning that researchers can identify a particular neuron in one sea hare (say, motor neuron L7G) and find the same neuron in the same place in another member of the species. This type of nervous system makes things much easier for a neuroscientist trying to understand how the brain encodes new memories.

Neuroscientists have documented each of the neurons involved in *Aplysia*'s gill-withdrawal reflex. The siphon contains 24 sensory neurons that are directly connected to 6 motor neurons that innervate the gill. Figure 3.10a shows a simplified scheme of this system of neurons, consisting of three sensory neurons S, T, and U and one motor neuron M. When the siphon is touched, sensory neuron S fires, releasing a neurotransmitter, *glutamate*, into the synapse (Figure 3.10b). Molecules of glutamate diffuse across the synapse to activate receptors in motor neuron M. If enough receptors are activated, neuron M fires, causing the muscles to retract the gill for a few seconds.

As simple as sea hares are, they are still capable of adapting their behavior in response to experience. *Aplysia* show habituation, sensitization, and several other forms of learning, just as rats and humans do. In *Aplysia*, however, scientists can actually watch the nervous system in action as these learning processes occur.

Habituation in Sea Hares

An initial, light touch on a sea hare's siphon will activate the gill-withdrawal response, but if the touch is repeated, the gill-withdrawal reflex gradually becomes weaker, or habituates. The amount of habituation is proportional to the intensity of the stimulus and the repetition rate. If a sufficiently light touch is delivered every minute, the withdrawal response habituates after 10 or 12 touches and can last for 10 to 15 minutes (Pinsker, Kupfermann, Castellucci, & Kandel, 1970).

In sea hares, we can see exactly what is causing this habituation. Refer back to the schematic diagram in Figure 3.10a. Recall that touching the siphon excites sensory neuron S, which releases the neurotransmitter glutamate, which in turn excites motor neuron M, which drives the withdrawal response (Figure 3.10b). With repeated stimulation, however, neuron S releases less glutamate (Figure 3.10c), decreasing the chance that neuron M will be excited enough to fire (Castellucci & Kandel, 1974). The reduction in glutamate release is evident even after a single touch and lasts for up to 10 minutes. This decrease in neurotransmitter release is associated with a decrease in the number of glutamate-containing vesicles positioned at release sites. Thus, in *Aplysia*, habituation can be explained as a form of **synaptic depression,** a reduction in synaptic transmission. This is exactly the sort of weakening of connections proposed by the dual process theory of habituation (see Figure 3.3b).

An important feature of habituation in sea hares is that it is **homosynaptic,** meaning that it involves only those synapses that were activated during the habituating event: changes in neuron S will not affect other sensory neurons, such as T or U in Figure 3.10a. In other words, a light touch to the tail or upper mantle still elicits the defensive gill withdrawal, even though a touch to the siphon is ignored. Even the responsiveness of the motor neuron M is not changed; in this case, habituation in the short term affects only how much neurotransmitter neuron S releases.

Long-term habituation in sea hares can often last much longer than 10 minutes, especially when exposures are spaced over several days (Cohen, Kaplan, Kandel, & Hawkins, 1997). How are the animals storing information about past exposures for such a long time? When a sea hare is repeatedly exposed to the same stimulus over several days, the actual number of connections between the affected sensory neurons and motor neurons decreases. Specifically, the number of presynaptic terminals in the sensory neurons of animals that have been repeatedly exposed to the same stimulus is reduced. Synaptic transmission in *Aplysia* can thus be depressed not only by decreases in neurotransmitter release but also by the elimination of synapses. This suggests that repeated experiences can lead not only to the weakening of connections, as suggested by the dual process theory of habituation, but also to their elimination.

Do the mechanisms of habituation in sea hares tell us anything about habituation in larger-brained animals? It is currently impossible to trace the entire neuronal circuit of habituation through the billions of neurons in a mammalian brain. However, neuroscientists have good reason to believe that the mechanisms of habituation documented in *Aplysia* occur in other species too. In fact, repeated stimulation of sensory neurons in other species, including crayfish and cats, also causes a reduction in neurotransmitter release. This suggests that at least some of the biological mechanisms of habituation are constant across species.

Sensitization in Sea Hares

What about sensitization, which, in contrast to habituation, causes increased responding to stimuli? *Aplysia* also provide a way to study the neural processes involved in this kind of learning. Suppose, instead of a light touch to the siphon, the researcher applies a more unpleasant stimulus: a mild electric shock to the tail that causes a large, sustained gill-withdrawal response. The aversive tail shock sensitizes subsequent responding, so that a weak touch to the siphon now produces a strengthened gill withdrawal.

To understand how this occurs, let's take the simplified circuit diagram from Figure 3.10a and add one more level of neural detail, as shown in Figure 3.11a. The tail shock activates sensory neuron T, which activates motor neuron M, causing the gill-withdrawal response. But because of the arousing nature of shocks, neuron T also activates modulatory interneurons, such as I_N. An

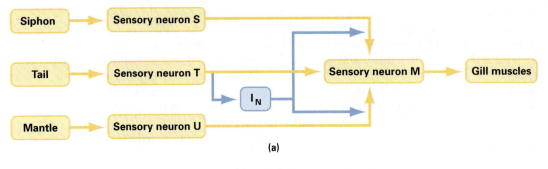

Figure 3.11 Sensitization in *Aplysia*
(a) A tail shock activates sensory neuron T, which activates motor neuron M, causing the motor response. T also activates an interneuron I_N, which delivers a neuromodulator (such as serotonin) to the axons of neurons S and U. (b) Subsequent activation of neuron S will cause a larger release of neurotransmitter (glutamate), leading to greater activation of neuron M than was previously evoked by S.

interneuron, as its name suggests, is a neuron that neither directly receives sensory inputs nor produces motor outputs but instead carries a message between two other neurons. A *modulatory interneuron* is an interneuron that alters the strength of the message being transmitted. You'll recall from Chapter 2 that *neuromodulators* are neurotransmitters that can affect activity in entire brain areas rather than just at a single synapse. In *Aplysia*, interneuron I_N connects neuron T to both S and U, communicating with them by releasing a neuromodulator such as *serotonin*. Serotonin increases the number of glutamate vesicles available to release glutamate from neuron S each time it fires. In effect, the interneuron does not tell S whether to fire; instead, it tells S, "When you do fire, fire strongly."

Suppose the sea hare now experiences a mild touch to the siphon. Before the tail shock, this mild touch would have caused neuron S to release neurotransmitter from a small number of vesicles, leading to a weak gill withdrawal (as in Figure 3.10b). But now, this mild touch causes neuron S to release neurotransmitter from a larger number of vesicles (Figure 3.11b), so that M is more likely to fire, leading to a stronger gill-withdrawal response (Brunelli, Castellucci, & Kandel, 1976; Castellucci & Kandel, 1976). In effect, the prior tail shock at T has put the slug on alert, making it sensitive to a subsequent light touch.

The key to sensitization is that it is **heterosynaptic,** meaning that it involves changes across several synapses, including synapses that were not activated by the sensitizing event. Because of this feature, a tail shock increases responses to any future stimulus. For example, if the experimenter touched the upper mantle (activating sensory neuron U) instead of the siphon (neuron S), the same overreaction would occur.

In effect, the tail shock has increased the sea hare's level of arousal, making it more likely to respond to any stimulus that follows. As with habituation, the degree of sensitization depends on the strength of the initial stimulus: a single mild shock can produce sensitization that lasts for minutes; four or five shocks together can produce sensitization that lasts two or more days (Marcus et al.,

1988; Squire & Kandel, 2000). Note that in the sea hare, sensitization does not engage a separate state system, as suggested by the dual process theory of habituation. Instead, interneurons that are part of the circuit that generates the reflexive response increase synaptic transmission. Nevertheless, two independent processes are associated with habituation and sensitization effects, and so the dual process theory of habituation does a good job of accounting for these effects in sea hares. Dual process theory was originally developed to explain habituation in mammals, so the fact that it can also capture many of the aspects of habituation and sensitization in a marine invertebrate suggests that many different species learn about repeated events in similar ways.

Test Your Knowledge

Synaptic Mechanisms of Learning in *Aplysia*

Habituation and sensitization have different effects on synaptic transmission in sea hares. For the following situations observed in sea hares, see if you can deduce whether habituation or sensitization has occurred and what is happening in the stimulus-response pathway. (Answers appear in the Answers section in the back of the book.)

1. Observations reveal that only one synapse, where once there were two, is now connecting a neuron that responds to stimulation of the tail to a neuron that contributes to the gill-withdrawal response.
2. Measurements of glutamate released around a motor neuron show that levels of glutamate are increasing over time.
3. Anatomical analyses of neural circuits reveal a larger number of synapses associated with the gill-withdrawal reflex circuit than are normally seen.
4. Recordings of motor neuron activity indicate that the neurons are firing less.

Perceptual Learning and Cortical Plasticity

When a sea hare learns about touches to parts of its body, its sensory neurons detect those touches the same way every time. Repeated touches change how strong the connections are between sensory neurons and motor neurons, but they do not change how the sensory receptors react to a touch—the amount of neural firing generated by sensory neurons with each touch is stable throughout habituation. Habituation occurs when a sea hare learns to ignore touches to its siphon. Perceptual learning, in contrast, involves increases in the ability to make distinctions between similar inputs. In perceptual learning, an individual learns to recognize stimulus differences that were not noticed before, and sensory neurons may change how they respond to events over time.

Unlike sea hares, which have only very simple neural circuits, your ability to distinguish different kinds of touches depends heavily on neurons within your somatosensory cortex. Sensory receptors in your skin send signals that pass up your spinal cord, through your thalamus, and into your somatosensory cortex (introduced in Chapter 2 and shown in Figure 2.7). Do you remember from Chapter 2 how the motor cortex contains a map of different regions of the body that it controls? It was called a *homunculus*. Somatosensory cortex has a similar homunculus that maps parts of the body receiving touch messages (Figure 3.12). So, whenever you touch something with your index finger, a specific set of neurons within your somatosensory cortex becomes active, and you perceive not only that your finger has contacted something, but what the surface that you have touched is like.

Figure 3.12 The homunculus corresponding to human somatosensory cortex Different regions of somatosensory cortex respond most strongly to touches of specific body parts. These regions are organized such that body parts close together activate adjacent regions of somatosensory cortex.

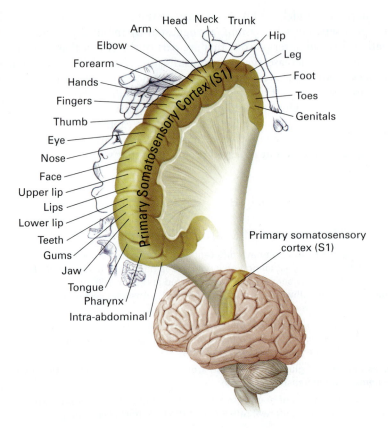

As described in Chapter 2, one of the most important jobs of the cerebral cortex is to process information about stimuli, and this includes distinguishing the features of perceived stimuli. *Sensory cortices* are especially important for making such distinctions, and the somatosensory cortex is an example. Sensory cortices are areas of the cerebral cortex that process visual stimuli, auditory stimuli, somatosensory (touch) stimuli, and so on. Within each of these brain regions, individual neurons respond to different stimulus features. For example, some neurons in your auditory cortex will fire strongly when you hear a high-pitched note, and others will fire strongly when you hear a low-pitched note.

The range of stimuli that cause a particular cortical neuron to fire is called the neuron's **receptive field.** Figure 3.13 shows the receptive field for one neuron in the auditory cortex of a guinea pig that was measured using single-cell recording techniques. This neuron fired when the guinea pig heard tones pitched between 0.7 and 3 kilohertz (kHz); this range of pitches is the neuron's receptive field. The neuron fired most when the guinea pig heard tones pitched near 0.9 kHz. Neuroscientists would say that this cortical neuron is *tuned* to 0.9 kHz, meaning that this pitch causes the most firing. In somatosensory cortex, the receptive field of a neuron is defined as the patch of skin or other tissue that when stimulated causes the neuron to fire. In general, the more neurons that are tuned to a particular type, source, or strength of stimulus (or any other feature of a stimulus), the better the organism will be able to make fine distinctions related to that stimulus. So, for example, in the body map shown in Figure 3.12, the region sensitive to touches on the thumb is larger than the region sensitive to touches on the neck; a larger region in the cortex means more neurons, with

Figure 3.13 Receptive field of a neuron in the auditory cortex of a guinea pig Receptive fields are identified by measuring the amount of neural activity produced in response to different stimuli—in this case, to sounds ranging from 0.1 to 100 kilohertz (kHz). This neuron responds most to 0.9 kHz, but it also responds to a narrow range of similarly pitched sounds, and this range constitutes the neuron's receptive field.

(Adapted from Weinberger, 2004.)

the result that the skin on the thumb is able to make finer distinctions than the skin on the neck is.

The spatial organization (body map) of somatosensory cortex shown in Figure 3.12 reflects the fact that neurons with similar receptive fields are often found clustered together in sensory cortices. In like manner, visual and auditory cortices also contain clusters of similarly tuned neurons. When these clusters are organized in predictable ways, the pattern of cortical organization is described as a *topographic map*, which simply means that cortical neurons that are physically close together are tuned to similar stimulus features. In topographic maps, neighboring cortical neurons have overlapping receptive fields. For example, if you collected recordings across the surface of a guinea pig's auditory cortex, you would find that adjacent neurons respond to gradually increasing or decreasing sound frequencies—neurons tuned to 0.9 kHz will be surrounded by neurons tuned to 0.8, 0.9, or 1.0 kHz. If you sat at a piano and played the keys one at a time from left to right up the keyboard, activity in your auditory cortex would gradually shift in a pattern that corresponds to the movement of your hand across the keyboard.

For most of the history of neuroscience, it was thought that neurons in sensory cortices responded to sensations in ways that were directly analogous to how piano strings respond to the pressing of piano keys. It was thought that every time a specific set of sensory receptors detected a stimulus, a particular set of cortical neurons became active. You may recall from Chapter 1 that René Descartes proposed that sensations cause this type of reflexive chain reaction. Neuroscientists were surprised to discover that in fact the receptive fields of neurons in sensory cortices change during early development and also after various injuries and as a result of repeated experiences. In other words, the topographic maps in your sensory cortices right now are not the same ones that were in your brain 10 years ago (although they are quite similar). The capacity for cortical receptive fields and cortical spatial organization to change as a result of experience is called **cortical plasticity.**

If what you perceive depends on how neurons in your sensory cortices are tuned and if the tuning of your sensory cortices changes over time, then what does this suggest about your perception? It suggests that your perception may also change over time—which is exactly what studies of perceptual learning show. The clearest evidence that repeated experiences can change perception by changing sensory cortices comes not from learning studies, however, but from studies of perceptual development.

Plasticity during Development

Normally, as young organisms develop, their ability to perceive differences in visual stimuli increases. Neurophysiological studies of neurons within the visual cortex of kittens show that their tuning becomes more selective over time and that topographic maps within visual cortex become more organized. If, however, a kitten's eye is sewn shut during development or if vision in an infant's eye is occluded by a cataract for several years, then even if vision in that eye is later restored, the acuity of that eye will be permanently degraded. Similarly, if young animals are experimentally deprived of vision in one eye, their cortical neurons will show less tuning to that eye than is seen in animals that grew up with both eyes functional. These findings suggest that normal development of visual cortical maps in mammals requires neural activity from both eyes. In other words, repeated visual experiences shape the organization of visual cortex during development, which in turn determines an organism's perception of the visual world (Morishita & Hensch, 2008).

If perceptual experiences change how sensory cortices respond to stimuli, what happens if stimulation from both eyes is cut off, such as when a person is born blind or loses his sight soon after birth? Neuroimaging studies show that the areas of visual cortex that normally respond to visual stimuli in sighted people will, in blind people, respond to sounds and tactile stimulation. For example, activity in the visual cortex is seen to increase in blind individuals during Braille reading and other tactile tasks but decreases in sighted individuals performing these same tasks (Lewis, Saenz, & Fine, 2010; Sadato et al., 1998).

Cortical plasticity produced by early blindness has recently been studied experimentally in developing opossums (Kahn & Krubitzer, 2002; Karlen, Kahn, & Krubitzer, 2006). Researchers blinded half of the animals at birth and then, when the animals reached adulthood, exposed both the blinded and sighted opossums to visual, auditory, and somatosensory inputs to measure between-group differences in cortical structure and receptive fields. Sighted opossums possessed distinct cortical regions that each were tuned exclusively either to visual, auditory, or somatosensory inputs. At the same time, receptive fields in other regions of the cortex were **multimodal,** meaning that neurons in those areas responded to inputs from more than one sensory modality—for example, visual *and* auditory stimuli. A different pattern was seen in opossums that had grown up blind. The cortical areas that were tuned exclusively to visual stimuli in sighted opossums had shrunk, and *within* those areas, some neurons now responded to auditory or somatosensory stimuli or both. In addition, the auditory and somatosensory areas of the cortex had increased beyond normal size. Most striking of all, the blinded opossums possessed a new cortical region with unique anatomical and physiological characteristics that didn't exist in any sighted opossum's brain.

Clearly, developmental experiences can have a huge effect on how neurons within sensory cortices respond to stimuli, influencing both the perception of sensory events and the development of responses to perceived events. In the case of opossums that developed without sight, the absence of vision radically changed the sensory experiences to which cortical neurons were exposed, and the opossums' brains changed accordingly. In all animals, not just those that have been blinded (or similarly injured) at birth, experience modifies sensory cortical maps. Your own cortical maps changed drastically during your infancy, and they will continue to change throughout your life, although you won't perceive that this is happening. In the Clinical Perspectives section, we describe how perceptual learning during development makes it possible for individuals to overcome sensory deficits such as blindness and deafness using new technologies.

Studies with opossums have revealed that the development of cortical structure and function depends on repeated experiences.

©Marion Wear/istockphoto

Hebbian Learning

You have now read about some of the evidence that neurons in sensory cortices change with experience, but what is the mechanism of this change? Several ideas have been proposed, but the most influential was suggested by psychologist Donald Hebb. In one of the most often quoted passages in neuroscience, Hebb wrote: "When an axon of cell A is near enough to excite a cell B and repeatedly or persistently takes part in firing it, some growth process or metabolic change takes place such that A's efficiency, as one of the cells firing B, is increased" (Hebb, 1949). A shorthand version of this "rule" that neuroscientists often use is *neurons that fire together, wire together.* One form of synaptic plasticity that seems to follow this rule is long-term potentiation (LTP), which, as you'll recall from Chapter 2, is thought to underlie many changes that occur in the brain during learning. Learning that involves strengthening connections between cells that work together (typically neurons) is called **Hebbian learning.**

Figure 3.14 shows a simple model of Hebbian learning. Eight hypothetical cortical neurons are shown, each with weak connections to surrounding neurons (Figure 3.14a). Now let's assume that some sensory stimulus evokes activation in a subset of these neurons that are tuned to features of this stimulus (solid circles in Figure 3.14a). As those neurons become active, they produce outputs that are transmitted to other nearby neurons. According to Hebb's rule—neurons that fire together, wire together—the connections between coactive neurons are strengthened as a result. Repeated coactivity of the same subset of neurons, in response to the same stimulus, has a cumulative effect, resulting in the strong connections (heavy lines) shown in Figure 3.14b. Thus, repeated exposure to a stimulus can strengthen connections within a distinctive subset of cortical neurons, and this subset can then provide an increasingly reliable basis for identifying the stimulus that is activating them. Hebbian learning provides a possible neural mechanism for the representational processes proposed in comparator models and differentiation theories of perceptual learning, described previously. Changing the connections between cortical neurons creates a pattern that makes a repeated stimulus more likely to be recognized and distinguished from other stimuli.

Hebbian learning can also explain how repeated exposures facilitate recognition (the priming effect). Suppose that once connections have been established between cortical neurons, the organism encounters an incomplete version of a familiar stimulus (Figure 3.14c). Only some of the subset of neurons that represents that familiar stimulus are activated at first (solid circles in Figure 3.14c), but the connections already established through repeated experiences will produce outputs that complete the familiar pattern, reconstructing Figure 3.14b. This kind of pattern completion may correspond to retrieval in the word-stem completion task described above. Priming might then be explained as a strengthening of existing connections between cortical neurons that lasts only as long as the priming effect. Similarly, recognition of distorted versions of a familiar stimulus, such as might occur when a blue jay perceives a camouflaged moth,

Figure 3.14 A simple model of Hebbian learning Circles correspond to cortical neurons, and lines denote connections between them. (a) Stimulus inputs activate a subset of the neurons (solid circles). (b) Connections between coactive neurons are strengthened (heavy lines). (c) After connections between coactive neurons have been established, an incomplete version of a familiar stimulus may activate just some of the neurons (solid circles) in the subset that represents the stimulus. Activation flows along the strengthened connections and ultimately retrieves the complete stimulus, resulting in the representation shown in (b).

(a)

(b)

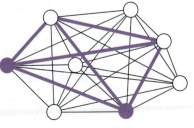

(c)

could also be facilitated by stored patterns encoded as connections between neurons that on a previous occasion were simultaneously active when moths were perceived. Thus, just as experiments with sea hares have provided a way to evaluate and extend the dual process theory of habituation, studies of cortical plasticity can potentially provide relevant information for assessing the adequacy of behavior-based models of perceptual learning and object recognition.

Cortical Changes in Adults after Exposure

During development, the arrival of inputs from different receptors determines how cortical neurons become tuned, as well as the proportion of available neurons that respond to a particular class of input. Someone born without vision is likely to have proportionately more neurons available to respond to tactile stimuli, and someone born deaf typically will come to have larger cortical regions sensitive to visual stimuli. Granted, these are extreme cases of depriving a brain of a particular class of input. What might happen in more subtle cases— for example, in a person who chooses to listen only to rap music, or to classical music, or to country music? Might the topographic map in the auditory cortex reflect the kinds of songs the person listens to the most? Is cortical plasticity only present during early development? How much exposure is required for the cortical neurons to become retuned?

Recent neuroimaging studies suggest that it is relatively easy to retune neurons within the sensory cortices of adults and that it can be done in less than a day. For example, simply touching a person's fingertip repeatedly with tiny pins was shown to improve the person's ability to distinguish subtle differences in the pins' positions. Initially, people were able to discriminate two simultaneous touches on the tip of their index finger, as long as the touches were spaced at least 1.1 mm apart (Figure 3.15a). After receiving 2 hours of exposure consisting of repeated simultaneous stimulation of two closely spaced points (0.25–3 mm apart) on the tip of their right index finger, participants' ability to discriminate touches improved (Dinse, Ragert, Pleger, Schwenkreis, & Tegenthoff, 2003; Hodzic, Veit, Karim, Erb, & Godde, 2004; Pilz, Veit, Braun, & Godde, 2004).

Like the experiment with squiggles described earlier (Figure 3.4), this study shows that humans can learn to make fine distinctions through mere repeated exposures. What's going on in the brain when this happens? Before repeated exposures, fMRI difference images showed that touching the right index finger resulted in localized activation within the somatosensory cortex (Figure 3.15b). After this finger was stimulated repeatedly for 2 hours, subsequent instances of stimulation activated a larger region of the somatosensory cortex than was observed before exposure (Figure 3.15c; Hodzic et al., 2004). Repeated touching of the fingertip led to both perceptual learning and cortical reorganization. In this case, the reorganization showed up in fMRI images as an increase in the size of the region of somatosensory cortex that was selectively activated during stimulation of the tip of the right index finger; thus, perceptual learning was associated with an increase in the number of cortical neurons tuned to touches of the fingertip.

This same phenomenon has also been examined using magnetoencephalographic (MEG) recordings of neural activity in somatosensory cortex. MEGs are similar to EEGs in that both reflect the activity of groups of neurons (unlike fMRI, which only measures blood oxygenation in the brain). The main difference between MEGs and EEGs is that MEGs measure small changes in magnetic fields rather than changes in electrical fields. MEG recordings showed that larger changes in somatosensory-cortex activity in response to tactile stimulation predicted larger improvements in discrimination abilities (Godde, Ehrhardt, & Braun, 2003). Together, these neuroimaging, neurophysiological, and behavioral

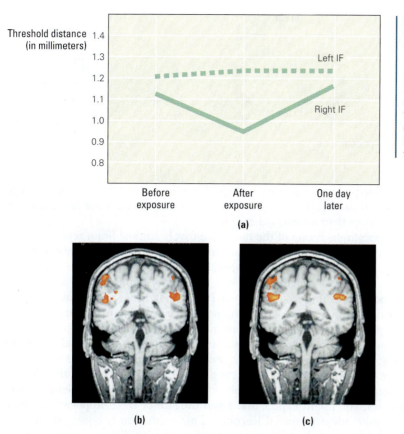

Threshold distance (in millimeters)

Before exposure — After exposure — One day later

Left IF

Right IF

(a)

(b)   (c)

Figure 3.15 **Cortical reorganization in humans after exposure** (a) Participants improved their ability to distinguish two separate touch points on their right index finger (Right IF) after 2 hours of passive exposure to stimulation of closely spaced points on that finger. (b) fMRI showing cortical activation patterns in somatosensory cortex during tactile stimulation of the right index finger before exposure. (c) After 2 hours of stimulation to the right index finger, activation in the left hemisphere (where the right finger is represented) has increased.

results suggest that perceptual learning and cortical changes occur in parallel and that both can occur after repeated exposures to inconsequential stimuli.

Given that perceptual learning after mere exposure is associated with cortical changes, might discrimination training also lead to similar kinds of cortical change? Several experiments have found that discrimination training does lead to cortical reorganization in adults (Fritz, David, Radtke-Schuller, Yin, & Shamma, 2010; Schiltz, Bodart, Michel, & Crommelinck, 2001; Schwartz, Maquet, & Frith, 2002). Many neuroscientists now believe that all forms of perceptual learning in mammals depend on cortical plasticity (Dinse & Merzenich, 2002; Kujala & Naatanen, 2010). In fact, almost every type of learning discussed in the subsequent chapters of this book has been shown to lead to retuning of cortical receptive fields (Hoffman & Logothetis, 2009; Weinberger, 2007). The role of cortical plasticity in learning and memory is further discussed in Chapter 6, on generalization, discrimination, and the representation of similarity.

The Hippocampus and Spatial Recognition

As mammals repeatedly experience sensory events, neurons in their sensory cortices gradually become tuned to specific features of those events. Might similar processes explain the kinds of latent learning observed when individuals actively explore the world around them? Researchers have attempted to answer this question by measuring and manipulating brain activity in rodents performing spatial tasks. Initially, the emphasis was on discovering where memories of mazes were stored in the cortex. Karl Lashley's failed attempt to locate cortical engrams for maze learning in rats (described in Chapter 2) represents one of the

(a) Monkey   **(b) Rat**   **(c) Bird**

Hippocampus

Hippocampus within medial temporal lobes

Hippocampus

Figure 3.16 The hippocampus in several types of animals Cross sections showing the hippocampus in a monkey, rat, and bird.

earliest attempts. Later neurophysiological studies of rats navigating through mazes revealed that spatial learning actually depends much more on activity in the hippocampus than on cortical engrams.

The hippocampus is one of the most extensively studied brain regions in the field of learning and memory. In humans and other primates, the hippocampus is a relatively small structure lying just beneath each temporal lobe (see Figure 2.3 and Figure 3.16a). In rodents, however, the hippocampus makes up a much larger proportion of the brain (Figure 3.16b). Many other vertebrates, including birds and reptiles, also possess a hippocampus. Although the hippocampus in birds is proportionately smaller than in rodents (Figure 3.16c), the absolute size of a bird's hippocampus is known to be important for spatial memory. Specifically, birds storing their food in many different locations for use in the winter have a hippocampus that is bigger than in related bird species that do not need to keep track of hidden food (Sherry & Hoshooley, 2010). Generalizing across species, you might expect that given the size of their hippocampus, rats should be quite adept at spatial learning. This prediction is borne out by the success with which rats learned to traverse thousands of different mazes during the early history of psychological research.

Identifying Places

As a first step toward understanding the role of the hippocampus in spatial learning, English neuroscientist John O'Keefe implanted electrodes in rats' hippocampal regions to record neuronal activity under various conditions (O'Keefe & Dostrovsky, 1971). When the rats were placed in an environment and allowed to explore freely, the investigators made a surprising discovery. Some hippocampal neurons seemed to fire only when a rat wandered into particular locations, and other hippocampal neurons fired only when the rat was in other locations. O'Keefe coined the term **place cells** to refer to neurons with such spatially tuned firing patterns. Each of these neurons had a certain preferred location to which it responded with maximal activity, and this location was termed the **place field** for that neuron (analogous to the receptive fields of sensory cortical neurons described above). The activity of these cells was so reliable that a blindfolded researcher could tell when a rat entered a particular region of the maze just by hearing the corresponding place cell begin to fire. O'Keefe suggested that place cells might form the basis for spatial learning and navigation.

How might place cells help with spatial navigation? If a certain neuron fires only when an individual is in a particular place, then that neuron might serve as an identifier for that place (much like road signs at street corners or mile markers along the highway). When the neuron fires, the brain would then "know" that the body is in a particular location. If you had enough place cells to code for every possible location you've ever visited—or ever might visit—you could work out where you are just by noting which place cell is firing. Of course, that would require an incredibly large number of place cells. Such a method, in which cells are kept on reserve to encode locations that you haven't yet visited, would be extremely wasteful. Instead, it would be smarter to create place cells as you need them. In other words, place fields should form during learning, as an animal explores its environment. This turns out to be the case.

An explanation of how place cells work must begin with a discussion of what defines a place. Put another way, what exactly determines whether a place cell will respond? Part of what leads a place cell to respond seems to be the animal's inner sense of its location in space: a rat's place cells often continue to respond in an orderly fashion even when the rat is running through a maze with the lights out. But place cell responses also depend heavily on visual inputs. For example, suppose a rat is allowed to explore a maze like the one shown in Figure 3.17a. This maze has three identical arms (labeled 1, 2, and 3 in the figure) differentiated by one salient visual cue: a card placed outside the maze between arms 2 and 3. After the initial exploration, various place cells in the rat's hippocampus will have place fields corresponding to parts of this maze. One hippocampal neuron, for example, had the place field shown in Figure 3.17b (darker areas indicate maximal firing; lighter areas, lesser firing). In other words, this place cell responded preferentially when the rat was in the southwest corner of the maze (as oriented in Figure 3.17a), at the outer edge of arm 2, on the side nearest the card (Lenck-Santini, Save, & Poucet, 2001).

Now suppose the experimenter takes the rat out of the maze and rotates the maze and card 120 degrees clockwise. What do you think will happen when the rat is put back in the maze (Figure 3.17c)? Will the place cell continue to fire when the rat is in the southwest corner of the maze? Or will it fire when the rat is at the end of arm 2, even though that is now the north-most corner of the maze? The answer is shown in Figure 3.17d: the place cell's preferred location has rotated along with the maze. In this particular case, since the three arms all look, smell, and feel pretty similar, the rat probably used the visual cue as a landmark. When the maze was rotated again, another 120 degrees clockwise, but the card was returned to its original place (Figure 3.17e), then the place

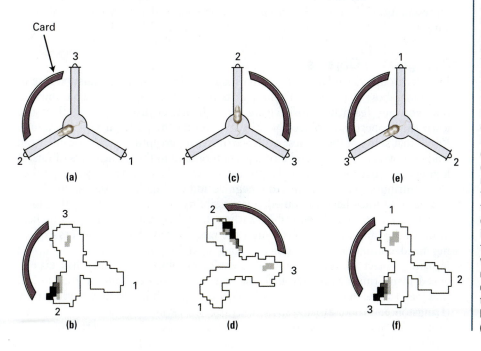

(a)   (c)   (e)

(b)   (d)   (f)

Figure 3.17 Effects of a visual landmark on a rat's place field Upper images show the rat's environment: a three-armed maze and a visual cue (a card, location marked in dark purple). Lower images show how a representative place cell fires in this environment: dark areas are regions that evoke heavy firing; lighter areas, regions that evoke lesser firing. (a, b) When the maze is in its initial position, this place cell fires maximally when the rat is in arm 2. (c, d) When maze and cue card are rotated 120 degrees clockwise, the place field is determined by visual cues; maximal firing still occurs in arm 2. (e, f) If the maze is rotated another 120 degrees but the card is returned to its original location, the place cell fires when the rat is in the southwest corner, even though this is now arm 3. In other words, place cell firing seems to depend on the rat's estimation of its location based on the visual landmark.

(Adapted from Lenck-Santini et al., 2001.)

cell again fired in the southwest corner of the maze, even though this was now arm 3 (Figure 3.17f). These findings illustrate the importance of visual landmarks (such as the card) in determining when a hippocampal place cell will fire. In addition to landmarks, some place cells in rats seem to be sensitive to other variables, such as the speed or direction in which a rat is moving. Thus, place cells respond like sensory cortical neurons with multimodal receptive fields.

Some place cells have place fields that are stable for months: if the rat is returned to the maze in Figure 3.17 after a long absence, the same place cell may still fire when the rat is in the same location as before. Research also shows that when place fields are unstable, spatial navigation is disrupted. The stability of place fields and their selectivity in terms of particular visual scenes are consistent with the idea that place cells provide the basis for a "cognitive map" that rats use to navigate through the world. But how, exactly, do place cells become tuned to a particular place?

One factor affecting the creation of place fields is experience. When rats repeatedly experience an environment, their place cells become increasingly tuned to locations within that environment (Lever, Wills, Cacucci, Burgess, & O'Keefe, 2002). Imagine the size of the dark place field in Figure 3.17 (b, d, and f) getting smaller and smaller, providing an increasingly precise and reliable report of where in the maze the rat is. This place-field shrinkage seems to correlate with rats' spatial navigation abilities in a maze; experiments in which rats' place-field shrinkage is disrupted (for example, by blocking inputs from the thalamus) show that the rats' spatial learning abilities decline (Cooper & Mizumori, 2001; Mizumori, Miya, & Ward, 1994; Rotenberg, Abel, Hawkins, Kandel, & Muller, 2000).

The findings presented above suggest that spatial learning that occurs during exploration is correlated with changes in the stability and selectivity of place cells (Rosenzweig, Redish, McNaughton, & Barnes, 2003). This phenomenon may explain how Tolman's rats were able to latently learn the layout of a complex maze even without associating specific locations with food rewards. Perhaps as the nonrewarded rats explored the maze, their place fields shrunk as much as (or more than) those of the rewarded rats, providing them with a precise representation of various locations within the maze that they could later take advantage of when the researchers initiated training with food.

Recognizing Objects

In order to use visual landmarks to navigate within a maze, rats must be able to recognize those landmarks. This suggests that as rats explore an environment, they not only learn how to navigate through that environment, but they also learn the properties of objects within and around the paths they are traveling. Recall that some of the earliest evidence of visual perceptual learning came from studies in which triangles and circles were mounted in the home cages of rats. If hippocampal neurons are sensitive to visual landmarks within a maze, might they also contribute to a rat's ability to recognize and distinguish those landmarks?

Recent studies have examined this possibility in rats performing the novel object recognition task described earlier. In initial experiments, researchers lesioned the hippocampus of rats after the rats had repeated experiences exploring fixed configurations of objects. Rats with hippocampal damage showed impaired object recognition memory, exploring objects that they had experienced many times as if they had not seen them before. Later studies found, however, that such lesions disrupted object recognition in certain situations only (Langston & Wood, 2010)—specifically, those in which memories of the position of the object and the context in which it was experienced were integrated.

These findings suggest that hippocampal neurons contribute to exploratory learning in ways that go beyond simply constructing spatial maps or identifying familiar objects. As you study further in this book, you will discover many more ways that the hippocampus and surrounding regions contribute to learning and memory.

Interim Summary

- In *Aplysia*, habituation is the result of synaptic depression in circuits that link sensory neurons to motor neurons. In contrast, sensitization in *Aplysia* reflects increases in synaptic transmission caused by the activation of interneurons.
- During perceptual learning, cortical neurons refine their responses to sensory inputs as discrimination abilities improve.
- In Hebbian learning, repeated exposures can strengthen associations between particular subsets of cortical neurons, causing neurons that fire together to wire together. This process can increase the ability to recognize repeated stimuli.
- Hippocampal place cells are neurons that become most active when an animal is at a particular location. These neurons may help animals identify and navigate through familiar environments.

3.3 Clinical Perspectives

Even when you are not consciously aware of it, perceptual learning influences every experience you have. From your ability to understand speech to your ability to find your way to school or work, every sensation and perception is influenced by the memories you've acquired through repeatedly experiencing similar stimuli. As noted earlier in this chapter, much of perceptual learning involves processing in sensory cortices. The cortical regions that process sensory information can be damaged through brain injury, and the result can be a fundamental change in how stimuli are perceived, processed, and learned about, which in turn will affect processes of habituation, perceptual learning, and familiarization.

Rehabilitation after Stroke: Habituation Gone Awry

The leading cause of brain damage in the United States is stroke. A **stroke** occurs when blood flow to some region of the brain stops or when an artery ruptures. Lack of blood causes neurons in the affected region to die, effectively creating a brain lesion. Immediately after a stroke, a patient often experiences large losses in perceptual function. For example, a patient may lose all sensation in one of his arms. Subsequently, although nothing may be wrong with the motor control of that arm, the patient may begin to ignore the desensitized arm and make greater use of the arm he can still feel. Over time, he may stop trying to use the desensitized arm altogether, a phenomenon called **learned non-use.** Effectively, the patient gets used to the lack of feeling in the dysfunctional arm and stops attempting to use it. In other words, the patient's repeated experiences with his or her desensitized arm leads to decreased use of that arm; learned non-use is a relatively clear case of habituation.

Monkeys show similar patterns of learned non-use when they lose sensation in a limb. For example, if somatosensory information from a monkey's

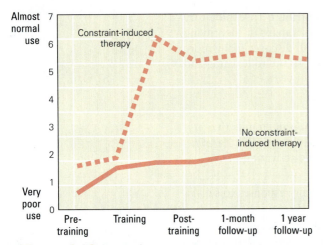

Figure 3.18 Overcoming learned non-use Patients with cortical lesions affecting one limb (e.g., an arm) often start using the unaffected limb in preference—a learned non-use of the affected limb. The graph shows results for two groups of patients who initially (pre-training) had very little use of one arm. One group underwent constraint-induced movement therapy, which forced them to use the affected arm for daily activities. These patients showed dramatic improvements in function of the injured arm compared with control patients not receiving this therapy.

(Adapted from Taub et al., 2002.)

right arm is blocked so that it cannot feel the arm, the monkey will stop using it, using the left arm instead. If the left arm is bound so that the monkey can no longer use it, however, the monkey may begin using the desensitized right arm, even if it has not used that arm for several years. After the monkey has become accustomed to using the right arm again, release of the left arm typically leads to the monkey's using both arms again, showing that it can overcome the learned non-use of the desensitized arm (Knapp, Taub, & Berman, 1963). One interpretation of this functional recovery is that binding the left arm created a new situation that dishabituated the monkey's responses to desensitization of an arm.

Techniques like those employed with the monkey are sometimes used in therapy for human stroke patients. For example, a patient who has lost the use of his left arm might consent to have his preferred right arm immobilized in a sling so that he is forced to try to use his left arm for eating, dressing, and other daily activities. As Figure 3.18 shows, patients receiving this kind of therapy, called **constraint-induced movement therapy**, often recover much more function in their affected arm than patients who are simply told to try to use their affected arm as often as possible (Taub, Uswatte, & Elbert, 2002; Wolf et al., 2010).

The idea behind constraint-induced movement therapy is to force the patient to use the affected arm as often as possible to encourage changes in cortex that compensate for stroke-related damage. This approach to generating cortical plasticity is similar to the approach used to change cortical processing in opossums during development, as described above. Recall that the newborn opossums were blinded so that cortical areas normally devoted to visual processing were instead reallocated to other sensory modalities. In stroke patients treated with constraint-induced movement therapy, just the opposite might happen. Because the part of the cortex that was devoted to processing sensory inputs from the arm is damaged, nearby undamaged cortical areas might take up some of the work that the damaged area once performed. Recent neuroimaging studies show that this therapy is associated with increases in the blood flowing to the sensory and motor cortex (Wittenberg & Schaechter, 2009) and that after constraint-induced movement therapy, structural changes are seen in these cortical regions that are not seen after other rehabilitation techniques (Gauthier et al., 2008). The therapy is thought to involve perceptual learning because patients must learn to make distinctions between sensations that are initially quite faint (and therefore difficult to discriminate).

Man-Machine Interfaces: Regaining Sensory Modalities through Perceptual Learning

If training can lead to cortical change that helps people recover motor functions after a brain injury, might it also enable people to develop perceptual abilities they don't have? For example, could discrimination training that leads to cortical change help someone who is deaf learn to hear? This is indeed possible and has in fact already been accomplished with sensory prostheses. **Sensory prostheses** are electromechanical devices that interface with the brain areas that normally process sensory information.

Transmitter coil

Receiver stimulator

Microphone

Behind-the-ear speech processor

Cochlea

Auditory nerve

Electrode array

Body-worn speech processor

Figure 3.19 Cochlear implant Cochlear implants use electricity to stimulate neurons in the auditory system, thereby creating virtual speech sounds in the brain. (Adapted from Clarke, 2002.)

To date, the most extensively developed sensory prosthetic technology is the **cochlear implant** (Figure 3.19). This device electrically stimulates auditory nerves to produce hearing sensations in profoundly deaf individuals, primarily to assist them in processing speech. Multiple electrodes implanted in the cochlea (the part of the ear that converts sounds into neural firing patterns) modify responses in the auditory nerve in ways that roughly simulate the neural activity normally produced by sounds. This technology is most effective in young children and in adults who have only recently lost their hearing. Conventional hearing aids amplify external sounds, but cochlear implants re-create the effects of sounds within the brain, generating "virtual sounds" from information about environmental sound that has been electronically detected and processed. The virtual speech sounds generated by cochlear implants are quite different from normal speech, so people using the implants must learn to discriminate between the new sounds before they can being to understand what they hear, an example of perceptual learning. Like most practice-based learning, speech perception by individuals with cochlear implants shows initial rapid improvement in the early months of use, followed by more gradual improvement over years (Clarke, 2002; Tajudeen, Waltzman, Jethanamest, & Svirsky, 2010).

It is likely that changes in speech-processing abilities after installation of a cochlear implant are the result of cortical plasticity, but this has yet to be experimentally demonstrated in humans. Neural activity generated by the implant may lead to changes in many areas of cortex, because the implant provides the brain with access not only to new sounds but also to all of the abilities that these sounds provide (such as the ability to engage in spoken conversations). Researchers have found that cochlear implants in deaf cats lead to massive changes in auditory cortex (Klinke, Kral, Heid, Tillein, &

Sensory prosthesis of the future? Researchers at Boston University are developing retinal implants that may provide blind users with virtual sight.

Courtesy of Boston Retinal Implant Project

Hartmann, 1999). After implantation, auditory cortex becomes organized differently from that of what is seen in deaf cats without implants and also from that of hearing cats, suggesting that the virtual sounds these cats hear are driving the observed changes in cortex.

Most current sensory prostheses are designed to replace lost abilities, but in principle, it should also be possible to use such devices to enhance existing capabilities or create new sensory abilities. No one knows how well cortical neurons would be able to process inputs from sensors detecting stimuli such as infrared light or ultrasonic sounds that humans are normally unable to perceive. Given how easily deaf people have learned to process novel inputs from cochlear implants, however, it seems likely that the human brain could accommodate a wide range of machine-provided inputs through perceptual learning.

Interim Summary

- Learned non-use of a desensitized limb can be overcome by constraint-induced movement therapy, which forces the individual to use the limb. Learned non-use can be viewed as a type of habituation, whereas constraint-induced movement therapy is an applied form of discrimination training that may lead to recovery through cortical plasticity.

- Sensory prostheses, such as cochlear implants, provide individuals with new sensory-processing capabilities. Training with a cochlear implant leads to perceptual learning that improves the user's ability to discriminate simulated speech sounds and also can lead to receptive field changes in auditory cortex.

▶ SYNTHESIS

Habituation, perceptual learning, and other phenomena that result from repeated exposures to stimuli are often described as the simplest forms of learning. This is partly because even the most primitive animals show habituation (even amoebas!). Moreover, neither perceptual learning nor habituation demands any obvious effort from the learner, although in the case of perceptual learning, practice can be beneficial. Nervous systems have evolved to collect information about what's new in the world and to recognize the familiar.

The processes involved in learning about repeated events can, however, be highly complex, involving the combined activities of multiple brain regions interacting in many different ways. A good example is the learning of landmarks for spatial navigation. Complex combinations of stimuli, including both visual patterns and specific movement patterns, determine how place cells in the hippocampus respond. Spatial learning can happen independent of observable responses, which means it is difficult for an observer to determine what another individual is learning about any particular set of landmarks. Who would guess that as you sit in a car staring out of the window, your brain is recording the locations of certain landmarks that can help you to find your way back to that location later?

Repeated experiences can slow down your ability to learn (in the case of habituation) or speed it up (in the case of priming and perceptual learning). They can also affect your responses to other, seemingly unrelated stimuli (as in the case of sensitization). For example, reading about the cannibalistic murderer Jeffrey Dahmer in the beginning of this chapter was probably novel in your experiences of reading psychology textbooks. If you have gotten used to experiencing the relatively predictable material within college textbooks (in other words, if you get bored reading textbooks), then this disturbing example may have caused your learned response to textbooks to dishabituate, which may have in turn increased your capacity to encode and remember the subsequent material, despite the fact that this material may have little to do with psychopathic killers. How is it that repeated exposures to stimuli can generate such a wide range of learning phenomena? Part of the answer, at least in mammals, is the contribution made by the cerebral cortex, one of the most complex structures in the brain. Experience-dependent changes in how cortical neurons respond to repeated events constitute one of several powerful mechanisms that seem to contribute to both perceptual learning and habituation.

Changes in behavior stemming from memories of repeated events have important implications for our daily lives, especially when the brain is not processing information the way it should. Understanding the mechanisms by which brains learn from repeated experiences can help clinicians interpret the effects of cortical damage and take steps to alleviate sensory deficits. The ability of brains to adapt in the ways described in this chapter may be the key to overcoming many mental deficits for which there are currently no cures. Thus, although habituation and perceptual learning can sometimes lead to negative outcomes (as in the circumstances surrounding Jeffrey Dahmer and in learned non-use), these processes also point to ways of rehabilitating patients and expanding people's perceptual abilities.

Key Terms

acoustic startle reflex, *p. 78*
Aplysia, *p. 97*
cochlear implant, *p. 113*
comparator model, *p. 89*
constraint-induced movement therapy, *p. 112*
cortical plasticity, *p. 103*
differentiation theory, *p. 90*
discrimination training, *p. 87*
dishabituation, *p. 79*

dual process theory, *p. 83*
familiarity, *p. 95*
habituation, *p. 77*
Hebbian learning, *p. 105*
heterosynaptic, *p. 100*
homosynaptic, *p. 99*
learned non-use, *p. 111*
learning specificity, *p. 88*
mere exposure learning, *p. 86*
multimodal, *p. 104*

novel object recognition, *p. 94*
orienting response, *p. 78*
perceptual learning, *p. 85*
place cell, *p. 108*
place field, *p. 108*
priming, *p. 95*
receptive field, *p. 102*
sensitization, *p. 82*
sensory prosthesis, *p. 112*

skin conductance response (SCR), *p. 82*
spatial learning, *p. 92*
spontaneous recovery, *p. 81*
stroke, *p. 111*
synaptic depression, *p. 99*
word-stem completion task, *p. 95*

Concept Check

1. A weight lifter repeatedly lifts a barbell. After several repetitions, he begins lifting it more slowly, until eventually he stops. Is this habituation?

2. A common example of sensitization is the experience of walking down a dark alleyway at night. The setting may produce feelings of nervousness, which lead to heightened arousal: you'll jump if you hear a noise behind you. Can you think of any situations in which people are intentionally sensitized?

3. After reading this chapter, you'll have learned at least some of the information it contains. If you read the chapter again, you may learn even more. Is this an example of learning from repeated events?

4. When structural MRIs of London taxi drivers were compared with those of control participants who did not drive taxis, researchers discovered that the average size of the hippocampus in the taxi drivers was larger than in the control participants and was correlated with the number of years they had been driving a taxi (Maguire et al., 2000). Why might that be?

Classical Conditioning

Learning to Predict Important Events

WHAT DO THESE TWO people have in common? Four-year-old Moira screams with delighted anticipation for ice cream when she hears the jingle of the vendor's truck in the distance; Chuck starts feeling anxious about the carpeting in his home when he sees rain clouds on the horizon and realizes that he left the windows open this morning. It's not immediately apparent, but a little investigation will show that the link connecting Moira and Chuck's reactions is Ivan Pavlov—or to be more precise, Ivan Pavlov's principle of classical conditioning. Moira and Chuck have both had their behaviors altered by classical (or "Pavlovian") conditioning.

Most people, even if they never took a psychology course, are vaguely aware of the story of Ivan Pavlov (1849–1936) and how he trained, or "conditioned," his dogs to salivate to cues such as bells or tones that predicted the impending delivery of food. Chapter 1 briefly introduced you to Pavlov and his training method; this chapter will explain why his work was so important and influential and why it continues to be relevant to experimental and clinical studies today.

Like many advances in science, Pavlov's discovery of classical conditioning was largely accidental. He was originally studying digestion, and he noticed that his dogs often started salivating even before they received their daily meat rations—when they saw the bowl that usually contained their food or when they heard the footsteps of the laboratory assistant who fed them (Pavlov, 1927). Initially, Pavlov viewed the premature salivation as a nuisance that interfered with his efforts to understand how the digestive system responds to

Behavioral Processes
Basic Concepts of Classical Conditioning
Error Correction and the Modulation of US Processing
Modulation of CS Processing
Further Facets of Conditioning

Brain Substrates
Mammalian Conditioning of Motor Reflexes
Brain Rhythms and Conditioning
Invertebrates and the Cellular Basis of Learning

Clinical Perspectives
Learning and Memory in Everyday Life: Extinguishing a Drug Habit

food. Soon, however, Pavlov realized that he had stumbled on a way of studying how associations are formed in the brain of a dog.

Pavlov and his assistants began a systematic study of factors that influence how an animal learns. By keeping the dogs in restraints and collecting saliva through a tube surgically inserted into their mouths (Figure 4.1), Pavlov could measure salivation in response to various cues. He began one study by first training a dog that a doorbell always preceded delivery of food; over many paired doorbell-food trials, the dog developed a stronger and stronger salivation response to the sound of the doorbell. This form of learning, in which an animal learns that one stimulus (such as a doorbell) predicts an upcoming important event (such as delivery of food), is known today as **classical conditioning** or **Pavlovian conditioning**.

There is much more to classical conditioning than dogs and saliva, however. This chapter will show why an understanding of classical "Pavlovian" conditioning (despite its seeming simplicity) is indispensable for building a behavioral and biological understanding of learning and memory. Moreover, classical conditioning is one of the few forms of learning for which the brain substrates have been worked out in precise detail, for every step, from the initial sensory input to the commands that drive the resulting motor responses. For these reasons, classical conditioning is avidly studied today by psychologists,

Figure 4.1 Pavlov's apparatus for studying learning
A restrained dog has a surgical tube inserted into its mouth to collect and measure salivation in response to meat placed in front of it or to a cue, such as a doorbell, that predicts delivery of the food.

neuroscientists, and clinical neuropsychologists, with implications far beyond what Pavlov could have anticipated when he made his accidental discovery almost one hundred years ago.

4.1 Behavioral Processes

Classical Pavlovian conditioning is a way of learning about one's environment. As a child, Moira learned that the distant sound of a certain jingle predicts the imminent arrival of an ice cream truck. Since she loves ice cream, she can exploit her foreknowledge of the truck's arrival by asking her mother for money now so she can be ready at the curb when the truck approaches. This is an example of learning to anticipate a positive event so as to take maximal advantage of it. Being able to anticipate negative events is also useful. If Chuck is surprised by a sudden rainstorm in midday, he must rush home from work to close all the windows to keep rain from blowing in and soaking his carpets. Had he anticipated the rainstorm earlier, Chuck could have closed the windows before he left for work.

This section begins by introducing the basic concepts and terminology of classical conditioning and then explores subsequent research into this type of learning. It describes an elegant and simple theory of conditioning, developed in the early 1970s, that helps explain a wide range of learning phenomena, and it discusses how conditioning behaviors seen in the simplest of animals help us understand the more complex cognitive behaviors observed in human learning. It ends by discussing several other facets of classical conditioning, including how attention can affect what is learned, how timing is important, and to what degree we may be biologically prepared to learn some things more easily than others.

Basic Concepts of Classical Conditioning

A dog will naturally salivate when it sees or smells food. No learning is needed for it to make this response. For this reason, Pavlov called the food an **unconditioned stimulus,** or **US,** meaning a stimulus that naturally—that is, without conditioning—evokes some response. Actually, Pavlov's term, translated from Russian, was "unconditional" (not unconditioned) stimulus, because these reflexive responses occurred unconditionally, that is, without any training or conditioning. However, the term was mistranslated into English almost one hundred years ago, and ever since then, English-speaking authors have been using the word "unconditioned" rather than "unconditional."

An unconditioned stimulus, such as food, evokes a natural response, such as salivation, which Pavlov called the **unconditioned response,** or **UR;** their relationship does not depend on learning. Similarly, Moira's craving for ice cream and Chuck's dismay at wet carpets in his house are natural—that is, unconditioned—responses to good and bad things in their lives. They both occur unconditionally without prior training. In contrast, a neutral stimulus, such as a bell that the dog has not heard before, evokes no such salivation by the dog (Figure 4.2a).

How Pavlov Conditioned Dogs to Salivate

After Pavlov put his dogs into the apparatus shown in Figure 4.1, he repeatedly paired the bell with food: each time the bell was rung, an assistant promptly delivered food to the dog. This resulted in the formerly neutral stimulus, the

Figure 4.2 Schematic illustration of Pavlov's experiment (a) Before training, food, an unconditioned stimulus (US), naturally evokes an unconditioned response (US), salivation. In contrast, a neutral stimulus, such as a bell, evokes no such response by the dog before training. (b) During training, the bell, formerly a neutral stimulus, becomes a conditioned stimulus (CS) when it is repeatedly paired with the food US to evoke a salivation UR. (c) After training, the bell, now a conditioned stimulus (CS), evokes a learned response, the conditioned response (CR) of salivation.

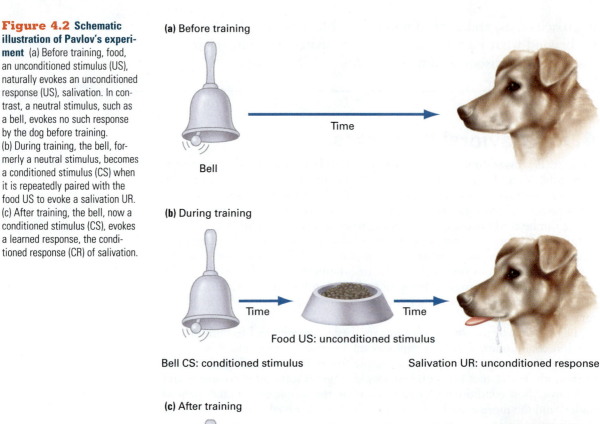

(a) Before training

Time

Bell

(b) During training

Time   Time

Food US: unconditioned stimulus

Bell CS: conditioned stimulus

Salivation UR: unconditioned response

(c) After training

Time

Bell CS: conditioned stimulus

Salivation CR: conditioned response

bell, becoming a **conditioned stimulus,** or **CS,** as illustrated in Figure 4.2b. After repeated presentations of the bell CS and the food US, the two became linked in the dog's mind. This training—or conditioning, as Pavlov called it—resulted in the dog learning something new: the bell predicts the food. We can evaluate the degree to which the dog learned this prediction—that is, how strongly it expects the food when it hears the bell—by measuring how much the dog salivates to the bell alone. This is shown in Figure 4.2c, in which the bell alone, the conditioned stimulus (CS), now evokes an anticipatory response, called the **conditioned response,** or **CR,** even in the absence of the food.

For Moira, the truck jingle is a conditioned stimulus (CS), which, after being repeatedly paired with the arrival of the ice cream truck, evokes an anticipatory conditioned response (CR) consisting of Moira asking her mother for money and running to the street corner. When this response has been fully learned, Moira will be waiting at the street corner, money in hand, when the unconditioned stimulus (US)—the ice cream truck—arrives at her house. For Chuck, the dark clouds in

Table 4.1

Terminology of Pavlovian conditioning, with examples

	Unconditioned stimulus, US	Unconditioned response, UR	Conditioned stimulus, CS	Conditioned response, CR
Pavlov's dog	Food	Salivation	Bell	Salivation
Moira	Ice cream truck	Appetite for ice cream	Truck jingle	Get money from Mom, run to corner before truck arrives
Chuck	Rain	Closing windows while carpets get wet	Dark clouds	Closing windows before the rain starts

the sky are an ominous conditioned stimulus (CS) that through his past experiences have become associated with subsequent heavy rains. These experiences have taught him a preparatory conditioned response (CR): to close all the windows in his house before the arrival of the rain, the unconditioned stimulus (US). In all three examples—Pavlov's dog, Moira, and Chuck—a learned association between a CS and subsequent US generates a CR that follows the CS. Table 4.1 reviews these terms and their relation to the three examples. We will continue to use all four terms—US, UR, CS, CR—throughout this chapter as well as the rest of this book, so it's a good idea to be sure you are comfortable with all four before moving on.

Test Your Knowledge

Classical Conditioning in Everyday Life

Identify the elements of classical conditioning (US, UR, CS, CR) in the following scenario. (Answers appear in the Answers section in the back of the book.)

Marian, who is on a tight budget, stayed in an inexpensive hotel, where she got bitten by bedbugs. Now every time she sees a commercial for that hotel, she develops an itch.

Appetitive Conditioning

When the US is a positive event (such as food delivery for Pavlov's dog or ice cream for Moira), the conditioning is called **appetitive conditioning.** In general, appetitive conditioning consists of learning to predict something that satisfies a desire or appetite. Food and sex are among the most powerful of appetitive USs. Michael Domjan and colleagues have studied male domesticated Japanese quail, who will copulate readily with a sexually receptive female (Figure 4.3). When an arbitrary stimulus, such as a light CS, is paired repeatedly with access to a sexually receptive female (the US), the male quail exhibits a CR of approaching and remaining near the light (Domjan, Lyons, North, & Bruell, 1986).

Aversive Conditioning

Chuck's learning that clouds predict rain damage to his home (if the windows are not shut) is an example of **aversive conditioning,** learning to avoid or minimize the consequences of an expected aversive event. Many of the procedures used for the experimental study of conditioning are examples of aversive conditioning.

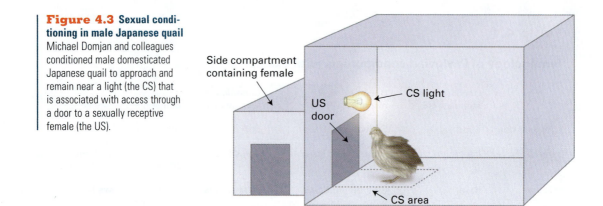

Figure 4.3 Sexual conditioning in male Japanese quail Michael Domjan and colleagues conditioned male domesticated Japanese quail to approach and remain near a light (the CS) that is associated with access through a door to a sexually receptive female (the US).

In Chapter 1 you read about both B. F. Skinner, the father of behaviorist approaches to the science of learning, and W. K. Estes, a founder of mathematical psychology and learning theory. In the early 1940s, Estes was a graduate student of Skinner's. At that time, the United States had not yet entered World War II. The Germans were using a new technology—rockets—to bomb England. As Londoners heard the whine of the rocket engines approaching, they stopped whatever they were doing—eating, walking, talking—and waited for the explosions. After the rockets dropped elsewhere and people realized they were safe, they resumed their interrupted activities.

Intrigued by these stories from London, Estes and Skinner developed a new conditioning procedure for rats that was similar, in some respects, to what they imagined Londoners were experiencing. This procedure, which they called the conditioned response (CR), was a technique for studying learned fear (Estes & Skinner, 1941). Estes and Skinner placed hungry rats in a cage that delivered food pellets whenever the rats pressed a lever. The cage also had a metal grid floor wired to deliver a mild shock to the rats' feet. Normally, the hungry rats busily pressed the lever to obtain food, but if the experimenters trained the rats to learn that a tone (the conditioned stimulus, or CS) predicted an upcoming shock (the unconditioned stimulus, or US), the rats would freeze (their conditioned response, CR) when they heard the tone, interrupting their lever presses and waiting for the shock. Measuring this freezing behavior allowed Estes to quantify trial-by-trial changes in the learned response. Within a few years, this conditioned emotional response procedure became one of the most widely used techniques for studying animal conditioning, and it is still in use today. In Chapter 10 you can read more about fear conditioning and how emotions, such as fear, influence learning and memory.

"Birds do it, bees do it, even educated fleas do it," wrote Cole Porter for the 1928 Broadway show *Paris*. Porter was, of course, referring to falling in love, but he could just as well have been writing about learning by classical conditioning. Even insects such as fleas and flies can be trained using classical conditioning methods. In fact, studies of classical conditioning of the fruit fly (*Drosophila*) have been enormously important for understanding the biology of learning (we'll see an example of such a study later in this chapter).

Figure 4.4 illustrates the behavioral procedure used in studies of fly conditioning (Dudai, Jan, Byers, Quinn, & Benzer, 1976). First the flies are placed in a container that contains one odor, designated odor 1 (Figure 4.4a), and nothing happens. Then the flies are exposed to another odor, odor 2, and in the presence of that odor (the CS), they are given a mild but aversive shock (the US). Later, the flies are placed in the middle of a container that has odor 1 at one end and

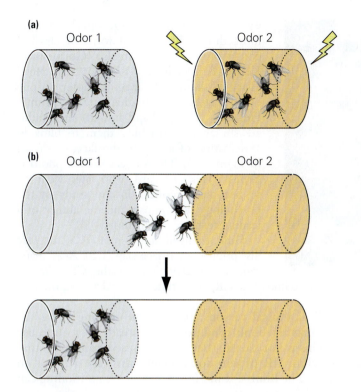

Figure 4.4 Odor conditioning in flies (a) Flies are placed sequentially in two different containers, first in one with odor 1, where they are not shocked, and then in another with odor 2, where they are shocked. (b) Later, they are placed in the middle of a container that has odor 1 at one end and odor 2 at the other end. The flies move toward odor 1, which was not associated with shock, indicating that they have learned the odor 2–shock association from their previous training.

odor 2 at the other end (Figure 4.4b). As the flies explore the container, they avoid the side where they smell odor 2 (which has been associated with shock) and gravitate toward the side where they smell odor 1 (which was not paired with shock). Like Chuck's keeping out the rain, the rats' and flies' avoidance of shocks are examples of aversive conditioning to predictors of a significant negative event.

Understanding the Conditioned Response

So far, we have introduced four different procedures for experimenting with classical conditioning. Two of these are appetitive conditioning procedures: Pavlov's original study with dogs and food and Domjan's studies of quails and sex. The other two are aversive conditioning procedures: the conditioned emotional response in which rats freeze when they hear a tone that predicts a shock (Estes & Skinner, 1941) and the fly shock preparation shown in Figure 4.4.

In each of these four cases, we can ask, why does the animal exhibit the conditioned response? In all four, the conditioned response can be understood as an anticipatory response that prepares the animal for the expected US, in much the same way that Moira prepares for the arrival of an anticipated ice cream truck or Chuck prepares for a predicted rainstorm. By moving away from the odor associated with shock, the fly is more likely to avoid being shocked. By salivating in anticipation of food, the dog is better prepared to efficiently digest the food. By freezing in anticipation of a shock, the rat is better prepared to ward off danger and also avoids having ongoing motor behaviors (such as eating) disrupted by the shock. By moving toward the light, the quail is all the sooner able to mount and copulate with the female.

Eyeblink Conditioning

Another widely studied form of aversive conditioning—one that induces an anticipatory defensive response much like Chuck's shutting his windows—is

Courtesy of Ernest Hilgard

Figure 4.5 **Face-slap eyeblink conditioning in the 1920s**
Clark Hull (standing with visor) and his young graduate student Ernest Hilgard (seated) in an early study of classical eyeblink conditioning at Yale University. Hull trained Hilgard to blink in anticipation of a slap to the face.

Figure 4.6 **Eyeblink conditioning in humans and rabbits**
(a) In human eyeblink conditioning, a tone CS is delivered through headphones. The US is a puff of air delivered through the rubber tube. The eyeblink CR is recorded by EMG electrodes placed above and below the eye. (b) In rabbit eyeblink conditioning, a similar rubber tube delivers the airpuff US to the rabbit in the restraining acrylic glass case; a photobeam measures the CR and UR.

eyeblink conditioning, perhaps the most thoroughly studied form of classical conditioning in mammals (Gormezano, Kehoe, & Marshall, 1983). You may recall Clark Hull of Yale from Chapter 1, one of the fathers of mathematical learning. He used (and perhaps abused) his graduate students by teaching them to blink in anticipation of a slap to the face, as shown in Figure 4.5. The subject in this photo is Ernest "Jack" Hilgard, who later went on to become a pioneer in the study of the psychology of hypnosis and the author of a leading textbook on memory.

Hull arranged for a tone (CS) to play just prior to each face slap (US). After many repeated presentations of the CS followed by the US, poor Jack began to blink (the CR) every time he heard a tone, whether or not it was followed by a slap.

For practical as well as ethical reasons, researchers no longer use the face slap as a US in human eyeblink conditioning. Instead, they often use an airpuff to the eye. This is not painful, but it does cause a reflexive—that is, unconditioned—eyeblink UR (if you don't believe this, ask a friend to blow lightly in your eye). The blink UR in human eyeblink conditioning can be measured in several different ways, one of which is through the use of electromyography (EMG) detectors of electrical activity of muscles, placed above and below the eye as shown in Figure 4.6a. The CS is a tone, typically delivered through headphones so that the volume can be regulated (and outside noises masked). With repeated pairings of the tone CS and airpuff US, subjects develop a CR: in this case, an anticipatory blink that occurs before US arrival, so that the eye is partially shut and partially protected when the airpuff occurs.

What is most important about eyeblink conditioning is the similarity of its appearance in many different species, so that the results found in one species can reasonably be expected to apply to others. Eyeblink conditioning has been shown in mice, rats, and monkeys, but one of the most common

(a)

Mark Gluck

(b)

Richard F. Thompson

animals for the study of eyeblink conditioning has been the rabbit, because of its propensity to sit still for long periods and to blink very little except when something bothers its eyes. Figure 4.6b shows a rabbit in a restraining acrylic glass case within which eyeblink conditioning is often conducted. The tube at the rabbit's left eye delivers the airpuff US while the eyeblink CR and UR are measured by photo beams.

With rabbits, just as with humans, the airpuff is the US, and the reflexive blink is the UR, as shown in Figure 4.7. Before training, the tone does not cause the rabbit to blink because it is a neutral stimulus, as shown in Figure 4.7a. However, if the airpuff US is repeatedly preceded by a tone, then the animal learns that the tone predicts the airpuff US and is a warning signal to get ready, as shown in Figure 4.7b. Eventually, the animal will blink as a response to the tone alone, as shown in Figure 4.7c. At this point, the tone has become a CS, and the anticipatory eyeblink is the CR.

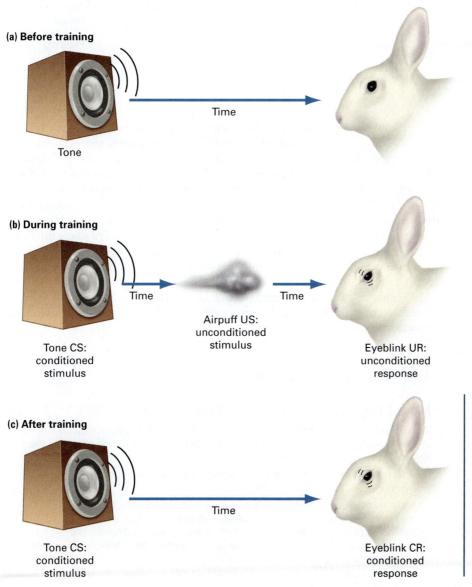

(a) Before training

Time

Tone

(b) During training

Time

Time

Tone CS: conditioned stimulus

Airpuff US: unconditioned stimulus

Eyeblink UR: unconditioned response

(c) After training

Time

Tone CS: conditioned stimulus

Eyeblink CR: conditioned response

Figure 4.7 Learning progression in rabbit eyeblink conditioning (a) Before training, the tone is a neutral stimulus that has no relevance to rabbit. (b) The tone CS followed by airpuff US causes an eyeblink UR in a naive rabbit. (c) The tone CS is followed by a blink CR in a rabbit that has undergone eyeblink conditioning. Compare these diagrams to Figure 4.2, showing analogous stages of Pavlov's conditioning procedure.

Table 4.2

Widely used classical conditioning procedures

	Appetitive conditioning			
	Unconditioned stimulus, US	Unconditioned response, UR	Conditioned stimulus, CS	Conditioned response, CR
Pavlov's dog	Food	Salivation	Bell	Salivation
Quail sex	Sexually available female	Approach, mounting, and copulation	Light	Approach
	Aversive conditioning			
Fly shock	Shock	Attempt to escape	Odor	Attempt to escape
Conditioned emotional response	Shock	Freezing	Tone	Freezing
Eyeblink conditioning	Airpuff	Blink	Tone	Blink

To the uninformed observer, the learned conditioned response, the eyeblink CR, is identical to the automatic unconditioned response, the eyeblink UR. However, the learned CR takes place during the warning period provided by the CS (analogous to a weather report predicting rain) in advance of the US and UR, adaptively protecting the eye from the onset of the airpuff. The same is true for Pavlov's original salivation study, in which the learned CR, salivation, is the same as the dog's natural unconditioned response to food, but it takes place *before* the food is presented, at the sound of the doorbell that predicts the food.

You have now been introduced to five different formats that are used for experiments in classical conditioning: two appetitive preparations and three aversive preparations. These are all reviewed in Table 4.2. To see if you really understand this material and can tell your USs, URs, CSs, and CRs apart, try to identify each in the real-world examples given in the accompanying Test Your Knowledge box.

Test Your Knowledge

More Classical Conditioning in Everyday Life

Are you sure you can tell the US, UR, CS, and CR apart? Test yourself by identifying each of them in the real-world situations described below. (Answers appear in the Answers section in the back of the book.)

1. Advertisements for a new sports car show a sexy model draped over the car's hood.

2. Mark loves pizza. When he was a boy, his parents frequently had it delivered to their home. Because the pizzas often arrived only lukewarm, his parents would put the pizza, still inside the box, into the oven to heat up. This caused the box to give off a smell of burning cardboard. Now, years later, whenever Mark smells cardboard burning, he gets hungry for pizza.

Learning a New Association

How, exactly, does learning progress in eyeblink conditioning or other classical conditioning procedures? Figure 4.8 shows an eyeblink CR becoming stronger over several days of training in a rabbit eyeblink-conditioning study. Each day, the animal received 80 training trials, each of which presented a tone followed shortly thereafter by an airpuff to the eye. The graphs in Figure 4.8 show the extent to which the rabbit's eyelid lowers at the start of different days during the experiment; the higher the curve, the farther the eyelid has shut. Note that on the beginning of day 1, the only response is the eyeblink UR that occurs *after* the onset of the airpuff US. However, with training, an eyeblink CR emerges. By day 3, there is movement of the eyelid before the US arrives. This anticipatory blink in response to the CS is the beginning of a CR. With further training, by about day 5, a strong anticipatory eyeblink CR occurs, timed so that the eyelid is safely closed before the airpuff US occurs.

In both rabbits and humans, eyeblink conditioning is a gradual process, occurring over many trials. Figure 4.9 shows trial-by-trial changes in the percentage of human participants and rabbits giving conditioned eyeblink responses in a study of tone-airpuff conditioning in both species. Although the graphs in the figure are not identical (humans learn faster), they are quite similar. Most important to note is that in both humans and rabbits, the percentage rises over time until most trials elicit an appropriately timed predictive eyeblink CR.

Figure 4.8 Acquisition of eyeblink conditioning response Development of a conditioned response as measured at the beginning of day 1, day 3, and day 5 of training, using a standard tone-airpuff trial sequence. On day 1, only a UR to the eyepuff is observed, but by day 3, an anticipatory eyeblink starts to emerge. By day 5, this anticipatory CR is strong and occurs reliably before the airpuff US.

Conditioned Compensatory Responses

Remember Chuck who learned (from past bad experiences) to notice signs of impending rain and close his windows in advance of it to protect his carpets? Chuck also has a swimming pool out back. If he were expecting heavy rains for several days, he might worry about the pool overflowing and damaging his lawn and house. Given the weather forecast, he might think it prudent to partially drain his pool, lowering the level a few inches before the rain arrives. When the rain does come, it will return the water level to the point it was at before he drained it, lessening the likelihood of an overflow. In this way, Chuck's preparatory response (preemptively lowering the water level in the pool) compensates for the expected rise in water level and ensures that the pool never gets too full.

An analogous conditioned compensatory response was demonstrated by two of Pavlov's colleagues more than 60 years ago (Subkov & Zilov, 1937). These researchers injected dogs on several occasions with adrenaline (also known as epinephrine), a chemical normally produced by the adrenal glands in response to stress or anxiety. The usual effect of adrenaline is an increase in heart rate. However, the dogs' heart rate increased less and less with each subsequent injection. Such a decrease in reaction to a drug, so that larger doses are required to achieve the original effect, is known as **tolerance.** What causes tolerance to develop?

To explore this question, the researchers placed their dogs on injection stands, where the dogs normally received the drug injection, but they administered a neutral inert substance rather than the adrenaline. The researchers observed that this caused the dogs' heart rate to *decrease*. Apparently, the various cues (the stand, the injection) that predicted the adrenaline injection triggered

Figure 4.9 **Learning curves for rabbit and human eyeblink conditioning**
(a) A learning curve showing the percent of rabbits giving CRs across blocks of training trials.
(b) Analogous learning curve for human eyeblink conditioning. Although these curves are qualitatively similar, they reflect different training regimes since the rabbits are usually trained in blocks of 1-hour trial sessions on successive days, while humans are trained in a single hour-long session.
(a) from Allen, Chelius, & Gluck, 2002;
(b) from Allen, Padilla, Myers, & Gluck, 2002.

a conditioned compensatory response that lowered the dogs' heart rate in anticipation of the adrenaline causing an increase in heart rate. Such automatic compensatory responses occur primarily in body systems that have a mechanism for **homeostasis,** the tendency of the body (including the brain) to gravitate toward a state of equilibrium or balance.

Much like the homeowner who acts to prevent the pool from overflowing during a storm, the dogs in these studies unconsciously used advance information about the forthcoming adrenaline injection to compensate for the drug's effect. The learned anticipatory decrease in heart rate combined with the increase produced by the drug resulted in a lower total increase in heart rate than was experienced on the first (unexpected) administration of adrenaline. Since the dogs had been conditioned to expect adrenaline after seeing cues such as the stand or the syringe, their bodies compensated by lowering their heart rates to maintain a constant level.

An addict's tolerance to drugs of abuse such as alcohol, cocaine, or ecstasy develops in the same way. As the addict's body adjusts to the drug effects (through expectation of the forthcoming "high"), larger and larger doses are required to produce the same high the addict experienced on first taking the drug. One way this happens is through conditioning: environmental cues that accompany drug use can classically condition the user to expect to receive the drug. In other words, the environmental cues (people, places, and so on) act like CSs associated with the drug (the US). The intense craving an addict feels in response to these cues is the CR and results from the body's conditioned compensatory response of lowering the levels of the brain chemicals enhanced by the drug in anticipation of the drug's arrival (more on this phenomenon in Chapter 5).

Like a rabbit that blinks to the same tone it was classically conditioned to years ago, a drug addict will respond to cues previously associated with drug use through prior conditioning, that is, the friends with whom this individual used to get high, the room where the drugs were used, and the sight of the various kinds of paraphernalia connected with drug use. Is it any wonder that recovery organizations such as Narcotics Anonymous and Alcoholics Anonymous emphasize cutting all ties with companions and locations formerly associated with the use of drugs?

Extinguishing an Old Association

What do you think would happen if Moira moved to a new neighborhood where jingling trucks sold not ice cream, which she loves, but broccoli, which she hates? If each time she heard the jingle, she got broccoli (rather than ice cream), you might expect that her excited reaction to the jingle would eventually disappear. In this case, a previously acquired association would become diminished through repeated presentation of the CS (jingle) in the absence of the US (ice cream), a process known as **extinction,** which was first described in the early studies of Pavlov, as noted in Chapter 1.

Once it is acquired, eyeblink conditioning can also undergo extinction if the former CS (tone) is presented repeatedly without an airpuff. Eventually, the rabbit (or person) that was formerly conditioned to blink to the tone begins to learn that the world has changed and the tone no longer predicts the US. Figure 4.10 shows what happens if, after 70 trials of eyeblink-conditioning acquisition training, rabbits are given 20 trials of tone-alone extinction trials (Moore & Gormezano, 1961).

It is tempting to think of the extinction in Figure 4.10 as simply the unraveling of acquisition. However, in recent years a consensus has been building in support of the idea that extinction is not just unlearning but rather a combination of unlearning and the learning of a new, opposing response to the CS. Specifically, it appears that during extinction, the CS acquires a second "don't respond" meaning that competes with the originally acquired "do respond" association. This suggests that even though the animal (or person) is no longer responding to the CS at the end of extinction training (as seen in Figure 4.10), the learned response is not gone, just unexpressed. Evidence for this view of extinction comes from studies that show that the original learned response can reappear if the animal is moved to another context (such as another room or testing chamber) or if a long time passes before the animal is retested with a presentation of the CS. The return of a CR after such a delay is an example of spontaneous recovery (which you previously encountered in Chapter 3, in our discussion of habituation): the tendency for a previously learned association to reappear after a period of extinction. This suggests that the association was dormant following extinction training, but not lost.

From what you have read so far in this section, it might appear that animals (and people) in conditioning studies are passively responding to what cues do, or do not, go together. However, as you will see in the discussions to follow, conditioning involves a much more subtle form of learning than was previously appreciated.

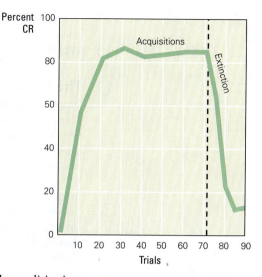

Figure 4.10 Acquisition and extinction of eyeblink conditioning Percent of rabbits exhibiting conditioned eyeblinks during 70 trials of acquisition and 20 trials of extinction.
Adapted from data in Moore & Gormezano, 1961.

Error Correction and the Modulation of US Processing

Chapter 1 introduced Aristotle's argument that contiguity—closeness in time and space—is necessary for a new association, such as that between a CS and US, to be learned. For most of the first half of the twentieth century, psychologists believed that contiguity was both necessary and sufficient: so long as a potential CS and a US occurred with little separation in time and space, animals and people were expected to form an association between them

(Hull, 1943). But would it really make sense for animals or people to learn associations between all the simultaneously occurring stimuli that they perceive? Would it even be possible?

The Informational Value of Cues

Imagine you are a struggling stock investor whose livelihood depends on correctly predicting whether the stock market will go up or down the next day. One morning Doris, an eager new stock analyst, walks into your office and says that if you hire her, she will tell you each day which way the next day's market will go. You agree, and during her first week of work, you are amazed to see that she is 100% accurate, correctly predicting each day whether the market will rise or fall. The next week, Herman comes to visit and offers you his services as a stock analyst to predict the market's movements. Would you hire him? Probably not, because he is redundant if you already have Doris; that is, Herman offers no value beyond what you are already getting from Doris. You might say that Doris's early success at predicting the stock market has blocked you from valuing Herman's similar, but redundant, ability to do the same.

A similar situation can occur in medical diagnosis. Consider a young physician who treated a patient who came into the emergency room on several occasions in January, each time with bad rash on his neck. She reviews what the patient ate the day before each outbreak. It turns out that each time the patient got a rash, he had eaten the same kind of chocolate that very morning. The physician suspects this may be the cause of the rash, an allergic reaction to the chocolate. The next month, the patient comes back to the emergency room, once again with this strange rash. Again the physician has him list everything he ate the day of the outbreak. This time, she notices that the patient ate both chocolate and red licorice just prior to his rash. Although it's possible that the licorice caused the rash, the physician dismisses this as unlikely, since she already believes that the chocolate is causing his rash and this theory is sufficient to explain the new outbreak. The physician's recommendation to her patient: avoid the chocolate, but licorice is probably okay.

In both of these examples, new information—or evidence—can be viewed in terms of its informational value, how much new predictive value it gives us relative to what we already know or believe. For the stock investor, Herman offers no additional aid in predicting the market beyond what Doris already tells him. For the emergency room physician, the presence of licorice offers no new explanatory value in understanding the cause of her patient's rashes given that she can already explain the rash as being caused by the chocolate candies. Research on learning has shown that humans and other animals are similarly sensitive to the informational value of cues in determining which associations they do or do not learn.

Early evidence for this sensitivity to the informational value of cues in human learning came from work by Gordon Bower and Tom Trabasso, who trained college students to categorize objects according to certain predefined rules (Bower & Trabasso, 1964). The students were presented with geometric figures varying in five dimensions: color, shape, number of internal lines, position of a dot, and position of a gap, as shown in Figure 4.11. Phase 1 of the experiment consisted of training the participants by asking them to guess whether each figure belonged to class A or class B; each time, they were told whether they had guessed correctly or not. For example, some participants were trained that all circular shapes belong in class A, while all triangular shapes belong in class B (and all other features are irrelevant), as illustrated by the two sample stimuli

(a) Phase 1 training   **(b)** Phase 2 training   **(c)** Testing

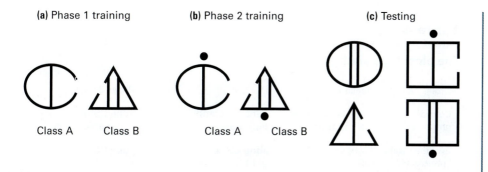

Class A   Class B   Class A   Class B

Figure 4.11 Human sensitivity to the informational value of cues (a) Examples of stimuli from phase 1 training of the Bower and Trabasso experiment, in which all circular shapes belong in class A and all triangular shapes belong in class B. (b) Examples of stimuli from phase 2. Participants are shown only circles and triangles, and the same circle → A/triangle → B rule still applies. However, now there is also a dot on the top of all class A items and a dot on the bottom of all class B items. (c) A final testing phase. Participants are given novel stimuli to see if they have learned that the dot-top → A/dot-bottom → B rule by itself can predict class membership.

Adapted from Bower & Trabasso, 1964.

shown in Figure 4.11a. Given enough trials with different stimuli, participants would deduce the rule: circle → A/triangle → B.

Once this lesson was mastered, the experimenter showed participants a slightly different set of figures: now all figures that were circular and thus belonged to class A had a dot on top, while all figures that were triangular and thus belonged to class B had a dot on the bottom (Figure 4.11b). This addition of a redundant cue in phase 2 (position of the dot) parallels the addition of the licorice stimulus in the second month of the physician trying to figure out what caused her patient's rash. Participants in the Bower and Trabasso study continued to perform well by using their old rule of sorting on the basis of shape; the question was whether they would also learn that the dot position by itself predicted class membership.

To test this, the experimenters used new figures, shown in Figure 4.11c. Given a figure with no dot, all participants continued to sort the circles into class A and the triangles into class B. However, when given a figure with a new shape (rectangle), none of the participants correctly sorted on the basis of dot position. Thus, these humans performed much like the physician (who dismissed the possibility that licorice could be causing her patient's rash), in that they displayed little or no response to the redundant cue added in phase 2. In effect, prior learning that the shape predicted class membership appears to have *blocked* subsequent learning that the dot position also predicts class membership. More recent studies have verified that this tendency to "tune out" information that is redundant with previously learned cues is pervasive in many forms of human learning (Kruschke, Kappenman, & Hetrick, 2005).

Kamin's Blocking Effect

In the late 1960s, just a few years after the Bower and Trabasso study was published, several studies of classical conditioning in animals made a similar point: for a potential CS to become associated with a US, the CS must provide valuable new information that helps an animal predict the future. Moreover, even if a given cue does predict a US, it may not become associated with that US if its usefulness has been preempted (blocked) by a co-occurring cue that has a longer history of predicting the US. Much as Doris's predictive value blocked the hiring of Herman, a prior-trained CS can block learning about another, redundant CS that is added later in training (Kamin, 1969).

In a classic study by Leon Kamin, rats were first trained that a light predicts a shock and later trained that a compound stimulus of a light and tone also predicts the shock (Kamin, 1969). Kamin found that, with this training, the rat will learn very little about the tone because the tone does not improve the rat's ability to predict the shock. This phenomenon is now known as **blocking**; it demonstrates that classical conditioning occurs only when a cue is both a useful and a nonredundant predictor of the future (Table 4.3).

Table 4.3

The blocking paradigm

Group	Phase 1	Phase 2	Phase 3 (test)
Control group	Rat sits in chamber; no training	Tone CS combined with light CS → shock US	Tone CS or light CS: medium CR
Experimental "pre-trained" group	Light CS → shock US	Tone CS combined with light CS → shock US	Tone CS : little or no CR (learning is "blocked")

Kamin's 1969 blocking study is worth describing in detail because of its influence on subsequent theories of learning. In this study, one group of rats (the control group) was trained with a compound cue consisting of a light and a tone; this cue was reliably followed by a shock (see Table 4.3, control group, phase 2). The light and tone constituted a compound CS that the rats learned to associate with the shock US. Later, these rats would give a medium-strong CR to either the tone alone or the light alone, though not as strong a response as to both the light and tone together.

Consider, however, the behavior of Kamin's second group of rats, identified as the experimental, or pre-trained, group in Table 4.3. These rats first received pre-training in which the light by itself predicted a shock (phase 1). From this training, they learned an association between the light CS and the shock US. Next (phase 2), they were given training that paired the light-and-tone compound cue and the shock, just like the control group animals had received. However, unlike the control rats, rats in the pre-trained group were already responding strongly to the light CS when they began the phase 2 compound training. For these rats, the additional presence of the tone provided no new information for predicting the US.

Phase 3 was a testing phase. When the pre-trained rats were tested with the light alone, they continued to exhibit a strong CR to the light, much as they had at the end of phase 1. However, in phase 3, if they were tested with the tone alone, they would give almost no response at all. This suggests that they learned almost nothing about the relationship between the tone and the US, despite the compound training received in phase 2, in which the tone was repeatedly followed by the US (Kamin, 1969). In contrast, rats in the control group, which did not receive phase 1 pre-training, exhibited significant (albeit medium-strength) CRs to both the light and the tone in phase 3. Thus, the blocking phenomenon, exhibited by the pre-trained rats, can be summarized as follows: prior training of the light → shock association during phase 1 blocks learning of the tone → shock association during compound (light + tone) training in phase 2. This is very similar to what happened with the emergency room physician. Having previously deduced that chocolate candies lead to a rash, she failed to credit the licorice with any rash-inducing properties when she later encountered both chocolate and licorice preceding the rash. That is, for this physician, learning the chocolate → rash association blocked learning of the redundant licorice → rash association.

The blocking paradigm demonstrates that contiguity between a cue and a US is not enough to elicit a CR, contrary to what Aristotle expected. For a stimulus to become associated with a US, it must impart reliable, useful, and nonredundant information (Kamin, 1969; Rescorla, 1968; Wagner, 1969). Apparently, "simple" Pavlovian conditioning is not as simple as psychologists once thought! In fact, rats (and other animals, including humans) appear to be very sophisticated statisticians. But how does one learn which are the most useful and informative cues to remember? The next discussion shows how some simple principles of learning result in learning only the most useful of associations.

Error-Correction Learning

"I have not failed," said Thomas Edison, "I've just found 10,000 ways that won't work." Like Edison, we can, and do, learn from our failures. Consider Herman, who we saw earlier didn't have much of a future as a stock analyst. His real passion is tennis, and he hopes to become a professional. He practices hours each day, focusing especially on his serve. His goal is to put the ball as far back in the serving zone as possible, but not so far that it goes over the line and is considered a fault. On his first serve of the day, he puts the ball into the middle of the serving zone (where his opponent could easily return it). To serve the next ball better, he adjusts his stance a little, throws the ball higher, and swings harder. This time the ball goes closer to the end of the zone. On the third serve, he throws the ball a little higher still and hits it just a bit harder. This time, however, the ball goes too far; it is a fault. In response to this error, Herman again adjusts his serve. He throws the ball a little less high and hits it a little softer than last time. This results in a perfect serve. After several tries, correcting his serve each time on the basis of how well he did previously, Herman has learned to hit a ball at the right height and strength to land just at the outer end of the service zone: not too close, and not too far.

Herman has learned through a process of trial and error, using a method called **error-correction learning,** in which the errors on each trial lead to small changes in performance that seek to reduce the error on the next trial. Error-correction learning can be summarized by describing three situations representing three types of errors Herman experienced: (1) when Herman hits the ball too close, he changes his next serve to hit the ball harder, so that it will land a little farther; (2) when Herman hits a perfect serve, he tries to do exactly the same thing the next time; and (3) when Herman hits the ball too far, he changes his next serve to hit the ball a little lighter so it lands a little closer next time. As we will see in the next discussion, this type of error-correction learning is very similar to how animals learn to adjust their expectations about which USs will follow each CS.

The Rescorla-Wagner Model

In the early 1970s, two psychologists at Yale, Robert Rescorla and Allan Wagner, were independently trying to understand Kamin's blocking effect and other related conditioning phenomena. Although the two researchers worked at the same university, they didn't realize that they were using the same approach to solve the same problem until they happened to take a train together to a conference and began chatting about their research. To their surprise, they realized that they had each come up with the same idea, and they decided to join forces.

Rescorla and Wagner's key idea was that the amount of change that occurs in the association between a CS and a US depends on a **prediction error,** the difference between whether the animal *expects* the US and whether the US

Table 4.4

Error correction and response in Rescorla-Wagner model and tennis

Conditioning error	Model response	Tennis error	Herman's response
Positive error: CS predicts nothing or too little, but US unexpectedly occurs or is unexpectedly strong	Increase association	Ball falls short	Increase strength of serve
No error: CS predicts US, and predicted US occurs	No learning	Ball lands perfectly	Do same thing next time
Negative error: CS predicts US, but no US occurs	Decrease association	Ball goes too far	Decrease strength of serve

actually occurs (Rescorla & Wagner, 1972). Rescorla and Wagner proposed that there are three key situations to consider in interpreting a prediction error, as summarized in Table 4.4; as you will see, these are very similar to the three ways Herman learned from past errors to improve his tennis serve.

Rescorla and Wagner argued that if either no CS or a novel CS is presented followed by a US, the US will be unexpected; this is considered a positive prediction error because there is more US than expected. The Rescorla-Wagner theory expects that the CS → US association should thus increase proportional to the degree that the US is surprising; that is, the larger the error, the greater the learning. This makes sense because if you failed to predict the US, you want to increase (move in a positive direction) your likelihood of predicting it in the future (given the same CS). It is similar to what Herman does when his serve is too short and he positively increases the strength of his serve to send it farther next time.

If, however, a well-trained CS is followed by the expected US, there is no error in prediction (the US was fully predicted by prior presentation of the CS), and thus no new learning is expected. This is similar to what happens when Herman makes a perfect serve; he doesn't want to change a thing from what he did last time. Finally, if the CS predicts a US and the US does not occur, the prediction error is considered negative, and Rescorla and Wagner expect it to be followed by a decrease in the CS → US association. This is similar to what happens when Herman hits the ball too far and he has to reduce the strength of his serve next time.

The real beauty and elegance of Rescorla and Wagner's approach is that to describe this process of learning by error correction, they devised a simple mathematical model that made only three assumptions:

1. *Each CS has an associative weight.* This weight is a value representing the strength of association between each cue and the US. In the blocking experiment described above and in Table 4.3, there would be two cue weights, one for light and one for tone, formalized as W_{Light} and W_{Tone} (and generalized as W_{Cue}), respectively. The "W" stands for the value of the weight for that cue. Think of these weights as numbers on a scale from 0 to 100 that indicate how strongly the CS predicts the US. An associative weight of 100 means that whenever the CS appears, the US will follow 100% of the time. If the weight is 90, then when the CS appears, there is a 90% chance the US will follow (and a 10% chance it will not), and so on. Before any training takes place, all associative weights are 0, meaning that when a potential CS first appears, there is no expectation that any US will follow. These associative weights change through learning as the animal discovers which stimuli predict the US and therefore which should have strong weights.

2. *The expectation of a US is based on a sum of weights for all the CSs present.* In phase 1 pre-training in the blocking experiment (see Table 4.3), when only the light is presented, the expectation of the US is W_{Light}. However, in the phase 2 compound training, when both the light and the tone are presented, the expectation of the US is the sum of the weights of both those cues: $W_{Light} + W_{Tone}$.

3. *Learning is proportional to the prediction error.* Prediction error is defined as the difference between the outcome the animal expects (the expectation calculated for the US) and what actually occurs (calculated as described below), as illustrated in Table 4.4. This difference is called the prediction error because it measures how much the animal's prediction differed from what really happened. Because learning is proportional to prediction error, a US that is totally unexpected causes a lot of learning, while a US that is only partially expected results in less learning.

Putting all of this together, the Rescorla-Wagner model says that the learning that takes place in a conditioning experiment can be predicted for each training trial by computing the prediction error, defined as

Prediction error = actual US − expected US

The *actual US* is defined as 100 if the US occurs and 0 if it does not. The *expected US* is the sum of the weights of all the cues presented on that trial. Thus, in the compound-cue training phase of the blocking experiment, expected US would be equal to the sum of the values of the weights for the light cue and the tone cue: $W_{Light} + W_{Tone}$.

Having defined prediction error, we can compute ΔW_{Cue}, the amount that each cue weight—whether for tone or light—will change on a trial due to learning. Remember that W_{Cue} is a number between 0 and 100 that specifies how strongly a particular cue predicts the US. If ΔW_{Cue} for a trial is greater than 0, then W_{Cue} goes up; if ΔW_{Cue} is less than 0, then W_{Cue} goes down. According to the Rescorla-Wagner model, ΔW_{Cue} is calculated as

$\Delta W_{Cue} = \beta \times$ prediction error

This equation says that the change in W_{Cue} on a trial is equal to a small constant β, called the "learning rate," multiplied by the prediction error. Later we will discuss some of the implications of different learning rates.

Test Your Knowledge

Computing the Prediction Error

What is the value of the prediction error if the actual US value is 90 and the expected US value 30? (Answer appears in the Answers section in the back of the book.)

Applying the Rescorla-Wagner Model to Learning a New Association

To see all of this in action, suppose an animal is trained over many trials that a light CS predicts a shock US, just like in phase 1 of the blocking study. Initially, W_{Light} is 0, meaning that the animal has no expectation of a shock US when it sees the light:

Expected US = W_{Light} = 0

and

Prediction error = actual US − expected US = 100 − 0 = 100

Once we know the prediction error, we know the direction in which to change the expectation: positive prediction errors lead to increases in association strength, while negative prediction errors lead to reductions in association strength. But how much should we increase (or decrease) the associations in response to these errors? This question is similar to the one Herman faces when he hits his tennis serve five feet too far. How much should he reduce the strength with which he hits the ball to correct this error? If he reduces it too little, he will continue to hit the ball too far. On the other hand, if he reduces the strengths of his serve too much, the ball may land too close to or even hit the net.

In the Rescorla-Wagner model, the degree to which the prediction error changes current association weights is known as the **learning rate,** a value that can range from 0 to 1 and controls how much learning takes place after each trial. A small learning rate means that the animal learns very slowly, which implies that changes in the weights will occur gradually over many trials. A large learning rate implies that learning takes place very quickly, with big jumps in the weights from one trial to another. In practical applications of the Rescorla-Wagner model, the learning rate is often derived by determining which value fits best with the learning curves observed in laboratory experiments. Different animals in different learning situations may have different learning rates. However, part of the power of the Rescorla-Wagner model is that many of its most important predictions are independent of the actual learning rate used. For the purposes of illustrating how the model works, we will assume here that the learning rate, β, is 0.2, which means that on each trial, the weights will change by 20% of the prediction error. Thus, on the first trial, where the light CS is paired with the US,

ΔW_{Light} = β × prediction error = 0.2 × 100 = 20

That means W_{Light} changes from 0 to 20. On the next trial, when the light appears again, the animal will now have a modest expectation of the US:

Expected US = W_{Light} = 20

Test Your Knowledge

The Learning Rate

1. Increasing the learning rate, β, in the Rescorla-Wagner model means that each training trial will have _____ (more/less) impact on the changes in associative weights.

2. If before a tone-shock training trial, W_{Light} = 20, and after the trial W_{Light} = 60, what was the learning rate used to compute the change in this associative weight?

(Answers appear in the Answers section in the back of the book.)

Not perfect, but better than before! Figure 4.12a plots the changes in W_{Light} over many trials. As you can see from Figure 4.12b, they are the same as the changes in expected US because there is only one cue and therefore only one weight used to calculate the expected US. The graphs show the values

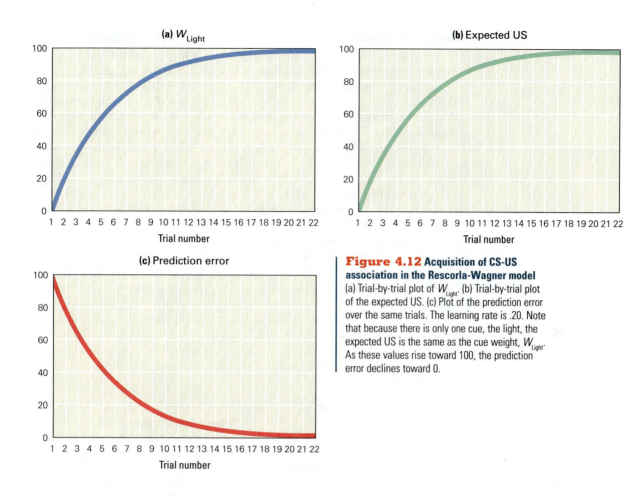

Figure 4.12 Acquisition of CS-US association in the Rescorla-Wagner model (a) Trial-by-trial plot of W_{Light}. (b) Trial-by-trial plot of the expected US. (c) Plot of the prediction error over the same trials. The learning rate is .20. Note that because there is only one cue, the light, the expected US is the same as the cue weight, W_{Light}. As these values rise toward 100, the prediction error declines toward 0.

increasing gradually until, after 20 trials, they equal 98.5 (just less than a perfect 100% prediction of shock). At this point, because the expected US is almost 100 and the actual US is 100 (the US is always present on these light → US trials), the prediction error will be reduced after 20 trials to nearly 0, as shown in Figure 4.12c; this outcome indicates that the animal has learned the task.

Rescorla and Wagner argued that this is the principle by which rabbits (and people and other animals) learn incrementally, trial by trial, to adjust their associations between a CS and a US. The Rescorla-Wagner model is called an error-correction rule because over many trials of learning, it reduces, or corrects, the likelihood of prediction errors.

Test Your Knowledge

The Rescorla-Wagner Model

1. When a subject has not yet been exposed to a neutral stimulus, such as a light or tone, what is the value of the expected US?

2. After repeated pairing of a previously neutral tone CS followed by a shock US, would you expect the prediction error to increase or decrease?

(Answers appear in the Answers section in the back of the book.)

Using the Rescorla-Wagner Model to Explain Blocking

Now we can show how the Rescorla-Wagner model explains the blocking paradigm described in Table 4.3. Rats in the control condition get no training at all in phase 1, so the values of W_{Light}, W_{Tone}, and the expected US all remain 0 throughout this phase (Figure 4.13a, left). In phase 2, where the tone-and-light compound cue is paired with the US, we see that the weights of both cues individually rise to 50, while the expected US (the sum of both weights) rises to 100, and then all stabilize at those values (Figure 4.13a, right). In a subsequent testing phase (phase 3 in Table 4.3), a medium-strong response is given to either the tone or the light if they are presented individually because W_{Light} and W_{Tone} each equal 50 at the end of phase 2.

For rats in the "pre-trained" condition of the blocking paradigm described in Table 4.3, the values change as plotted in Figure 4.13b. In phase 1, the animals experience light → US conditioning. By the end of phase 1, W_{Light} is equal to about 100, so whenever the light is presented, the animal scores a perfect 100% in predicting that the US will follow. Because no tone is presented in phase 1, W_{Tone} remains 0 throughout that part of the experiment. In phase 2, the tone CS and light CS are presented together as a compound. With W_{Light} already equal to 100, prediction of the US is perfect, so the prediction error is 0. Therefore, by equation 1 above, there is no further change to any of the weights. The weight of W_{Tone} will be stuck at 0 and will never change, no matter how many times the tone-light compound is paired with the shock. As a result, in phase 3, the testing

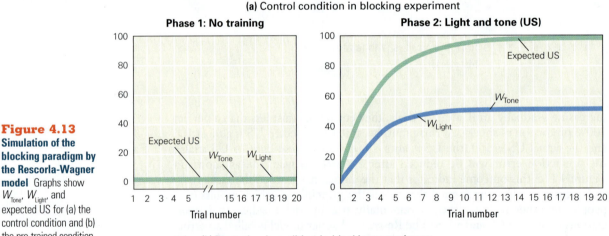

(a) Control condition in blocking experiment

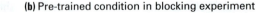

Figure 4.13
Simulation of the blocking paradigm by the Rescorla-Wagner model Graphs show W_{Tone}, W_{Light}, and expected US for (a) the control condition and (b) the pre-trained condition.

(b) Pre-trained condition in blocking experiment

phase, these rats will give a strong response to the light but little or no response to the tone, exactly as Kamin found in his classic study and as summarized in Table 4.3. This use of the Rescorla-Wagner rule to explain Kamin's blocking effect demonstrates the more general conclusion that for a potential CS to become associated with a US, the CS must provide valuable new information that helps an animal or a person predict the future.

Influence of the Rescorla-Wagner Model

More than four decades after its publication, the Rescorla-Wagner model is generally acknowledged as the most influential formal model of learning. Its broad acceptance is due to its elegant simplicity and to the fact that it explains a wide range of previously puzzling empirical results. One hallmark of a successful model is that it reveals underlying connections between a series of observations that initially seemed unrelated or even contradictory.

The Rescorla-Wagner model also made surprising predictions about how animals would behave in new experimental procedures, and experimenters rushed to test those predictions. This is another feature of a successful model: it should allow scientists to make predictions that could not otherwise be foreseen without the model. Ideally, modeling and empirical work should constitute a cycle in which the model makes predictions that, when tested, provide new empirical data. If the data match the predictions, the model is supported. If not, then the model must be revised. The revised model then generates new predictions, and the cycle continues.

Owing to its simplicity, the Rescorla-Wagner model cannot account for every kind of learning, and should not be expected to. However, many researchers have devoted their careers to showing how one or another addition to the model would allow it to explain a wider range of phenomena. With so many additions, the model may be in danger of losing some of its simplicity and appeal. Nevertheless, the Rescorla-Wagner model has been the starting point from which many other promising models have been built, including the models of human learning discussed below.

Error Correction in Human Category Learning

Do concepts such as blocking and conditioning models such as the Rescorla-Wagner model apply only to classical conditioning, or might they also provide insights into higher forms of human cognition and behavior, especially those that involve prediction or categorization? We saw a hint that the latter might be true in the earlier review of the Bower and Trabasso study of a blocking-like effect on human learning. More generally, we can ask, to what extent are the cognitive processes of human learning analogous to the more elementary learning mechanisms studied in animal conditioning experiments?

Although the fields of animal and human learning were originally closely intertwined, they became largely divorced from each other in the late 1960s and early 1970s. Animal learning at that time remained primarily concerned with elementary associative learning, while human learning studies focused more on memory abilities, characterized in terms of information processing and rule-based symbol manipulation, approaches borrowed from the emerging field of artificial intelligence. Ironically, this schism occurred just as animal learning theory was being reinvigorated by the new Rescorla-Wagner model in the early 1970s.

In the late 1980s, the expanding impact of computer simulations of network models of human learning (also called connectionist models) revived interest in relating human cognition to elementary associative learning processes. Some of this work was discussed in Chapter 1, when we reviewed David Rumelhart's

Figure 4.14 **A sample training trial in Gluck and Bower's probabilistic categorization task** On a particular learning trial, a research subject would see some symptoms (e.g., bloody nose and stomach cramp) and make a diagnosis, and then be given feedback as to whether or not the diagnosis was correct.

contributions to the field. Because of the growth of these connectionist network models in cognitive psychology, interest in simpler associative processes, such as classical conditioning, led to a revival of interest in the Rescorla-Wagner model. The connectionist network models adapted their association weights using a generalized (and more powerful) variation on the Rescorla-Wagner model, thereby showing how many complex human abilities (including speech recognition, motor control, and category learning) might emerge from configurations of elementary associations similar to those studied in conditioning experiments.

One example of this link between conditioning and cognition is a simple neural network model developed by Mark Gluck and Gordon Bower to model how people learn to form categories (Gluck & Bower, 1988). In this study, college students were asked to learn how to diagnose patients suffering from one of two nasty-sounding (but fictitious) diseases—midosis or burlosis. The students reviewed medical records of fictitious patients, who were each suffering from one or more of the following symptoms: bloody nose, stomach cramps, puffy eyes, discolored gums. During the study, each student reviewed several hundred medical charts, proposed a diagnosis for each patient, and then was told the correct diagnosis (Figure 4.14). The students initially had to guess, but with practice they were able to diagnose the fictitious patients quite accurately. The fact that the different symptoms were differentially diagnostic of the two diseases helped them guess. Bloody noses were very common in burlosis patients but rare in midosis, while discolored gums were common in midosis patients but rare in burlosis. The other two symptoms, stomach cramps and puffy eyes, were only moderately diagnostic of either disease.

This kind of learning can be modeled using the network in Figure 4.15. The four symptoms are represented by four input nodes at the bottom of the network, and the two disease categories correspond to the two output nodes at the top of the network. The weights of the arrows leading from the symptoms to the diseases are updated according to the learning rule from the Rescorla-Wagner model, much as if the symptoms were CSs and the diseases were alternate USs.

Learning and performance in the model works as follows. As the subject learns the correct associations, the connections between nodes and diseases acquire weights which capture the true diagnisticity of each cue for each disease. For example, presentation to a research subject of the chart of a patient with the symptoms "bloody nose" and "stomach cramp" (as in Figure 4.14)

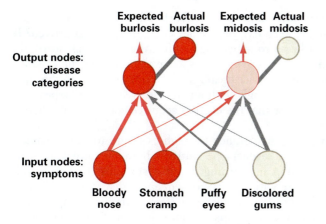

Output nodes: disease categories

Input nodes: symptoms

Expected burlosis — Actual burlosis — Expected midosis — Actual midosis

Bloody nose — Stomach cramp — Puffy eyes — Discolored gums

Figure 4.15 **Gluck and Bower's network model of category learning** The arrows from bloody nose and stomach cramp to burlosis and from puffy eyes and discolored gums to midosis are thick, indicating highly diagnostic relationships (that is, heavily weighted cues). The other cues are of only moderate diagnosticity. This figure shows a trial in which a patient presents with two symptoms, bloody nose and stomach cramp; thus, these two input nodes are active (dark red). The other two input nodes represent symptoms that are not present (puffy eyes and discolored gums), and these nodes are inactive (gray). Relative activation levels (dark red and light red) of the two "expected" category nodes are based only on the weight of the input (the current associative weights of these cues) flowing up the arrows from the active and present symptoms (bloody nose and stomach cramp).

Adapted from Gluck & Bower, 1988.

is modeled in Figure 4.15 by turning "on" the corresponding input nodes. Activating these two input nodes causes simulated neural activity to travel up four weighted connections, shown as arrows: two to burlosis and two to midosis (Figure 4.15). On this trial, burlosis is the correct label, indicated by the very dark "actual burlosis" node. The model is more likely to diagnose the patient as having the disease with the higher activation, namely, burlosis, which in fact is the correct diagnosis.

By analogy with the Rescorla-Wagner model, these output-node activations are equivalent to the network's *expectation* of one disease versus another. After a student guesses at a diagnosis and is told the correct answer, learning in that student is modeled by having the network modify the weights so as to reduce future error, in accordance with the Rescorla-Wagner model's error-correction learning rule. The network model shown in Figure 4.15 incorporates nothing more than the learning principle of the Rescorla-Wagner conditioning model. At the same time, this "animal conditioning" model of human cognition accounts for variations in how the participants classified different patient charts. The model correctly predicted the percent of participants who would classify each of the 14 possible symptom charts as being midosis versus burlosis and also predicted how well the participants were later able to make judgments about the probabilities of the two diseases when they only knew one of the symptoms.

Modulation of CS Processing

Despite the many successes of the Gluck and Bower model in predicting human cognitive data, several limitations of the model became evident in further studies of human category learning. In particular, as a model of category learning, it fails to account for people's ability to actively focus their attention on one or another symptom (such as bloody nose or stomach cramp) or to shift or refocus this attention during learning. These limitations echo similar problems of the Rescorla-Wagner model (on which the Gluck and Bower model is based), specifically its inability to account for how attention to stimuli is modulated during learning, especially when animals or people are repeatedly exposed to stimuli that have no consequence.

To better understand where and how the Rescorla-Wagner model (and by analogy the Gluck and Bower model) fall short in accounting for attentional changes, let's consider the example of Moira, the little girl at the beginning of the chapter who learned to run to the corner with money each time she heard the ice cream truck jingle in the distance. What do you think would have happened if, soon after she arrived in the neighborhood, she continued to hear the jingle off in the distance each day, but the ice cream truck never arrived? If weeks later the truck did begin to appear again after the jingle was heard, do you think Moira would so quickly learn to associate the jingle in the distance with the forthcoming arrival of the ice cream truck? Prior exposure to the cue's having been irrelevant (like the jingle without the ice cream truck appearing) retards our ability to learn later that the cue has acquired some new predictive or associative relevance.

This learning about a cue's irrelevance through exposure to the cue alone (with no associated significant event) is quantified by a measure known as **latent inhibition,** a reduction in learning about a stimulus (CS) to which there has been prior exposure without any consequence (that is, no US). The name refers to the fact that the exposure latently (that is, implicitly) appears to inhibit later learning about the cue. This phenomenon was first described in the animal conditioning literature by Robert Lubow and Ulrich Moore (Lubow & Moore, 1959). Lubow and Moore's study was conducted using sheep and goats; however, for consistency with the rest of this chapter (and to facilitate comparison with other studies previously discussed), we will describe their latent inhibition paradigm using rabbit eyeblink conditioning, which has reliably produced the same results.

Latent inhibition studies use two groups of subjects: the first group, the control group, receives no pre-training, and the second group does receive pre-exposure training, as summarized in Table 4.5. Control animals simply sit in their chambers until they are ready for the critical phase 2, in which they are trained to associate a tone CS with an airpuff-in-the-eye US. In contrast, animals in the pre-exposed group are repeatedly exposed to a tone with no US in phase 1 before they undergo the same tone training in phase 2 as the control animals do. Thus, the only difference between the two groups is that one group is pre-exposed to the tone in phase 1.

As illustrated in Figure 4.16, rabbits in the pre-exposed group learn to associate the tone with a puff of air much more slowly in phase 2 than do rabbits in the control group (Shohamy, Allen, &

Table 4.5

The latent inhibition paradigm

Group	Phase 1	Phase 2
Control group	Animal sits in chamber	Tone CS → shock US
Experimental "pre-trained" group	Tone CS presented (but not US)	

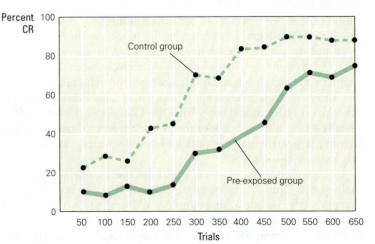

Figure 4.16 Latent inhibition in rabbit eyeblink conditioning This graph shows the percent of trials producing CRs in each block of 50 trials during the common phase 2 tone-airpuff training of the rabbits in the study. The rabbits in the control group (dotted line) learned rapidly. In contrast, the rabbits in the pre-exposed group (solid line), who had previously experienced 850 trials of tone-alone presentations in phase 1, learned much more slowly.

Adapted from Shohamy et al., 2000.

Gluck, 2000). The same kind of slow learning following CS pre-exposure is seen in a variety of species; for example, it is seen in human eyeblink conditioning as well (Lubow, 1973).

Latent inhibition—that is, impaired learning following cue pre-exposure—is problematic for the Rescorla-Wagner model: there is no surprise during the first phase of tone-alone exposure and thus no prediction error. Therefore, the Rescorla-Wagner model expects no learning to occur in phase 1. Thus, the Rescorla-Wagner model makes the incorrect prediction that the pre-exposed group should be no different from the control group at the start of phase 2, a prediction clearly disconfirmed by Lubow's studies, as well as by the data in Figure 4.16.

Latent inhibition and similar paradigms that involve learning during mere exposure to apparently neutral cues suggest that there is more going on during conditioning than the error-driven learning characterized by the Rescorla-Wagner model. Chapter 3 introduced some of these non-associative mechanisms, such as habituation and sensitization. To account for latent inhibition and other phenomena beyond the scope of the Rescorla-Wagner model, several alternative theories of conditioning have been proposed, and these are described next.

An Attentional Approach to Stimulus Selection

The Rescorla-Wagner model is often called a **US modulation theory** of learning because it proposes that the manner in which the US is processed determines what stimuli become associated with that US. Thus, in the Rescorla-Wagner model, the ability of the US to promote learning is modulated by how unexpected the US is, given the potential CS that precedes it. The error-correction principle of learning described above—the core idea behind the Rescorla-Wagner model—is that error modulates the ability of a US to promote learning about the CSs that preceded it.

An alternative class of learning theories focuses instead on the CSs, suggesting various mechanisms that modulate (either increase or reduce) the ease with which potential CSs can be incorporated into an association. For this reason, they are referred to as **CS modulation theories:** they propose that the way attention to different CSs is modulated determines which of them become associated with the US. One such theory, presented by Nicholas Mackintosh in the early 1970s, is based on the observation that people and animals have a limited capacity for processing incoming information (Mackintosh, 1975). This limited capacity means that paying attention to one stimulus diminishes (and hence modulates) our ability to attend to other stimuli.

Remember the blocking analogy in which Doris was the first to establish herself as a reliable predictor of the stock market so that later, when Herman showed up, you gave him little credit for making equally successful predictions? The Rescorla-Wagner model argues that this outcome is due to the stock market (the US) already being well predicted by Doris (the first CS), so that no additional value (no learning) is attached to Herman (a potential second CS). However, Mackintosh's view of blocking is quite different. He argues that you come to devote all of your attention to Doris because she has a long history of predicting the stock market, and therefore you have no attention left to pay to Herman. The core idea of the Mackintosh theory is that a previously conditioned stimulus derives its salience from its past success as a predictor of important events (Mackintosh, 1975), and this happens at the expense of other co-occurring cues that don't get access to your limited pool of attention. In essence, Rescorla and Wagner's model lets Herman come in for an interview but doesn't consider him valuable for predicting the market, while Mackintosh's model never lets Herman in the door.

In addition to Mackintosh, several other learning theorists, most notably John Pearce and Geoffrey Hall, have proposed alternative hypotheses of how CS salience is modulated during training (Pearce & Hall, 1980). All of these models share the basic underlying idea that the changes in weighting of the CS are due to modulations of the CS, not of the US. We turn next to review one of the situations in which the CS-modulation theory of Mackintosh does a better job than the US-modulation theory of Rescorla and Wagner in explaining some aspects of learning phenomena.

An Attentional Explanation of Latent Inhibition

Recall that the Rescorla-Wagner model cannot explain cue–pre-exposure phenomena such as latent inhibition because, as a US modulation theory of learning, it only explains learning that takes place when a US is present or when previously trained cues predict the US. Thus, the Rescorla-Wagner model suggests incorrectly that no learning takes place when a neutral (previously untrained) cue is presented. In contrast, Mackintosh's model predicts that the salience of a tone as a potential CS will decrease when the tone is presented without any US because the tone develops a history of predicting nothing. According to Mackintosh, the animal treats these tone-alone trials as if they were the little boy who cried wolf. Eventually the tones (like the boy) are ignored because they don't reliably predict that anything bad or good is about to happen.

Although these CS modulation models have had many successes, especially in explaining behavioral phenomena that are not explained by the Rescorla-Wagner model, they have had less of an impact on the field of learning and memory, in part because they are more complex than the Rescorla-Wagner model and because they don't explain as broad a range of behaviors. Moreover, as discussed earlier in this chapter, the Rescorla-Wagner model has been especially influential because it works on the same fundamental principle as the learning algorithms employed in the connectionist network models of human memory used by cognitive psychologists, including both the models of David Rumelhart and colleagues described in Chapter 1 (Rumelhart & McClelland, 1986) and the category learning model of Gluck and Bower (1988) discussed above.

Which view is correct, the CS modulation or the US modulation approach to conditioning? For many years the two camps were viewed as being in direct conflict, with each entrenched on a different side of the Atlantic Ocean: the US modulation view predominated in the United States (where Rescorla and Wagner worked), while the CS modulation view predominated in the United Kingdom (where Mackintosh, Pearce, and Hall worked). However, behavioral and biological studies of conditioning now suggest that *both* views are probably correct; that is, there are likely to be both CS modulation and US modulation mechanisms engaged in learning. As you will see in Section 4.2, part of what has helped resolve this debate is new data from neuroscience that have identified differential neural substrates for these two types of learning processes. This is one more example of the many areas where new forms of data from neuroscience have informed and helped resolve long-standing questions in psychology.

Test Your Knowledge

Contrasting the Rescorla-Wagner and Mackintosh Models

1. Fill in the blanks: The Rescorla-Wagner model explains conditioning as modulation of the effectiveness of the _____ for learning, while the Mackintosh model explains conditioning through modulation of attention to the _____ .

2. Which of these explanations of Connie's behavior would be best explained by the Rescorla-Wagner model? Which would be better explained by the Mackintosh model?

   a. Connie loved the oatmeal raisin cookies so much, she devoted all of her attention to them. She didn't even bother tasting the chocolate chip cookies.

   b. Connie was happy eating only the oatmeal raisin cookies, and she didn't feel any need to begin eating a new type of cookie.

(Answers appear in the Answers section in the back of the book.)

Further Facets of Conditioning

Both the US-modulation model of Rescorla and Wagner and the CS-modulation model of Mackintosh have been influential in enhancing our understanding of associative learning (Rescorla & Wagner, 1972; Mackintosh, 1975). They are powerful models precisely because they reduce the behavioral process of learning to its essential elements so that we can see the underlying, fundamental principles at work. However, as a result of such simplification, these models necessarily ignore many of the more subtle facets of conditioning, such as the role of timing in conditioning and the importance of innate biases for associating different stimulus cues.

Timing

The Rescorla-Wagner model and the Mackintosh model both treat classical conditioning as if it were always composed of a series of discrete trials that occur one after the other. Moreover, these **trial-level models** treat each trial as a single event, resulting in a single change in learning. In reality, conditioning is more complex, and a trial consists of many events that can vary in different ways from trial to trial. For example, these models don't describe the timing of the animal's response within a given trial: does the CR occur right after the CS begins, or is it delayed until just before the US occurs? This information is lost in a trial-level model that only describes the aggregate effect of a training trial in terms of an overall association strength. Thus, one cost of having a simple and powerful model is that it can't account for every detail of the animal's behavior.

One important aspect of many conditioning studies is the temporal relationship between the CS and the US. Figure 4.17a illustrates eyeblink conditioning that is conducted using an approach known as **delay conditioning,** in which the tone CS continues throughout the trial and only ends once the US has occurred (this is, in fact, how all of the animals were trained in the rabbit eyeblink conditioning studies reported so far in this chapter). The term "delay" refers to the delay from time of onset of the CS to the onset of the US (as opposed to them occurring simultaneously). Another form of conditioning also includes a delay, but here the CS is first turned off before the US begins. This training procedure is called **trace conditioning** and is represented in Figure 4.17b; it uses a shorter CS that terminates some time before the onset of the US, requiring the animal to maintain a memory "trace" of the CS to associate with the subsequently

Figure 4.17 Delay and trace forms of eyeblink conditioning (a) In delay conditioning, the CS continues throughout the training trial and only terminates when the US terminates. (b) In trace conditioning, a short CS is followed by a gap before the US occurs. (c) The percentage of conditioned eyeblinks as a function of the length of the interval between the onset of CS and the US in a delay-conditioning experiment. Adapted from McAllister, 1953.

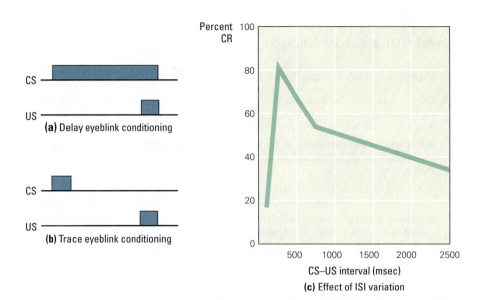

(a) Delay eyeblink conditioning

(b) Trace eyeblink conditioning

(c) Effect of ISI variation

arriving US. Although many trial-level learning models treat these types of conditioning as if they were equivalent, many studies have shown that learning behaviors, and the neural substrates associated with them, can be quite different for trace and delay-training procedures.

Even within a simple delay-training procedure such as that shown in Figure 4.17a, variations in the **interstimulus interval (ISI)**, the temporal gap between the onset of the CS and the onset of the US, can have significant effects. For eyeblink conditioning in the rabbit, the optimal ISI for fastest learning is about one-quarter of a second (250 msec), as shown in Figure 4.17c. Shorter or longer intervals make learning more difficult for the animal and necessitate additional training trials. One of the remarkable aspects of rabbit eyeblink conditioning is that the timing of the CR corresponds exactly to the ISI (see Figure 4.8), so that the eyelid is maximally closed at precisely the moment the onset of the US is expected.

Researchers have begun to integrate both US- and CS-modulation learning theories into unified learning theories that also accommodate some of the subtle temporal aspects of learning. One notable early example is the work of Allan Wagner, who proposed a model called SOP (sometimes opponent process) that allows both for error-correction learning (US modulation) and for changes in the salience of CS cues (CS modulation), with these events occurring at different times through different processes (Wagner, 1981). Other researchers, too, have argued that a full understanding of classical conditioning must involve closer attention to the subtle timing interactions that occur during and between trials (Gallistel & Gibbon, 2000). The need for a better understanding of the role of timing in learning is one of the challenges at the forefront of current learning research.

Associative Bias and Ecological Constraints

The formal learning models described above imply that any arbitrary cue (such as a tone or a light) can be associated with any outcome, be it a shock or food. But is that really true? Consider Garfield, who came down with the flu soon after eating oysters for dinner. The same evening that he ate the oysters, he also went to the movies with his date and saw a romantic comedy. Later that night, he woke up with a terrible stomachache. Both eating the oysters and watching the romantic comedy were events that preceded the illness. But whereas Garfield hasn't been able to eat oysters since that evening, he has not stopped going to see romantic comedies. What this suggests is that not all cues are equally likely to be associated with every outcome. Rather, it appears that there is an associative bias whereby some cues (such as food) are more likely to be associated with some outcomes (such as illness).

This was strikingly demonstrated in a study of **conditioned taste aversion** by John Garcia and R. A. Koelling, in which rats learned to avoid specific tastes (Garcia & Koelling, 1966). Garcia and Koelling trained rats with compound stimuli consisting of an unfamiliar taste and an unfamiliar tone (a rat's version of Garfield watching a romantic comedy while eating oysters). One group of rats was then injected with a poison that made them ill. A second group of rats was given an electric shock instead (Table 4.6). Which cue would the rats in each group "blame" for their illness or shock, the taste or the tone stimulus? To see which cues were most readily associated with which outcomes, the experimenters subsequently tested the rats with each of the cues independently: on some test trials the rats were given food with the same novel taste but no tone, while on other test trials, the rats were presented with the tone but no food.

What the researchers found was that the rats in the poison group were far more likely to associate the taste stimulus with the poison than to associate the tone with the poison (much as Garfield would be more likely to blame oysters rather than romantic comedies for his illness). In contrast, the rats in the shock group were more fearful in the presence of the tone stimulus than when they encountered the taste stimulus. Garcia and his colleagues concluded that taste is a more effective stimulus for learning to predict illness but that an audio cue is more effective for learning to predict a shock. Clearly, rats, like people, have prior biases about what should predict what. This isn't to say that you couldn't be trained to throw up at romantic comedy movies, but it would be much harder (and require more training) than learning to avoid the taste of oysters.

Remember the quail that were trained to associate a light with sex? Although the quail were able to learn this association following many trials of training, Domjan and colleagues found that quail could be conditioned much faster and more robustly if the CS, rather than being an arbitrary cue like a light, were something that is naturally associated in the wild with available females. These cues included the sight of a female at a distance or the sight of a female's head when the rest of her body is hidden in the underbrush (Cusato & Domjan, 1998).

Why are both Garfield and Garcia's rats more likely to associate food, rather than other cues, with getting sick? The answer may have to do with the potential *causal* relationship between eating food and getting sick that is a very real part of a person's or other animal's natural environment. In contrast, there is unlikely to be a natural causal relationship between watching a movie (good or bad) or hearing a tone and getting sick. Perhaps a sensitivity to the likely causal relationships is what guides and biases associative learning in animals. The best predictors of future events are the causes of those events, or at least their detectable indices (Dickinson, 1980). Thus, it would make evolutionary sense for humans and other animals to be biased toward learning associations that correspond to causal relationships in the ecological niches in which the animals live and evolve.

Table 4.6

The Garcia-Koelling taste-aversion study

Group	Phase 1	Phase 2
Poison group	Tone + taste → poison	Tone → ?
Shock group	Tone + taste → shock	Taste → ?

Interim Summary

- Classical conditioning involves learning about the predictive nature of stimuli in the environment, that is, what cues predict desirable or undesirable events. If an unconditioned stimulus, US, is repeatedly and reliably preceded by a neutral stimulus, such as a bell, that neutral stimulus can become a conditioned stimulus, or CS, that evokes an anticipatory response, called the conditioned response, or CR. Conditioned responses are anticipatory responses that prepare an animal for the expected US.

- The pairing of a potential CS with a US is not sufficient for conditioning to occur. Rather, for a CS to become associated with a US, it must provide valuable new information that helps an animal predict the future. Even if a given cue is predictive of a US, it may not become associated with that US if its usefulness has been preempted ("blocked") by a co-occurring cue that has a longer history of predicting the US.

- Rescorla and Wagner (1972) argue that learning should occur in proportion to the degree to which the US is unexpected when it is experienced. A key assumption in the Rescorla-Wagner model is that when there are multiple CS cues present, the expectation (or prediction) of the US is calculated as the sum of the weights of all of the cues present on that trial.

- CS-modulation theories of learning (like Mackintosh's model) presume that limits in attentional capacity cause attention to one stimulus to decrease our ability to attend to other stimuli. In contrast, the Rescorla-Wagner model is a US-modulation theory of learning because it describes the learning of associations as depending on how accurately the US is predicted based on all available information. Current behavioral and biological studies of conditioning now suggest that both CS-modulation and US-modulation mechanisms are likely to be involved in learning.

- Taste is more effective than an audiovisual stimulus for learning to predict illness, while an audiovisual cue is more effective for learning to predict a shock. One interpretation of this difference is the potential causal relationship between eating food and getting sick that is part of the animal's natural ecological environment.

4.2 Brain Substrates

Pavlov was a physiologist. When he discovered associative learning in his dogs in the early 1900s, he was naturally interested in understanding the brain mechanisms responsible for it. He even conducted a few experiments examining how cortical lesions affect conditioning. However, at the beginning of the last century, the technology for observing the brain's inner workings was not highly developed. Only in recent years have scientists gained knowledge and techniques that allow detailed study of the neural circuits for conditioning. We review here two neural systems, one in mammals and the other in invertebrates, that illustrate how studies of the neural bases of conditioning have yielded insights into the circuits, cells, molecules, and genes controlling the formation of new memories.

Mammalian Conditioning of Motor Reflexes

As you saw in Figure 2.4, the **cerebellum** sits just behind and slightly below the rest of the brain and looks like a miniature brain itself. In fact, the name *cerebellum* is Latin for "little brain."

In the early 1980s, Richard Thompson and his coworkers made a startling discovery: small lesions in the cerebellum of rabbits permanently prevented the acquisition of new classically conditioned eyeblink responses and abolished retention of previously learned responses (Thompson, 1986). Thompson and his colleagues have studied the cerebellum and its role in motor-reflex conditioning for more than 25 years. Their work provides an instructive example of how support for a theory can be strengthened by converging evidence from a variety of scientific methods, such as electrophysiological recordings, brain stimulation, experimental lesions, temporary inactivation of brain structures, and genetically mutated animals.

The cerebellum has two main regions, as shown in Figure 4.18. Lying along its top surface is the *cerebellar cortex*, which contains certain large, drop-shaped, densely branching neurons called **Purkinje cells.** Beneath the cerebellar cortex lies a collection of cells called the *cerebellar deep nuclei*, one of which is the **interpositus nucleus.** There are two major sensory-input pathways to the cerebellum:

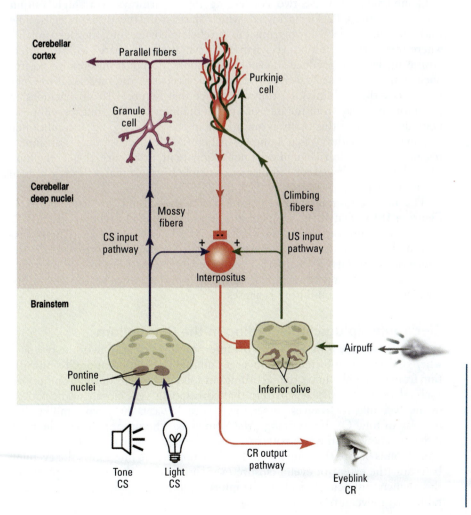

Figure 4.18 Cerebellar circuits for motor-reflex conditioning in mammals A schematic diagram of the cerebellar circuits for conditioning. The CS input pathway is purple, the CR output pathway is red, and the US input pathway is green. Excitatory synapses are shown as arrows, and inhibitory synapses terminate with a rectangle.

the CS input pathway and the US input pathway. The CS input pathway is shown in purple in Figure 4.18. (Not all the cells in the cerebellum are shown here, only the cells and pathways critical for understanding the cerebellar circuits for motor-reflex conditioning.) CS pathways from elsewhere in the brain project first to an area in the brainstem called the pontine nuclei. The pontine nuclei have different subregions for each kind of sensory stimulation. Thus, a tone CS would travel to one area of the pontine nuclei and a light CS to another. This CS information then travels up to the deep nuclei of the cerebellum along axon tracts called the mossy fibers, which branch in two directions. One branch makes contact with the interpositus nucleus. The other branch projects up toward the cerebellar cortex (by way of the granule cells and other cells not shown), across the parallel fibers, and connects to the dendrites of the Purkinje cells.

The second sensory-input pathway, shown in green, is the US pathway. An airpuff US to the eye activates neurons in the **inferior olive**—a structure in the lower part of the brainstem—which in turn activates the interpositus nucleus. In addition, a second branch of the pathway from the inferior olive projects up to the cerebellar cortex by means of the climbing fibers (Figure 4.18). Each climbing fiber extends to and wraps around a Purkinje cell. The climbing fibers have a very strong excitatory effect on the Purkinje cells, indicated in Figure 4.18 by the large arrowhead at this synaptic junction.

Complementing these two converging input pathways is a single output pathway for the CR, shown in red, which starts from the Purkinje cells. The Purkinje cells project down from the cerebellar cortex into the deep nuclei, where they form an inhibitory synapse (shown as a red square) with the interpositus nucleus. To produce an eyeblink response, output from the interpositus nucleus travels (via several other intermediary cells) to the muscles in the eye to generate the eyeblink CR. You may notice that Figure 4.18 also includes an inhibitory pathway from the interpositus to the inferior olive, but we will postpone discussion of this pathway until later in the chapter. The unconditioned response (UR) pathway is not shown in Figure 4.18 because that is an innate response; it is not learned and does not originate in, or require, the cerebellum. Instead, it is a reflex circuit, similar in principle to the spinal reflexes you read about in Chapter 2.

The most important thing to note about this circuit (as diagrammed in Figure 4.18) is that there are two sites in the cerebellum where CS and US information converge and, thus, where information about the CS-US association might be stored: (1) the Purkinje cells in the cerebellar cortex and (2) the interpositus nucleus. These two sites of convergence are intimately interconnected in the output pathway: the Purkinje cells project down to the interpositus nucleus with strong inhibitory synapses.

Electrophysiological Recording in the Cerebellum

When an electrode is inserted into the interpositus nucleus (one of the two sites where CS and US information converge and the final exit point of CR information from the cerebellum), the recordings of spiking neurons during conditioned eyeblink responses display a pattern that corresponds very closely to the pattern of the eyeblinks themselves, as seen in Figure 4.19a, taken from a rabbit after one day of tone CS-US training (McCormick & Thompson, 1984). The main difference between the two patterns is that the neural activity occurs just a few milliseconds before the actual behavior. The upper blue line shows the eyeblink behavior (the extent of eyelid closure over time), while the lower graph shows the frequency of neuron firing in the interpositus nucleus, averaged over several rabbits and several trials.

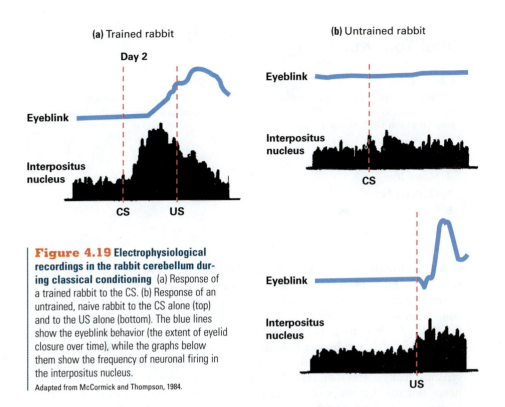

(a) Trained rabbit

Day 2

Eyeblink

Interpositus
nucleus

CS   US

(b) Untrained rabbit

Eyeblink

Interpositus
nucleus

CS

Eyeblink

Interpositus
nucleus

US

Figure 4.19 **Electrophysiological recordings in the rabbit cerebellum during classical conditioning** (a) Response of a trained rabbit to the CS. (b) Response of an untrained, naive rabbit to the CS alone (top) and to the US alone (bottom). The blue lines show the eyeblink behavior (the extent of eyelid closure over time), while the graphs below them show the frequency of neuronal firing in the interpositus nucleus.
Adapted from McCormick and Thompson, 1984.

Researchers have also recorded unpaired-CS or US-alone trials in naive rabbits. In both cases, where there is no CR, there is no activity in the interpositus nucleus, as seen in Figure 4.19b. The lack of substantial interpositus activity in a US-alone trial (despite a strong eyeblink UR) confirms that the cerebellum is responsible for conditioned eyeblink CRs only and not for the unconditioned eyeblink URs.

Figure 4.20 shows the firing rates recorded for a single Purkinje cell in a well-trained rabbit, with the time of the CS onset and the US indicated below. Purkinje cells spontaneously fire all the time, even when nothing is happening. However, in a well-trained animal, many of these cells *decrease* their firing in response to the tone CS, as shown in Figure 4.20. Why would the Purkinje cells turn off in response to a CS? Looking back at the diagram of cerebellar circuitry in Figure 4.18, note that Purkinje cells *inhibit* the interpositus nucleus, the major output pathway driving the conditioned motor response. Shutting off the Purkinje cells removes inhibition from the interpositus, freeing the interpositus to fire (as in Figure 4.19a).

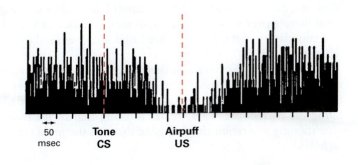

50
msec

Tone
CS

Airpuff
US

Figure 4.20 **Purkinje cell activity in a well-trained rabbit** The Purkinje cell's normal high rate of firing is halted in response to the CS and resumes after the US has occurred.
Data from R. F. Thompson.

Test Your Knowledge

Cerebellar Anatomy

For each cerebellar region or pathway below, identify whether its most critical involvement is in the US, UR, CS, or CR pathway. (Answers appear in the Answers section in the back of the book.)

1. Inferior olive
2. Pontine nuclei
3. Mossy fibers
4. Climbing fibers
5. Interpositus nucleus

Brain Stimulation as a Substitute for Behavioral Training

What if we knew exactly which pathways in your brain would change as a result of reading the words on this page? If so, we might be able to put electrodes in your brain and electrically stimulate those pathways in just the right pattern, at just the right time, to mimic the effect of reading this text. If that were possible, you wouldn't have to bother reading this book any further or studying for the final exam. Instead, you could stimulate a few neural pathways, create a little synaptic change, and then take the final exam and score an A+, even if you had never opened the textbook or sat through your professor's lectures! Science fiction, right? Unfortunately, it is still a fantasy because we don't yet know exactly where or in what way complex learning is stored in the brain. However, for simpler forms of learning, like eyeblink conditioning, this scenario is not only possible, it's been done.

Through electrical brain stimulation of the CS and US pathways shown in Figure 4.19, an experimenter can create conditioned eyeblink responses in the rabbit that are indistinguishable from those arising from behavioral training.

Recall that different parts of the pontine nuclei respond to different kinds of sensory input, such as auditory tones or visual signals, as illustrated in Figure 4.18. It is even possible to find a specific region in the pontine nuclei that responds to a *particular* tone. As a result, it is possible to condition rabbits merely by pairing electrical stimulation of the pontine nuclei (CS) with electrical stimulation of the inferior olive (US), that is, without presenting any external stimuli (airpuff or tone). After training with this type of brain stimulation, rabbits give precisely timed, reliable eyeblink responses the very first time they hear an actual tone corresponding to the pontine nuclear region that was stimulated, just as if they had been trained all along with tones and airpuffs (Steinmetz et al., 1989).

In these studies, direct stimulation of the inferior olive causes the rabbit to blink and can be substituted for an airpuff US, as shown in Figure 4.21. Similar conditioning over 4 days of training is seen whether an airpuff US (dashed line) or a stimulation of the inferior olive (solid line) was used (Steinmetz, Lavond, & Thompson, 1989).

Thus, rabbits that have had their inferior olives and pontine nuclei electrically stimulated will "pass the eyeblink test" much as if they had gone through days of tone-airpuff training. Like the science fantasy alluded to earlier, stimulating the correct pathways creates learning that seems indistinguishable from conditioning in a rabbit that has gone through the usual training with tones and airpuffs.

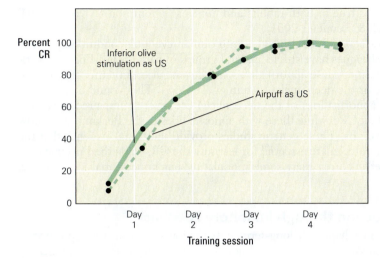

Percent CR

Figure 4.21 Substituting stimulation of the inferior olive for a US Similar conditioning over 4 days of training is seen whether an airpuff (dotted line) or a stimulation of the inferior olive (solid line) was used as the US.
Adapted from Steinmetz et al., 1989.

Impaired Conditioning following Cerebellar Damage

Another experimental approach for investigating the neural bases of classical conditioning is to introduce brain lesions—that is, to selectively remove small areas of the brain—and observe the consequences. Recall that the interpositus nucleus (see Figure 4.19) projects information about the CR out of the cerebellum. Thus, without the interpositus nucleus, you would expect that there could be no CR. This is exactly what Thompson and colleagues found: removing even 1 cubic millimeter of tissue from the interpositus nucleus completely and permanently abolished all previously learned conditioned responses and prevented all future eyeblink learning.

In contrast to lesions of the interpositus, which totally abolish learned eyeblink CRs, lesions of the cerebellar cortex (including the Purkinje cells) disrupt, but do not eliminate, eyeblink conditioning. Animals with lesions of the cerebellar cortex show small, poorly timed conditioned CRs (Perret, Ruiz, & Mauk, 1993). Recently, researchers have developed mutant mice with a genetic variation that causes selective degeneration of Purkinje cells. These mutant mice are slow at learning eyeblink conditioning, much like animals that have their cerebellar cortex physically removed (Chen, Bao, Lockard, Kim, & Thompson, 1996). Together, these lesion and mutant studies provide strong converging evidence that the interpositus nucleus is involved in the formation and execution of the conditioned response, while the cerebellar cortex is involved in response timing.

Given the critical role of the cerebellum in motor-reflex conditioning, it is not surprising that patients with cerebellar damage display significant deficits in acquiring the eyeblink conditioning. Such patients are slower to learn the CR and show low overall frequency and abnormal timing of CRs (Daum et al., 1993). Interestingly, patients who have undergone surgery that spares the deep nuclei are able to acquire a little conditioning, while patients with more extensive cerebellar damage show no conditioning at all. It is important to note that cerebellar damage does not impair all forms of associative learning. For example, cerebellar patients perform within the normal range on learning verbal associations, such as matching names with faces, which suggests that other areas of the brain play a role in these more abstract tasks (Daum et al., 1993). There is also a clear lateralization of cerebellar involvement in eyeblink conditioning: damage to the left cerebellum interferes only with conditioning to the left eye, while damage to the right cerebellum interferes only with conditioning to the right eye; this is true in both rabbits and humans (Thompson & Krupa, 1994; Woodruff-Pak & Lemieux, 2001).

Genetics offers additional insights into human eyeblink conditioning. Irene Daum and colleagues have studied several groups of patients in whom chromosomal irregularities cause abnormalities and degeneration in either the cortical Purkinje cells or the deep nuclei (Daum et al., 1993). They found that patients with genetic abnormalities of the deep nuclei are severely impaired at acquiring the eyeblink CRs, while those with abnormalities in the Purkinje cells show more mixed results. These genetic studies provide additional evidence that the deep cerebellar nuclei are essential for learning the CR, while the Purkinje cells in the cerebellar cortex exert some modulating but nonessential influence on this learning.

Error Correction through Inhibitory Feedback

As described in Chapter 2, long-term potentiation (LTP) of a synapse occurs when simultaneous activity in two adjoining neurons leads to a strengthening of the connecting synapse. LTP is a mechanism for synaptic change that occurs whenever two adjoining neurons fire at the same time and is thus much simpler than the error-correcting rule of the Rescorla-Wagner model, in which associative changes depend on many inputs (such as all the CSs present on a trial). Given its complexity, the Rescorla-Wagner model of learning probably does not describe what takes place in a learning brain at the cellular level, but the error-correction mechanisms the model predicts do appear to emerge from brain circuits.

If you look again at the cerebellar network in Figure 4.18, you will see an additional pathway within the cerebellum we have not yet discussed. This inhibitory feedback pathway projects from the interpositus nucleus to the inferior olive. In a well-trained animal, the production of a CR, through activation of the interpositus nucleus, will in turn inhibit the inferior olive from sending US information to the Purkinje cells in the cerebellar cortex (Sears & Steinmetz, 1991). This means that activity in the inferior olive will reflect the actual US minus (due to inhibition) the expected US, where the expected US is measured by the interpositus activity that drives the CR. Actual US minus expected US: sound familiar? It should. This is the same difference (actual US minus expected US) that the Rescorla-Wagner model uses to calculate the prediction error on a trial, which is then used to determine how much weight should accrue to the CS association.

If the inferior olive is where the brain codes the prediction error during conditioning, then we should be able to predict changes in the firing of the inferior olive based on the Rescorla-Wagner model (Gluck, Reifsnider, & Thompson, 1990; Gluck, Allen, Myers, & Thompson, 2001). Recall from Figure 4.12c that during CS-US acquisition training, the prediction error diminishes on each successive learning trial. Thus, we should expect to see inferior olive activity in response to the US diminish the more the US is predicted by the trained CS. Eventually, when the CR is well learned, there should be very little activity in the inferior olive (that is, when error in the Rescorla-Wagner model is close to zero). What happens matches the predictions exactly: inferior olive activity starts off high early in training and then gradually diminishes as the conditioned response is acquired (Sears & Steinmetz, 1991).

This interpretation of how the cerebellar circuits compute the changes in association weight called for in the Rescorla-Wagner model implies that Kamin's blocking effect (the clearest experimental evidence for error-correction learning) should depend on the inhibitory pathway from the interpositus to the inferior olive. This prediction was confirmed in a study by Thompson and colleagues. The researchers first trained rabbits to give reliable eyeblink responses to a tone CS and then injected a drug into the interpositus that temporarily disabled the inhibitory connection from the interpositus to the inferior olive. With this pathway disabled, they predicted, the inferior olive's activity would reflect the presence of the actual US and no longer the expected US.

The rabbits were then given phase 2 blocking training, in which a compound tone-and-light CS was paired with the US. The rabbits showed high inferior olive activity whenever the US was presented, whether or not a conditioned response was generated. As a result, in phase 3, the rabbits gave a strong response to the light CS. In other words, by disabling that one inhibitory pathway which is essential for the actual US minus expected US computation, Thompson and colleagues were able to "*block* blocking" (Kim, Krupa, & Thompson, 1998). These and related results suggest that the cerebellar–inferior olive circuit plays a role in the execution of Rescorla and Wagner's error-correction rule.

The Hippocampus in CS Modulation

Error correction as explained by the Rescorla-Wagner model is only one mechanism at work in classical conditioning. Another, CS modulation, was suggested, as noted above, by the theories of Mackintosh and of Pearce and Hall. Here we briefly discuss some of the brain systems that appear to govern these mechanisms for modulating the processing of CS cues.

As you learned in Chapter 2, the hippocampus is a string-bean–shaped structure that lies, in humans, just inward from the ears. Figure 4.22 shows the hippocampus in several different species.

The hippocampus is not necessary for learning new conditioned responses. For example, animals or humans with hippocampal damage are able to learn a basic conditioned eyeblink response quite normally. Nevertheless, electrophysiological recordings of animals show that the hippocampus is very active during conditioning, especially early in training. What role does the hippocampus play in conditioning? One way to find possible clues to its role is to look at more complex conditioning paradigms, such as latent inhibition (described in Table 4.5). As you learned in Section 4.1, latent inhibition is demonstrated when, before training, an organism is exposed to a cue unassociated with a US; later, during conditioning, the organism is then slow to learn that the cue does predict a US.

As you also learned, the Rescorla-Wagner model is *not* able to explain the phenomenon of latent inhibition. If the Rescorla-Wagner model's error-correction process cannot explain latent inhibition and if the cerebellum implements the error-correction principle, then perhaps other brain regions involved in classical conditioning besides the cerebellum are responsible for

Figure 4.22 The hippocampus in several species of animals, including humans. The medial (inner) part of the temporal lobes contains the hippocampus, the amygdala, and several nearby cortical areas, including the entorhinal cortex, perirhinal cortex, and parahippocampal cortex.

(a) HUMAN

Hippocampus with medial temporal lobes

(b) RAT

Hippocampus

(c) BIRD

Hippocampus

latent inhibition. Might the hippocampus be such a region? If so, then the animal learning theories that capture behavioral phenomena other than error-correction learning might provide us with some ideas of what the hippocampus may do during classical conditioning.

The CS modulation theories of Mackintosh and of Pearce and Hall, discussed earlier in this chapter, suggest that to find the system responsible for latent inhibition and related phenomena, we should look for a system involved in determining the salience of sensory cues. If the hippocampus is needed for CS modulation effects in classical conditioning, then an animal *without* a hippocampus should *not* exhibit CS modulation effects such as latent inhibition. In fact, this is exactly what researchers have found: removing the hippocampus (and associated cortical input regions) eliminates the latent inhibition effect in classical conditioning of the rabbit eyeblink reflex (Solomon & Moore, 1975; Shohamy, Allen, & Gluck, 2000).

Many other behavioral phenomena that cannot be explained by the Rescorla-Wagner model are also found to disappear in animals that have lesions to the hippocampus and surrounding brain regions. This suggests that the Rescorla-Wagner model may be better described as a model of the cerebellar contributions to motor-reflex conditioning in hippocampal-lesioned animals than as a model of conditioning in healthy, intact animals. That is to say, the model applies best to the brain regions responsible for error-correction learning, such as the cerebellum, but does not explain the additional contributions of the hippocampus.

What functional role, then, does the hippocampus play in classical conditioning of motor reflexes such as the eyeblink response? If the hippocampus is necessary for latent inhibition and other forms of CS modulation, we might infer that the hippocampus plays a role in determining how sensory cues are processed before they are used by the cerebellum to form long-term memory traces.

Further discussion of the role of the hippocampus in processing sensory relationships while remembering new facts and events will be discussed in Chapter 6. Later, in Chapter 9, we describe some specific theories about how the hippocampus modulates sensory processing in various forms of learning and memory. We turn next, however, to describing some exciting new developments in learning theory that suggest how brain rhythms, including those produced during sleep, can affect the hippocampus and conditioning.

Brain Rhythms and Conditioning

A growing body of evidence suggests that oscillating waves of synchronized electrical activity in the hippocampus are necessary for the storage of new information. Neuroscientists believe that these waves, called theta waves, represent a "ready state" for learning. When the hippocampus is in a theta state, waves of synchronized neural firing travel back and forth across the hippocampus, about 7 times a second (Buzsáki, 2002), as seen on the left side of Figure 4.23.

Early evidence for the role of theta waves in learning comes from studies done in the 1970s by Steven Berry and Richard Thompson (Berry & Thompson, 1978). By inserting recording electrodes into a rabbit's hippocampus, they were able to detect this rhythm and identify the behaviors corresponding to the theta state in the rabbit's hippocampus. Their study showed that rabbits exhibiting theta activity just before an eyeblink-conditioning experiment learned faster than

Figure 4.23 Theta wave and sharp wave brain rhythms in the hippocampus Two fundamentally different and antagonistic patterns characterize network activity in the hippocampus. Rhythmic theta oscillations (7–9 Hz) are associated with exploration (left) and REM sleep, whereas irregular sharp waves (right) are present during more sedentary behaviors such as eating, drinking, and slow-wave sleep.
From Buzsáki, 1989.

Exploration   Immobility

rabbits that did not. In a more recent study, Berry and colleagues extended this finding by monitoring the rabbit's hippocampus throughout the experiment. The electrode was connected to a computer that generated the tone-airpuff trials, allowing each trial to be triggered by the presence of theta activity in the hippocampus (Seager, Johnson, Chabot, Asaka, & Berry, 2002). As shown in Figure 4.24, rabbits trained in this way learned much faster than a control group of rabbits whose trials were random and not triggered by theta waves. They also learned faster than rabbits that were explicitly not in a theta state when the tone CSs were presented.

Figure 4.24 Eyeblink conditioning synchronized to theta vs. non-theta conditions Percent CRs in five-trial blocks across days of training. Rabbits in the theta condition gave significantly higher percentages of CRs than rabbits in the non-theta condition.

From Seager, Johnson, Chabot, Asaka, & Berry, 2002.

Imagine how helpful it would be if your professor could monitor your hippocampal theta waves, presenting you with new information only when a little green "ready to learn" light on your forehead turns on to indicate that you are in a receptive theta state. Perhaps you, like the theta-triggered rabbits, could learn twice as much in a day as you do now.

But why does the theta rhythm enhance learning? That is a major unsolved mystery in the neurobiology of learning and memory. Gyorgy Buzsáki, a leading researcher in the study of the role of theta waves, argues that they play a crucial role in the communication between the hippocampus, where memories are first encoded and temporarily stored, and other areas of the brain where memories are stored for the long term (Buzsáki, 2002). Theta waves, produced when animals are exploring and learning about their environment, represent what Buzsáki describes as the "input" phase of learning, during which external information is organized and stored in the hippocampus. When there is a break in this input stream, he argues, the hippocampus shifts into a "broadcast" phase, in which irregular sharp waves of activity transmit a condensed version of the new information to other brain areas responsible for long-term storage (Buzsáki, 1989). By storing information during the breaks between periods of new exploration and input, the hippocampus readies itself to receive the next batch of new information. Buzsáki's work suggests that the hippocampus efficiently alternates between data-collection phases (theta) and data archiving (sharp waves). This theory still leaves us with the mystery of how the theta rhythms enable the hippocampus to store new information and, in doing so, facilitate classical conditioning and other forms of learning.

Invertebrates and the Cellular Basis of Learning

Chapter 3 introduced you to the sea snail *Aplysia* and studies by Eric Kandel and colleagues on the neural substrates of two forms of non-associative learning: habituation and sensitization. To briefly recap, habituation occurs when *Aplysia*'s siphon (see Figure 3.9) is repeatedly but lightly touched. Initially this results in a gill-withdrawal reflex. However, each subsequent stimulation of the siphon elicits a progressively smaller response. The circuit for this learned response includes a sensory neuron (activated by touching the siphon) that makes an excitatory synapse with a motor neuron that controls the gill withdrawal (see Figure 3.10). The neural mechanism for habituation is thought to be a progressive decrease in the number of neurotransmitter (in this case, glutamate) vesicles available in the sensory neuron's axon for each successive stimulation of the siphon. In contrast, sensitization is a global increase in responding to all or most stimuli following an unpleasant stimulus, such as an electric shock to *Aplysia*'s tail. The tail shock activates modulatory interneurons that release serotonin onto the axon terminals of all the sensory neurons that project to the gill-withdrawal motor neuron. Serotonin increases the number of glutamate vesicles released when the sensory

Table 4.7

Varieties of learning in *Aplysia*

Type of learning	Associative	Stimulus specific	Mechanism(s)	Duration of effect
Habituation	No	Yes	Decrease in glutamate	Short-term cellular process
Sensitization	No	No	Serotonin-induced increase in glutamate	Short-term cellular process
Classical conditioning	Yes	Yes	1. Presynaptic-activity-dependent enhancement of glutamate release from sensory neuron 2. Postsynaptic change in receptors of motor neuron 3. A cascade of intracellular molecular events that activate genes in the neuron's nucleus, causing an increase in the number of sensory-motor synapses	Short-term cellular process Long-term structural change

neuron is stimulated. This results in the generalized (non–stimulus-specific) increase in gill withdrawal elicited by all future stimuli, including touches on either the siphon or the mantle. The top two entries in Table 4.7 summarize the key differences between these two forms of non-associative learning.

What do you think would happen if both kinds of stimuli—touching the siphon and shocking the tail—were repeatedly paired? Tom Carew, in collaboration with Kandel and other colleagues, showed that *Aplysia*'s siphon-withdrawal reflex can be classically conditioned, as illustrated in Figure 4.25a. When touching the siphon (a potential CS) is repeatedly paired with shocking the tail (the US), an enhanced siphon withdrawal (CR) results in response to subsequent touches of the siphon (Carew, Hawkins, & Kandel, 1983). The enhanced siphon-withdrawal response to the siphon-touch CS following paired training is considerably greater than the generalized sensitization that occurs from presentation of the tail shock alone. Moreover, this classically conditioned siphon-withdrawal CR is also specific to the siphon and does not generalize to other stimuli, such as a touch on the mantle.

What happens inside the nervous system of *Aplysia* when these two stimuli are paired? Kandel and colleagues demonstrated that paired training produces an increase in the glutamate vesicles that are released in the siphon's synapse on the motor neuron, much like an exaggerated form of the mechanism for sensitization described in Chapter 3 (Hawkins, Abrams, Carew, & Kandel, 1983). This implies that a cellular mechanism for classical conditioning can be understood as an elaboration of the same cellular mechanism used for sensitization.

The pairing-specific enhancement of glutamate release in the sensory neuron synapse is called an **activity-dependent enhancement** because it depends on activation of the sensory neuron prior to the administration of the US. Earlier in this chapter, we discussed how classical conditioning of the rabbit eyeblink response is sensitive to the order and timing of the tone CS and the airpuff US. The same holds true for conditioning of *Aplysia*'s siphon withdrawal: conditioning occurs only if the siphon-touch CS is presented about half a second before the tail-shock US. If the US occurs much later (more than 2 seconds after the CS) or before the CS, nothing other than nonspecific sensitization will occur. Thus, after sensory stimulation, whatever process occurs within the neuron to prime the neuron for an increase in glutamate release has a time course of about a half a second.

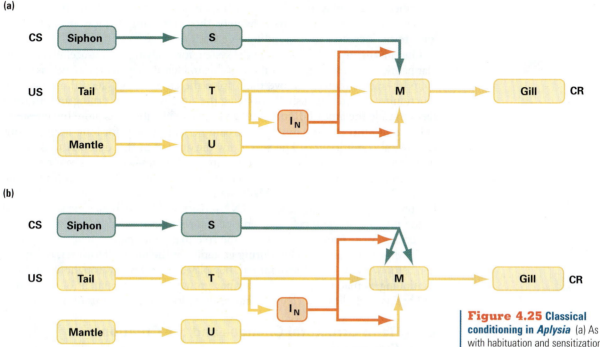

(a)

(b)

Figure 4.25 Classical conditioning in **Aplysia** (a) As with habituation and sensitization, classical conditioning (a CR) in *Aplysia* results when three sensory pathways—the siphon (CS), the tail (US), and the mantle—converge on the gill-withdrawal motor neuron (M). The tail pathway includes a secondary pathway through an interneuron (I_N), and this releases serotonin onto the other sensory synapses when the tail is shocked. (b) Long-lasting forms of classical conditioning require the formation of new synapses (the dark green arrow heads) between the sensory neurons of the siphon and the motor neuron. The new synapses are created through a molecular cascade set in motion by the serotonin released by the interneuron.

To summarize, Kandel and colleagues demonstrated that activation of *Aplysia*'s sensory neuron has at least three consequences. First, it causes the motor neuron to fire, by the release of the neurotransmitter glutamate into the synapse. Second, it causes a short-term decrease in glutamate vesicles available for any subsequent stimulation of the sensory neuron, resulting in habituation. Third, it primes the synapse, through a series of intracellular events lasting about half a second, so that a subsequent presentation of the neurotransmitter serotonin (released following activation of an aversive tail shock) creates an increase in future glutamate release—resulting in a classically conditioned increase in gill withdrawal following pairing of the sensory stimulus (the CS) and the tail shock (the US).

Presynaptic versus Postsynaptic Changes during Learning

This activity-dependent enhancement of the sensory neuron's release of glutamate onto the motor neuron is a presynaptic form of synaptic plasticity, because like the mechanism for sensitization discussed in Chapter 3, it involves a change in the sensory neuron. However, the story is actually more complicated. Later studies demonstrated that there is also a postsynaptic mechanism for conditioning that involves changes in neurotransmitter receptors on the motor neuron (Bao, Kandel, & Hawkins, 1998). Thus, the mechanisms for classical conditioning in *Aplysia* involve both presynaptic and postsynaptic changes in the circuits connecting the CS and the CR, as summarized in Table 4.7.

As discussed in Chapter 3, the known neural mechanisms for habituation and sensitization are relatively short-lived forms of learning, usually lasting only a few minutes (or a few hours at most). If, as suggested above, classical conditioning in *Aplysia* is built up from the synaptic plasticity mechanisms that mediate habituation and sensitization, shouldn't classical conditioning be similarly short-lived? In fact, behavioral studies of gill withdrawal in *Aplysia*, eyeblink conditioning in rabbits and many other forms of conditioning clearly demonstrate that classically conditioned responses can be maintained for far longer—days, weeks, months, or more. This suggests that the short-term synaptic changes described above may be only one component of the neural mechanisms for classical conditioning in *Aplysia*, namely, those resulting in short-term, but not long-term, increases in responding to a CS.

One advantage of *Aplysia* as a model system for studying the intracellular molecular pathways of learning is that it is possible to identify key neurons (such as entire memory-trace circuits), remove them from the animals, and keep those neurons functioning in a culture dish. By isolating the key circuits for learning and studying them outside the animal, Kandel and colleagues were able to explore the question, What long-term changes in *Aplysia* circuitry could account for long-lasting forms of classical conditioning? The search for the answer to this question took scientists back to the very origins of who we are—our genes—and has given rise to an important new field, the molecular genetics of memory (and also won Kandel the Nobel Prize for Physiology or Medicine in 2001). As we review in more detail in Chapter 12, genes are stretches of DNA molecules (deoxyribonucleic acid), found in the nucleus of every cell, that encode information needed to produce protein molecules. Most people are aware of the role that genes play in determining how our bodies and brains develop during gestation in the uterus. However, our genes don't stop working after birth; rather, they play a critical role throughout our lives, continuing to maintain and guide further growth and development of our bodies and brains, including the changes that result in long-lasting forms of memory.

Long-Term Structural Changes and the Creation of New Synapses

Using recent advances in molecular biology techniques, Kandel and colleagues were able to show that the serotonin released by *Aplysia*'s interneurons following a tail-shock US does more than cause a short-term increase in the sensory neuron's release of glutamate; it also launches a cascade of intracellular molecular events that set the stage for long-term structural changes in the neuron. Following multiple pairings of the CS and US, protein molecules in the sensory neuron's synapse travel back up the axon of the sensory neuron all the way to the cell body. There they switch on genes inside the nucleus of the neuron that in turn set in motion the growth of new synapses (Figure 4.25b).

More recent work by Kandel and others has identified two proteins that are found inside neurons and that play critical regulatory roles in this synapse-creation process. The first protein, CREB-1, activates genes in the neuron's nucleus that initiate the growth of new synapses. The second protein, CREB-2, plays an opponent role, inhibiting the actions of CREB-1. The creation of new synapses during learning requires a cascade of processes inside the cell that activate CREB-1 and suppress CREB-2.

What do you think would happen if functioning of the CREB-1 protein was impaired? Kandel and colleagues demonstrated that if CREB-1 is rendered inactive by injection of molecules into the neuron that compete with CREB's ability to activate genes for new synapses, the circuits subsequently fail to show long-lasting forms of associative learning (Dash, Hochner, & Kandel, 1990). Most important, the inactivation of CREB-1 does not affect the short-lasting forms of learning that depend only on increased glutamate release. This study provided critical evidence for a dissociation between short-lasting forms of learning, which do not require the CREB-1 protein, and long-lasting forms, which do.

In a related study, Kandel and colleagues showed that removing the influence of the opponent protein, CREB-2, had the opposite effect: with the CREB-2 inactivated, long-lasting learning occurs rapidly at the sensory neurons, after even a single exposure to serotonin (Bartsch et al., 1995). The role of CREB molecules in modulating long-lasting forms of memory is not limited to *Aplysia*;

increasing CREB-1 in fruit flies (*Drosophila*) allows them to learn much more rapidly than usual, while increasing their CREB-2 blocks the formation of long-term memories, such as those produced in the odor-conditioning task described earlier in this chapter (Yin et al., 1994). The CREB molecules also play a critical role in mammals' learning; studies in mice have shown that activity of CREB-1 in the hippocampus is critical to long-lasting but not short-term increases in neuron-to-neuron associations based on LTP (Bourtchuladze et al., 1994).

Studies of classical conditioning in *Aplysia* have demonstrated that anatomical changes in neural circuits, including the growth or deletion of synapses, are characteristic of long-lasting forms of memory. In contrast, short-term, labile forms of memory are associated with temporary intracellular changes within existing anatomical pathways, including shifts in the location, size, or number of neurotransmitter vesicles, which alter synaptic transmission efficacy. Thus, as was also discussed in Chapter 3, the transition from short-term to long-term learning may be characterized as a shift from transmission-process–based changes within the neuron to structural changes within the neural circuits (see Table 4.7).

Test Your Knowledge

Cellular Bases of Invertebrate Conditioning

Fill in the blanks:

1. Initially, activation of the *Aplysia* sensory neuron causes a _____ neuron to fire, followed by a short-term decrease in _____ vesicles available for subsequent stimulation, resulting in short-term _____.

2. Subsequent and repeated activation of the sensory neuron paired with an aversive tail shock causes a(n) _____ in glutamate release, resulting in a pairing-specific _____.

3. Two proteins in *Aplysia* have opposite effects on long-term memory formation: _____ activates the growth of new synapses, while _____ inhibits this growth.

(Answers appear in the Answers section in the back of the book.)

Interim Summary

- There are two sites in the cerebellum where CS and US information converges and that might potentially be locations for the storage of the CS-US association: (1) the Purkinje cells in the cerebellar cortex and (2) the interpositus nucleus. The interpositus nucleus is the only output pathway from the cerebellum; it is the route through which the learned response travels to the motor systems that control behavior, such as an eyeblink CR.

- The inferior olive is believed to compute the degree to which a US is unexpected, providing the information necessary to implement Rescorla and Wagner's principle of error-correction learning in the cerebellum.

- The hippocampus is a structure underlying some of the CS-modulation effects in conditioning. This is consistent with data showing that an animal without a hippocampus does not exhibit CS-modulation effects such as latent inhibition.

- Rabbits learn faster if training is synchronized to present CSs during the periods of theta rhythm in the hippocampus, possibly because the theta rhythm occurs preferentially when the hippocampus is in input mode.

- Kandel and colleagues demonstrated that activation of *Aplysia*'s sensory neuron by an external stimulation (such as presentation of a stimulus cue) primes the synapse, through a series of intracellular events lasting about half a second, so that a subsequent presentation of serotonin (released following activation of an aversive tail shock) creates an increase in future glutamate release, resulting in a classically conditioned increase in gill withdrawal.

- After multiple pairings of the CS and US in *Aplysia*, protein molecules in the sensory neuron's synapse travel back up the axon of the sensory neuron all the way to the cell body. There they activate genes inside the nucleus of the neuron that in turn set in motion the growth of new synapses.

4.3 Clinical Perspectives

In this final section of the chapter, we focus on ways in which drug addiction and drug abuse are intimately linked to classical conditioning. The role of learning and memory in drug addiction is a fascinating topic that we consider from several viewpoints in this textbook. In Chapter 5, we will explore the neural mechanisms of reward that are impaired by most drugs of abuse. Chapter 8 discusses the role of the frontal lobes as the brain's executive controller, their importance in inhibiting inappropriate behaviors, and how this role is compromised in drug addicts. In the following discussion of clinical perspectives on classical conditioning, we will discuss how the behavioral and biological mechanisms of classical conditioning influence various aspects of drug addiction and abuse.

Recall the discussion, earlier in this chapter, about how tolerance to drugs such as cocaine or heroin reflects the addict's conditioned drug expectation, in response to environmental cues that, through the process of homeostasis, induces an intense craving for the drug. What are the potential consequences of such conditioned tolerance? One consequence is that victims of heroin overdose are rarely novice users (Siegel, 2001). Rather, they tend to be long-time heroin addicts who have developed a high degree of tolerance to the drug but make the mistake of taking their usual dose in an unusual setting.

For example, the situational cues that result in conditioned drug tolerance can include the room in which the drug is usually taken. You may recall reports of rock stars and others dying of heroin overdoses in hotel bathrooms, which were most likely far different from the settings in which they were used to taking their drug. What might have happened is that they overdosed on what was otherwise their normal dosage of drug because, in this novel setting, their body was not prepared for the large influx of drug that occurred. Different methods of drug injection are another form of environmental cue that can become associated with drug expectation. One longtime heroin addict is reported to have died of an overdose when, looking for an accessible blood vein, he injected himself in his penis for the first time (Winek, Wahaba, & Rozin, 1999). Without the compensatory response to customary cues, the net effect of his usual dose was far greater than he was used to and resulted in his death (for reports of similar real-life cases, see Siegel, 2001; Siegel & Ellsworth, 1986).

An unusual taste to a drink can serve as a novel situational cue influencing the effects of alcohol on the brain. This was confirmed in a study in which college students showed greater cognitive and motor impairments when they consumed a given amount of alcohol in an unusual drink (in this case, a blue, peppermint-flavored beverage) than when they had the same amount of alcohol in a familiar drink, such as beer (Remington, Roberts, & Glauthier, 1977). Perhaps this is yet another reason why people get wilder at holiday parties, when they are drinking alcohol in sweet and bubbly holiday punches.

Research has demonstrated conditioned tolerance in a wide variety of animal species. For example, Shepard Siegel and colleagues examined the effect of cues when heroin is administered to rats (Siegel, Hinson, Krank, & McCully, 1982).

Siegel gave three groups of rats a fairly large (for their body weight) dose of heroin. The first group of rats had previously received a lower dose of heroin, administered in the same cage and room where they were later tested with the larger dose (the "same-tested" group in Figure 4.26). The second group of rats had also previously received the lower dose of heroin, but in a different cage and room (the "different-tested" group). Finally, the "first-time tested" group of rats were receiving heroin for the first time.

As shown in Figure 4.26, Siegel and colleagues found that the large dose of heroin almost always (96% of the time) resulted in a fatal overdose in the "first-time tested" rats. In contrast, the "different-tested" group showed some evidence of tolerance; only 64% of these rats suffered a fatal overdose. But the "same-tested" rats, who were tested in the same environment in which they had previously been administered low doses of heroin, had a mortality rate of only 32%. Thus, these rats were protected from overdose by the conditioned tolerance that they learned during the administration of lower doses of heroin in the same setting.

If drug tolerance is a form of classical conditioning, you might expect that the same rules and principles would apply to it as to eyeblink and other forms of conditioning. This appears to be the case. Recall the paradigm of latent inhibition discussed earlier and shown in Table 4.5: pre-exposure to a CS delays subsequent learning of a CS-US association. If this latent inhibition effect applies to drug tolerance, then pre-exposing an animal to the cues that predict drug delivery should slow down development of learned tolerance to the drug. To test latent inhibition in the context of drug use, researchers have given animals an injection of an inert placebo to pre-expose them to the contextual cues (the sound and feel of getting an injection) of drug use. This pre-exposure does prove to slow down, by latent inhibition, the development of a cue-drug association where the cue is the CS and the drug is the US. In fact, this is exactly what Siegel and colleagues found in studies of morphine tolerance in rats (Siegel, 1983).

Such results provide compelling evidence for the applicability of Pavlovian analyses to learned drug tolerance. They suggest that drug tolerance and the loss of drug tolerance in novel drug-taking environments are mediated by basic processes of classical Pavlovian conditioning.

As you recall from Section 4.1, an extinction paradigm should eliminate (or at least reduce) the association between conditioned cues and conditioned response when the cues are repeatedly presented alone and not paired with the prior US. If drug craving is viewed as a conditioned response, then the same principle of extinction should also apply, and indeed it does. In carefully controlled laboratory studies, rats that became addicted to alcohol showed significant extinction of this addiction through repeated nonreinforced exposure to experimentally manipulated cues that had previously been paired with administration of alcohol (Krank & Wall, 1990). In real life, however, it is very hard to both identify and extinguish all the cues that have become associated with drug use.

Eventually, these and other studies, by deepening scientists' understanding of the role of classical conditioning in drug addiction, may provide new tools to help drug addicts overcome their addiction. For example, perhaps further research on the extinction of conditioned responses will shed light on why addicts so often relapse when they are trying to kick their drug habit. You can read more about this mechanism in "Learning and Memory in Everyday Life: Extinguishing a Drug Habit."

Figure 4.26 A study of drug tolerance Rats in the "first-time tested" group, which received no prior heroin, showed the highest percentage of fatal overdose. Of those rats who had received a smaller prior dose, the ones tested in the same cage as previously ("same-tested") showed the lowest level of overdoses, while the ones tested in a different cage ("different-tested") showed an intermediate level of overdosing.
From Siegel et al., 1982.

Extinguishing a Drug Habit

Even in a well-controlled laboratory, extinguishing a cue and keeping it extinguished turns out to be extremely difficult. Mark Bouton and colleagues, studying the extinction of conditioned responses in rats, demonstrated that manipulations such as changing the context, or just waiting a specific period, often result in the extinguished cues reacquiring their conditioned associative properties (Bouton, 2000). Is it any surprise, then, that efforts to adapt extinction methods to therapy for drug addiction have yielded only mixed results at best (Carroll, 1999; Siegel & Ramos, 2002)? The fact that the addict remains susceptible to the first drink or smoke suggests that to extinguish the drug associations, we would have to include small doses of the drugs during cue-exposure therapy to better reproduce and extinguish the cravings. Clearly, such a procedure would result in many practical and legal difficulties. Nevertheless, Bouton's work suggests four principles that can help guide anyone trying to extinguish a habit or association. They are

1. Since extinction effects are highly context-sensitive, cue-exposure therapy should be conducted in as many different contexts as possible, including those that are part of the patient's everyday life. This will prevent the extinction of drug craving from becoming dependent on any one context (such as a drug rehab center).
2. The extinction training should be spread out over time rather than conducted all at once because time serves as a powerful context. A 2-week stint in a rehab clinic may not be enough to make a long-term difference. Multiple therapy sessions at different times and in different contexts are more effective.
3. Whenever possible, the cue-exposure therapy should take place in the same contexts in which the original drug habits were acquired. Thus, it is better to go through the cue-exposure therapy at home rather than in a very unfamiliar setting, such as a drug rehabilitation center.
4. Since drug use itself is part of the context for further drug taking, extinction therapy can be more effective if it includes small amounts of drug use during cue exposure.

Interim Summary

- The situational cues that result in conditioned drug tolerance can be any sensory cues associated with drug use, including the feel of the needle and the method of injection.
- Rats are protected from overdose by the conditioned tolerance that they learned during the administration of lower doses of heroin in the same setting.
- Addiction can be partially reduced through Pavlovian extinction: rats who became addicted to alcohol showed significant extinction of this addiction through repeated nonreinforced exposure to experimentally manipulated cues that had previously been paired with administration of alcohol.

▶ SYNTHESIS

Classical conditioning is far more than just another behavioral process or tool for investigating brain systems: it is the mother of all memory systems. Evidence of classical "Pavlovian" conditioning surrounds us every day. Like Moira, who runs to the curb when she hears the musical jingle of an ice cream truck, and like Garfield, who has sworn off oysters, everyone has been conditioned by cues in the environment to predict what might follow next.

In recent years, classical conditioning experiments have moved to the forefront of research into the physiological bases of learning because of the exquisite control they afford over what stimuli are presented as cues and because of the highly refined behavioral analyses and models that have been developed as a result. Building on these analyses and models, biological research has shown how different forms of classical conditioning are mediated by different brain systems, leading to fundamental insights into the neurobiology of learning and often providing tools that help us understand various clinical brain disorders.

Psychological studies of conditioning have resulted in elegant mathematical theories of learning, especially the error-correcting model of Rescorla and Wagner, which continue to influence and guide research into the neural bases of conditioning in a broad range of brain systems, including the cerebellum, the amygdala (to be discussed in the context of fear conditioning in Chapter 10), and the role of dopamine in reward prediction (see Chapter 5). Links between conditioning and complex forms of cognition, such as category learning, help us see how mechanisms for learning studied in simple animal circuits can provide insights into the behavioral and neural bases of human cognition. The studies in animals also illustrate the general biological principle that evolution does not work like an engineer, creating new specialized systems for each new function. Rather, evolution works more like a tinkerer, using preexisting components, in slightly modified form, to perform new functions. The behavioral and biological processes for classical conditioning are the basic building blocks, the biological alphabet, from which more complex forms of learning emerge in all species, including humans.

Key Terms

activity-dependent enhancement, *p. 158*

appetitive conditioning, *p. 121*

aversive conditioning, *p. 121*

blocking, *p. 131*

cerebellum, *p. 149*

classical conditioning, *p. 118*

conditioned response (CR), *p. 120*

conditioned stimulus (CS), *p. 120*

conditioned taste aversion, *p. 147*

CS modulation theory, *p. 143*

delay conditioning, *p. 145*

error-correction learning, *p. 133*

extinction, *p. 129*

eyeblink conditioning, *p. 124*

homeostasis, *p. 128*

inferior olive, *p. 150*

interpositus nucleus, *p. 149*

interstimulus interval (ISI), *p. 146*

latent inhibition, *p. 142*

learning rate, *p. 136*

Pavlovian conditioning, *p. 118*

prediction error, *p. 133*

Purkinje cells, *p. 149*

tolerance, *p. 127*

trace conditioning, *p. 145*

trial-level model, *p. 145*

unconditioned response (UR), *p. 119*

unconditioned stimulus (US), *p. 119*

US modulation theory, *p. 143*

Concept Check

1. Following acquisition training with a tone predicting an airpuff, the Rescorla-Wagner model predicts that W_{Tone} will equal 100. What would happen, according to the model, if we then began extinction training, presenting the tone CS without administering an airpuff US? Assuming a learning rate of 0.2, compute the values of W_{Tone}, expected US, actual US, prediction error, and the change in W_{Tone} for the first five trials of extinction training.

2. Returning to our stock analysts Doris and Herman, consider what would happen if Doris showed up every day to work, but Herman only came in every now and then. On the days that Doris works alone, she does a great job of predicting the stock market. But on the days that Herman shows up, the pair of them do a lousy job. What would you think about Herman? You'd probably conclude that he is no great asset. In fact, worse than being a do-nothing, he seems to interfere with Doris's ability to perform. You might even say that Herman *inhibits* Doris's predictive value. This is similar to what occurs in conditioning procedures where a tone cue is always followed by the US except when the tone appears as part of a compound tone-and-light stimulus. On these compound trials, no US occurs. What does the Rescorla-Wagner model predict will happen to the associations during this training?

3. The true test of a new theory is how well it predicts previously unobserved phenomena, especially when the predictions are not obvious or are counterintuitive. A striking example of this kind of success occurred when Rescorla sought in the following way to test the limits of what the Rescorla-Wagner model could predict: in phase 1, he trained a group of animals with a tone followed by a US in half of the trials and with a light followed by a US in the other half (Rescorla, 1976). Then in phase 2, he presented these two cues simultaneously, as a tone-and-light compound, and followed this compound cue with a US. Later, Rescorla tested the animals. What did the Rescorla-Wagner model predict for this study?

Operant Conditioning

Learning the Outcome of Behaviors

MOST CHILDREN ARE TOILET TRAINED as toddlers. A few lucky kids seem to grasp the idea almost intuitively; others are prone to wetting accidents during the early school years. But, for most children, learning occurs over a span of days or weeks.

Consider toddler Annie. After she has had a drink and her bladder is likely to be full, her parents put her on a toddler-size potty seat and wait for nature to run its course. When Annie successfully uses the potty, her parents provide verbal praise ("What a good girl you are, Annie!"), a gold sticker, or even a small toy. When a wetting accident occurs, her parents may admonish her ("Mommy is very disappointed in you, Annie"). Gradually, the toddler learns that using the potty will result in the reward of parental approval and failing to do so will result in parental disapproval. Eventually, the behavior becomes automatic enough that Annie continues to use the potty seat and finally the toilet, even though she no longer receives an explicit reward for doing so.

This kind of learning is an example of **operant conditioning:** the process whereby organisms learn to make or refrain from making certain responses in order to obtain or avoid certain outcomes. The learning is called "operant" because the organism "operates" on the environment to determine what outcome occurs. Operant conditioning is sometimes also called *instrumental conditioning*, meaning that the organism's behavior is "instrumental" in producing the outcome.

Operant conditioning is a deceptively simple-sounding process, but it can be used to train fantastically complex behaviors. In the days before computer animation, most television ads that featured real animals singing, dancing, or otherwise pitching a product depended on operant conditioning. A famous animal act from the 1950s, "Priscilla, the Fastidious Pig," featured a pig whose routine included turning on the radio, eating breakfast at a table, picking up dirty clothes and putting them in a hamper, running the vacuum cleaner, and—of course—picking out her favorite brand of pig chow (Breland & Breland, 1951). By the end of this chapter, you should have a pretty good idea of how to train your own pig to do the same.

5.1 Behavioral Processes

Humans have been using the principles of operant conditioning as long as there have been sheep to herd, horses to ride, and toddlers to toilet train. But it wasn't until the end of the nineteenth century (about the same time that Ivan Pavlov was "discovering" classical conditioning) that Edward Thorndike first tried to systematically explore how animals learn new behaviors.

The "Discovery" of Operant Conditioning

In Chapter 1, you read about Edward Thorndike and his studies of how cats learned to escape from puzzle boxes, such as the one shown in Figure 5.1a. The puzzle boxes were made from fruit crates, each with a door that could be opened from the inside if the animal executed the correct sequence of pressing levers, pulling ropes, and stepping on pedals (Thorndike, 1898, 1911, 1932). When Thorndike would put a cat in such a box for the first time, the animal would hiss, claw at the walls, and generally try to fight its way free. Eventually, the cat would accidentally perform the movements needed to open the door and get out. Thorndike recorded how long it took the animal to escape and then returned the cat to the box to try again. After a few experiences in the box, a cat typically learned the sequence of moves that allowed it to escape. Figure 5.1b shows the data from one cat; after a dozen or so trials in the box, the cat was able to get out almost immediately.

Thorndike concluded that when an animal's response was followed by a satisfying outcome (such as escaping from a puzzle box or obtaining food), then

Figure 5.1 Thorndike's studies of animal learning
(a) One of Thorndike's puzzle boxes. (b) Data from one cat that learned to escape from the puzzle box efficiently after a few experiences.
[Data from (Thorndike, 1911).]

(a)

Time to escape (in seconds)

Trials

(b)

Yale University Library

Box C.

the probability of that response occurring again in the future would increase. Alternatively, if the response was followed by an unsatisfying outcome (such as an electric shock), then the probability of that response occurring again would decrease. Thorndike formalized this idea in his *law of effect*. As you read in Chapter 1, the law of effect states that, given a particular stimulus (designated S), a response (R) that leads to a desirable or pleasant outcome will tend to increase in frequency, strengthening the S-R association and making it more likely that S will evoke the same R in future. On the other hand, if R leads to an undesirable or unpleasant outcome, R will tend to decrease in frequency, weakening the S-R association.

But, as you also read in Chapter 1, Edward Tolman argued that the S-R framework was too limiting; Tolman believed that animals make responses because they (in some sense) understand the consequences that will follow actions. According to Tolman, animals make response R to obtain outcome O, learning an R-O association. Various studies have provided evidence that both S-R and R-O learning occur, but they may be localized in different parts of the brain (more on that in the Brain Substrates section later in this chapter). For now, we'll formalize operant conditioning as a three-way association:

Stimulus S → Response R → Outcome O

In the case of a puzzle box, S is the box, R is the sequence of movements needed to open the door, and O is escape. The S-R association is strengthened when R is followed by a desirable outcome O.

Classical versus Operant Conditioning

A few decades after Thorndike published his original account of operant conditioning, B. F. Skinner read it, along with Pavlov's work on classical conditioning, and concluded that these two types of learning were fundamentally different (Skinner, 1938). In classical conditioning, organisms experience an outcome (the unconditioned stimulus, or US) whether or not they have learned the conditioned response (CR). In operant conditioning, by contrast, the outcome O is wholly dependent on whether the organism performs the response R.

For example, in classical conditioning of the eyeblink response, a rabbit may hear a tone (the conditioned stimulus, or CS) that is reliably followed by an airpuff US, and the rabbit may learn to make an eyeblink CR to the tone. The airpuff follows the tone whether or not the CR occurs—so this paradigm is classical conditioning. By contrast, a cat placed in a puzzle box (S) must learn to make a series of responses (R) in order to escape and obtain food (O). If the responses R are not made, the outcome O doesn't occur. Therefore, this paradigm is operant conditioning. Whenever you have to decide whether a paradigm is operant or classical, focus on the outcome. If the outcome occurs regardless of responding, then the paradigm is classical; if it is contingent on a response, then the paradigm is operant.

Differences aside, operant and classical conditioning share many characteristics, including a negatively accelerated learning curve: Figure 5.1 shows that the time to escape from a puzzle box decreases rapidly in the first few trials and then levels off; similar learning curves occur in classical conditioning (as you saw back in Figure 4.7). Both operant and classical conditioning also show extinction: a tendency for learned responses to extinguish if no longer paired with an outcome. Researchers who want to investigate a particular phenomenon such as extinction or latent inhibition are generally free to use either classical or operant conditioning, depending on which is more convenient and what specific hypothesis they are testing.

Test Your Knowledge

Is It Classical or Operant?

In classical conditioning, the outcome (US) follows the stimulus (CS) whether or not a learned response (CR) is made. In operant conditioning, the outcome (O) only follows the stimulus (S) if a particular response (R) is made. Analyze the following scenarios to check whether you understand the difference. (Answers appear in the Answers section in the back of the book.)

1. Since retiring, Jim spends a lot of time sitting on his back porch, watching the birds and whistling. One day, he scatters crumbs, and birds come and eat them. The next day, he sits and whistles and strews crumbs, and the birds return. After a few days, as soon as Jim sits outside and starts whistling, the birds arrive.

2. Shevonne's dog Snoopy is afraid of thunder. Snoopy has learned that lightning always precedes thunder, so whenever Snoopy sees lightning, he runs and hides under the bed.

3. Michael takes a new job close to home, and now he can walk to work. On the first morning, there are clouds in the sky. Michael gets very wet on the way to work. On the next morning, there are also clouds in the sky. Michael brings his umbrella along, just in case. When it rains, he stays dry. After that, Michael carries his umbrella to work anytime the sky looks cloudy.

4. In Carlos's apartment building, whenever someone flushes the toilet, the shower water becomes scalding hot and causes him to flinch. Now whenever he's in the shower and hears the noise of flushing, he automatically flinches, knowing he's about to feel the hot water.

Free-Operant Learning

Chapter 1 introduced B. F. Skinner as the "radical behaviorist." Skinner was attracted to Thorndike's work, with its promise of animal responses that could be measured and evaluated without requiring speculation about the animal's mental states. But Skinner thought he could refine Thorndike's techniques. Thorndike's procedures were characterized by **discrete trial paradigms,** meaning that the experimenter defined the beginning and end of each trial. For example, on one trial with the puzzle box, the experimenter would pick up a cat, put it in the box, shut the door, and record how long it took the cat to escape. He would then pick up the cat and return it to the box to start the next trial. Similarly, when testing rats in a maze, the experimenter would place a rat at the start of the maze and record how long it took the rat to reach the goal. He would then pick up the rat and return it to the start to begin the next trial. Each trial is separate, or discrete, and the experimenter decides when and how often to begin a new trial.

Skinner developed a maze with a return ramp so that the animal could finish one trial in the maze, collect the food, and then run back to the beginning of the maze by itself to start the next trial—and obtain the next piece of food. Part of Skinner's intention was to automate data collection so that the experimenter no longer had to intervene at the end of each trial by returning the rat to the starting position for the next trial. But a side effect was that the animal—not the experimenter—now controlled its own rate of responding, by how quickly or slowly it ran around to start the next trial. Skinner referred to this type of setup as a **free-operant paradigm,** meaning that the animal could operate the apparatus freely, whenever it chose—as distinct from the discrete trials paradigm, where trials were controlled by the experimenter.

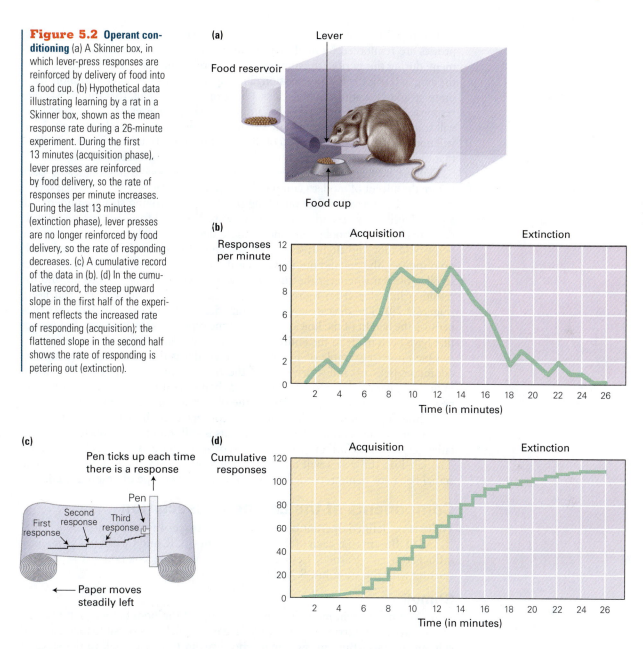

Figure 5.2 Operant conditioning (a) A Skinner box, in which lever-press responses are reinforced by delivery of food into a food cup. (b) Hypothetical data illustrating learning by a rat in a Skinner box, shown as the mean response rate during a 26-minute experiment. During the first 13 minutes (acquisition phase), lever presses are reinforced by food delivery, so the rate of responses per minute increases. During the last 13 minutes (extinction phase), lever presses are no longer reinforced by food delivery, so the rate of responding decreases. (c) A cumulative record of the data in (b). (d) In the cumulative record, the steep upward slope in the first half of the experiment reflects the increased rate of responding (acquisition); the flattened slope in the second half shows the rate of responding is petering out (extinction).

Skinner also devised a cage—now commonly called a **Skinner box**—with a trough in one wall through which food could be delivered automatically (Figure 5.2a). The box contained a mechanism, such as a lever or a pressure-sensitive disk, that controlled the delivery of food. When the animal pressed the lever or tapped the disk, food dropped into the trough. As the animal explored its cage, eventually it would accidentally manipulate the lever or disk and receive the food. Over time, as animals learned the relationship between response R (pressing the lever or disk) and outcome O (obtaining food), they would dramatically increase their rate of responding. The process of providing an outcome for a behavior that increases the probability of that behavior is called **reinforcement.** The opposite process would occur if the outcome were, for example, an electric shock; formally, **punishment** is the process of providing outcomes for a behavior that decrease the probability of that behavior.

Figure 5.2b shows example data from a free-operant experiment in which lever presses are reinforced by food delivery during the first 13 minutes of the experiment; during this period, the number of lever presses increases rapidly with time as the animal learns the R-O association. The experiment can be made a bit more elaborate by adding a stimulus S, such as a light on the cage wall, that signals whether response R will be reinforced: for example, pressing the lever while the light is on will trigger food delivery (outcome O), whereas lever presses while the light is off will not. Finally, minutes 14 to 26 of the experiment illustrated in Figure 5.2b show that the response extinguishes if it no longer produces reinforcement.

Skinner next invented a means of recording responses automatically. Back before the advent of modern computers, mechanical devices such as the one shown in Figure 5.2c recorded data on a long piece of paper rolling steadily underneath a pen. (Until fairly recently, such devices were also used for seismographs and lie detectors.) Skinner hooked up one of these devices to a Skinner box so that the pen would move up slightly each time the animal responded. If the animal made no responses, the pen did not move, thus drawing a long straight line as the paper scrolled by. But whenever the animal made a response, the pen ticked up, and the resulting line sloped up more steeply as responses were made faster and faster (Figure 5.2d). The device shown in Figure 5.2c is called a **cumulative recorder** because the height of the line at any given time represents the number of responses that have been made in the entire experiment (cumulatively) up to that time.

One modern example of a cumulative recorder is the odometer in a car. The odometer ticks off miles driven, and the ticks occur faster if you drive faster. When you park the car for the night and then start it up the next morning, the new mileage is added right on top of the old for a cumulative record.

Although pen-and-paper cumulative recorders aren't in general use anymore, data from operant-conditioning experiments is still sometimes reported as cumulative responses (as in Figure 5.2d) instead of as response rates (as in Figure 5.2b). The label on the y axis will tell you which kind of data you're looking at. The actual behavior being recorded is the same whichever type of graph is used.

Components of the Learned Association

We've now defined operant conditioning as a three-way association between S, R, and O. But, in fact, each of these components (S, R, and O) can independently influence what's learned. Let's consider each of these components separately, starting with the stimulus, S.

Stimuli

At a swim meet, swimmers line up at the edge of the pool before each race. At the sound of the starting whistle, they dive in as quickly as possible to get a good start in the race. But any swimmer who dives in too early (before the starting whistle) may be penalized or even disqualified. The outcome varies, depending on whether the dive occurs before or after the whistle.

Discriminative stimuli are stimuli that signal whether a particular response will lead to a particular outcome. As you read in Chapter 4, a stimulus can be any object or event that the organism can detect. For the swimmers, the starting whistle is a discriminative stimulus signaling that dive responses will now result in a favorable outcome:

S (starting whistle) → R (dive) → O (good start in the race)

In a Skinner box, a light may be used as a discriminative stimulus: lever-press responses while the light is on result in the outcome of food delivery, and lever presses while the light is off do not:

S (light on) → R (press lever) → O (get food)

As the S-R-O notation suggests, the stimulus is the first part of the chain that triggers the response and leads to the outcome. Sometimes, the S-R association is so strong that the stimulus S seems to evoke the learned response R automatically no matter what other options are available. In one striking example, well-trained rats in a familiar maze ran right through a pile of food on their way to the goal box (Stoltz & Lott, 1964). Apparently, the discriminative stimulus of the maze environment S was so strongly associated with the maze-running response R that unexpected food encountered along the way couldn't disrupt the S-R association. Such behavior is sometimes called a *habit slip*. People exhibit habit slips all the time, particularly when drowsy or distracted. Perhaps you've started making a phone call and mistakenly dialed a familiar number (your best friend or your mother) instead of the number you intended to dial, or perhaps you've awoken bright and early one morning and started dressing for class only to realize it's a weekend and you can stay in bed.

Habit slips aren't the only occasions on which organisms sometimes make seemingly irrational responses to discriminative stimuli. In one study, hungry pigeons in a Skinner box were first trained to peck at a lighted disk to obtain access to grain in a feeder. The box also contained a little food cup that was initially empty. But after the pecking response was well learned, the cup was filled with grain. You might expect that the pigeons would now ignore the disk and instead gorge on the free grain. Instead, as Figure 5.3 shows, the pigeons continued to peck vigorously to obtain grain from the feeder. Although they did sometimes eat free grain from the cup, they got most of their food by pecking for it (Neuringer, 1969). Rats that have been trained to press a lever to obtain food show a similar behavior: they will often continue to work to obtain food in preference to eating identical food from a freely available source (Neuringer, 1969; Stephens, Metze, & Craig, 1975). This behavior has been nicknamed the *Protestant ethic effect* because it echoes the religious precept that rewards should be earned and that hard workers are morally superior to freeloaders.

Children, too, show the Protestant ethic effect. In one study, children sat at one end of a large box with a lever that they could press to obtain marbles; they were instructed to obtain as many marbles as possible because the marbles could be exchanged for a toy later. After the children obtained five marbles this way, the experimenter seated them at the other end of the box, where marbles occasionally dropped into a tray without requiring any lever pressing. The children were then allowed to choose where to sit. Most of the children spent the majority of their time sitting in front of the lever and "working" for marbles rather than sitting at the other end of the box and simply collecting the marbles as they appeared (Singh, 1970). Just like habit slips, the Protestant ethic effect shows how strongly discriminative stimuli can evoke the associated responses, overruling other possible behaviors.

Responses

In operant conditioning, the organism learns to make a specific response to achieve (or avoid) a particular outcome. A response is defined not by a particular pattern of motor actions, however, but by the outcome it produces. For example, a rat in a Skinner box may receive access to food when it presses a lever:

S (lever in box) → R (press lever) → O (get food)

As long as the lever is pressed, the food arrives—whether the rat presses the lever with its left front paw, its right front paw, or even its nose—anything that depresses the lever enough to trigger the food delivery device. In another example,

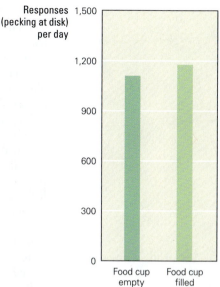

Figure 5.3 **The Protestant ethic effect** Pigeons were first trained to peck at a lighted disk; pecking responses were reinforced with access to grain in a feeder. During training, there was also an empty food cup in the chamber. Later, the cup was filled with grain. Despite the presence of freely available food in the cup, pigeons continued to peck just as vigorously to obtain grain from the feeder.

[Adapted from Neuringer, 1969.]

Karl Lashley trained rats to run through shallow water in a maze, making a correct series of turns to reach the goal; later, he raised the water level so that the animals had to swim. The rats continued to navigate to the goal, even though swimming involved a new set of motor responses that the rats had never executed in this environment (Lashley, 1924). Similarly, Annie's parents may reinforce neatness in their older daughter, Becky, by providing an allowance if Becky cleans her room; the precise sequence of movements by which Becky accomplishes this are unimportant as long as the clothes come off the floor and the toys are put away.

But how do Becky and the animals learn that their responses lead to particular outcomes in the first place? As an extreme case, consider Priscilla, the Fastidious Pig. If it took Thorndike's cats several hours to stumble across the response that opened a puzzle box door, one can only imagine how long it might have taken Priscilla to accidentally run a vacuum cleaner and discover that her trainers would reinforce this behavior.

As you may have guessed, researchers and animal trainers who want to elicit complex behaviors rarely rely on accidents. Instead, they use a process called **shaping,** in which successive approximations to the desired response are reinforced. For example, when a rat is first placed in a Skinner box, it may perform any of its natural behaviors: grooming, exploring, or just sitting quietly. When the rat happens to wander near the food tray, the experimenter drops in a piece of food. The rat eats the food and starts to learn an association between the tray and food. After a few such trials, the rat starts spending all its time near the food tray. The experimenter then changes the rules so that being near the food tray isn't enough: now, the rat must also be near the lever before food is dropped. Soon, the rat learns to loiter in the vicinity of the lever. Once the rat has learned this, the rules change again: food is dropped only if the animal is actually touching the lever, then only if the animal is rearing up and touching the lever, then only if the animal is pressing down on the lever. Gradually, by a series of successive approximations, the desired response is learned: the rat presses the lever to obtain food.

If you think this sounds like a difficult and time-consuming process, you're right. Shaping requires considerable skill on the part of the experimenter, who must decide how fast to proceed, how hard to make each new stage, and even whether to back up a few steps if the animal appears to be getting confused. Some researchers have proposed standardized methods and criteria that can help optimize shaping techniques (e.g., Galbicka, 1994). Still, the difficulties of shaping are one reason that people often pay professional animal trainers to housebreak puppies.

Annie's parents use a similar shaping procedure when first introducing the potty seat. When they think Annie might be ready to use the potty seat, they put her on it; if she does use the potty seat successfully, they reinforce this behavior with praise. Gradually, through a series of progressive approximations, Annie learns to approach the potty and perform the response on her own.

The utility of shaping in humans is not limited to toilet training. Kindergarten teachers may use shaping to teach handwriting: children receive reinforcement (food treats, gold stars, or verbal praise) first for scribbling with crayons, then for producing lines that approximate letters, then for drawing recognizable letters, and so on. Physical therapists use shaping to help patients recover the use of limbs—for example, requiring a patient first to open and close the hands, then progressively working up to the fine motor control needed to grasp and use a spoon. Shaping has even been used in speech therapy for children with autism: therapists first reinforce any vocalizations, then reinforce only vocalizations that sound like words, and eventually reinforce actual word production (Lovaas, 1987). Shaping is also used to train service animals, including guide dogs for the blind and sniffer dogs that detect explosives or contraband at airports and border crossings (see "Learning and

Memory in Everyday Life" below, for more on how sniffer dogs are trained).

A related technique is **chaining,** in which organisms are gradually trained to execute complicated sequences of discrete responses. Skinner once trained a rat to pull a string that released a marble, then to pick up the marble with its fore-paws, carry it over to a tube, and drop the marble inside the tube (Skinner, 1938). Skinner couldn't have trained such a complex sequence of responses all at once. Instead, he added "links" to the chain of learned responses one at a time: he first trained the rat to pull the string, then trained it to pull the string and pick up the marble, and so on. Sometimes, it is more effective to train the steps in reverse order, in a process called *backward chaining*: first train the rat to drop the marble in the tube, then train the rat to carry the marble to the tube and drop it in, and so on. At each stage, the rat must perform a progressively longer sequence of responses to gain its food.

Chaining is a useful technique for training humans, too. Workers learning to manufacture items are often taught the process one step at a time (Walls, Zane, & Ellis, 1981), trainee pilots may master landing sequences by practicing pro-gressively longer sequences on a flight simulator (Wightman & Sistrunk, 1987), and budding pianists may learn keyboard techniques starting with one or two fingers, then one hand, and finally both hands (Ash & Holding, 1990).

Twiggy is a squirrel who water-skis behind a miniature remote-controlled speedboat at a water park in Florida. How do you think she was trained to do this trick?

AP/Wide World Photos

LEARNING AND MEMORY IN EVERYDAY LIFE

Bomb-Detecting Dogs

If you've traveled by air in the last few years, then your luggage has probably been inspected by specially trained sniffer dogs, now commonly used at air-ports and border crossings to help authori-ties detect smuggled drugs, explosives, and other illegal substances. Rescue workers also use trained dogs at disaster sites to help locate human remains or trapped survivors. In airports, the sniffer dogs can search baggage in a fraction of the time it would take a human, without requiring any high-tech machinery. And the dogs aren't only fast, they're sensitive: they can detect faint odors even if the target substance is sealed inside plastic or smeared with chocolate to disguise the scent.

So how are sniffer dogs taught their jobs? By the basic principles of operant conditioning. Training usually starts with positive reinforcement, in which a puppy learns to fetch a toy to obtain a reward such as playtime with the trainer, which

most dogs find highly enjoyable. Then the toy is doused with the scent of explo-sives or drugs—whatever the dog will be trained to detect. Each time the dog retrieves the toy and gets a rewarding bout of playtime, the association between odor, retrieval, and reward is strength-ened. As training continues, the dog may be required to sniff out other objects doused with the same odor so that the dog learns to retrieve any object with the target scent. Still later, a verbal command may be added ("Go find!") to indicate that the dog is to begin searching. At this point, the verbal command acts as a discrimina-tive stimulus:

S ("Go find!") → R (find an object with target scent) → O (playtime)

As training continues, a new response may be shaped so that instead of retriev-ing the scented object, the dog simply sits when the odor is detected. This allows the dog to discreetly signal to the handler,

who can then take appropriate action without unnecessarily alerting passersby.

The exact number of sniffer dogs cur-rently in use at U.S. airports and the exact fashion in which they are deployed is considered sensitive information, but a December 2009 report from CNN.com esti-mated that about 700 bomb-sniffing dogs were employed at U.S. airports at that time (Conder & Finnstrom, 2009), and the 2011 budget of the Department of Homeland Security requested support for 275 addi-tional teams to be distributed among 94 airports. The dogs' record isn't perfect: now and then the news media report that an airport has been shut down for several hours after a false alarm by a sniffer dog or that sniffer dogs failed to distinguish the scents of explosive materials in a series of planned tests. On the other hand, advocates believe that the dogs provide an effective and cost-efficient layer of security in the screening process.

Reinforcers

So far we've discussed outcomes fairly loosely, but now let's get to a formal definition of the two kinds of outcome that can occur in operant conditioning: reinforcers and punishers. A **reinforcer** is a consequence of behavior that leads to increased likelihood of that behavior in the future. For example, food is a reinforcer to a hungry animal, and the animal will repeat behaviors that result in access to food. Food, water, sleep, the need to maintain a comfortable temperature, and sex are all examples of **primary reinforcers**, meaning that organisms have innate drives to obtain these things and therefore to repeat behaviors that provide access to these things. Psychologist Clark Hull's **drive reduction theory** proposed that all learning reflects the innate, biological need to reduce these drives by obtaining primary reinforcers (Hull, 1943, 1952). The motivation to obtain primary reinforcers was a key variable in Hull's equations with which, as you read in Chapter 1, he hoped to explain all learning.

One complication is that primary reinforcers are not always reinforcing. Thirsty animals will work to obtain access to water, a primary reinforcer; but once they've drunk to satiation, further water is not reinforcing. In addition, all primary reinforcers are not created equal. Hungry animals will work to obtain food, but they will work even harder for food they like. For example, rats will run a maze faster for bread and milk (which they find especially tasty) than for sunflower seeds, even though the seeds satiate hunger just as effectively (Simmons, 1924). Similarly, human infants will suck an artificial nipple more vigorously for sweetened water than for plain water, even though both liquids reduce thirst equally (Kobre & Lipsitt, 1972).

In addition to primary reinforcers, learning can also be driven by **secondary reinforcers**, which are reinforcers that initially have no intrinsic value but that have been paired with (or predict the arrival of) primary reinforcers (Shahan, 2010). The best example of a secondary reinforcer is money. Money itself has no biologically reinforcing properties, but it can be exchanged for any number of primary reinforcers, including food, shelter, and even sex (millionaires tend to attract potential mates much more easily than paupers do). People may work for food only so long as they are hungry, but they will work indefinitely for secondary reinforcers; as Donald Trump and Bill Gates demonstrate, you can never have too much money. For a student, grades can function as secondary reinforcers: an A won't feed you if you're hungry or warm you if you're cold, but good grades can (eventually) be exchanged for a degree, which in turn can be exchanged for a good job, resulting in money, which in turn can be exchanged for primary reinforcers.

Secondary reinforcement is often used in prisons, psychiatric hospitals, and other institutions where the staff have to motivate inmates to behave well and to perform chores such as making beds or taking medications. Each desired behavior is reinforced with a token, and tokens can then be exchanged for privileges (say, access to the telephone or group activities). Such arrangements are called *token economies* since the tokens function in the same way as money does in the outside world (Hackenberg, 2009). Token economies have also been used with some success to modify behavior in children with intellectual disability or with autism (Matson & Boisjoli, 2009); even nonverbal children may be able to learn that certain responses result in acquisition of tokens, which in turn can be exchanged for candy or toys.

Animals, too, will work for secondary reinforcers. For example, trainers can use secondary reinforcement to teach dolphins to do tricks. The trainer first pairs a whistle sound with food reinforcement until the dolphin has learned an association between whistle and food; at this point, the whistle has become a secondary reinforcer, and it can be used to maintain the behavior

African pouched rats have been trained to sniff out buried land mines left over from the civil war in coastal Mozambique. Guided by little harnesses, the rats scamper around the minefield without detonating the mines and give a decisive scratch with both forepaws when they smell an explosive. They are trained by food reinforcement (pieces of banana) paired with a clicker, but eventually they work for clicker reinforcement alone.

Reuters/Howard Burditt/Landov

(Pryor, Haag, & O'Reilly, 1969). Horse trainers often use a similar technique, pairing a clicking noise with oats and then eventually using the clicking noise alone (Skinner, 1951). In both cases, as long as the secondary reinforcer is occasionally followed by food, the behavior is maintained.

Secondary reinforcers are particularly useful in animal training because the animal trainer can deliver clicker reinforcement immediately without waiting till the trick is finished; the more quickly the response is followed by reinforcement, the more effective the reinforcement is. Another benefit of secondary reinforcers is that, although animals will not work for food unless they're hungry, they—like money-seeking humans—may continue to work indefinitely for secondary reinforcers.

The standard explanation of secondary reinforcement is that, by virtue of being paired with a primary reinforcer (such as food), secondary reinforcers (such as the clicker) became reinforcers themselves, which the organism will work to obtain. Some evidence supports this view. However, other research suggests that animals aren't "fooled" into thinking that the secondary reinforcers are worth working to obtain; rather, the secondary reinforcers provide informational feedback or "signposts" that behavior is on the right track for obtaining the primary reinforcer: "Keep executing this response, and you'll eventually get food" (Shahan, 2010). This is similar to the behavior of a prison inmate who completes chores not because he is particularly motivated to obtain tokens per se, but because he knows that the acquisition of tokens is a way to obtain things that he does like.

The story doesn't end with primary and secondary reinforcers. As you'll read below, later experiments showed that the definition of reinforcer must even be extended to include the opportunity to engage in various activities: for example, when Becky's parents tell her, "You can watch TV after you've finished your homework," the opportunity to watch TV becomes a reinforcer for the behavior of completing homework.

Although many things can function as reinforcers, the identity of the reinforcer does matter. The organism learns that response R results not just in any random outcome but in a particular outcome O. A switch in the outcome may produce a change in responding. For example, hungry deer will eat food pellets strongly flavored with tannin, a bitter taste that they normally dislike, but deer that first eat from a bowl of weakly flavored pellets and are then switched to a bowl with the strongly flavored pellets eat less from the second bowl than deer that had been given the strongly flavored pellets all along (Bergvall, Rautio, Luotola, & Leimar, 2007). Similarly, while rats can be trained to make lever-press responses to obtain either food pellets or water sweetened with sucrose, they tend to prefer the latter. If the sweetened water is used as the reinforcer during the first half of each training session and food pellets as the reinforcer during the second half of each session, rats typically make many more responses during the first half of the session (Weatherly, Plumm, Smith, & Roberts, 2002). These phenomena are examples of *negative contrast*: organisms given a less preferred reinforcer in place of an expected and preferred reinforcer will respond less strongly for the less preferred reinforcer than if they had been given that less preferred reinforcer all along (Flaherty, 1982).

Negative contrast can be observed in humans, too. In one classic study, infants would suck a nipple providing either plain water or sweetened water, but the sweetened water (Figure 5.4, dark green line) elicited a higher rate of responding than plain water (light green line). Thus, sweetened water was a preferred reinforcer. If infants were started on sweetened water for the first session, then switched to plain water in session 2, the sucking response plummeted (red line)—so that

Figure 5.4 The negative contrast effect A normally acceptable reinforcer elicits less responding if a preferred reinforcer is expected: human infants will suck at a higher rate for sucrose-sweetened water (dark green) than for plain water (light green), indicating that sweetened water is a preferred reinforcer. But infants who receive sweetened water in session 1 and are then switched to plain water in session 2 (red line) will suck less vigorously in session 2 than the infants who received plain water all along. [Data from Kobre and Lipsitt, 1972.]

those infants sucked less plain water in session 2 than the infants who received plain water all along (Kobre & Lipsitt, 1972). Similar negative contrast effects can be observed in children who go trick or treating expecting candy and instead get pennies (which they would usually appreciate) and in game-show contestants who hope to win the $1 million grand prize and instead dejectedly settle for a consolation prize such as a new car or a trip to Hawaii.

Punishers

As noted earlier, reinforcers are not the only kind of outcome. There are also **punishers:** consequences of a behavior that lead to decreased likelihood of that behavior in the future. Common punishers for animals include pain, loud noises, and exposure to predators (or even the scent of predators). Common punishers for humans are monetary fines, social disapproval, and jail time. A rat will learn to stop pressing a lever if it receives an electric shock for doing so; Becky will learn to stop teasing her younger sister, Annie, if the teasing is always punished by parental scolding.

On the basis of a few early experiments, both Thorndike (1932) and Skinner (1938, 1953) concluded that punishment was not nearly as effective as reinforcement at controlling behavior. Modern researchers generally disagree, finding that punishment—if applied correctly—can be very effective indeed (see Staddon, 1995, for a review). The problem is that there are several factors that determine how effective the punishment will be. We describe four of the most important factors here.

1. Discriminative stimuli for punishment can encourage cheating. Remember how discriminative stimuli can signal to an organism whether an operant response will be reinforced? Discriminative stimuli can also signal whether a response will be punished. For a speeding driver, the sight of a police car is a discriminative stimulus for punishment: speeding in the presence of this stimulus will probably be punished. But speeding in the absence of a police car will probably not be punished. In this case, punishment doesn't train the driver not to speed—it only teaches him to suppress speeding in the presence of police cars. When no police car is visible, speeding may resume. In effect, the driver has learned to cheat—speeding only when the discriminative stimulus for punishment is absent. Similarly, the dominant male in a group of chimpanzees may punish females for mating with any other males—but when his back is turned, the females often sneak off into the bushes with lower-ranking males. And rats that have been trained to eat no more than four pellets at a time will happily eat all the food in sight if no human is watching (Davis, 1989).

2. Concurrent reinforcement can undermine the punishment. The effects of punishment can be counteracted if reinforcement occurs along with the punishment. Suppose a rat first learns to press a lever for food but later learns that lever presses are punished by shock. Unless the rat has another way to obtain food, it is likely to keep pressing the lever to obtain food reinforcement in spite of the punishing effects of shock. Similarly, a child who is reprimanded for talking in class will suppress this behavior much less if the behavior is simultaneously reinforced by approval from classmates. And although a speeding driver risks a hefty ticket, the effects of this punisher may be counteracted by the reinforcing fun of driving fast.

3. Punishment leads to more variable behavior. According to the law of effect, reinforcement of a particular response R increases the probability that the same response R will occur in the future, whereas punishment of R decreases the probability that R will occur in the future. But this does not tell us what response will occur instead of R. In fact, punishment tends to produce variation in behavior as the organism explores other possible responses. That's okay if the primary goal is simply to eliminate an undesired response (such as training a child not to go near a hot stove). But it's not a particularly good way to train desired behaviors. If the goal of conditioning is to shape behavior in a predetermined way, then reinforcing the desired response generally produces much faster learning than simply punishing alternate, undesired responses.

4. Initial intensity matters. Punishment is most effective if a strong punisher is used from the outset. In one study, rats received a shock as they ran through a maze to the goal box (Brown, 1969). The shock was initially delivered at the lowest intensities (1 or 2 volts) and had little effect on behavior. Gradually, across several days, shock intensity increased to 40 volts. Behavior was essentially unaffected, even though naive rats given a 40-volt shock would stop running immediately. Apparently, early weak shocks made rats insensitive to later, stronger ones. The effectiveness of the strong shock was completely undermined by starting weak and working up from there.

Unfortunately, the principle of intense punishment for a first offense often conflicts with our sense of what is appropriate and fair. Instead, humans have a tendency to start with a mild punisher and work up to more intense punishments for repeated offenses. A child who misbehaves in class may first receive a warning, then a scolding, then detention, then expulsion. The expulsion, when it comes, may be much less effective at deterring future misbehavior because of the prior, milder punishments. Similarly, a speeding driver may not be deterred much by a hefty $500 ticket if he is already accustomed to paying lesser fines. In each case, the prior weak punishers may undermine the effectiveness of the severe punisher when it finally comes. (See "Learning and Memory in Everyday Life" below for more discussion of the problems with punishment.)

▶ **LEARNING AND MEMORY IN EVERYDAY LIFE**

The Problem with Punishment

In the United States, 94% of parents of toddlers report that they use spanking or other forms of physical punishment to discourage unwanted behaviors (Kazdin & Benjet, 2003). There is no question that physical punishment is an effective technique for reducing the frequency of an unwanted response. Spanking is a form of punishment that even a very young child can understand, and it can effectively modify behavior.

But physical punishment is controversial. Many people believe that hitting a child is never justifiable. Some studies have suggested that children who are spanked can develop emotional problems, including aggression and stress (Gershoff, 2002), although other studies have found that occasional mild spanking does not cause any lasting harm (Baumrind, 2002; Larzelere, 2000).

Parents who want to avoid spanking have other options. Punishment does not have to cause physical pain to be effective. Scolding is a form of punishment that does not cause physical harm; other methods are time-out, grounding, and withholding of allowance.

But there is still the problem that punishment is hard to apply effectively. Let's take a hypothetical example. Shawn has two busy working parents, and he has to compete with his older siblings for the parents' attention. When Shawn is well behaved, his siblings tend to get most of the parental attention, but when Shawn breaks china, fights with his brothers, or causes trouble at school, the parental spotlight shines on him. Although they may think they are punishing Shawn, his parents are actually reinforcing his bad behavior by giving him attention when he misbehaves.

What's to be done? For one thing, Shawn's parents should punish unwanted behavior with a minimum of fuss so that the offender gets less attention—and less reinforcement—for it. They can also reduce unwanted behavior by *differential reinforcement of alternative behaviors*, particularly behaviors that are incompatible with the undesired ones. If the child has a choice between performing a behavior that will result in reinforcement and performing one that will result in punishment, the reinforced behavior should win out. This means that Shawn's parents have to commit the extra time and effort to pay more attention to their youngest child, not just punishing him when he's bad but rewarding him when he's good. The payoff may be a well-behaved child and a happier family while avoiding many of the problems of punishment.

Putting It All Together: Building the S-R-O Association

Now that you've learned about stimulus, response, and outcome in some detail, let's explore the ways they can be arranged. An experimenter can vary several factors: the temporal spacing between S and R and O, whether the outcome is added or subtracted following the response, and even the regularity with which the outcome follows the response. The rules determining when outcomes are delivered in an experiment are called **reinforcement schedules.**

Timing Affects Learning

In most of the operant-conditioning examples presented so far, the outcome (reinforcer or punisher) has immediately followed the response. For example, as soon as the rat presses a lever, food drops into the Skinner box; as soon as a dolphin executes a trick, the trainer provides whistle reinforcement; as soon as Becky teases her sister, her parents scold her.

Normally, immediate outcomes produce the fastest learning. This principle—that operant conditioning is faster if the R-O interval is short—is similar to the principle of temporal contiguity in classical conditioning, which you read about in Chapter 4. In classical conditioning, learning is fastest when the CS and US are closely related in time. Similarly, in operant conditioning, if there is a significant delay between response and reinforcement, learning decreases. If there is no delay, then the odds are good that the most recent behavior will be identified as the response that caused the outcome. But if there is a long delay, it is more likely that other behaviors have crept in during the interval; now these are more likely to be associated with the outcome. To illustrate this idea, Figure 5.5 shows that rats learn a lever-pressing task quickly when the delay between response and food delivery is 0 seconds but are slower to learn the association if the delay is 4 seconds; if the delay is 10 seconds, there seems to be little learning at all (Schlinger & Blakely, 1994).

Temporal contiguity of response and outcome also has an impact on the effectiveness of punishment. Punishers are most effective if there is no delay between response and outcome. A dog is more easily housebroken if punished for each accident on the rug immediately after it occurs; if the dog's owner doesn't find the evidence until a few hours later, the dog will probably not associate the punishment with the earlier accident, and so the punishment will be much less effective.

Human society often employs delayed punishment. Criminals may not come to trial—much less serve their sentence—until months or years after committing the crime. A middle school student who misbehaves in the morning and receives

Figure 5.5 The delay between response and outcome affects speed of learning Rats were trained to lever-press, with food reinforcement delivered immediately or after a short delay. Rats learned more quickly with no delay than with 4-second delays, and rats with 10-second delays hardly ever pressed the lever, as indicated by a nearly flat cumulative response curve.
[Adapted from Schlinger & Blakely, 1994.]

detention after school experiences a delay of several hours between response and outcome. These delays undermine the punishment's effectiveness, and may weaken learning.

The time lag between response and outcome is an important factor in **self-control,** an organism's willingness to forgo a small immediate reward in favor of a larger future reward. For example, suppose a pigeon can choose to peck at one key for a small, immediate food reinforcement or at a second key for a larger food reinforcement that arrives 6 seconds later. Under these circumstances, pigeons almost always choose the small, immediate reinforcement—even though overall, they obtain less food this way (Green, Fischer, Perlow, & Sherman, 1981).

The same trade-off occurs in humans: it is easy to convince a student to study if a test is coming up tomorrow; it is harder if the exam is not for 5 weeks. The delay between response (studying) and reinforcement (good grade) makes the reinforcement less effective in eliciting the response. Similarly, one reason a weight-loss diet is difficult to maintain is that, at each meal, the dieter has to choose between the immediate reward of a dessert and the delayed reward of weight loss.

The ability to wait for a delayed reinforcement differs across individuals and across the age span. When asked, "Would you rather receive $500 today or $1,000 in one year?" adults in their sixties are likely to choose the larger, delayed reward; college students are somewhat less likely to choose the delayed reward; and 12-year-olds almost never choose the delayed reward—preferring immediate gratification (Green, Fry, & Myerson, 1994).

One way of improving an individual's ability to wait for a reward is to induce the person to make a *precommitment*, that is, to make a choice that is difficult to change later. So, for example, a student may be more likely to study early in the semester if he joins a weekly study group, in which case he will experience peer pressure to attend the group and to study a little each week. A dieter may be less likely to cheat on her diet if she first empties the kitchen of chips and ice cream so that when the cravings hit, it will be difficult for her to sneak some junk food. These precommitments do not make it impossible to get the immediate reward (the student can skip a study meeting, and the dieter can drive to the supermarket to buy ice cream), but they make it harder to get the immediate reward, and the individual is consequently more likely to stick by an earlier decision to wait for the later, larger reward.

Outcomes Can Be Added or Subtracted

Toddler Annie learns that, in the presence of the potty seat (S), emptying her bladder (R) will result in the reinforcement of parental praise (O); when S is absent, the same response R will result in the punishment of parental disapproval (O). Note that in both these examples, the outcome is something "added" to Annie's environment:

S (potty present) → R (emptying bladder) → O (praise)

S (potty absent) → R (emptying bladder) → O (disapproval)

For that reason, these paradigms are technically called **positive reinforcement** and **positive punishment.** Note that here the word "positive" doesn't mean "good"; instead it means "added" in the mathematical sense (like a positive number). In positive reinforcement, performance of the response causes the reinforcer to be "added" to the environment; in positive punishment, the response must be withheld, or else the punisher is "added" to the environment.

But there are also learning situations in which the outcome is taken away from or "subtracted" from the environment. In **negative reinforcement,** behavior is encouraged (reinforced) because it causes something to be subtracted from the environment. Thus, if you have a headache, you can take aspirin to make the headache go away:

S (headache) → R (take aspirin) → O (no more headache)

The net result is that you are more likely to take aspirin again next time you have a headache, so this scenario is an example of reinforcement. The outcome, though, is not something added but something subtracted: the headache is taken away. Similarly, a rat can be placed in a chamber with an electrified floor grid from which it receives electric shocks. The rat can escape these shocks by climbing onto a wooden platform. In this case, the response is climbing, and the outcome is escape from shock—shock has been subtracted (negative) from the rat's immediate environment:

S (shock) → R (climb) → O (no more shock)

The net result is that the rat is more likely to climb the platform in the future. In other words, the climbing response has been reinforced. Because the outcome involves a subtraction (shock is taken away), this is an example of negative reinforcement. Negative reinforcement is sometimes called *escape* or *avoidance* training because the response causes an escape from, or avoidance of, something aversive (such as headache or shock).

Just as behavior can be reinforced by taking bad things away, so behavior can be punished by taking good things away. This kind of paradigm is called **negative punishment** because something is subtracted (negative) from the environment, and this subtraction punishes the behavior. Again, as with negative reinforcement, the word "negative" does not mean "bad"; it means "subtraction" in a mathematical sense. (Negative punishment is also sometimes called *omission training* because the response R results in something being "omitted from" the environment.) For example, if Becky displays aggressive behavior toward other children during recess, the teacher may make Becky sit by herself while the other children play:

S (recess) → R (aggressive behavior) → O (loss of playtime)

The net effect is that Becky may be less likely to display aggressive behavior in the future. This kind of negative punishment is sometimes called a "time-out": Becky is punished by time away from a normally reinforcing activity. Time-outs work only if the activity being restricted is something reinforcing. A time-out from an activity the child doesn't like may actually serve to reinforce, rather than reduce, the bad behavior that earned the time-out!

Negative punishment is widely applied in human society: teenagers may be grounded for staying out too late, drivers may have their licenses suspended for speeding, and people who don't pay their credit card bills on time may have their credit rating reduced, decreasing their ability to get credit in the future. In each case, an undesirable behavior is punished by revoking privileges in the hope of decreasing the likelihood that such behavior will occur again in the future.

Table 5.1 summarizes the four types of training. Keep in mind that the terms "reinforcement" and "punishment" describe whether the response increases (reinforcement) or decreases (punishment) as a result of training. The terms "positive" and "negative" describe whether the outcome is added (positive) or taken away (negative).

Laboratory experiments often fit neatly into the grid shown in Table 5.1, but real life is more complicated. Sometimes it is difficult to determine whether an individual is learning because of reinforcement or punishment or both. For

Table 5.1

Operant conditioning paradigms

	Response increases (reinforcement)	Response decreases (punishment)
Outcome is added (positive)	Positive reinforcement *Example: Clean room → get weekly allowance*	Positive punishment *Example: Tease little sister → receive parental scolding*
Outcome is removed (negative)	Negative reinforcement (escape/avoidance training) *Example: Take aspirin → headache goes away*	Negative punishment (omission training) *Example: Fight with other children → time-out from play*

example, when students study for an exam, are they working to obtain a good grade (positive reinforcement) or to avoid flunking (negative reinforcement)? It could be either—or both. Similarly, a child who misbehaves may receive both a scolding (positive punishment) and a time-out (negative punishment), and both considerations may motivate her to keep bad behavior to a minimum.

Test Your Knowledge

Reinforcement vs. Punishment

It's easy to confuse the ideas of negative reinforcement, positive punishment, and so on, since we often use the words "positive" and "negative" to mean "good" and "bad." Don't fall into this trap! In operant conditioning, "positive" and "negative" mean "added" and "subtracted," regardless of whether this addition or subtraction is pleasant or unpleasant.

You can determine what kind of paradigm you're dealing with by asking yourself whether the outcome is added to (positive) or subtracted from (negative) the environment and whether the outcome causes responding to increase (reinforcement) or decrease (punishment).

Try your hand at the following scenarios, and see if you can tell whether each is an example of positive reinforcement, negative reinforcement, positive punishment, or negative punishment. For each scenario, ask yourself: (a) Who does the learning? (b) What is the stimulus? (c) What is the response? (d) What is the outcome? (e) Is the outcome something added or taken away? (f) Does the response increase or decrease as a result of learning? (Answers appear in the Answers section in the back of the book.)

1. At the grocery store, 2-year-old Lucy sees candy and wants it. Her mother says no, and Lucy starts to cry. The situation quickly escalates into a full-blown temper tantrum. Eventually, Lucy's mother relents and buys Lucy some candy. The next time they go shopping, Lucy sees candy and immediately throws another tantrum. This time, she obtains the candy quickly.

2. An interesting aspect of conditioning is that sometimes more than one person is doing the learning. Scenario 1 is presented from Lucy's point of view. But consider the same story from the mother's point of view: Susan takes her toddler on

a shopping trip. The child sees candy, wants it, and throws a tantrum. Overtired and in a rush, Susan gives the child some candy, and the tantrum stops. On the next trip, as soon as the child starts a preliminary wail, Susan quickly hands over some candy to stop the screaming.

3. Shevonne installs an electric fence system around the perimeter of her yard and gives her dog Snoopy a collar that makes a high-pitched noise whenever he gets too close to the boundary. The first time Snoopy strays out of bounds, the noise plays and distresses him. Soon, Snoopy learns to avoid the noise by staying inside the yard.

4. Miguel is a wide receiver on a college football team. During a close game, an opposing player tackles him roughly, and Miguel starts a fistfight in retaliation. Considering this behavior unacceptable, the coach revokes Miguel's playing privileges for a week. When allowed to rejoin the team, Miguel is again tackled roughly. This time, he reacts by shouting at the opposing player and protesting to the referee—but stops short of starting another fistfight.

Reinforcement Need Not Follow Every Response

In addition to controlling whether a response results in reinforcement or punishment being added or taken away and whether the outcome ensues immediately or after a delay, an experimenter can also control the frequency with which these outcomes are delivered. So far, almost all of the examples in this chapter have been ones in which the outcome reliably follows the response. For example, whenever the rat presses a lever, it gets food; whenever Annie uses the potty, she gets praise; and so on. These examples illustrate **continuous reinforcement schedules,** meaning that each response R is always followed by the outcome O.

But in some situations, a response must be repeated multiple times before resulting in the expected outcome. For example, Becky has to clean her room 7 days in a row to obtain her weekly allowance (seven responses for one reinforcement), and a baseball player is allowed to swing and miss three times before he strikes out (three responses for one punishment). In the laboratory, an experimenter can devise a schedule defining exactly when outcomes are delivered. Patterns in which an outcome follows a response less than 100 percent of the time are called **partial reinforcement schedules** (or *intermittent reinforcement schedules*). The term "reinforcement schedule" is used for simplicity because these schedules can be applied either to reinforcement (Becky's weekly allowance) or to punishment (three strikes and you're out). There are four basic types of partial reinforcement schedule.

1. Fixed-ratio (FR) schedule. In an FR schedule, some fixed number of responses must be made before a reinforcer is delivered. For example, if a rat must press a lever five times to obtain one food pellet, the ratio of responses to reinforcers is 5:1; this is often called an FR 5 schedule. Using this same notation, continuous reinforcement can be expressed as an FR 1 schedule: every (one) response results in reinforcement. Ratios can gradually be increased—for example, by starting with an FR 1 schedule and working up through an FR 5 schedule to an FR 50 schedule and so on. In fact, animals can be trained to make several hundred responses for each reinforcement on an FR schedule.

Rats on an FR schedule show a characteristic pattern of steady responding leading up to the reinforcement, followed by a few seconds with no responding. This short break in responding after a reinforcement is called the **postreinforcement pause.** This pattern of responding under an FR schedule is most easily seen using a graph of cumulative responding (the type introduced in

(a) Fixed-ratio (FR) and variable-ratio (VR) schedules

(b) Fixed-interval (FI) and variable-interval (VI) schedules

Figure 5.6

Reinforcement schedules In each figure, data show cumulative responding by a hypothetical rat; arrows indicate food delivery (reinforcement). (a) An FR 5 schedule (reinforcement after every fifth response) produces a pattern of steady responding leading up to each reinforcement, with a short postreinforcement pause (flat line) following each delivery of food. A VR 5 schedule (reinforcement after every fifth response, on average) produces fast and steady responding, with little or no postreinforcement pause—because the next response could produce another reinforcement. (b) An FI 10-sec schedule (reinforcement for the first response after a 10-second interval) produces a scalloped curve. After each postreinforcement pause, the response rate gradually increases until the next reinforcement arrives. A VI 10-sec schedule (reinforcement for the first response after a 10-second interval, on average) produces steady responding, with no postreinforcement pause, as the rat keeps checking to see whether a new reinforcement is available yet.

Figure 5.2c), which is one reason why some researchers continue to display data in this format. Figure 5.6a shows the hypothetical behavior of a rat trained to respond on an FR 5 schedule: steady response rates leading up to each reinforcement, followed by a brief pause before another round of responding begins in order to obtain a new reinforcement.

During the postreinforcement pause, it seems almost as if the animal is pausing to take a breath before its next bout of responding. And in fact, the length of the postreinforcement pause is related to the number of responses required to obtain the next reinforcement: thus, the postreinforcement pause when an animal is on an FR 50 schedule is longer than when the animal is on an FR 5 schedule. In effect, the rat is behaving like a human teenager who does a short chore (say, taking out the trash) the first time his mother asks but procrastinates for hours before starting a really time-consuming chore (mowing the lawn).

Examples of fixed-ratio schedules in human life include factory workers who get paid a flat fee for every 100 pieces they turn out and migrant farmworkers who get paid a fixed amount for every bushel of apples picked. In fact, such workers tend to show behavior similar to that of rats on an FR schedule—steady bursts of responding followed by postreinforcement pauses: the workers complete a batch, take a few minutes for a coffee break, and then start in again. A similar phenomenon occurs in readers, who may complete a chapter or a fixed number of pages before putting the book aside. Novelists often try to combat this "postreinforcement pause" by ending each chapter with an exciting cliffhanger so that readers will keep turning pages to see what happens next.

2. Fixed-interval (FI) schedule. Whereas an FR schedule provides reinforcement after a fixed *number* of responses, an FI schedule reinforces the first response after a fixed *amount of time*. For example, on an FI 10-sec schedule, the rat is reinforced for the first response it makes after an interval of 10 seconds

What kind of learning is going on here?

since the last reinforcement. Importantly, the reinforcement is not automatically obtained after the fixed interval; it merely becomes available to be earned—the organism must still respond in order to actually receive that reinforcement. Once the interval has elapsed, the reinforcement remains available until the response occurs and the reinforcement is obtained. At that point, the clock starts ticking on the next fixed interval until the next reinforcement becomes available.

Under these circumstances, the most efficient strategy on the rat's part would be to wait exactly 10 seconds after each reinforcement, then respond once to obtain the next reinforcement. Earlier responses (before the 10 seconds have elapsed) are wasted effort. However, Figure 5.6b shows how an animal on an FI schedule actually behaves: each reinforcement is followed by a period of few or no responses, but the animal's rate of responding gradually increases as the end of the interval nears. Presumably, animals (including humans) cannot judge time intervals perfectly, so they estimate as well as they can how much time has passed and err a little on the side of wishful thinking by responding too soon. The result is a characteristic "scalloped" cumulative response curve, as illustrated in Figure 5.6b.

An example of fixed-interval reinforcement is seen when you bake a cake without a timer. You know from the recipe that the cake needs to bake for 30 minutes. Because you don't have a timer, you have to estimate when the cake's done—you don't want it to burn. There is little point in checking after the first 5 or 10 minutes, but it might be worth checking after you estimate that 20 or 25 minutes have passed. And as the elapsed time gets closer and closer to 30 minutes, you might check more and more frequently, not wanting to leave the cake in too long. In this example, the response is checking on the cake, the reinforcement is taking out a perfectly baked cake, and only the response that occurs immediately after the end of the baking interval is reinforced—the rest are "wasted" responses.

3. Variable-ratio (VR) schedule. A VR schedule provides reinforcement after a certain average number of responses. For example, whereas an FR 5 schedule produces reinforcement after every fifth response, a VR 5 schedule produces reinforcement after every 5 responses, *on average*. Thus, the responder never knows exactly when a reinforcement is coming. As a result, there is a steady, high rate of responding even immediately after a reinforcement is delivered because the very next response just might result in another reinforcement (Figure 5.6a). Thus, the VR schedule eliminates (or greatly reduces) the postreinforcement pause observed under FR schedules.

A real-life example of a VR schedule could be a slot machine. Even if you know that, on average, the slot machine pays off on every tenth game (in a generous casino), you don't know exactly which games will pay off. Even if you have just won a game, the very next game might be a winner, too, so there is a strong incentive to keep playing.

4. Variable-interval (VI) schedule. Whereas an FI schedule reinforces the first response after a particular time interval, a VI schedule reinforces the first response after an interval that averages a particular length of time. So, for example, a VI 10-sec schedule reinforces the first response after an interval that is 10 seconds *on average*—but the actual interval might be longer or shorter on any particular trial.

In the VI schedule, as in the VR schedule, the responder never knows exactly when the next reinforcement is coming: a response a few seconds after the previous reinforcement just might be reinforced, too. Thus, the response rate of animals under a VI schedule is usually steadier than under an FI schedule since the animals check periodically to see whether reinforcement is available (Figure 5.6b).

An everyday example of the effect of a VI schedule is demonstrated by Tom, a college student whose girlfriend is studying abroad for a semester. She's promised to keep in touch through daily online posts, but sometimes she posts in the morning, sometimes in the evening—and sometimes more than once a day. Tom loves her and wants to read her posts as soon as they arrive, but he also doesn't want to spend 24 hours a day mooning in front of the computer waiting for the next post to come. A sensible compromise is for Tom to check online every few hours. This minimizes the time unread posts will sit waiting for him while leaving him free to go pursue other interests in the meantime. Notice that this is a VI schedule, not a VR schedule, because the rate at which Tom checks online doesn't make the posts appear any faster. Once a new post does appear, it sits there waiting until Tom logs in; his next response is rewarded since he gets to read the note.

Just as VR schedules tend to produce higher rates of responding than FR schedules, so VI schedules tend to produce higher rates of responding than FI schedules. For example, if Tom's girlfriend posts every day at the fixed time of 2 p.m., Tom will tend to check online once every day at about that time; if she posts at variable times, he is likely to check much more often just in case a new post is waiting.

Choice Behavior

In addition to continuous and partial reinforcement schedules, there are also **concurrent reinforcement schedules,** in which the organism can make any of several possible responses, each leading to a different outcome. These allow researchers to examine how organisms choose to divide their time and efforts among different options. For example, suppose a pigeon is placed in a chamber with two keys, key A and key B. Pecking on key A is reinforced on a VI 2-min schedule, and pecking on key B is reinforced on a VI 1-min schedule. In other words, the pigeon can obtain food by pecking on A at 2-minute intervals or by pecking on B at 1-minute intervals. What should the pigeon do?

Within a 2-minute interval, the pigeon can get two food pellets for pecking on B but only one for pecking on A. So, you might think that the pigeon would concentrate on B and ignore A. On the other hand, if the experiment goes on for longer than 2 minutes, there is a food pellet waiting to be delivered as soon as the pigeon pecks at A—and this pellet will never be obtained if the pigeon ignores A completely. Therefore, the optimal behavior is some strategy that allows the pigeon to maximize the amount of food it can get from both keys, probably by spending the most effort on B but occasionally switching over to A just to check. In fact, this is more or less what animals do. This behavior is analogous to channel surfing in humans: confronted with several possibly entertaining television programs, a typical response is to watch the preferred program but switch over to other choices during the commercials just in case something interesting is going on.

Variable-Interval Schedules and the Matching Law

Let's look more closely at the pigeon given a choice between key A on a VI 2-min schedule and key B on a VI 1-min schedule. Can we be more precise about the pigeon's allocation of time? One way to discover the pigeon's strategy is simply to let the pigeon peck away for a few minutes, according to its own preference, and then calculate the proportion of time it spent on key A versus key B. In fact, such calculations show that a pigeon will spend about 33% of its time pecking on A and about 67% of its time pecking on B—or about twice the time on B as on A (Herrnstein, 1961). Note that this ratio is identical to the relative rate of reinforcement on the two keys since B is reinforced twice as often as A.

The **matching law of choice behavior** states that, given two responses that are reinforced on VI schedules, an organism's relative rate of making each response will (approximately) match the relative rate of reinforcement for that response (Herrnstein, 1961):

$$\frac{\text{rate of response A}}{\text{rate of response B}} = \frac{\text{rate of VI reinforcement for A}}{\text{rate of VI reinforcement for B}}$$

Figure 5.7 shows data from one pigeon responding on a range of reinforcement schedules for two keys, A and B (Herrnstein, 1961). The horizontal axis shows the *relative rate of reinforcement* on A. If the relative rate of reinforcement on A is 20%, then the relative rate of reinforcement on B is 80%, and B is reinforced four times as often as A; if the relative rate of reinforcement on A is 50%, then the relative rate of reinforcement on B is also 50%, and so on. The matching law predicts that the rate of responding on A should be approximately equal to the relative rate of reinforcement on A; this behavior would result in the yellow line in Figure 5.7. The pigeon's actual behavior (green line) is quite similar: the rate of pecking on A is approximately equal to the relative rate of reinforcement on A for a whole range of possible VI schedules.

Of course, even within a lab experiment, a rat or pigeon has more options than just pecking one of two keys: it will spend some of its time eating the food it earns, and it can even take a break and spend some of its time grooming, exploring, or sitting quietly. Nevertheless, as Figure 5.7 illustrates, the matching law is a fairly good description of how the animal will allot its time and effort among a set of possible responses.

Behavioral Economics and the Bliss Point

A pigeon confronted with two keys is the simplest possible example of a choice situation. Outside the laboratory, choices are far more complicated. A college student has to divide her allotted studying time among different classes according to how that studying is likely to pay off best, and she has to divide her total time among studying, sleeping, eating, socializing, and so forth. Farmers have to decide how to distribute their acreage between stable crops that will survive rough weather and higher-risk, higher-payoff specialty crops in order to maximize expected profit. A dieter who is allowed a fixed number of calories per day must decide whether to eat several low-calorie meals or splurge on a bowl of ice cream (and then survive on water and lettuce for the rest of the day).

Behavioral economics is the study of how organisms allocate their time and resources among possible options. For example, a worker who makes $3,000 a month after taxes can distribute this income on rent, food, new clothes, savings, and so on. If she lives in a very expensive apartment, there is less money available for fancy food and new clothes; if she rents a less expensive apartment, she has more money to spend on other things. How does she choose?

Figure 5.7 Choice behavior A pigeon is presented with two keys, A and B, each reinforced on a different variable-interval (VI) schedule. The matching law predicts that the rate of responding (pecking) on A versus B should approximately equal the relative rate of reinforcement on A versus B for a whole range of possible reinforcement schedules. The actual behavior of the pigeon closely approximates this prediction. [Adapted from Herrnstein, 1961.]

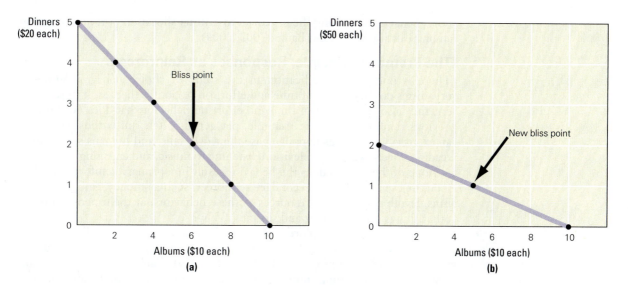

(a)

(b)

Figure 5.8 Behavioral economics (a) A student with $100 income per week may choose to distribute it between downloading new albums ($10 apiece) and eating out ($20 per meal); any point on the line will satisfy the budgetary criteria. The bliss point is the point at which this particular student gets maximum subjective value for his money. (b) The bliss point may shift as conditions change—for example, if the cost of eating out increases to $50.

Economic theory predicts that each consumer will allocate resources in a way that maximizes her "subjective value," or relative satisfaction. (In microeconomics, the word "utility" is used instead of "subjective value.") The value is subjective because it differs from person to person: one individual may find much subjective value in an expensive apartment, but another may find more subjective value in having extra money to buy clothes and food. The particular allocation of resources that provides maximal subjective value to an individual is called the **bliss point** (Allison, 1983; Timberlake, 1980). We determine an individual's bliss point simply by recording what that individual chooses to do. For example, suppose Jamie, a college student, has a part-time job and takes home about $100 a week. Assuming that Jamie has no other expenses, he can spend this money on his hobby of collecting new music (downloading albums at, say, $10 apiece from an online store) or going out to dinner (say, $20 at a local restaurant). Each week, he can spend the full $100 on 10 albums or he can eat out 5 times—or any other combination that adds up to $100.

Figure 5.8a shows Jamie's possible options. So, given these options, what does Jamie actually do? Most weeks, he eats out twice and downloads six albums. This point (shown in Figure 5.8a) is Jamie's bliss point—the distribution of expenditures that (apparently) results in maximum subjective value for this individual: he gets plenty of new music and also gets to eat out frequently. Of course, both the curve and the bliss point can shift if economic conditions change: if the restaurant raises its prices ($50 for dinner), then Jamie may shift to one dinner out and five albums per week—resulting in the new bliss point shown in Figure 5.8b.

Animals show similar patterns of compromise between existing options. For example, a pet cat can distribute its time among eating, drinking, sleeping, grooming, and playing with its favorite toys. The amount of time it spends on each behavior defines that animal's bliss point. An untrained rat in a Skinner box will spend some amount of time grooming, exploring, sitting quietly—and a very small amount of time pressing the lever. However, after the rat learns that lever pressing results in food (and assuming that the animal is hungry), it will begin to spend more of its time on lever pressing (and eating) and proportionately less on other activities, because the subjective value of pressing the lever has been increased. From the behavioral economics perspective, then, operant conditioning is not so much training an organism to execute a specific novel behavior as causing the organism to shift its allocation of time and energy among existing behaviors (Baum, 2002, 2004).

The Premack Principle: Responses as Reinforcers

There is one final complication in the study of choice behavior: although organisms do spend a lot of time and effort on responses that result in reinforcers, they also spend a lot of time and effort on behavior that does not produce obvious reinforcement. For example, pet gerbils often run enthusiastically in an exercise wheel, dogs happily chase their own tails, and humans spend hours reading novels, watching television, listening to music, and engaging in hobbies. In none of these cases does the behavior result in a primary reinforcer, such as food, or even an obvious secondary reinforcer, such as money. And yet organisms devote considerable resources to these behaviors, at the expense of doing other things such as eating and sleeping. Why?

This question was explored by David Premack, a student of B. F. Skinner (Premack, 1959, 1961, 1962). Premack gave a group of rats free access to drinking water and a running wheel (Premack, 1959). Each rat spent some time drinking and some time running, but on average rats spent more time running than drinking. Then Premack restricted the rats' access to the wheel: they were allowed to run only after they had drunk a certain amount of water. The rats soon learned the R-O association and started drinking water (R) in order to gain access to the wheel (O). Unsurprisingly, the total amount of running decreased because the rats now had to work to obtain access to the wheel. But the total amount of drinking increased because the rats now performed this behavior more often in order to gain access to the wheel. In effect, the activity of running was acting as a reinforcer, and it was increasing the probability of an otherwise infrequent behavior, drinking.

Premack went on to show a similar pattern in human children (Premack, 1959). He put the children in a room that contained a pinball machine and a bowl of candy, and he recorded how much time each child spent playing pinball and eating candy. Some of the children spent more time playing pinball. Premack then restricted access to the pinball machine, allowing these children to play (O) only after they had eaten some candy (R). Candy eating increased, showing that access to the preferred activity (pinball) could reinforce the less preferred activity (candy eating). Conversely, other children who preferred eating candy in the first place would start to play more pinball if access to the candy was made contingent on playing pinball.

Thus, in both rats and children, the opportunity to perform a highly frequent behavior can reinforce a less frequent behavior. This idea came to be known as the **Premack principle.** Examples of the Premack principle abound in human life. For example, left to their own devices, most children will spend more time watching television than doing their homework. Thus, watching television is a preferred activity, and it can be used to reinforce the less preferred activity of homework. The parent restricts television time, making it contingent on homework. As a consequence, the child spends more time doing homework than he would have if television had not been restricted.

A later extension of the Premack principle, the **response deprivation hypothesis,** suggests that the critical variable is not which response is normally more frequent but merely which response has been restricted: by restricting the ability to execute almost any response, you can make the opportunity to perform that response reinforcing (Allison, 1993; Timberlake & Allison, 1974). For example, perhaps you have a chore, such as cleaning your room or doing laundry, that you normally detest. But if access to this activity is restricted, it can become reinforcing. If you have been studying for several hours straight, the idea of "taking a break" to clean your room or do the laundry can begin to look downright attractive. If so, you've experienced the Premack principle at work.

Interim Summary

- In operant conditioning, organisms learn to make responses in order to obtain or avoid outcomes: Stimulus S → Response R → Outcome O.

- An outcome that an organism will work to obtain is called a reinforcer; an outcome that an organism will work to avoid is called a punisher.

- In operant conditioning, the outcome (reinforcement or punishment) occurs only if the organism makes the response. In classical conditioning, by contrast, the unconditioned stimulus (US) occurs whether or not the organism makes a conditioned response (CR).

- The four basic types of operant paradigm are positive reinforcement, negative reinforcement, positive punishment, and negative punishment. The words "positive" and "negative" denote whether the outcome is added or subtracted; "reinforcement" and "punishment" denote whether the response increases or decreases as a result of learning.

- Schedules of reinforcement define whether the outcome O follows every response R, is available after some (fixed or variable) number of responses, or is available only after some (fixed or variable) time interval.

- Behavioral economics is the study of how organisms choose to allocate their time and resources among various responses that result in different outcomes.

- The Premack principle states that the opportunity to perform a highly frequent behavior can reinforce performance of a less frequent behavior. The response deprivation hypothesis states that any behavior can be reinforcing if the opportunity to perform that behavior is restricted.

5.2 Brain Substrates

The previous section defined operant conditioning as learning an association between a stimulus S, response R, and outcome O. In studying such associations, neuroscientists are discovering that the parts of the brain that link stimuli with responses (S-R learning) are different from the parts of the brain that link responses with expected outcomes (R-O) learning. Although many brain areas play a role in these processes, two key areas are the dorsal striatum, which appears to be particularly important for S-R learning, and the orbitofrontal cortex, which appears important for learning about expected outcomes.

The Dorsal Striatum and Stimulus-Response (S-R) Learning

Voluntary motor responses occur when neurons in the motor cortex send messages to motor neurons in the muscles that control movements. The motor cortex receives its primary inputs from cortical areas that process sensory information, such as the visual cortex (V1) and the somatosensory cortex (S1), and also from the frontal cortex. Thus, when you see a book, this visual stimulus is registered by your visual cortex. If you decide to pick up the book, this

Dorsal striatum

Orbitofrontal cortex

Figure 5.9 Some brain substrates of operant conditioning During operant conditioning, the dorsal striatum may help create links between the sensory cortex and the motor cortex so that stimuli can elicit appropriate motor responses (S-R learning). Parts of the frontal cortex, including the orbitofrontal cortex, may play a role in learning that specific responses lead to particular outcomes (R-O learning).

"decision" is made in your frontal cortex, and signals from both the visual cortex and the frontal cortex travel to the motor cortex, which integrates these signals and produces the appropriate instructions, resulting in your picking up the book.

Information from the sensory cortex to the motor cortex can also travel via an indirect route, through the **basal ganglia.** The basal ganglia are a collection of *ganglia* (clusters of neurons) that lie at the base of the forebrain. One part of the basal ganglia is the **dorsal striatum** (Figure 5.9), which can be further subdivided into the *caudate nucleus* and the *putamen*. The dorsal striatum receives highly processed stimulus information from sensory cortical areas and projects to the motor cortex, which produces a behavioral response.

The dorsal striatum plays a critical role in operant conditioning, particularly if discriminative stimuli are involved. Rats with lesions of the dorsal striatum can learn a simple R-O association (e.g., lever-press R to obtain food O) as well as control rats can. But if discriminative stimuli are added (e.g., lever-press R is reinforced only in the presence of a light S), then the lesioned rats are markedly impaired (Featherstone & McDonald, 2004). In humans, too, individuals with damage or disruption to the striatum due to Parkinson's disease or Huntington's disease show deficits in the ability to associate a stimulus with a correct response (Ashby & Waldron, 2000; Robbins, 1996). In short, the dorsal striatum appears necessary for learning S-R associations based on feedback about reinforcement and punishment (McDonald & White, 1994; O'Doherty et al., 2004).

S-R associations that depend on the dorsal striatum tend to be relatively automatic or habitual (Balleine, Daw, & O'Doherty, 2008). Remember the well-trained rats, discussed earlier in this chapter, who would run right through a pile of food on their way to a goal box in the maze? That behavior probably reflects S-R learning in the striatum, making the maze running automatic even when other behaviors (such as pausing to eat) would have resulted in reward. Similarly, the Protestant ethic effect, when children and rats continue making a learned response even if they no longer need to work to obtain a desired outcome, may reflect habitual responding based on S-R associations in the dorsal striatum. In both cases, the actions are based on a history of learning in which those responses resulted in desirable outcomes, but after a long period of training, the responses are performed even though the outcome is no longer contingent on that action.

The Orbitofrontal Cortex and Learning to Predict Outcomes

S-R learning is, of course, only half the picture in operant conditioning. Organisms learn to predict that particular responses R will result in particular outcomes O. For example, you read about the negative contrast effect in the Behavioral Processes section earlier in this chapter: monkeys may shriek in annoyance if their response earns them a less preferred food than the one they expected, and trick-or-treaters may feel cheated if they receive pennies rather than the expected candy. Such results show that organisms don't make responses blindly but make them in anticipation of particular outcomes.

Several brain areas appear to be involved in learning to predict the outcomes of behavior. Among these are parts of the *prefrontal cortex*, including the **orbitofrontal cortex,** which lies at the underside of the front of the brain in primates (Figure 5.9) and appears to contribute to goal-directed behavior by representing predicted outcomes (Schoenbaum, Roesch, Stalnaker, & Takahashi, 2009; Tanaka, Balleine, & O'Doherty, 2008). The orbitofrontal cortex receives inputs conveying the full range of sensory modalities (sight, touch, sound, etc.) and also visceral sensations (including hunger and thirst), allowing this brain area to integrate many types of information; outputs from the orbitofrontal cortex travel to the striatum, where they can help determine which motor responses are executed.

One reason for believing that the orbitofrontal cortex plays a role in predicting the outcome of responses comes from lesion studies. Animals (including people) with orbitofrontal lesions tend to show inflexible or inappropriate responding (Murray, O'Doherty, & Schoenbaum, 2007). For example, monkeys can be taught a discrimination task in which two cues S1 and S2 are presented; choosing S1 produces reward, but choosing S2 produces no reward or even punishment:

S1 → R → reward

S2 → R → no reward

Monkeys with orbitofrontal lesions can learn to respond to S1 and not to respond to S2, indicating that they are quite capable of learning S → R associations (presumably mediated by their intact dorsal striatum and motor cortex). But if the contingencies are then reversed, so that responses to S2 rather than S1 are rewarded, the lesioned monkeys are much slower to adapt their responses than control monkeys (Izquierdo, Suda, & Murray, 2004). Similar reversal impairments occur when the orbitofrontal cortex is damaged in other species, including rats, cats, and humans (Murray et al. 2007). These results suggest that orbitofrontal cortex is important for associating responses with particular outcomes.

A second reason for believing that the orbitofrontal cortex plays a role in predicting outcomes of actions comes from neuronal recordings. Thirsty rats can be trained on a discrimination task in which S1 and S2 are odors, the response R is to poke the nose into a nearby water cup, and the two possible outcomes are a tasty sucrose solution or a bitter quinine solution:

odor 1 → R → (delay) → sucrose (reward)

odor 2 → R → (delay) → quinine (punisher)

Here, a short delay (typically less than a second) is introduced between the response and the outcome, during which period the animal is "expecting" the outcome. During this delay, some neurons in orbitofrontal cortex fire differently, depending on whether a reward or punisher is expected (Schoenbaum, Chiba, & Gallagher, 1998). Figure 5.10a shows an example of the firing patterns of one neuron in the orbitofrontal cortex of a rat learning such a task. This particular neuron fires strongly if the rat has just made a (mistaken) response to odor 2 and is expecting quinine but less strongly if the rat has just made a response to odor 1 and is expecting sucrose. Thus, this neuron appears to be coding expectation of the punisher rather than the reward. If the contingencies are reversed, so that odor 1 now predicts quinine and odor 2 now predicts sucrose, such neurons often alter their responses to reflect the new contingencies (Stalnaker, Franz, Singh, & Schoenbaum, 2007).

There is some evidence that different subareas in the orbitofrontal cortex represent pleasant versus aversive outcomes. Specifically, the medial portion

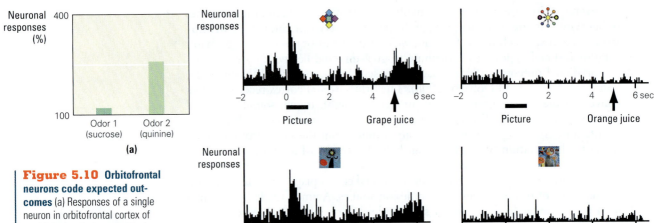

Figure 5.10 Orbitofrontal neurons code expected outcomes (a) Responses of a single neuron in orbitofrontal cortex of a rat learning that responding to odor 1 produces sucrose while responding to odor 2 produces quinine. Responses are shown during the delay between response and outcome. This neuron shows very little increase above baseline (100%) after the rat has responded to odor 1 but a strong increase after the rat has (mistakenly) responded to odor 2. Thus, this neuron appears to code for expectation of quinine. (b) A single neuron in orbitofrontal cortex of a monkey trained that some pictures predict rewarding of a response by grape juice but others predict that the response will be rewarded by orange juice. The figure shows four sample pictures, each presented for 1 second, with juice delivered 4 seconds later. Below each picture is a histogram in which the height of the bars indicates strength of neural responding. This neuron responds strongly while grape-juice-predicting stimuli appear and again when grape juice is delivered, but not while orange-juice-predicting pictures appear or when orange juice is delivered. Thus, this neuron codes not only expectation of reward but expectation of a specific outcome: grape juice.

[(a) Adapted from Schoenbaum et al., 1998, Figure 3a. (b) Adapted from Tremblay & Schultz, 1999, Figure 3b, Courtesy of Wolfram Schultz.]

of the orbitofrontal cortex may process information about reinforcers, and the lateral portion may process information about punishers (Kringelbach & Rolls, 2004). For example, in one study, Dana Small and colleagues used PET to scan the brains of volunteers while they ate pieces of chocolate. After eating each piece, the volunteers gave ratings of how much they liked the chocolate and how much they wanted another piece (using a scale from "I really want another piece" to "Eating more would make me sick"). Volunteers who reported wanting the chocolate had heightened activity in the medial area of the orbitofrontal cortex, but those who reported satiety had heightened activity in the lateral orbitofrontal cortex (Small, Zatorre, Dagher, Evans, & Jones-Gotman, 2001). Remember the Premack principle, in which the reinforcement value of an activity can change, depending on whether access to that activity is restricted? Here, just the opposite occurs: even chocolate can cease to be rewarding if you're forced to consume enough of it.

The responses of orbitofrontal neurons don't only code whether the upcoming outcome is expected to be generally pleasant or generally aversive; some neurons appear to code the actual identity of the expected outcome. Thus, monkeys can be trained with a set of pictures that predict whether the upcoming reward will be grape juice or orange juice. Figure 5.10b shows the responses of a single neuron that became active whenever pictures that predicted grape juice were presented but not when pictures predicting orange juice were presented (Tremblay & Schultz, 1999). This same neuron also fired during the actual delivery of grape juice but not orange juice.

Orbitofrontal cortex neurons may also play a role in helping us select between potential actions based on their expected consequences. When monkeys are trained to choose between two responses that result in different outcomes (say, water vs. Kool-Aid), most individual monkeys have a preference for one beverage over another. Given a choice between licking to obtain water or Kool-Aid, a particular monkey will alter his responses based on the amount of each he will get. If response R1 produces 1 cc of water and response R2 produces 1 cc of Kool-Aid, he may choose to lick to obtain the sugary Kool-Aid. But if R1 produces 6 cc of water, he may choose that option instead. In fact, the likelihood that the monkey will make response R1 depends on the trade-off between his individual preference of beverage and the relative amount of each he would obtain, resulting in choice behavior very much like that of the pigeon of Figure 5.7. Neurons in the monkey's orbitofrontal cortex respond with a strength proportional to the perceived value of each choice (Padoa-Schioppa & Assad, 2006).

Remember college student Jamie, who could spend his weekly income by distributing it among choices such as music purchases and restaurant dinners? Possibly, neurons in Jamie's orbitofrontal cortex were helping him to evaluate the potential outcomes of his actions and to choose between them. When dinners were cheap, certain of these neurons may have responded strongly, indicating that dinners were the preferred choice. But when the cost of dining out rose, the same neurons may have responded more weakly, leading Jamie to prefer the opposite alternative for spending his money.

Mechanisms of Reinforcement Signaling in the Brain

The previous section suggested that neurons in the orbitofrontal cortex code not only the identity of an outcome (e.g., grape juice vs. orange juice) but also whether that outcome is reinforcing or not (e.g., water flavored with sucrose vs. quinine). This distinction is critical: if an outcome is reinforcing, the S-R association should be strengthened, increasing the likelihood that S elicits R in the future; if it is a punisher, the association should be weakened, decreasing the likelihood of R. What signals in the brain determine whether an outcome is a reinforcer or a punisher?

"Wanting" and "Liking" in the Brain

In 1954, James Olds was experimenting with delivering electrical stimulation to the rat brain. He inserted an electrode into an area that researchers now believe to have been the lateral hypothalamus. Olds waited until the rat wandered into one corner of the experimental chamber, and then he applied a brief electrical current. After a few minutes of wandering around the chamber, the rat came back to the same corner, where Olds gave it a second stimulation. The rat caught on quickly and began to hang around that corner of the chamber, apparently hoping for more electrical stimulation (Olds, 1955). Thus, electrical stimulation to this area of the brain seemed to be acting much like a reinforcer: increasing the probability of certain responses (in this case, hanging around the correct location).

Olds was intrigued, to say the least. He rigged a Skinner box so that the rats could press a lever to turn on the electrical stimulation. The rats were soon lever pressing at a furious rate: as many as 700 times an hour (Olds, 1958). If allowed, rats would press the lever continuously for up to 48 hours, until they collapsed from physical exhaustion! Given a choice between electrical stimulation and food, the rats would literally starve themselves, preferring the stimulation (Routtenberg & Lindy, 1965).

Later studies identified that rats would work for electrical stimulation in several brain areas, including the **ventral tegmental area (VTA),** a small region in the midbrain of rats, humans, and other mammals (Figure 5.11). The electrodes in Olds's original studies were probably stimulating hypothalamic neurons that project to the VTA, so that the electrical current was indirectly activating this area. Because VTA stimulation was such a powerful reinforcer, some researchers inferred that the rats "liked" the stimulation, and the VTA and other areas of the brain where electrical stimulation was effective became informally known as "pleasure centers."

Figure 5.11 The ventral tegmental area (VTA) and substantia nigra pars compacta (SNc) The VTA (part of the midbrain) and the SNc (a part of the basal ganglia) are small regions containing neurons that project dopamine to many brain areas, including the dorsal striatum and frontal cortex.

Frontal cortex

Dorsal striatum

Substantia nigra pars compacta (SNc)

Ventral tegmental area (VTA)

The idea of "pleasure centers," although obviously attractive, is something of an oversimplification. For one thing, rats lever pressing for electrical brain stimulation don't tend to act as if they're enjoying it; they tend to become agitated and may bite the lever instead of simply pressing it, or even scratch the walls or show other behaviors such as eating, fighting, or shredding of nesting material. This is more like the behavior of an excited animal than one who is enjoying food. Skinner, of course, would caution that we can't infer what an animal might be feeling just by watching its behaviors. Nevertheless, some researchers have suggested that electrical brain stimulation causes not pleasure but rather excitement or anticipation of reinforcement—much like the anticipation we experience when expecting a good meal or a big present (Flynn, 1972).

Currently, many researchers believe that we have separate brain systems for signaling **hedonic value**—meaning the "goodness" of a reinforcer, or how much we "like" it—that are distinct from those signaling **motivational value**—meaning how much we "want" a reinforcer and how hard we are willing to work to obtain it. No matter how much we may "like" chocolate cake, most of us will not be very motivated to obtain more if we have just eaten three slices; similarly, Olds's rats doubtless still "liked" food and rest, but they were more motivated to obtain electric brain stimulation, even when starving and exhausted. In these examples, provision of a "liked" reinforcer isn't enough to evoke responding. Only when "wanting" and "liking" signals are both present will the arrival of the reinforcer evoke responding and strengthen the S-R association.

Dopamine: How the Brain Signals "Wanting"?

The neurotransmitter dopamine is produced by neurons in several areas of the brain, including the ventral tegmental area (VTA), which projects to the frontal cortex (among other places), and also including the nearby **substantia nigra pars compacta (SNc),** which is a part of the basal ganglia that projects to the striatum. As you read above, the dorsal striatum is an important site of S-R association, and the orbitofrontal cortex (and other frontal areas) are important for R-O associations, so dopaminergic neurons in the VTA/SNc are a good place to start looking at how the brain signals motivational value.

In rats, dopamine release from the VTA/SNc is triggered by encounters with food, sex, drugs of abuse, and secondary reinforcers. In humans, PET and fMRI studies have shown that presentation of juice, cocaine, money, humor, and even video games causes heightened activity in dopamine target sites such as the striatum (Berridge & Robinson, 1998; Knutson, Fong, Adams, Varner, & Hommer, 2001; Mobbs, Greicius, Abdel-Azim, Menon, & Reiss, 2003). Even in invertebrates, such as the sea slug *Aplysia*, dopamine is released in conjunction with positive reinforcement during operant conditioning (Brembs, 2003; Nargeot, Baxter, Patterson, & Byrne, 1999).

On the other hand, drugs that interfere with dopamine production or transmission reduce responding in a trained animal. For example, in one study, healthy rats were trained to press a lever to obtain food (Wise, Spindler, de Wit, & Gerber, 1978). After training, the rats were split into three groups. One was a control group that continued to receive food as a reinforcement for lever pressing; unsurprisingly, these rats kept responding at high rates (Figure 5.12, dark green line). A second control group (light green line) stopped receiving food reinforcement for lever presses; in this group, as you'd expect, responding gradually extinguished. Rats in the third group (red line) were given pimozide, a drug that blocks dopamine receptors. These rats continued to receive food when they pressed the lever, but their responding started to extinguish anyway. In fact, responding by the rats receiving pimozide was indistinguishable from

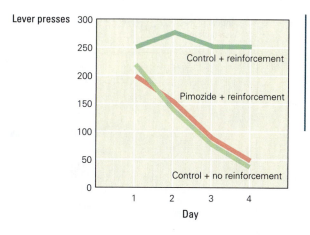

Lever presses

Control + reinforcement

Pimozide + reinforcement

Control + no reinforcement

Day

Figure 5.12 **Extinction mimicry** After being trained to lever-press for food, healthy rats continue to respond vigorously as long as lever pressing is reinforced with food (control + reinforcement). If food is not delivered (control + no reinforcement), healthy rats gradually stop responding; this is the process of extinction. Rats given the dopamine blocker pimozide gradually stop responding too, even though they are still obtaining food when they lever-press (pimozide + reinforcement); this is extinction mimicry.

[Data from Wise et al., 1978.]

that by control rats no longer receiving reinforcement. This effect is called *extinction mimicry* since the response in pimozide-treated rats seemed to be extinguishing, too, even though the animals were still receiving food for their lever presses.

Why might extinction mimicry occur? The simplest explanation of Figure 5.12 might be that the rats given pimozide simply stopped "liking" the taste of food. However, most researchers now believe that dopamine does not directly signal hedonic value. For example, Parkinson's disease damages dopamine-producing neurons that project to the striatum. But when patients with Parkinson's disease are asked to rate the perceived pleasantness of sweet and salty tastes, their ratings are the same as those of healthy people. Apparently, the dopamine reduction in these patients causes no loss of the ability to "like" pleasurable stimuli (Travers et al., 1993).

Researchers can infer degree of liking in nonhuman animals by watching the animals' reaction to various tastes. When a sweet substance is placed in a rat's mouth, the animal shows a recognizable cluster of responses that include rhythmic movements of the mouth and protrusion of the tongue. This is sometimes called the hedonic or "yum" reaction. A bitter taste elicits a different cluster: gapes, shakes of the head, and wiping of the face with paws (the aversive or "ugh" reaction). Rats given injections of a drug that destroys dopaminergic neurons exhibit hedonic and aversive responses that are just as strong as or stronger than those of control rats (Berridge & Robinson, 1998). This suggests that rats with damaged dopamine systems continue to "like" and "dislike" food just as much as control rats do. What seems to change is their willingness to work for it.

The **incentive salience hypothesis of dopamine function** states that the role of dopamine in operant conditioning is to signal how much the animal "wants" a particular outcome—how motivated it is to work for it. According to this hypothesis, the incentive salience of food and other reinforcers—their ability to attract attention and motivate responding—is reduced in dopamine-depleted animals (Berridge, 1996; Berridge, 2007; Berridge & Robinson, 1998). Given a choice between competing alternatives, normal animals will tend to choose a preferred reinforcer, even at the cost of a little extra work. In contrast, dopamine-depleted animals are still perfectly willing to eat a preferred food if it is placed in front of them, but they are unwilling to work hard to earn it (Salamone, Arizzi, Sandoval, Cervone, & Aberman, 2002). Under this hypothesis, the pimozide-drugged rats (Figure 5.12) still "liked" the food they earned; they were just unmotivated to work for it by lever pressing.

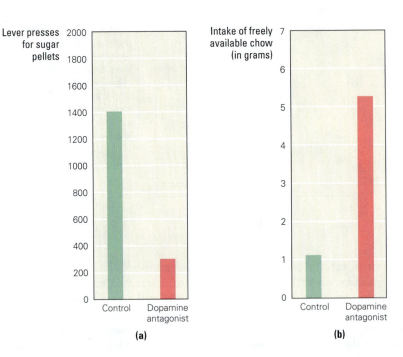

Figure 5.13 Dopamine and incentive salience If rat chow is freely available but sugar pellets (which rats prefer) have to be "earned" by pressing a lever, control rats will spend most of their time working for sugar pellets and eating relatively little free chow. Rats given a dopamine antagonist are much less willing to work for the sugar pellets and instead settle for eating the freely available chow.

[Adapted from Salamone et al., 2002.]

A good example of this is seen in experiments where rats can choose to work for different types of food. For example, most healthy rats prefer sugar pellets to rat chow, and they will work for the pellets by lever pressing, even if chow is freely available (Figure 5.13, green bars). Rats given a dopamine antagonist also prefer sugar to rat chow if both are freely available. But if they have to work for the sugar pellets by lever pressing, they mostly settle for the free chow instead (Salamone et al., 2002). You can think of this as an inversion of the Protestant ethic effect: animals with normal dopamine levels prefer to work to obtain their preferred food; animals with reduced dopamine prefer not to work, even if this results in inferior food.

Dopamine seems to affect incentive salience in humans, too. For example, the drug amphetamine can produce pleasurable feelings in humans, and these pleasurable feelings are not altered if the human is also given the dopamine-blocker pimozide (Brauer & de Wit, 1996, 1997). But the pimozide does suppress cravings for the amphetamine high. In other words, interfering with the dopamine system reduces "wanting" but not "liking" of amphetamine.

Conversely, increasing brain dopamine levels can increase craving. For example, in one study, humans with cocaine addiction volunteered to participate in a study where they were given the drug pergolide, which increases brain dopamine levels; the participants reported an increased craving for cocaine but no increase in the self-reported "high" from cocaine (Haney, Foltin, & Fischman, 1998). Thus, stimulating the dopamine system increases "wanting" but not "liking" of cocaine.

In addition to evidence that dopamine signals "wanting," there is also considerable evidence that dopamine helps strengthen learning of S-R associations during operant conditioning (Wickens, 2009). Although dopamine isn't required for new learning, studies show that increases in brain dopamine levels (through drug administration or by presenting a reward) do tend to enhance new S-R learning (Wise, 2004). Dopamine generally promotes synaptic plasticity, possibly by increasing the ability of the presynaptic neuron to activate the target neuron, and since (as you read in Chapter 2) neurons that fire together wire together, this tends in turn to strengthen the synaptic connection between those neurons (Jay, 2003). However, the effects of dopamine on neurons are notoriously variable and complicated, and a great deal remains to be clarified about this neurotransmitter and its role in learning.

Endogenous Opioids: How the Brain Signals "Liking"?

If dopamine signals "wanting," then what signals "liking" in the brain? Probably the best-studied candidate is the opioid system. Opiate receptors in the brain were discovered quite by accident in the 1970s by researchers trying to figure out how heroin and morphine work. Heroin and morphine belong to a class of drugs called *opiates*, which bind to a class of neuronal receptors called *opiate receptors*. Rather than assume that the brain evolved special receptors to respond to heroin and morphine, researchers suspected there might be naturally occurring brain chemicals that also activate the opiate receptors. They found a class of brain chemicals, named the **endogenous opioids,** that are naturally occurring neurotransmitter-like substances (peptides) with many of the same effects as opiate drugs. (The word "endogenous" means "originating on the inside"; "opioid" means "opiate-like.") Endogenous opioids are distributed throughout the central nervous system, and when released into the body, they have a wide range of effects, including lessening the normal perception of pain and producing feelings of euphoria.

Although there is still a great deal to be learned about the endogenous opioids, many researchers believe these substances may mediate hedonic value, or "liking." If so, the reason that heroin and morphine are so intensely pleasurable could be that they happen to activate the same brain receptors as the endogenous opioids do.

For example, morphine makes sweet food taste sweeter and bitter food taste less bitter (Rideout & Parker, 1996). It can also make pain feel less painful; morphine is used medically for patients who are enduring extreme, long-term pain (in cases where the benefits of relieving suffering are considered to outweigh the risks of morphine addiction). These patients usually report that they still feel the pain but that it doesn't trouble them as much as it did before.

Endogenous opioids are released in response to primary reinforcers, such as food, water, and sex, and they may be released in response to secondary reinforcers and pleasurable behaviors, too (Le Merrer, Becker, Befort, & Kieffer, 2009). Differences in the amount of endogenous opioid released, and in the specific opiate receptors they activate, may also help determine an organism's preference for one reinforcer over another (Le Merrer, Becker, Befort, & Kieffer, 2009), and this may contribute to effects such as you saw in Figure 5.4, where infants worked harder to obtain sweetened water, even though less tasty plain water satisfies thirst just as effectively. Just like infants, rats normally prefer sweetened to plain water, but rats given the opioid antagonist naloxone choose the sweetened water much less often than control rats (Hayward, Schaich-Borg, Pintar, & Low, 2006). The abrupt switch from high opiate activity produced by the taste of sweetened water to low opiate activity produced by the taste of plain water may partially explain the drop in responding observed in the negative contrast effect. Individual variations in the opiate system may underlie one individual's preference for vanilla over chocolate—and may therefore help determine subjective value—affecting our choice behavior, as well as the location of our individual "bliss points."

How Do "Wanting" and "Liking" Interact?

Given that "wanting" seems to be signaled by dopamine and "liking" by the endogenous opioids and that both contribute to driving behavior, how do these two brain systems interact? The answer is not yet clear. One possibility is that some endogenous opioids may modulate dopamine release. For example, some neurons in the VTA have opiate receptors on their dendrites that, when activated, could affect those neurons' normal tendency to release dopamine. In this model, the endogenous opioids would signal "liking," which in turn would affect the VTA's ability to signal information about "wanting." But other studies have suggested that different subpopulations of dopamine neurons might exist, conveying salience ("wanting") and valence ("liking") separately (Matsumoto & Hikosaka, 2009). The picture is complicated because some drugs, such as heroin, may manipulate both pathways: activating the "liking" system to produce a pleasurable high, while also activating the "wanting" system to produce a craving for more of the drug and the high.

Interim Summary

- The dorsal striatum is an important brain substrate for storing stimulus–response (S-R) associations; striatal-mediated S-R associations may be relatively automatic and habitual.

- The orbitofrontal cortex may be an important brain substrate for storing response–outcome (R-O) associations and in helping organisms to choose particular responses based on the expected outcomes of those actions.

- Reinforcers and punishers may activate neurons in the ventral tegmental area (VTA) and substantia nigra pars compacta (SNc), which project dopamine to the dorsal striatum, frontal cortex, and elsewhere. Interrupting these pathways, by lesions or drugs, disrupts operant conditioning.

- The incentive salience hypothesis suggests that dopamine modulates "wanting" rather than "liking"—determining how hard an organism is willing to work for a reinforcement. Dopamine also affects plasticity, possibly helping to create or strengthen S-R associations in the dorsal striatum and elsewhere.

- The endogenous opioids, which are mimicked by many highly addictive drugs, may signal the hedonic value ("liking") of reinforcers and punishers such as food and pain.

5.3 Clinical Perspectives

Through the brain's reinforcement system, animals are hardwired to seek and obtain the things they need for survival (food, water, sleep, etc.) and to avoid those things that threaten survival (pain, sickness, predators, etc.). The pleasure that we feel when we eat fatty food ensures that we are sufficiently motivated to repeat the experience. The human brain evolved millennia ago, when our ancestors had to forage for food and could never be sure when they'd find their next meal. Fat could be stored in the body and used for energy later, when food was scarce. Under these conditions, seeking out fatty foods was a good strategy for survival. In twenty-first-century America, food is easier for most of us to obtain, but our biological drives have not changed, and many of us—still driven to obtain the taste of fatty foods—have become dangerously overweight. This is one way in which the brain's powerful reinforcement system can go awry.

Drug addiction represents another way in which the reinforcement system can malfunction (or, rather, function only too well). You read in Chapter 4 how classical conditioning can contribute to drug addiction. Another large piece of the addiction puzzle is operant conditioning: learned responding to obtain a particular kind of reinforcement. Insights from operant conditioning theory may deepen our understanding of addiction and lead to more effective treatments.

Drug Addiction

We all know people who are "addicted" to their morning cup of coffee, their afternoon chocolate bar, or even their favorite television show. Such people experience intense cravings for the addictive substance between uses and may experience withdrawal symptoms if the addictive substance is taken away. Someone who is addicted to her morning coffee may show signs of withdrawal (crankiness, sleepiness, headaches, difficulty paying attention) if she goes without. However, in most cases, such everyday addictions are not serious enough to interfere with our lives or our health.

Medically, **pathological addiction** is defined as a strong habit (or compulsion) that is maintained despite known harmful consequences (Berke, 2003; Leshner, 1999; McLellan, Lewis, O'Brien, & Kleber, 2000). The difference between pathological addiction and simple habit is largely one of degree. A coffee drinker may be sleepy or cranky until she gets her morning caffeine, and she may have trouble kicking the habit, but this would not usually be considered a pathological addiction unless she drank enough coffee to cause harmful medical consequences or to interfere with her normal life (for example, if she failed to pay the rent because she's spending all her income at Starbucks).

By contrast, a person is diagnosed as pathologically addicted to cocaine if he is unable to quit, suffers withdrawal symptoms between highs, and is obsessed with obtaining his next hit of the drug, to the point where he starts neglecting other aspects of his life—such as his family and his job—because nothing else is as important to him as cocaine. Alcohol can drive pathological addiction in the same way: an alcoholic may be unable to give up drinking, even though it has cost him his job and his family. A rat that starves rather than cease performing the response that brings it electrical brain stimulation could be considered pathologically addicted to the stimulation.

Remember the college student Jamie who had to choose how to allocate his resources between eating out and downloading music (Figure 5.8)? We can think of a person with addiction as having similar choices for allocating resources (time, money, effort) and increasingly choosing the addictive substance at the expense of all other options.

Many individuals with pathological addictions want to quit and try very hard to overcome their addictions. Unfortunately, there are several processes working against them. Addiction may involve not only seeking the "high" but also avoiding the adverse effects of withdrawal from the drug. In a sense, the high provides a positive reinforcement, and the avoidance of withdrawal symptoms provides a negative reinforcement—and both processes reinforce the drug-taking responses.

Many highly addictive drugs are opiates, meaning that they target opiate receptors in the brain. Heroin and morphine are two examples of opiate drugs. Other commonly abused drugs, including amphetamines and cocaine, work by increasing brain dopamine levels. Recall from Chapter 2 that neurons communicate when the presynaptic neuron releases molecules of a neurotransmitter into the synapse, and these neurotransmitter molecules activate receptors on the postsynaptic neuron (Figure 5.14a). Amphetamine causes dopaminergic neurons to release higher levels of dopamine. Cocaine works by blocking dopamine reuptake, so that dopamine remains in the synapse longer before being reabsorbed. In both cases, the effect is to increase the amount of dopamine available

Figure 5.14 **The effects of amphetamine and cocaine on dopaminergic neurons** (a) A presynaptic dopamine-producing neuron releases dopamine into the synapse (1). These molecules activate dopamine receptors on the postsynaptic neuron (2). Unused molecules are either broken down (3) or taken back into the presynaptic neuron, a process called reuptake (4). (b) Amphetamine works by causing dopaminergic neurons to make and release more dopamine (1). Cocaine works by blocking the reuptake of unused dopamine molecules (4). Both drugs thus increase the amount of dopamine in the synapse, increasing the chance that dopamine molecules will activate receptors on the postsynaptic neuron (2).

to activate the postsynaptic neuron (Figure 5.14b). Both amphetamine and cocaine can be used as reinforcers. Thus, for example, rats and mice will learn to lever-press vigorously for injections of amphetamine or cocaine (McBride, Murphy, & Ikemoto, 1999).

One interesting aspect of cocaine and amphetamine use is that, although "liking" seems to be critical in the early stages of drug use, people with long-term addictions often report that they no longer experience an appreciable high from the drug but crave it anyway—as if their "wanting" system has disconnected from their "liking" system and has run amok. In fact, individuals who have taken a dose of cocaine or amphetamine don't typically report feeling happy or pleasured—they feel aroused or excited. These facts fit nicely with the incentive salience hypothesis, which proposes that dopamine is involved in "wanting" but not necessarily in "liking."

In summary, drug addiction results from several factors, including positive reinforcement (the pleasurable high), negative reinforcement (avoiding withdrawal), and malfunction of the dopaminergic "wanting" system (the craving). As you read in Chapter 4, long-term drug use can also cause physiological changes in the synapse so that ever-larger doses of drug are needed to get the same effect. Of course, the relative role of each of these factors varies among individuals as a function of genetics, personality, and experience. Some people become strongly addicted to drugs after a single use, some become addicted over time, and a very few individuals can use drugs over a long period without developing pathological addictions. As yet there is no way to predict whether a particular individual who starts using a particular drug will become addicted or how difficult it will be for that individual to break free of addiction.

Behavioral Addiction

Most researchers believe that drugs such as heroin and cocaine interact with the brain's reinforcement system and that drug addiction is driven by both a craving for the high and a desire to avoid painful withdrawal. For some people, behaviors such as skydiving or winning at gambling can provide highs that are just as reinforcing as drugs—and just as addicting. **Behavioral addictions** are addictions to behaviors, rather than drugs, that produce reinforcements or highs, as well as cravings and withdrawal symptoms when the behavior is prevented.

Perhaps the most widely agreed-on example of a behavioral addiction is compulsive gambling. Many people gamble occasionally, buying a weekly lottery ticket, playing online poker once in a while, or going on occasional weekend trips to Las Vegas or Atlantic City. These people pay their money, have their fun, and then walk away. But other people get hooked: they start to gamble more and more often, risking progressively larger sums of money until nothing is as important as the chance to gamble. Up to about 1.6% of the general population may suffer from compulsive gambling at some point in their lifetime, and the problem may be even more widespread in particular groups, such as African Americans and college students (Potenza, Kosten, & Rounsaville, 2001).

Skinner suggested that one reason gambling is so seductive is that it is often reinforced on a VR schedule, as we described earlier: you can never be sure when the next big payoff will come, which makes it easy to talk yourself into playing just one more time, then just one more time . . . (Skinner, 1953). Each big win provides a powerful reinforcement of the gambling behavior.

Gambling is not the only behavior that can affect the brain's reinforcement system and become addictive. Examples of other behavioral addictions are compulsive eating, sex addiction, compulsive exercising, kleptomania, compulsive shopping—the list goes on and on. In each of these cases, the addicted person experiences a high from the behavior, followed by craving for another high, and withdrawal symptoms if the behavior is prevented. Some researchers even class romantic infatuation as a type of behavioral addiction, in which lovers devote large amounts of time and attention to their beloved, often at the expense of other activities and responsibilities—and suffer withdrawal when separated or rejected (see "Learning and Memory in Everyday Life" on the next page for more discussion of the addictive properties of romantic love).

It increasingly seems that behavioral addictions may reflect dysfunction in the same brain substrates affected by drug addictions. Modern research using fMRI has documented that gambling activates the brain in much the same pattern as seen when people with cocaine addiction receive an infusion of the drug (Breiter, Aharon, Kahneman, Dale, & Shizgal, 2001). Similarly, mice selectively bred for excessive exercise show greater concentrations of dopamine in the dorsal striatum, as do mice selectively bred for overeating (Mathes et al., 2010).

These results suggest there is a general reinforcement system in the brain, activated in similar ways for different categories of reinforcers, including primary reinforcers (food), secondary reinforcers (money), and drugs (cocaine)

For some, gambling is an occasional, harmless pastime. For others, it can develop into a pathological addiction.

Everynight Images/Alamy

Addicted to Love?

Thinking about the object of his desire, Sam's heart starts to pound, his palms get sweaty, and he feels excitement and anticipation. Denied access, he becomes irritable, has trouble sleeping, and develops an overwhelming obsession that swamps all other interests.

Based on the above description, Sam might be a cocaine addict. Or he might just be passionately in love. Humans viewing pictures of their beloved show increased brain activity in areas including the dorsal striatum, the VTA/SNc, and the orbitofrontal cortex (Aron et al., 2005; Xu et al., 2010). These are some of the same brain areas activated by addictive drugs such as cocaine and amphetamine, and they are different from the brain areas activated by sexual arousal, indicating that romantic love is more than just a drive to obtain sex (Fisher, Aron, & Brown, 2005). Viewing pictures of a romantic partner can even produce pain relief, apparently by activating reward centers in the brain that overrule the simultaneous processing of pain (Younger, Aron, Parke, Chatterjee, & Mackey, 2010).

If romantic love activates the same reward circuits as cocaine, can it be just as addictive? Individuals experiencing intense romantic infatuation can display behaviors reminiscent of drug seeking: pursuit of the beloved to the exclusion of other activities, obsessive and intrusive thoughts, and even impulsiveness and poor decision making—leading, for example, to crimes of passion (Frascella, Potenza, Brown, & Childress, 2010). On the other hand, just because romantic love shares some brain circuitry with cocaine and can elicit some of the same behaviors doesn't necessarily justify calling love an "addictive substance." Not everything that elicits reward-seeking behavior or that provokes withdrawal symptoms qualifies for that label. (You seek out water when you're thirsty, and you experience distress if you go too long without; yet would you consider yourself "addicted" to water?) Many experts believe that the depression and grief that accompany a breakup are a normal part of life—not evidence of an addictive disorder.

Nonetheless, some individuals do display excessive devotion to their beloved and experience severe withdrawal symptoms after romantic rejection, including clinical depression and (in rare cases) suicide or homicide. It is possible that, just as some individuals can try cocaine and walk away while others become pathologically addicted, so too some individuals can survive a painful breakup while others remain trapped in a state of loss. Debate continues regarding whether such individuals should be diagnosed with a pathological addiction (Reynaud, Karila, Blecha, & Benyamina, 2010).

As research elucidates the brain substrates of drug addiction and suggests therapies (including medication) to reduce the cravings associated with drug withdrawal, should we consider using the same medications to help reduce cravings following romantic rejection? If you've ever had your heart broken by a failed romance, would you have taken advantage of such a treatment if it existed?

(Breiter et al., 2001). If so, a better understanding of the biochemical and behavioral principles underlying drug addiction may also help in the treatment of individuals suffering from behavioral addictions.

Treatments for Addiction

Until fairly recently, addiction was generally considered to be a character flaw. People thought all a person had to do was display enough willpower to stay away from the addictive substance (whether a crack pipe, a gambling table, or a pack of cigarettes). Nowadays, it's more widely appreciated that the intensity of the cravings experienced in addiction, not to mention the often excruciating physical pain of withdrawal, make it impossible for many people to break free of addiction without outside help.

Currently, in the United States, the vast majority of treatment plans for addiction include cognitive therapy, often centered on self-help sessions with a support group (such as Alcoholics Anonymous and its many spin-off organizations— Gamblers Anonymous, Narcotics Anonymous, Overeaters Anonymous, and so on). Medical treatment may also help. For example, naltrexone is a drug that blocks opiate receptors, presumably decreasing the ability of heroin to bind to those receptors and cause a hedonic reaction. In some studies, people with heroin addiction who had undergone detoxification were able to stay off heroin longer if they received continuing treatment that included naltrexone (Kirchmayer et al., 2002; Rawson & Tennant, 1984), and compulsive gamblers have also reported reductions in gambling urges following naltrexone treatment (Grant, Kim, & Hartman, 2008). These studies generally take place over a short period (typically a few weeks or months), and it is not yet clear how well naltrexone's effects hold over the long term or how likely patients are to relapse if treatment is discontinued.

The behavioral principles of operant conditioning suggest some other therapies to help fight addiction. Addiction could be considered as a strong S-R-O association, with sets of environmental stimuli (S) that trigger the addictive behavior (R), resulting in the reinforcing outcome (O) of a "high" or a reduced craving or both. When we look at addiction this way, the challenge for treatment is to break or reduce the strength of the conditioned association. Perhaps the most obvious approach is simple *extinction*: if response R stops producing outcome O, the frequency of R should decline. This is one way of interpreting the effectiveness of naltrexone: once the brain's reinforcement system is blocked, subsequent heroin (or gambling) doesn't produce the outcome that it used to, so the response (drug taking or gambling) should decline.

Another conditioning-based method for combating addictions and habits is *distancing*: avoiding the stimuli that trigger the unwanted response. For example, a cigarette smoker who is struggling to quit and who gets the urge to light up whenever she hangs out with friends who are heavy smokers should try to avoid those situations. If the S is never present, the R may never be triggered.

A third method is *reinforcement of alternate behaviors*, which you read about previously in the context of childrearing (see "Learning and Memory in Everyday Life" on page 179). If the smoker makes it through a whole week without a cigarette, she can reinforce her own behavior by treating herself to a favorite food or activity. Friends can also help by praising the nonsmoking behavior (one aspect of Alcoholics Anonymous is the social reinforcement provided by the group for each week the alcoholic stays sober). Some programs for heroin addicts reinforce abstinence with actual monetary vouchers, providing yet another form of reinforcement for the alternative behavior of not using the drug (Preston, Umbricht, & Epstein, 2000).

A final conditioning-inspired technique is *delayed reinforcement*: whenever the smoker gets the urge to light up, she can impose a fixed delay (e.g., an hour) before giving in to it. Recall that increasing the delay between response and outcome weakens learning of the R-O association (see Figure 5.5). Imposing long delays between cravings and cigarettes may similarly weaken the association and will also, by default, reduce the total number of cigarettes smoked per day.

These and other behavioral approaches can be used in combination, increasing the chances of success. But even with all these behavioral therapies, addicted cigarette smokers (and alcoholics and drug users and gamblers) can still have a very hard time kicking their habits. Currently, the most successful approaches appear to be those that combine cognitive therapy (including counseling and support groups) with behavioral therapy based on conditioning principles—and medication for the most extreme cases (Legg & Gotestam, 1991).

Interim Summary

- Addictive drugs (heroin, cocaine, etc.) may hijack the brain's reinforcement system and can produce psychological as well as physiological addiction.
- Behavioral addictions may reflect the same brain processes as drug addictions.

▪ Among the treatments for people with addictions are cognitive therapies, medications, and behavioral therapies, including principles learned from operant conditioning.

▶ SYNTHESIS

Remember Priscilla, the Fastidious Pig? Her trainers taught her to turn on the radio, eat breakfast at a table, put away dirty clothes, and run a vacuum cleaner. They did this using the basic principles of operant conditioning: shaping one element of the routine, reinforcing the response with a bit of food each time the animal approximated a desired behavior, and then chaining the various elements of the routine together. The same general principles applied to Annie, the toilet-trained toddler: her parents shaped the desired response (use of the potty seat), reinforcing this behavior by verbal praise and punishing alternate responses with scolding.

Operant conditioning is a powerful form of learning that can be applied to adult humans, as well as infants and pets. You can even use it on yourself if you want to break a bad habit or reinforce good study habits. And the applications have been implicitly appreciated at least since the time of the ancient Greeks; in *Lysistrata*, a play by Aristophanes, the women of Athens agree to withhold sexual favors from their men until the men call off a frivolous war with Sparta—a clear example of negative punishment.

Many brain areas participate in operant conditioning. S-R associations may be stored in connections between sensory and motor cortex and in the dorsal striatum; predictions about the outcome O that will follow R depend on frontal areas, including the orbitofrontal cortex. The brain also seems to have a general-purpose reinforcement system—including the VTA/SNc dopaminergic system—that helps strengthen the S-R connection and also allows the organism to choose between competing responses that result in different predicted outcomes. Many kinds of addiction, including drug addictions and behavioral addictions, may result when chemicals or behaviors interfere with this reinforcement system; behavioral therapy for addiction is a clear application of operant conditioning procedures to help improve people's lives. Operant conditioning also forms the basis for behavioral economics, the study of how individuals allocate their time and energy among different available responses.

The bottom line: operant conditioning isn't just for circus animals. People use many operant conditioning techniques in daily life without even realizing it. By understanding the underlying principles, you can use them much more effectively.

"Oh, not bad. The light comes on, I press a bar, they write me a check. How about you?"

Key Terms

basal ganglia, *p. 192*

behavioral addiction, *p. 202*

behavioral economics, *p. 188*

bliss point, *p. 189*

chaining, *p. 175*

concurrent reinforcement schedule, *p. 187*

continuous reinforcement schedule, *p. 184*

cumulative recorder, *p. 172*

discrete trial paradigm, *p. 170*

discriminative stimuli, *p. 172*

dorsal striatum, *p. 192*

drive reduction theory, *p. 176*

endogenous opioids, *p. 199*

fixed-interval (FI) schedule, *p. 185*

fixed-ratio (FR) schedule, *p. 184*

free-operant paradigm, *p. 170*

hedonic value of a stimulus, *p. 196*

incentive salience hypothesis of dopamine function, *p. 197*

matching law of choice behavior, *p. 188*

motivational value of a stimulus, *p. 196*

negative punishment, *p. 182*

negative reinforcement, *p. 182*

operant conditioning, *p. 167*

orbitofrontal cortex, *p. 193*

partial reinforcement schedule, *p. 184*

pathological addiction, *p. 201*

positive punishment, *p. 181*

positive reinforcement, *p. 181*

postreinforcement pause, *p. 184*

Premack principle, *p. 190*

primary reinforcers, *p. 176*

punisher, *p. 178*

punishment, *p. 171*

reinforcement, *p. 171*

reinforcement schedule, *p. 180*

reinforcer, *p. 176*

response deprivation hypothesis, *p. 190*

secondary reinforcers, *p. 176*

self control, *p. 181*

shaping, *p. 174*

Skinner box, *p. 171*

substantia nigra pars compacta (SNc), *p. 196*

variable-interval (VI) schedule, *p. 186*

variable-ratio (VR) schedule, *p. 186*

ventral tegmental area (VTA), *p. 195*

Concept Check

1. A new kindergarten teacher wants to train her pupils to put away toys after playtime. Suggest three conditioning techniques she could use to train this behavior.

2. An employer wants to start testing her employees for drugs. She hopes that the threat of such tests will encourage employees to avoid drug use. According to the principles of conditioning, what would be the best way to schedule these drug tests?

3. Some researchers believe that organisms are biased to engage in behaviors that allow them to "control" their environment. How could this idea explain superstitious behavior? How could it explain the Protestant ethic effect?

4. Imagine that the police raid a house party and find the crowd taking an unfamiliar kind of drug. The users are sitting in front of a TV enthusiastically munching on stale bread and laughing hysterically at an old sitcom. Even without submitting samples of the drug to a laboratory, what might we hypothesize about the mechanisms by which this drug works?

CHAPTER 6

Generalization and Discrimination Learning

SITTING IN HER HIGH CHAIR, two-year-old Sabrina picks up a small piece of green broccoli from her plate and puts it in her mouth. Then, scrunching up her nose in disgust, she spits the broccoli out onto the floor and begins to pick through her plate for something else to try. Soon she comes upon another vegetable. In shape and size it resembles the broccoli, but it is white, not green. If the white cauliflower tastes anything like the green broccoli, Sabrina would certainly want to avoid it. But she is hungry, and if the white cauliflower tastes good to her (in contrast to the green broccoli), she'd love to eat it. Sabrina faces what philosophers and psychologists have long understood to be a fundamental challenge for learning: how and when to generalize. **Generalization** is the transfer of past learning to new situations and problems.

If, after tasting (and spitting out) the green broccoli, Sabrina assumes that all vegetables taste terrible, she might find herself missing out on lots of wonderful foods to enjoy. On the other hand, if she assumes that only vegetables that look exactly like the green broccoli are distasteful, she may suffer over and over again from eating related but not quite identical vegetables whose flavors are similar. Sabrina is faced with the core issue of generalization: the need to find an appropriate balance between *specificity*, deciding how narrowly a rule applies (for example, deciding that only green-broccoli-like vegetables are nasty tasting), and *generality*, deciding how broadly a rule applies (for example, assuming all vegetables will taste nasty).

As her palate matures and her experience with different foods expands, Sabrina learns to recognize the similarities and differences between vegetables—to treat some of them the same (generalization) while discriminating between those she considers delicious and those she finds unappetizing. **Discrimination** is the perception of differences between stimuli.

This chapter considers the behavioral and biological principles of generalization and discrimination and how they allow us to apply past learning to novel future situations. Our ability to function in a complex world and deal with novel challenges depends on our ability to form categories, recognize similarities between events or objects, make generalizations, and discriminate between members of different categories.

Generalization is seen in all the forms of learning and memory presented in this book. In classical Pavlovian conditioning, such as the rabbit eyeblink conditioning described in Chapter 4, rabbits that are trained to blink to a 1,000-Hz tone will generalize this learning, to some degree, to a 900-Hz tone and other tones of similar frequency. In operant conditioning, such as training pigeons to peck lighted keys for food as described in Chapter 5 and discussed again below, a pigeon that has been trained to peck a yellow light for food will generalize this learning, to some degree, from yellow to orange lights.

This chapter provides a broad, integrative overview of what is known about the behavioral and neural bases of generalization as well as the brain disorders that interfere with our ability to effectively generalize from old experiences to new ones. Life never replays exactly the same events, with exactly the same objects or circumstances that you have experienced before. To adapt—to survive and prosper—you need to apply what you have learned in the past to novel situations that may be similar, but not identical, to what you have previously experienced. The "Learning and Memory in Everyday Life" box on the next page describes how companies such as Amazon.com have learned to generalize for much the same adaptive purpose.

6.1 Behavioral Processes

Two scenarios are possible given Sabrina's dilemma of whether or not to eat the white cauliflower, with its similarity in shape to the green broccoli she dislikes. Either eating the two vegetables will have the same outcome—and the cauliflower will taste bad to her—or eating the two vegetables will lead to different outcomes, and she'll find the white cauliflower, unlike the green broccoli, to be yummy. These are special cases of the more general problem of generalization, schematized in Table 6.1. The discussion in the next few pages is organized around this table, addressing in turn each of the four situations it describes.

How Does Amazon.com Know What You Want to Buy Next?

Have you ever had the pleasure of meeting someone and discovering you have many interests and tastes in common? You both like the same obscure music, enjoy the same French films, and read many of the same books. Finding someone like this is like finding your doppelganger (your phantom twin or double), and once you have found such a person and confirmed that you like the same 10 of the books that you discussed, you would take very seriously his recommendation of a book that is unfamiliar to you.

Amazon.com and other websites attempt to achieve much the same thing when they use a form of generalization to predict what books you might want to buy from them. They do it by trying to find as many of your doppelgangers as possible among their other customers. The process they use, called *collaborative filtering,* is an automatic filtering (or making predictions) based on information from a large number of other people's past behaviors. In essence, collaborative filtering works by creating a very detailed stereotype of what kind of reader you are.

Once Amazon.com has found a sufficiently large number of like-minded individuals among its customers, it collates their purchasing histories to find books they have not yet purchased but that were purchased by one or more other individuals like them. Thus, by profiling you and creating a mini-category of individuals similar to you, Amazon.com seeks to generalize from your past behaviors to what you might do in the future. In this way, Amazon.com and other websites not only increase their ability to sell large numbers of books but also help you discover the hidden gems you might miss if you never met your own personal doppelganger.

Table 6.1

Alternatives for generalization about and discrimination between two stimuli

	Same outcome	Different outcomes
Similar stimuli	Similar stimuli → same outcome *Broccoli and cauliflower → nasty*	Similar stimuli → different outcomes *Broccoli → nasty, cauliflower → yummy*
Dissimilar stimuli	Dissimilar stimuli → same outcome *Broccoli and red peppers → nasty*	Dissimilar stimuli → different outcomes *Broccoli → nasty, red pepper → yummy*

As we examine each of these facets of generalization, we will see how the efforts of psychologists to understand them led to models that accomplished two things. First, the models allowed psychologists to formulate general principles of behavior and predict, often with quantitative detail, the behaviors to be expected in a wide range of learning and memory experiments. Second, these models—originally posited as abstract theories about networks of associations—identified, years in advance, the basic mechanisms that brains use to accomplish these processes, which we will describe in Section 6.2.

Our first discussion concerns the learning that occurs when similar stimuli predict similar outcomes or consequences, such as when a child decides that both the broccoli and the cauliflower are nasty tasting, corresponding to the top-left quadrant of Table 6.1. The key questions that psychologists have asked about these situations are (1) how do people mentally represent the fact that two entities, such as broccoli and cauliflower, are similar, and (2) when we know two things are similar, what are our expectations for how likely they are to lead to the same outcome?

When Similar Stimuli Predict Similar Outcomes

Using a situation comparable in structure to the problem of Sabrina and her vegetables, Harry Guttman and Norman Kalish trained pigeons to peck at a yellow light for food reinforcement (Guttman & Kalish, 1956). They then tested what the pigeons had learned by showing them, in each of a succession of test trials, a single colored light that was either green, yellow, orange, or one of the in-between colors yellow-green or yellow-orange. By counting how often the pigeons pecked at each color, the investigators were able to measure how the similarity of the color to the yellow training stimulus affected the amount of pecking. Because the sensation of color results from physically different wavelengths of light—for example, yellow light has a wavelength of 580 nanometers (nm)—researchers can compare colors in terms of wavelengths. In this case, the colors ranged along a physical continuum from green (520 nm) to orange (620 nm).

Figure 6.1 shows how the pigeons responded. Not surprisingly, the pigeons pecked most at the stimulus on which they were trained: the yellow light, with its wavelength of 580 nm. However, the pigeons also responded to lights of other colors. Lights most similar to yellow (as measured by wavelength) produced the next-highest levels of responding. As the colors grew increasingly different from the original training stimulus (yellow), responding decreased rapidly.

The curve seen in Figure 6.1 is a **generalization gradient,** a curve showing how changes in the physical properties of stimuli (plotted on the horizontal axis) correspond to changes in responding (plotted on the vertical axis). The curve is called a "gradient" because it generally shows that an animal's response changes in a graded fashion that depends on the degree of similarity between a test stimulus and the original training stimulus. After training in which a single stimulus (such as a light of a particular color) has been reinforced repeatedly, generalization gradients around that trained stimulus show a peak, or point of maximal responding, corresponding to the original stimulus on which the animal was trained. This responding drops off rapidly as the test stimuli become less and less similar to the training stimulus.

From looking at a generalization gradient, you can deduce to what degree animals (including people) expect similar outcomes for stimuli that vary in some physical property, such as light wavelength. Thus, a generalization gradient is often taken to be a measure of the animal's or person's perception of similarity, in that if two stimuli are perceived as being highly similar (or identical) there will be significant generalization between them.

Figure 6.1 Stimulus-generalization gradients in pigeons Pigeons were trained to peck at a yellow light, having a wavelength of about 580 nm. When the pigeons were tested with other colors of light, their response rates decreased as the colors (wavelengths) departed farther from the trained color.
Adapted from Guttman & Kalish, 1956, pp. 79–88.

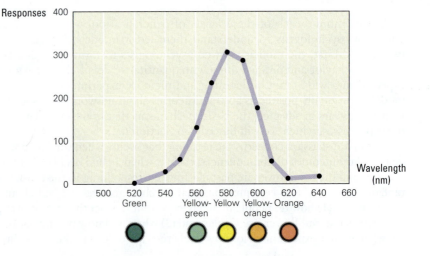

Generalization gradients have been studied for stimuli that vary in height, angle, size, or tone frequency. The generalization gradient in Figure 6.1 represents typical behavior for many different stimuli and across a broad range of generalization experiments. The fundamental characteristic of these generalization gradients is that they decline rapidly on either side of the peak. Roger Shepard, an influential American cognitive psychologist, described this feature of generalization gradients as one of the most constant basic laws of psychology (Shepard, 1987).

Generalization as a Search for Similar Consequences

Why should a pigeon that has been trained to peck at a yellow light respond to an orange light at all? Could the pigeon be making a mistake—confusing the orange light and the yellow light or failing to tell them apart? Probably not. Pigeons can easily be trained to discriminate yellow from orange. One explanation for generalized responding is that pigeons (and all animals, including humans) are savvy estimators of the probability of future events.

Imagine you are prospecting for gold and you find a mountain stream that yields bountiful quantities of ore. After you've taken all the gold from that one stream, you wonder where you might find more. If you are optimistic, you imagine that you have stumbled onto a fabulous mother lode and that all the streams in the entire valley are filled with gold. At your most pessimistic, you realize that there may only be gold in this one particular stream. Alternatively, the truth lies between these two extremes, and there is gold in just a few more streams in the valley.

Your initial discovery of gold in one stream does not tell you the size or shape of the gold-producing region or the location of its boundaries. All you know is that this one particular stream that yielded gold lies inside a gold-producing region of unknown extent. According to Roger Shepard, the fundamental challenge of generalization—for the gold miner, for Sabrina, and for Guttman and Kalish's light-pecking pigeons—is to identify the set of all stimuli that have the same consequence as the training stimulus. Shepard called this set the **consequential region** (Shepard, 1987). In Shepard's view, the generalization gradient in Figure 6.1 reflects the pigeon's best estimate of the probability that novel stimuli will have the same consequence as a training stimulus. The pigeon, Shepard argues, is not *confusing* a yellow-orange 600-nm light with the original yellow 580-nm light; rather, the pigeon, by responding at about 50% of its original rate to the yellow-orange light, is implicitly showing that it *expects*, based on what it learned from pecking the yellow light (which always resulted in food), that there is an even chance that pecking the yellow-orange light will yield the same food delivery. The shape of generalization gradients, Shepard argued, suggests that animals (including people) consistently expect that the chance that two stimuli will have the same consequence drops off sharply as the stimuli become more distinct. This implies that you can view generalization gradients as an attempt to predict, based on past experience, the likelihood that the consequences of one stimulus will also be the same as that of other, similar stimuli.

The Challenge of Incorporating Similarity into Learning Models

Chapter 4 described formal models of classical conditioning, such as the Rescorla-Wagner model, in which networks of associations (each with an associative weight) link stimuli (lights and tones) to outcomes (airpuffs or shocks). In the studies that led to these models, the stimuli were highly distinct, with little perceptual similarity between them. When two stimuli were employed, they were usually from two different modalities, such as a light and a tone. But what if the stimuli in a conditioning experiment are two tones of similar frequency or two lights of similar wavelength? The application of Rescorla and Wagner's associative learning model from Chapter 4 to Guttman and Kalish's pigeon experiment (which used similarly colored lights) provides a good illustration of how easily the Rescorla-Wagner model falls apart and makes erroneous predictions unless you incorporate an additional assumption about how to represent the physical similarity of different stimuli.

Recall from Chapter 4 that when learning involves multiple cues, the Rescorla-Wagner model can be visualized as a simple one-layer network with links from the various cues to the possible outcomes, as was illustrated in Figure 4.15 (Gluck & Bower, 1988a). Each presentation of a trial was modeled by activating the corresponding input node for each stimulus cue (such as a tone), which then caused activation to travel through links to an output node (e.g., the prediction of the airpuff) while being multiplied by the associative weight on each link. When activation from a given input node reaches an output node, it is added to the incoming activations (multiplied by weights) of all the other active stimulus cues on that trial. Learning resulted when the associative weights on the links were modified at the end of each trial so as to reduce the likelihood of a future mismatch (or "error") between the network's prediction for an outcome (the activation in the output nodes) and the actual outcome that was presented as feedback on that trial by the experimenter. Thus, as described in Chapter 4, the Rescorla-Wagner model details a process whereby an animal or person learns to minimize the difference between what actually happens (the airpuff) and their expectation of that outcome. It is that expectation of the airpuff outcome that generates an anticipatory conditioned response, such as an eyeblink.

In our earlier applications of this model to classical conditioning, you saw how a tone and a light were identified as two distinct stimuli, each with an associative weight communicated from a corresponding input node to an output node that produced the conditioned response. To apply the same idea to Guttman and Kalish's operant pigeon paradigm, we'd need five input nodes, one for each of the five discrete colors that might be presented.

Figure 6.2a shows how one might model stimulus generalization using a simple network that has a single input node for each possible color of light (five are shown). This is called a **discrete-component representation,** meaning that each possible stimulus is represented by its own unique node (or "component") in the model. The network also contains a single output node for the response and has weights from the input nodes to the output node that are modifiable by learning, according to a learning algorithm such as the Rescorla-Wagner rule. Each of the input nodes in Figure 6.2a represents a different color of light (for example, green, yellow, or orange). Depending on the pattern of inputs, activity may be evoked in the output node; strong activity in this output node will cause the model to generate a response.

Figure 6.2 A model of stimulus generalization, using discrete-component representations A first attempt to model stimulus generalization would have one input node for each possible color of light, making this a discrete-component representation. Active nodes and weights are shown in red. (a) The network is first trained to respond to a yellow light, which activates the "yellow" input node. At the end of training, the weight from the "yellow" input node to the output node is strong (illustrated by a thick red line). (b) When a novel yellow-orange light is presented to the network, the yellow-orange light activates a different input node. This input node has never had its weight strengthened, and so it does not cause activation in the output node. Thus, the discrete-component network does not produce any response to the yellow-orange light despite the similarity to the trained yellow light. This model does *not* account for the generalization gradient seen in pigeons that is shown in Figure 6.1.

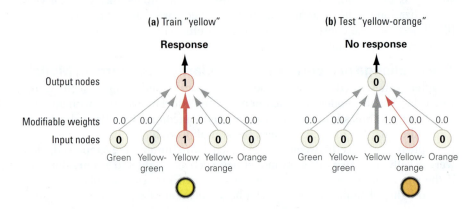

Before training, the weights from all the input nodes to the output node are set to 0.0, meaning that there are no prior associations between any of the lights and the response. Each training trial is modeled by activating the yellow-light input node, letting the activation from that node be multiplied by the yellow-response associative weight and then updating this weight based on the difference between the actual output activation and the ideal output activation (1 in this case because it should respond on every trial with the light cue). If the model is given repeated training trials of this sort over and over, in which the yellow light is presented followed by a reward, then the weight of the association connecting the yellow node to the response node will increase until it has a value of close to 1.0. Figure 6.2a displays the weight from the yellow node as being thicker than the others, to represent this greater weight.

Figure 6.2b shows what happens when this model is now tested with presentation of a novel yellow-orange light. There is still a strong 1.0 weight from the yellow node to the output node (because of the previous training), but that weight is not active (because a pure yellow light is not presented during this new test trial). Instead, only the yellow-orange input node is active, and it causes no activity in the output node because the weight from this input node is still 0.0. Thus, the model will produce no response to the yellow-orange light, even though that stimulus is very similar to the trained yellow light. In fact, this model will produce no response to any stimulus other than the original yellow training stimulus and so shows no generalization. The result would be a generalization gradient as shown in Figure 6.3: the model produces strong (about 80%) responding to the yellow test stimulus but no (0%) responding to any other color. This does not look like the more gently sloping generalization gradient obtained from Guttman and Kalish's pigeons, seen in Figure 6.1. Clearly, the model in Figure 6.2 is wrong: it predicts a generalization gradient that is totally at odds with what Guttman and Kalish actually found.

This analysis suggests that the simple models based on the Rescorla-Wagner rule are limited in scope. They are useful for describing, understanding, and predicting how organisms learn about highly dissimilar stimuli, such as a tone and a light, but they don't work as well with stimuli that have some inherent similarity, such as lights of different colors. Do we throw out the old models when we run into a problem like this and simply assume that the Rescorla-Wagner rule is wrong? Not necessarily. Instead, given the otherwise wide range of success of this learning model, researchers have tried to extend it to account for generalization gradients. In this way, simple models can be considered to

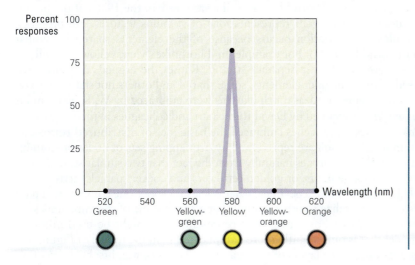

Figure 6.3 The generalization gradient produced by the discrete-component network of Figure 6.2 The discrete-component network gives no response to the yellow-orange light despite the similarity in color to the previously trained yellow light. It only responds to the trained "yellow" stimulus. In other words, this simple network fails to show a smooth generalization gradient like that shown by the pigeons in Figure 6.1.

be preliminary steps toward a more complete understanding of learning and memory that builds, cumulatively, on past progress.

The learning model shown in Figure 6.2 uses the simplest-possible scheme for representing stimuli: a discrete-component representation in which each distinct stimulus is represented by a single input node that is then connected, by a modifiable weight to an output node. Discrete-component representations are applicable to situations in which the similarity between cues is small enough that there is negligible transfer of response from one to another. This was the case in the experiments discussed previously in Chapters 4 and 5, many of which used just a single tone or light. However, discrete-component representations fail in cases where stimuli have a high degree of physical similarity, since the models then produce unrealistic generalization gradients like the one shown in Figure 6.3.

Before moving on, let's consider how different kinds of representations can have different degrees of usefulness depending on the task, whether in our models, in our mental activities, or in the actual physical workings of our brain. Let's compare some of the different kinds of representations you use in everyday life. The letters in these words on the page, for example, are representations of sounds, and the words themselves represent ideas and concepts. To represent Rachel, a student at Rutgers University, the government may use her nine-digit Social Security number, 015-88-6999; the university uses her student ID number, and the phone company her mobile phone number. Each of these representations was chosen to suit a particular need. However, what is appropriate for use as a representation in one context may not be appropriate in others. Of particular importance to our discussions in this chapter is the fact that different representations in different contexts yield different patterns of similarity: Rachel is most similar to Reyna when their names are spoken aloud (even if they have very different Social Security numbers). However, to the government, Rachel may be more similar to Elizabeth, whose social security number, 016-88-6999, differs by only one digit from Rachel's.

With this deeper appreciation for the effect of context on similarity between representations, we next explore how psychological theorists have grappled with the limitations of various representation schemes in learning models and how their solutions changed modern approaches to understanding the interplay between similarity, representation, and generalization.

Shared Elements and Distributed Representations

Recall from Chapters 1 and 5 the work of Edward Thorndike, whose *law of effect* states that the probability of a response will increase or decrease depending on the outcomes that follow. Thorndike was well aware back in the 1920s of the limitations of discrete-component representations of stimulus features. He proposed that stimulus generalization occurs because of the elements shared by similar stimuli (Thorndike, 1923). For example, in Thorndike's view, yellow and yellow-orange are not two totally separate stimuli. Rather, he argued, they are each composed of many distinct elements, some shared and others not shared. As you read back in Chapter 1, ideas much like this were embraced by W. K. Estes in his *stimulus sampling theory* and by David Rumelhart and colleagues in their *connectionist models*. All these approaches embraced the basic idea of **distributed representations,** in which stimuli are represented by overlapping sets of nodes or stimulus elements. Similarity emerges naturally from the fact that two similar stimuli (such as yellow and orange lights, or golden retrievers and cocker spaniels) activate elements belonging to both sets. Thus, what is learned about one stimulus will tend to transfer or generalize to other stimuli that activate some of the same nodes.

Figure 6.4a shows how distributed representations might be used in a network model that is only slightly more complicated than the model of Figure 6.2. This network has three layers of nodes and two layers of weights; by convention

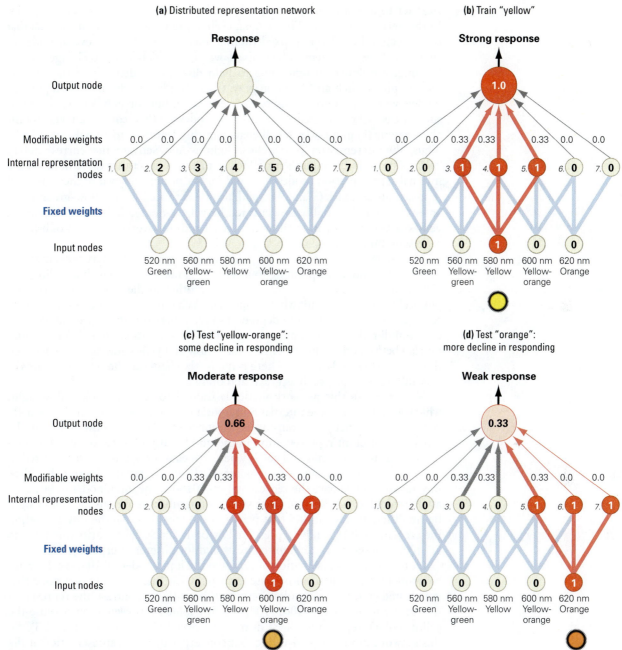

Figure 6.4 A network model using distributed representations (a) Presentation of a colored light activates a unique node in the input layer of the network. Each input layer node is connected, through fixed (nonmodifiable) weights—shown in light blue—to several nodes in the internal representation. The seven (numbered 1 to 7) nodes in the internal representation are then connected, by modifiable weights, shown in gray, to a single output node. (b) First, the network is trained to respond to yellow light. Presentation of the stimulus activates the corresponding input node, which activates three nodes in the internal representation (3, 4, 5), which connect to the output node. If the yellow light is repeatedly paired with a reward, weights from these three active internal-representation nodes to the output node are strengthened. (c) Next, the network is tested with a similar stimulus (a yellow-orange light) that activates internal nodes 4, 5, and 6. Because yellow-orange and yellow share two overlapping internal representation nodes (4 and 5), some response activation is produced at the output node. (d) An even more different color, orange, evokes even less overlap in the internal representation nodes because it shares only one common internal node (5), and thus orange evokes only weak response activation.

we refer to it as a two-layer network, counting the number of layers of nodes. In the network model in Figure 6.4a, each stimulus activates an *input node* that is connected, by a layer of fixed (nonmodifiable) weights, to several nodes in an *internal representation*. These fixed weights, which do not change during learning, are drawn in light blue to help distinguish them from the modifiable weights, which are shown in gray. (Later, we'll consider more complicated models where the lower weights can be trained, but for now let's stick to this simpler case.) The internal representation nodes are then connected, via modifiable weights (in gray), which will change during learning, to a final *output* node. Thus, the presentation of a yellow light would activate the corresponding "yellow" node in the input layer, which in turn would activate three nodes at the internal representation (nodes 3, 4, and 5), but notice that two of these internal representation nodes (3 and 4) could also be activated by a yellow-green light, and nodes 4 and 5 could also activated by yellow-orange light. In this manner, yellow-green, yellow, and yellow-orange all activate overlapping sets of internal representation nodes.

The nodes in Figure 6.4a are laid out as a **topographic representation,** meaning that nodes responding to physically similar stimuli (such as yellow and yellow-orange light) are placed next to each other in the model. However, the physical layout itself is not what's important. What is important to a topographical representation is that the degree of overlap between the representations of two stimuli reflects their physical similarity. Thus, in Figure 6.4a, there is more overlap between the representations for yellow and yellow-orange than between those for yellow and orange. There is no overlap between the representations of very different colors, such as green and orange.

Now suppose this network model is trained to respond to a yellow light, which activates the three internal representation nodes as shown in Figure 6.4b. Note that this network transforms a representation of yellow light on the input to a different representation in the middle. If you were to view the input nodes as a string of ones and zeros where 1 means a node is on (colored red in Figure 6.4b) and 0 means a node is off (outlined in gray in Figure 6.4b), then this network transforms the representation 00100 at the input nodes to 0011100 at the middle nodes. Both of these strings of numbers represent the yellow light but in different ways at different places in the model (much the way Rachel, in the earlier example, can be represented by both her Social Security number and her phone number, in different contexts and for different purposes).

Note that the representation of yellow at the input nodes (00100) is a discrete-component representation because each light has one and only one node that is activated (and no other colors activate this node). In contrast, the representation at the middle nodes (0011100) is a distributed representation because the yellow color's representation is distributed over three nodes (3, 4, and 5). So this network can be viewed as one that converts a discrete representation at the input nodes to a distributed representation at the middle nodes. As you will see next, this distributed representation allows the model to account for similarity and generalization.

One way of determining how much the active weights should be increased is to use the Rescorla-Wagner learning rule. As you read in Chapter 4, this rule states that weights should be changed in proportion to the error on each trial (with error defined as the mismatch between the outcome that occurred and the actual response activation, which is equivalent to the outcome that was predicted). Following many trials of training in which yellow is paired with reward, the weights from the three active nodes would each come to equal 0.33, as shown in Figure 6.4b, illustrated by the thickened lines connecting internal representation nodes 3, 4, and 5 to the output node. Presentation of a yellow light now activates nodes 3, 4, and 5, which in turn results in a net response activation of 1.0 in the output node, that being the sum of these three weights. (Note that the weights from internal representation nodes that have never been activated or associated with reward remain at their initial value of 0.)

Compare the distributed network in Figure 6.4b, which was trained to respond to a yellow light, with the discrete-component network from Figure 6.2b, which was trained with the very same stimulus and outcome pairings. In the distributed network of Figure 6.4b, the learning is distributed over weights from three internal representation nodes, each with a trained weight of 0.33; in contrast, the discrete-component network in Figure 6.2 localizes this same respond-to-yellow rule into a single weight of 1.0 from one input node. Both network models give a response of 1.0 when the original yellow light is presented.

The difference between the distributed network of Figure 6.4 and the discrete-component network of Figure 6.2 becomes apparent only on presentation of stimuli that are similar—but not identical—to the trained stimulus. The distributed network is able to generalize. This generalization behavior can be assessed by testing a yellow-orange light, as shown in Figure 6.4c. Here, yellow-orange activates an internal representation that has considerable overlap with the representation activated by the trained yellow light. Specifically, both nodes 4 and 5 are also activated by the yellow-orange light, and each of these internal representation nodes will contribute to partially activate the output node. As a result, a reasonably strong output node activation of 0.66 results, proportional to the two-thirds degree of overlap between the representations for yellow and yellow-orange light. If the same network was tested with orange light, there would be less overlap with the representation of yellow light and a consequently weaker response of 0.33 (as shown in Figure 6.4d).

Figure 6.5 shows that when this model is used to generate responses to a series of novel lights, it produces a stimulus-generalization gradient that decreases smoothly for stimuli of increasing distance from the trained stimulus, similar to the pigeons' generalization gradient shown in Figure 6.1. This ability to capture animals' and humans' natural tendency to generalize—that is, to treat similar stimuli similarly—contrasts markedly with the (lack of a) generalization gradient in Figure 6.3, which was produced using the network that had only discrete-component representation. Thus, even though the two models can learn the same initial task (respond to yellow light), they differ considerably in their generalization performance.

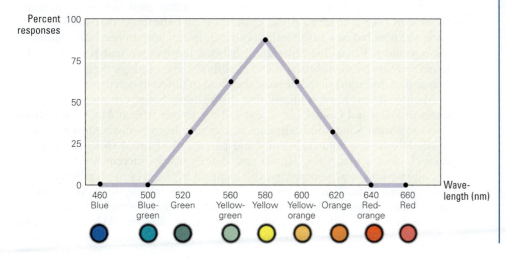

Percent responses — 100, 75, 50, 25, 0

Wavelength (nm): 460 Blue, 500 Blue-green, 520 Green, 560 Yellow-green, 580 Yellow, 600 Yellow-orange, 620 Orange, 640 Red-orange, 660 Red

Figure 6.5
Stimulus-generalization gradient produced by the distributed representation model of Figure 6.4 The trained network in Figure 6.4 generates this stimulus-generalization gradient, which shows peak responding to the trained stimulus, yellow, and decreased responses for stimuli that are increasingly different from the trained stimulus. This smooth gradient is similar in shape to the ones seen in animals (including humans), such as that obtained from pigeons, shown in Figure 6.1.

The generalization gradients in Figures 6.5 and 6.1 are not identical. The network model responds more strongly to orange light than the pigeons do. The exact width and shape of the generalization gradient produced by a model can, however, be manipulated by varying the number and amount of overlap of nodes in the model. Nevertheless, the overall shape makes the necessary point. Distributed-representation systems capture a fundamental property of learning: humans and other organisms tend, all other things being equal, to treat similar events similarly and to expect similar stimuli to have similar consequences. As you will read in Section 6.2, these early theoretical notions of shared elements and distributed representations within psychological models presciently anticipated later findings by neuroscientists demonstrating that, indeed, there are overlapping neural networks in our brains for similar stimuli.

Test Your Knowledge

Discrete or Distributed Representation Models?

Which of the following learning experiments can be understood and modeled using a discrete-component representation of the stimuli? Which require a distributed representation with overlapping patterns of elements? (Answers appear in the Answers section in the back of the book.)

1. A low-frequency tone predicts a shock and a high-frequency tone predicts a shock, but a light predicts food. Test: What does a medium-frequency tone predict?

2. Patients in a hospital that has the walls painted blue take 2 days, on average, to recover and be discharged, while patients in a hospital that has red walls take 4 days to recover and be discharged. Test: How many days would you expect it to take for patients in a hospital with green walls to recover?

When Similar Stimuli Predict Different Outcomes

Remember Sabrina, the fussy two-year-old from the beginning of this chapter? She is faced with a problem similar to that of Guttman and Kalish's pigeons. If green broccoli tastes awful to her, she may assume that a similar-shaped vegetable, such as cauliflower, has a good chance of being equally unappealing to her as well. On the basis of this prediction, she may decide it isn't worth the risk of experiencing another icky taste to eat the cauliflower. . . *unless* she is really hungry and there are few other options for her at that meal. If hunger motivates Sabrina to take a chance on the cauliflower and she finds that she loves the taste, she now has new information: broccoli tastes nasty to her, but cauliflower tastes yummy. From this experience, Sabrina has learned that it is important to *discriminate* between broccoli and cauliflower even though they have similar shapes (but different colors) because they lead to different outcomes when eaten.

Many children learn similarly fine distinctions. Some can discriminate the tastes of Pepsi and Coca-Cola or can tell the french fries at McDonald's from those at Burger King. Similarly, gem cutters may learn to distinguish diamonds of subtly different color or quality and parents of identical twins learn to tell their children apart. A dog fancier can identify many different breeds of terriers, all of whom may appear virtually identical in the eyes of a cat fancier who couldn't care less. Two objects or substances that initially seem very similar, or even indistinguishable, eventually come to be distinguishable when each is repeatedly paired with a different label, name, or outcome. What determines whether two stimuli are to be treated as similar (generalization) or different (discrimination)? This is a fundamental problem in psychology, and the ensuing discussion reviews some of what psychologists have learned about it from years of careful studies of generalization in animals and humans.

Discrimination Training and Learned Specificity

Chapter 3 introduced discrimination training with examples of people learning to increase their sensitivity to subtle variations in stimuli. We turn now to look more closely at this phenomenon and what it tells us about mechanisms for learning and generalization. One important study in this area, conducted by Herbert Jenkins, a Canadian psychologist, was based on the behavior of two groups of pigeons. One group received standard training in which a 1,000-hertz (Hz) tone signaled that pecking a key would result in food delivery (Jenkins & Harrison, 1962). Because the birds only received the food after pecking the key, the food reinforcement was contingent on the birds' behavior. Recall from Chapter 5 that this operant conditioning can be described as

S (1,000-Hz tone) → **R (key peck)** → **O (food)**

The second group of pigeons received **discrimination training,** in which one of two different (but similar) stimuli was presented on each trial. For these pigeons, the 1,000-Hz tone signaled that a key peck would result in food reinforcement, but another, very similar tone of 950 Hz signaled that a key peck would *not* result in food reinforcement:

S (1,000-Hz tone) → **R (key peck)** → **O (food)**

S (950-Hz tone) → **R (key peck)** → **O (no food)**

Following this training, both groups of pigeons were given test trials with new tones, ranging from very low frequency (300 Hz) tones to very high frequency (3,500 Hz) tones. The experimenters measured how frequently the birds pecked in response to each test tone. As shown in Figure 6.6a, the group receiving training with a single tone showed a broad, bell-shaped generalization gradient similar to what Guttman and Kalish found for light stimuli (see Figure 6.1).

Figure 6.6 Generalization gradients following discrimination training (a) Data from study in which one group of pigeons learned that a 1,000-Hz tone signaled that key pecks would be reinforced; these birds showed a typical generalization gradient when tested with novel tones. A second group of pigeons learned that the 1,000-Hz tone signaled that pecks would be rewarded but that the (very similar) 950-Hz tone signaled no reward ("discrimination training"); these birds showed a much steeper generalization gradient.
Adapted from Jenkins and Harrison, 1962.

(b) Examples of the prototypical category A and category B exemplars used in the Wills and McLaren (1997) categorization study, and a graph showing generalization gradients following discrimination versus A-only training.
Adapted from Wills & McLaren, 1997.

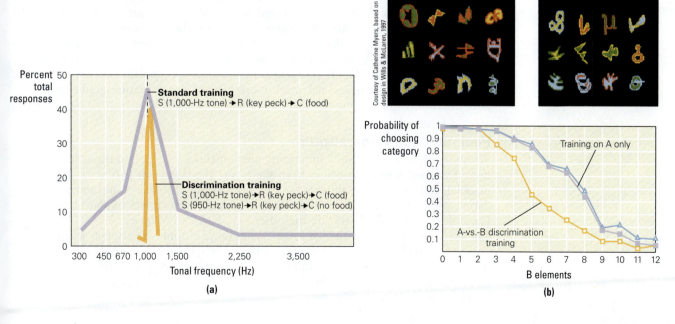

(a)

(b)

In contrast, the pigeons given discrimination training showed a different pattern of generalization. Their generalization gradient was much steeper, centered immediately around the 1,000-Hz tone and dropping off much more rapidly—so that they were not responding at all to the nearby 950-Hz tone or to any other tones higher or lower than 1,000 Hz. The difference in shape of the two generalization gradients in Figure 6.6a shows that with discrimination training, the generalization gradient can change to reflect more specific (more narrowly focused) responding to the reinforcing stimulus. In fact, the generalization gradient following discrimination training in Figure 6.6a looks very much like the gradient in Figure 6.3, which illustrated what a component-representation model predicts when there is no overlap in **stimulus representations**. This suggests that Figure 6.3 wasn't wrong; it was just an illustration of what happens after discrimination training when the stimuli do not have overlapping representations.

A similar difference between the generalization gradients that emerge from training with a single stimulus as compared to discrimination training can also be seen in studies of human category learning in which people are shown visual stimuli consisting of sets of abstract geometric elements (Wills & McLaren, 1997). Each subject was presented with two 12-member sets of abstract geometric elements. One of the sets was presented as a prototypical exemplar of category A, and a distinct set of 12 was presented as prototypical of category B (Figure 6.6b). Other, potential exemplars were constructed with different mixtures of the elements, some from the prototypical A exemplar and some from the prototypical B exemplar. An exemplar was considered to be a member of category A if it possessed at least 8 out of the 12 elements from the category A prototype.

Participants in this study were assigned to one of two types of training. Participants who received discrimination training were shown many examples of category A and many examples of category B, with each example labeled according to its correct category assignment. Other participants did not receive discrimination training but instead were only shown exemplars from category A. After receiving one or the other form of training, participants were given a subsequent generalization test in which they were asked to judge whether unlabeled exemplars were members of category A. As you can see from the curves in Figure 6.6b, people who were trained only with the category A stimulus showed broader generalization gradients than those who received A-versus-B discrimination training, endorsing more of the ambiguous exemplars as being members of category A. This pattern of data echoes the pattern seen in Herbert Jenkins's pigeon study (Figure 6.6a): broad generalization gradients after standard acquisition training and narrower, more focused generalization gradients after discrimination training.

Peak Shifts in Generalization

To understand another very important phenomenon in generalization, let's meet Lisa and consider a conundrum she faces. She decides it is time to get married, and so she goes online to look for prospective husbands at an Internet dating site. Of the first four bachelors she meets, the two whom she likes, Ian and Jim, are both 5′10″ tall; the other two, Bart and Mauricio, are 5′11″, and she does not fancy either of them. What do you think will happen when she comes upon the profile of Marcus, who is 5′9″? Would you expect her to like Marcus as much as Ian or Jim (both 5′10″), whom she previously found to be acceptable, or will she be disposed to like Marcus even more than any of the others?

S+ peak: 550 nm

Responses

S− Group

S+ control group

S+ Wavelength (nm)

Figure 6.7 Peak shift following discrimination training along a physical continuum Pigeons were reinforced for pecking in the presence of a 550-nm light and then were divided into two groups. One group received only this training (the control, or S+, group), while the other received discrimination training in which the 550-nm lights were positively reinforced while a similar 555-nm light was negatively reinforced (the S− group).
Adapted from Hanson, 1959, *Journal of Experimental Psychology, 58*, pp. 321–333.

One study (Hanson, 1959) looked at this very issue, albeit using pigeons and colored lights, not marital prospects. Pigeons were trained to peck at a 550-nm light (for which they received food reward) until they were responding reliably and consistently to this stimulus (a form of operant conditioning). Some of these pigeons (the control group, also called the S+ group) received only this training, while another group (the experimental group, or S−) were given additional discrimination trials with a very similar light, at 555 nm, that was not reinforced. Both groups of pigeons were later tested with probe trials using a full range of different-colored lights, measuring from 480 to 620 nm. The results are shown in Figure 6.7.

As you can see, the peak responding of the experimental animals shifted away from the nonreinforced stimulus, an effect that is therefore called peak shift. It has been observed in many different discrimination paradigms in which stimuli vary along some physical continuum, such as color, brightness, tone, pitch, tilt, or numerosity. Experimental studies of peak shifts in learning are not limited to pigeons pecking, either. Peak shift effects have been observed in bees (Lynn, Cnaani, & Papaj, 2005), horses (Dougherty & Lewis, 1991), rats, goldfish, guinea pigs, chickens, pigeons, and humans (Purtle, 1973). Studies in humans have found evidence of peak shift effects in discriminating complex categories (McLaren & Mackintosh, 2002; Wills & Mackintosh, 1998), pictures of faces that morph along a complex visuospatial dimension (Spetch, Cheng, & Clifford, 2004), and complex acoustic sounds that vary in time (Wisniewski, Church, & Mercado, 2009).

Why does peak shift occur so ubiquitously in animal and human discrimination learning? Kenneth Spence (1937) suggested an interpretation of the peak shift phenomenon that demonstrates how it might arise from the summation of cue-outcome associations.

As schematized in Figure 6.8, Spence proposed that a positive generalization gradient develops around S+ and that an inhibitory gradient develops around S−, each emerging as a result of the fact that each of the two stimuli activates a range of elements shared with stimuli above and below it, as hypothesized in Figure 6.4. If the net associative strength for any test stimulus is the difference between the excitatory gradient formed around S+ and the inhibitory gradient formed around S− and if these two gradients overlap considerably, then the greatest net positive strength will be to the left of S+ because this region is both close to S+ (550) and farther away from S− (555). The peak shift is the

Figure 6.8 Spence's theory of peak shifts Spence argued that the peak shift arises through the combination of excitatory and inhibitory stimulus-generalization gradients that are established around the S+ and S−, respectively. The net association is presumed to be the sum of these gradients, calculated by subtracting the level of inhibition from the level of excitation at each point along the stimulus domain. The peak shift is the movement between the previous maximal responding to S+ at the right vertical line to the new point of maximal responding at the left vertical line.

movement between the previous maximal responding to S+ at the red vertical line to the new point of maximal responding at the blue vertical line shown in Figure 6.8. This is analogous to arguing that Lisa will like 5′9″ Marcus the most because he is very similar to the 5′10″ men she liked (Ian and Jim) and very dissimilar from the 5′11″ Mauricio and Bart, whom she rejected.

Peak Shift and the Rescorla-Wagner Model in Fixed-Ratio Operant Conditioning

Another form of peak shift can be seen in a very clever study by Donald S. Blough in which hungry pigeons were trained to peck keys illuminated with different lights (Blough, 1975). Key pecks to lights at wavelengths below 597 nm were reinforced with a food reward on 1/12 of the trials, whereas key pecks to lights that were above 597 nm were reinforced with a food reward on 1/3 of the trials. As you may recall from Chapter 5, this is a form of fixed ratio (FR) operant conditioning. In this case, two different fixed-ratio schedules were used—one for below 597 nm and one for above 597 nm. According to the matching law of probabilistic reinforcement (see Chapter 4), you might expect pigeons to peck at lights below 597 nm 1/12 (8.3%) of the time and to peck at lights above this wavelength 1/3 (33%) of the time. This is approximately what Blough found. But more interesting were the peak-shift bulges (identified by arrows) in rates of responding seen on either side of 597 nm, as shown in Figure 6.9a.

Blough (1975) elaborated on the key idea of Spence's theory to show how this peak-shift-like effect could emerge from interaction between the shared-elements mechanism for similarity (presented above) and the error-correction learning mechanisms of the Rescorla-Wagner learning rule (introduced in Chapter 4). In the analysis of his pigeon data, Blough points out that a very important property of the Rescorla-Wagner model is its expectation that

Figure 6.9 Peak shift effect in fixed ratio conditioning (a) Response rates of three pigeons to lights varying in wavelength. The vertical line separates the high- and low-reinforcement stimuli. Note the trough and peak to the left and right of that line in both graphs (identified by the arrows), a peak-shift-like effect seen in this form of fixed ratio operant conditioning. (b) Predicted output node activations from the Rescorla-Wagner rule for discrimination training applied to a stimulus continuum.

Adapted from Blough, 1975.

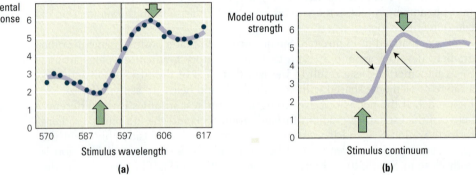

co-occurring cues will compete to predict the outcome. This can be illustrated by the following example: imagine you are training to compete in a kayak race. To enhance your training, your coach puts you in a two-person boat with someone who is so inept that he often paddles backward (when you are trying to go forward). After a month of training with this partner, during which you must paddle extra hard to overcome his backward strokes, you would surely become superbly conditioned. If, after this month of training, you then moved to a one-person kayak that you paddle by yourself, you would likely be faster and stronger than other paddlers who had trained alone or with partners who were helpful.

A similar effect happens in classical conditioning. If cue A is first trained as a conditioned inhibitor of the US (that is, A predicts absence of the US) and then A is paired with a new, unfamiliar cue, B, and both together are repeatedly associated with the US, B will become superconditioned to the US; that is, it will come to overpredict the US. By analogy to the example above, the conditioned inhibitor, cue A, is like the backward paddler, who makes you (like cue B) have to paddle extra hard to get where you are going. The net expectation of a US in the Rescorla-Wagner model is calculated as the sum of the weights of the CSs that are present, in much the same way that the net forward speed of a kayak is the sum of the paddling strengths of the kayakers. In this way, the Rescorla-Wagner model expects that cue B will have a weight greater than 1 because it has had to overcome the negative weight of cue A, with which it was paired during training. This same principle of superconditioning (of you as a superpaddler or cue B as a superpredictor of the US) and how it emerges from the weight summation and cue-competition property of the Rescorla-Wagner model is key to understanding Blough's study and how he explained his data using a combination of shared elements and the Rescorla-Wagner model.

Figure 6.9b shows predictions of the Rescorla-Wagner model from Blough (1975) in which the training stimuli are represented by a distributed "shared elements" scheme much as illustrated earlier in Figure 6.4. This modeling predicts a slight "peak" or "trough" on either side of the 597-nm transition point, as shown in Figure 6.9b (indicated by vertical green arrows). The presence of these "shoulders" on the response curve is a subtle consequence of the cue competition that occurs in the Rescorla-Wagner model when the weights of two (or more) cues summate to predict the outcome. The trough and peak in the model results shown in Figure 6.9b depict responses that are superconditioned to be even lower or higher than the other elements on the same side of the transition point. In contrast, the parts of the curve that are closer to the transition point (indicated by the red arrows) along the continuum have intermediate values because they tend to be responses to the distributed activation that "bleeds" across the transition point—that is, the responses identified by the red arrows are close enough to the transition point that they get some of their reinforcement from lights below 597 nm (reinforced 1/12 time) as well as from lights that are reinforced more often (1/3) of the time, being above the 597-nm transition point. Because the stimuli near the transition point are, in effect, spoiled by being dragged down (or up) by signals on the other (wrong) side of the transition point, the stimuli a little farther away from the transition point—which are too far away to incur this spoiling effect from the other side—have to become superconditioned to make up the difference, creating the exaggerated superconditioned trough and peak indicated by the green arrows. In essence, the stimuli near the transition point (red arrows) are like paddlers who sometimes paddle in the wrong direction, requiring the other elements with which they are often paired (coactivated) to become superconditioned.

In addition to providing another example of the pervasive peak-shift effect, Blough's study and analysis show how two of the most important theories in associative learning—shared-elements representation for similar stimuli and the error-correction learning of the Rescorla-Wagner model—can be combined to help us understand subtle but important properties of learning.

Discrimination Training with Multiple Dimensions: Implications for Attention Allocation

Although many studies of learning and discrimination employ stimuli that differ on only one dimension (such as tone amplitude or color), other studies have used more complex stimuli that can vary on two or more dimensions. In one such study of human category learning, participants were first trained to categorize squares into two groups, category A or category B, based on either their size or brightness (Goldstone, 1994). Sixteen stimuli were provided in the form of squares that varied according to four levels of size and four levels of brightness. On each trial, a subject would see one of these 16 squares and be asked to categorize it as an A or a B. For half the participants, the size of the square determined if it was A or B, and for the other half of the participants, the brightness of the square determined its category membership.

Figure 6.10 shows you the full array of all 16 squares that were used in the experiment (although only one of these was shown on each training trial). For the participants who were trained to categorize the squares according to brightness, the brighter squares (in rows B3 and B4) belonged to category A, and the darker squares (in rows B1 and B2) belonged to category B. Other participants were trained to categorize based on size rather than brightness, with the larger squares (columns S3 and S4) belonging to one category and the smaller squares (columns S1 and S2) belonging to the other.

After this training, all participants were asked to judge the perceived similarities or differences between selected squares: "Are these two squares physically identical?" Of particular interest were the comparisons of squares that differed only in size, such as the square at B2–S2 versus the square at B2–S3, which are the same brightness (B2), or squares that differed only in brightness—such as square B2–S2 versus square B3–S2, which are the same size (S2). Participants who had been initially trained to make brightness discriminations, as illustrated in Figure 6.10, were far less likely to confuse squares that differed in brightness (for example, B2–S2 versus B3–S2) and more likely to confuse squares that differed in size (for example, B2–S2 versus B2–S3).

Figure 6.10 Stimuli for discrimination of squares on the basis of size or brightness The 16 stimuli were constructed using squares that varied according to four levels of size and four levels of brightness. Some participants were trained that the eight brightest squares belonged to category A and the eight darkest belonged to category B, as shown here. Other participants were trained to categorize the same squares based on size (small versus large) rather than brightness.

Adapted from Goldstone, 1994.

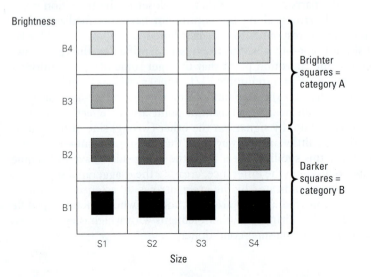

In contrast, participants who were initially trained in size discrimination showed the opposite pattern: they showed much more confusion of similar brightnesses and far less confusion of similar sizes. Thus, people who had been trained on one dimension (whether size or brightness) were subsequently more able to make fine distinctions between stimuli that differ along that dimension than between stimuli that differ along a different, untrained dimension. For example, if you were a trained mycologist (mushroom expert), you might be on the lookout for certain shapes that are indicative of poisonous mushrooms but pay less attention to size or color of the mushrooms if these vary widely across both poisonous and edible mushrooms. The aforementioned study, and the mushroom example, show that, through learning, the degree to which people generalize on the basis of specific stimuli can be adapted to different contexts. In other words, generalization gradients can be modified by experience (learning) so that the organism pays attention to whatever are the most relevant stimulus dimensions in a given situation.

Negative Patterning: Differentiating Configural Cues from Their Individual Components

Another complication of generalization can occur with compound stimuli composed of different features or attributes. Consider, for example, what happens when Sabrina starts playing with boys. She might learn from experience on the playground that freckle-faced boys are usually bratty and that red-haired boys are also bratty. Given these two associations, you might expect her to be especially wary of a new boy she meets one day who is both red haired and freckle faced. Based on her past experiences, she expects him to be really horrid because he has both of the attributes she associates with brattiness. All other things being equal, we, like Sabrina, tend to assume that combinations of cues will have consequences that combine, and possibly summate, what is known about the individual cues.

But is this always the case? What if a certain combination of cues implies something totally different from what the individual cues mean? For example, you know what the letter "c" sounds like and you know what the letter "h" sounds like, but when you see these two letters together as "ch," they represent quite a different sound. Thus, readers of English learn that certain combinations of letters can sound very different than their component letters. Consider another example, from driving a car. While waiting at an intersection, you notice that the antique Citroën car in front of you has its *left* rear red taillight flashing, signaling the car is about to turn left (Figure 6.11a). If its *right* rear red taillight were flashing, you would assume the driver intends to turn right (Figure 6.11b).

Figure 6.11 The challenge of interpreting combined cues (a) Left blinking light means left turn, (b) right blinking light means right turn, (c) both lights blinking means that the driver has turned on the hazard lights.

Mark Gluck

(a)   (b)   (c)

But what if both taillights were flashing, as in Figure 6.11c? Although either the left or the right turn signal flashing indicates an imminent turn, both taillights flashing together certainly does not indicate a combination of two turns. Instead, twin flashing taillights signal a hazard; the car is proceeding slowly or is disabled. Although our tendency may be to assume that what is true of component features presented individually is also true of their combination, clearly it is possible to override this tendency to generalize from components to compounds, as do automobile drivers who learn that the combination of both left and right lights flashing means something quite different from either of them flashing alone.

This kind of situation, where cue combinations have radically different meanings than their components, has been extensively studied with both animal and human learning tasks. Suppose, for example, that a rabbit in a classical conditioning study is trained to expect that either a tone or a light, presented alone, predicts an airpuff US to the eye but that there will be *no* airpuff US if the tone and light appear together. To respond appropriately, the animal must learn to respond with a blink to the individual tone cue or light cue but to withhold responding to the compound tone-and-light cue. This task is known as **negative patterning** because the response to the individual cues is positive while the response to the compound (i.e., the "pattern") is negative (no response).

Because both the tone and the light cues are part of the tone-and-light compound, there is a natural tendency for the animal to generalize from the component cues to the compound cue and vice versa. However, this natural tendency to generalize from component features to compounds doesn't work in this case because the components and the compound are associated with very different outcomes. Negative patterning is difficult to learn because it requires suppressing the natural tendency to generalize about similar stimuli.

With training, the negative-patterning task can be mastered by many animals, including humans. Figure 6.12 shows an example of negative patterning in rabbit eyeblink conditioning (Kehoe, 1988). After only a few blocks of training, the animals learn to give strong responses both to the tone alone and to the light alone. In addition, during this early phase of training, the rabbits make the mistake of overgeneralizing from the components to the compound, giving incorrect strong responses to the compound tone-and-light stimulus. Only with extensive further training do the rabbits begin to suppress responding to the tone-and-light compound.

Can associative-network learning models such as those in illustrated in Figure 6.2 (with discrete-component representation) or Figure 6.4 (with distributed representations to indicate stimulus similarity) provide an explanation of how

Figure 6.12 Negative patterning in rabbit eyeblink conditioning Negative patterning requires learning to respond to two cues (a tone and light) when presented separately but to withhold the response when the two cues are presented together.
Adapted from Kehoe, 1988.

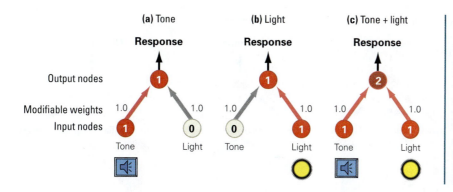

Figure 6.13 **Failure of a single-layer network with discrete-component representations to learn negative patterning** (a) For the tone cue to correctly generate a strong response, the connection from that input to the output must be strongly weighted. (b) For the light cue to correctly generate a strong response, the connection from that input to the output must also be strongly weighted. (c) Consequently, when both tone and light cues are present, the network will incorrectly give a strong response.

rabbits and other animals learn negative patterning? Figure 6.13 illustrates why single-layer network models, like those in Figure 6.2, using discrete-component representations cannot learn the negative-patterning problem. To produce correct responding to the tone alone, the weight from the input unit encoding tone must be strengthened to 1.0. (Figure 6.13a). To produce correct responding to the light alone, the weight from the input unit encoding light must also be strengthened to 1.0 (Figure 6.13b). But this means that if the tone and light are presented together, activation will flow through both those modifiable weighted connections and produce strong responding to the compound—stronger responding, in fact, than to either component alone (Figure 6.13c).

All the weights could be decreased, of course, to reduce the level of response to the compound in Figure 6.13c, but this would also, incorrectly, reduce responding to the individual components. In fact, there is no way to assign association weights in the network of Figure 6.10 that would make the network respond correctly to all three different types of training trials.

One way to resolve this dilemma is to use a two-layer network, as shown in Figure 6.14. This network has two layers of weights (but three layers of nodes); the critical additions are the three nodes in its internal representation layer. One of these nodes (designated "Tone only") becomes active whenever the tone is present, and another ("Light only") becomes active whenever the light is present. To solve negative patterning (and other similar tasks), the internal layer of nodes of this model also contains a new type of node, called a **configural node.** This node (labeled "Tone + light") acts as a detector for the unique configuration (or combination) of two cues. It will fire only if *all* of the inputs are active, that is, when *both* tone and light are present.

Configural nodes are equivalent to what engineers call an "AND" gate because they respond only when all the inputs are active. For example, a configural node might fire when tone *and light are present but not when only one or the other of these two cues is present.* Note that these configural ("AND") nodes are very different from the nodes in Figure 6.4, which capture similarity through overlapping representations. The reason the shared nodes in Figure 6.4 are able to capture the fact that orange and yellow are similar is that these shared nodes are active when either orange or yellow is present. As such, the nodes in Figure 6.4 are equivalent to what engineers call an "OR" gate because they fire if one *or* the other input is present. Just as engineers have long appreciated that they need both "AND" and "OR" gates to build a broad range of complex circuits in hardware, evolution appears to have similarly constructed neural systems capable of encoding both types of logical operations.

Configural "AND" nodes, which require all their inputs to be on in order to fire, are indicated in Figure 6.14 by a double circle to distinguish them from

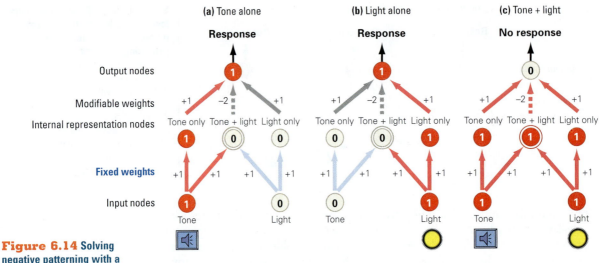

Figure 6.14 Solving negative patterning with a network model A multilayer network in which one node in the internal representation layer (labeled "Tone only") becomes active whenever the tone is present, while another ("Light only") becomes active whenever the light is present, and a third, configural, node ("Tone + light") becomes active when both tone and light are present but not when either alone is present. The configural node is represented by a double circle (one inside the other). (a) When the tone alone is present, the tone-only node becomes active, sending an excitatory signal (+1) to the output node, and the network generates a response. (b) When the light alone is present, the light-only node becomes active, sending an excitatory signal (+1) to the output node, and the network generates a response. (c) When both tone and light are present, the tone + light configural node is also activated. This node sends strong inhibitory signals to the output node (of −2), counteracting the excitatory (+1) signals from the tone-only and light-only nodes, so the net activation of the output node is 0, and the network correctly generates no response.

the shared nodes in Figure 6.4 that represent the "OR" function (that of firing when any of the inputs are present). Figure 6.14 shows how such a network might look after it has been trained to solve the negative-patterning problem. Figure 6.14a shows that when the tone (alone) is present, the tone-only node in the internal representation layer becomes active and in turn activates the output node. Similarly, in Figure 6.14b, the light by itself activates the light-only node, which subsequently activates the output node. However, when both tone and light are present (Figure 6.14c), all three internal representation layer nodes are activated. The tone-only and light-only internal nodes each have a linkage weight of +1 to the output node so their activation together would tend to cause—contrary to the rules—an output activation of 2 (their sum). However, the connection of the tone-and-light compound node to the output node is given a *negative* weight of −2. Therefore, when the configural node is activated, it cancels out the effects of the tone-only and light-only nodes, for a net output activation of (+1) + (+1) + (−2), or 0, as shown in Figure 6.14c. Thus, the network correctly responds to either cue alone, but (equally correctly) not to the compound, solving the negative patterning problem. This shows how and why it is important to have the ability to respond to, and represent, the presence of unique configuration stimuli.

Negative patterning is just one example of a larger class of learning phenomena that involve configurations of stimuli and that cannot be explained using single-layer networks or networks whose internal nodes are "OR" nodes only. To master configural learning tasks, an animal must be sensitive to the unique configurations (or combinations) of the stimulus cues, above and beyond what it knows about the individual stimulus components.

Configural Learning in Categorization

Configural learning is especially important in **category learning,** the process by which animals and humans learn to classify stimuli into different categories. Chapter 4 reviewed work by Mark Gluck and Gordon Bower that utilized simple networks based on the Rescorla-Wagner model to capture some aspects of how people learn to categorize multidimensional stimuli (Gluck & Bower, 1988a). As you will recall, these studies showed that people acquire feature-category associations in much the same way that animals acquire CS → US associations in classical conditioning.

One of their studies tested people's ability to learn to diagnose fictitious medical patients. On each trial, participants were given the description of a patient who had one or more symptoms. The participants were then asked to determine, based on that pattern of symptoms, whether the patient had a particular disease. Gluck and Bower's original model for this task (shown in Figure 4.15) looked much like the associative network in Figure 6.2, with discrete-component representations for each input symptom and one layer of modifiable associative weights connecting those inputs to an output node. However, just like the network in Figure 6.2, this category-learning model could only capture learning for tasks in which there were no important configural relationships among the cues. To ensure that their model could solve complex multi-cue tasks such as negative patterning, Gluck and Bower later added configural nodes to their category-learning model (Gluck & Bower, 1988b; Gluck, Bower, & Hee, 1989).

As an example of how such a model could work, Figure 6.15a shows a network that can learn to diagnose hypothetical patients based on three symptoms: fever, ache, and soreness. Each symptom has its own input node that is active whenever the symptom is present. This network also has one internal representation

Figure 6.15 A configural-node model of category learning
(a) This multilayer network is used to diagnose the presence or absence of a disease, either by the occurrence of individual symptoms or by combinations of symptoms. For simplicity, the numbers corresponding to weight strengths are omitted from this figure; instead, line thickness approximates the strength of the connections. Upper-layer weights (gray) are modifiable, but the lower-layer weights (blue) are fixed. A double circle indicates a configural node, meaning one that is activated if and only if all the weights of connections leading into the node are active themselves. This kind of multilayer network with configural nodes shows behaviors that are similar to those of humans learning the same task. (b) The presence of both fever and soreness produces strong activation in the output node, resulting in a diagnosis that the disease is present. (c) An alternative approach to a network with large numbers of preexisting nodes in the internal representation layer (to capture every possible stimulus configuration) is a more flexible network that has fewer nodes in the internal representation layer but is able to "create" configural nodes as needed. A specialized learning algorithm is required to determine when and which types of configural nodes are required for each problem.

node for each individual symptom as well as internal representation nodes for each possible combination of two or more symptoms. A double circle indicates a configural node, meaning one that is activated if and only if all the weights of connections leading into the node are active themselves. The output node is used to make a prediction of disease: when the output node is highly active, the diagnosis is that the disease is present; otherwise, the diagnosis is that the disease is absent. For instance, if a patient reports fever and soreness, the internal-layer nodes corresponding to these individual symptoms are activated as are nodes corresponding to the configuration of fever and soreness combined, as shown in Figure 6.15b. This leads to strong activation of the output node, resulting in a diagnosis that the disease is present.

There is, however, a critical drawback to this configural representation. Note that the disease-diagnosis network of Figure 6.15a and Figure 6.15b has one internal-layer node for each symptom and another for each possible combination of symptoms. When there are only three symptoms, the model need only keep track of the weights of eight nodes. If the patient exhibited 10 symptoms, however, more than one thousand internal-layer nodes would be required to encode every possible combination of symptoms. Unfortunately, the problems that confront us in the real world consist of numerous stimuli occurring alone or in combination. The number of nodes needed in a network to encode all possible combinations of all possible stimuli would be vast—too many for even a powerful computer to handle. And yet only a small fraction of these combinations will ever actually occur. This dilemma, called **combinatorial explosion,** stems from the rapid expansion of resources required to encode configurations as their number of component features increases.

An alternative to the configural-node network model of Figure 6.15a would be a network like the one shown in Figure 6.15c. This alternative has a smaller number of nodes in the internal representation layer, but those nodes can be assigned the role of configural nodes when needed. The problem of how a network might designate new configural nodes as needed puzzled researchers for many years. However, in the mid-1980s, David Rumelhart and his colleagues, about whom you read in Chapter 1, developed sophisticated new learning algorithms to show how the problem might be solved (Rumelhart & McClelland, 1986). In Figure 6.15c, for example, the network has two layers of modifiable weights—one layer going from the input nodes to the internal nodes and another layer going from the internal nodes to the output node. When experience shows a particular combination of stimuli (for example, fever + ache) to be useful for the purposes of solving a problem, changes in the values of the lower-layer weights can cause the network to adapt so that in the future, a particular internal node will become active only when that specific combination of inputs is present. This advance in learning theory created an explosion of research in network models for learning, memory, and other aspects of cognition.

Test Your Knowledge

Configural Representation of Cues

If we construct an associative network model that uses pair-wise configural cues to discriminate among the eight different objects that can be formed from three binary dimensions—*small/large, black/white,* and *circle/square* (i.e., small black circle, small black square, small white circle, etc.)—what are all the pair-wise configural cues that would be needed in the model to represent all the various configural cues that could be formed? (Answers appear in the Answers section in the back of the book.)

When Dissimilar Stimuli Predict the Same Outcome

So far in this chapter, we have discussed the process of learning in cases of similar stimuli that lead to similar consequences (and dissimilar stimuli that lead to different consequences). We have also discussed the process of learning in cases of similar stimuli that lead to different consequences. But there's a third possibility: what happens when two dissimilar stimuli predict the same outcome? As you will see next, generalization can even occur when physical similarities between the stimuli are absent.

One way in which generalization can extend to dissimilar stimuli is through frequent pairing, or co-occurrence. William James (1890) argued that if all cold objects were wet and all wet objects were cold, the two characteristics would be viewed as a single concept; the presence of one (for example, wet) would imply the presence of the other (that is, cold). James concluded that organisms would tend to cluster, or treat equivalently, stimulus features that tend to co-occur. More recently, in his historical novel *The Alienist*, author Caleb Carr told the story of a nineteenth-century forensic psychologist, a former student of William James at Harvard, who uses this very example from James's Introductory Psychology lectures to hunt for a serial murderer who is terrorizing New York City. The criminal had a childhood history of being beaten by the people he loved, and as a consequence he came to view violence and love as so intertwined that when one was present, he expected or exhibited the other, beating to death any woman he loved and loving any woman whom he beat.

Much common wisdom is based on examples of this kind of clustering, such as "where there's smoke, there's fire." The same kind of clustering of stimuli based on common outcomes or consequences can be demonstrated in the learning laboratory, as seen in the following discussions of sensory preconditioning and acquired equivalence.

Sensory Preconditioning: Co-occurrence and Stimulus Generalization

One way in which co-occurrence of two stimuli can lead to generalization is through a training procedure known as **sensory preconditioning**, in which the prior presentation of two stimuli together, as a compound, results in a later tendency for any learning about one of these stimuli to generalize to the other.

In the laboratory, sensory preconditioning is usually tested in three phases, as summarized in Table 6.2. In phase 1, animals in the compound-exposure group (that is, the experimental group) are first exposed to a compound of two stimuli, such as a tone and a light presented simultaneously. In phase 2, the animals learn that one of the stimuli by itself (such as a light) predicts an important consequence (such as a blink-evoking airpuff), and they eventually give a blink response to the light. In phase 3, the animals are then exposed to the tone only.

Table 6.2

Sensory preconditioning

Group	Phase 1	Phase 2	Phase 3: Test
Compound exposure	Tone + light (together)	Light → Airpuff ⇒ Blink!	Tone ⇒ Blink!
Separate exposure (control group)	Tone, light (separately)	Light → Airpuff ⇒ Blink!	Tone ⇒ No blink

Most will show at least some response to the tone. In contrast, a second (control) group of animals are given exposure to the tone and light separately in phase 1. They are then given phase 2 training identical to the phase 2 training given the other group: they learn that the light by itself predicts the airpuff. But when tested with the tone alone in phase 3, these animals show little or no response (Thompson, 1972).

It seems that the compound exposure in phase 1 establishes an association between the tone and light. In phase 2, the light becomes associated with the airpuff, and this learning is indirectly transferred to the tone too. This transfer can be interpreted as a *meaning-based generalization* because the tone and light are assumed to have the same meaning (that is, they both predict the airpuff) even though they do not have any relevant physical similarity. A meaning-based generalization can be contrasted with a *similarity-based generalization*, which arises naturally between two stimuli that are physically similar. Sensory preconditioning shows that co-occurrence of two stimuli is sufficient to produce meaning-based generalization from one stimulus to the other.

Acquired Equivalence: Novel Similar Predictions Based on Prior Similar Consequences

Another form of meaning-based generalization can occur when two non-combined stimuli share the same consequence, that is, predict the same outcome. In this case, it is possible for generalization to occur between two very dissimilar stimuli even if they never co-occur. Consider two girls, Mandy and Kamila, who look nothing alike but who both love hamsters. Later you learn that Mandy's favorite fish is a guppy. Given that Mandy and Kamila have similar taste in pet rodents, you might expect that Kamila will also like Mandy's favorite pet fish.

Geoffrey Hall and colleagues have found a similar form of generalization in their studies with pigeons (Bonardi, Rey, Richmond, & Hall, 1993; Hall, Ray, & Bonardi, 1993). In one study, they trained pigeons to peck at a light that changed between six different colors, identified as A1, A2, B1, B2, X1, Y1. The researchers then trained the animals to associate the four two-color sequences A1–X1, A2–X1, B1–Y1, and B2–Y1 with the arrival of a food reward (Table 6.3, left column).

In effect, the colors A1 and A2 were "equivalent" because they were both paired with X1. Likewise, colors B1 and B2 were equivalent in their pairing with Y1. Next, the pigeons learned that pecking to A1 alone resulted in food; in contrast, no food followed pecks to B1 alone (Table 6.3, middle column). In phase 3, the pigeons were tested for response to A2 and B2. The birds responded strongly to A2 but not to B2 (Table 6.2, right column), suggesting that the birds had learned equivalencies in phase 1 between A1 and A2 and between B1 and B2.

Table 6.3

Acquired equivalence

Phase 1 Training	Phase 2 Training	Phase 3: Test
A1 → X1 → food	A1 → food	A2: strong pecking response
A2 → X1 → food		
B1 → Y1 → food	B1 → no food	B2: no strong response
B2 → Y1 → food		

After phase 1 training that A2 was "equivalent" to A1 and phase 2 training that responses to A1 resulted in food, the birds expected that responses to A2 would also result in food. Hall and colleagues called this behavior **acquired equivalence** because prior training that two stimuli were equivalent increased the amount of generalization between them—even if those stimuli were superficially dissimilar. Similar effects have been shown in humans (Spiker, 1956) and rats (Honey & Hall, 1991; Hall & Honey, 1989). In summary, although physical similarity is a frequent cause of generalization, generalization may also have other causes. Animals and people can learn to generalize from one stimulus to another that is superficially dissimilar if the stimuli have a history of co-occurring or of predicting the same consequence.

Test Your Knowledge

Discriminating between Generalization Paradigms

To be sure that you have learned to discriminate between the various behavioral paradigms of generalization, see if you can assign each of the following four paradigms to the real-world example that best exemplifies it in the numbered list below. (Answers appear in the Answers section in the back of the book.)

   a. Discrimination training

   b. Negative patterning

   c. Sensory preconditioning

   d. Acquired equivalence

1. Elizabeth is quite impressed by men who, on a first date, bring her either candy or flowers. However, if a man shows up with both, she is turned off, feeling he is coming on too strong.

2. As a child, Samson learned that people who have deep voices also tend to have beards. When he later discovered that men with beards are strong, he inferred that a deep voice was also likely a sign of strength.

3. By playing snippets of music by Brahms, then Schubert, and then Brahms again, a music teacher is able to teach his class how to recognize the style of each.

4. Mark and Kaori enjoy many of the same foods and people. Based on this observation, Mark guesses that Kaori will also like a particular song of which he is fond.

Categorization, Generalization, and Decision Making

The formation of categories is a basic cognitive process through which people organize, describe, and generalize about the world. Categories help us make inferences about objects and events in the world and guide us in predicting the future. The study of how people learn categories, especially in cases where there is only a fuzzy or probabilistic relationship between the features and categories in question, has been a rich domain for applying principles of conditioning to understand human learning and cognition.

Probabilistic Category Learning and Transfer Generalization

Recall from Chapter 4 (as well as earlier in this chapter) the studies of probabilistic category learning by Gluck and Bower (1988) in which college students learned about two categories of fictitious diseases, burlosis and midosis. The students in that study reviewed medical records of fictitious patients who were each exhibiting one or more of the following symptoms: bloody nose, stomach cramps, puffy eyes, discolored gums. By repeatedly studying these patient charts, the students learned through trial and error to do a reasonably good job of predicting who had burlosis and who had midosis. That is, given a list of all of a patient's symptoms, the participants in the study were soon able to predict with reasonable accuracy the probability that the patient had midosis versus burlosis. How did they learn this? Gluck and Bower argued that they learned this task much like animals in conditioning experiments, by applying the principles of error-correction learning (formalized by the Rescorla-Wagner model) to learning the association weights connecting the symptoms to the diseases. When presented with a new patient who has a bloody nose and stomach cramp, the student participants would access their memory for four associations, the associations connecting each of the two symptoms to each of the two diseases. If the sum of the association weights to burlosis was greater than the sum of the weights for midosis, the participants were more likely to diagnose the patient as having burlosis. Figure 4.15 showed that a model of this learning process does a very good job of predicting the frequency with which participants in the study diagnosed a particular patient as having burlosis versus midosis.

However, the ability of participants in the Gluck and Bower experiment to learn to diagnose patients' disease categories based on their patient charts was only the first half of the experiment. What was particularly striking was how badly these participants did on a subsequent transfer generalization task where they had to apply what they had previously learned about midosis and burlosis but do so in a novel way. To understand how and why they generalized poorly, we need to discuss in more detail the nature of the categories used in this experiment. One critical feature of these categories was that one of them occurred three times as frequently as the other. To reflect this difference, we will refer to the more common disease category as C and to the rarer disease category as R (these categories were randomly called burlosis or midosis for different participants). There were four symptoms used in the experiment, which we will refer to as symptoms 1 through 4 (in the study, four symptom names were randomly assigned for each participant).

Figure 6.16a shows the probabilities (*P*) of each of the four symptoms given each of the two categories. From this graph, you see that a patient who suffered from the rare disease (R) has a .69 probability of having symptom 1. In contrast, a patient with the common disease had only a .20 probability of having symptom 1. These figures and the graph give a measure of *P*(symptom|disease), the probability of a particular symptom being present given that you know the disease category. Thus, symptom 1 was far more frequent in patients with the rare disease than in patients with the common disease. However, recall that the common disease occurred on three times as many trials as the rare disease. This means that on any randomly selected training trial, there was a 25% chance of the patient having the rare disease but a 75% chance of the patient having the common disease. These measures are referred to as the base-rate frequencies of each of the two diseases. If you knew nothing about the symptoms in a patient's chart, then you should predict that the patient has a .75 probability of having the common disease and a .25 probability of having the rare disease because these reflect the base-rate frequencies with which each disease occurs in the population.

Bayes's theorem, a statistical rule used to determine inverse probabilities, allows us to combine the information about the probability of the symptoms given the disease (the statistics plotted in Figure 6.16a) with the base-rate frequencies of the two diseases to compute the independent diagnosticity of each symptom for each disease, that is, the probability of the disease given the symptom, or *P*(disease|symptom), as shown in Figure 6.16b. The most striking thing about Figure 6.16b is that for any single symptom, the objective probability of

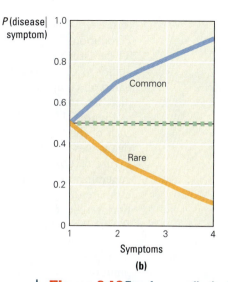

Figure 6.16 Transfer generalization in the Gluck and Bower (1988) study of probabilistic category learning
(a) The probabilities of each of the four symptoms occurring in patients suffering from each of the two diseases. The lower-numbered symptoms were more typical of the rare disease, whereas the higher-numbered symptoms were more typical of the common disease. (b). Conditional probabilities of each of the two diseases given the presence of each of the symptoms, computed from the left-hand side by using the ratio of the base-rate frequency for the two categories (3:1) and Bayes's theorem. (c). Results and predictions for the transfer generalization phase of the study. The objective probabilities of the rare disease given each of the symptoms are shown as a dashed line (with the scale along the left vertical axis). The predictions of the neural-network model, which learns according to the Rescorla-Wagner theory (see Chapter 4), are shown as shaded areas above or below the middle axis to indicate that they are to be interpreted as relative to the scale on the right, which ranges from positive value to negative values around the "0" point, which corresponds to the 50% (.50) mark on the left. The observed means of the subjects' actual estimates of P(rare disease | each symptom)—the measure of generalization—are shown as a solid line (with the scale along the left vertical axis ranging from 0.0 to 1.0).

the rare disease is always less than or equal to the probability of the common disease. This may seem counterintuitive at first. We know that symptom 1 is far more typical of patients with the rare disease than the common disease, so it might seem intuitively plausible that if all you knew about a patient was that he had symptom 1, you should expect the patient to be suffering from the rare disease. In fact, this is not true, given that if you are told a patient is exhibiting symptom 1 (and you know nothing else about what other symptoms they do or don't have), this patient is actually equally likely to be suffering from the common disease as from the rare disease, as shown in Figure 6.16b: P(rare disease | symptom 1) and P(common disease | symptom 1) are both equal to .5.

After training, subjects in the Gluck and Bower (1988) experiment were tested by being asked to estimate directly the probability that a patient exhibiting a particular symptom was suffering from one or the other disease. For each symptom and disease, subjects were asked, "Of all the patients in the hospital exhibiting [symptom], what percent of those patients would you expect to suffer from [disease]?" They then gave numerical estimates of P(rare disease | symptom) and P(common disease | symptom) on a 0-to-1 scale for each of the four symptoms. These estimates were the data of primary interest in evaluating the participants' ability to generalize (from their trial-and-error training at diagnosing patients based on complete charts) so as to make probability estimates based on incomplete information, that is, based only on the status of a single symptom.

Figure 6.16c graphs three measures of the likelihood of the rare disease given each of the four symptoms, obtained by three different methods: the "normative values" are the correct probabilities derived through statistics (taken from Figure 6.16b), the "data" are the actual estimates given by the subjects in the generalization phase of the Gluck and Bower study, and the "predictions" are estimates derived from the network model of Figure 4.15 using the final association weights from the Rescorla-Wagner learning rule as the basis for inferring P(rare disease | symptom); they are shown as shaded areas to indicate that they are to be evaluated by reference to the right axis, which has values that range from positive to negative around a "0" point that corresponds to the .50 (50%) point on the left axis. The most striking difference between the normative probability measures (the correct answers people should have given, shown by the dashed line) and the data from the Gluck and Bower study for what people actually estimated was for symptom 1. As you can see from Figure 6.16c, participants in the study estimated P(rare disease | symptom 1) as being .67 when in fact the correct answer, as noted earlier, is .50. The results indicate that people are very poor at making these kinds of probability estimates when the base rates for the two categories are very different, a finding that echoes an often-described failure in decision making known as base-rate neglect (Kahneman & Tversky, 1973).

Why did the participants in the Gluck and Bower study make this error? The authors argue that their network model, in which associations are learned using the Rescorla-Wagner conditioning model, leads people to acquire associations that are very good at predicting the correct disease but only when applied in the context in which the training occurred—that is, to patterns of symptoms in complete patient charts. The failure of generalization occurs when these associative weights are used to make estimates of conditional probabilities given only partial information, namely, the information about the presence of only one of the symptoms with no information about the other symptoms. Thus, one moral of this study is that the accuracy of people's information about a category may be very tightly bound to the particular way they learned the properties of that category. Such learning may not generalize well if a subsequent transfer task challenges the learners to apply their knowledge in novel ways.

Decision-Making Errors in Misapplications of Generalization

Categories, and the generalizations we make based on them, can lead us astray if we don't use them correctly. One of the most common misuses of generalization comes from faulty inverse reasoning about categories. For example, records show that almost 80% of the players in the National Basketball Association are black (Thomas, 2002). It is therefore an accurate generalization about the category of professional basketball players to say that most are black. However, the inverse is not true: most black men are not professional (or even amateur) basketball players. Nevertheless, in a broad range of situations, people routinely misinterpret probabilities and statistics in this way (Bar-Hillel, 1984).

The problem of faulty inverse reasoning is especially prevalent in medical diagnoses. For example, a woman with breast cancer is very likely to have a positive reading on a mammogram test. But the inverse assumption is false: a woman with a positive reading on her mammogram does not necessarily have a high probability of having breast cancer; this is because the test has a tendency to produce a high rate of false positives. Thus, many women who test positive actually do not have cancer. Unfortunately, people often mistakenly confuse the probability that a member of a category has a particular feature (e.g., that NBA players are black or that women with breast cancer have positive mammograms) with the inverse relationship, the probability that a particular feature is predictive of category membership (e.g., being black predicts NBA membership or having a positive mammogram predicts the presence of breast cancer), especially when the categories in question (e.g., African Americans or women with breast cancer) are not frequent in the general population. The Gluck and Bower study (1988) showed how this faulty inverse reasoning can also emerge with artificially learned categories. The failure of subjects in their study to differentiate between the P(symptom|disease) in Figure 6.16a and the P(disease|symptom) in Figure 6.16b is reminiscent of the prediction error in the examples of NBA players and positive tests for breast cancer.

Education and expertise do not make a person immune to this kind of faulty inverse reasoning from otherwise valid generalizations. By confusing the two relationships, physicians often assume that a woman who has a positive mammogram probably has breast cancer, a mistake in logical inference that can result in women undergoing needless biopsies and surgery (Eddy, 1982). Few of us, in fact, are immune from decision-making errors due to generalizations, a point highlighted in the Learning and Memory in Everyday Life box on pages 240–241.

Interim Summary

- Generalization enables us to apply prior experience to new situations. However, it requires finding an appropriate balance between specificity (knowing how narrowly a rule applies) and generality (knowing how broadly the rule applies).

- Generalization gradients show the strength of an organism's expectation that the consequences of one stimulus will follow other, similar stimuli. Through discrimination training, the generalization gradient can be modified to allow an organism to distinguish (and respond differently to) highly similar stimuli.

- Different models of generalization represent stimuli in different ways. A discrete-component representation depicts each stimulus (or stimulus feature) as one node (or network component). Such representations only apply to situations in which the similarity between the stimuli is small enough that learning about one stimulus should not transfer appreciably to the others. In contrast, distributed representations, in which stimuli are represented by sets of nodes (that overlap when the stimuli share some of the same features or elements), provide a framework for modeling stimulus similarity and generalization.

- The problem of generalization is really four different subproblems—what happens when stimuli (or events) are similar, what happens when they are dissimilar, what happens when the outcomes (or consequences) are similar, and what happens when they are dissimilar.

- Categories enable us to make inferences—that is, generalizations—about members of categories and guide us in predicting the future (to the extent possible), leading us to formulate expectations about the likely behaviors or properties of new experiences, events, or people.

- One of the most common misuses of generalizations comes from faulty inverse reasoning about categories. Even fundamentally accurate generalizations based on categories of events or people can be used to draw inaccurate conclusions if the information they convey about the category is misapplied.

Stereotypes and Generalizing about Other People

When our behavior toward another person is based on his or her belonging to a category defined by race, ethnicity, national origin, gender, religion, or age, we are implicitly making a generalization. In such cases, our generalization is likely to be a stereotype, a standard generalization, or set of beliefs, about the personal attributes of a group of people (Ashmore & Del Boca, 1981). In this essay, we discuss two key questions about stereotypes and how they relate to psychological principles of categorization, discrimination learning, and generalization. First, how do we learn stereotypes of categories of people? Second, how accurate, in general, are stereotypes?

1. How do we learn stereotypes of other people?

Although some of our stereotypes come from direct personal experience, many stereotypes are socially communicated through secondhand reports in books and movies, which may or may not be accurate (for more on the psychology and neuroscience of social learning, see Chapter 11). If the only Colombians you ever hear of are those who are portrayed as drug dealers on TV, it might not be surprising if you come to intuitively assume that this stereotype applies to most or even many people from that country. Stereotyped ideas may also be transmitted through the news media because of their strong tendencies to simplify and to report salient negative events. One black man being arrested for robbery may make the 6 p.m. news; 10 black men working late at their investment banks on Wall Street does not.

Keep in mind that in the process of acquiring stereotypes, people are filtering what they pay attention to through the lens of their own needs and self-interest, a process that may bias or distort stereotypes. We have a vested interest in believing good things about our own group in comparison with other groups. Once people have formed a negative stereotype about members of another group, they are more likely to pay attention to examples that confirm this stereotype and to try to explain away any alternate explanations and disconfirming examples (Pettigrew, 1979).

Also remember, as you saw in the Chapter 5 discussion of operant conditioning, that learning is limited by the fact that organisms learn only about the outcomes of the actions they choose to perform; they do not learn about the outcomes of actions that they do not perform. Thus, you might continue for years to do fine in business by hiring only people who have a Harvard degree, never realizing that you would have done better had you hired the brilliant superstar from Howard University whom you didn't bother to interview.

2. How accurate are stereotypes and the generalizations we make about categories of people?

Consider a commonly held stereotype about a particular category of dogs. It is said that pit bulls are a dangerous breed. To decide whether this generalization is true, we must first agree on what we mean by it. Do we mean that (a) all pit bulls are dangerous, (b) that most pit bulls are dangerous, or (c) that more pit bulls than, say, poodles are dangerous? In fact, the interpretation most in line with psychological and linguistic research into generalizations is

6.2 Brain Substrates

Why devote a whole chapter to generalization? As was noted in the introduction, generalization is the payoff for learning. A medical student may be exposed to many rules and examples during her years of training, but there is no way she can study every possible kind of patient that she might ever meet. Rather, as she approaches each new and novel patient in her practice, she will have to decide when and in what ways their particular symptoms and case histories are like and unlike the examples and principles she studied in medical school.

The psychological theories described in the last section were developed to explain the four kinds of generalization we explored there. These theories were, for many years, just abstractions—tools that psychologists used to help organize, understand, and predict behavioral phenomena. As you read in the previous section, many of these theories were developed as simple models of how relationships between stimuli and outcomes might be represented—that is "encoded"—in the patterns of mental activity or structure of associative networks. Although these associative network theories from psychology were originally abstract tools for describing and explaining behavior, they have in recent years become increasingly useful to neuroscientists as a blueprint for how the brain might accomplish similar processes, which is the focus of our inquiries in this section.

(c): when we say "pit bulls are dangerous dogs," we mean that pit bulls are more dangerous than most other breeds of dog. Under this interpretation, a generalization about pit bulls as dangerous could be accurate even if only 10% of pit bulls are dangerous so long as this is higher than the percent of dogs of other breeds that are dangerous (which, for example, might be only 2% of dogs overall). "Pit bulls are dangerous dogs" is a valid stereotype if knowing that a dog is a pit bull increases (by five times, in this hypothetical example) our expectation that the dog will be dangerous and thus increases our ability to evaluate possible outcomes and act accordingly.

This interpretation of the stereotype about pit bulls is consistent with a broad range of psychological studies in animals and humans with regard to when, and why, categories—and hence generalizations—are formed. The idea that a category or generalization's value is based on its informational utility is, in fact, the same analysis that Robert Rescorla applied to his study of contingency learning in rats (Rescorla, 1968). Rescorla showed that rats will learn a tone → shock association so long as the frequency of shocks following the tone is higher than the frequency of shocks experienced otherwise. The statistical contingency between shocks and the tones is the ratio of the frequency of shocks occurring preceded by the tone divided by the frequency of shocks occurring without the tone. The higher the contingency of shock on the occurrence of the tone, the more useful the tone is as a predictor of the shock. Rescorla showed that it is the contingency of shock on tones (rather than the overall frequency of tones and shocks appearing together) that determines what and how fast an animal will learn about the tone. Thus, a rat has categorized tones as predictors of shocks because doing so provides it with valuable information that enables it to better anticipate and prepare for future shocks. Note that this will occur even if shocks only occur on 10% of the trials in which a tone is present so long as the shocks occur alone even less frequently, for example, only 2% of the time. Thus, a rat responds with fear to a tone even when 90% of the time this is the wrong response so long as the cost (in terms of wasted fear) of these errors is less than the cost of being unexpectedly shocked. Many prejudicial behaviors toward individuals might also be understood as resulting from a similar cost-benefit comparison.

The ability of rats to sense the informational value of cues is a fundamental feature of associative learning found in all species. Humans are also sensitive to the informational value of cues for organizing and interpreting the world around us, using them as the basis for the formation of new categories (Gluck & Bower, 1988a; Corter & Gluck, 1992). This sensitivity suggests that we, like rats, are more likely to develop categories when perceivable cues (such as racial, ethnic, gender, or national identity) are statistically predictive of other variables of interest to us, such as income level, crime rate, or amount of education. The critical issue in stereotypes is the same one that defines all the core psychological issues reviewed in this chapter: Stereotypes enable us to apply prior experience to new situations. However, using them appropriately requires finding a balance between specificity (knowing how narrowly a stereotype applies) and generality (knowing how broadly it applies).

One of the ideas we'll be considering is represented by artist Saul Steinberg's most famous cover for the *New Yorker* magazine (Figure 6.17), caricaturing his view of a typical New York City dweller's mental map of the world. Within this depiction of New York City, Ninth and Tenth Avenues are drawn in such fine detail that they take up half the map. The rest of the country, the area between New Jersey and California, is represented as a largely barren desert marked by a few scattered rocks and hills.

This painting satirizes the belief of many New Yorkers that they are living in the most important place in the world. It also illustrates an important psychological principle. Fine distinctions that are meaningful to New Yorkers, such as the differences between fashionable street addresses, are emphasized and highly elaborated in their mental maps; that is, these places are physically spread out and detailed within this drawing. At the same time, distinctions that may be irrelevant to the typical New Yorker, such as the difference between Illinois and Indiana, are de-emphasized and compressed into less space on the map.

The idea that representations of important places are elaborated with fine details and take up lots of space, while representations of less important places lack definition, may sound familiar to you. In Chapter 2, you read about motor and sensory maps in the cortex and how the area in the cortex devoted to each

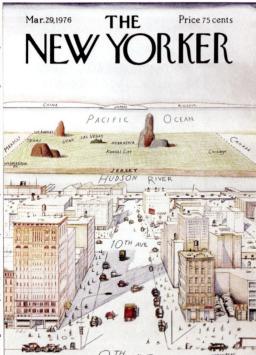

Figure 6.17 **Caricature of a New York City resident's mental map of the United States** Regions that are important to a New Yorker, such as Ninth and Tenth Avenues, are exaggerated in this representation, while other regions, such as the entire Midwest, are disproportionately small.

body part relates in extent to the levels of sensitivity and fine motor control of that body part (a topic that was revisited in Chapter 3, where you read about cortical maps and how they expand with extensive practice, as seen in violin players). The basic principle explored in those discussions was that regions of the cerebral cortex that mediate a highly practiced skill can expand with practice, while regions that are less used may even shrink.

What does this have to do with generalization? As described by the models in Section 6.1, representations directly influence generalization behaviors. If the drawing in Figure 6.17 were, indeed, an accurate representation of a New Yorker's mental map of the world, what would that imply? Based on this representation, you might expect a New Yorker to make very few generalizations grouping one neighborhood with a nearby one in New York despite their proximity. A New Yorker can discriminate between real estate prices on Central Park West (expensive) and those on Columbus Avenue (much cheaper), even though these two streets are actually only a few hundred yards apart (and even though a midwesterner would consider both of them expensive to live on). In other words, a New Yorker is unlikely to generalize from one to the other and make the mistake of expecting that an apartment for sale on Central Park West would cost the same as an identical apartment one block over on Columbus Avenue (but if you find one that does, grab it!).

The preceding example might suggest that New Yorkers are pretty knowledgeable people (and, indeed, they like to think so). However, everything changes when they are tested on their knowledge of the Midwest. For a New Yorker with a mental map like Figure 6.17, all the Midwest states are functionally equivalent. If you tell this New Yorker that Kansas has lots of corn farms, he will probably assume the same must surely be true of Iowa and Illinois. In other words, a New Yorker who has identical (or very similar) mental representations of these states will automatically generalize from one midwestern state to another and have great difficulty telling them apart.

Are New Yorkers unusual in having such a warped view of the world, with extreme generalization in some areas and extreme discrimination in others? To some extent, we all create similarly idiosyncratic worldviews, with uniquely distorted representations; distinctions important to us are enhanced, while less relevant ones are de-emphasized. For example, students asked to sketch a map of the world tend to draw their home region disproportionately large—and in the center of the map. Figure 6.18 is an actual map drawn by a student from Illinois, who overemphasized Illinois relative to the rest of the country, omitted most other states (including New York!), and enlarged North America relative to the other continents. Many American students have this tendency. In contrast, European students tend to draw Eurocentric maps, while students from Australia are naturally more likely to place Australia and Asia in the center.

These kinds of representational distortions, although sometimes comic in their egocentricity, are actually very useful. A similar process allows a violinist to devote more of her cerebral cortex to the fine control of her left hand, which must perform the demanding work of holding down different combinations of strings on the proper frets of the instrument, as compared with her right hand, which is only used for the less intricate movements of drawing the bow back

Reproduced from Solso, R. (1991). Cognitive psychology. Boston: Allyn

Figure 6.18
Representational distortion: the Midwest version A student from Chicago, when asked to sketch a map of the world, drew his home state disproportionately large and omitted most of the other states. He also drew North America larger than the other continents.

and forth across the strings. With only a finite number of neurons available to control all our behaviors, it makes sense to allocate them efficiently according to which distinctions are, and are not, most needed.

The studies reviewed in the first part of this Brain Substrates section will relate the plasticity of the sensory cortices to behavioral properties of stimulus generalization and discrimination learning. The section concludes with a look at the special role of the hippocampal region in stimulus generalization.

Cortical Representations and Generalization

Chapter 3 discussed three main findings about perceptual learning and cortical plasticity. First, when perceptual learning occurs in humans, cortical changes accompany the enhanced discrimination abilities. Second, the selectivity of individual cortical neurons in responding to specific stimulus features can be modified through experience. Third, learning can change the spatial organization of interconnected neurons in the sensory cortex. Each of these principles of perceptual learning and cortical plasticity has a bearing on the generalization and discrimination behaviors described above in the Behavioral Processes section of this chapter, especially with regard to what happens to mapping in the brain when similar stimuli are associated with similar outcomes and what happens when these mappings are altered through discrimination training so that similar stimuli come to be associated with different outcomes. The overlapping and distributed representations for similar stimuli that you saw modeled in Figure 6.4 return in the discussion below, to model the cortical representations of tones of different frequencies in the auditory cortex.

Cortical Representations of Sensory Stimuli

Let's begin our discussion of cortical representations by reviewing some basic features of cortical anatomy. Recall that initial cortical processing of sensory information occurs in a region dedicated to the sensory modality in question: primary visual cortex (or V1) for vision, primary auditory cortex (or A1) for sounds, primary somatosensory cortex (S1) for touch, and so on. From these initial processing regions, sensory information progresses to higher sensory areas that integrate it with other information, first within and then across sensory modalities. Many primary sensory cortical areas are organized topographically (as described in Chapters 2 and 3). This means that each region of the cortex responds preferentially to a particular type of stimulus and neighboring cortical

Figure 6.19 A topographic map of a primary sensory region in cortex Different neurons on the surface of the primary sensory cortex, S1, respond to touch stimuli on different parts of the body, as seen previously in Chapter 2. Neurons in each area respond most to input received from the body parts shown above them. As a result, these areas form a distorted map of the body, often termed a homunculus.

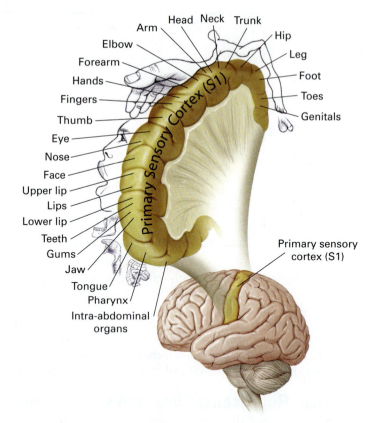

regions respond to similar stimuli. It is therefore possible to draw various "maps" on the cortical surface by studying the responses of different cortical regions.

For example, as described in Chapter 2, S1 is a thin strip of cortex running down each side of the human brain (Figure 6.19). Some neurons respond primarily to stimulation on a particular finger, some primarily to touch on a certain region of the face, and so on. If this procedure is followed for a large number of S1 neurons, it is possible to draw a "map" of the body on S1, with each body part lying over the cortical region that shows the greatest response when touched (Figure 6.19).

To some extent, adjacent areas within S1 contain neurons that respond to neighboring areas of the body (albeit with some discontinuities; for example, Figure 6.19 shows that the parts of S1 that respond to sensations on the fingers lie near those that respond to sensations on the forehead). Parts of the body that are especially sensitive to touch, such as fingers and lips, activate larger areas of S1. The result is a *homunculus*, a distorted neural representation of the human figure with exaggerated hands and lips but a greatly shrunken torso, as shown in Figure 6.19. This figure of a human is distorted in much the same way as the *New Yorker* cover in Figure 6.17: regions where fine discriminations are important (such as sensations on the fingertips) are disproportionately large and detailed.

The primary somatosensory cortex in other animals shows similar organization, with the homunculus replaced by a distorted figure of the species in question, altered to reflect body areas important to that animal. For instance, primates receive a great deal of touch information through their fingers and lips, which are disproportionately elaborated in their cortical map. Rats receive a great deal of information from the displacement of their whiskers, meaning that a rat's whisker area is disproportionately represented on its cortical map.

The primary auditory cortex (A1) lies near the top of the temporal lobe in humans, and it too is organized as a topographic map, as shown in Figure 6.20. In A1, however, neurons respond to sound instead of touch stimulation. Areas of A1 that are adjacent to each other respond to similar frequencies. Each neuron in the auditory cortex responds most to one particular tone, as was discussed in Chapter 3.

We know what these auditory maps look like because of studies that recorded how often a single neuron fires in response to tones of different frequencies. Figure 3.13 presented data collected from such an electrophysiology experiment. This information represents the **receptive field** for a neuron, meaning the range (or "field") of physical stimuli that activate it. The wider a neuron's receptive field is, the broader the range of physical stimuli that will activate the neuron.

Primary auditory cortex

Secondary auditory cortex

Figure 6.20 A **topographic map of the primary auditory cortex** In the primary auditory cortex, neurons respond to auditory stimuli of different frequencies. Areas lying adjacent to each other respond to similar frequencies.

Shared-Elements Models of Receptive Fields

How well does the functioning of receptive fields of neurons match the theories of generalization described in the section on behavioral processes? If the brain is organized to use distributed representations, then physically similar stimuli, such as two tones with similar frequencies, will activate common nodes, or neurons. In other words, two similar tones—of 550 Hz and 560 Hz, for example—should cause overlapping sets of neurons to fire.

Figure 6.21a shows how brain organization might resemble the distributed-component representation (or "shared elements") model from the Behavioral Processes section. A 550-Hz tone might activate sensory receptors in the ear that travel to primary auditory cortex (A1) and there activate three nodes—numbers 2, 3, and 4 in Figure 6.21a. Activation from A1 neurons might then travel (through one or more way stations in the brain) to activate other neurons (possibly in the motor cortex) that can execute a learned behavioral response. A 560-Hz tone activates a different subset of A1 neurons—numbers 3, 4, and 5 in Figure 6.21b. These subsets overlap, in that both of them contain neurons 3 and 4, as shown in Figure 6.21c. Thus, learning about the 550-Hz tone is highly likely to generalize to the 560-Hz tone. This diagram is much the same as the illustration used in the Behavioral Processes section (see Figure 6.4) to show how a shared-elements representation of yellow and orange explains pigeons' generalization between these two physically similar stimuli.

This simplified network may explain why cortical neurons display receptive fields. For each tone in a continuum, you can ask how a particular A1 neuron, such as neuron 3, will respond. The curve in Figure 6.22 shows the results we'd expect. The neuron's best frequency is 550 Hz; similar tones also activate this neuron, although not as strongly as a tone of 550 Hz. The result is a generalization gradient that looks very like the actual receptive fields obtained during cortical mapping studies, like the one shown earlier in Figure 3.13.

Topographic Organization and Generalization

The idea of topographic organization was a central part of Pavlov's theories of learning in the early 1920s, but it remained only a theoretical conjecture until nearly a half a century later. In the 1960s, Richard Thompson established a direct relationship between behavioral properties of auditory generalization and certain anatomical and physical properties of the auditory cortex (Thompson, 1962).

A common experimental finding was that cats trained to respond to a tone of a particular frequency would show a generalization gradient to tones of other

Figure 6.21 A shared-elements network model of generalization within auditory cortex This network has a series of input nodes that each respond to one sound frequency and that each activate a distributed representation in the nodes of the internal representation layer. (For simplicity, only a few of the weights are shown here.) (a) A 550-Hz tone activates nodes 2, 3, and 4 in the internal representation layer. (b) A similar, 560-Hz tone activates nodes 3, 4, and 5. (c) The overlap between these two distributed representations determines the degree to which learning about one tone will generalize to the other.

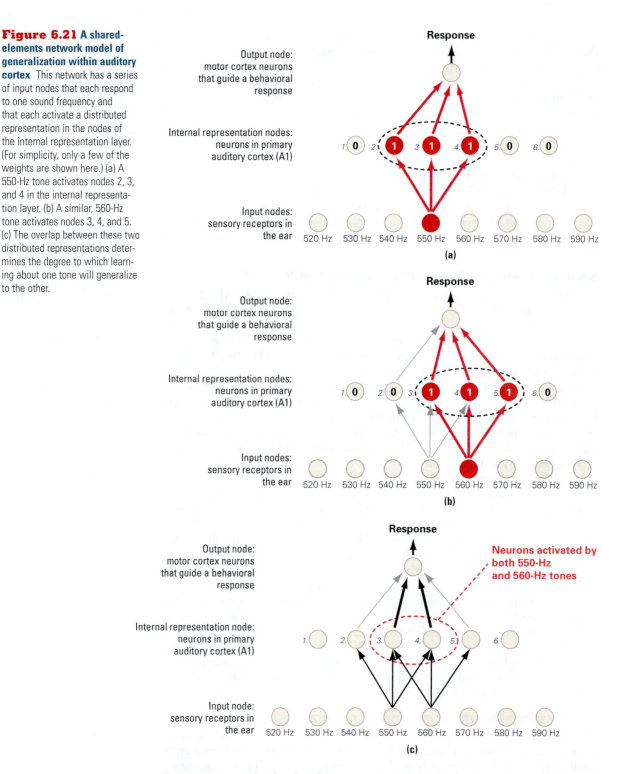

frequencies, much like the sloping gradient seen in Figure 6.1. However, after Thompson removed the primary auditory cortex (A1) of some of the cats, they responded equivalently to all tones, even those separated by 5 octaves or more! This experiment demonstrated that A1 was necessary for the production of appropriate generalization gradients to auditory stimuli (Thompson, 1965). The

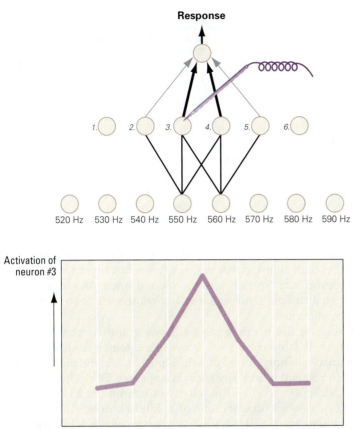

Response

520 Hz 530 Hz 540 Hz 550 Hz 560 Hz 570 Hz 580 Hz 590 Hz

Activation of neuron #3

520 Hz 530 Hz 540 Hz 550 Hz 560 Hz 570 Hz 580 Hz

Figure 6.22 A simulated electrophysiology study The activity of node or neuron #3 is recorded for each of the tones between 520 Hz and 580 Hz; the frequency leading to the strongest response is 550 Hz.

indiscriminate behavior of the lesioned cats reflected massive overgeneralization resulting in a flat generalization gradient. As a control study, Thompson also tested cats who had undergone removal of primary somatosensory cortex (area S1) instead. These animals showed normal generalization behavior to tones, indicating that the auditory overgeneralization occurred specifically in animals with A1 lesions. Similar overgeneralization of visual stimuli has been reported in monkeys with damage to V1, the primary visual cortex (Thompson, 1965).

These studies suggest that, although it is possible for an animal to learn to respond to stimuli while lacking the corresponding areas of sensory cortex, an intact sensory cortex for that stimulus type is essential for normal generalization. Thus, without A1, animals can learn to respond to the presence of a tone but cannot respond precisely to a *specific* tone. In other words, without the primary sensory cortex, animals overgeneralize and have difficulty discriminating stimuli in the corresponding sensory modality. What these studies do not show is whether the receptive sets of neurons in the brain can be changed as a result of learning and experience. This question is addressed in more recent research, as we see below.

Plasticity of Cortical Representations

We saw in earlier chapters that if a particular part of the body receives frequent stimulation, the corresponding parts of the somatosensory map will grow and expand (at the expense of adjacent cortical areas, which compensate by contracting). Lack of stimulation or use can cause change of a different kind in cortical representations, with disused cortical areas shrinking. For example, when a limb

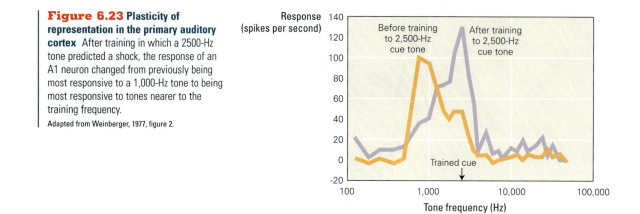

Figure 6.23 Plasticity of representation in the primary auditory cortex After training in which a 2500-Hz tone predicted a shock, the response of an A1 neuron changed from previously being most responsive to a 1,000-Hz tone to being most responsive to tones nearer to the training frequency.

Adapted from Weinberger, 1977, figure 2.

is amputated, the part of S1 representing the lost limb does not receive any more sensory input. Rather than allowing that region of cortex to remain idle, nearby areas of the homunculus may "spread" into the vacated space. As a result, those areas acquire increased cortical representation and consequent increased sensitivity to stimulation and touch.

In seminal studies on the neural bases of learning and cortical plasticity, Norman Weinberger and his colleagues recorded responses from individual neurons in the primary auditory cortex of guinea pigs before and after the animals were trained to respond to auditory cues (Weinberger, 1993). In one study, Weinberger and colleagues recorded the activity of neurons in A1 before and after the animals experienced presentations of a 2500-Hz tone paired with a shock. Through training, many neurons changed their receptive field to become most responsive to tones near the training frequency of 2,500 Hz. One such neuron is shown in Figure 6.23. This neuron, which had originally responded most strongly to tones of about 1,000 Hz, now responded most strongly to tones of the trained frequency. If enough neurons were to show this type of change, the overall result could amount to cortical remapping that allows a larger area of A1 to respond to the trained frequency. These cortical changes occurred quickly, after as few as five pairings of the tone and shock.

In another study, Weinberger showed that if a tone is repeatedly presented alone (as in habituation, described in Chapter 3), then the opposite effect occurs: there is a decrease in neuronal responding to this frequency (Condon & Weinberger, 1991). Moreover, if the tone and shock are both presented but not paired (that is, if they are presented separately), then no significant changes are observed in the neurons' responses to tones (Bakin & Weinberger, 1990). This result indicates that the cortical plasticity is a result of the tone-shock pairing. It implies that stimulus presentation alone doesn't drive cortical plasticity; the stimulus has to be meaningfully related to ensuing consequences, such as a shock.

If cortical change occurs because a stimulus in one sensory modality is meaningfully related to—or in other words, is predictive of—a salient consequence (such as food or shock) in a different sensory modality, how did information about that consequence reach the primary sensory cortex of the first modality in order to produce the change there? After all, A1 is specialized to process information about sounds, but food is a gustatory (taste) stimulus and shocks are somatosensory, not auditory, stimuli, and yet, the findings in Figure 6.23 clearly indicate that pairing a tone with a shock *does* bring about a change in auditory cortex.

Weinberger has argued that A1 does not receive specific information about somatosensory or gustatory stimuli but instead only receives information that some sort of salient event has occurred (Weinberger, 2004). This information is enough to instigate cortical remapping and expand the representation of the cue stimulus. The primary sensory cortices (A1, V1, S1, and so on) only determine which stimuli deserve expanded representation within that primary cortex and which do not.

How does the brain determine whether a stimulus merits cortical remapping, without necessarily specifying exactly why? It turns out that several brain regions may serve this function. The basal forebrain is a group of nuclei important for learning and memory; damage to it can produce *anterograde amnesia*, which is a severe impairment in forming new fact and event memories (more on this in Chapter 7). Many cortical mapping researchers have focused on a small group of neurons located in an area of the basal forebrain called the **nucleus basalis** (Figure 6.24). The nucleus basalis projects to all areas of the cortex and to the amygdala. When nucleus basalis neurons are activated, they release **acetylcholine (ACh)**, a neurotransmitter that has many functions in the brain, including the promotion of neuronal plasticity. In summary, the nucleus basalis functions to enable cortical plasticity: when a CS is paired with a US, the nucleus basalis becomes active and delivers acetylcholine to the cortex, enabling cortical remapping to enlarge the representation of that CS (Weinberger, 2003).

But how does the nucleus basalis "know" when to become active? It receives the information through connections from areas such as the *amygdala*, which codes emotional information such as discomfort and pain (for example, from an electric shock) and pleasure (from food). (The function of the amygdala is discussed further in Chapter 10.) Several studies have confirmed that the nucleus basalis can play a role in mediating cortical plasticity. Most important, experiments show that if a tone is paired with nucleus basalis stimulation—rather than with a "real" consequence, such as food or shock—cortical remapping occurs to enhance response to that tone (Bakin & Weinberger, 1990; Kilgard & Merzenich, 1998).

These findings are very exciting because of their implications for rehabilitation after cortical damage. It may eventually be possible to use judicious stimulation of the nucleus basalis to encourage cortical remapping in individuals who have lost the use of one of their cortical areas. Although that is still far in the future, Michael Merzenich and colleagues have shown that strategic application of behavioral training procedures that encourage cortical remapping can be used to remediate certain types of brain disorders in people.

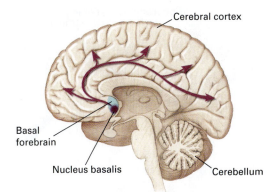

Figure 6.24 The role of the nucleus basalis in cortical plasticity This medial view of the human brain shows the nucleus basalis within the basal forebrain. Neurons in the nucleus basalis transmit the neurotransmitter acetylcholine throughout the cerebral cortex.

Test Your Knowledge

Cortical Plasticity and Generalization

1. Removing the auditory cortex of a cat results in (increases/decreases) in generalization among tones of different frequency.

2. Repeated unreinforced presentation of a tone CS would cause (more/fewer) neurons in the auditory cortex to respond to the tone.

(Answers appear in the Answers section in the back of the book.)

Figure 6.25 The hippocampal region in rats and the analogous medial temporal lobe in humans. (a) The hippocampus and broader hippocampal region in rats. (b) The hippocampus and broader medial temporal lobe in humans.

Generalization and the Hippocampal Region

Recall the configural representations modeled in Figures 6.14 and 6.15; these represent an essential form of learning in which a unique combination of two (or more) cues acquires a meaning distinct from that of the component cues. You can view this as a form of learning that requires sensitivity to the relationship between two sensory cues. Other forms of learning and generalization that involve relationships between sensory cues are the sensory preconditioning and acquired-equivalence processes also discussed in Section 6.1. Learning about relationships among stimuli in the environment is part of the special role in learning and conditioning served by the hippocampus and related structures, referred to as the **hippocampal region** in rats and other small animals and as the **medial temporal lobe** in humans (Figure 6.25).

Effect of Damage to the Hippocampal Region

To examine the role of the hippocampal region in generalization, we must return to the procedure for sensory preconditioning summarized in Table 6.2. In the first phase of sensory-preconditioning experiments, animals in the compound exposure group are exposed to a combination of two stimuli, such as a tone and a light, presented together. Control group animals are exposed to each stimulus separately. In phase 2, presentation of one of the stimuli by itself—say, the light—predicts a salient event, such as a blink-evoking airpuff; control animals and compound exposure animals learn to respond to the light with an eyeblink. Finally, in phase 3, the two groups of animals are tested with the other stimulus (in this case, the tone) alone. Normal animals of the compound exposure group will give a significant eyeblink response to the tone in phase 3, indicating that they have generalized the training from the tone to the light based on the prior co-occurrence of tone and light (Figure 6.26). By contrast, normal animals of the control group, given separate exposure to the tone and light in phase 1, show little or no responding to the tone in phase 3.

The results are different, however, for animals with damage to their hippocampal region. Rabbits with surgically created lesions in the fornix (part of the hippocampal region) display no sensory preconditioning (Figure 6.26; Port & Patterson, 1984). That is, lesioned animals in the compound exposure group show no more transfer in phase 3 than animals in the separate exposure group. It seems that an intact and functioning hippocampal region is needed for generalizing between stimuli that have co-occurred in the past.

Similarly, in a study of acquired equivalence using rats (see Table 6.3 on page 234), researchers found that rats with hippocampal region damage—specifically lesions of the entorhinal cortex, which lies next to the hippocampus—show impaired acquired equivalence: they can learn the associations in phases 1 and 2 but show no generalization in phase 3 (Coutureau et al., 2002). Here again, animal lesion studies show that the hippocampal region is critical for meaning-based generalization.

Other evidence supporting a key role for the hippocampal region in generalization comes from studies of latent inhibition, a classical conditioning paradigm in which learning a CS-US association is slower in animals given prior exposure to the CS (*CS exposure* condition) compared with animals given equivalent prior

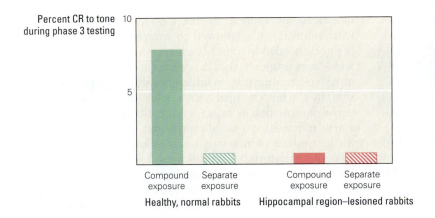

Percent CR to tone during phase 3 testing

Healthy, normal rabbits — Compound exposure / Separate exposure

Hippocampal region–lesioned rabbits — Compound exposure / Separate exposure

Figure 6.26 **The hippocampal region and sensory preconditioning** In rabbit eyeblink conditioning, hippocampal damage abolishes the sensory preconditioning effect, so that lesioned rabbits given compound exposure to tone and light in phase 1 show no more response to the tone in phase 3 than do rabbits given separate exposure.

Drawn from data presented in Port & Patterson, 1984.

exposure to the context alone (*sit exposure* condition). This is essentially a generalization task in which the CS-exposed animals are tricked into overgeneralizing from phase 1 (where there is no US) to phase 2 (where the CS now does predict a US).

One such finding is shown in Figure 6.27, from a study of rabbit eyeblink conditioning by Daphna Shohamy and colleagues (Shohamy, Allen, & Gluck, 2000), who demonstrated that latent inhibition in rabbit eyeblink conditioning is eliminated by hippocampal region damage—specifically, a lesion of the entorhinal cortex. One interpretation of latent inhibition is that the experimental procedure manipulates the relationship between the stimulus cue and the context during pre-exposure. According to this view, in the CS-exposed group, the CS is generalized to the context during phase 1 and therefore is harder to discriminate from the context in phase 2, when the animal has to learn to respond to the CS in the context but not to the CS alone. Consistent with this idea, other studies have shown that latent inhibition is highly context sensitive and requires that the animal be exposed (phase 1) and trained (phase 2) in the same context (Lubow, 1989).

In summary, studies of hippocampal region lesions in animals, using three different experimental paradigms—sensory preconditioning, acquired equivalence, and latent inhibition—all converge to suggest that this brain region is critical for stimulus generalization, especially when that generalization involves learning relationships between different stimuli.

Modeling the Role of the Hippocampus in Adaptive Representations

The data described above suggest that the hippocampal region is involved in even the most elementary forms of associative learning, including classical conditioning. (Chapter 7 shows how the hippocampus and related structures in the medial temporal lobe are critical for learning about facts and events, too.) This does not mean that the hippocampal region is *necessary* for learning a stimulus-response association. Instead, the hippocampal region appears to be critically involved in developing new representations. Mark Gluck and Catherine Myers proposed a model in which the hippocampal region operates as an "information gateway" during associative learning, storing new representations of events that are experienced (Gluck & Myers, 1993, 2001). In their model,

Figure 6.27 **Latent inhibition in rabbit eyeblink conditioning** Latent inhibition in rabbit eyeblink conditioning is eliminated by hippocampal region damage, specifically a lesion of the entorhinal cortex. Control rabbits in the "sit exposure" condition (solid green bar), who did not receive any preexposure to the tones, produced many more eyeblink CRs during subsequent tone-airpuff training than control rabbits, who had been previously exposed to the tone (green-striped bar). In contrast, animals with entorhinal cortex (EC) lesions (shown in red) showed no such effect. In fact, the rabbits with EC lesions in the "CS exposure" group (red-striped bar) learned better than control rabbits in the equivalent CS exposure group (green-striped bar). Brain damage actually helped these rabbits learn faster.

Adapted from Shohamy, Allen, & Gluck, 2000.

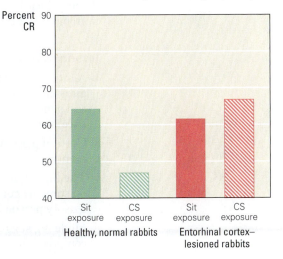

Percent CR

Healthy, normal rabbits — Sit exposure / CS exposure

Entorhinal cortex–lesioned rabbits — Sit exposure / CS exposure

Cerebellum and cortex

Long-term memory for associations

Hippocampal region

New representations
1. *Compression if unimportant or redundant*
2. *Differentiation if useful*

Figure 6.28 Gluck and Myers's model of hippocampal region function in learning The hippocampal region (on right) compresses and differentiates representations of new events so that these optimized representations can be transmitted (indicated by red arrow) to other brain regions, such as the cerebellum and cortex (on the left).

illustrated in Figure 6.28, the hippocampal region selects what information is allowed to enter memory and how it is to be encoded by other brain regions. Specifically, Gluck and Myers proposed that the representation of unimportant or redundant information undergoes shrinkage (or compression) by the hippocampal region, while the representation of useful information is expanded (or differentiated), creating a new, efficient, optimized representation that encodes only the key aspects of incoming information.

Remember Figure 6.17, caricaturing a typical New Yorker's mental map of the world? This image captures just the kind of compression (for example, of the entire Midwest into a small, barren strip) and expansion (for example, the exaggerated detail of Ninth and Tenth Avenues) that Gluck and Myers propose are dependent on the hippocampal region. In their model, these representational changes are computed in the hippocampal region and then used by other brain regions, such as the cerebral cortex and the cerebellum, where the stimulus-response associations that control motor outputs are actually stored.

Gluck and Myers applied their model of the hippocampal region's role in conditioning to a broad range of experimental findings, including the studies of sensory preconditioning and latent inhibition summarized above. In both cases, they showed that the learning displayed by healthy, normal animals was similar to how the model behaved when the representational compression and differentiation processes were turned on. In contrast, when these hippocampal-dependent changes in representation were turned off, the resulting "lesioned" model provided a good description of the altered learning seen in animals with lesions to their hippocampal region, as in the studies of sensory preconditioning, acquired equivalence, and latent inhibition reviewed above (Gluck & Myers, 2001).

Further evidence implicating hippocampal region function in the modification of stimulus representations comes from functional brain imaging. The model predicts that the hippocampal region should be very active early in training, when subjects are learning about stimulus-stimulus regularities and developing new stimulus representations, but should be less active later in training, when other brain regions (such as the cerebellum and cerebral cortex) are using these representations to perform the behavioral response. As predicted, a functional magnetic resonance imaging (fMRI) study of normal humans learning a probabilistic categorization task (similar to Gluck and Bower's study of medical diagnoses, described earlier) found that activity in the hippocampal region was high early in training and then tapered off as the task was learned (Poldrack et al., 2001).

Interim Summary

▪ Although animals can learn to respond to auditory stimuli without the primary auditory cortex, an intact A1 is essential for normal auditory learning and generalization. Without A1, animals can learn to respond to the presence of a tone but cannot respond precisely to a specific tone.

▪ Cortical plasticity is driven by the correlations between stimuli and salient events.

▪ The hippocampal region plays a key role in forms of learning that depend on stimulus generalization, including the classical conditioning paradigms of sensory preconditioning and latent inhibition.

▪ Modeling suggests that one role of the hippocampal region is to bring about compression or differentiation of stimulus representations as appropriate.

6.3 Clinical Perspectives

Given what animal studies have shown about the importance of the hippocampal region in generalization, it will not surprise you to learn that damage or dysfunction in the hippocampal region in humans can also have deleterious consequences for learning and generalization. We discuss here evidence that hippocampal dysfunction in the mental disorder schizophrenia leads to significant changes in how patients with this disorder learn and generalize, impairing their interaction with the world, especially in novel situations. Other disorders that disrupt the hippocampal region include amnesia (discussed in Chapter 7) and Alzheimer's disease (discussed in Chapter 12). The hippocampus is not, however, the only brain region affected by schizophrenia—schizophrenia is a complex and heterogeneous disorder that involves many brain areas. Chapter 9 addresses some of the ways in which frontal lobe dysfunction impairs other aspects of learning, memory, and attention that are pertinent to schizophrenia.

Figure 6.29 The shape of the hippocampus in schizo-phrenia Three-dimensional volume rendering of hippocampi (with the amygdala at the front) as seen from the front of the brain in both a normal subject (a) and an age-matched schizophrenic patient (b). Note the smaller hippocampi and amygdalae in the schizo-phrenic patient, especially on the left (right side of image, as is the convention for clinical scans used by radiologists).

Image reconstruction and figure courtesy of Martha Shenton and Robert McCarley. As reproduced in Heckers, 2001.

Schizophrenia is a heterogeneous and severe mental disorder with symptoms of hallucinations, delusions, flattened affect, and social impairment. Functional brain imaging studies have shown reduced hippocampal activity in patients with schizophrenia (Heckers et al., 1998), while a wide range of structural and func-tional brain imaging studies have identified abnormalities in the hippocampus as a core feature of the illness, present from the onset and, to a lesser degree, in first-degree relatives of people with schizophrenia (Heckers, 2001). In par-ticular, people with schizophrenia show hippocampal shape abnormalities, most notably an overall smaller volume, as illustrated in the three-dimensional ren-derings of hippocampi in controls and patients shown in Figure 6.29.

More recently, studies of associative learning and generalization have shown that most patients with schizophrenia are able to learn simple associations but are markedly impaired when these associations must be transferred to a new context (Polgár et al., 2007) or flexibly modified in some other way (Waltz & Gold, 2007). We turn next to several studies that help us understand how some of the cognitive impairments in schizophrenia may be related to dysfunction in the hippocampus.

Acquired-Equivalence Studies in Schizophrenia

Catherine Myers and colleagues have adapted the acquired-equivalence procedure from animal conditioning for use with humans (Myers et al., 2003). In consider-ation of the data that the hippocampal region in rats is essential for acquired equiv-alence (Coutureau et al., 2002), Myers and colleagues applied their human version of the task to the study of generalization impairments in people with schizophrenia.

On each trial in the Myers et al. human-acquired equivalence tasks, participants see a cartoon face and two colored fish and are asked to learn which fish each per-son prefers, as shown in Figure 6.30. In phase 1, for example, the participants might be asked to learn that one person (a brown-haired girl) prefers blue fish over green fish and that another person (a blond-haired woman) also prefers blue fish over green fish (Figure 6.30, left). In other words, participants should gradually learn that these two people are equivalent in the sense that they are to be paired with the same fish. In phase 2, participants learn some new information: the brown-haired girl also prefers red fish over yellow fish (Figure 6.30, center). Finally, phase 3 is a testing phase, in which participants are quizzed on all the pairings they've learned so far. Intermixed with this testing are some critical pairings that the participants have never seen before. For example, they are shown a blond-haired woman and asked if she is likely to prefer a red or a yellow fish (Figure 6.30, right).

Figure 6.30 An acquired equivalence task for humans The figure shows a schematic diagram of the task's three phases. On each trial of the task, participants must choose which of two fish they think the person will prefer.
Adapted from Myers et al., 2003.

Phase 1: equivalence training   Phase 2: train new outcome   Phase 3: transfer

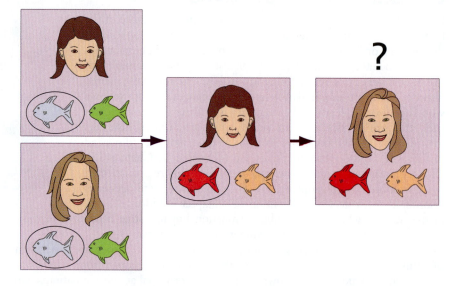

Healthy adults reliably judge that the blond-haired woman prefers red fish over yellow fish, even though they've never specifically been taught this (Myers et al., 2003). In essence, participants in this study are showing acquired equivalence: when they learn that two people show an equivalent pattern of past preferences (as in phase 1) and one of the two prefers the red fish over the yellow fish (in phase 2), then they judge that the other person will probably prefer the red fish over the yellow as well.

How do people with schizophrenia perform on this task? Szabolcs Kéri and colleagues in Hungary have conducted several studies using the task from Figure 6.30, comparing patients with schizophrenia with healthy control subjects (Kéri et al., 2005; Farkas et al., 2008). The deficit observed in the transfer generalization phase for new pairs in Figure 6.31 suggests that hippocampal region–dependent functions are indeed impaired in schizophrenia. More recently, Daphna Shohamy and colleagues presented data showing that antipsychotic medications partially remediate the acquired-equivalence deficits in people with schizophrenia, suggesting that these medications either enhance hippocampal region function directly or else indirectly enhance the ability of the hippocampal region to cooperate with other brain regions (Shohamy et al., 2010).

To further clarify the role of the hippocampal region in generalization, Shohamy and Anthony Wagner studied brain activity in healthy undergraduates with fMRI while using a variant on the Myers et al. acquired-equivalence procedure illustrated in Figure 6.30. As shown in Figure 6.32, they found that the

Figure 6.31 Acquired equivalence data from people with schizophrenia When tested on the acquired-equivalence task from Figure 6.30, patients with schizophrenia (SZ) are normal at learning and retention of associations but are impaired at transfer generalization as compared with matched healthy controls (HC).
Adapted from data presented in Kéri et al., 2005.

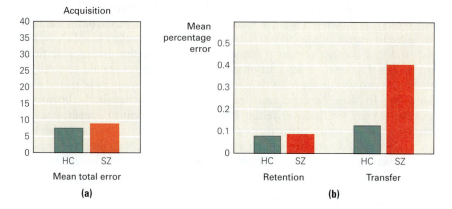

magnitude of activation increase in the hippocampus (as well as in the midbrain) during phase 1 training correlated with subsequent accuracy on the generalization trials at test. Interestingly, they found no such correlation between hippocampal activation during the generalization trials and the accuracy on those trials. Their finding that the critical hippocampal activity occurred during learning, not activation, confirms Gluck and Myers's prediction that the hippocampal role in acquired equivalence is to lay down an appropriate stimulus representation during learning that permits subsequent use of this learning in a broader, more flexible range of future transfer situations.

Other Studies of Transfer Generalization in Schizophrenia

Acquired equivalence is not the only task that has been used to study the role of the hippocampal region in generalization in people with schizophrenia. Other studies of people with schizophrenia have shown that they are impaired at transitive inference, a form of hippocampal-region-dependent reasoning in which learned information is used to guide later inferences. If you learn that Liz is smarter than Alice and Alice is smarter than Isabel, then by transitive inference, you would infer that Liz is smarter than Isabel. Using ">" to represent "is smarter than," we would write this inference as "if Liz > Alice and Alice > Isabel, then Liz > Isabel."

In a study of this kind of learning and transitive inference, patients and healthy controls were trained on a series of learned discriminations that were hierarchically organized according to the pattern A > B, B > C, C > D, and D > E (Titone, Ditman, Holzman, Eichenbaum, & Levy, 2004). They were then tested on each of these four training pairs as well as on two novel "inference" pairs. The novel pairs, consisting of stimuli the participants had seen before but that had not previously been paired, were AE, which can be evaluated without consideration of hierarchical relations (because A and E only appear in one type of relationship, superior or inferior to another cue), and BD, which can only be evaluated by hierarchical relations because both B an D have previously been shown in superior and inferior relationships to other cues. Schizophrenia patients and controls successfully learned the training pairs and correctly responded to the nonrelational AE pair. However, the schizophrenia patients were less accurate than controls in responding to the relational BD pair, consistent with the hypothesis that higher-level memory processes associated with relational memory organization, and its role in supporting generalization from training to transfer tasks, are impaired in schizophrenia.

Kéri and colleagues have also studied transfer generalization in schizophrenia, using a task in which participants navigate a cartoon character, Kilroy, through a sequence of four rooms by learning to choose the unlocked door from three colored doors in each room. In the training phase, each stimulus leading to reward (unlocked door in each room) is trained via feedback until the complete sequence is learned (Figure 6.33). Note that on each run through the experiment, the location of each of the colored doors moves around, and it is color, not location, that is the cue to be learned. In the transfer generalization phase, the decision-making context is manipulated so that a given room will contain a door whose color was correct in another room although it is not the correct door in the new room. Compared with healthy controls, patients with schizophrenia were markedly impaired at the transfer generalization of the previously learned rules to rooms with these different alternative options, even when they had successfully learned the initial training phase (Polgár et al., 2009).

Figure 6.32 Individual differences in acquired equivalence learning in healthy subjects (a) Brain image showing the hippocampus activation that was correlated with transfer generalization performance. (b) Brain activation signal during learning correlated with accuracy in tests of transfer generalization across all subjects in the Shohamy and Wagner study.

Adapted from data presented in Shohamy & Wagner, 2008.

Figure 6.33 The chaining task used to study learning and generalization in schizophrenia Upper row, left panel: At the start of the experiment, participants choose among the closed doors in room 1. Upper row, right panel: Choosing the purple door is incorrect and results in no exit. Lower row, left panel: Choosing the yellow door in room 1 is correct, and Kilroy goes outside. Lower row, right panel: In room 2, the participant chose the correct door (on right), allowing Kilroy to enter into room 1.

Adapted from Polgár et al., 2009.

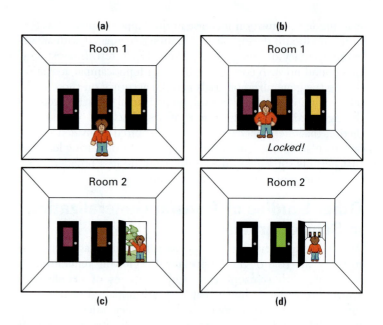

Test Your Knowledge

Schizophrenia, the Hippocampus, and Generalization

In phase 1 of a study, a person with schizophrenia hears a tone played over and over 10 times with nothing following it. Later, this same tone is repeatedly followed by a mild shock. Do you think the person would learn the tone-shock association faster or slower than a healthy control subject? (Answer appears in the Answers section in the back of the book.)

Interim Summary

- People with schizophrenia show deficits in generalization, consistent with their impaired medial temporal lobe function.
- Generalization deficits in acquired equivalence are probably linked to impaired hippocampal function during learning, as shown by functional brain-imaging studies.

▶ SYNTHESIS

Since we last saw her, two-year-old Sabrina has wiggled out of her high chair, walked across the kitchen, and sneaked out the back door. While exploring the backyard, she came across a small brown dog blocking her path. It turns to Sabrina and begins to growl. Sabrina has never seen this dog before. He looks something like her own friendly dog, Max, of whom she is quite fond, but this dog is new to her. Should Sabrina approach the dog or flee?

Sabrina's visual cortex registered the visual information about the animal's brown fur, and her auditory cortex picked up the growling sound. Because her dog, Max, is brown, the brown-detecting regions of Sabrina's visual cortex are highly sensitive and enlarged and can quickly detect and recognize Max when he comes into the room. On the basis of this dog's similar color to Max, she is disposed to generalize her positive feelings toward Max to this new dog and view him as friendly. At the same time, Sabrina's auditory cortex is highly attuned to Max's unique bark, and this dog sounds less like Max and more like the snarling and scary dogs she sometimes sees in Central Park. On the basis of bark, she is inclined to discriminate this dog as being different from Max and potentially dangerous. As such, the information from her visual cortex and auditory cortex are suggesting conflicting tendencies: one suggests generalization and the other discrimination.

However, as her primary sensory cortices are processing the sights and sounds associated with this new dog, Sabrina's hippocampal region is combining the information with other information about the overall context in which this event is occurring: the backyard of her home in New Rochelle, on a warm summer day. The combination of this contextual information along with the visual and auditory cues about the animal allows Sabrina's hippocampus to detect an important pattern: her father's friends often visit during the summer with their dogs so that all can enjoy the lovely frontage on Long Island Sound. Based on this configuration of local contextual information (the place and the season) and the sight and sound of the animal, Sabrina infers that this particular dog is more likely to be friendly than aggressive. She reaches out and pets him, and he rolls over to let her scratch his belly. Like Sabrina, your ability to discriminate and generalize, to recognize friend from foe will govern your choices—and determine what you learn from each experience.

Key Terms

acetylcholine (ACh), *p. 249*	discrimination, *p. 210*	generalization, *p. 209*	receptive field, *p. 245*
acquired equivalence, *p. 235*	discrimination training, *p. 221*	generalization gradient, *p. 212*	sensory preconditioning, *p. 233*
category learning, *p. 230*	discrete-component representation, *p. 214*	hippocampal region, *p. 250*	stimulus representation, *p. 222*
combinatorial explosion, *p. 232*	distributed representation, *p. 216*	medial temporal lobe, *p. 250*	temporal lobe, *p. 250*
configural node, *p. 229*		negative patterning, *p. 228*	topographic representation, *p. 218*
consequential region, *p. 213*		nucleus basalis, *p. 249*	

Concept Check

Consider the following experiment, conducted by Robert Rescorla in 1976: In phase 1, he trained rats to associate a yellow light (the CS) with a US (Rescorla, 1976). After all the rats were fully trained and giving reliable CRs to the yellow light, he divided the animals into two groups. Rats in the experimental group received a second phase of training with an orange light as the CS until they learned to give reliable CRs. The control rats, however, continued to be trained with the yellow-light CS. Finally, in the third test phase of the experiment, all animals were exposed to a yellow light as the possible CS. What do you predict occurred in phase 3: did the rats in the experimental group give a larger or smaller response to the yellow light compared with the rats in the control group?

Why? And what does this suggest about the best way for you to prepare for your tennis tournament?

Hint: In keeping with the shared-elements approach of Thorndike and Estes, designate X as a shared element common to both yellow lights and orange lights (capturing the similarity of these two cues) and designate Y and O as the elements unique to yellow and orange lights, respectively. Thus, the yellow light can be viewed as a compound cue YX, and the orange light can be viewed as a compound cue OX. Using this shared-elements representation for these two similar stimuli, apply the Rescorla-Wagner model to each of the three phases of the experiment and predict which group should give a stronger response to the yellow light in phase 3.

Episodic and Semantic Memory

Memory for Facts and Events

FOR OVER 50 YEARS, THE IDENTITY of the man known only by the initials H.M. was one of the most closely guarded secrets in psychology. Before H.M., many scientists held to Karl Lashley's view, described in Chapter 2, that memory is encoded in a distributed fashion across the brain. But the results of the experiments in which H.M. participated revolutionized scientific thinking by documenting that the formation of new fact and event memories depends on distinct brain regions, separate from the brain regions that mediate other cognitive functions and other kinds of memory.

H.M.'s troubles began in childhood. By the age of 10, he was having epileptic seizures, during which the neurons in his brain fired wildly and uncontrollably. By age 16, the seizures were frequent and debilitating. Severe attacks, during which he might convulse and lose consciousness, occurred weekly; minor attacks occurred up to 10 times a day. H.M. struggled to complete high school, finally graduating at age 21, but the seizures were so frequent and so severe that he had difficulty holding a simple job. His doctors put him on a near-toxic diet of anticonvulsant drugs, but still the seizures continued.

In 1953, in desperation, H.M. and his family agreed to try brain surgery. At the time, doctors knew that, in many epileptic patients, seizures start in either the left or right hemisphere, usually in the **medial temporal lobes,** the inner (or medial) surfaces of the temporal lobes, which contain the **hippocampus,** the *amygdala,* and several nearby cortical areas. Doctors had found that surgical removal of the medial temporal lobe from the hemisphere where the seizures originated could eliminate the source of the problem and cure the

Behavioral Processes
Features of Episodic and Semantic Memories

Encoding New Memories

Retrieving Existing Memories

Learning and Memory in Everyday Life: Total Recall! The Truth about Extraordinary Memorizers

When Memory Fails

Learning and Memory in Everyday Life: Remembering Computer Passwords

Memory Consolidation and Reconsolidation

Brain Substrates
The Cerebral Cortex and Semantic Memory

The Medial Temporal Lobes and Memory Storage

The Frontal Cortex and Memory Storage and Retrieval

Subcortical Structures Involved in Episodic and Semantic Memory

Clinical Perspectives
Transient Global Amnesia

Functional Amnesia

epilepsy in these patients. Because H.M.'s seizures were so severe, and because their precise origin could not be determined, the doctors decided to remove his medial temporal lobes bilaterally (Corkin, Amaral, Gonzalez, Johnson, & Hyman, 1997).

Medically, the operation was a success: H.M.'s seizures declined drastically in frequency and severity. But there was a terrible cost. H.M. developed **amnesia,** or memory loss. Specifically, he lost the ability to form new memories for facts and events (Scoville & Milner, 1957). He could no longer remember what he had eaten for breakfast or why he was in the hospital. He could spend all morning working intensively with a psychologist and then take a break for lunch; an hour later he would not recognize the psychologist at all (Haglund & Collett, 1996). When H.M. found out that a favorite uncle had died, he experienced intense grief—then forgot. Again and again, he asked after the uncle and reacted with surprise and fresh grief every time he was told of the death (Milner, 1966). H.M. himself was painfully aware of his poor memory and described his life as constantly waking from a dream he couldn't remember (Milner, Corkin, & Teuber, 1968).

Despite his devastated memory, H.M.'s personality was basically unchanged, and after the operation his IQ actually went up—probably because, without constant seizures, he could now concentrate better on whatever he was doing. He could no longer follow the plot of a television show, because the commercials would interrupt his memory of the story line, but he could still amuse himself solving crossword puzzles. As long as H.M. paid attention to a task, he could perform well; as soon as he turned his attention to something else, the information vanished. H.M. was living proof that the ability to form new fact and event memories depends on the medial temporal lobes but that many other kinds of memory (and cognitive function) do not.

On December 2, 2008, H.M. passed away, and—by prior agreement—the details of his identity were finally released to the public. Scientists and students of the brain finally learned the name— Henry Gustav Molaison (pronounced "Mollisson")—and saw the face of the man who has taught us so much about memory and the brain. Even in death, H.M. continues to contribute. His brain was donated to science, and a team of

Henry Molaison, known to brain researchers everywhere as H.M. This photo was taken when he was in high school, shortly before he underwent the surgery that would destroy his ability to form new memories of facts and events.

© Suzanne Corkin, used with permission of The Wylie Agency LLC researchers at the University of California–San Diego began digitizing images of the preserved tissue to create a "virtual" map that will eventually be available on the Internet for others to study (you can check on the project's current status online at thebrainobservatory.ucsd.edu).

Fortunately, amnesia as severe as H.M.'s is extraordinarily rare. But amnesia does occur, sometimes as the result of a brain injury and sometimes as the result of disease or extreme stress. Some patients, like H.M., lose the ability to form new memories. In other cases, patients lose memories of a specific past event or—rarer still—lose all memories of their identity and personal history. Cases such as these remind us that our memories—the facts we know and the autobiographical events we remember—define us.

7.1 Behavioral Processes

Think back to the day of your high school graduation. Where was the ceremony held? Who sat near you? What were you wearing? Did a local celebrity speak? Did the school band perform? What were your feelings—pride, excitement, or perhaps impatience for the ceremony to end so you could celebrate with your friends?

These details of your graduation constitute an **episodic memory:** a memory for a specific autobiographical event (Tulving, 1972, 1983; Tulving, 2002). An episodic memory includes information about the spatial and temporal context: where and when the event occurred.

Related to, though distinct from, episodic memories are **semantic memories:** memories for facts and general knowledge about the world, as well as for personal information such as your own name and your favorite food. Unlike episodic memory, semantic memory is *not* tagged in time and space. For example, if asked to name the first president of the United States, you probably know the answer. But you may not remember exactly where or when you first learned the information. Whereas episodic memory is what we "remember," semantic memory is what we "know" (Tulving, 1985).

Features of Episodic and Semantic Memories

Episodic and semantic memories share two key features (Table 7.1). First, both episodic and semantic memories can be communicated flexibly, in different formats than the one in which they were originally acquired. When you remember an episodic memory—say, the memory of your graduation—you can describe the details you recall, even if you've never tried putting them into words before. Similarly, if someone were to show you a photo of the graduation taken from a different vantage point (perhaps taken from the stage rather than from where you and your classmates were seated), you would probably be able to recognize the scene, even though you had never seen it in quite this way.

Semantic memory can also be communicated flexibly. If someone asks you how to get from your home to class, you can answer by giving verbal directions or by drawing a map, even though you may never have attempted to put the information into these specific formats before. Similarly, after studying a list

Table 7.1

Comparing and Contrasting Episodic and Semantic Memory

Episodic Memory Event-related: "I remember"	Semantic Memory Factual: "I know"	Same (✓) or Different (✗)
Can be communicated flexibly—in a format other than that in which it was acquired	Can be communicated flexibly—in a format other than that in which it was acquired	✓
Consciously accessible (you know that you know)	Consciously accessible (you know that you know)	✓
Tagged with spatial and temporal context	**Not necessarily** tagged with spatial or temporal context	✗
Must be **autobiographical**	Can be **personal or general** information	✗
Learned in a **single exposure**; can be weakened by exposure to similar events	Can be learned in a single exposure, but can also be **strengthened by repetition**	✗

of historical facts, you can generally communicate that knowledge on an exam, whether the format is true/false, multiple choice, or essay questions.

The issue of flexibility may seem trivial, but some memories are hard to communicate in ways other than how they were originally learned. For example, in Chapter 8, you'll read about perceptual-motor skills, like tying your shoes. You can probably tie a shoe easily, but imagine someone asked you for a short description of how to do it. Odds are you'd find it difficult to comply—you might even have to go through the hand movements to remind yourself what comes next. Skill memories are generally not easy to communicate flexibly in the same way that episodic and semantic memories are.

The second key commonality between episodic and semantic memories is that both are consciously accessible. When someone asks you about a specific fact or event, you know whether you know the answer or not. If someone asks you the name of the first U.S. president, you not only know the answer, you know that you know. Even if the answer has temporarily slipped your mind, you know that sooner or later you'll recall it. On the other hand, if someone asks you the atomic weight of boron, you know right away that you don't know (unless you're a chemistry major). This phenomenon is sometimes called *metamemory*: our knowledge of, and ability to think about, our own memories. You've used metamemory every time you studied for a test and judged that you had successfully mastered the new material.

Because of these similarities between episodic and semantic memory, some researchers use the term **declarative memory** as a broader term that includes both episodic and semantic memory, reflecting the fact that it is easy to verbalize ("declare") or otherwise communicate your knowledge (J. Anderson, 1976; Cohen & Squire, 1980; Squire, Knowlton, & Musen, 1993). Other kinds of memory—grouped under the heading **nondeclarative memory**—are not always easy to communicate (Squire & Knowlton, 1995). Skill learning is one kind of nondeclarative memory, as is classical conditioning.

Other researchers use the term **explicit memory** (Graf & Schacter, 1985; Schacter, 1987), to reflect the fact that episodic and semantic information is consciously accessible or "explicit" (you know that you know); by comparison, **implicit memory** is memory that you may not be aware you've acquired. For example, H.M. (who couldn't acquire new episodic or semantic memories) could learn new skills such as reading mirror-reversed text (Gabrieli, Corkin, Mickel, & Crowden, 1993). Just like the performance of healthy control patients, H.M.'s performance slowly improved with practice. But when asked about these new skills, H.M. reported having no conscious memories of the training sessions and no knowledge of his new skill. Thus, this learning was implicit.

H.M. is a special case, of course; most of us, while practicing new skills, will also form consciously available episodic and semantic memories of what we're learning. In fact, it's proven extraordinarily difficult to disentangle explicit and implicit learning in healthy adults (Shanks, 2010). What H.M.'s case demonstrates is that conscious awareness is not absolutely *necessary* for implicit memories to form.

What Distinguishes Episodic from Semantic Memory?

Despite their similarities, episodic and semantic memory have several contrasting properties (Table 7.1). First, episodic memories concern specific events that occurred at a particular place and time: you must remember when and where those events occurred. Semantic memories involve factual information: you need not remember where and when you learned this information—only the fact itself.

Second, episodic memory is always autobiographical: the event you recall must have happened to you. Semantic memory can be personal (remembering your name or your favorite flavor of ice cream), but it can also be general factual information (remembering the atomic weight of boron or the name of the first U.S. president).

Third, by definition, episodic memory is acquired in a single exposure: the event itself. In principle, semantic memories can be acquired in a single exposure too, particularly if the information is sufficiently interesting or important. For example, it might take you several exposures to memorize the Latin word for "arch"—*fornix*—unless you are also told that, in ancient Rome, prostitutes used to ply their trade under arches, which is where we get the modern word "fornicate." Such extra information, which relates the vocabulary item to other information you know, may help you remember the word after only a single exposure.

But ordinary semantic information generally needs a few additional exposures before being fully acquired. So, for example, you may have to study a Latin vocabulary list several times before you have all the items memorized. In general, repeated exposures to a single fact *strengthen* semantic memory for that fact (Linton, 1982); by contrast, repeated exposure to very similar events may *weaken* episodic memory for any one of those events (Figure 7.1). If you park your car in the same large parking lot every day, you may confuse the episodic memories of all the prior, highly similar parking events, making it hard to remember exactly where you parked the car today. This is one reason why any large parking lot contains a number of people walking around with panicked expressions on their faces.

Which Comes First, Episodic or Semantic Memory?

The exact relationship between episodic and semantic memory is a matter of intense debate. The distinction between episodic memory and semantic memory was first made by psychologist Endel Tulving, who argues that episodic memory grows out of semantic memory (Tulving, 2002). According to this view, an organism has to have a certain amount of semantic information before episodic memories can be built on that framework. If you don't know what a graduation is, you can hardly have an episodic memory for any specific graduation—even your own.

An alternative possibility is that semantic memory is information we have encountered repeatedly—so often that the actual learning episodes are blurred and only the semantic "fact" content remains (Conway, 2009). For example, if you remember the very first time you learned about George Washington, then you have an episodic memory for that event—perhaps it was a history class. But if

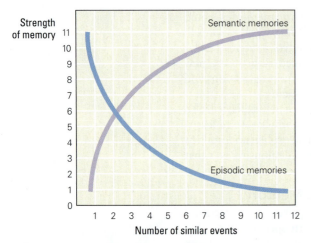

Figure 7.1 Episodic and semantic memory In general, semantic memory is strengthened by repetition, but episodic memory may be weakened by repeated exposure to similar events.

you have heard about George Washington in many different classes and have also read about him in books and seen television depictions, then you have accumulated a general store of knowledge about the first U.S. president, whether or not you remember the individual episodes.

A third possibility is that episodic and semantic memory are fundamentally interdependent: each can affect the other (Greenberg & Verfaellie, 2010). On the one hand, episodic memories will be formed more strongly, and last longer, when there is a rich background of semantic information to help us recognize and encode aspects of the event; on the other hand, semantic memories will be formed more strongly, and last longer, when we have a distinct episodic memory of the context in which we encountered the information (Neath, 2010). Under this view, it may be most useful not to think about declarative memories as being either strictly episodic or strictly semantic but to acknowledge that many of our memories include both episodic and semantic content.

Can Nonhumans Have Episodic and Semantic Memory?

The easiest way to assess semantic memory in humans is by question-and-answer. If an experimenter asks you the name of the first U.S. president and you reply "George Washington," then the experimenter can safely conclude that you have a semantic memory of that fact. Things get a little more problematic with nonhuman animals; we can't ask a rat to name the president. But we can assess semantic memory in other ways. For example, Figure 7.2 shows a *radial arm maze*: a maze with a central area from which several arms branch off like the spokes of a wheel. The top of the maze is open so that a rat placed in the maze can see out and use landmarks in the room, such as the placement of windows or posters, to help navigate.

A radial arm maze can be used to assess many kinds of learning and memory. In one version, researchers put food at the end of one arm (the "goal arm") and place the rat at the end of a different arm (the "start arm"). The rat is then allowed to roam the maze until it finds and consumes the food. Over many such trials, the rat learns where the food is located, and when it is placed in the start arm, it will run directly to the goal arm. If a well-trained rat is placed in a new start arm and still runs to the food—via a route it has never used before—then researchers conclude that the rat "knows" where the food is and can use this information flexibly in new ways (such as using a new route to get there). Thus, most researchers would agree that this is an example of semantic memory in rats.

Figure 7.2 The radial arm maze After many trials in which the rat is allowed to explore the maze until it finds food located at the end of the "goal arm," it will eventually learn to run straight to the goal arm, indicating it has semantic memory for where the food is located in the maze.

Episodic memory is harder to assess in animals. In fact, some researchers have explicitly argued that animals cannot maintain episodic memories, at least not in the way that humans do (Roberts & Feeney, 2009; Tulving, 2002). Endel Tulving, in particular, has argued that episodic memory requires "mental time travel," a re-experiencing of the event in memory; this in turn requires a conscious sense of self, as well as a subjective sense of time passing, which—Tulving argues—have not been demonstrated in nonhumans (Tulving, 2002). But other researchers argue that there is mounting evidence that animals can indeed form "episodic-like" memories for specific events, including information about the spatial and temporal context in which those events occurred (Clayton, Yu, & Dickinson, 2001; Crystal, 2010; Bennett Schwartz & Evans, 2001).

For example, gorillas seem to remember specific autobiographical events, and they can communicate this information flexibly to human testers. One gorilla, King, was taught to "name" various fruits and humans by using cards with drawings that represented the fruits and humans (Schwartz, Colon, Sanchez, Rodriguez, & Evans, 2002). This general knowledge about how to use the cards qualifies as semantic memory. Researchers then attempted to assess whether King could remember distinct autobiographical episodes. During the day, King received various pieces of fruit from different human handlers. Twenty-four hours later, when asked (via the cards) who had given him a particular fruit the day before, King could use the cards to name the correct human. Because King had eaten several fruits and interacted with other humans during the course of the day, his performance seems to demonstrate that he had episodic-like memory for the events of the prior day—remembering not just that he ate fruit but the specific type of fruit, who gave it to him, and approximately when this happened. And he could communicate this behavior to the experimenters, using abstract symbols on cards. This behavior seems to satisfy the criteria for an episodic memory (Schwartz & Evans, 2001).

Birds may also be able to remember specific events and how long ago they happened. Scrub jays, for example, bury extra food in caches so they can retrieve it later. These birds accurately remember their cache locations and will return to those locations later even if an experimenter has secretly removed the food in the meantime to ensure that the birds can't use scent to find the buried food. To test episodic-like memory, Nicola Clayton and her colleagues allowed scrub jays to cache worms and nuts in sand-filled compartments of an ice cube tray (Figure 7.3a). The birds were then allowed to recover food either 4 hours or 124 hours later. Normally, scrub jays prefer worms to nuts, and when tested after a 4-hour interval, they chose to recover the worms more often than the nuts (Figure 7.3b). But worms decay over a 124-hour interval, and nuts do not. And, indeed, when tested at a 124-hour interval, the birds typically preferred to recover the nuts (Clayton & Dickinson, 1999). These results suggest that scrub jays can remember not only where they have stored food but what type of food was stored and how long ago (Clayton, Yu, & Dickinson, 2001; Griffiths, Dickinson, & Clayton, 1999). Rats, dolphins, and pigeons may have similar abilities to remember specific events, including when and where the events took place (Kart-Teke, De Souza Silva, Huston, & Dere, 2006; Mercado, Murray, Uyeyama, Pack, & Herman, 1998; Zentall, Singer, & Stagner, 2008).

Some researchers go even further, arguing that some nonhuman animals (rats, dolphins, nonhuman primates, and some birds) do have a subjective sense of self and of time, and that their behavior demonstrates they can indeed mentally re-create autobiographical events from their own past and imagine their own future (Dere, Kart-Tecke, Huston, & De Souza Silva, 2006; Zentall, 2006).

Figure 7.3 Episodic-like memory in birds (a) Scrub jays were permitted to cache worms and nuts in the compartments of sand-filled ice cube trays. (b) Four hours later, the birds tended to dig in the compartments where they had buried worms (their favorite food). But after a delay of 124 hours, during which time the worms would have rotted, the birds went after the nuts instead. This suggests that the birds remembered what they had buried where and how long ago—an "episodic-like" memory.

(a) Adapted from Griffiths et al., 1999; (b) adapted from Roberts, 2002.

(a)

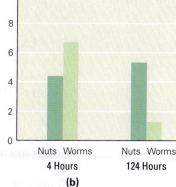

(b)

For the rest of this chapter, we'll adopt the convention of referring to "episodic-like" memories in nonhuman animals if those memories include what-where-when information about the spatial and temporal context in which the episode occurred (Crystal, 2010; Eacott & Easton, 2010; Wang & Morris, 2010). Use of the term "episodic-like" (rather than just "episodic") acknowledges that we cannot directly ask non-verbal animals about their subjective sense of self, or their ability to perform "mental time travel." In the absence of direct evidence on these points, controversy continues over whether nonhuman animals can form true episodic memories or whether this ability is uniquely human.

Test Your Knowledge

Episodic versus Semantic Memory

Episodic memories are memories for autobiographical events, set in a particular time and spatial location; semantic memories are memories for fact or general knowledge about the world, independent of when and how this information was acquired. Sometimes, though, the line between the two is blurred. A single behavior can contain components of both semantic and episodic information. Read the following scenarios to check whether you understand the difference. (Answers appear in the Answers section in the back of the book.)

1. A college senior is helping a new student learn her way around campus. When the tour finishes, the newcomer asks where she can buy a cup of coffee. The senior thinks for a moment, then says that the coffee is better at a nearby Starbucks than at the student center. Is this an example of semantic or of episodic memory?

2. The senior walks into his Latin vocabulary exam later that day. The first phrase to be translated is *carpe diem*. This is an easy one; he knows the answer is "seize the day," even though he can't remember exactly where he first heard this expression. Is this student using semantic or episodic memory?

3. The second phrase to be translated is *ne tentes, aut perfice*. This is harder; the student can remember studying the phrase, and he even recalls that the phrase was printed in black ink on the lower left of a page in his textbook, but he can't recall the translation. Is the student using semantic or episodic memory?

Encoding New Memories

Much of the time, the formation of new episodic and semantic memories seems automatic and effortless. For example, you probably remember a great deal of information about your high school graduation even if you did not spend the day consciously trying to memorize the details so you could recall them later. On the other hand, every student who's ever studied for a test knows that some type of information are easier to learn than others. Here are three basic principles that govern how successfully a new episodic or semantic memory is *encoded*, or stored in memory.

Mere Exposure to Information Does Not Guarantee Memory

On the principle that practice makes perfect, you might think that the best way to learn new information is to study, study, study. But the truth is a little more complicated. Mere repeated exposure to information is not enough to guarantee memory. One telling example of this occurred when BBC Radio in the United Kingdom was planning to change its broadcast frequency. The BBC saturated the airwaves with announcements informing listeners about the new station call numbers. A survey of radio listeners who had heard the announcement at least 25 times a day for many weeks found that less than a quarter of these individuals had learned the new call numbers (Bekerian & Baddeley, 1980). Just presenting the information again and again wasn't enough to guarantee that listeners would remember.

Memory for visual details can be just as bad. Here's a quick test: try to remember what a U.S. penny looks like. You probably remember that Lincoln's face appears on the front, but can you remember whether he's facing to the left or the right? If you're not sure, you're not alone. Few U.S. students can accurately draw a penny; in fact, few can even pick out an accurate drawing from among a set of fakes (Nickerson & Adams, 1979). Residents of other countries are just as poor at remembering details of their own national currency (Jones, 1990; Martin & Jones, 1995). Most of us handle money every day and are quite capable of recognizing coins when we see them. Yet most of us have remarkably poor memory for the details of what these familiar objects actually look like.

Can you pick out the correct drawing of a penny? Most people have very poor ability to recognize the details of a coin face, though they see and handle the coin every day. Adapted from Nickerson & Adams, 1979.

In short, sheer repetition of either verbal or visual information isn't enough to ensure its being remembered. So what does determine whether information gets encoded and retained?

Memory Is Better for Information That Relates to Prior Knowledge

Earlier in the chapter, you read that the Latin word for "arc" or "arch" is *fornix*. To help make this information memorable, we presented the tidbit about Roman prostitutes. The idea was to provide a link between *fornix* and "fornication" (a word you already know), which should help you remember better than if you were just trying to memorize an otherwise meaningless Latin word.

A basic principle of memory is that new information is easier to remember if you can relate it to things you already know. In a classic study, John Bransford and Marcia Johnson read the following paragraph to a group of research participants:

> **If the balloons popped, the sound wouldn't be able to carry since everything would be too far away from the correct floor. A closed window would also prevent the sound from carrying since most buildings tend to be well insulated. Since the whole operation depends on a steady flow of electricity, a break in the middle of the wire would also cause problems. Of course, the fellow could shout, but the human voice is not loud enough to carry that far. An additional problem is that a string could break on the instrument. Then there could be no accompaniment to the message. It is clear that the best situation would involve less distance. Then there would be fewer potential problems. With face-to-face contact, the least number of things could go wrong.**

Presented in this way, the paragraph makes little sense. Not surprisingly, Bransford and Johnson found that, on testing, most people could recall only about 20% of the ideas in the paragraph (Figure 7.4a) (Bransford & Johnson, 1972). However, a second group of people saw the sketch shown in Figure 7.4b before hearing the paragraph. The sketch shows a man serenading a woman at a high window. If you read the paragraph again in the light of this background information, you will find that it makes more sense. Indeed, people who saw the picture first were able to recall twice as much about the paragraph. Importantly, the effect of background information on memory is limited to the process of encoding; it does not help with recall. Thus, people who heard the paragraph before they viewed the picture did not recall the information any better than people who never saw the picture at all (Figure 7.4a). Only people who knew the background information ahead of time remembered the paragraph well.

Figure 7.4 The effects of organization on memory An experimenter read aloud to participants a short story describing a scene. (a) Participants who heard the paragraph alone ("No picture") recalled few items, but participants who saw the picture in (b) and then heard the paragraph ("Picture before story") recalled more items. Participants who saw the picture only after hearing the paragraph ("Picture after story") performed no better than those who had never seen the picture.

(a) Data from and (b) adapted from Bransford and Johnson, 1972.

This principle has clear implications for optimizing study habits. In general, you will remember textbook material better if you take the time to scan a chapter first to get a sense of the major points before reading the details. This is also the reason that many professors encourage students to complete assigned readings before each lecture. With this preparation, the students' minds are better able to encode the information presented in the lecture.

Deeper Processing at Encoding Improves Recognition Later

A third important principle is that the more deeply you analyze information, the more likely you are to successfully encode the information in memory. Specifically, the **depth-of-processing effect** is the finding that, in general, deeper processing at encoding of new information improves the ability to remember that information later. (Craik & Lockhart, 1972; Craik & Tulving, 1975). If you think about the word *fornix* and its relationship to "fornication," you're processing the word more deeply than if you just tried to memorize the fact that *fornix* = "arch." Many experiments have shown that people remember words better if they're forced to think about the semantic content (meaning) of the words rather than simply asked to memorize them without such efforts.

In one such study, participants saw a list of adjectives. For some of the words, participants were instructed to generate a mental image (for DIRTY they might imagine a garbage dump); for others, participants were asked to imagine pronouncing the word backward (for HAPPY they might say YIP-PAH). Presumably, the "image" condition required thinking deeply about the meaning of the word, but the "pronounce" condition required only superficial thinking about how the letters were arranged. Later, the participants were shown a second list and asked to identify those words they had studied earlier (Figure 7.5). Just as you'd expect, the deeply processed "image" words were better recognized than the superficially processed "pronounce" words (Davachi, Mitchell, & Wagner, 2003).

(a) Recognition performance

(b) Brain activity (fMRI)

Left frontal cortex

Left Hemisphere

Underside

Left hippocampus

Science Magazine/Courtesy of Anthony D. Wagner

Figure 7.5 Depth-of-processing effect Participants were shown words and asked either to generate a mental image of a place described by the word (the "image" condition) or to imagine pronouncing the word backward (the "pronounce" condition). (a) Later, when shown a second list and asked whether or not each word had been previously viewed, participants recognized many more words from the "image" condition than from the "pronounce" condition. (b) fMRI scans conducted during the encoding phase of this task revealed several brain areas (red) that were significantly more active during the "image" condition than during the "pronounce" condition.

(a) Data from and (b) adapted from Davachi et al., 2003.

One criticism of the depth-of-processing idea is that it is vague. How, exactly, can we be sure whether individuals are processing information "deeply" or "superficially"? Just because an experimenter asks participants to process words superficially, how can we know they are not thinking about the meaning of the word too? And, for that matter, how can we be sure that thinking about word meanings requires deeper processing than pronouncing words backward?

It is hard to answer these questions by using purely behavioral measures, but functional neuroimaging provides some clues. Lila Davachi and her colleagues used functional magnetic resonance imaging (fMRI) to look at brain activity during either the "image" condition or the "pronounce" condition (Davachi, Mitchell, & Wagner, 2003). The "pronounce" activity pattern was then subtracted from the "image" activity pattern to produce the difference images shown in Figure 7.5b. Overall, participants' brains were much more active during the "image" trials than during the "pronounce" trials. This suggests that the brain is indeed working harder during the "image" condition. Brain areas where activity during the "image" condition was particularly high included the left frontal cortex and the left hippocampus. Later in this chapter, we'll talk more about these brain areas and their roles in episodic and semantic memory; for now, though, simply note that the psychological concepts of deep versus superficial processing seem to correspond to physiological measures of how hard the brain is working to encode new information.

Retrieving Existing Memories

Of course, successfully encoding a new memory is only half the battle; the other half is successfully accessing, or retrieving, that memory when we want it. You've probably experienced the "tip-of-the-tongue" phenomenon, when you were trying to summon a word or a name from memory that you were sure you knew but simply couldn't retrieve at the moment. In these cases, the information is not permanently lost, only temporarily inaccessible. You may succeed in recalling the information later, often after you've turned your attention to something else. Why can we retrieve stored memories at some times, yet at other times they elude us? Like encoding, successful retrieving is governed by several basic principles. We'll present two key principles below.

Memory Retrieval Is Better When Study and Test Conditions Match

One factor in our ability to retrieve a memory is the degree to which the current context resembles the context in which the information was originally acquired. The **transfer-appropriate processing effect** refers to the finding that retrieval is more likely to be successful if the cues available at recall are similar to those that were available at encoding. For example, suppose you are initially shown a series of pictures of objects (a dog, a house, and so on) and then later are given a recognition test in which some of the objects are presented as pictures and some as words. Which objects do you think you'd remember best? Most people show better recognition if the format is the same at encoding as at testing: if objects presented as words are tested as words, and objects presented as pictures are tested as pictures (Köhler, Moscovitch, Winocur, & McIntosh, 2000). Performance is worse when the encoding and testing formats differ.

Some researchers have argued that the depth-of-processing effect, whereby "deeper" processing leads to better memory than "superficial" processing, is really a transfer-appropriate processing effect in disguise. People who process a word "deeply," thinking about its meaning and visualizing it, may indeed be better at a standard visual recognition test (as you saw in Figure 7.5a). But people asked to merely rhyme a word—a "superficial" processing task that doesn't involve thinking about the word's semantic meaning—actually perform better if the later memory test involves rhyming recognition (Morris, Bransford, & Franks, 1977). In short, deep processing during encoding may help only if the test also requires deep processing. If the test instead involves the physical attributes or sounds of a word, superficial processing may be preferable!

Transfer-appropriate processing involves not only the physical appearance of the stimuli but also the physical context in which memory is stored and retrieved. Have you ever been at the gym or the supermarket and run into someone you know from school and been temporarily unable to recognize that person in the unusual setting? You may even have struggled to chat for a while (without admitting you couldn't remember exactly who this person was) before something "clicked" and the memory fell into place. If you've ever had this type of experience, then you already know the powerful effect of physical context on memory retrieval.

In a famous demonstration of this principle, researchers tested memory in members of a diving club (Godden & Baddeley, 1975). Some of the divers were asked to learn a list of 40 words while on dry land; the remainder learned the list underwater. The divers were then tested on their recall of the words. Divers who were tested in the same environment where they had studied the list (either on land or underwater) could remember more words than those who were trained in one environment and tested in the other. Similarly, students who learn a list either standing up or sitting down will later recall a few more words if they are in the same position during testing (Godden & Baddely, 1975). A list learned while classical or jazz music plays will be remembered better if the same music plays during recall (Smith, 1985). In each case, recall is slightly better if the retrieval conditions are similar to the encoding conditions.

So, does this mean that studying in the same room where you will take a test will improve your performance? Not necessarily. A large study of 5,000 college students found no effect on performance when final exams were administered in the same room where the course had been taught or in a novel classroom (Saufley, Otaka, & Bavaresco, 1985). (This may be because most classrooms are pretty much alike; taking the exam in a novel classroom may be much less disruptive to retrieval than taking the exam underwater.) But there are other ways to use the principles of transfer-appropriate processing to your advantage. For example, suppose you can study for an exam either by taking online multiple-choice tests or by recruiting a friend to ask you open-ended questions from your class notes. If you know that the professor usually gives essay exams, which study method should you use? The best way to prepare for a test is by processing the material in a way that is similar to how you expect to be tested on it, making the study and recall formats as similar as possible (Butler & Roediger, 2007).

More Cues Mean Better Recall

Of course, many formats are available for testing memory. The first and most obvious is **free recall,** in which you are simply asked an open-ended question and you supply the answer from memory (What is the Latin word for "arch"?). A second possibility is **cued recall,** in which you are given some kind of a prompt or clue to the correct answer (What is the Latin word for "arch"? f____). A third possibility is **recognition,** in which you pick out the correct answer from a list of possible options (What is the Latin word for "arch"? A = *fenestra*, B = *fornix*, or C = *fundus*).

In general, free recall is harder than cued recall, which in turn is harder than recognition. This ranking directly reflects the number of cues available to jog the memory. In free recall, the tester provides no (or minimal) explicit cues, in cued recall, the tester provides at least some kind of cue, and in recognition, the entire item is provided. In one study, when asked to recall the names of their high school classmates, recent graduates could, on average, produce about 50% of the names; individuals who had graduated several decades earlier could produce only about 20 to 30% of the names. But when shown a list of names and asked to recognize which people had been classmates, recent graduates could get about 90% correct, and even long-ago graduates got about 85% correct (Bahrick, Bahrick, & Wittlinger, 1975).

Most people instinctively understand that free recall is harder than recognition. This is one reason why many students prefer exams containing multiple choice rather than essay questions (recognition as opposed to free recall). Of course, professors understand this too, and they usually compensate by designing multiple-choice questions to include choices that can easily be mistaken for the correct response if a student hasn't studied the material closely. (Have you ever wished you were better at memorization? See "Learning and Memory in Everyday Life" below.)

> ### LEARNING AND MEMORY IN EVERYDAY LIFE
>
> ## Total Recall! The Truth about Extraordinary Memorizers
>
> We have all heard stories about people who have phenomenal memory abilities. Probably the most famous expert memorizer was a Russian newspaper reporter named S. Shereshevskii (more commonly known as S.). Russian neuropsychologist Aleksandr Luria could read S. a list of 70 words, which S. could then repeat accurately from memory: "15 years later," Luria wrote, "S would sit with his eyes closed, pause, then comment: 'Yes, yes . . . This was a series you gave me once in your apartment. You were sitting at the table and I in the rocking chair . . . You were wearing a gray suit . . .' And with that he would reel off the series precisely as I had given it to him at the earlier session" (Luria, 1982 [1968], p. 384). Other famous memorizers include basketball great Jerry Lucas, who amazed his teammates by memorizing portions of the New York City phone book.
>
> How could such feats be possible? S. visualized stimuli mentally, in great detail, and these images helped him recall information later. Jerry Lucas also formed unusual visual images of the to-be-remembered information, making it more memorable and easier to recall. Such strategies are examples of **mnemonics** (pronounced "nee-MON-ics"), which are techniques that make information easier to memorize. You yourself may have used simple mnemonic devices such as the acronym ROY G. BIV (to remember the colors of the spectrum: red, orange, yellow, green, blue, indigo, violet) or the rhyme "Thirty days hath September . . ."
>
> (to remember the number of days in each month).
>
> Most world-class memory performers use mnemonics of one sort or another. A recent neuroimaging study of exceptional memorizers found no differences in brain anatomy between exceptional memory performers and people with average memories (Maguire, Valentine, Wilding, & Kapur, 2003). The implication is that almost anyone could attain a "world-class memory" by mastering the right mnemonic system (Ericsson, 2003). Unfortunately, there is no evidence that such memory masters are any better than the rest of us at memory challenges in the real world, such as remembering where we parked the car or when someone's birthday is.

When Memory Fails

You've just read about some basic principles affecting encoding and retrieval of episodic and semantic memories. At each stage, various conditions (how the material is presented, whether you're underwater, etc.) can help or hinder the process. When you consider all the opportunities for failure, it is amazing how often our memories serve us well.

But there are many situations in which episodic and event memory do fail us. The tip-of-the-tongue phenomenon, mentioned above, is an example of a temporary failure: the memory is inaccessible at the moment but may resurface later. In other cases, though, memories are truly lost or corrupted. Many failures of memory reflect one of four basic phenomena: simple forgetting, interference from other memories, memory misattribution, and false memory. We'll discuss these in more detail next.

Forgetting

It's probably obvious that you are more likely to remember things that happened recently than things that happened long ago. For example, you probably remember most of the events that have happened to you today, but you probably don't remember most of what happened to you on, say, July 16, 2003. However, if someone had questioned you on July 17, 2003, you probably could have reported the prior day's events in great detail. Somehow, that information has trickled away during the interval. What governs how fast we forget?

As you read back in Chapter 1, Hermann Ebbinghaus conducted a series of early studies to quantify human learning and forgetting. Ebbinghaus memorized lists of nonsense words and then tested his own memory for the items. He concluded that most forgetting occurs in the first few hours or days after learning (Ebbinghaus, 1885/1964). Information that survives the critical first few days might last in memory indefinitely.

Ebbinghaus's basic finding has since been replicated in a variety of studies. For example, in the 1980s, memory researcher Larry Squire developed a test in which people were queried about television shows that had aired for a single season from 1 to 15 years earlier (Squire, 1989). (In those days, there were still a relatively small number of television networks, and most people were familiar with most programs that aired.) On average, people did quite well at this test of semantic memory. Most people could correctly recognize the names of more than 75% of TV shows that had aired in the prior year, although they recognized progressively fewer shows from earlier years (Figure 7.6a). Most

Figure 7.6 Two kinds of forgetting (a) Passive forgetting occurs as a function of time: older information is more likely to be forgotten than more recently acquired information. Here, people tested in the 1980s could correctly recognize the names of more TV shows that had aired in the prior year than of shows that had aired a decade previously.
Adapted from Squire, 1989.
(b) Directed forgetting occurs when we intentionally try to suppress memory. Here, participants' memory was worse for studied word pairs they had been instructed to forget than for pairs they'd been instructed to remember or control pairs they hadn't seen since the original study phase.
Data from Anderson et al., 2004.

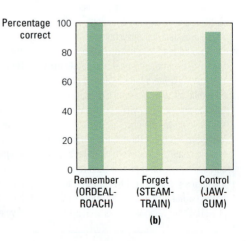

(a)

(b)

forgetting occurred within the first decade, so people remembered almost as many TV shows from 15 years ago as from 10 years ago.

We normally think of forgetting as a passive process, in which old memories—particularly those we haven't accessed in a while—just quietly fade away. But we may have more power over what we remember (and forget) than we realize. **Directed forgetting** (or *intentional forgetting*) occurs when information is forgotten on demand. For example, Michael Anderson and colleagues trained participants on a series of word pairs: ORDEAL-ROACH, STEAM-TRAIN, JAW-GUM, and so on (M. Anderson et al., 2004). Next, he showed the participants some of the studied words. For some words (ORDEAL), people were now asked to *remember* the associate (ROACH). For others (STEAM), they were now asked to try to *forget* the associate (TRAIN). Later, Anderson tested memory for all the studied words (Figure 7.6b). People were less able to remember the words they'd tried to forget than those they'd tried to remember or those they hadn't seen since original training (GUM). Note that in the Forget condition of Figure 7.6b, people still remembered about 50% of the items on average. Thus, directed forgetting isn't perfect. But these results suggest that we have some control over what we do and don't forget. Some studies have even shown that intentional forgetting can extend to autobiographical events: participants who kept a daily diary and were then instructed to forget the previous week's events subsequently recalled fewer events than participants who kept a diary but did not receive instructions to forget (Joslyn & Oakes, 2005).

Obviously, intentional forgetting in the laboratory may be very different from forgetting in real life. Nevertheless, the fact that it is theoretically possible to intentionally forget unwanted information may help explain some real-world cases of memory suppression in which individuals forget highly traumatic and unpleasant events such as war, rape, or natural disasters. And it may be possible to exploit this ability in developing therapy for psychiatric disorders in which people suffer from intrusive and unwanted thoughts, such as posttraumatic stress disorder and obsessive-compulsive disorder. In this way, the "memory failure" of forgetting may actually have some psychological benefits.

Interference

Remember the parking lot example, in which memories of prior days' parking locations disrupt your ability to recall where you parked the car today? This is an example of **interference:** when two memories overlap in content, the strength of either or both memories may be reduced.

Suppose you're participating in a memory experiment and the experimenter asks you to learn a list of word pairs—say, List 1 in Figure 7.7. You might practice this list, repeating it aloud, until you have it memorized. Then, after some delay, the experimenter gives you a test of cued recall: given the stems (e.g., DOG-____), fill in the appropriate associate (CHAIR) for each stem.

Now suppose the experimenter asks you to memorize a second list, List 2 in Figure 7.7. Note that some of the items (DOG, SHIRT) appear in both lists. As you attempt to learn the new pair DOG-WINDOW, the stem (DOG) will stimulate recall of the old associate (CHAIR). This may interfere with your learning of List 2, and when it comes time to test your memory for List 2, you may mistakenly respond with the old associate (CHAIR) instead of the new one (WINDOW). This process, whereby old information can disrupt new learning, is called **proactive interference** (J. Anderson, 1981; Wickelgren, 1966).

The opposite process also occurs: suppose that, after heavy practice with List 2, you try to go back and recall List 1. Now, when the experimenter prompts DOG-____, you might recall WINDOW from List 2 instead of CHAIR from List 1. This process, whereby new information can disrupt old

Figure 7.7 Two kinds of interference Imagine you are asked to learn the word pairs in List 1 and then the word pairs in List 2. After that, if you are asked to recall List 2, older items from List 1 may interfere (proactive interference). Conversely, if you are asked to recall List 1, newer items from List 2 may interfere (retroactive interference).

Proactive interference: Previously acquired information interferes with new learning

List 1
DOG-CHAIR
AXE-SNOW
SHIRT-TREE
(etc.)

List 2
DOG-WINDOW
TRUCK-SMILE
SHIRT-BROOM
(etc.)

Task: Recall List 2
DOG-_____?

Old learning interferes with new
Mistaken response: CHAIR

Retroactive interference: Recently acquired information interferes with old memory

Task: Recall List 1
DOG-_____?

New learning interferes with old
Mistaken response: WINDOW

learning, is called **retroactive interference.** A simple mnemonic to help you remember the difference between proactive interference and retroactive interference is that *PRoactive* interference means *PReviously acquired* information is at fault; *REtroactive* interference means *REcently acquired* information is at fault.

Proactive and retroactive interference occur in many real-life contexts. For example, the last time you changed a frequently used computer password, you probably went through a phase during which you sometimes typed the old password by mistake. This is an example of *proactive* interference, as memory of the *previous* password interfered with your ability to retrieve memory for the new one. On the other hand, once you had successfully mastered the new password, you might have had some trouble remembering the password you used to use. This is an example of *retroactive* interference, as memory of the *recently* acquired password interfered with your ability to remember the old one. (For help creating memorable passwords that at the same time are hard to crack, see "Learning and Memory in Everyday Life" on page 275.)

Memory Misattribution

Another kind of memory failure is **misattribution,** which occurs when we remember information but mistakenly associate it with an incorrect source (Schacter, Harbluk, & McLachlan, 1984). For example, we may think we remember a childhood party when what we really remember is what we later saw in a home movie of the event. A related phenomenon is **source amnesia,** which occurs when we remember information but cannot remember the source at all. For example, we may read some gossip in a trashy tabloid and, even though we know better than to take such reading material seriously, we may later remember the gossip but forget the dubious source—and thus give the rumor more credence than it deserves.

Such memory misattribution crops up fairly often in real life and may be particularly pronounced as people get older. One famous example involves former U.S. president Ronald Reagan. During his campaigns, Reagan often told an inspiring story about a World War II gunner who was unable to eject after his plane was hit by enemy fire. The gunner's commander, who could have parachuted to safety, refused to abandon his injured comrade. "Never mind, son," he

LEARNING AND MEMORY IN EVERYDAY LIFE

Remembering Computer Passwords

Almost everyone who has Internet access has to remember multiple passwords—for email accounts, bank and credit card accounts, household wireless server . . . the list goes on and on. Each online system may have its own set of rules for choosing an acceptable password—a minimum or maximum number of characters, required inclusion (or exclusion) of numbers, capital letters, and punctuation marks—so that a password accepted by one system may be rejected by another. On top of all this, some systems require that passwords be changed every few months.

Survey after survey reports that trying to remember all those passwords is the number-one frustration for users of online services. Many people, overwhelmed at the task, wind up writing their passwords down—creating just the kind of security risk that passwords are intended to avoid. Other people settle for memorable but hackable passwords; in early 2010, the New York Times reported that the most popular account password was "123456," closely followed by "abc123" and "password" (Vance, 2010).

You probably know that you're supposed to avoid easy-to-guess passwords that include your name, date of birth, or other personal information that can be gleaned from your Facebook profile (favorite band or pets' names). But the more complicated the password you choose, the harder it is to remember, right?

Not necessarily. And what you know about memory can help. Here are three tips for creating memorable computer passwords that are still hard for others to crack.

1. Remember that memory is better for information that you can link to items you already know. So, don't choose random, hard-to-remember passwords ("6ws@ij444"). Choose passwords that have some meaning for you—such as a favorite song lyric or movie quote: "Toto, I've got a feeling we're not in Kansas anymore!" Meaningful phrases are easier to remember than random strings of characters.

2. Choose long passwords. The truth is that it's the length, not the oddness, of a password that makes it harder for hackers to crack. Longer passwords are also easier to remember because they have more semantic content. If the account requires shorter passwords, try just the first letters of each word: "T,Igafwni Ka!"—complete with capitals and punctuation.

3. Use cued recall. If you must write a note to help you remember your passwords, use a clue, not the whole password ("Clue: Wizard of Oz"). The cue will help jog your memory while still making it hard for anyone who finds the note to pin down exactly what your password is.

---

said, "we'll ride it down together." The commander was posthumously awarded the Congressional Medal of Honor for his bravery.

Only later did anyone wonder how the heroic words had been recorded, given that both commander and gunner had presumably perished in the crash. Journalists began to dig deeper and found no recorded Medal of Honor winner who fit the profile of Reagan's hero. In fact, the touching scene was the fictional climax of a 1944 movie, *Wing and a Prayer*. Apparently, Reagan remembered the story but had misremembered its source.

A special kind of memory misattribution is *cryptomnesia*, in which a person mistakenly thinks that his thoughts are novel or original when he's actually remembering information he learned somewhere else. Cryptomnesia can lead to inadvertent plagiarism: a student reads a sentence in a textbook and remembers it; later, when the sentence pops to mind, it "feels" new and gets included in a term paper. The student may honestly think this is an original idea—but if the instructor has read the same textbook, accusations of plagiarism will follow.

Cryptomnesia has been studied scientifically, using a variant of the game Boggle (Marsh & Bower, 1993). Research participants were given 16 letters, from which to form as many words as they could. In the experiment, the participants played against a computer, with human and computer taking turns to generate words. Later, the participants were asked to write down all the words they had generated (but not the words generated by the computer). Participants remembered many of the words they had generated—but about 10% of the words they wrote down had in fact been generated by the computer.

Doonesbury©1994 G. B. Trudeau Reprinted with permission of Universal Press Syndicate

Why might someone mistakenly think he had attended a highly publicized event?

One famous example of cryptomnesia occurred in the early 1970s, when ex-Beatle George Harrison released the hit single "My Sweet Lord" and was sued for copyright infringement because the tune was so similar to an earlier song, the Chiffons' "He's So Fine." Harrison argued that "My Sweet Lord" was his own creation and denied any plagiarism, although he admitted to having heard the Chiffons' song. A judge ruled that Harrison had indeed been influenced by his memories of the earlier song, although the judge was convinced that Harrison's plagiarism was unintentional. Apparently, the ex-Beatle had suffered cryptomnesia: remembering the melody and mistakenly thinking he had composed it himself.

False Memory

Memory misattribution is a case of good memory gone bad: for example, Reagan's story about the heroic World War II commander was a perfectly valid memory—Reagan's error was in forgetting that it was a scene from a movie, not from real life. In contrast, **false memories** are memories of events that never actually happened.

Elizabeth Loftus and her colleagues have conducted several studies in which they intentionally "implanted" false memories in ordinary people. For example, in one study the researchers invented several fictitious events, such as getting lost in a shopping mall or surviving a vicious animal attack, and then told research participants that these events had happened to them as children (Loftus & Pickrell, 1995). Family members (who had agreed to collaborate) also spoke about the events as if they had really happened. Sure enough, a few days later, about 25% of the participants seemed to believe the events were real—and even "remembered" additional details that had not been present in the original story.

In another study, Kimberley Wade and her colleagues pasted childhood photos of their adult research participants into a photograph of a hot-air balloon ride. Figure 7.8 shows how one such photo was constructed. The researchers then showed participants the doctored photos and asked them to describe everything they could remember about the fictitious ride. After three such sessions, about half the people in the study claimed to remember having taken the ride—even though none had ever been in a hot-air balloon (Wade, Garry, Read, & Lindsay, 2002).

(a)   (b)

Figure 7.8 Creating false memories in the laboratory Researchers pasted childhood pictures (left) of adult participants into a photograph of a hot-air balloon ride (right). When prompted to recall details of the trip, about half the participants claimed they could remember the episode—even though none had ever been in a hot-air balloon.

Reprinted with permission from Wade et al., 2002.

False memories tend to occur when people are prompted to imagine missing details; later, they may mistakenly remember those details as the truth—a form of memory misattribution. The more that people imagine an event, the more likely they are to subsequently believe it really happened (Goff & Roediger, 1998; Thomas & Loftus, 2002).

Researchers can even elicit false memories in the laboratory simply by asking people to learn lists of words that share a particular implicit theme (Deese, 1959; Roediger & McDermott, 1995). For example, a word list based on the theme "sweet" might contain words such as CANDY, SUGAR, HONEY, and TASTE but not the word SWEET itself. Figure 7.9 shows data from one such study. In general, when participants are given a second list and asked to recognize the studied words, they correctly identify the studied words and correctly reject (fail to recognize) novel, unrelated words (e.g., DOG, HOUSE, or TOMATO). But participants also often claim to recognize the theme word (SWEET) even though that wasn't on the original list. Apparently, while learning such a list, people encode the semantic meaning of the words—the theme—and this leads them to believe they have actually seen the theme word (Cabeza, Rao, Wagner, Mayer, & Schacter, 2001).

If false memory occurs in the real world at anything like the rate observed in the laboratory, it could be a very commonplace, widespread phenomenon. This should be a matter of public concern. For example, if an eyewitness is shown a picture of a suspect in a criminal case, the witness's memory of that picture may become confused with the actual memory of the crime, leading the witness to "recognize" the suspect as the perpetrator even though the suspect is innocent. A similar recognition error occurred when a woman who had been raped identified psychologist Donald Thompson as her attacker (Thompson, 1988). Fortunately for Thompson, he had an iron-clad alibi: he was appearing on live TV at the time the rape occurred. Apparently, the woman had been watching TV just before the assault and mistakenly associated her memory of Thompson's face with the event of the rape.

Elizabeth Loftus and other false-memory researchers have been vocal in warning that eyewitness memory is more prone to error than most people realize. They and other experts on eyewitness testimony argue that the types of procedures that induce false memory in the lab (such

Figure 7.9 False memory for studied words People were first asked to learn lists of words organized around an unstated theme (such as "sweet"). Later, participants were generally accurate at recognizing the studied words and at rejecting (failing to recognize) novel, unrelated words. But they would also claim to recognize the unstudied theme words.

Data from Cabeza et al., 2001.

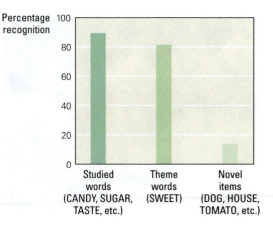

as showing a witness the photo of a suspect or asking her to imagine missing details of the witnessed event) must be scrupulously avoided in the justice system to minimize convictions based on false memory (Loftus, 1996, 2003; Radelet, 2002; Wells, Memon, & Penrod, 2006). And such convictions may be all too frequent. One study reviewed 62 cases in which people were convicted of crimes and later exonerated based on DNA evidence (Neufield & Dwyer, 2000). In more than 80% of these cases, the crucial evidence leading to conviction was eyewitness testimony, where witnesses had mistakenly identified people later proven to be innocent.

Memory Consolidation and Reconsolidation

Passive-forgetting curves, such as the one shown in Figure 7.6a, suggest that, if you can still remember a fact or event after a few months, then the odds are good that you'll remember it permanently (or at least for a very long time). One implication of this finding is that semantic and episodic memories have a **consolidation period:** a time window during which new memories are vulnerable and easily lost (Dudai, 2004; McGaugh, 2000; Ribot, 1882).

In an early demonstration of this principle, Carl Duncan trained rats to make a simple conditioned response. He then gave the rats **electroconvulsive shock,** a brief pulse of electricity passed through the brain via electrodes on each side of the head. If the shock was given 20 seconds after the end of training, the rats' memory of the conditioned response was severely disrupted. However, if the shock was given an hour or more after training, there was little disruption. Intermediate delays produced intermediate levels of disruption (Duncan, 1949). Thus, the consolidation period for this type of learning in rats appears to extend for a few minutes; older memories (from several hours ago) are relatively stable and difficult to disrupt; more recent memories (from less than a minute ago) are highly vulnerable to disruption.

Electroconvulsive shock is sometimes administered to humans to provide temporary relief from certain kinds of mental illness, particularly severe depression. Patients are given general anesthesia and a muscle relaxant beforehand. The entire procedure, called *electroconvulsive therapy*, or *ECT*, takes about 30 minutes. No one knows exactly why ECT relieves depression, but patients often experience relief for weeks or even months afterward (Glass, 2001; National Institutes of Health Consensus Conference, 1985).

By studying patients who are undergoing ECT, researchers have been able to investigate the effects of electroconvulsive shock on human memory. For example, Larry Squire and his colleagues administered the TV-show test to patients with severe depression (Squire, Slater, & Chace, 1975; Squire, Slater, & Miller, 1981). Before an ECT session, the patients remembered recent shows (from 2 to 3 years earlier) very well and older shows (from 8–15 years earlier) less well (Figure 7.10). This is similar to the performance of healthy adults, which you saw in Figure 7.6a. A week after ECT, the patients retook the TV-show test. Almost invariably, they had forgotten some of the information they'd reported earlier, especially memories for shows that had aired within the last few years; older memories (>3 years) were generally unaffected. A similar pattern was seen for autobiographical memories. Other kinds of memory, such as newly acquired motor skills, seem to be spared by ECT (Squire, Cohen, & Zouzounis, 1984; Vakil et al., 2000).

Electroconvulsive therapy is sometimes used to treat patients with severe depression.

Will McIntyre/Photo Researchers, Inc.

For most patients who undergo ECT, many of the disrupted episodic and semantic memories return with time. Typically, only the memories for a short period before and after the ECT session are gone forever. For many patients, this limited memory loss is a small price to pay for relief from the debilitation of severe depression.

The idea of a consolidation period, during which new memories are vulnerable to disruption, is attractive because it accounts for a great deal of data from animals and humans. Recently, though, new data is resurrecting an old idea that no memory, however ancient, is really permanent and immutable (Nadel & Land, 2000; Nader & Hardt, 2009; Nader, Schafe, & LeDoux, 2000a). For example, it has long been known that, if an old memory is recalled just before electroconvulsive shock is administered, it can be disrupted too (e.g., Misanin, Miller, & Lewis, 1968). Modern research is extending these early findings to show that old memories can also be disrupted if they are recalled just before administration of drugs that block the formation or maintenance of synaptic connections (Nader, Schafe, & LeDoux, 2000b; Przybyslawsky & Sara, 1997). Apparently, each time an old (presumably consolidated) memory is recalled or reactivated, it may become vulnerable again and need to be *"reconsolidated"*—just like a brand-new memory. Why might this be? Memory is not static, like a printed record, but dynamic. Each time we retrieve an old memory, we can modify it by integrating new information into it (Dudai, 2004; Sara, 2000; Wang & Morris, 2010). This opens the door to potential disruption—but it also allows existing memories to be continually updated, refined, and elaborated based on new experiences.

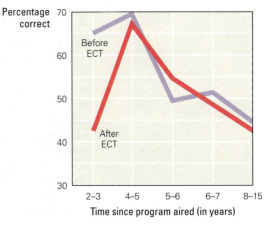

Figure 7.10 Effects of ECT on memory Before electroconvulsive shock therapy (ECT), patients with depression show a forgetting curve (purple line) similar to that of nondepressed adults. After the patients undergo ECT (red line), retrieval of recent memories is temporarily disrupted.

Adapted from Squire et al., 1975.

Interim Summary

- Episodic memory is memory for specific autobiographical events that occurred in a unique spatial and temporal context; it is information we "remember."

- Semantic memory is memory for facts and general information about the world and does not necessarily include information about where or when the memory was originally acquired; it is information we "know."

- Both episodic and semantic memories can be flexibly communicated in ways other than those in which they were originally acquired, and both are available to conscious recollection.

- Researchers still debate whether nonhuman animals can have true episodic memories; some believe this faculty belongs to humans alone, but others cite mounting evidence for "episodic-like" memory in nonhuman species.

- Several principles govern the encoding of new memories: (1) Mere exposure to information does not guarantee memory. (2) Memory for new information is stronger if it can be related to existing knowledge. (3) Memory is also affected by depth of processing at encoding.

- Successful retrieval of existing memories is more likely if (1) encoding and retrieval conditions match (transfer-appropriate processing) and (2) if more cues are available to prompt recall.

- Memory can also "fail" in many ways because of simple forgetting, interference, memory misattribution, and creation of false memories.

7.2 Brain Substrates

Functions as complex as semantic and episodic memory depend on many interacting brain systems, and scientists are still a long way from fully understanding them all. At present, most researchers agree that semantic memories are stored in the cerebral cortex. Similarly, most researchers agree that the encoding of new episodic memories depends on the hippocampus, but there's ongoing debate about whether semantic memories require the hippocampus and about whether the hippocampal role is limited to encoding or whether the hippocampus is required throughout the life of an episodic memory. Finally, many other brain structures, including the frontal lobes, the basal forebrain, and the diencephalon, have roles in modulating the storage, maintenance, and retrieval of semantic and episodic memories, but the exact nature of these roles is still under study.

The Cerebral Cortex and Semantic Memory

In the 1930s, a neurosurgeon named Wilder Penfield was preparing epileptic patients for brain surgery; Penfield planned to surgically destroy the brain areas where the seizures originated. A few decades later, surgeons would try Penfield's procedure to treat H.M. But unlike H.M., whose seizures could not be localized to a single source, many of Penfield's patients had seizures that appeared to originate the in the cerebral cortex. Before operating, Penfield removed pieces of the patients' skull to expose the cerebral cortex, then stimulated different areas of cortex with an electrical probe to see how the person would respond (Penfield & Boldrey, 1937; Penfield & Rasmussen, 1950). Each of Penfield's patients was given local anesthesia to prevent pain from the incision but was otherwise fully conscious. The probe itself didn't cause pain because the brain itself contains no pain receptors. The idea was to accurately identify the parts of the brain where the seizures were originating so Penfield could target them more accurately for surgery and reduce side effects. At the same time, he realized he had an important opportunity to map the cortex of living humans.

When Penfield touched an electrode to areas in the parietal lobe, the patient might report "feeling" a localized numbness or tingling in the skin. When the electrode touched areas of cortex in the occipital lobe, the patient might report "seeing" a flashing light; when the electrode touched areas in the superior temporal lobe, the patient might report "hearing" a buzzing noise. These results contributed greatly to scientific understanding of how different areas of cerebral cortex process information from different sensory modalities; in fact, the "motor homunculus" (which you saw in Figure 2.14) that maps the function of motor cortex was based on Penfield's drawings.

As you've read in earlier chapters, the cerebral cortex can be divided into different regions, some of which are specialized to process particular kinds of sensory information. These include the somatosensory cortex in the parietal lobe, the visual cortex in the occipital lobe, and the auditory cortex in the temporal lobe. Cortical areas that specialize in one kind of sensory information are often grouped under the heading of **sensory cortex.** Other cortical areas (e.g., those shown in pale pink in Figure 7.11) are called **association cortex,** meaning they are involved in associating information within and across modalities. Association cortex helps us link the word "dog" with the visual image of a dog and with semantic information about what dogs are like as well as with linguistic information about how to pronounce and recognize the spoken word itself. Thus, cerebral cortex is a primary storage site for many kinds of semantic information.

Somatosensory cortex:
Parietal lobe

Auditory cortex:
Superior temporal lobe

Visual cortex:
Occipital lobe

Figure 7.11 **Semantic memory and the cerebral cortex** Some areas of the cerebral cortex specialize in processing specific kinds of sensory information; these include areas in the parietal lobe (somatosensory cortex), the occipital lobe (visual cortex), and the superior temporal lobe (auditory cortex). Many of the remaining cortical areas are association areas that link information within and across modalities, forming a basic substrate for semantic information.

People with cortical damage can display various kinds of **agnosia,** relatively selective disruption of the ability to process a particular kind of semantic information. ("Agnosia" is from the Greek for "not knowing.") For example, patients with *auditory agnosia for speech* can "hear" sounds and echo them, but they are unable to understand the meaning of spoken words—though they can often recognize written words (Bauer & McDonald, 2003). These patients may describe hearing their native language as if it were a foreign tongue—little more than a stream of unintelligible gibberish. Patients with *associative visual agnosia* have difficulty recognizing and naming objects, even though they can "see" the objects (and can usually copy them accurately). If such a patient is shown a pen or a cup, she may be unable to name it or say what it is used for—though she may be able to name the object based on feel if it is placed in her hand (Farah, 2003). In contrast, patients with *tactile agnosia* may be able to recognize an object by sight or description but not by feel (Caselli, 2003). In each case, the agnosia results from the loss of semantic knowledge linking the perception of an object (through sight, sound, or touch) with its identity (or name or function).

Some types of sensory agnosias are caused by damage to the corresponding areas of sensory cortex (see Figure 7.11). Thus, for example, patients with associative visual agnosia often have damage to cortex in the inferior temporal lobe, those with auditory agnosia for speech often have damage to the cortex in the superior temporal lobe, and those with tactile agnosia often have damage to the cortex in the parietal lobe (Zeki, 1993).

But sometimes, individual patients show agnosias that are much more specific. For example, one man developed a peculiar kind of visual agnosia that left him unable to name living things and foods though he could successfully name inanimate objects (Warrington & Shallice, 1984). Another man developed a form of auditory agnosia that left him able to use and comprehend nouns—but not verbs (McCarthy & Warrington, 1985). And one woman showed a selective deficit when asked questions about the physical attributes of animals ("What color is an elephant?") although she could correctly answer questions about nonphysical attributes such as whether the animals are kept as pets or used as food (Hart & Gordon, 1992).

Such agnosias seem to suggest that specific categories of semantic knowledge are stored in unique places in the brain, so that a cortical lesion can destroy knowledge for a particular kind of object (foods, say, or verbs) but not closely related objects. This may seem counterintuitive, especially given what you read in Chapter 2 about Lashley's theory of equipotentiality. But recent studies suggest that this may be the case after all. Just as in Penfield's time, modern patients

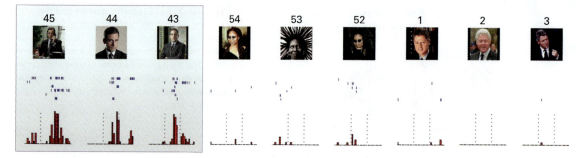

Figure 7.12 Category-sensitive neurons in the human brain A patient with electrodes implanted in the right hippocampus was shown photos of famous celebrities and landmarks, including the nine photos shown here (Quiroga et al., 2005). The response of a single neuron to each photo appears below it, with the height of the red bars indicating the strength of the neuron's response. This neuron responded strongly to pictures of actor Steve Carell (pictures 43–45) but not to photos of other celebrities such as Whoopi Goldberg (pictures 52–54) or Bill Clinton (pictures 1–3).

Adapted from Quiroga et al., 2008, Figure 1.

sometimes have intracranial electrodes implanted for clinical reasons, and some of these patients are willing to undergo memory testing while the electrodes are in place. In these studies, patients are shown different types of pictures, and the responses of individual neurons to each picture can be recorded. Some neurons respond to many pictures; others respond to none. But some neurons respond to pictures of particular categories of objects, such as animals, faces, or houses (Krieman, Koch, & Fried, 2000). Some neurons respond to sad faces but not happy, angry, or neutral faces (Fried, MacDonald, & Wilson, 1997). And some neurons even respond to pictures of one person but not others (Quiroga, Reddy, Kreiman, Koch, & Fried, 2005).

For example, Figure 7.12 shows some sample responses of a single neuron in the right hippocampus of one patient. This neuron fired strongly in response to photos of actor Steve Carell but was nearly silent in response to photos of other celebrities such as Whoopi Goldberg or Bill Clinton. Another patient had a neuron that responded to photos of Jennifer Aniston and Lisa Kudrow, both actresses in the TV series *Friends*; a different neuron in the same patient responded to pictures of the Eiffel Tower and the Tower of Pisa but not to other famous landmarks (Quiroga, Reddy, Kreiman, Koch, & Fried, 2005).

In nonhuman primates too, individual neurons in various areas of cortex in the frontal and temporal lobes can show surprising selectivity. To take just one example, Edmund Rolls and colleagues (Thorpe, Rolls, & Maddison, 1983) recorded neurons in the orbitofrontal cortex of rhesus monkeys, a small area located at the base of the frontal lobes; out of 494 neurons analyzed, they found 26 that responded selectively to visual stimuli representing food; even more striking, four neurons responded most strongly to oranges, four responded to peanuts, two responded to bananas, and one responded to raisins.

Remarkable as these results are, the fact that the neuron from Figure 7.12 responded "only" to Steve Carell in the experiment doesn't mean that we have individual neurons each specialized to detect images of a single person (one neuron for Steve Carell, one for Jennifer Aniston, one for your grandmother, and so on). In fact, there might be many other people or objects—not explicitly tested in the experiment—that would also elicit a response from that neuron. Most researchers believe it is more likely that we have networks of neurons that respond primarily to information representing simple, familiar categories, such as TV-sitcom actors, large pointy landmarks, or bananas. This way, loss of a single brain cell wouldn't erase all memories of the category, but when larger networks are damaged, semantic information about those categories might be lost. So perhaps it isn't quite so surprising that human patients with localized brain damage can sometimes show very selective agnosia—just as if the networks of neurons encoding a particular category of semantic knowledge had been selectively destroyed.

The Medial Temporal Lobes and Memory Storage

The medial temporal lobes in humans contain the hippocampus, the amygdala, and nearby cortical areas, including the entorhinal cortex and the perirhinal cortex (Figure 7.13). Chapter 3 described the role of the hippocampus in spatial learning, and Chapter 4 described the role of the hippocampus in certain forms of classical conditioning. But in fact, the most widely studied role of the human hippocampus is in the storage of new episodic and semantic memories, and the most obvious impairment in humans with damage to the medial temporal lobe is the loss of this function. At the start of this chapter, you read about H.M., the man who became amnesic after bilateral surgical removal of his medial temporal lobes. In their original report, William Beecher Scoville and Brenda Milner argued that it was specifically the lesion of the hippocampus, rather than the loss of other medial temporal lobe structures that were removed, that caused H.M.'s amnesia (Scoville & Milner, 1957). Before H.M., other neurologists, such as John Hughlings Jackson in the late 1800s and Vladimir Bekhterev in the early 1900s, had noted the role of the medial temporal lobes in memory, and Wilder Penfield had observed memory deficits in his patients with temporal lobe epilepsy. But H.M.'s case provided especially strong, widely accepted evidence for this idea—partly because of the severity of his impairment and partly because of H.M.'s decades-long willingness to participate in all kinds of memory tests that carefully documented exactly what he could and couldn't learn and remember.

Obviously, after H.M., no more surgeries were performed to remove the medial temporal lobes bilaterally in humans (although unilateral surgeries, which don't cause severe amnesia, are still sometimes performed for patients with intractable epilepsy). Unfortunately, bilateral medial temporal lobe damage does occur in humans as a result of various other kinds of injury and disease. For example, another patient, E.P., suffered bilateral medial temporal lobe damage as a result of viral encephalitis. (Like H.M., E.P. is known by his initials to protect his privacy.) When viewed on structural MRI, E.P.'s brain damage looked strikingly similar to H.M.'s—and he showed a very similar pattern of memory impairment (Stefanacci, Buffalo, Schmolck, & Squire, 2000). And patient R.B., who suffered a brain infection that damaged his hippocampus bilaterally, provided strong evidence that damage limited to the hippocampus (rather than the additional medial temporal lobe structures that were damaged in H.M. and E.P.) was indeed sufficient to disrupt memory (Zola-Morgan, Squire, & Amaral, 1986).

Figure 7.13 The medial temporal lobe in humans The medial (inner) portion of the temporal lobes contains the hippocampus, the amygdala, and several other cortical areas, including the entorhinal cortex and the perirhinal cortex.

Amygdala

Hippocampus

Entorhinal cortex

Perirhinal cortex

Hippocampus

By studying memory in such patients, as well as in nonhuman animals with medial temporal lobe lesion or dysfunction, neuroscientists are building up a picture of the role this brain area plays in memory.

The Hippocampus Is Critical for Forming New Episodic Memory

The most profound and noticeable memory impairment observed in patients such as H.M. and E.P. is **anterograde amnesia,** a severe loss of the ability to form new episodic and semantic memories. When questioned about autobiographical events, E.P. could remember his childhood, his marriage, and his travels during World War II. But he could not recall what he had done the day before or almost anything that had happened to him since the onset of his amnesia in 1992. Within a one-hour session, he might repeat the same anecdotes over and over as many as 10 times, unaware that he had told the stories before. In 1993, a year after the onset of E.P.'s amnesia, he and his family moved to a new home in California, but after seven years of living there, he could not draw a floor plan of the new house, describe how to get to the grocery store, or even point in the direction of the Pacific Ocean, which was less than two miles from his home (Stefanacci, Buffalo, Schmolck, & Squire, 2000).

Like H.M., E.P. participated in a large number of memory tests. A standard test of visual memory uses the complex figure shown in Figure 7.14a. Participants are first asked to copy the figure and then to draw it from memory 10 to 15 minutes later. Healthy adults can usually copy the figure quite accurately and manage to reproduce the figure from memory reasonably well after the delay (Figure 7.14b). E.P. could copy the drawing without difficulty, but after the delay, he had no memory of the picture at all (Figure 7.14c). His memory for verbal information was similarly poor: immediately after listening to a short story, he could only recall about 10% of the words or concepts; 15 minutes later, he could remember nothing about it.

Like H.M., animals with broad lesions of the hippocampal region have difficulty learning new information (Mishkin, 1978; Squire, 1992). They are especially impaired at episodic-like learning that involves memory of unique events set in a particular scene (Gaffan & Hornak, 1997; Gaffan & Parker, 1996). For example, the radial maze shown in Figure 7.2 can be used for a task in which researchers place a piece of food at the end of every arm and then place a hungry rat in center of the maze. The rat has a few minutes in which to obtain all the food it can. Notice that once a rat has entered a given arm and eaten the food there, subsequent entries into the same arm are a waste of time. Therefore, the

Figure 7.14 Anterograde amnesia in patient E.P. Shown a complex figure (a), a healthy control participant can generally copy it accurately (b, top) and can do a reasonably good job if asked to draw the figure from memory 15 minutes later (b, bottom). Patient E.P. could also copy the drawing well (c, top), but asked to draw it from memory after the delay, he had essentially forgotten everything about it (c, bottom).

Adapted from Stefanacci et al., 2000, Figure 7.

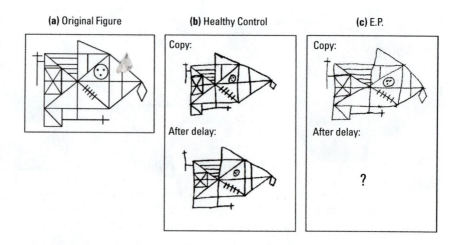

(a) Original Figure   **(b)** Healthy Control   **(c)** E.P.

rat can solve this task most efficiently by visiting each arm exactly once. This requires that the rat remember where it's already been. But if the task is given on several successive days, the rat will have to remember which arms it's already visited so far today, distinct from the memories of prior days on which the rat entered those arms and found food there. Proactive interference affects rats in a radial arm maze, just as it affects humans in a parking lot! The only way out of this dilemma is to remember the spatial and temporal context of visits—namely, whether a specific arm was visited yet *today*, as distinct from all other visits on all other days. In other words, this task requires "episodic-like" memory, a memory of not just what happened but when. After several days of training, healthy rats learn to navigate the radial arm maze very efficiently: they collect all eight rewards, and in the process, they make very few erroneous reentries into previously visited arms. In contrast, rats with hippocampal lesions make many more errors: they repeatedly reenter previously visited arms, apparently aware that there is food to be found but unable to remember which arms they've already visited on this particular day (Cassel et al., 1998; Jarrard, Okaichi, Steward, & Goldschmidt, 1984; Olton, 1983).

In birds, hippocampal-region damage also disrupts episodic-like learning. Remember the scrub jays, who bury food in caches and then return to the caches later? When the birds' hippocampal region is lesioned, they lose the ability to locate their caches (Capaldi, Robinson, & Fahrback, 1999). They continue to store new food, but they quickly forget where they've put it; they search almost at random—much like the lesioned rat running around the radial maze.

Are There Different Brain Substrates for Episodic and Semantic Memory?

Most researchers agree that the hippocampus is necessary for acquiring new episodic information about autobiographical events. But there is tantalizing evidence that some patients with damage limited to the hippocampus that spares other medial temporal lobe areas can still acquire semantic information.

A classic example is the patient known as Beth. Beth was born without a heartbeat. The delivery team resuscitated her, but she continued to have seizures for the next few weeks. After that, her condition stabilized, and she seemed to grow into a normal little girl. It wasn't until age 5, when Beth started school, that her family noticed she was amnesic. Beth has almost no memory for any autobiographical events. She cannot remember the day's activities, reliably report a telephone conversation, or follow the plot of a television program. When Beth was 14 years old, a structural MRI showed that her hippocampus was much smaller than normal on both sides; other parts of her brain—including the rest of her medial temporal lobes—looked normal (Gadian et al., 2000; Vargha-Khadem et al., 1997).

Given what we know about the hippocampus, Beth's episodic memory difficulties are not too surprising. What is surprising is that Beth progressed relatively successfully through school, getting average grades and even participating in extracurricular activities. She was competent in language and speech and could read and write nearly as well as her peers. She scored well on tests of vocabulary and intelligence. When asked general knowledge questions, Beth could give a reasonable answer—indicating that she had as much semantic knowledge as any other girl of her age.

Because Beth's hippocampal damage occurred at birth, all of this semantic knowledge was, by definition, acquired after the onset of her amnesia. Farina Vargha-Khadem and her colleagues working with Beth concluded that the hippocampus is critically necessary for the acquisition of new autobiographical or episodic information (of which Beth has none) but not for new semantic information (of which Beth has plenty). Instead, Vargha-Khadem and her colleagues conclude that semantic learning depends on medial temporal areas, including the entorhinal cortex and perirhinal cortex, that were spared in Beth (Vargha-Khadem et al., 1997). This is why Beth could pass her high school classes.

Remember the debate that you read about above in the Behavioral Processes section about whether episodic memories depend on semantic memories or vice versa? Beth's case seems consistent with the view that episodic memories depend on semantic memories (so you can't have an episodic memory for your graduation unless you have knowledge about what graduations are). According to this view, episodic memories are semantic memories that have context information added on, courtesy of the hippocampus. With no hippocampus, patients such as Beth can remember the information but can't record the autobiographical context in which those memories were formed (Tulving & Markowitsch, 1998).

But remember that other researchers believe that semantic memories are built up through repetition and rehearsal of many individual episodes. In other words, if you hear a fact once and remember it, you may have an episodic memory for the learning experience, but if you hear the same fact many times in many different spatial and temporal contexts, the episodes may blur together until only the fact remains. If semantic memories are based on episodic memories, then you would expect people with hippocampal damage to show impairments at learning new factual information because they don't have their episodic memory to help. In fact, many amnesic patients with brain damage relatively limited to the hippocampus are profoundly impaired in learning new semantic information as well as episodic information (Manns, Hopkins, & Squire, 2003). For example, as you've already read, E.P. couldn't sketch the floor plan of his new home, even after living there for several years, and H.M. couldn't name the current U.S. president. These cases suggest that Beth might be a special case and that—for most patients—damage to the medial temporal lobes devastates both episodic and semantic memory.

The debate continues.

Functional Neuroimaging of the Healthy Hippocampal Region

Our knowledge of the role of the hippocampal region in new memory formation is not limited to studies of humans and other animals with brain damage. Functional neuroimaging studies allow us to see the hippocampus in action in brains with normal memory function. For example, Anthony Wagner and his colleagues have used a *subsequent memory* paradigm (Wagner et al., 1998). Participants first view a list of words and are asked to categorize each word as abstract or concrete; fMRI is used to take images of brain activity during this initial phase. This phase is called an "incidental encoding" phase because any learning about the words is incidental to the task at hand. Next, the researchers administer a surprise recognition test: showing the participants a new list of words and asking them to identify which words were on the previous list. As you might expect, people correctly recognize some of the words but not all of them. The important finding is that fMRI activity during the incidental encoding phase differs for words that will be successfully recognized later compared with words that will not. In effect, researchers viewing the fMRI of a participant's brain during incidental encoding can predict with reasonably accuracy whether that word will be recalled or forgotten later. Specifically, Figure 7.15a shows that the left medial temporal lobe is more active during incidental encoding of words that are subsequently remembered compared with words that are subsequently forgotten. (There is a similar effect in the left frontal cortex, shown in Figure 7.15b; we'll return to this later in the chapter.)

Figure 7.15 The "subsequent memory" paradigm Brain imaging (fMRI) records activity while participants make categorization judgments on a series of words. Later, participants are given a recognition test; typically, they correctly recognize some but not all of the previously viewed words. Some areas of the brain, including the left medial temporal lobe (a) and left prefrontal cortex (b), are more active during initial viewing of words that will subsequently be remembered compared with initial viewing of words that will subsequently be forgotten.

(a, b) Adapted from Wagner et al., 1998.

(a) Medial temporal lobe

(b) Frontal lobe

Science Magazine/
Courtesy of Anthony D. Wagner

Similar studies, in which the stimuli are pictures, also show that the medial temporal lobe is more active during incidental encoding of pictures that will be remembered than pictures that will be forgotten—but whereas words tend to activate only the left medial temporal lobe, pictures tend to activate the medial temporal lobe bilaterally (Brewer, Zhao, Desmond, Glover, & Gabrieli, 1998).

These studies suggest that pictures and words that are processed more elaborately in the medial temporal lobes (visible as increased temporal lobe activity on fMRI) are more likely to be encoded and remembered later. This may underlie the depth-of-processing effect, in which "imaging" a word produces better memory than merely "pronouncing" a word backward (Figure 7.5a). And the hippocampus itself may play a crucial role in the what-happened-where aspect of episodic memory. When the experimenters asked people to remember not only the word but also where they'd heard it—during the "image" condition or the "pronounce" condition—the hippocampus was more active when both word and source were recalled than when the word was recalled without the source (Davachi, Mitchell, & Wagner, 2003). Apparently, the hippocampus helps bind together the memory of an object (such as a word) with the unique spatial and temporal context in which that object was experienced. This seems to occur in rats and monkeys as well as humans (Eichenbaum, 2000; Gaffan & Parker, 1996; Honey, Watt, & Good, 1998).

Other functional neuroimaging studies have considered false memory, the "remembering" of events that never actually occurred. In the false-memory test described earlier, in which people study a list of words related to an unnamed theme word (Figure 7.9), fMRI during the recognition phase shows a striking pattern. Several brain areas are more active for studied list words than for novel words, but the (unstudied) theme words evokes high activity too (Cabeza & Nyberg, 2000). This could explain why people are prone to falsely recognize the theme words.

The hippocampus is one of the brain areas that is "fooled" into responding as strongly to the theme words as to the studied list words. But a small area in the medial temporal lobe shows a different pattern. A region of cortex called the posterior parahippocampal gyrus, located just behind the hippocampus, also responds more strongly to studied words than to novel words, but it does not respond strongly to the (unstudied) theme words. Apparently, this small brain region is able to correctly distinguish true episodic memories from false ones (Cabeza, Rao, Wagner, Mayer, & Schacter, 2001; Okado & Stark, 2003)—at least in the lab. If this finding extends to false memories outside the lab, it may have real-world application, particularly for court cases in which a witness claims to remember details of a crime and the defense charges that the memory is a false one. Maybe someday the defense will be able to present an fMRI of a witness's brain as evidence that the witness may not have experienced the event the way she or he is recalling it. For now, though, nobody has developed a foolproof brain-mapping procedure for distinguishing a true from a false memory.

The Hippocampus and Cortex Interact during Memory Consolidation

In the late 1800s, French philosopher Theodore Ribot noticed that individuals with head injury often developed **retrograde amnesia,** loss of memories for events that occurred before the injury (Ribot, 1882). This is in contrast to anterograde amnesia, in which patients lose the ability to form memories for events that occurred after the injury. Typically, retrograde amnesia follows a pattern called the **Ribot gradient:** retrograde memory loss is worse for events that occurred shortly before the injury than for events that occurred in the distant

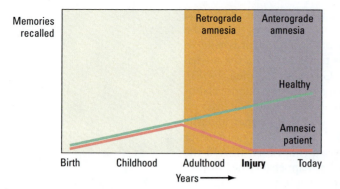

Figure 7.16 Retrograde and anterograde amnesia A healthy adult (green line) may be able to recall most of what happened today and will recall progressively less about events that happened weeks, months, and years ago. In contrast, a person with bilateral hippocampal damage (red line) may suffer anterograde amnesia, a loss of the ability to form new episodic and semantic memories since the injury, as well as retrograde amnesia, or memory loss for events that occurred days or weeks before the injury. If the brain damage extends beyond the hippocampus into nearby cortex, retrograde amnesia may be much more severe and may extend back for decades or longer.

past. For example, a man who hit his head during a car accident might lose all memories of the accident itself and might also have some disruption of memories from the minutes or hours before the accident, but he would have relatively little disruption of memories for events that occurred months or years earlier (Figure 7.16). The Ribot gradient also describes the effects of electroconvulsive shock, which preferentially disrupts recently formed memories (see Figure 7.10).

People with bilateral medial temporal lobe damage generally show some retrograde amnesia along with their anterograde amnesia. These patients don't forget their own identity—H.M. could remember his name and his childhood—but patients often lose memories for events that happened some time before the brain damage, and this retrograde amnesia can affect information acquired decades earlier (Manns, Hopkins, & Squire, 2003). For example, as you read above, patient E.P. suffered bilateral medial temporal lobe damage that left him with dense anterograde amnesia, meaning that he could recall almost nothing that had happened to him since 1992. In addition, E.P. displayed retrograde amnesia. His memory for childhood events was excellent—as good as that of healthy control patients of the same age. But when asked about adulthood events that had occurred decades before his encephalitis, E.P. remembered significantly less than the control patients (Reed & Squire, 1998; Stefanacci, Buffalo, Schmolck, & Squire, 2000).

You've already read about the consolidation period, during which new memories are especially vulnerable to disruption. E.P.'s case suggests that the consolidation period may last for decades, because he lost memories of at least some decades-old events. So just how long is the consolidation period in humans? How long before a new memory becomes independent of the medial temporal lobes and is "safely" stored in sensory and association cortex?

Experts disagree on the answer. One position, sometimes called **standard consolidation theory,** holds that the hippocampus and related medial temporal lobe structures are required for the initial storage and retrieval of an episodic memory but that their contribution diminishes over time until the cortex is capable of retrieving the memory without hippocampal help (Dudai, 2004; McGaugh, 2000; Squire, 1992). This view conceptualizes an episodic memory as consisting of many components (sight, sound, texture, context, etc.) that are stored in different areas of the cortex (Figure 7.17a). Initially, all of these components are linked together via the hippocampus into a unified episodic memory (Figure 7.17b). Over time, through the process of consolidation, the components can form direct connections with one another and no longer need hippocampal mediation (Figure 7.17c). If the hippocampus is damaged, older memories would be more likely to have such connections, and thus be more likely to survive, than new memories. This would explain the temporal gradient of retrograde amnesia observed in many amnesic patients with medial temporal lobe damage.

According to standard consolidation theory, patients with brain damage strictly limited to the hippocampus should have profound anterograde amnesia but relatively little retrograde amnesia. And indeed, there is some evidence that the extent of retrograde amnesia in a particular patient reflects the size of the brain lesion. In other words, individuals with damage limited to the hippocampus (such as R.B.) may have retrograde amnesia that extends back a year or

Components of an
episodic memory

Hippocampus

(a)   (b)   (c)

Figure 7.17 Standard consolidation theory (a) An episodic memory consists of many components, such as sight, sound, texture, and other features, stored in sensory and association cortex. (b) Initially, the hippocampal region helps link these components into a single episodic memory. (c) Over time, the components become linked to one another directly, and hippocampal involvement is no longer required.

two, but individuals with broader medial temporal damage (such as E.P.) may have retrograde amnesia that extends back many years, perhaps decades (Nadel, Samsonovich, Ryan, & Moscovitch, 2000; Reed & Squire, 1998). Retrograde amnesia may be greatest of all in individuals whose brain damage extends beyond the medial temporal lobe and into other areas of cerebral cortex—where semantic and episodic memories are normally stored (Bayley, Gold, Hopkins, & Squire, 2005).

On the other hand, in some cases of amnesia, patients have severe retrograde memory loss that extends as far back as childhood and is not temporally graded (Nadel & Moscovitch, 1997). To account for such extensive retrograde amnesia, Morris Moscovitch and Lynn Nadel have argued that the hippocampus mediates storage and retrieval throughout the entire lifetime of an episodic memory (Moscovitch & Nadel, 1998; Nadel & Moscovitch, 2001). According to this **multiple memory trace theory,** episodic memories are encoded by an ensemble of hippocampal and cortical networks, and the cortical networks never, in normal circumstances, become fully independent of the hippocampal networks. According to this view, individuals with hippocampal damage effectively lose all their episodic memories (Nadel, Samsonovich, Ryan, & Moscovitch, 2000). Such individuals might be able to rehearse a piece of autobiographical information so many times that it becomes a semantic memory. But this is a far cry from how people normally recall episodic memories. It would be equivalent to a person "remembering" the day she was born because she's heard the family stories so often. She has semantic information about the event and knows it happened to her, but that isn't quite the same thing as remembering the event firsthand. In short, according to this view, individuals with medial temporal lobe damage lose the capacity for "mental time travel" and with it the capacity for episodic memory (Steinvorth, Levine, & Corkin, 2005).

Various studies have attempted to test the predictions of standard consolidation theory against those of multiple memory trace theory. For example, standard consolidation theory predicts that in normal memory function, hippocampal activity should be greatest for recently acquired memories (which are still dependent on the hippocampus) and lowest for very old memories (which should be fully consolidated and independent of the hippocampus). Some studies have shown just this. Christine Smith and Larry Squire asked individuals to recall important news events from 1 to 30 years ago while undergoing fMRI to measure brain activity. They found that activity in the hippocampus does indeed gradually decrease as the age of the semantic memory increases from 1 to 12 years and remains low during recall of memories from 13 to 30 years ago, suggesting that the consolidation period may last over a decade but does eventually end (Smith & Squire, 2009). Other brain areas, including cortical areas in the frontal lobe, temporal lobe, and parietal lobe, showed the opposite pattern—higher activity for old than for new memories—consistent with the idea that these brain areas, and not the medial temporal lobes, are the eventual storage site of semantic memories. Other studies have similarly found that hippocampal activity decreases with the age of an episodic memory, which is evidence in favor of standard consolidation theory (Addis, Moscovitch, Crawley, & McAndrews, 2004; Takashima et al., 2006). But still other studies have found equal hippocampal activation for recent and remote memories, which is evidence in favor of multiple memory trace theory (Bernard et al., 2004; Kapur, Friston, Young, Frith, & Frackowiak, 1995; Maguire, 2001).

At this point, it remains an open question whether standard consolidation theory or multiple memory trace theory provides a better description of the hippocampal role in memory (Wang & Morris, 2010). The concept of reconsolidation may help to unify the two theories (Hardt, Einarsson, & Nader, 2010). As described earlier in this chapter, the idea of reconsolidation predicts that each time an old memory is recalled, it may become vulnerable to disruption again until it is reconsolidated. When it is recalled, a new episodic memory of this recall event may be created—with the help of the hippocampus. Thus, perhaps memories do consolidate outside the hippocampus, but only until they are recalled—and a memory that has been recalled many times may indeed have multiple memory traces, many of which are still dependent on the hippocampus.

The Frontal Cortex and Memory Storage and Retrieval

The **frontal cortex,** those regions of cortex that lie within the frontal lobes, may help determine what information we store (and remember) and what information we don't store (and therefore forget). Recall that Wagner's subsequent memory study found heightened medial temporal lobe activity during the incidental encoding of words that would subsequently be remembered (Figure 7.15a). As Figure 7.15b showed, the left frontal lobe was also more active during incidental encoding of subsequently remembered information (Wagner et al., 1998).

Other areas in the prefrontal cortex may suppress hippocampal activity, inhibiting storage and retrieval of "unwanted" memories. For example, in the directed forgetting task of Figure 7.6b, participants studied words and then were asked to explicitly try to remember or forget each one. Later, participants' memory was worse for items they'd been instructed to forget than for items they'd been instructed to remember (or items they hadn't seen since the original study phase).

What could underlie this effect? Michael Anderson and colleagues collected fMRI data while participants were trying to remember or forget the word associates. As Figure 7.18 shows, the hippocampus was more active during the remember trials than during the forget trials; this is not particularly surprising given the role of the hippocampus in memory (M. Anderson et al., 2004). More surprising was the finding that several areas in the prefrontal cortex were more active during the *forget* trials than during the remember trials. One possible explanation is that certain areas of prefrontal cortex inhibit the hippocampus, and so their heightened activity during intentional forgetting suppresses hippocampal memory encoding. And indeed, the greater the prefrontal activation in a

More active during "forget" than "remember"

More active during "remember" than "forget"

Courtesy of Dr. Michael Anderson, University of Oregon and Dr. Jeffrey Cooper, Stanford University

Figure 7.18 **Directed forgetting** fMRI images show the hippocampus to be less active (blue) while people were actively trying to forget than while they were actively trying to remember. Several prefrontal areas, however, were more active (yellow) while participants were trying to forget.
Adapted from Anderson et al., 2004.

participant during a given trial, the more likely the participant was to forget that word on the final test. The specific prefrontal areas activated during intentional forgetting are slightly different from those that are active during intentional remembering (Wylie, Foxe, & Taylor, 2008).

These and similar experiments strongly suggest that the frontal lobes contribute to determining what new information gets encoded as episodic and semantic memories and what gets forgotten. The frontal lobes may also help us bind contextual information to event memory, allowing us to form episodic memories that encode not only what happened but also where and when the episode took place (Schacter & Curran, 1995).

In keeping with these ideas, you might expect that people with frontal-lobe damage would be especially prone to source amnesia—an inability to remember where and when an event occurred. And this seems to be the case: individuals with frontal-lobe damage may be able to remember a story but not whether it occurred in their own past, or on television, or in their imagination (Kapur & Coughlan, 1980). Source amnesia is generally not as devastating as the all-out memory failure of anterograde amnesia or retrograde amnesia, but it can still be a serious problem if a person can't reliably tell the difference between a fictional story and a real-life experience.

Subcortical Structures Involved in Episodic and Semantic Memory

Two other brain structures deserve special mention in the context of episodic and semantic memory: the basal forebrain and the diencephalon (Figure 7.19). The **basal forebrain** is a collection of structures that lie—as the

Frontal cortex

Fornix

Mediodorsal nucleus of the thalamus

Mammillary body

Basal forebrain
Hypothalamus
Amygdala
Hippocampus

Figure 7.19 The basal forebrain and diencephalon Structures in the diencephalon (including the mediodorsal nucleus of the thalamus and the mammillary bodies) and in the basal forebrain connect with the hippocampus via a fiber bundle called the fornix. Damage to either the diencephalon or the basal forebrain can cause anterograde amnesia that resembles the effects of hippocampal damage.

name suggests—at the base of the forebrain. Structures of the basal forebrain include the *nucleus basalis* and the *medial septal nuclei*, which contain neurons that produce the neuromodulator *acetylcholine* and distribute it throughout the brain. The **diencephalon** is an area near the core of the brain, just above the brainstem, that includes the *thalamus*, the *hypothalamus*, and the *mammillary bodies* (which are sometimes considered to be part of the hypothalamus). The thalamus consists of several nuclei, many of which help relay sensory information from sensory receptors to the appropriate areas of sensory cortex; the hypothalamus plays an important role in regulating involuntary functions such as heartbeat, appetite, temperature control, and the wake/sleep cycle. (The function of the mammillary bodies isn't clear, although, as you'll read below, they play a role in memory.) Parts of the basal forebrain and diencephalon connect with the hippocampus via an arch-like fiber bundle called (you guessed it) the **fornix.** Damage to the basal forebrain, the diencephalon, or the fornix can result in amnesia.

The Basal Forebrain May Help Determine what the Hippocampus Stores

The basal forebrain receives blood and oxygen from a small artery, the anterior communicating artery (ACoA). The ACoA is a common site of *aneurysm*, a type of stroke in which an artery wall balloons out under pressure and may even rupture. ACoA aneurysm rupture may cause damage to the basal forebrain, and survivors often have anterograde amnesia very similar to that caused by medial temporal lobe damage (DeLuca & Diamond, 1995).

Why should basal forebrain damage cause amnesia? As you read in Chapter 2, neurotransmitters such as GABA and neuromodulators such as acetylcholine are critical for proper brain function. The medial septum, a group of cells in the basal forebrain, sends acetylcholine and GABA to the hippocampus, where they affect the activity and synaptic plasticity of hippocampal neurons. Thus, these projections may help determine whether and when the hippocampus will process and store information (Buzsaki & Gage, 1989; Damasio, Graff-Radford, Eslinger, Damasio, & Kassell, 1985; Hasselmo, 1999; Myers, Ermita, Hasselmo, & Gluck, 1998). This could explain why basal forebrain damage leads to amnesia: although the hippocampus is undamaged, it can't work effectively without neuromodulation from the basal forebrain telling it when to store new information.

When questioned about past events, many individuals with basal forebrain damage will respond with highly detailed but false memories, a phenomenon called **confabulation.** For example, asked what he did yesterday, a patient may say that he went into the office for a few hours, met an old friend for lunch, and then did some grocery shopping on the way home; the story may sound perfectly convincing except for the fact that the patient has been in the hospital for the past two weeks!

Individuals who confabulate are not lying. Rather, they seem to believe the stories they've made up and are often sincerely confused when confronted with proof that the stories are false. Some examples of confabulation seem to be no more than a kind of source amnesia. In the above example, the patient can't remember what he did yesterday because of his amnesia. But he can retrieve a plausible answer from old memory. Consistent with this idea, confabulation typically appears in patients in whom the damage from the aneurysm rupture extends beyond the basal forebrain and into the frontal cortex. Apparently, the basal forebrain damage leaves patients unable to store new memories; when questioned about recent events, they can't remember but may retrieve a plausible answer—and the frontal cortex damage leaves them with a kind of source amnesia, unable to determine whether it's old or new (DeLuca, 2000). In many patients, confabulation is most severe immediately after the aneurysm but tends to decrease as time passes; the amnesia, however, is generally permanent.

The Diencephalon May Help Guide Consolidation

Over a century ago, doctors noted memory problems in individuals with **Korsakoff's disease,** a condition caused by a deficiency in thiamine (a B vitamin) that sometimes accompanies chronic alcohol abuse (Kopelman, Thomson, Guerrini, & Marshall, 2009). Korsakoff's disease consistently damages two areas of the diencephalon: the mammillary bodies and part of the thalamus (specifically, the *mediodorsal nucleus of the thalamus*), although other brain regions may be damaged too. In many cases of Korsakoff's, patients develop the same kind of anterograde amnesia and time-graded retrograde amnesia observed in H.M. and other individuals with medial temporal lobe damage—even though patients with Korsakoff's have no direct damage to their medial temporal lobes. Some people with damage to the thalamus due to other causes also show anterograde amnesia with time-graded retrograde amnesia (Collinson, Meyyappan, & Rosenfeld, 2009; Hampstead & Koffler, 2009; Kapur, Thompson, Cook, Lang, & Brice, 1996), as do rats given conjoint lesions to the mammillary bodies and the mediodorsal nucleus of the thalamus (Aggleton & Mishkin, 1983; Mair, Knoth, Rabchenuk, & Langlais, 1991).

It is still unclear why diencephalic damage causes amnesia. Because the mammillary bodies and thalamic nuclei are anatomically connected to both the cerebral cortex and the medial temporal lobes, one possibility is that the diencephalic structures help mediate the interaction between the frontal cortex and the hippocampus during memory storage and consolidation, so that diencephalic damage disrupts this interaction (Collinson, Meyyappan, & Rosenfeld, 2009). Consistent with this idea, patients with Korsakoff's disease may also confabulate, providing detailed and fictitious stories when questioned about events they've forgotten—again suggesting a failure to distinguish between old and new memories.

Many questions remain unanswered about diencephalic amnesia and basal forebrain amnesia and about their relation to medial temporal amnesia. But these different classes of amnesia provide compelling evidence that memory is a function of the whole brain. Many structures—including the hippocampus, cortex, diencephalon, and basal forebrain—must all be working well and working together for episodic and semantic memory to function properly.

Interim Summary

- Semantic memories seem to be stored in the cortex; to some extent, specific kinds of semantic information are stored in the cortical areas devoted to processing that kind of information (visual, auditory, etc.).

- The hippocampal region (which lies in the medial temporal lobe in humans and other primates) is important for new episodic memory formation; patients with bilateral hippocampal-region damage show anterograde amnesia (loss of ability to encode new episodic and semantic memories); they may also show retrograde amnesia (disruption of old memories acquired before the damage).

- In healthy humans, functional neuroimaging shows that the hippocampal region is especially active during encoding of information that will be successfully remembered later.

- Some researchers believe that while the hippocampus is required for new episodic memory formation, other areas of the medial temporal lobes are sufficient to store new semantic memories; other researchers believe that the hippocampus is necessary for both episodic and semantic memory formation.

- Debate continues over whether episodic memories ever become fully independent of the hippocampus.

- Besides the hippocampal region, brain areas involved in episodic and semantic memory include the frontal cortex (especially important for determining what information gets stored and for remembering source information), the basal forebrain (which may help guide how the hippocampus stores new information), and the diencephalon (which may mediate communication between the hippocampus and the frontal cortex).

7.3 Clinical Perspectives

Patients such as H.M. and E.P. have permanent memory loss caused by identifiable brain damage. E.P.'s amnesia, for example, can be traced directly to medial temporal lobe damage dating to his bout with herpes encephalitis, and H.M.'s amnesia stems from his brain surgery. Once the medial temporal lobes are damaged or destroyed, the lost memories cannot be recovered.

In other cases, however, the memory dysfunction may not be permanent. You've already learned about one kind of "temporary amnesia" in patients who undergo electroconvulsive shock therapy. These patients typically experience anterograde amnesia for the events of the ECT session and retrograde amnesia for events that happened a short time before the session. But their memory machinery is not permanently damaged. After a few hours, their brains are again able to encode new memories and retrieve old ones. This section reviews two other kinds of amnesia that do not involve permanent disruption of the ability to store memories: transient global amnesia (TGA) and functional amnesia.

Transient Global Amnesia

As its name suggests, **transient global amnesia (TGA)** is a transient, or temporary, disruption of memory (Brand & Markowitsch, 2004; M. Kritchevsky, Squire, & Zouzounis, 1988; Markowitsch, 1983; Shekhar, 2008). Typically, TGA starts suddenly, persists for several hours, and then gradually dissipates over the course of a day or so. During the amnesic episode, the patient shows severe anterograde amnesia. There is usually also some degree of retrograde amnesia for events that occurred within the preceding decade or so (Kritchevsky & Squire, 1989; Kritchevsky, Squire, & Zouzounis, 1988).

Transient global amnesia is one of the more common forms of amnesia; annual incidence has been estimated at about 5 cases per 100,000 people per year in the United States (Miller, Petersen, Metter, Millikan, & Yanagihara, 1987). Despite the prevalence, TGA is difficult to study because it doesn't usually last long. But there are a few well-documented cases in the literature. One such case involves a 38-year-old man, S.G., who underwent brain surgery (Kapur, Millar, Abbott, & Carter, 1998). The surgery seemed to go smoothly, but there may have been some complication that temporarily reduced blood flow to his brain. When S.G. woke up, he knew his own name but did not remember his occupation, the month, or how long he had been in the hospital.

The onset of S.G.'s amnesia occurred around 12:30 p.m. Memory researchers rushed to the scene, and S.G. agreed to an extensive battery of testing.

(a) S.G.'s anterograde amnesia: Score on memory for a story just read

(b) S.G.'s retrograde amnesia: Score on memory for personal semantic information

Time since onset of TGA (in hours)

At about 3 p.m., S.G. showed profound anterograde amnesia: he could listen to a short story, but a few minutes later he would recall only a few words of it (Figure 7.20a). S.G. also showed retrograde amnesia. Given a questionnaire about jobs he had held, places he had lived, and other personal semantic information, he could provide only a few answers (Figure 7.20b). (The correct answers were verified by S.G.'s fiancée.) S.G.'s memory was similarly poor for recent public events, although it was better for events that had happened at least a few decades before.

Researchers continued to test S.G. every few hours through the afternoon and evening; gradually, his anterograde and retrograde amnesia lessened. By noon of the next day, 24 hours after the onset of amnesia, S.G.'s memory had returned to normal, except for a slight retrograde amnesia for events that had occurred shortly before the surgery. The TGA was over; S.G.'s brain seemed to be back in working order.

Why might TGA occur? Like S.G., many individuals with TGA probably experience a temporary interruption of blood flow to the brain from a head injury, a hypoglycemic episode (low blood sugar), or a heart attack or stroke. (In a few cases, migraine headaches are implicated.) As in ECT, the temporary disruption in neuronal activity might completely erase unconsolidated memories of recent events but merely limit access to fully consolidated older memories. When the blood flow resumes, so does the brain function.

Studies using neuroimaging methods such as positron emission tomography (PET) and magnetic resonance imaging (MRI) suggest that some individuals with TGA show small abnormalities in the hippocampus (Gonzalez-Martinez, Comte, de Verbizier, & Carlander, 2010; Yang, Kim, Kim, Kwak, & Han, 2009); in some cases, these abnormalities are no longer detectable on follow-up imaging two months after the TGA (Alberici et al., 2008; Della Marca et al., 2010). While this may not explain all cases of TGA, it suggests that the temporary disruption of memory storage and recall may reflect temporary disruption of the hippocampus.

Functional Amnesia

In the 2002 film *The Bourne Identity*, Jason Bourne (played by Matt Damon) awakes on a fishing boat with no memory of his own name, his past, or why he has the number of a Swiss bank account implanted in his hip. Through the movie,

Figure 7.20 Transient global amnesia (TGA) (a) Patient S.G., 2.5 hours after the onset of amnesia, could remember almost nothing from a story he'd heard a few minutes ago. By 24 hours after onset, however, his performance improved, and he scored even better than the average expected from a same-age healthy control patient (dotted line). (b) Similarly, 2.5 hours after the onset of his amnesia, S.G. showed severe retrograde amnesia for autobiographical information; his memories returned to normal 24 hours later.
(a, b) Adapted from Kapur et al., 1998.

Bourne struggles to regain his memories while staying one step ahead of the CIA agents who are trying to kill him. Such memory loss has formed the basis of countless books, movies, and plays, from Alfred Hitchcock's 1945 classic *Spellbound*, to 2007's *Spider-Man 3*, in which villain Harry Osborn temporarily forgets his identity as the Green Goblin, to an episode of *The Simpsons* in which Marge develops amnesia and loses all memories of her dysfunctional animated family.

Such total memory loss can also happen in real life, although it is far rarer than Hollywood might lead you to believe. **Functional amnesia** (sometimes called *psychogenic amnesia*) is a sudden, massive retrograde memory loss that seems to result from psychological causes, in contrast to *organic amnesia*, which arises from obvious physical causes, such as brain injury (Mark Kritchevsky, Chang, & Squire, 2004; Schacter & Kihlstrom, 1989). One type of functional amnesia is *dissociative amnesia*, in which patients lose memory of a specific, traumatic event; an even more dramatic form of functional amnesia is *dissociative fugue*, in which patients lose all memory of their identity. Dissociative fugue is extraordinarily rare. Moreover, some individuals who claim to have lost their memory will later admit to faking functional amnesia in order to avoid dealing with a difficult situation such as a crime or a relationship problem (Jenkins, Kapur, & Kopelman, 2009). Some cases, however, do seem to involve genuine memory loss.

Daniel Schacter records one case of functional amnesia involving a 21-year-old man, P.N., who was admitted to the hospital complaining of back pains (Schacter, Wang, Tulving, & Freedman, 1982). When questioned about his identity, P.N. could not remember his name or anything about his past except that he had once been given the nickname "Lumberjack." Schacter later concluded that P.N. had developed functional amnesia following the death of his grandfather, to whom P.N. had been close. P.N.'s extreme grief was the psychological trauma that triggered the memory loss.

In contrast to P.N.'s severe retrograde amnesia for autobiographical events, his semantic memories were intact: both his language functions and knowledge about the world seemed normal. However, P.N. also showed anterograde amnesia, having difficulty remembering new information for more than a few minutes at a time. The functional amnesia persisted for about a week until P.N. happened to watch a television show that included a funeral scene; as if by magic, lost memories came flooding back, and P.N. recalled his own identity and history. Only the memories of events that occurred during P.N.'s amnesia were permanently lost, possibly because his anterograde amnesia had prevented those memories from being successfully stored in the first place.

Not all cases of functional amnesia resolve so well. Mark Kritchevsky and his colleagues studied 10 individuals with functional amnesia; all were unable to report their names or personal histories (Kritchevsky, Chang, & Squire, 2004). One of these patients later admitted to feigning his amnesia, and Kritchevsky and colleagues suspected a second may have been feigning too. But of the eight patients whose amnesia seemed genuine, only one fully recovered all the lost memories, and a few patients never recovered any memories at all, even 2 or more years after the onset of their amnesia. Currently, there is no way to predict when or whether a particular patient will recover his memory.

Given that patients with functional amnesia have no known brain damage, what could cause this syndrome? Functional imaging may provide some clues. In one study using PET, an individual with functional amnesia had abnormal activity patterns in areas of the medial temporal lobes and the diencephalon; these abnormalities disappeared when the amnesia resolved (Markowitsch et al., 1998). This suggests that functional amnesia may result from a (possibly temporary) malfunction of the brain areas normally involved in episodic memory storage and retrieval. Another study using functional magnetic resonance imaging (fMRI) showed that when two people with functional amnesia "failed to recognize" individuals with whom they were actually acquainted, there was increased activity in the prefrontal cortex and decreased activity in the hippocampus (Kikuchi et al., 2010). This is the same basic pattern observed during directed forgetting in healthy adults (see Figure 7.18) and suggests that—consciously or unconsciously—the patients may have been suppressing the activity of the hippocampus in recalling information. Interestingly, when one patient's amnesia resolved, the abnormal pattern of prefrontal activation disappeared.

Together, these imaging results suggest that functional amnesia may reflect dysfunction of the same brain regions that are damaged in organic amnesia (Ouellet, Rouleau, Labrecque, Bernier, & Scherzer, 2008). The major differences would be that, whereas organic amnesia is brought on by a physiological injury, functional amnesia is brought on by a psychological trauma, and so—because there is no permanent injury to the brain—it may be possible for patients with functional amnesia to recover both their brain function and their memories in a way that would be impossible for patients such as H.M. and E.P.

Interim Summary

- Transient global amnesia (TGA) is a temporary disruption of memory that may be due to temporarily reduced blood flow. During a TGA episode, a patient shows severe anterograde amnesia and usually some degree of retrograde amnesia, but memory typically returns to normal over the course of a day or so.

- In functional amnesia, patients lose memory for specific episodes in their lives or may even lose their identity. This very rare form of amnesia seems to result from psychological trauma rather than any physical cause.

Test Your Knowledge

Don't Forget Your Amnesias

"Amnesia" is a general term for memory loss. For each specific type of amnesia listed below, can you remember what kind of information is lost or disrupted, as well as what kind of brain damage might be responsible? (Answers appear in the Answers section in the back of the book.)

1. Anterograde amnesia
2. Functional amnesia
3. Retrograde amnesia
4. Source amnesia
5. Transient global amnesia (TGA)

▶ SYNTHESIS

In the Clinical Perspectives section of this chapter, we mentioned a few examples of the many movie and television characters who have been depicted as developing amnesia. Knowing what you now know about memory and amnesia, you should be able to assess the plausibility of these characters—as well as of amnesia portrayals in other movies, TV shows, and books.

The vast majority of these, like Jason Bourne in *The Bourne Identity*, are afflicted with functional amnesia—usually a complete loss of identity caused by psychological trauma rather than physical brain damage. These characters typically maintain their semantic memory, as well as their skills. This profile is roughly similar to that observed in real-world patients such as P.N., whose functional amnesia stripped him of his personal history, though his general knowledge about the world seemed intact. Jason Bourne (like the protagonists of many other amnesia stories) spends much of the movie trying to solve the mystery of what triggered his amnesia, as well as trying to recover his lost identity. In this sense, *The Bourne Identity* and other "lost identity" stories share many features with real-world cases of functional amnesia. Where these stories depart from reality is mainly in their resolution: in many a soap opera, the heroine who has lost her memory following a blow to the head needs nothing more than a second blow to bring the memories flooding back. In the real world, head injuries don't cure functional amnesia. Some patients recover spontaneously, but others recover slowly or not at all.

Organic amnesia is a much less common plot device than functional amnesia. Exceptions include the 2000 film *Memento*, a psychological thriller featuring a protagonist who suffers from anterograde amnesia, and Pixar's 2003 *Finding Nemo*, featuring an animated fish (voiced by Ellen DeGeneres) with the same disorder. In both these cases, the characters are intelligent and motivated individuals who are unable to acquire new episodic or semantic memory; anything they learn or do is forgotten within a few minutes. While *Finding Nemo* doesn't explore the medical causes underlying amnesia, *Memento*'s protagonist explains that he developed his condition following a head injury that damaged his hippocampus. These fictional characters share many characteristics with real-world amnesic patients such as H.M. and E.P., who developed anterograde amnesia following medial temporal lobe damage. However, real-world patients such as H.M. and E.P. usually have at least some retrograde amnesia as well—loss of some (and often quite a lot) of their memories from before the brain damage.

Yet another class of memory-related plots revolves around false memories. For example, the 1990 sci-fi classic *Total Recall* (Lion's Gate) stars Arnold Schwarzenegger as a construction worker who pays to have memories of an expensive trip to Mars implanted in his brain—at a fraction of the time and cost that it would take to actually vacation on another planet. In the classic film *The Manchurian Candidate* (1962, Metro-Goldwyn-Mayer, starring Frank Sinatra; remade in 2004 by Universal Studios, starring Denzel Washington), an evil corporation uses brainwashing and hypnotism to implant false memories. These stories are obviously science fiction, but the phenomenon of false memories is science fact: researchers can implant false memories that feel as rich and real as true memories—so real that research participants will often argue when researchers attempt to explain the hoax. False memories lead to exciting adventures in the movies, but they can lead to serious real-world problems too, as when eyewitnesses confuse memories of a crime scene with pictures of a suspect aired on the nightly news.

In all of these plots, the drama springs from a universal sense that our episodic and semantic memories—the facts we know and the events we've experienced—make us who we are. It is easy to empathize with a character whose autobiographical memories have been stripped away, because we can imagine the devastating impact.

On a more mundane level, everyone experiences occasional failures of episodic and semantic memory. Some of these failures, such as forgetting where we parked the car or blanking on the name of someone we meet unexpectedly at the gym, are just a normal part of everyday life. Some of us have experienced an episode of TGA following a sports injury, have fallen prey to cryptomnesia while writing a term paper, or suffer from source amnesia for a childhood event that we don't really remember but have seen in home movies or heard about at family get-togethers. Most of the time, our access to episodic and semantic memory is effortless, and our memories are long lasting and largely accurate—but at the same time, our memory processes may fail more often than we like. Understanding these processes may help us improve their function while giving us—like Jason Bourne and his fellows—a better appreciation of the episodic and semantic memories we do possess.

Key Terms

agnosia, *p. 281*
amnesia, *p. 260*
anterograde amnesia, *p. 284*
association cortex, *p. 280*
basal forebrain, *p. 291*
confabulation, *p. 292*
consolidation period, *p. 278*
cued recall, *p. 271*
declarative memory, *p. 262*
depth-of-processing effect, *p. 268*
diencephalon, *p. 292*

directed forgetting, *p. 273*
electroconvulsive shock, *p. 278*
episodic memory, *p. 261*
explicit memory, *p. 262*
false memory, *p. 276*
fornix, *p. 292*
free recall, *p. 271*
frontal cortex, *p. 290*
functional amnesia, *p. 296*
hippocampus, *p. 259*
implicit memory, *p. 262*
interference, *p. 273*

Korsakoff's disease, *p. 293*
medial temporal lobes, *p. 259*
misattribution, *p. 274*
mnemonics, *p. 271*
multiple memory trace theory, *p. 289*
nondeclarative memory, *p. 262*
proactive interference, *p. 273*
recognition, *p. 271*
retroactive interference, *p. 274*
retrograde amnesia, *p. 287*
Ribot gradient, *p. 287*

semantic memory, *p. 261*
sensory cortex, *p. 280*
source amnesia, *p. 274*
standard consolidation theory, *p. 288*
transfer-appropriate processing effect, *p. 269*
transient global amnesia (TGA), *p. 294*

Concept Check

1. Suppose you join a club with six members, and you want to remember each member's name for the next meeting. What are three ways, based on the principles described in this chapter, that you can improve your likelihood of remembering the names?

2. A semantic memory is a memory for a fact without memory of the spatial and temporal context in which that fact was learned. How does this differ from source amnesia?

3. Failures of episodic and semantic memory can be annoying, but they serve a purpose. Why might it be desirable for an organism to be able to forget some information?

4. In adult humans with normal memory function, fMRI shows that the hippocampus is active even for retrieval of very old autobiographical information (Ryan et al., 2001). Does this prove that autobiographical memories always remain at least partially dependent on the hippocampus?

5. Suppose you are working in an emergency room when a man comes in who claims to have forgotten his entire identity. What questions would you ask the friend who drove him to the hospital? What tests might you conduct to find out what's going on?

CHAPTER 8

Skill Memory

Learning by Doing

"When starting a kiss, the rule of thumb is to start slow. This just makes sense, and it lets everyone get used to the dynamics of that particular kiss. A slow start is a good introduction . . . and sometimes the kiss should just stay slow. Jumping into rapid tongue maneuvers can scare your partner, and is rude to boot. Athletes always warm up before moving onto serious play . . . why should kissing be any different?"

("Kissing 101," Hays, Allen, & Hanish, 2005)

DO YOU REMEMBER YOUR FIRST KISS? For some, it is a magical memory. For others, it was an awkward experience in which a single thought kept recurring: "Am I doing this right?" Kissing is simple enough in concept. Take your lips and press them against someone else's lips. What could be easier? After just a few experiences with bad kissers, however, a person realizes that simple as kissing appears, it is not an ability humans are born with. By the same token, a single encounter with an especially good kisser is enough to make you appreciate that kissing well requires some skill.

The success of a first kiss may depend in part on the setting and the partner, but most young people are savvy enough to know that they need to practice if they want their first real kiss to be a good one. Practice might consist of kissing one's own hand or arm, a pillow, or a stuffed animal. The hope is that these practice sessions will provide an edge when a real opportunity comes along. Practicing by kissing your hand or arm is a good strategy because that way you get feedback about what your lips feel like. Taking a class might also help, but you will not become an adept kisser by memorizing lists of rules about how to kiss. To become an expert,

Behavioral Processes
Kinds of Skill Memories
Expertise and Talent
Learning and Memory in Everyday Life: Are Some Cognitive Skills Easier for Men Than Women?
Practice
Transfer of Training
Models of Skill Memory

Brain Substrates
The Basal Ganglia and Skill Learning
Learning and Memory in Everyday Life: Are Video Games Good for the Brain?
Cortical Representations of Skills
The Cerebellum and Timing

Clinical Perspectives
Apraxia
Huntington's Disease
Parkinson's Disease

you need to get in there and kiss (a lot), you need to get feedback about your kissing, and most important, your brain has to store memories of your kissing successes and failures. Some of what you learn about kissing can be shared verbally, but a lot of what you learn will be easier to demonstrate than to explain. You might not think of making out as "practicing a skill," but your kissing experiences can change your abilities whether you are aware of it or not. And, with enough practice, you might even become an expert.

This chapter describes how repeated experiences can incrementally enhance the performance of a skill by gradually modifying memories of how the skill can best be executed. As you will discover, repeated experiences not only can change how a person performs a skill, they also can change the structure of the brain circuits that are used to perform that skill. Skill memories are formed and processed by several brain regions, including the basal ganglia, the cerebral cortex, and the cerebellum. People with damage in one or more of these brain regions have trouble learning new skills as well as performing skills already learned.

8.1 Behavioral Processes

The previous chapter dealt with memories for events and facts—in other words, information a person remembers and knows. Skill memories, in contrast, relate to what a person knows how to do. By reading this sentence, you are exercising skills that you learned a long time ago. Reading may seem so effortless now that you can hardly recall the challenge of acquiring this complex ability. When you turn a page, highlight a sentence, type or write notes, or think about what you'll need to do to remember the contents of this chapter, you are accessing memories of several different skills.

Kinds of Skill Memories

A **skill** is an ability to perform a task that has been honed through learning. Skill memories are similar in many respects to memories for events (sometimes called episodic memories) and facts (semantic memories), but they also possess some unique qualities (Table 8.1). Like memories for facts, skill memories are long lasting and improved by repeated experiences. Unlike memories for events and facts, however, skill memories can't always be verbalized; moreover, skill memories may be acquired and retrieved without conscious awareness. As you'll recall from Chapter 7, psychologists sometimes classify skill memories as *nondeclarative* memories because these memories are not easily put into words—skill learning is also sometimes referred to as *procedural learning*.

Skills can be learned in many ways, but the most common methods involve practice and the observation of others performing skills. Chapter 5 describes one technique, *operant conditioning*, that is commonly used to train animals to perform skills. Pressing a lever, pecking a key, or rolling over on command might seem like trivially easy abilities for an animal to learn, but it is clear that these abilities improve with practice. Not all skills are difficult to learn or

Table 8.1

Comparison of memories for skills, events, and facts

Skill memories	Memories for events and facts
1. Are difficult to convey except by direct demonstration	1. Can be communicated flexibly, in different formats
2. May be acquired without awareness	2. Have content that is consciously accessible
3. Require several repetitions	3. Can be acquired in a single exposure

impressive to watch, and the fact that an animal can be trained to perform a task with automated techniques does not disqualify that ability from being classified as a skill. Operant conditioning is an effective method for training new skills, but it is not the only way. Furthermore, how an individual is trained is not the only factor that determines what an individual's memories for skills are like or what skills the person is capable of learning. This section looks at different kinds of skill memories, exploring how performance of skills (recall of skill memories) varies and what factors determine how performance varies. Contemporary researchers generally classify skills into two basic types: perceptual-motor skills and cognitive skills (Gabrieli, 1998; K. M. Newell, 1991; Rosenbaum, Carlson, & Gilmore, 2001; van Lehn, 1996; Voss & Wiley, 1995).

Perceptual-Motor Skills

The kinds of skills you are probably most aware of are those that athletes demonstrate when they compete or that musicians reveal when they perform. More mundane skills include opening and closing doors, driving a car, dancing, drinking out of a glass, and snapping your fingers. These are all examples of **perceptual-motor skills:** learned movement patterns guided by sensory inputs.

Consider dancing. An important part of dancing is being able to move your body in certain established patterns. This requires significant voluntary control of your movements. If you can't control where your arms go, you'll end up being more of a spectacle than a dance sensation. Dancing is more than just repeatedly moving your feet and arms in a pattern, however; you also have to move to the beat (that is, respond to timed auditory inputs). In addition, some well-established dances, such as the Hokey Pokey, require specific movements to be performed at specific points in a song. The goal in learning these kinds of dances is to perform a consistent sequence of movements in a prescribed way. Professional ballet dancers, too, learn precisely choreographed dance sequences. Psychologists classify skills such as ballet dancing, which consist of performing a predefined sequence of movements, as **closed skills.** Other kinds of dancing, such as salsa or swing dancing, also involve particular movement patterns, but dancers may vary the way they combine these movements when they dance, at least in social dance settings. Such dances depend to some extent on the dancers' predicting (or directing) their partner's next move. Researchers classify skills that require participants to respond based on predictions about the changing demands of the environment as **open skills.**

These classifications apply to a wide range of perceptual-motor skills. For example, athletes who are gymnasts or divers are perfecting closed skills, whereas athletes who participate in coordinated team sports, such as soccer or hockey, depend heavily on open skills. Dogs can learn to catch a Frisbee (an open skill), and they can also learn to play dead (a closed skill). Catching a Frisbee is an open skill because many environmental variables—such as quality and distance of the throw, wind speed, and terrain characteristics—determine which movements the dog must make to perform the skill successfully. Most perceptual-motor skills contain aspects of both closed skills and open skills, and so it is better to think of any particular skill as lying somewhere along a continuum from open to closed (Magill, 1993).

Research on perceptual-motor skills typically focuses on much less complex skills than those needed to dance or play soccer. Skills studied in the laboratory might consist of pressing buttons quickly or tracking the position of a moving object (Doyon, Penhune, & Ungerleider, 2003). It's not that knowing how a person learns to dance is uninteresting to psychologists. Rather, research psychologists want to keep things as simple as possible so they can control the relevant variables more precisely. This gives them a better chance of understanding how experience affects an individual's ability to perform a particular skill. For example, it is much easier to assess quantitatively whether someone's tracking abilities are improving than to measure improvements in their dancing abilities.

Cognitive Skills

There is no limit to the list of abilities that you could potentially improve with practice. How about playing cards, budgeting your money, taking standardized tests, or managing your time? These particular examples are all **cognitive skills,** which require you to solve problems or apply strategies rather than to move your body based on what you perceive (Ackerman, 2007; Ackerman, Kanfer, & Goff, 1995; J. R. Anderson, Fincham, & Douglass, 1997; Singley & Anderson, 1989). Researchers often conduct experiments on cognitive skills that participants can learn relatively quickly, such as those used to solve simple puzzles like the Tower of Hanoi (Figure 8.1). In this puzzle, the objective is to move different-size disks from one peg to another, one disk at a time (we discuss this task in greater detail in Chapter 9). The puzzle would be trivially easy except that the rules forbid you to put a larger disk on top of a smaller one. The numbered sequence in Figure 8.1 shows one solution to the puzzle. Normally, people get better at solving this puzzle with practice. This is not because they are getting better at physically moving the disks from one peg to another (a perceptual-motor skill), but because they are learning new strategies for moving the disks so that they end up in the desired position (J. R. Anderson, 1982).

Psychologists usually associate cognitive skills with the ability to reason and solve problems or to perform tasks that require sorting through large amounts of knowledge (such as writing a textbook). Descartes proposed that the ability to reason is what distinguishes humans from other animals. Descartes would probably have been willing to accept that dogs can store memories for how to perform perceptual-motor skills such as how to catch a Frisbee, but he would have considered it impossible for a dog or any other nonhuman animal to learn a cognitive skill. Following Descartes's lead,

Figure 8.1 **The Tower of Hanoi puzzle** The objective of this task is to move all the disks from the leftmost peg to the rightmost peg, one disk at a time, without placing a larger disk on a smaller disk. The numbered sequence shows one way of doing this. The ability to solve such puzzles is a cognitive skill.

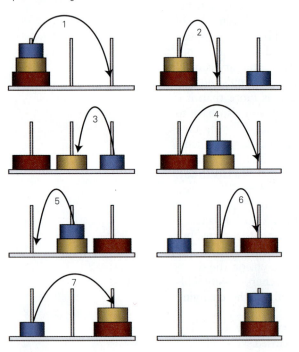

many psychologists assume that only humans can reason or perform complex cognitive tasks. Consequently, most of what is currently known about cognitive skills comes from studies of humans.

Humans are not the only animals that can learn cognitive skills, however. For instance, it was once thought that only humans used tools and that this particular problem-solving ability played a key role in the evolution of the human mind. But in the past two decades, psychologists and animal behavior researchers have described tool use in many animals, including elephants, apes, octopuses, birds, otters, and dolphins (Beck, 1980; Hart, 2001; Hunt, Corballis, & Gray, 2001; Krutzen et al., 2005; Whiten et al., 1999). In the lab, experimenters have taught primates and other animals to use various tools. There is also recent evidence that animals in the wild can teach themselves to use tools—for example, dolphins have learned to use a sponge while foraging (Krutzen et al., 2005), as shown in Figure 8.2. Researchers have also observed chimpanzees in the wild that learn how to use stones to crack nuts (Whiten & Boesch, 2001). Tool use is an ability that typically involves both perceptual-motor and cognitive skills. Movement patterns required for using a tool improve with practice as does the recognition that a particular tool (or strategy) can be useful in solving various problems.

Clearer evidence of cognitive skills in nonhumans comes from laboratory studies showing that various species can learn to perform cognitive tasks on command. In one study, mentioned briefly in Chapter 7, dolphins learned to repeat whatever action they had performed most recently when instructed to do so by a trainer (Mercado, Murray, Uyeyama, Pack, & Herman, 1998). Most of the "tricks" that you may have seen dolphins performing on TV or in oceanariums are closed perceptual-motor skills. The trainer gives a signal, and in response the dolphin performs a particular movement sequence. When a dolphin is instructed to repeat an action, however, the signal to do so is not associated with one particular motor response. Almost any action a dolphin can perform could be a correct response to such an instruction, depending on what the dolphin was doing before the instruction was given. To successfully follow a "repeat" instruction, the dolphin must actively recall its recent actions. Recall and reenactment of past episodes is a cognitive skill—it can be improved through practice (Brehmer, Li, Muller, von Oertzen, & Lindenberger, 2007). By successfully learning to repeat actions on command, dolphins have demonstrated that they can perform the cognitive skill of recalling past events.

Some animals can use tools and learn complex cognitive tasks more flexibly and imaginatively than others. By comparing different animals' abilities to learn perceptual-motor and cognitive skills and by exploring which neural systems they use when forming and retrieving memories of different skills, scientists are beginning to gain a clearer understanding of the brain systems underlying skill memories (Mercado, 2008).

Historically, philosophers and psychologists have distinguished perceptual-motor skills from cognitive skills. However, recent evidence suggests there are many more similarities in how humans learn and remember both types of skills than was previously thought (Rosenbaum, Carlson, & Gilmore, 2001). Furthermore, many skills involve both cognitive and perceptual-motor components. Professional athletes in team sports have to make split-second decisions about which of several possible actions they will take and keep in mind the idiosyncratic strengths and weaknesses of individual competitors. Olympic gymnasts must maintain focus and poise while under tremendous pressure. As you read

Lars Bedjer

Figure 8.2 Dolphins using tools Some dolphins in Australia have taken to carrying around sponges when they are foraging. Researchers suspect that the dolphins use the sponges as tools to protect themselves against injuries from sea urchins and other spiny sea creatures as they probe the seafloor for food.

this chapter, consider what, if anything, makes memories of perceptual-motor skills different from memories of cognitive skills. Is it how they are learned, how they are remembered, how they are forgotten, or something else? Perhaps the differences lie not in how a person forms and recalls these memories but where in the brain the memories are formed and recalled. We will return to these questions about how and where memories for skills are processed later, in the Brain Substrates section.

Now that you know how researchers classify different kinds of skills, let's consider the question of what allows some individuals to excel at a particular skill. You won't be surprised to hear that practice is an important factor. We'll examine how different kinds of practice affect performance and retention of skill memories and why individuals who are great at one skill are not necessarily as good at other, similar skills. We'll also describe a classic psychological model of skill learning.

Test Your Knowledge

Open and Closed Skills

Psychologists classify skills in many ways. One conventional scheme for classifying perceptual-motor skills is the extent to which skills are open or closed. Open skills involve movements that are modified based on predictions about environmental demands, and closed skills depend on performing predefined movements that, ideally, never vary. Try to label each of the following perceptual-motor skills as either an open or a closed skill, considering all the possible contexts in which the skills might be performed. (Answers appear in the Answers section in the back of the book.)

1. A sea lion balancing a ball
2. A girl swimming
3. A young man kissing
4. A bear catching a fish
5. A fish catching insects
6. A boy playing a piano
7. A young woman throwing darts

Expertise and Talent

You might be able to dance as well as an all-star basketball player, a virtuoso pianist, or a Nobel Prize–winning scientist, but they clearly have mastered other skills at a level that would be difficult for you to match—unless you happen to belong to one of those categories. Different individuals start with different capabilities, and the extent to which practice can improve their performance levels also varies from one person to the next. People who seem to master a skill with little effort (the way Mozart mastered anything related to music) are often described as having a **talent** or "gift" for that skill, and people who perform a skill better than most are considered to be **experts.** The people who start off performing a skill well are often those who end up becoming experts (Howard, 2009), but someone who initially has little ability to perform a skill may, with practice, become better at that skill than someone who seemed destined to become a star. So, if your significant other is currently lacking in the kissing department, don't lose hope! Additional practice (or guidance) may yet unleash his or her full potential.

What role does talent play in achieving expertise in cognitive or perceptual-motor skills? Even child prodigies are not born able to perform the skills that make them famous. Like everyone else, they learn to perform these skills. Mozart's father, a professional musician, trained Mozart extensively from a young age. So it's difficult to determine to what extent Mozart's musical abilities were a result of his musical talents versus his father's teaching abilities and persistence. Most modern research equates talent with genetic predispositions that positively affect an individual's abilities.

Psychologists have attempted to gauge the role of genetics in skill learning and performance by conducting studies with twins—some identical (sharing 100% of their genes) and some fraternal (sharing, like other siblings, 50% of their genes)—who were raised in different homes. Other twin studies look at the differences between twins reared together.

In one large study of twins reared apart, researchers at the University of Minnesota trained participants to perform a skill in which they had to keep the end of a pointed stick, called a stylus, above a target drawn on the edge of a rotating disk, as shown in Figure 8.3a (Fox, Hershberger, & Bouchard, 1996). Researchers frequently use this task, known as the **rotary pursuit task,** to study perceptual-motor skill learning. The task requires precise hand-eye

(a)

(b)

(c)

Figure 8.3 **Effects of practice on performance of the rotary pursuit task** (a) In the rotary pursuit task, a person gradually learns to keep a stylus above a particular point on a rotating disk. (b) With repeated trials, individuals become better at keeping the stylus over the target. (c) In studies of how twins perform on this task, correlations between the performances of identical twins increased slightly as training progressed, indicating that, after training, the accuracy at tracking a rotating target is similar for each twin. In contrast, correlations between the performances of fraternal twins decreased with training, indicating that their capacity to track the rotating target becomes less similar with practice. These findings suggest that practice decreases the effects of previous experience (i.e., nurture) on motor performance and increases the effects of genetic influences (nature).

(b, c) Adapted from Fox et al., 1996.

coordination. When individuals first attempt the rotary pursuit task, they generally show some ability to keep the stylus over the target but often have to adjust the speed and trajectory of their arm movements to correct for errors (such as lagging behind the target). With additional practice, most individuals rapidly improve their accuracy, increasing the amount of time they can keep the stylus tip over the target (Figure 8.3b).

The researchers found that when they trained twins to perform the rotary pursuit task, identical twins' abilities to keep the stylus on the target became more similar as training progressed, whereas fraternal twins' abilities became more dissimilar. That is, during training, the performance of one twin became more correlated with the performance of the second twin when the two twins shared 100% of their genes (Figure 8.3c). Put another way, if you were to view videos of the participants' hands after training as they attempted to keep the stylus above the rotating target, you would judge the movements of identical twins' hands to be the most similar. Their movements might remind you of synchronized swimming. In the case of fraternal twins, however, you would probably judge their movements after training to be dissimilar. For example, one twin might keep the stylus over the target continuously, while the other twin might have to increase her speed a bit every few seconds to catch up with the target.

One interpretation of these data is that, during the experiment, practice decreases the effects of participants' prior experiences on the accuracy of their tracking movements and increases the effects of genetic influences. In other words, the more practice people have, the more their differences are due to genetic differences. Identical twins have identical genes, so when practice increases the role of their genes in behavior, their behavior becomes closer to identical. Because fraternal twins have different genes, increasing the role of their genes in behavior makes their behavior more different. Researchers have tested for such effects only in tasks, such as the rotary pursuit task, that require individuals to learn simple perceptual-motor skills. It is possible, however, that practice has similar effects on more complex perceptual-motor and cognitive skills. For example, perhaps you possess hidden talents that you're unaware of because you have never practiced the skills that require those talents or have not practiced them enough. Perhaps future genetic analyses will discover biological correlates of specific talents, thus permitting identification of individuals who have inherited propensities to perform certain skills exceptionally well. (See "Learning and Memory in Everyday Life" on page 310 for a brief look at whether men and women are born with different innate abilities in what they can learn.)

Some psychologists argue that talent plays no role in expertise and that practice alone determines who will become an expert (Ericsson, Krampe, & Tesch-Romer, 1993; Ericsson & Lehman, 1996). In particular, it has been argued that the amount of deliberate practice is the main determinant of skill level and that a minimum of 10,000 hours of practice is what is required for an individual to become an expert at a particular skill. This viewpoint has been challenged by studies showing that mastery of skills at an early age (for example, playing chess or a musical instrument) is predictive of which individuals will reach the highest levels of performance (Howard, 2009), even among individuals having similar amounts of experience. Until more is known about how practice affects skill memories, it will be difficult to reliably predict either an individual's maximum level of skill performance or the amount of practice someone needs to reach peak performance. In any case, scientists investigating skill memory in experts suggest that, for all individuals, the total amount of practice is critical in predicting whether a person will be an expert at performing a particular skill.

Researchers studying expertise have occasionally examined the abilities of athletes, chess masters, or other professional game players. There are several reasons for this. First, people who learn to play games outside a research lab serve as good examples of "real world" skill learning. Second, it is relatively easy to find people with widely varying levels of expertise in sports or games such as chess, and individual variations in ability often can be quantitatively assessed based on performance in competitions. Finally, sports and games require a variety of perceptual-motor and cognitive skills, making them useful for investigating many different psychological phenomena.

Kasparov falls to Deep Blue.
Computers can now perform many tasks as well as or better than experts.

A person must practice thousands of hours to become a master chess player, learning more than 50,000 "rules" for playing chess in the process (Simon & Gilmartin, 1973). Researchers studying expert chess players found that experts and less experienced players scan the game board (a visual-motor skill) differently (Charness, Reingold, Pomplun, & Stampe, 2001). When chess masters look at chess pieces, their eyes move rapidly to focus on a small number of locations on the board, whereas amateur chess players typically scan larger numbers of locations and do so more slowly. When experts stop moving their eyes, they are more likely than non-experts to focus on empty squares or on strategically relevant chess pieces.

Differences in visual processing are also seen in athletes. Inexperienced soccer players tend to watch the ball and the player who is passing it, whereas expert players focus more on the movements of players who do not have the ball (Williams, Davids, Burwitz, & Williams, 1992). A recent study of expert basketball players found that experts were better able to predict the outcome of a shot based on viewing a player's movements before the ball was released than were amateur players or professional spectators (Aglioti, Cesari, Romani, & Urgesi, 2008). These studies suggest that *perceptual learning* (discussed in Chapter 3) may contribute to the superior abilities of experts.

Humans may need to practice many hours to become experts at chess, but practice is not a universally necessary prerequisite for expert chess performance. Computer programmers have designed software that can compete with the best chess players. For example, Deep Blue, a chess-playing computer designed by IBM, defeated world champion Garry Kasparov in 1997. Computers access large databases of stored information to replicate some of the abilities of human experts. If a skill is an ability that improves with practice, chess-playing computers can be considered experts without skills, unless they are programmed to improve their performance based on past experiences. Although humans also make use of large amounts of information in performing certain skills, the way their brains store and access information differs greatly from the way computers do this. For example, if one computer can be programmed to perform a particular task, the same ability is usually easy to replicate in another computer. If only humans could acquire abilities so easily! For better or for worse, information can't yet be copied from one brain to another. If you want to become an expert at a particular skill, you'll probably have to do it the old-fashioned way: practice, practice, practice.

Are Some Cognitive Skills Easier for Men Than Women?

In 2005, the president of Harvard University, Larry Summers, provoked a national uproar when he suggested that one reason why there are more men than women in top-tier science and engineering positions is because of "different availability of aptitude at the high end." Essentially, he was suggesting that among the most scientifically or technologically talented people that are born, there are more men than women. If this claim had been made in relation to athletic skills, then it probably would not have made a ripple, because one need only consult the record books (or rosters of professional sports leagues) to see that the fastest sprints, highest jumps, and longest shot puts were all performed by men. This does not mean that men are able to learn to perform all (or even most) perceptual-motor skills at levels beyond what is possible for women, but it certainly supports the idea that there are some biological qualities (e.g., strength and height) that give men an edge when

it comes to reaching the upper echelons of athletic performance. Might something similar be true for cognitive skill learning by males?

If one examines the historical record of scientific and technological achievements, then it is clear that men have received more accolades and high-level positions than women. Unlike the findings in modern sports, however, this pattern could easily reflect sociocultural constraints rather than intrinsic differences in mental capacities. Stronger evidence of sex differences in cognitive performance come from standardized high school achievement exams such as the Advanced Placement (AP) tests. In these tests, substantially more men receive high scores in Calculus, Chemistry, and Physics despite the fact that more women take the tests (Ackerman, 2006). These data do not show that men are better able to learn about scientific topics, but they do show that men currently are

acquiring more cognitive skills related to retrieving and applying scientific knowledge during their early education. In general, greater facility with scientific knowledge will make learning related cognitive skills in college courses easier, and in this sense, scientific and technological skills will be easier for the most capable male undergraduates to learn than they will be for the most capable females. However, there is currently no way to assess whether these differences in performance reflect differences in the intellectual talents of men versus women or whether they reflect differences in the interests, motivation, instruction, or practice of men versus women when learning about science and technology. Until more is known about how neural mechanisms constrain learning capacity, it may be impossible to assess which features of male or female brains might enhance (or depress) learning of different cognitive skills.

Practice

In the 2010 movie *The Karate Kid*, a young boy asks a kung fu master to give him a crash course in martial arts. The master reluctantly agrees and begins by making the student repeatedly drop his coat on the floor, pick it up, put it on, take it off, and hang it up on a peg. This goes on for several days. The student does as he is told and later discovers that the movements he has been laboriously repeating are the kung fu movements that he needs to perform to defend himself. Because he has repeated these movements thousands of times, he is able to reproduce them rapidly and effortlessly. He (supposedly) has learned the skills of kung fu without even knowing it!

The portrayal of the relationship between practice and skill memories in this movie is similar to several early psychological theories of skill learning. The basic idea is that the more times you perform a skill, the faster or better you'll be able to perform it in the future. Is this how practice works? Or is there more to practice than just repetition? To address this issue, Edward Thorndike conducted experiments in which he repeatedly asked blindfolded individuals to draw a line exactly 3 inches long (Thorndike, 1927). Half of the participants were told when their line was within one eighth of an inch of the target length, and the other half were not given any feedback about their lines. Both groups drew the same number of lines during the experiment, but only the participants who received feedback improved in accuracy as the experiment progressed. This simple study suggests that repeatedly hanging up a coat is probably not a good way to learn kung fu moves. Feedback about performance, what researchers in the field usually call **knowledge of results,** is critical to the effectiveness of practice (Butki & Hoffman, 2003; Ferrari, 1999; Liu & Wrisberg, 1997; A. P. Turner & Martinek, 1999; Weeks & Kordus, 1998). Coaches, professors, and kung fu instructors all provide learners with knowledge of the results of practice (including studying), which can play a major role in how an individual's skills improve.

Acquiring Skills

The earliest detailed studies of how practice affects performance were conducted by military researchers who were interested in the high-speed, high-precision performance of perceptual-motor skills such as tracking and reacting to targets (these studies are reviewed by Holding, 1981). One of the basic findings from this early research was that the extent to which practice can lead to further improvements decreases with extent of practice. For example, Figure 8.4a shows that as participants practiced a reading task, the amount of time they spent reading each page decreased (A. Newell & Rosenbaum, 1981). Early in training, participants showed large gains in reading speed, but after this initial improvement, additional training led to much smaller increases in speed. Figure 8.3b shows a similar acquisition pattern for individuals learning the rotary pursuit task—the initial gain in performance is the largest. This pattern is known as the **power law of learning.** It holds for a wide range of cognitive and perceptual-motor skills, both in humans and in other species.

When you first learned to use a computer keyboard, you had to search for keys, and the number of words you could type per minute was probably low. After your first year of using a keyboard, you probably had doubled or tripled the number of words you could type per minute. If your typing speed doubled after every year of practice, you would be typing incredibly fast by now! The power law of learning, however, predicts that this won't happen. According to the power law, each additional year of practice after the first produces smaller increases in typing speed; learning occurs quickly at first, but then gets slower.

It may seem obvious that as you become more proficient at a skill, there is less room for improvement. What is surprising about the power law of learning is that the rate at which practice loses its ability to improve performance does

Figure 8.4 Effects of practice and feedback on skill performance (a) As training on a reading task progressed, improvements in reading speed became smaller. (b) After improvement slows, new sources of feedback can lead to a new burst of rapid improvement. In this graph, after his initial rate of improvement in speed of kicking had begun to slow, a participant was shown a film of optimum kicking. The film helped him improve his own kicking speed.

(a) Adapted from Singley and Anderson, 1989; (b) adapted from Hatze, 1976.

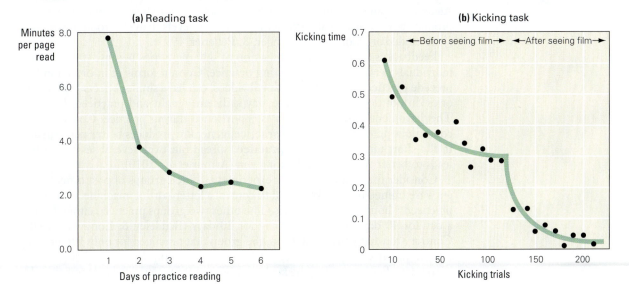

(a) Reading task

Minutes per page read

Days of practice reading

(b) Kicking task

Kicking time

←Before seeing film→ ←After seeing film→

Kicking trials

not depend on either the skill being practiced or the type of animal learning the skill. In many cases, psychologists can use a simple mathematical function (called a power function) to describe how rapidly individuals will acquire a skill; the number of additional practice trials necessary to improve a skill almost inevitably increases dramatically as the number of completed practice trials increases.

The power law of learning provides a useful description of how practice generally affects performance. It is possible to overcome this law, however, and enhance the effects of practice. For example, in one experiment, researchers asked a participant to kick a target as rapidly as possible. With visual feedback about his kicking speed, the participant was able to increase that speed, and his pattern of improvement was exactly what the power law of learning would predict (Hatze, 1976). When the man stopped improving, the researchers showed him a film comparing his movements with movements known to minimize kicking time. After seeing the film, the man improved his kicking speed considerably (Figure 8.4b). This is an example of *observational learning*, a topic we discuss in detail in Chapter 11. The participant observing the film formed memories of the observed performance techniques that he later used to improve his own performance. These memories can be viewed as an additional source of feedback about how successfully he was performing the kicking skill relative to what is physically possible.

All feedback is not equally helpful, and the kinds of feedback provided can strongly determine how practice affects performance. The secret to improvement is to discover what kinds of feedback will maximize the benefits of practicing a particular skill. Experiments show that frequent feedback in simple perceptual-motor tasks leads to good performance in the short term but mediocre performance in the long term, whereas infrequent feedback leads to mediocre performance in the short term but better performance in the long term (Schmidt & Wulf, 1997; Schmidt, Young, Swinnen, & Shapiro, 1989). For the most part, however, instructors, coaches, and their students discover through trial and error what types of feedback work best in each situation. For example, dance instructors have discovered that the visual feedback provided by mirrors enhances the effects of practicing dance movements, and most dance studios now have mirrors on the walls. Can you think of any similar advances that college professors have made in the last century in providing feedback to improve students' cognitive skills? One example might be online tutorials that provide immediate feedback about the accuracy of students' responses to intermittent quizzes; some research suggests that these can produce faster learning and greater achievement levels than classroom instruction (J. R. Anderson, Corbett, Koedinger, & Pelletier, 1995).

Feedback is critical to the acquisition of skill memories because it affects how individuals perform the skills during practice. Certain forms of information that precede practice, such as instructional videos, can have similar effects. Skill memories do not depend only on the way skills are taught and practiced, however. They also depend on how effort is apportioned during practice. Concentrated, continuous practice, or **massed practice,** generally produces better performance in the short term, but **spaced practice,** spread out over several sessions, often leads to better retention in the long run (Arthur et al., 2010).

Consider the following classic experiment. Three groups of post office workers were trained to use a keyboard to control a letter-sorting machine. One group practiced 1 hour a day for 60 days. The other two groups practiced either 2 hours a day for 40 days or 4 hours a day for 20 days (Baddeley & Longman, 1978). Contrary to what you might guess, the group that practiced for only 1 hour a day (spaced practice) required fewer total hours of training than any other group to become proficient at using the keyboard (Figure 8.5). The downside was that this group had to be trained over a longer period—two months instead of one. Interestingly, when participants were surveyed about their satisfaction with their training schedule, those trained for 1 hour a day were the least satisfied, while those trained for 4 hours a day were the most satisfied, suggesting that satisfaction with a training program (or course) may not be a very good measure of the learning achieved in that program. Although researchers have conducted many studies to determine what kinds of practice schedules lead to optimal learning and performance, there is still no consensus about how to identify the best schedule for any given individual attempting to learn any given skill.

Researchers also observe differences in the outcomes after equal amounts of practice when they compare different kinds of practice (as opposed to different schedules of practice). In this case, the comparison is between practice with a very limited set of materials and skills, a process called **constant practice,** and practice with more varied materials and skills, a process called **variable practice.** Constant practice consists of repeatedly practicing the same skill—for example, repeatedly attempting to throw a dart at the bull's-eye of a dartboard under fixed lighting conditions or attempting to master a single trick shot in pool. Variable practice consists of practicing a skill in a wider variety of conditions, such as attempting to hit each number sequentially on a dartboard under various levels of lighting or trying to improve one's performance at interviews by applying for a diverse range of jobs. Several studies have shown that variable practice leads to better performance in later tests. In one such study, individuals tracked targets that were moving along various paths. People who used variable practice to learn this task performed better, both in training sessions and in later tests, than individuals who trained with constant practice (Wulf & Schmidt, 1997). Variable practice is not always more effective than constant practice, however (van Rossum, 1990); researchers have not discovered how to reliably predict when variable practice will lead to better learning and performance. Researchers and coaches alike continue to vigorously debate which schedules and which types of practice are most effective.

Implicit Learning

When you acquire a skill, it is usually because you have made an effort to learn the skill over time. If you learn a skill and are able to verbalize how it is done, the process is called **explicit learning** (which creates *explicit memories*, described in Chapter 7). In some cases, however, individuals can learn to perform certain skills without ever being aware that learning has occurred. You probably wouldn't be able to master kung fu without knowing that you're learning the moves, but you might be able to learn to be a better kisser without being aware that you're improving. Learning of the second sort, called **implicit learning,** probably happens to you more often than you think. Implicit learning produces *implicit memories*, which were defined in Chapter 7 as memories that are acquired without conscious awareness. Given this lack of conscious awareness, you'd be hard pressed to estimate how many skills you've acquired in this way. For all you know, you're implicitly learning right now!

Implicit skill learning comes in at least two forms (Knowlton et al., 1996; Pohl, McDowd, Filion, Richards, & Stiers, 2001; Willingham, 1999; Wulf & Schmidt,

Figure 8.5 Benefits of spaced practice versus massed practice The performance of post office workers using a keyboard to control a letter-sorting machine improved at different rates depending on their training schedules. Workers who practiced for 1 hour a day for 60 days (spaced practice) improved their performance more per hour of practice than workers who practiced for 2 or 4 hours a day. Although the group with spaced practice learned the task in fewer total hours, the training took longer (2 months). Adapted from Baddeley and Longman, 1978.

1997). One form of implicit learning is seen in individuals with anterograde amnesia. We described in Chapter 7 the problems that individuals with anterograde amnesia have with learning and remembering events and facts. However, such individuals can nevertheless acquire skills relatively normally, showing improvement from one session to the next even if they show no awareness that they have practiced or observed the skill in the past (Cohen, Poldrack, & Eichenbaum, 1997; Seger, 1994; Sun, Slusarz, & Terry, 2005). Individuals with anterograde amnesia make an effort to learn the skill during each session but always think they are trying it for the first time. The fact that their performance improves with each session demonstrates that they are forming skill memories even though they can't verbally describe their prior practice sessions. H.M., the patient with amnesia whom we introduced in Chapter 7, was able to learn new perceptual-motor skills, but he did not know that he had learned them (Corkin, 2002; Gabrieli, Corkin, Mickel, & Growdon, 1993; Tranel, Damasio, Damasio, & Brandt, 1994). In a second type of implicit learning, individuals perform some task, such as washing windows, and incidentally learn an underlying skill that facilitates their performance; maybe they learn that circular rubbing movements shine the window brighter and faster than random rubbing. The learners may or may not realize that they have discovered a faster, better manner of execution. Implicit skill learning occurs without the learner being consciously aware that he or she is improving. The main difference between the two forms described above is that amnesiacs intentionally try to learn the skill (but are unaware of improvements across training sessions), whereas implicit learning typically occurs unintentionally.

A task that psychologists commonly use to study implicit skill learning is the **serial reaction time task,** in which participants learn to press one of four keys as soon as a visual cue (a light) indicates which key to press (Figure 8.6a). The computer presents the visual cues in long sequences that are either unpredictably ordered (the so-called random condition) or ordered in a fixed sequence of about 12 cues (called the sequential or implicit learning condition). For example, if we designate the four keys from right to left as A through D, then the fixed sequence might be ABADBCDACBDC. Participants eventually begin to get a feel for the repeating sequential patterns and anticipate which key to press next, as reflected by faster reaction times for implicitly learned sequences relative to random sequences (Figure 8.6b). When researchers interview participants after training, however, they typically show no awareness that any of the sequences were repeating patterns (Exner, Koschack, & Irle, 2002). In other words, they have learned the sequences without knowing that they learned them, making their learning implicit.

As mentioned earlier in this chapter and in Chapter 7, people (especially experts) often have difficulty verbalizing what they have learned after mastering

Figure 8.6 Serial reaction time task in the study of implicit learning (a) In a serial reaction time task, participants learn to press keys as rapidly as possible in response to visual cues provided on a computer screen. (b) Participants' reaction times are slower when the cues are presented in random order than when they are presented in a fixed sequence. Quicker reaction times for the sequential cues indicate that the participants implicitly learned to anticipate which key they needed to press next even though their verbal reports reveal no awareness that there was a fixed sequence.

Adapted from Robertson, 2007.

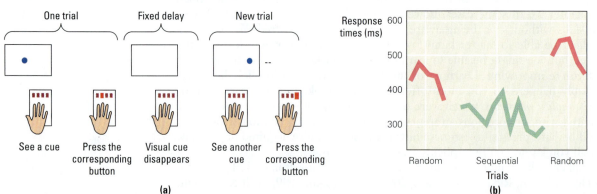

a perceptual-motor skill. This might seem to suggest that perceptual-motor skills are more likely than cognitive skills to be learned implicitly. But people can also acquire many components of cognitive skills through implicit learning. No one becomes a chess grand master simply by reading the rules of chess and listening to other players explaining why they made particular moves. Mathematical whizzes do not become experts by simply hearing about mathematical axioms and proofs (Lewis, 1981). Development of both of these skills requires extensive practice during which implicit learning undoubtedly occurs. In the case of cognitive skill acquisition, it is difficult to assess which abilities are improving independent of awareness because the changes in thinking produced by practice are not easy to observe. Moreover, the learner would, by definition, be unaware of these changes and therefore unable to report them. Consequently, there is currently no way to assess whether implicit learning is more likely to occur during the learning of perceptual-motor skills than cognitive skills.

The distinction between implicit and explicit learning—one being unconscious, whereas the other occurs with conscious awareness—suggests they may be two quite different modes of learning. Moreover, there is evidence suggesting that conscious awareness may be a prerequisite for acquiring skills to a certain level. For example, elite athletes may consent to endure grueling practice sessions not because they enjoy such practicing or because they are more talented and therefore have greater endurance than other athletes but because they are more aware of the necessity of such practice regimens for achieving the highest levels of performance (Yarrow, Brown, & Krakauer, 2009). Nevertheless, recent research suggests that the distinction between "aware" learning versus "unaware" learning may not be as sharp as the current descriptions imply (Robertson, 2007; Song, 2009). Currently, there are no definitive methods for showing that an individual is unaware during learning (Hannula, Simons, & Cohen, 2005). It is possible that there is no threshold point at which an unaware learner is transformed into an aware learner and that, instead, a continuum of awareness exists throughout the learning process. For example, you might become aware that you are improving at a skill before realizing what it is that you are doing differently, or you might be aware that your attempts at improving a skill (say, getting a date) are not working without recognizing what you are doing wrong. In this case, implicit and explicit learning would correspond to points along a continuum of awareness rather than to two different kinds of learning.

Test Your Knowledge

Tasks That Test Skill Memory

Several tasks are commonly used to investigate different phenomena related to skill memory, including the rotary pursuit task, the Tower of Hanoi, and the serial reaction time task. Try to identify which aspects of skill memories each of these three tasks might be useful for testing. (Answers appear in the Answers section in the back of the book.)

Retention and Forgetting

Like the strength of memories for facts and events, the memorability of a skill—how well the skill, after being acquired, is performed on a later occasion—depends on the complexity of the skill, how well the skill memory was encoded in the first place, how often the skill has subsequently been performed, and the conditions in which recall is attempted (Arthur, Bennett, Stanush, & McNelly,

1998). The common wisdom that you never forget how to ride a bicycle once you learn to do it is not accurate. Although skill memories can last a lifetime, they do deteriorate with non-use. Generally, retention of perceptual-motor skills is better than retention of cognitive skills, but unless you actively maintain your bike-riding skills, the skill memories you created when you first learned to ride will gradually deteriorate.

Researchers have studied the forgetting of events and facts much more than they have studied the forgetting of skills. Perhaps this is because if someone loses the ability to do something, it is hard to judge whether he has forgotten how to do it, or forgotten that he knows how to do it, or lost the physical control or strength necessary to perform what he recalls. Loss of motor control does not imply that a skill memory is forgotten. To the outside observer, however, it may be impossible to distinguish whether someone knows how to perform a skill but has impaired movement abilities or has forgotten how to perform the skill.

Psychologists call loss of a skill through non-use **skill decay.** Most of the data collected so far indicate that skill decay follows patterns similar to those seen in the forgetting of memories for events and facts. Motor deficits and injuries (including brain damage) can clearly affect skill decay because they are likely to lead to non-use of learned skills.

In some ways, forgetting a skill is like learning it in reverse. Not performing the skill is almost the opposite of practice: if you don't use it, you lose it. Most forgetting occurs soon after the last performance of the skill; as time goes by, less and less forgetting occurs. Thus, forgetting curves are similar to learning curves. Forgetting occurs quickly at first, then gets slower (as is seen with memories for lists of nonsense words in Figure 1.5 and for passive forgetting of television shows in Figure 7.6).

Does the passage of time simply cause a skill to be "unlearned"? It often may seem this way, but forgetting can also result when new memories interfere with the recollection of old memories. As time passes, you perform more new skills, creating more memories that potentially interfere with the recollection of earlier skill memories. (Recall from Chapter 7 that interference and decay are also involved in the forgetting of memories for events and facts.) Much of this interference can occur without any awareness on the part of the person attempting to recall a skill. For example, you might have difficulty recalling some of the dances you learned when you were younger but easily recall dance steps you learned recently. Rather than thinking this recent learning is hampering your ability to perform the old dances, you'd probably assume that you can't remember an older dance simply because it has been so long since you last did it. However, there is no subjective way for you to distinguish whether your forgetting is due to the passage of time or due to interference.

Recently, researchers observed that interference of skill memories can occur even within a single day. Students trained to perform a finger-tapping task, similar to the serial reaction time task discussed above, demonstrated more rapid and accurate pressing times after a period of sleep (Walker, Brakefield, Hobson, & Stickgold, 2003; Walker, Brakefield, Morgan, Hobson, & Stickgold, 2002; Walker, Brakefield, Seidman, et al., 2003). This simple task qualifies as a perceptual-motor skill because the students' ability to perform it improved with practice. If students learned to press keys in two different sequences on the same day, sleep-dependent enhancement of their performance was seen only for the *second* sequence learned. However, if participants learned the second sequence one day after the first sequence, sleep enhanced the performance of both sequences. Interestingly, if on the second day the students reviewed the first day's sequence immediately before learning the new sequence, then on the third day sleep enhanced their accuracy on only the second sequence. Thus, not only can practicing two skills on the same day interfere with retention of memories for the first skill, but reviewing a recently learned skill before beginning to practice a new one can interfere with subsequent recall of the skill that was reviewed! These findings highlight the intimate relationship between skill acquisition and skill recall and the fragile nature of newly acquired skill memories. Note, however, that athletes and musicians commonly practice multiple skills in parallel with no obvious evidence of interference, and variable practice generally leads to better long-term performance than constant practice. Thus, skills more complex or more distinctive than learning sequences of finger movements may be less susceptible to interference effects.

Research has also shown that a major determinant of whether a person will recall a particular skill is the similarity between the retrieval conditions and the conditions the person experienced while learning the skill. In many situations, of course, the conditions under which a skill must be recalled are *not* the same as the training conditions. In this case, trained performance must "transfer" to the novel conditions.

Transfer of Training

Skills are often highly restricted in terms of how they can be applied (Brady, 2008; Goodwin, Eckerson, & Voll, 2001; Goodwin & Meeuwsen, 1995; Ma, Trombly, & Robinson-Podolski, 1999). You may have mastered the culinary skills needed to make great Italian food, but this will not make you a great sushi chef. In some cases, skill memories are so specific that the introduction of additional informative cues can disrupt performance. For example, after individuals were trained to touch a target with a stylus without visual feedback about their arm movements, their performance was *worse* when researchers allowed them to see their arm moving as they carried out the task (Proteau, Marteniuk, & Levesque, 1992). Most people normally use visual feedback when learning to aim at a target, so it is surprising that providing such feedback can interfere with the skill memory.

In other cases, skills seem to transfer to novel situations relatively easily. For example, you learned to write with your right or left hand, and you may even have practiced with each hand, but have you ever written with your mouth or feet? If you try, you will discover that you can write semi-legible text using these and other body parts. You are able to transfer what you have learned about writing with one hand to other body parts despite large differences in the specific movements you must perform to do so. In sports, teams spend much of their time practicing in scrimmages, with the hope that these experiences will transfer positively to similar situations in real games. If skills learned during practice did not transfer to real games, it is unlikely that so many coaches in so many different sports would train their teams in this way.

The restricted applicability of some learned skills to specific situations is known as **transfer specificity.** This phenomenon led Thorndike to propose that the transfer of learned abilities to novel situations depends on the number of elements in the new situation that are identical to those in the situation in which the skills were encoded (Thorndike & Woodworth, 1901). Thorndike's proposal, called the **identical elements theory,** provides one possible account of why transfer specificity occurs. It predicts that a tennis player who trained on hard courts might suffer a bit the first time she attempted to play on a clay court and would

Will practicing cricket on the beach help this woman improve her stroke in tennis or her swing in softball?

Paul Jones/Getty Images

do progressively worse as the game was changed from tennis to badminton or table tennis. Conceptually, transfer specificity is closely related to transfer-appropriate processing, which was described in Chapter 7. The main differences between the two stem from whether the memories being recalled are memories of skills or memories of facts and events.

When you perform a skill that you have learned in the past, you are generalizing from a past experience to the present (discussed in detail in Chapter 6). From this perspective, every performance of a skill involves transfer of training. For example, each time you open a door, you are making use of memories you acquired by opening doors in the past. Practice improves performance and recall and thus increases the stability and reliability of skill memories over time. How might elements of skill memories be made stable? Current theoretical models of skill acquisition suggest that an individual stabilizes skill memories by converting them from memories for events and facts into memories for predefined sequences of actions called *motor programs* (J. R. Anderson, 1982), as discussed below.

Models of Skill Memory

In previous chapters, we described how psychologists have developed quantitative models of learning and memory to describe incremental patterns of behavioral change. Such models are useful for describing how individual experiences cumulatively affect behavior. Scientists studying skill memories have developed similar models of acquisition, but most models of skill memory focus on shifts in how individuals improve skills with extensive practice rather than on trial-by-trial changes in performance.

Motor Programs and Rules

When you practice a skill, you probably do so because you want to become better at performing that skill. To most people, "becoming better" means that their performance becomes more controlled and effortless. Say the skill you are practicing is juggling. The goal is to keep the objects moving in the air and in and out of your hands. Ideally, you'd probably like to be able to juggle while casually talking to a friend. In this case, your friend would know you are an expert juggler because you don't need to pay attention to what you are doing. The skill has become automatic. Some might even say that your juggling actions have become reflexive. Reflexes, however, are inborn, involuntary responses to stimuli, distinct from highly learned responses. Sequences of movements that an organism can perform virtually automatically (with minimal attention) are called **motor programs**—they are also sometimes referred to as *habits* (James, 1890; Graybiel, 2008). Unlike reflexes, motor programs can be either inborn or learned. Releasing an arrow from a bow is not an inborn reflex, but for the expert archer it has become as automatic and precise as a reflex. More complex action sequences such as juggling can also become motor programs.

One way to determine whether a skill has become a motor program is to remove the stimulus during the action sequence and observe the results. For example, if someone grabs one of the balls in midair as you are juggling, does your arm still "catch and throw" the nonexistent ball? If so, it suggests that your juggling skill has become a motor program. In Chapter 5, we described rats that had learned to run down an alley to receive food and became so accustomed to doing this that they actually would run over a pile of food to reach the end of the alley; in this case, running down the alley had become a motor program.

Classifying highly learned perceptual-motor skills as motor programs is straightforward, but what about highly learned cognitive skills? Might they also, with extended practice, become motor programs? The surprising answer is yes. Think back to when you learned the multiplication tables. This probably required some practice, but now if someone asks you, "What is two times three?" you will respond promptly: "Six." You no longer need to think about quantities at all. You perceive the spoken words, and your brain automatically generates the motor sequence to produce the appropriate spoken word in response. Similarly, in the laboratory, once a person has solved the Tower of Hanoi problem many times, she has learned that particular movement sequences always lead to the solution. Eventually, practicing enables her to perform these motor sequences rapidly, without thinking about which disk goes where. In both cases, a cognitive skill has become a motor program.

The learning of new skills often begins with a set of instructions. You give your great-uncle a new microwave oven and later discover that he refuses to set the time on the display. Why? Because he lost the instructions and, without them, he doesn't know how to do it. The makers of the oven predicted that your great-uncle might not possess this skill, and so they provided written rules—a list of steps to follow to display the correct time. In a perfect world, your great-uncle would have read the manual and acquired the skills necessary to set the time on the microwave oven. Without the manual, the oven controls might be confusing, making his first attempts at setting the time awkward and possibly unsuccessful. Once you locate the manual online, he can follow the instructions relatively easily. However, at a later date, when he wants to reset the time, he might not be able to find the file containing the instructions and may try to recall the steps from memory. Because he will depend on his memories for events and facts to perform the skill, you could say that his skill memories are his memories of the instructions or of a past episode. In other words, skill memories can be memories for events and facts!

Following a recipe in a cookbook provides another example of how memories for facts can serve as skill memories. A recipe teaches you the facts you need to know to prepare a certain dish: what ingredients you need, in what proportions, and how to combine them. However, after some practice—with baking cookies, for example—you may no longer need to depend as heavily on the written "rules."

How can skill memories lead to reflex-like automatic movements but also consist of remembered events and facts? A classic model proposed by Paul Fitts in 1964 suggests that this is possible because practice transforms rules into motor programs.

Stages of Acquisition

Fitts proposed that skill learning includes an initial period when an individual must exert some effort to encode a skill, acquiring information through observation, instruction, trial and error, or some combination of these methods (Fitts, 1964). This period is followed by stages in which performance of the skill becomes more "automatic," or habitual. Fitts called the first stage of skill learning the **cognitive stage,** to emphasize the active thinking required to encode the skill. When your great-uncle is setting the time on the microwave based on instructions or memories of the steps that were previously successful, he is in the cognitive stage of skill acquisition. During this stage, he bases his performance on what he knows, as well as on his ability to control his movements and thoughts so

Simon had mastered clicking his mouse while he slept, but he would soon learn this was useless without the correct posture.

Patrick Hickey/cartoonstock.com

as to accomplish specific goals. If you're learning to play a new sport—let's say cricket—then you will initially have to find out what the rules are and keep them constantly in mind to avoid breaking them. This, too, corresponds to the cognitive stage of skill learning.

Humans are likely to depend on memories of verbalizable facts or rules at this stage, but this is not what happens in other animals. A monkey can also learn to change the time on a microwave oven if motivated to do so, but the goals and strategies the monkey employs to learn this skill are very different from the goals and strategies available to your great-uncle. Researchers do not yet know the degree to which memories for facts or events are important for skill acquisition in nonhumans or preverbal children as compared with adult humans.

Fitts called the second stage in his model of skill acquisition the **associative stage.** During this stage, learners begin using stereotyped actions when performing the skill and rely less on actively recalled memories of rules. The first few times you play a video game, for example, you may need to keep reminding yourself about the combinations of controller movements or button presses or both that are necessary to produce certain outcomes. Eventually, you no longer need to think about these combinations. When you decide that you want a particular action to occur on the screen, your hands do what is necessary to make it happen. How do they do this? Your brain has encoded specific combinations and is recalling them as directed. What began as a process of understanding and following verbalizable rules has become a process of remembering and reenacting previously performed actions.

Of course, mastering the skills needed to play a video game requires far more than simply memorizing hand movements. You must be able to produce very rapid sequences of precisely timed combinations of those movements to achieve specific outcomes. To reach high levels of performance, your movement patterns must become quick and effortless. In Fitts's model, this level of skill is represented by the third stage, the **autonomous stage**—the stage at which the skill or subcomponents of the skill have become motor programs. At this stage it may be impossible to verbalize in any detail the specific movements being performed, and performance may have become much less dependent on verbalizable memories for events and facts. In fact, at this stage, thinking too much about what you are doing when you perform a skill can actually impair performance—a phenomenon related to "choking" under pressure. If you can juggle while having a casual conversation, you have reached the autonomous stage. You can perform the skill without paying much attention to what you're doing, and if someone unexpectedly snatches a ball, your arms will continue to move as if the missing ball were still there.

In the autonomous stage, the actions of a monkey trained to set the time on a microwave oven might be almost identical to the actions performed by your great-uncle when he is setting the time. The monkey and your great-uncle may have learned this skill through different strategies, but their end performance is very similar (perhaps identical, depending on how much your great-uncle looks like a monkey). But even if the observable skills look the same, the memories underlying the skills may be very different. Comparing neural activity in your great-uncle and in the monkey would be one way to determine whether they are accessing information similarly while performing the same skill.

Fitts's model of skill acquisition (summarized in Table 8.2) provides a useful framework for relating skill performance to practice. Although psychologists have developed this model extensively over the past 50 years, many recent versions retain the same basic progression of stages (Ackerman, 2007). The "three stages" are, of course, abstractions. There is generally no single performance that can be identified as the last performance belonging to, say, stage one. Additionally, the three-stage model of skill acquisition is primarily descriptive. It

Table 8.2

Fitts's three-stage model of skill learning

Stage	Characteristics	Example
1. Cognitive stage	Performance is based on verbalizable rules.	Using written instructions to set up a tent
2. Associative stage	Actions become stereotyped.	Setting up a tent in a fixed sequence, without instructions
3. Autonomous stage	Movements seem automatic.	Setting up a tent while carrying on a discussion about politics

won't help you predict how much practice you need to convert your skill memories into motor programs or give you pointers about how and when you should practice. The model does suggest, however, that learned abilities may rely on different kinds of memory as practice progresses. Different kinds of memory may in turn require different kinds of neural processing or activation of different brain regions. The following section discusses what scientists have learned about the neural activity associated with skill acquisition.

Interim Summary

- A skill is an ability that has been honed through learning. Skills that consist of producing pre-defined movements are called closed skills; skills in which movements are situation dependent are called open skills.

- Practice can decrease the effects of past learning on motor performance and increase the effects of genetic influences. Feedback about performance, or knowledge of results, is critical to the effectiveness of practice.

- The power law of learning, which holds for a wide range of cognitive and perceptual-motor skills, states that the extent to which practice can lead to further improvements decreases with extended practice.

- Concentrated, continuous practice generally produces better performance in the short term, but practice that is spaced out over several sessions leads to faster learning per unit of time spent practicing and better skill retention in the long run.

- Repetition of a skill under fixed conditions, called constant practice, often does not improve performance as much as practicing the skill in varying contexts, called variable practice.

- Implicit learning, which is the learning of skills without an awareness of learning, is often tested with the serial reaction time task and is generally preserved in patients with anterograde amnesia, who cannot acquire new explicit memories.

- Thorndike's identical elements theory proposes that the degree to which skills transfer to novel situations depends on the number of elements that are identical between the learning context and the novel situation.

- In Fitts's model, skills are learned in three stages: the cognitive stage, when skill performance requires active thinking; the associative stage, when the skill is performed using stereotyped actions; and the autonomous stage, when the skill has become a motor program.

8.2 Brain Substrates

What neural systems do humans and other animals need to acquire memories of perceptual-motor and cognitive skills? Is there something special about the human brain that makes acquisition of new skills easier for humans than it is for other animals? Or do humans use the same neural systems to learn skills as other animals do, but in slightly different ways? How might we judge whether the skill memories that underlie a dolphin's ability to use a sponge differ from the skill memories a human uses to wash windows?

Neuroscientists have used neuroimaging and neurophysiological recordings to monitor brain activity in humans and other animals during the acquisition and performance of skills. These techniques have enabled researchers to identify several brain regions involved in the formation and recall of skill memories. Scientists have also compared brain activity in experts and amateurs performing various skills, as well as in individuals before and after they have learned a particular skill. Neuropsychological studies of skill learning by patients with brain damage are also an important source of information. Through these kinds of research, researchers hope to associate stages of skill acquisition with changes in brain structure and activity.

All movements and postures require coordinated muscle activity. As you saw in Chapter 2, a major function of the nervous system is to initiate and control patterns of muscle activity. The spinal cord and brainstem play a critical role in the performance of perceptual-motor skills by controlling and coordinating movements. Brain regions dedicated to sensation and perception, including the sensory cortices, are also involved, processing information that contributes to the guidance of movements. Of these, the somatosensory and visual systems (described in Chapter 2) are particularly important for learning perceptual-motor skills. Remember the experiment described earlier in this chapter in which researchers instructed the participant to kick a target as quickly as possible? He improved at the task by processing visual feedback about how effectively he was coordinating the muscles in his leg.

In this section we describe how practicing skills can change neural circuits. Although you can form skill memories in ways other than practice (such as studying videos of expert athletes or kissers), neuroscientists have focused much of their effort on understanding the incremental effects of practice on brain activity during skill learning. Sensory processing and motor control by circuits in the spinal cord are clearly necessary for learning and performing perceptual-motor skills. However, the core elements of skill learning seem to depend in particular on three other areas of the brain (introduced in Chapter 2 and discussed in Chapters 3 through 7): the basal ganglia, the cerebral cortex, and the cerebellum (Figure 8.7). When any of these brain regions becomes dysfunctional, the performance and learning of both cognitive and perceptual-motor skills become seriously impaired, a topic we will return to in the final section of this chapter.

Figure 8.7 Brain regions that contribute to skill learning Skill-memory systems in the brain include the basal ganglia, cerebral cortex, and cerebellum. These three regions modulate the control of movements by circuits in the brainstem and spinal cord.

Cerebral cortex
Basal ganglia
Brainstem
Cerebellum
Spinal cord

The Basal Ganglia and Skill Learning

Basal ganglia is one of the few names for a brain structure that literally describe the region (or in this case regions) to which they refer. You may recall from Chapter 5 that the **basal ganglia** are a collection of *ganglia* (clusters of neurons) that lie at the *base* of the forebrain (the most prominent part of the human brain).

The basal ganglia are positioned close to the hippocampus (see Figure 2.3). Like the hippocampus, the basal ganglia receive large numbers of inputs from cortical neurons. In fact, most cortical areas send inputs to the basal ganglia. These inputs provide the basal ganglia with information about what is happening in the world—in particular, about the sensory stimuli the person is experiencing. Many of these cortical inputs are initially processed by the striatum, a subregion of the basal ganglia that we describe in greater detail in Chapter 5, as it is known to play an important role in operant conditioning. The basal ganglia send output signals mainly to the thalamus (affecting interactions between neurons in the thalamus and motor cortex) and to the brainstem (influencing signals sent to the spinal cord). By modulating these motor control circuits, the basal ganglia play a role in initiating and maintaining movement.

The basal ganglia are particularly important for controlling the velocity, direction, and amplitude of movements, as well as for preparing to move (Desmurget, Grafton, Vindras, Grea, & Turner, 2003; Graybiel, 1995; R. S. Turner, Grafton, Votaw, Delong, & Hoffman, 1998). For example, suppose you are performing the rotary pursuit task. You need to move your arm in a circle at a velocity matching that of the rotating target. In this task, your basal ganglia will use information from your visual system about the movements of the target, the stylus, and your arm, as well as information from your somatosensory system about the position of your arm, to help control the direction and velocity of your arm movements. Similarly, if you dive into a pool to retrieve a coin, your basal ganglia will help you avoid colliding with the bottom of the pool.

Given all the interconnections between the basal ganglia and motor systems, it's not surprising that disruption of activity in the basal ganglia impairs skill learning. Such disruption does not, however, seem to affect the formation and recall of memories for events and facts. Consider the case of Muhammad Ali. Ali was one of the most agile and skilled boxers of his era, but his career was ended by a gradual loss of motor control and coordination. Doctors identified these deficits as resulting from Parkinson's disease, a disorder that disables basal ganglia circuits (we discuss this disease in more detail later in the chapter). Over time, the loss of basal ganglia function resulting from Parkinson's disease affects even the most basic of skills, such as walking. Whereas H.M.'s hippocampal damage (described in Chapter 7) prevented him from reporting on his past experiences, Muhammad Ali's basal ganglia dysfunction hinders his use of skill memories and his ability to learn new skills; it has not affected his memory for facts or events.

Many researchers suspect that processing in the basal ganglia is a key step in forming skill memories, although how it contributes is still debated (Barnes, Kubota, Hu, Jin, & Graybiel, 2005; Graybiel, 2005, 2008). Most researchers agree, however, that practicing a skill can change how basal ganglia circuits participate in the performance of that skill and that synaptic plasticity is a basic neural mechanism enabling such changes (Conn, Battaglia, Marino, & Nicoletti, 2005; Graybiel, 2008). We describe here experimental results that show the importance of the basal ganglia not only for performing skills but also for forming and accessing skill memories.

Learning Deficits after Lesions

Much of what is known about the role of basal ganglia in skill learning comes from studies of rats learning to navigate mazes, such as the radial maze shown in Figure 7.2. In the standard radial maze task, rats learn to search the arms in the maze for food without repeating visits to the arms they have already searched. This task simulates some features of natural foraging (because food does not magically reappear at locations where a rat has just eaten) and has often been used to test rats' memories for events and locations (discussed in Chapter 7). However, the entrances to the arms of the maze are all very similar, so unless the rat remembers specifically which arms it has visited, it is likely to go to the same arm more than once. In early sessions, this is just what rats do. They often go to the same arm multiple times and consequently waste a lot of time running back and forth along arms that contain no food. With practice, the rats learn that they can get more food for their effort by keeping track of where they have been, and they make fewer repeat visits to the same arm—their performance improves incrementally with practice, and so their ability to navigate through the maze is a skill. Food acts as a kind of feedback in the radial maze task, in that correct performance leads to food.

To learn to navigate the radial maze efficiently, rats must remember certain aspects of past events. Not surprisingly, rats with hippocampal damage have major problems with this task (Figure 8.8a). Even after many sessions, they continue to visit arms they have visited before. In contrast, rats with basal ganglia damage learn this task as easily as rats with no brain damage. This shows that basal ganglia damage does not disrupt rats' memories for events, nor does it prevent them from performing the skills necessary to find food in a radial maze.

Researchers can modify the radial maze task slightly to make it less dependent on memories of past events. If instead of putting food in all the arms, the experimenter places food only in arms that are illuminated, rats quickly learn to avoid the nonilluminated arms (Figure 8.8b). Rats with hippocampal damage can learn this version of the task because they only need to associate light with food, which does not require keeping track of arms they've visited. Surprisingly, rats with basal ganglia damage have difficulty learning this "simpler" version of the task. They continue to search nonilluminated arms even though they never find food in those arms (Packard, Hirsh, & White, 1989). Basal ganglia damage seems to prevent rats from learning the perceptual-motor skill of avoiding dark arms and entering illuminated arms.

Rats with brain damage show similar learning deficits in another task: the Morris water maze. In the standard version of this maze, experimenters fill a circular tank with murky water. They then place rats in the tank, and the rats must swim around until they discover a platform hidden just beneath the water surface. Once a rat finds the platform, it no longer has to swim, and the trial is over. Researchers measure the time it takes a rat to find the platform and use this as a measure of learning. Intact rats gradually learn the location of the hidden platform after repeated trials in the tank. In this case, the skill the rats have learned is to direct their swimming movements based on visual cues present around the tank. With practice, rats become better at selecting which directions to swim given their observations of which cues are currently visible. (Compare this task with the situation faced by

Figure 8.8 Effects of brain damage on rats' learning in a radial maze (a) When placed in a maze with food at the end of each arm, intact control rats learn, over repeated trials, to avoid revisiting arms they have already visited. Rats with basal ganglia damage can also learn this, but rats with a dysfunctional hippocampus cannot. (b) Intact rats can also learn to enter only the illuminated arms in a radial maze. Rats with hippocampal damage can learn this, too, but rats with basal ganglia damage cannot. This result shows that basal ganglia damage can disrupt perceptual-motor skill learning.

Adapted from Packard et al., 1989.

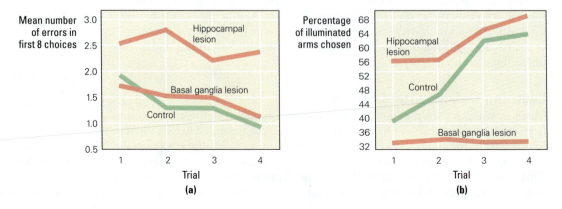

humans asked to solve the Tower of Hanoi puzzle. In both cases, participants have to learn which direction to move to reach a predefined goal that cannot be directly perceived.) Rats with hippocampal damage have severe difficulties learning this standard task but have no problem learning the task if the platform is visible above the surface of the water. Rats with basal ganglia damage can learn to swim to the location of the platform whether it is visible or not. This seems to suggest that basal ganglia damage does not affect a rat's ability to learn this task.

Tests of transfer of training, however, tell a different story. If experimenters move a visible platform in the Morris water maze to a new location during testing, rats with hippocampal damage (or no damage) swim directly to the platform to escape the water. Rats with basal ganglia damage, however, swim to where the platform used to be and only afterward do they find the platform in its new location (McDonald & White, 1994). One interpretation of this finding is that rats with basal ganglia damage have difficulty learning to swim toward a platform to escape the water (even when the platform is clearly visible) and instead learn to swim to a particular location in the tank to escape the water. This study illustrates that just because two animals may seem to be performing a skill in the same way doesn't mean that their skill memories and their ability to use those memories in novel situations are equivalent.

The findings from these experiments with rats illustrate the effects of damage to the basal ganglia on the formation of skill memories. Such studies have led researchers to conclude that the basal ganglia are particularly important in perceptual-motor learning that involves generating motor responses based on specific environmental cues. The basic assumption behind such research is that

---

LEARNING AND MEMORY IN EVERYDAY LIFE

Are Video Games Good for the Brain?

Since the advent of television, people have been spending much of their lives staring at the glow of a rectangular screen. Video games have transformed passive viewing into an interactive process, and today's video games are as complex as any sport, card game, or board game. Video games are quickly replacing other recreational activities as the preferred pastime of children around the world. Many parents are concerned that this new pastime is turning children's brains into mush and that the skills acquired by playing such games are worthless. What is actually going on? Does video game playing have a negative impact on a person's mental capacities?

Video games have some advantages over traditional games. They offer a wide variety of experiences and options, they build expertise without requiring instruction from an expert, they present minimal risk of injury, and they can be played in any weather at any time. On the other hand, video games are blamed for provoking teen violence, contributing to obesity and a general lack of physical fitness, reducing literacy, decreasing opportunities for face-to-face interactions with family members and peers, and occupying children's minds with useless information (see C. A. Anderson & Bushman, 2001, for a review of the scientific literature on this topic).

The question of whether video games are good or bad for your brain has received little scientific study. One recent series of experiments found that college students who played high-action video games such as Grand Theft Auto 3, Crazy Taxi, Counter-Strike, and Spider-Man at least 1 hour a day, at least 4 days a week, for at least 6 months had increased visual attention abilities compared with students who did not play video games (Green & Bavelier, 2003). The benefits of playing fast-action games included increased visual capacity and enhanced spatial attention, with an increased ability to apprehend and count sets of visual stimuli. Interestingly, a control group that spent the same amount of time playing a non-action video game, Tetris, showed no enhancement in visual attention.

Based on the limited evidence available so far, it seems that the effects of video games on your brain are like the effects of bread on your body. The amount of bread you eat can influence what you look like to some extent and might affect how healthy you are, but it will not strongly determine how your body functions or what your mental and physical capacities are. And the kind of bread you eat can make a difference. Of course, in the case of video games, it is too early to say which games are the whole wheat bread and which are the Texas toast.

there is nothing unique about the way the basal ganglia function in rats learning to navigate mazes, and consequently basal ganglia damage should disrupt skill learning in similar ways in humans. Conversely, enhanced basal ganglia function may facilitate skill learning. For example, researchers found that individuals with larger basal ganglia were the quickest to improve at the video game Space Fortress (Erickson et al., 2010). (See "Learning and Memory in Everyday Life" on the previous page for more insight into how video game playing might in turn affect brain function.)

Neural Activity during Perceptual-Motor-Skill Learning

Measures of neural activity in the basal ganglia during learning provide further clues about the role of the basal ganglia in the formation of skill memories. Experimenters can train rats to turn right or left in a T-shaped maze in response to a sound cue that the rats hear just before reaching the intersection where they must turn (Figure 8.9). For example, an experimenter releases a rat in the maze, and then a computer plays a specific sound instructing the rat to make a right turn. If the rat turns to the right, the experimenter gives the rat food (as discussed in Chapter 5, this is a particularly effective form of feedback). With practice, rats learn to perform this simple perceptual-motor skill accurately. In a recent experiment, researchers implanted electrodes in the basal ganglia of rats before training them in the T maze. They then recorded how neurons in the basal ganglia fired as rats learned the task (Jog, Kubota, Connolly, Hillegaart, & Graybiel, 1999).

These recordings revealed four basic patterns of neural activity in the basal ganglia when rats were in the T maze: (1) some neurons fired most at the start of a trial, when the rat was first released into the maze; (2) some fired most when the instructional sound was broadcast; (3) some responded strongly when the rat turned right or left; and (4) some fired at the end of a trial, when the rat received food. During the early stages of learning, about half of the recorded basal ganglia neurons showed one of these four patterns of activity. Most of these neurons fired only when a rat turned right or left in the maze (Figure 8.9a). The other half of the recorded neurons fired in ways that were not clearly related to the rats' movements or experiences in the maze. As the rats' performance improved with practice, the percentage of neurons that showed task-related activity patterns increased to about 90%, with most neurons firing strongly at the beginning and at the end of the task rather than during turning (Figure 8.9b). These measurements show that neural activity in the basal ganglia changes during the learning of a perceptual-motor skill, suggesting that encoding or control of skills by the basal ganglia changes as learning progresses.

The increased neural activity seen in the beginning and end states during the maze task suggests that the basal ganglia developed (or monitored) a motor plan that the rat's brain initiated at the beginning of each trial. The motor plan then directed the rat's movements until the trial ended (Graybiel, 2008). This hypothetical process is consistent with Fitts's model of skill learning, in which automatically engaged motor programs gradually replace active control of movements (Fitts, 1964). Someone learning to juggle might show similar changes in basal ganglia activity—that is, if we

Figure 8.9 Changes in basal ganglia firing patterns during skill learning (a) Researchers implanted electrodes in rats' basal ganglia, then trained the rats to turn right or left in a T maze after hearing a tone instruction. Early in training, 50% of basal ganglia neurons fired strongly (indicated by the lightning bolt) when the rats chose which direction to turn. (b) As training progressed, basal ganglia neurons began to fire mainly at the beginning and end of the rats' movements through the maze; finally, more than 90% of neurons fired almost exclusively when rats were at these positions.

Adapted from Jog et al., 1999.

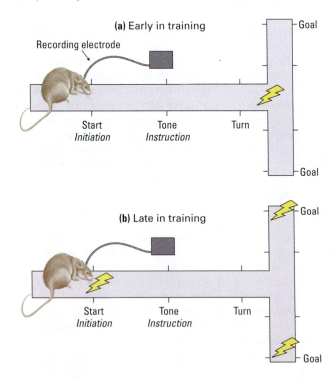

could record signals from her neurons, which is not yet possible. In a novice juggler, still in the cognitive stage of skill acquisition, basal ganglia neurons might fire most strongly when the balls are in the air (when an action must be chosen based on visual information). In an expert juggler, who has reached the autonomous stage of skill learning, basal ganglia neurons might fire most strongly when she is catching and tossing the balls.

Earlier in the chapter, we raised the question of whether cognitive skills might involve some of the same brain regions and neural mechanisms as perceptual-motor skills. The data presented above show that the basal ganglia contribute to learning of perceptual-motor skills. Do they also contribute to cognitive skill learning?

Brain Activity during Cognitive Skill Learning

Neuroimaging studies of the human brain reveal that the basal ganglia are indeed active when participants learn cognitive skills (Poldrack, Prabhakaran, Seger, & Gabrieli, 1999; Poldrack et al., 2001). In these experiments, participants learned to perform a classification task in which a computer presented them with sets of cards and then instructed them to guess what the weather would be, based on the patterns displayed on the cards (Figure 8.10a). Each card showed a unique pattern of colored shapes. Some patterns appeared when rain was likely, and others appeared when the weather was likely to be sunny. As each card was presented on-screen, participants predicted either good or bad (sunny or rainy) weather by pressing one of two keys. The computer then determined and reported the actual weather outcome based on the patterns on the cards. Participants had to learn through trial and error which patterns predicted which kind of weather (Knowlton, Squire, & Gluck, 1994). The task mimics real-world weather prediction in that no combination of "patterns" (that is, of cloud cover, temperature, wind, and so on) is 100% predictive of the weather that will follow; meteorologists must develop a wide range of cognitive skills to accurately forecast the weather. For participants in this study, the task may have seemed more like reading tarot cards than learning a cognitive skill, but the participants usually did improve at this task with practice.

Although each card was associated with the likelihood that a particular kind of weather would occur, there was no simple rule that participants could use to

Figure 8.10
Neuroimaging during learning of the weather prediction task (a) A participant, lying with his head in the MRI scanner, is shown a set of cards on-screen that he must use to judge what weather conditions are likely to occur. Different patterns correspond to different predictions; for example, the pattern of squares on the leftmost card shown here predicts a 60% chance of rain. The participant is not given this information but must figure out through trial and error which patterns indicate a high chance of rain. (b) During the weather prediction task in a well-trained subject, fMRI difference images show increased activation (orange) in the basal ganglia.
(b) Adapted from Poldrack et al., 2001.

Basal ganglia

Russell Poldrack

Increased brain activation

(a)　　　　　　(b)

make accurate predictions. Instead, to improve at the task, participants gradually had to learn which cards *tended* to predict certain types of weather. Brain-imaging data showed increased activity in the basal ganglia as individuals learned to make these judgments (Figure 8.10b). This and similar imaging studies suggest that the basal ganglia contribute to both cognitive and perceptual-motor-skill learning. But how do they contribute?

Despite considerable evidence that the basal ganglia enable skill learning, their specific function in this process is still unclear. Because the basal ganglia are involved in the control and planning of movements, it is possible that damage to the basal ganglia leads to changes in performance that impair learning processes in other brain regions: if you can't control how your arms are moving, you will have difficulty learning how to juggle. Consequently, changes in skill learning caused by lesions to the basal ganglia, as seen in rats learning the radial maze task, do not definitively prove that this region is critical for encoding or retrieving skill memories. Similarly, learning-dependent changes in the activity of basal ganglia neurons, as seen in rats learning to follow instructions in a T maze, could reflect changes in the information coming from the sensory cortex rather than changes generated by the basal ganglia.

Are basal ganglia neurons doing most of whatever is required to form memories of skills, or are other brain regions such as the cortex and cerebellum doing the bulk of the encoding and retrieval? Is it possible that the basal ganglia contribute no more to skill-memory formation than do other brain regions but that they (the basal ganglia) are specialized for specific aspects of the learning process? We need to take a closer look at different cortical regions during and after practice sessions to shed light on these issues.

Cortical Representations of Skills

How important is the cerebral cortex for the learning and performance of skills? Given that most animals don't have a cerebral cortex and that animals born with a cortex can continue to perform many actions after surgical removal of all their cortical neurons, you might conclude that the cerebral cortex isn't very important for either learning or performing skills. In fact, mammals are the only animals that make extensive use of cortical circuits for any purpose, so whatever the role of the cerebral cortex in skill memory, it probably plays this role most extensively in mammals. Coincidentally (or not), mammals are highly flexible, relative to most other species, when it comes to learning new skills.

Neural circuits in your cerebral cortex that become active when you run, jump, or sing are continuously changing over time in ways that may enhance your ability to perform these actions. From this perspective, skill memories are the neural outcomes of repeated performances. A simple analogy is the way your muscles and performance change in response to a bodybuilding regimen. Just as increasing the strength and flexibility of your leg muscles can affect how well you jump, changing patterns of activity in your cortex through practice and performance may also influence your jumping ability.

Cortical Expansion

If cortical networks are like brain "muscles," then you'd expect that practicing different skills should affect different cortical regions, just as different physical exercises affect different muscle groups. This seems to be true. Regions of the cerebral cortex involved in performing a particular skill often expand in area with practice, while regions that are less relevant to the skill show fewer changes. Neuroimaging techniques such as fMRI reveal this expansion by showing increased blood flow to particular regions. For example, brain-imaging studies of professional violinists showed that the cortical activation evoked in the somatosensory cortex during use of the fingers that control note sequences was more extensive than in nonviolinists (Elbert, Pantev, Wienbruch, Rockstroh, & Taub, 1995). Interestingly, the cortical maps of violinists' bow hands (on which the fingers always move together) showed no such elaborations: the cortical changes were specific to the hand that moves the fingers separately. Similar differences in cortical activation have also been observed in the motor cortices of expert racquetball players when they use their playing hand versus their nonplaying hand (Pearce, Thickbroom, Byrnes, & Mastaglia, 2000).

Although expansion of cortical regions is usually associated with superior performance, there is some evidence that too much expansion can cause problems. In a disorder called *musician's dystonia*, extensive practice playing an instrument can lead to a reduction or loss of motor control. Recent experimental work indicates that this loss of control reflects excessive reorganization of the motor cortex (Rosenkranz, Butler, Williamon, & Rothwell, 2009).

Measures of blood flow reveal larger areas of activation in sensory and motor cortices after extensive practice, which implies that experience is affecting cortical circuits. These measures do not reveal what physical changes occur, however. Recent studies using structural MRI techniques indicate that practice can actually change the amount of cortical gray matter, which is where the cell bodies of neurons are found. For example, after about 3 months of training, people who learned to juggle three balls continuously for at least 1 minute showed a 3% increase in gray matter in areas of the visual cortex that respond to motion (Draganski et al., 2004). In fact, changes in gray matter can be observed as early as 7 days after training begins (Driemeyer, Boyke, Gaser, Buchel, & May, 2008). No comparable structural changes were observed in the motor cortex, basal ganglia, or cerebellum. It is not known whether this expansion of gray matter reflected changes in the number or size of synapses, changes in the number of glia (the cells providing functional and structural support to neurons), or changes in the size of cortical neurons.

Like neuroimaging studies in humans, electrophysiological studies in monkeys show that practice can expand cortical representations. In one such study, researchers trained monkeys to perform a tactile discrimination task (Recanzone, Merzenich, Jenkins, Grajski, & Dinse, 1992). The task required the monkey to release a handgrip whenever it felt a stimulus on its fingertip that differed from a standard stimulus. During each trial, the monkey initially felt a vibration having a certain fixed speed for about half a second on one of its fingers. This initial tactile stimulus, always the same, provided a standard for comparison. The initial stimulus was followed by a half-second interval of no stimulation and then a series of one to four additional vibrating stimuli, each vibrating either at the same rate as the standard or faster. The monkey was given fruit juice if it released the handgrip when vibrations were faster than the standard. This task is similar to the T maze task described earlier, in which researchers recorded the activity of basal ganglia neurons in a rat as it learned to turn right or left in response to acoustic cues. Both the T maze and the tactile discrimination task require the animal to perform one of two responses (in one task, turn right or turn left; in the other, grip or release) based on specific cues provided to a single sensory modality (sound in one task, touch in the other). These two tasks might not seem to require much skill compared with the musical performances of professional violinists or the physical feats of professional athletes, but it is important to keep in mind that these animals would never perform the trained actions in the wild. The criterion for whether an ability is a skill is not how hard it would be for a human to perform but whether the ability can be improved through experience.

When a monkey learned to respond to a vibrating tactile stimulus that predicted the delivery of juice, the area of the somatosensory cortex that processed the cue increased. As a result, monkeys that learned the tactile discrimination task had enlarged cortical representations for the finger they used to inspect tactile stimuli. Studies such as this show that perceptual-motor-skill learning is often associated with expansion of representations within the sensory cortex involved in performing the skill. Similarly, practicing a perceptual-motor skill can cause representations within the motor cortex to expand. For example, electrical stimulation of the motor cortex (a technique introduced in Chapter 2) in monkeys trained to retrieve a small object showed that the area of the cortex that controlled movements of the fingers expanded (Nudo, Milliken, Jenkins, & Merzenich, 1996). In monkeys that learned to turn a key with their forearm, cortical representation of the forearm expanded. Researchers don't know how many different cortical regions are modified during learning of a particular skill, but the current assumption is that any cortical networks that contribute to performance of the skill are likely to be modified as training improves (or degrades) performance. Researchers also have yet to determine exactly how the expansion of cortical representations occurs, but most neuroscientists believe that representational expansion reflects the strengthening and weakening of connections within the cortex resulting from synaptic plasticity (basic mechanisms of synaptic plasticity are described in Chapter 2).

Are Skill Memories Stored in the Cerebral Cortex?

Many experiments have shown that cortical networks change as skill learning progresses, but this tells us only that the two phenomena are correlated, not that changes in the cerebral cortex actually cause the improved performance. Such studies also do not establish that skill memories are stored in cortical networks. As you saw earlier, changes in neural activity in the basal ganglia also take place during skill learning. The cerebral cortex clearly contributes to skill learning and performance, but knowing this is not the same as knowing what cortical circuits do during skill learning.

One way to get closer to understanding the cortical contribution to skill learning is to measure cortical activity during training. Much of what is known about skill learning pertains to how different practice regimens relate to differences in skill acquisition and forgetting. If it were possible to show that cortical changes parallel known behavioral patterns or that improvements in performance can be predicted from cortical changes, we could be more certain that skill levels and cortical activity are closely related. Initial investigations in this direction suggest that the behavioral stages of skill acquisition are indeed paralleled by changes in cortical activity.

Data from brain-imaging studies show that when people begin learning a motor skill that requires sequential finger movements, the part of the motor cortex activated during performance of the task increases rapidly during the first training session and more gradually in later sessions. Avi Karni and colleagues required participants to touch each of their fingers to their thumb in a fixed sequence as rapidly and accurately as possible (Karni et al., 1998). In parallel with the changes seen in the motor cortex during training, participants' performance of this task improved rapidly in early sessions and more gradually in later sessions (Figure 8.11a), consistent with the power law of learning. Imaging data collected over 6 weeks of training suggested that practice beyond the third week

(a)

(b)
Trained sequence   Untrained sequence

Increased activation

Decreased activation

Copyright 1998 National Academy of Sciences, U.S.A

Figure 8.11 Changes in skill performance and associated motor cortex during training (a) Participants who practiced performing a sequence of finger movements gradually increased the rate and accuracy with which they could perform this skill. The plot shows average scores for the group of participants. (b) After training, fMRI scans revealed that the area of motor cortex activated when participants performed the practiced sequence expanded (left panel) relative to the region activated when they performed an untrained sequence of identical finger movements (right panel).
Adapted from Karni et al., 1998.

of training (after performance had stabilized) resulted in additional increases in the representation of learned movements in the motor cortex.

Overall, the region of motor cortex activated during performance of the practiced sequence expanded relative to the area activated by different, untrained sequences of finger movements (Figure 8.11b). Karni and colleagues hypothesized that the period of "fast learning" involves processes that select and establish the optimal plans for performing a particular task, whereas the subsequent slower stages of learning reflect long-term structural changes of basic motor control circuits in the cortex. Recent data from studies of perceptual-motor skill learning in rats are consistent with this interpretation. Rats trained in a reaching task showed significant differences in their motor map only after practicing the task for at least 10 days (Kleim et al., 2004). This finding suggests that structural changes in the cortex reflect the enhancement of skill memories during later stages of training.

A wide variety of sensory and motor events activate circuits in the cerebral cortex, so it is not surprising that these brain regions contribute to skill learning and performance. However, the respective roles of the cortex and basal ganglia in forming and recalling skill memories remain to be assessed and will require studying the interactions between the cerebral cortex and the basal ganglia while individuals are learning various perceptual-motor and cognitive skills.

Test Your Knowledge

Which Cortical Regions Change during Skill Learning?

As skill learning progresses, cortical regions change in ways that mimic patterns of skill acquisition. Based on what is known from neurophysiological experiments with monkeys and from behavioral experiments with humans, what cortical regions do you think might show different activation levels in a chess grand master compared with a beginner? (Answers appear in the Answers section in the back of the book.)

The Cerebellum and Timing

What about skill learning in animals such as birds and fish that don't have much cortex? Researchers can train pigeons to perform a wide range of perceptual-motor skills, and fish can rapidly learn to navigate mazes. Animals without much cortex must rely on evolutionarily older parts of the brain to learn skills. One region that seems to be particularly important in this process is the cerebellum. You may recall from Chapter 4 that the cerebellum plays a key role in learning to predict important events, especially in the formation, execution, and timing of conditioned responses. These functions also are important for skill learning.

The cerebellum is probably one of the most basic neural systems involved in encoding and retrieving skill memories. Even animals as lowly as fish and frogs, which may seem to have little potential for skill learning, have a cerebellum. Although you aren't likely to see a fish or a frog performing in a circus, this doesn't mean these animals cannot learn perceptual-motor skills; for example, with practice, fish can learn to press little levers for food. You are more likely to have seen parrots riding tricycles or heard them producing intelligible sentences. Birds, too, have a cerebellum, which may facilitate their ability to learn such tricks. In fact, most animals that have a spine also have a cerebellum. Yet there are relatively few studies of cerebellar function in nonmammals. Consequently, much less is known about how the cerebellum contributes to skill-memory formation in animals possessing little cortex than is known about cerebellar function in mammals with lots of cortex.

Most of the inputs to the cerebellum are from the spinal cord, sensory systems, or cerebral cortex, and most of the output signals from the cerebellum go to the spinal cord or to motor systems in the cerebral cortex. Experiments conducted in the early 1800s showed that cerebellar lesions impair the performance of motor sequences. People with cerebellar damage, for example, have difficulty playing a musical instrument or writing. Collectively, these anatomical and neuropsychological data indicate that the cerebellum contributes to the performance of perceptual-motor skills in mammals. Because the structure of the cerebellum is organized similarly across different species, it is presumed to serve similar functions in both mammals and nonmammals (Lalonde & Botez, 1990).

Other evidence suggests that, in addition to facilitating the performance of skills, the cerebellum is involved in forming memories for skills. The cerebellum appears to be especially important for learning movement sequences that require precise timing, such as acrobatics, dancing, or competitive team sports. A person with cerebellar damage might be able to learn new dance moves but would probably have trouble learning to synchronize those moves to musical rhythms. For example, early brain-imaging studies of systems involved in motor learning showed that there is a sudden increase in cerebellar activity when humans begin learning to perform sequences of finger movements (Friston, Frith, Passingham,

Liddle, & Frackowiak, 1992). Similarly, rats that learn complex motor skills to navigate an obstacle course (for example, balancing on tightropes and seesaws) develop predictable physiological changes in cerebellar neural circuitry, such as increased numbers of synapses (Kleim et al., 1997). Cerebellar changes in acrobatic rats seem to depend on skill learning rather than on activity levels because rats that run in an exercise wheel for the same amount of time do not show such changes. Furthermore, recent studies found that rats depended on cerebellar processing even when they learned to perform a task by simply watching other rats perform the task (Leggio et al., 2000). Rats that received cerebellar lesions after observing other rats navigate a maze benefited from those observations when they were later trained in the maze, whereas rats that received lesions before observing other rats traverse the maze did not benefit from their observations. Recent studies in humans similarly found cerebellar involvement during observational learning of a perceptual-motor skill (Torriero et al., 2011), further suggesting that memories of skills either performed or witnessed depend at least in part on cerebellar processing.

The cerebellum is also important for tasks that involve aiming at or tracking a target. A task that psychologists commonly use to assess such abilities is **mirror tracing.** In this task, individuals learn to trace drawings by looking in a mirror to observe their hand and the figure to be traced, which are otherwise hidden from view (Figure 8.12a). It's hard to draw well under these conditions, but if the cerebellum is working properly, the participant can eventually learn to perform this task well. In contrast, a person with cerebellar damage would find this task to be quite difficult. It took patients with cerebellar damage twice as long to trace images shown in a mirror as individuals without damage (Figure 8.12b), even after several sessions of training (Laforce & Doyon, 2001).

It is interesting to note in Figure 8.12b that the *rate* of learning for patients with cerebellar damage was comparable with that of the control group. This seems to suggest that learning in the patients with cerebellar damage was similar to that of the control group and that the patients simply performed more poorly. However, subsequent transfer tests in which both groups traced more complex figures revealed that the individuals in the control group benefited more from their training experiences than did the individuals with cerebellar damage. Thus, although both groups were learning at a similar rate, they were not transferring the mirror-tracing skill in the same way. This finding is similar

Figure 8.12 The mirror-tracing task (a) In this task, participants learn to trace a figure using only a mirror reflection of their hand and the figure for guidance. (b) Cerebellar lesions disrupt performance of the mirror tracing task. Note, however, that the rate of learning is the same for individuals with and without cerebellar lesions.

(b) Adapted from Laforce and Doyon, 2001.

(a)

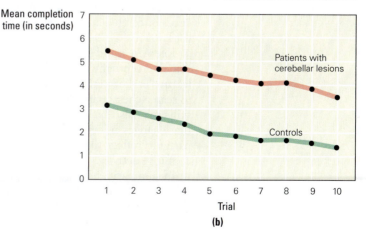

(b)

Figure 8.13 Cerebellar activation during cognitive skill learning fMRI imaging studies shows that after the learning of a mirror-reading task, activity in the right cerebellum increased (a) and activity in the left cerebellum decreased (b).
Adapted from Poldrack and Gabrieli, 2001.

Right cerebellum

(a) Learning-related increase

Left cerebellum

Increased activation

Decreased activation

(b) Learning-related decrease

to that in the study described earlier in which rats with basal ganglia lesions seemed to have learned to find a visible platform in the Morris water maze in the same way as intact rats but then performed differently when the platform was moved to a new location.

So far, we have discussed how the cerebellum contributes to perceptual-motor-skill learning. Recent brain-imaging studies show that activity in the cerebellum also changes when individuals learn certain cognitive skills, such as **mirror reading.** In the mirror-reading task, individuals learn to read mirror-reversed text. Researchers found that cerebellar changes that occur during learning of the mirror-reading task are *lateralized*—that is, are different in each hemisphere (Figure 8.13), with the left cerebellum showing decreased activity and the right cerebellum showing increased activity with training (Poldrack & Gabrieli, 2001). Were you assuming that both sides of your brain are doing the same thing while you're reading this chapter? niaga knihT. How such hemisphere-specific differences in cerebellar processing contribute to skill learning or performance is not yet known.

Keep in mind that almost all cognitive skills require the performance of some perceptually guided movements, if only eye movements. For example, we learned earlier in this chapter that chess masters move their eyes more efficiently to scan a chessboard than do less experienced players. Similar perceptual-motor skills may also be important for tasks such as mirror reading. So, it is possible that changes in cerebellar activity during the learning of cognitive skills might partially reflect the learning of motor sequences required for performing the cognitive activity.

In summary, then, the cerebellum, cerebral cortex, and basal ganglia are each critical, in different ways, to skill learning. If you're having trouble learning a skill, which part of your brain should you blame? There is no cut-and-dried division of labor between these three brain regions that would allow you to identify the culprit. The importance of each for encoding or performing any given skill probably depends on the particular skill and your level of expertise. Nevertheless, the cerebellum seems most critical for timing; the cerebral cortex, most critical for controlling complex action sequences; and the basal ganglia, most critical for linking sensory events to responses. Knowing this, which brain region do you think would be most important for learning to run down stairs? The answer is probably all three, at different points in the learning process (Hubert et al., 2007; Steele & Penhune, 2010; Yin et al., 2009). Early on, the cerebellum, visual cortex, and motor cortex may work together to coordinate the timing and sequencing of leg movements. After extensive practice, the basal ganglia may begin to initiate and control more-automatic sequences of leg movements. How these three brain regions work together during the acquisition and retention of skill memories is a question that researchers are still attempting to answer.

One feature that all three systems have in common is that skill learning is associated with gradual changes in the firing of neurons in these areas during performance of the skill. This finding means that practice can change the structure of neural circuits to make the control and coordination of movements (or thoughts, in the case of cognitive skills) more accurate and efficient. The most likely mechanism for such changes is synaptic plasticity. Understanding how and when the brain is able to adjust specific synapses within and between the cerebellum, basal ganglia, and cortex will clarify how humans and other animals learn skills.

Interim Summary

- Skill learning depends on three brain areas: the basal ganglia, the cerebral cortex, and the cerebellum.
- Studies of how rats with basal ganglia damage learn to navigate mazes suggest that the basal ganglia are critical for learning to generate motor responses based on environmental cues.
- Neural response patterns in the basal ganglia change during the learning of a perceptual-motor skill, suggesting that representations of that skill are dynamically modified as learning proceeds. The basal ganglia are also activated when people learn cognitive skills such as the weather prediction task.
- Regions of the somatosensory cortex and motor cortex needed to perform a particular skill expand with practice, but regions that are less relevant show fewer, if any, changes.
- The cerebellum is especially critical for learning and performing movement sequences that require precise timing, such as dancing, and tasks that involve tracking a target, as in mirror tracing.
- The cerebral cortex is mainly involved in controlling complex actions, and the basal ganglia link sensory events to responses.

8.3 Clinical Perspectives

In Chapter 7 you learned how damage to the hippocampus and surrounding brain regions can disrupt memories for events and facts. Damage to the cerebral cortex and basal ganglia resulting from injury or disease can similarly interfere with the formation and use of skill memories. In this section we explore the types of deficits caused by damage and dysfunction in these two brain regions.

The disorders reviewed here have a major impact on society, affecting millions of individuals. Experiments conducted with groups of patients who have these disorders provide unique opportunities for understanding how the neural systems involved in skill learning can be disrupted. Unlike the various types of amnesia, in which memory loss can be measured with standard tests, the effects of brain dysfunction on skill learning are difficult to distinguish from impairments to skill performance. Nevertheless, clinical studies of patients with skill deficits provide clues about the neural systems responsible for skill learning—information that would be difficult or impossible to obtain through experiments with unimpaired individuals.

Apraxia

Damage to the cerebral cortex, especially the parietal lobe of the left hemisphere (Figure 8.14), can lead to problems in the coordination of purposeful, skilled movements. This kind of deficit is called **apraxia.** The most common causes of apraxia are sharp blows to the head (a typical occurrence in motorcycle accidents) and interruption of blood supply to neurons (as occurs during a stroke). Tests for apraxia generally include asking patients to perform or mimic specific gestures. A patient with apraxia can usually voluntarily perform the individual steps that make up the movement or gesture requested by the experimenter, but most such patients cannot combine these steps in appropriately sequenced and coordinated patterns when instructed to do so (Gross & Grossman, 2008).

The position and extent of cerebral cortical damage determine what abilities are affected. For example, in patients with left parietal lesions, the greatest impairment is in the ability to imitate actions, whereas in patients with lesions in more frontal areas, the greatest loss is in the ability to pantomime actions that involve the use of both hands (Halsband et al., 2001). Sometimes patients are unable to perform a skill with one hand and yet can perform it quite easily with the other. These patients understand what the neuropsychologist is instructing them to do, but they are unable to comply.

Early case studies describing patients with apraxia, such as the description below, give some sense of the severe problems associated with the disorder:

> The patient is requested to light a candle in its holder. He takes the match, holds it with both hands without doing anything further with it. When asked again, he takes the match upside down in his hand and tries to bore it into the candle. . . . A box of matches is put in his hand. He takes a match out and brushes his beard with it, and does the same thing when given a burning match. (quoted in Brown, 1988)

Cortical damage clearly causes deficits in skill performance. For example, researchers have found that apraxia can affect individuals' abilities to perform both perceptual-motor skills and cognitive skills (Leiguarda & Marsden, 2000; Zadikoff & Lang, 2005). What is less clear is how the cortical damage might be affecting the memories of skills that are lost or the ability to form new memories. One hypothesis for why individuals with apraxia have difficulty performing skills is that they cannot flexibly access memories of how to perform those actions (Rothi, Ochipa, & Heilman, 1991). For example, patients with apraxia who were unable to pantomime gestures such as flipping a coin also had difficulty

Figure 8.14 Cortical lesions in the parietal lobes Regions in blue represent lesions in the parietal lobe that are associated with apraxia.

Adapted from Sirigu et al., 2004.

Lesion

Lesions

identifying when an actor in a film performed a specific gesture, such as opening a door (Heilman, Rothi, & Valenstein, 1982). This inability to recognize actions suggests that these patients have not simply lost the ability to generate certain actions but instead can no longer access memories of those actions.

Studies of skill learning in patients with apraxia suggest that cortical damage interferes with the control and execution of skills more than with the learning and recalling of skills. For example, with practice, such patients can improve at performing skills, and their rate of improvement is comparable with that of unimpaired individuals. The highest level of performance they can reach, however, may be lower than the levels at which unimpaired individuals can perform with no training (Jacobs et al., 1999). How well someone with apraxia can learn a particular task seems to depend on both the nature of the person's deficits and the nature of the task. It remains unclear whether learning in individuals with apraxia occurs through the same neural processes as in unimpaired individuals. Patients with apraxia might make do with a subset of these processes, or they might use alternative mechanisms, such as adopting different strategies during practice sessions. Possibly the reduced amount of cortical tissue in relevant regions limits the amount of cortical expansion that is possible, effectively limiting the potential benefits of practice.

One way to investigate the conditions leading to apraxia is to create temporary states of apraxia in healthy individuals by inactivating cortical circuits and then to examine the effect on skill learning and recall. This strategy has recently been made possible by *transcranial magnetic stimulation* (TMS; Figure 8.15), a procedure in which a brief magnetic pulse (or series of pulses) applied to the scalp produces small electrical currents in the brain that affect normal patterns of activity over an area of about 1 square centimeter (this technique was described in Chapter 2). The effect lasts for just a few tens of milliseconds, but if timed properly, it can temporarily impair skill learning and performance. Researchers can disrupt activity in different cortical regions simply by changing the position of the stimulating device. Transcranial magnetic stimulation is a powerful way of studying how cortical deficits affect the formation and recall of skill memories.

Currently, the main technique for helping patients with apraxia overcome their deficits is behavioral training that involves extensive repetitive practice. Knowing how different variables such as feedback, pacing, and variety of practice can influence learning (as described previously in the Behavioral Processes section) is important for developing appropriate behavioral therapies. Future advances in understanding the cortical networks contributing to skill memory will probably suggest important ways of enhancing existing treatments for apraxia as well as ways of developing new ones.

Huntington's Disease

Huntington's disease is an inherited disorder that causes gradual damage to neurons throughout the brain, especially in the basal ganglia and cerebral cortex. The disease leads to a range of psychological problems (including mood disorders, hypersexuality, depression, and psychosis) and a gradual loss of

Figure 8.15 Using TMS to modulate cortical activity This technique enables researchers to disrupt cortical activity in volunteers to temporarily simulate conditions such as apraxia.

Wire coil

Pulsed magnetic field

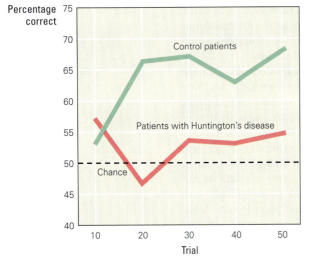

Figure 8.16 **Impaired skill learning in people with Huntington's disease** This graph traces accuracy in performing the weather prediction task. People with Huntington's had problems learning this task compared with the control group, which consisted of healthy elderly individuals.

Adapted from Knowlton et al., 1996.

motor abilities over a period of about 15 years. Facial twitching usually signals the onset of the disease. As Huntington's progresses, other parts of the body begin to shake, and this eventually interferes with normal movement.

Patients with Huntington's disease show a number of memory deficits, some affecting skill memory (Doyon et al., 2009; Gabrieli, Stebbins, Singh, Willingham, & Goetz, 1997). Such patients can learn new perceptual-motor and cognitive skills (with performance depending on how far the disease has progressed), but they generally learn more slowly than healthy individuals (Ghilardi et al., 2008; Willingham & Koroshetz, 1993). People with Huntington's have particular difficulty learning tasks that require planning and sequencing of actions, and they cannot perform the mirror reading or weather prediction tasks (described above) as well as healthy individuals (Knowlton et al., 1996). For example, Barbara Knowlton and colleagues found that an experimental group of 13 patients with Huntington's disease who were tested on the weather prediction task showed no signs of learning after 150 trials, whereas a control group of 12 healthy people rapidly improved at the task (Figure 8.16). Recall that experimental studies with animals show that lesions of the basal ganglia can greatly impair skill learning. The basal ganglia damage in patients with Huntington's may explain why they find the weather prediction task so difficult to learn. However, they can learn some other cognitive skills that require similar abilities, such as the Tower of Hanoi task (Butters, Wolfe, Martone, Granholm, & Cermak, 1985), so possibly it is only certain aspects of learning particular tasks that are impaired.

Individuals with Huntington's disease typically show large deficits in perceptual-motor-skill learning that seem to be related to problems with retrieval and decreased storage capacity. They have difficulty learning the serial reaction time task, the rotary pursuit task, and most other skills that require aiming at or tracking a target. However, it is difficult to determine to what extent deficits in learning of perceptual-motor skills are a direct result of cortical or basal ganglia damage as opposed to being a side effect of patients' inability to move normally. Imagine trying to learn to throw darts with someone randomly pushing your arm. You would probably have problems improving your throw under those conditions—not because you've lost the ability to store and recall memories of past attempts but because you don't have control of your movements. It's also not easy to know how the combination of abnormal psychological states and damaged neural systems might affect learning in people with Huntington's. A recent behavioral study found, however, that both explicit and implicit components of a motor sequence learning task were impaired even before people with Huntington's showed any clinical symptoms of the disease, suggesting that learning deficits are not simply a side effect of motor control problems or abnormal psychological states (Ghilardi et al., 2008). Additionally, experiments in which transcranial magnetic stimulation was used to change activity in the motor cortex of presymptomatic individuals with Huntingon's showed abnormal cortical plasticity (Orth et al., 2010), consistent with the idea that perceptual-motor-skill learning may be impaired at an early stage in the development of the disease.

Scientists have made great progress in using genetic markers to diagnose Huntington's disease, but prevention and treatment of symptoms are still rudimentary. Using knowledge about the genetic abnormalities found in people with Huntington's, researchers have produced mice and fruit flies with similar genetic abnormalities (Nishimura et al., 2010; Simmons et al., 2009). Experiments with these genetically engineered animals may provide critical new information about how Huntington's disease affects skill-memory systems and how the deficits caused by this disorder might be overcome. For example, recent experiments with Huntington's disease mice have revealed severe deficits in perceptual-motor-skill learning and in the changes in cortical circuits that should occur during learning (Mazarakis et al., 2005). Synaptic plasticity mechanisms such as long-term potentiation and long-term depression (see the discussion of synaptic plasticity in Chapter 2) are also abnormal in these mice (Cummings et al., 2007; Nithianantharajah, Barkus, Vijiaratnam, Clement, & Hannan, 2009). Thus, learning and memory deficits in patients with Huntington's may reflect not only basal ganglia damage but also more fundamental deficits in the ability to modify synapses based on experience.

Parkinson's Disease

Parkinson's disease is another nervous system disease involving disruptions in the normal functions of the basal ganglia and progressive deterioration of motor control (Delong & Wichmann, 2007; Redgrave et al., 2010). Unlike Huntington's disease, however, Parkinson's does not seem, in most cases, to be the result of heritable genetic abnormalities or to involve large-scale neuronal death in either the cerebral cortex or the basal ganglia. The main brain damage associated with Parkinson's disease is a reduction in the number of dopaminergic neurons in the substantia nigra pars compacta (SNc) that control activity in the basal ganglia (see discussion of the striatum in Chapter 5). Neurons in the SNc normally determine the levels of dopamine in the basal ganglia, and when these neurons are gone, dopamine levels are greatly reduced.

Patients with Parkinson's disease show increasing muscular rigidity and muscle tremors and are generally impaired at initiating movements. Symptoms of the disease usually do not appear until after the age of 50 but can arise much earlier. Not surprisingly, people with Parkinson's have many of the same skill-learning impairments as people with Huntington's disease. Both conditions make it harder to learn certain perceptual-motor tasks, such as the serial reaction time task and tracking tasks (including the rotary pursuit task). On the other hand, individuals with Parkinson's can learn some skills, such as mirror reading, that cause problems for those with Huntington's (Koenig, Thomas-Anterion, & Laurent, 1999). This suggests that although both diseases affect processing in the basal ganglia and cerebral cortex, the damage each causes leads to different but overlapping deficits in skill-memory systems. Researchers recently have suggested that Parkinson's disease may selectively disrupt circuits in the basal ganglia that contribute to the learning and performance of closed skills, especially those that have reached the autonomous stage of learning, where movements normally would be automatic (Redgrave et al., 2010).

Currently, the main treatments for Parkinson's disease are drug therapies to counteract the reduced levels of dopamine and surgical procedures to counteract the disruption caused by lack of dopamine in the basal ganglia. One recently developed surgical technique, **deep brain stimulation,** has become the most effective neurosurgical technique for treating Parkinson's, but scientists are still not sure why it works (Benabid, 2003; Naskar, Sood, Goyal, & Dhara, 2010). It delivers an electrical current through one or more electrodes permanently implanted deep in the patient's brain. Neurosurgeons place the ends of the

Electrode

Thalamus

Implanted
stimulator

Figure 8.17 Deep brain stimulation for treatment of Parkinson's disease Neurosurgeons position the tip of an electrode in a brain location (such as the thalamus) that, on stimulation, will affect neural activity in the basal ganglia–cortical loop. An implanted stimulator periodically passes current through this electrode to temporarily relieve symptoms of Parkinson's disease.

electrodes near neurons that are part of the basal ganglia–cortical loop (for example, in the thalamus or basal ganglia), as shown in Figure 8.17. When electrical current from an implanted stimulator passes through these electrodes, many of the motor symptoms associated with Parkinson's disease, such as tremors, disappear within seconds, although they eventually return. One theory of how this technique works is that without proper levels of dopamine, interactions between neurons in the cerebral cortex and the basal ganglia become locked into fixed patterns (Dowsey-Limousin & Pollak, 2001). This creates a situation similar to the endless back and forth of young children arguing (Child 1: "No, you be quiet!" Child 2: "No, you be quiet!" Child 1: "No, you . . ."—ad infinitum) and disrupts the control of movements. Stimulation from the electrode is thought to quiet both brain regions, allowing normal brain activity to resume.

A more recent proposal is that deep brain stimulation replaces disruptive activity in the basal ganglia–cortical loop with a new pattern of activity that is less disruptive (Naskar et al., 2010). This new approach to treating Parkinson's disease illustrates how increased knowledge of the brain systems underlying skill memories can help doctors repair these systems when things go awry.

Interim Summary

- Apraxia results from damage to cortical regions, which leads to difficulties in producing purposeful movements and can disrupt the execution of learned skills.

- Huntington's disease damages the basal ganglia and the cerebral cortex, producing motor symptoms as well as large deficits in perceptual-motor skill learning that seem to be related to problems with retrieval and decreased storage capacity.

- Parkinson's disease involves both disruptions in the normal functioning of the basal ganglia and progressive deterioration of motor control and skill-learning abilities.

▶ SYNTHESIS

Kissing requires both perceptual-motor and cognitive skills, acquired and improved through observation and practice. Differentiating the cognitive aspects from the perceptual-motor ones can be difficult, as this chapter shows. Cognitive skills often depend on perceptual-motor skills (and vice versa) and may even become transformed into perceptual-motor skills over time.

Certainly, one cognitive aspect of kissing is the use of social skills to motivate someone to want to kiss you or be kissed by you. Once you solve this problem—which in some cases may be as strategically challenging as a chess game—you face the perceptual-motor challenge of coordinating your own kissing movements with those of your partner, based on what you perceive of your partner's maneuvers. Your skills at this point will depend on how much and how often you have practiced, as well as on the types of feedback you have received from past partners. Perhaps you are in the cognitive stage of learning to kiss, still thinking carefully about each move you make, or perhaps in the associative stage, feeling comfortable with your performance but knowing there is room for improvement and still having to keep in mind things to avoid. Possibly you are at the autonomous stage of skill acquisition, having become an expert—your kissing makes use of various motor programs that you perform without thinking in response to sensory stimuli. If you are an experienced kisser, the skill memories you rely on are dependent on the coordination of several brain regions, including the basal ganglia, the cerebral cortex, and the cerebellum.

In short, there is more to kissing than simply recalling and executing a fixed series of movements. Kissing is an open skill in which the recent actions and reactions of your partner provide important feedback that you can use to guide your own actions. Keeping track of what has happened in the recent past is thus a key component of skillful kissing. The ability to maintain and flexibly use memories of the recent past requires input from brain regions other than those we have focused on thus far in our discussion of skill learning and performance. You will learn more about these kinds of memories and their neural substrates in the next chapter, on working memory.

Key Terms

apraxia, *p. 336*	deep brain stimulation, *p. 339*	mirror reading, *p. 334*	serial reaction time task, *p. 314*
associative stage, *p. 320*	explicit learning, *p. 313*	mirror tracing, *p. 333*	skill, *p. 302*
autonomous stage, *p. 320*	expert, *p. 306*	motor program, *p. 318*	skill decay, *p. 316*
basal ganglia, *p. 322*	Huntington's disease, *p. 337*	open skill, *p. 303*	spaced practice, *p. 312*
closed skill, *p. 303*	identical elements theory, *p. 317*	Parkinson's disease, *p. 339*	talent, *p. 306*
cognitive skill, *p. 304*	implicit learning, *p. 313*	perceptual-motor skill, *p. 303*	transfer specificity, *p. 317*
cognitive stage, *p. 319*	knowledge of results, *p. 311*	power law of learning, *p. 311*	variable practice, *p. 313*
constant practice, *p. 313*	massed practice, *p. 312*	rotary pursuit task, *p. 307*	

Concept Check

1. A teenage girl wants to improve her kissing skills but doesn't want to practice with lots of different boys because of the possible harm to her reputation. What are some strategies she might try for learning these skills?

2. A graduate student who believes his pet tarantula is exceptionally bright wants to prove to the world that spiders can reason and solve problems. How might he convince others that he is correct?

3. Some researchers believe that the right kinds and amounts of practice can make anyone an expert. What sort of experimental evidence might convince these researchers that there is such a thing as talent?

4. According to Fitts's model of skill learning, individuals must go through an initial cognitive stage before they can master a skill. Does this imply that for a fish to learn to press a lever, it must first think about what is required to perform the task?

5. Neuroscience research has shown that regions in the somatosensory cortex and motor cortex expand in parallel with learning of perceptual-motor skills. Does this mean that practicing a skill causes regions of cortex not involved in performing that skill to shrink?

6. Patients with Huntington's or Parkinson's disease are often also diagnosed as having apraxia. Why might this be?

Working Memory and Cognitive Control

T IS TUESDAY AT 9:10 A.M., AND ROBERTA must rush if she is going to make it across campus in time for her 9:30 a.m. French class and still do several errands along the way. She has only 20 minutes to get cash from the bank machine, sign up for the afternoon yoga class, and drop off her biology homework, which is due by 10:00 a.m. Before heading out the door, Roberta grabs the various things she will need for the rest of the day, including her yoga mat and iPad (for last-minute cramming for this afternoon's quiz). The sign-up sheet for the yoga class is in the student center, which is near the biology building and close to where her French class is being held. It is quicker, she figures, to go to the bank machine first, as that requires just a short detour from her dorm room. Punching in her four-digit PIN, she withdraws cash from the ATM and then heads to the student center. After signing up for yoga, she starts to walk to French class when, *zut alors!*, she realizes she forgot one of her errands. She doubles back quickly to the biology department, drops off her homework there, and then heads on to French.

Behavioral Processes
Transient Memories
Working Memory
Cognitive Control and the Central Executive

Brain Substrates
The Frontal Lobes and Consequences of Frontal-Lobe Damage
Frontal Brain Activity during Working-Memory Tasks
Mapping Executive Processing and Working Memory onto PFC Anatomy

Learning and Memory in Everyday Life: Improving Your Working Memory
Prefrontal Control of Long-Term Declarative Memory

Clinical Perspectives
Schizophrenia
Attention Deficit/Hyperactivity Disorder

As she walks toward the French class building, Roberta remembers that today's class has been moved from the usual room on the third floor to the large auditorium in the basement, where they will have a guest speaker. She is so used to running up the stairs every Tuesday and Thursday that she has to struggle to remember that today she needs to bypass those stairs and take the elevator to the basement instead.

Slipping into the back of the auditorium, Roberta listens with half an ear to the speaker. Some of the material he is presenting is new, but when he covers topics that are familiar from her own past reading, she switches her attention to her iPad, lying discretely in her lap, so she can review the chemistry text for the upcoming quiz and also chat on Facebook with her roommates about the party this coming Friday. It isn't the perfect situation for learning about French literature, studying chemistry, or planning what to wear Friday night, but by switching back and forth between the three, she manages to make some progress on all these tasks.

A day in the life of a college student is taxing indeed. To keep track of all her activities and commitments and deal efficiently with emergencies and last-minute changes, Roberta needs something like a mental blackboard. In fact, that is a good description of her **working memory,** the active and temporary representation of information that is maintained for the short term in Roberta's mind to help her think and allow her to decide what to do next. As she attends to her various responsibilities during the day, Roberta's ability to control the flow of information into and out of her working memory is critical to the multitasking and planning she has to do to thrive in her sophomore year of college. **Cognitive control** is the manipulation and application of working memory for planning, task switching, attention, stimulus selection, and the inhibition of inappropriate reflexive behaviors. Thus this chapter is about both working memory itself and the broader range of cognitive control tasks in which working memory plays a crucial role.

9.1 Behavioral Processes

Psychologists have long recognized that memory consists of multiple stores, or repositories, although demarcating the exact distinctions between these stores has proven difficult. Most would agree that the three main distinctions to make are between **sensory memory,** where information automatically and rapidly decays; **short-term memory (STM),** where information can be maintained as long as it is rehearsed or consciously attended to; and **long-term memory (LTM),** where memories can be retained for long periods, possibly permanently, without requiring ongoing maintenance or conscious attention. This view was laid out in an influential model by Richard Atkinson and Richard Shiffrin and is diagrammed in Figure 9.1 (Atkinson & Shiffrin, 1968). In this conceptualization of the stages of memory, short-term memory is the part of the memory system used as a temporary storage area and as the site of working memory operations.

The episodic and semantic memories discussed in Chapter 7 are long-term memories, which may last for hours, days, or even years. (They are represented in Figure 9.1 by the panel at the far right.) In contrast, the memories that are the main focus of this chapter—short-term memories—are transient, existing briefly for seconds or minutes at most. These temporary memories are crucial for performing many high-level cognitive control functions, such as planning, organization, and task management.

Figure 9.1 The Atkinson–Shiffrin model of memory
Richard Atkinson and Richard Shiffrin's model depicted incoming information as flowing first into sensory memory (shown as having distinct visual, auditory, and haptic, i.e., touch, registers). Elements of sensory information that are attended to are then transitioned to short-term memory (STM). From there they go through various control processes and in some cases are transferred into long-term memory (LTM).

Transient Memories

Transient memories are short-lasting mental representations, sometimes persisting for only a few seconds. The Atkinson–Shiffrin model describes two types of transient memory—sensory memory and short-term memory—and sees them as corresponding to the first two stages through which information from the world enters our consciousness and potentially becomes part of our long-term memory.

Sensory Memory

Sensory memories are brief, transient sensations of what you have just perceived when you have seen, heard, touched, smelled, or tasted something. Considerable research has been devoted to understanding how sensory memories are held in the mind so that they are accessible for further processing. Take a quick look at the table of letters in Figure 9.2; just glance at it for a second, no more. Now, without looking back at the figure, try to remember as many of the letters as you can. You probably only recalled four or five letters, or about 30 to 40% of the total array.

Based on this exercise, you might imagine that four or five items are the limit of your **visual sensory memory,** the temporary storage in sensory memory for information perceived by your visual system. Perhaps, however, you felt as if your eyes saw more than four or five letters, but you just couldn't recall more of them. In a seminal 1960 paper, George Sperling conducted a study confirming that you probably did, very briefly, register more than just the few items you were able to recall. Sperling presented people with a 3-by-4 visual array much

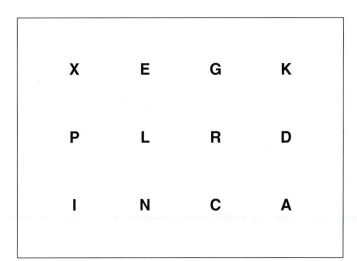

Figure 9.2 The Sperling task These three rows of four letters each are similar to the array George Sperling used in his studies of visual sensory memory (Sperling, 1960). How many of the letters did you remember after glancing at them for a second?

like that shown in Figure 9.2. He then played one of three tones after the array was removed. A high tone indicated that participants were to report the first row of letters, a medium tone corresponded to the middle row, and a low tone corresponded to the bottom row.

When this partial report procedure was used, participants were able to report about 75% of the letters. Note that this is about double the number of letters recalled when people are simply asked to report as many letters as they can after the array is removed. What accounts for this doubled recall in Sperling's partial report procedure? Sperling interpreted it as meaning that people have a visual memory that persists for a very short time—less than a second—but includes *all* the items recently seen.

If there is rapidly decaying sensory memory for visual information, you might imagine that there would also be an analogous rapidly decaying sensory memory for other sensory modalities, such as touch, smell, and hearing. Indeed, there have been studies showing similar phenomena with auditory memory (Moray, Bates, & Barnett, 1965). As illustrated in Figure 9.1, there is a form of sensory memory for each sensory modality (auditory, visual, haptic, i.e., touch, etc.), which lasts very briefly and captures raw incoming sensory stimuli so that they can be processed and passed on to the short-term memory store, from which it may later be entered into long-term memory.

Short-Term Memory

Consider the common experience of looking up a phone number and then repeating it over and over to yourself as you prepare to press the buttons on your phone. The phone number has already been recognized and registered by sensory memory, but now it is the job of your short-term memory to maintain this information temporarily through active rehearsal. William James, whom you read about in Chapter 1, described short-term memory as being of limited capacity, effortlessly available, and fleeting in contrast to long-term memories, which are permanent memories of the past, retrieved with effort, and of potentially unlimited capacity (James, 1890). Short-term memory was, in James's view, the essence of our active conscious awareness. As summarized in Table 9.1, short-term memory and long-term memory can be distinguished in several ways.

Your ability to hold on to this information in short-term memory is limited in several ways. First, as James noted, your memory is limited in capacity; a 10-digit phone number is a lot of information to keep in mind, even more so if you also have to remember a 4-digit extension. In Chapter 1 you read about

Table 9.1

Behavioral distinctions between short-term memory (STM) and long-term memory (LTM)

STM	LTM
Active contents of consciousness	Not currently in consciousness
Access is rapid	Access is slower
Capacity is limited	Capacity is unlimited
Forgotten quickly	Forgotten more slowly

the classic studies of George Miller, who in the early 1950s suggested that the capacity of short-term memory is about 7 items, a number he described as "the magic number 7" because it recurred so frequently in studies of memory capacity (Miller, 1956). Actually, Miller argued that there are a range of short-term memory capacities centered on 5 items but ranging from about 5 to 9 in most people (with the lower limits being more common).

Short-term memory is also limited to what you can pay attention to. If you get distracted by something else, you are likely to forget all or some of the phone number as you walk across the room to get your phone: that's why you rehearse it over and over in your head. By continuing to rehearse the number, you could potentially remember it indefinitely, as long as you do nothing else. Of course, there are plenty of things that could distract you and interrupt this rehearsal. If your roommate asks you a question—such as, "When is the chemistry exam?"—your rehearsal might be interrupted just long enough for you to forget some or all of the phone number. If you do forget it, you have to go back to look up the number again.

The capacity of short-term memory is also determined by how we encode the information we try to retain. As noted above, most people can only keep about half a dozen random numbers in short-term memory. Given this limited capacity for short-term memory, you might think it impossible to keep the following 12 digits in mind without memorizing them: 181217761492. Actually, it is quite easy, because you really only need to remember three historic dates: the war between the United States and Great Britain (1812), the signing of the U.S. Declaration of Independence (1776), and Columbus's discovery of America (1492). Miller argued that the limit to short-term memory was not an absolute amount of information (or digits) but rather a limit in the number of unique concepts or links to long-term memory that could be held active. Miller argued that recoding of information is key to optimizing the amount of information that can be maintained in short-term memory. As Miller wrote in his 1956 paper, "recoding is an extremely powerful weapon for increasing the amount of information that we can deal with."

It is no accident that 10-digit American phone numbers are broken into three chunks of three, three, and four digits, respectively. Chunking is an essential tool for controlling our short-term memory and using it effectively to store, temporarily, as much information as possible. Note that in the case of storing three historically significant dates to increase capacity to 12 digits, you must utilize your long-term memory to retrieve the dates from your knowledge of American history. As you will read later, these interactions between short-term memory and long-term memory are critically important.

Working Memory

Rehearsal is an important part of how we keep information active and accessible within short-term memory. As you walk across the room from your computer—where you found the phone number—to the phone, you rehearse the number to keep from forgetting it. Your goal isn't necessarily to store the phone number in your long-term memory (although that might be useful for future reference); rather, your immediate aim is to remember the number just long enough to get to your phone and make the call.

"These drugs will affect your short-term memory, so you better pay me now."

Paul Taylor/CartoonResource.com

Short-term memory used in this way serves as a buffer, or temporary holding station, maintaining information for a brief period before it is manipulated or otherwise used to affect behavior. It is when short-term memory is employed in this fashion that it is referred to as our working memory. Thus, working memory involves the temporary retention of information just experienced or just retrieved from long-term memory. When information is maintained in working memory, it can be manipulated in ways that make it useful for goal-directed behavior, such as making decisions and retrieving other information from long-term memory. These processes will be described in more detail below.

Baddeley's Working-Memory Model

Alan Baddeley, an English psychologist, proposed an influential model of working memory illustrated in Figure 9.3 (Baddeley & Hitch, 1974). It can be viewed as an alternate (and more detailed) version of what goes on inside the STM/working-memory box in Figure 9.1 Baddeley's model includes two independent short-term memory buffers: the visuospatial sketchpad and the phonological loop. The **visuospatial sketchpad** holds visual and spatial images for manipulation. The **phonological loop** does the same for auditory memories, maintaining them by means of internal (subvocal) speech rehearsal (much like a "loop" of a tape recording that goes around and around, playing the same song over and over). A key feature of Baddeley's theory was that visuospatial information and verbal-phonological information are stored separately in working memory.

A third component of Baddeley's model is the **central executive,** which monitors and manipulates both of these working-memory buffers, providing cognitive control of working memory. The central executive's manipulations include adding to and deleting from the items in the buffers, selecting among the items in order to guide behavior, retrieving information from long-term memory, and transferring information from the visuospatial sketchpad and phonological loop to long-term memory. In these ways, the central executive manages the work that takes place in short-term memory and the traffic of information back and forth between short-term and long-term memory.

Figure 9.3 highlights two important distinctions made by Baddeley's model. First, it distinguishes between two general processes of working memory: manipulation (which depends on the central executive) and maintenance (which requires only rehearsal of information in the two memory buffers). Second, it

Figure 9.3 Baddeley's working-memory model This model consists of two material-specific temporary stores for short-term maintenance of information—a visuospatial sketchpad for object and location information and a phonological loop for verbal material—that are controlled by a central executive. Baddeley's model can be viewed as depicting what goes on inside the STM box in Figure 9.1.

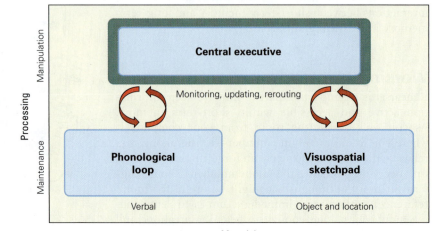

identifies the memory buffers as being material specific: one stores verbal material and the other stores object and location material. We will proceed now with a discussion of the two memory buffers: the phonological loop and the visuospatial sketchpad. Later, in the Brain Substrates section, we will discuss recent data from neuroscience suggesting how both the material-specific and process-specific dichotomies in Baddeley's model of working memory have guided research on the brain mechanisms of working memory and cognitive control.

The idea of material-specific buffers in short-term memory received support from a series of studies of selective interference. These studies posited that if two tasks are using the same processing mechanism, they should interfere with each other if performed at the same time. Indeed, a wide range of studies show that verbal tasks interfere with verbal short-term memory but not visual short-term memory, and visual tasks interfere with visual short-term memory but not verbal short-term memory, lending support to the notion that working memory contains independent, material-specific systems for verbal and visual memories. The following paragraphs review some of this data.

The Phonological Loop

Read this list of seven numbers: 5 6 2 8 1 7 3. Now look away for 5 seconds and then repeat the list out loud. How did you solve the problem of remembering the numbers in this digit-span test? Most likely, you rehearsed them silently in your mind during the interval. In fact, if you didn't rehearse the numbers, you probably would have been unable to remember them. Without rehearsal, most people retain about 2 seconds' worth of information in their phonological memory, which gives most people enough time to remember about 5 to 7 items, Miller's magic number 7. Because of this time limit, people with slow rates of speech but normal intelligence do worse on short-term verbal memory tasks than people of normal intelligence who speak at a normal rate (Raine et al., 1991). (A person's internal speech proceeds at about the same rate as the person's speech spoken aloud.) This internal, unspoken speech used during rehearsal is key to the phonological loop and verbal working memory.

In fact, if this internal rehearsal is disrupted or eliminated, phonological storage cannot occur. For instance, if you were to say out loud, "good morning, good morning . . ." during the delay period while you were trying to remember the list of numbers in the digit-span test, your ability to internally rehearse would be greatly disrupted, impairing your ability to recall the seven numbers. On the other hand, tapping your fingers (a motor task) does not interfere with internal vocal rehearsal because it requires different modalities of processing, speech versus motor.

Additional insights into the processes for internal rehearsal in short-term memory come from studies where people are asked to remember lists of words. For example, which list do you think would be easier to remember?

> List 1: **bat, hit, top, cat, door**

> List 2: **university, expedition, conversation, destination, auditorium**

Most people would say the first is easier. As the length of the words increases, the number of words you can remember declines; this is known as the **word-length effect**. Short, one-syllable words like "bat" and "hit" are easier to rehearse in working memory than longer, multisyllable words like "university" and "auditorium." Longer words take longer to rehearse (Baddeley, Thomson, & Buchanan, 1975).

The Visuospatial Sketchpad

The visuospatial sketchpad in Baddeley's model of working memory (see Figure 9.3) is a mental workspace for storing and manipulating visual and spatial information. Here is an example of it in use: without writing anything down, picture a 4-by-4 grid (16 squares) in your mind and imagine a "1" in the square that is the second column of the second row. Then place a 2 to the right of that. Next, in the square above the 2, put a 3, and to the right of that put a 4. Below the 4, put a 5 and below that, a 6, and then to the left of that, a 7. Now, what number is just above the 7? To correctly answer this question ("2"), you had to use your visuospatial sketchpad.

Just as the phonological loop has a 2-second time limit, the visuospatial sketchpad also has a limited capacity. The two capacities, however, are independent: filling up one does not much affect the capacity of the other. Dual-task experiments, in which subjects are asked to maintain information in the visuospatial sketchpad while simultaneously carrying out a secondary task using the other modality—such as retaining an auditory list of words in the phonological loop—provide evidence for the independence of these two memory buffers.

For example, Lee Brooks used a dual-task paradigm in which people were shown a block-capital letter "F" and were then asked to visualize this letter (from memory) and imagine an asterisk traveling around the edge of it (Figure 9.4a; Brooks, 1968). When the imaginary asterisk reaches a corner, it turns left or right to continue following the outline of the letter F. At each such turning point, the people were asked to indicate whether or not the asterisk was at a corner at the extreme top or bottom of the F (for example, the point at the F's upper right) or at one of the in-between corners. The crucial manipulation was that the participants were divided into three groups, and each group was assigned a different way of signaling. The *vocal group* signaled their answer to each question with a verbal "yes" or "no," the *tapping group* signaled with one tap for yes and two taps for no, and the *pointing group* pointed to a visual array of Y's and N's on a screen. Of the three groups, the pointing group performed most slowly, suggesting that the visuospatial demands of pointing at the appropriate symbol interfered with the visuospatial memory task (Figure 9.4b).

Because visual memory can be easily studied in a wide range of species, it has become the modality of choice for many carefully controlled laboratory experiments on working memory in animals. For example, in an early study of spatial working memory, Carlyle Jacobsen trained monkeys on a delayed spatial-response task (Jacobsen, 1936). Each monkey watched food being placed in either the left or the right of two bins. Next, an opaque screen came down and blocked the monkey's view of the bins for several seconds or minutes. When the screen was removed, the bins now had lids hiding the food. To be marked

Figure 9.4 **A dual-task experiment** (a) Participants were asked to imagine an asterisk traveling along the periphery of a letter "F." Whenever the asterisk was turning a corner, they were to signal whether it was turning at a corner on the extreme top or bottom of the letter or at some point in between. (b) Reaction times varied depending on whether subjects signaled vocally (fastest times), by tapping (intermediate times), or by pointing at symbols on a screen (slowest times).
Adapted from Brooks, 1968.

(a)

(b)

Monkey moves sample object for reward.

(a)

Screen obscures monkey's view during delay.

(b)

Monkey chooses novel nonmatch object.

(c)

Courtesy of David Yu, Mortimer Mishkin, and Janita Turchi, Laboratory of Neuropsychology, NIMH/NIH/DHHS.

correct, the monkey first had to remember in which bin the food had been stored and then displace the lid of just that bin to retrieve the reward.

The **delayed nonmatch-to-sample (DNMS) task** is another test of visual memory. Each trial involves remembering some novel object. Figure 9.5a shows Pygmalion, a rhesus monkey in Mortimer Mishkin's laboratory at the National Institute of Mental Health. He is shown a novel "sample" object, a blue ring, under which he finds a food reward, such as a peanut or a banana pellet. Afterward, an opaque black screen obscures Pygmalion's view (Figure 9.5b) for a delay period ranging from seconds to minutes, depending on the experiment design. During this delay period, the experimenters introduce a new object, a red disk. When the screen is raised, Pygmalion sees both objects, one on the right and the other on the left. As shown in Figure 9.5c, Pygmalion has learned that a reward will now be found under the red disk because this is the novel object, a "nonmatch" to the sample object he saw previously. Training on this delayed nonmatch-to-sample task continues for several trials, each of which involves two objects not used in previous trials. Thus, the next trial might involve a yellow box as the sample and a green disk as the novel object. Over many such trials, the correct answer is sometimes on the left and sometimes on the right so that spatial location will not be a useful cue.

Because each trial uses a new set of objects, the monkeys must learn to remember which unique sample they saw previously and hold this memory in their visuospatial memory buffer until presented with the choice of that previous sample and the novel object. With short delays, the DNMS task can be used to assess working memory; with longer delays, however, the same task has also been used to study long-term memory.

Cognitive Control and the Central Executive

Most of the tasks described in the preceding section require the person or animal simply to maintain some word, digit, object, sound, or location in working memory during a delay period. But there is much more to working memory than just the maintenance of phonological or visuospatial memories: there is the far more complex and involved process of *manipulating* working memory. It is this

Figure 9.5 Delayed nonmatch-to-sample task
(a) A monkey is shown a sample object, here a blue ring, and finds a reward under it. (b) During the delay period, an opaque black screen blocks the monkey's view of any test objects. (c) The monkey is shown two objects, the blue ring from before (the sample) and a new object, a red disk. The food reward is hidden under the new object, the nonmatch to the original sample. The monkey chooses the nonmatch.

Table 9.2

Cognitive control through the manipulation of working memory

Behaviors	Tasks used to explore these behaviors
Controlled updating of short-term memory	*N*-back task, self-ordered search
Setting goals and planning	Tower of Hanoi
Task switching	Wisconsin Card Sorting Test
Stimulus attention and response inhibition	Stroop task

manipulation of working memory that allows for the control of various aspects of higher-order cognition and leads us to the second major topic of this chapter, cognitive control.

We saw earlier, for example, that Roberta has to keep several of her day's goals in mind: get cash, prepare for yoga, study for chemistry, and listen to a French lecture. Balancing these multiple goals requires her to switch her attention back and forth between activities as the situation requires: during French class she discretely reads a bit of chemistry while periodically looking at the teacher to follow some of the French lecture. Her working memory is constantly being updated and reorganized to accomplish different and competing tasks. New tasks are constantly added, as when Roberta's boyfriend text-messages her to find out where she wants to go for dinner. All of these tasks require the cognitive-control function of her working memory's central executive.

Of the three components of Baddeley's model, the central executive is the most important, the most complex, and the least well understood. What is common to all the functions of the central executive is that they involve the *manipulation* of information in short-term memory, including adding or removing items, reordering items, and using working memory to guide other behaviors. Through this manipulation of information held in short-term memory, the central executive goes beyond simple rehearsal to become, in effect, the *working* component of working memory. Researchers have found evidence of cognitive control in many behaviors, including, but not limited to, (1) controlled updating of short-term memory buffers, (2) setting goals and planning, (3) task switching, and (4) stimulus attention and response inhibition. We will discuss each of these in turn in the following pages, and they are summarized in Table 9.2. This list of behaviors may seem, at first glance, like a random selection of activities, but they all depend on the controlled manipulation of working memory. The list is by no means exhaustive—there are many other behaviors that involve working-memory manipulation—but these four examples serve to illustrate the breadth and diversity of mental activities that involve working memory and cognitive control.

Controlled Updating of Short-Term Memory Buffers

The central executive for working memory functions much like a manager at a large corporation who is responsible for assigning specific people to certain jobs at particular times. On Monday, he might tell Mike to work the front desk and Stephanie to work on the sales floor. Come Tuesday, however, he might fire Mike, promote Stephanie to the front desk, and then hire Kristy to work on the sales floor. In an analogous fashion, the central executive for working memory updates working memory by receiving and evaluating sensory information, moving items into and retrieving them from long-term memory, and deciding which memories are needed for which tasks.

To study the controlled updating of working memory, researchers often use what is called a 2-back test. In a 2-back test, a participant is read a seemingly random list of items, usually numbers. A certain item—let's say the number 7—is designated as the "target." Whenever the target number 7 is read, the participant is to respond with the number that was read *two numbers previously* (hence the name 2-back). Sound tough? Try it. If the numbers read aloud are 4 8 3 7 8 2 5 6 7 8 0 2 4 6 7 3 9 . . . , what would the correct responses be? (Answer: "8" to the first 7, "5" to the second 7, and "4" to the third 7.)

To succeed at this task, the participant must constantly keep track of the last two numbers that were read: the 1-back and 2-back numbers. As each new number is read, a new 1-back number must be stored and the old 1-back number must be shifted to the 2-back slot, replacing the previous 2-back number in working memory. In addition, each number must be checked as it is read to see if it is the target number. If it *is* the target number, the participant has to respond with the 2-back number; if it isn't the target number, the participant says nothing. Not easy!

Performing the 2-back task requires active maintenance of many kinds of items in working memory. First are the target number and the rules for performing the task, both of which stay constant throughout the experiment. Second, the last two numbers that were read must always be remembered in case the next number is the target number. These two items change in identity, priority, or both with each new number that is read and must be regularly updated in working memory.

What might happen to your performance on this type of task if you were asked to repeat the 3-back or 4-back number instead of the 2-back number? Although the 2-back task is the most commonly used variation, this class of tasks is generally called *N*-back because *N* can be any number. The larger *N* is, the greater the challenge. The *N*-back task taps into many aspects of the central executive's manipulation of working memory, including online storage of recent information, selective attention, remembering task demands, and updating and reorganizing stored items. For this reason, it is considered an excellent tool for assessing the central executive. We will discuss several experimental studies of the *N*-back task in the Brain Substrates section.

A more common situation faced by your own central executive is the need to keep track of the various everyday tasks you need to perform: What have you done already? What remains to be accomplished? For example, if you have lost your eyeglasses *somewhere* in your home, you might search every room for them. While it may not matter which rooms you search first, you do want to keep track of the rooms so as not to waste time searching where you have already been. Self-ordered tasks that ask people to keep track of their previous responses (analogous to keeping track of the rooms they already searched) are another tool that can be used to assess the central executive's manipulation of working memory.

Michael Petrides, at McGill University in Canada, developed self-ordered memory tasks in studying the behavioral and neural bases of working memory (Petrides & Milner, 1982; Petrides, 2000). In the human version of this task, people are shown a stack of cards, each containing the same set of items but in a

Figure 9.6 A self-ordered memory task for humans
Sample cards from a self-ordered search task for humans (Petrides & Milner, 1982). Participants are presented with a stack of cards, each containing all the items in the target set but in different random order. Participants must point to a different item on each card without repeating any of the items.
Adapted from Petrides, 2000.

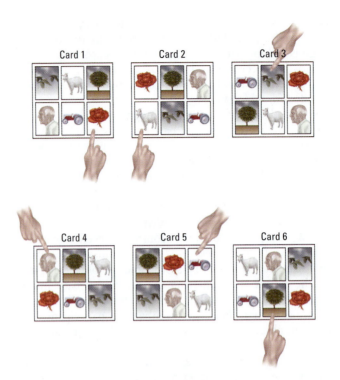

different order. In the example shown in Figure 9.6, there are six items on each card. In card 1, the drawing of a rose (to which the subject is pointing) appears in the lower right corner, while in card 2 the rose is in the upper left corner, and in card 3 it is in the upper right corner.

The experiment proceeds as follows: On trial 1 a participant is shown the first card and is asked to choose any of the six items on it. The participant in Figure 9.6 has chosen the rose. This card is then flipped over. Next, on trial 2, the participant is shown the second card (with the same six items in a different order) and is asked to choose any of the five items not yet selected. In Figure 9.6, the participant has chosen the goat. This second card is then flipped over. Then the participant is shown the third card and must pick any of the four remaining items that were not chosen on the previous two cards, that is, any image except the rose or the goat. This self-ordered task continues until the participant has pointed to all six different items without repeating any. Note that this task requires the participants to monitor (keep track of) the information being held in short-term memory and decide what to keep there given the current task.

This task is appealing to researchers who want to understand working memory in both human and nonhuman primates because it can also be studied in monkeys, as shown in Figure 9.7 (Petrides & Milner, 1982). On the first trial, a monkey sees a row of three nonmatching containers, each of which contains a reward, and selects the reward from one of them. Following this step, an opaque screen is placed between the monkey and the containers for 10 seconds, and the containers are shuffled so that on the second trial the monkey sees the same containers in a new order. Now the monkey must choose one of the other containers in order to get a reward. Like the human self-ordered task described above, this task requires the monkey to remember the items chosen previously. On the third trial, the monkey has to choose again, with only one remaining container still baited with a reward. Because this kind of working-memory task

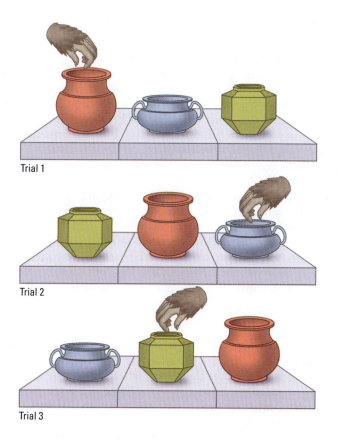

Trial 1

Trial 2

Trial 3

Figure 9.7 A self-ordered memory task for monkeys The monkey sees three distinct containers and selects a reward from one of them. Their order is shuffled on each trial, and the monkey must remember which containers have had rewards removed so that on subsequent trials the monkey does not pick a previously chosen (and hence empty) container.

can be performed by both monkeys and humans, it is useful for comparative studies of the neural substrates of working memory, as will be described later in the Brain Substrates section.

Setting Goals and Planning

As Roberta prepared for the school day ahead of her, she had to be aware of her immediate goals (getting to French class on time in the morning) as well as her goals for later that afternoon (taking yoga). To make sure she could take a yoga class in the afternoon, she had to (1) search through her closet to find her yoga mat and (2) stop by the student center to sign up for the yoga class. Only then would she go to French class. Roberta's busy schedule requires her to keep track of many goals at once and to juggle them in her mind as the day passes, noting which tasks have been accomplished and which are left to be done, and of those left to be done, which should be done next. Keeping track of goals, planning how to achieve them, and determining priorities all draw heavily on the central executive of working memory.

The French mathematician Edouard Lucas invented a game back in 1883 that requires many of these same planning and goal-setting abilities. The game is based on an ancient legend about a temple in India, where the puzzle was used to develop mental discipline in young priests. A stack of 64 gold disks, each slightly smaller than the one beneath, were all stacked on a large pole. The young priest's assignment was to transfer all 64 disks from the first pole to a second and, finally, to a third pole by moving one disk at a time and only placing smaller disks on top of larger disks. According to the legend, if any priest ever solved the problem, the temple would crumble into dust, and the world would vanish. Perhaps one reason the world still exists today, thousands of years later, is that even if a very smart and quick priest were to move one disk per second, solving this task with 64 disks would take him 580 billion years.

Lucas called his simplified three-disk version, which was marketed as a board game, the Tower of Hanoi. You were briefly introduced to it in Chapter 8. At the game's start, the three disks are placed on the left-most of three pegs, arranged by increasing size from bottom to top, as was shown in Figure 8.1 (see p. 304): a small blue disk on top of a medium yellow disk on top of a large red disk. In order to move the disks properly and solve the puzzle, it helps to establish subgoals, such as getting the large red disk over to the right-most peg, a maneuver that takes four moves.

Solving the Tower of Hanoi requires a great deal of manipulation of working memory because you must remember at least three things at all times: (1) what subgoals have been accomplished, (2) what subgoals remain, and (3) what is the next subgoal to be addressed. After each move, some of these will be updated and changed, while others will stay the same. This kind of goal-directed controlled updating of short-term memory is exactly the kind of task that places a heavy load on your central executive. It is hard enough to do with the real disks and pegs.

Task Switching

In French class, Roberta listens with one ear to her professor. When the material in the lecture is familiar, she switches her attention to her chemistry reading. This kind of task switching requires the manipulation of working memory because Roberta must pay attention to the task she is doing at a given moment while at the same time monitoring external cues for information that may signal the need to switch to another task.

A commonly used procedure for studying task switching in the laboratory is the Wisconsin Card Sorting Test, in which people are shown cards with graphics that differ in three characteristics, or dimensions: color, shape, and number. One sample card might have three red circles, while another card might have one yellow triangle. On each trial they are told to guess which of four piles a particular card goes on, and then they are informed if their choice is correct or not. In this way, people learn which of the three dimensions they should be paying attention to in order to sort the cards correctly: for example, a person might learn it is correct for all the blue cards to go on one pile, all the yellow cards on another, and so forth, as illustrated in Figure 9.8a. Later, however, after the person has discovered this sorting rule, the task changes without warning and the subject receives positive feedback only when she sorts the cards by another rule. For example, if the original rule was to sort by color, now the rule might switch to sorting by shape, making a pile for circles, a pile for squares, and so on, as shown in Figure 9.8b. This task taps into people's working memory and **executive control** because it requires not only learning a rule and keeping it in mind while they sort, but also learning to change the rule and keep track of the new one without confusing it with the old.

Stimulus Selection and Response Inhibition

While visiting Los Angeles, California, from his home in England, Trevor walks to an intersection and prepares to cross the street. He automatically begins turning his head toward the right to check for oncoming cars but quickly reminds himself that he is in the United States and oncoming cars will come from the left, not the right. In this situation, information about his current context has inhibited Trevor's ingrained, reflexive response and redirected his attention. Trevor's well-functioning central executive allows him to inhibit a

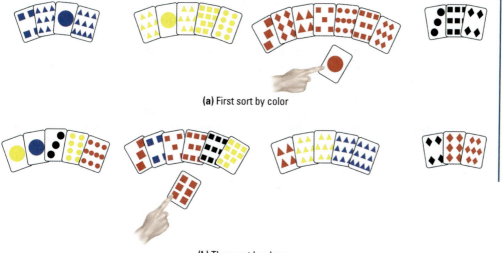

(a) First sort by color

(b) Then sort by shape

Figure 9.8 The **Wisconsin Card Sorting Test** (a) In this example, participants are first rewarded for sorting by color, so that there are blue, yellow, red, and black piles. (b) Later, they are rewarded for sorting by shape instead, so that there are separate piles for circles, squares, triangles, and diamonds.

habitual response that he has developed and shift his attention to an alternative, context-specific rule ("look left when crossing streets in the United States") that he must remember—perhaps by repeated rehearsal when walking through Los Angeles—as long as he remains in the United States. Given how difficult it is to suppress these well-learned reflexive responses, it is not surprising that many London intersections have a "Look Right" sign painted on the curb in an attempt to reduce the number of American and European visitors who mistakenly look left before walking into oncoming traffic.

Don Norman and Tim Shallice (1980/1986) proposed that situations like these highlight the distinction between two types of processes—automatic ones and willed, or controlled, ones—that occur in parallel, competing to influence our behaviors. Automatic processes are triggered by situational cues, such as approaching a street, which to an Englishman like Trevor elicits an overlearned quick turn to the right to look for oncoming cars. These automatic responses are deeply ingrained and reflexive and typically occur with minimal conscious awareness; they do not generally interfere with other concurrent activities (like talking to a friend with whom we are walking). In contrast, willed, or controlled, actions are mediated by what Norman and Shallice described as the *supervisory attentional system*, which modifies behavior when the automatic responses are inappropriate, inhibits automatic routines in favor of more appropriate behaviors, and changes the prioritization of cues for attention.

A well-known test of how well a person's control processes can direct attention to stimuli and inhibit inappropriate automatic responses is the Stroop task (Stroop, 1935), which creates a laboratory situation analogous to Trevor's trying to adapt to the traffic patterns in the United States. The Stroop task consists of a series of names of colors, each printed in a color that is *different* from the color being named (Figure 9.9). The word "green" might be printed in red ink, the word "blue" in green ink, the word "black" in blue ink, and so forth. The task is to look at each word in turn and say the color it is printed in, ignoring what the word happens to say.

Because people usually respond automatically to a written word by reading it, the Stroop task is very difficult to perform smoothly. Try it and you will see how hard it is to overcome the almost irresistible urge to read what the words say. To perform the task rapidly, you must inhibit your automatic impulse to

Figure 9.9 The **Stroop task** The names of colors are printed from top to bottom, each in a color that does not correspond to the name. The task is to recite the colors that the words are printed in (color of ink) without being distracted by what the words say.

Green
Blue
Black
Red
Orange
Purple
White
Yellow

read the words and instead keep a context-specific goal in your working memory to remind you of the task at hand: to attend to the ink color alone, much as Trevor must keep in mind the rule "look left for cars" when he is crossing the road in the United States. Thus, the Stroop task requires inhibiting currently inappropriate automatic reflexive responses while attending to the task-specific aspects of a stimulus. The Stroop task illustrates the fundamental competition within our brains over the control of our behaviors and thoughts. The various inputs competing for our attention at any given moment include both bottom-up processes that are stimulus-driven (potentially eliciting automatic reflexes and well-learned responses) and top-down processes that are goal-directed and require selective attention to specific aspects of our environment. Although the simple hardwired, reflexive responses are useful for many situations that require rapid responding and minimal conscious effort, they are insufficient for dealing with the more complex facets of our dynamic world, where long-range planning, goals, and the ability to foresee future consequences are necessary (Miller & Wallis, 2008).

Are Working Memory and Cognitive Control the Keys to Intelligence?

Intelligence, defined as the capacity for learning, reasoning, and understanding, is a familiar enough term, but the concept itself is often poorly understood. Intelligent people are frequently described as "quick," but a growing body of research suggests that intelligence has less to do with brain speed and more to do with executive control of working memory.

Assessing students' working memory using a delayed recall task, Meredyth Daneman and Patricia Carpenter found a strong correlation between working-memory scores and verbal SAT tests of reading comprehension, often viewed as an approximate indication of intelligence (Daneman & Carpenter, 1980), although others have argued it is simply an indicator of expected performance in college.

However, the relationship between working memory and intelligence does not depend only on verbal intelligence. Carpenter and her colleagues used puzzles based on standard non-verbal tests of intelligence, the Raven Progressive Matrices, that employ two-dimensional visual analogy problems in which the participant is directed to select the design that completes each pattern. The illustrative example shown in Figure 9.10 is a 3-by-3 array of geometric figures with one in the lower-right-hand corner missing. Participants must pick which of the six alternatives at the bottom best fits the pattern. What is the pattern? Note that each figure varies on two dimensions: the color (black, gray, or white) and the number of triangles (1, 2, or 3). Moreover, no row or column has two figures with the same number of triangles or the same color. To complete this pattern, the figure in the lower right would have to be white (there is no white figure in the third row or third column) and contain two triangles (there is no figure with two triangles in the third row or third column). Thus, the correct answer is #5, two white triangles.

An enormous range of difficulty can be introduced into this kind of task simply by increasing the complexity of the patterns or the number of components. Carpenter and colleagues showed that being able to juggle many rules in one's head is correlated with scoring high on non-verbal tests of intelligence. These kinds of evidence suggest that general intelligence, as detected by intelligence tests, is not just a matter of thinking or responding quickly. Rather, general intelligence appears to be associated with a strong working memory, especially the control and manipulation of larger numbers of rules, concepts, goals, and ideas.

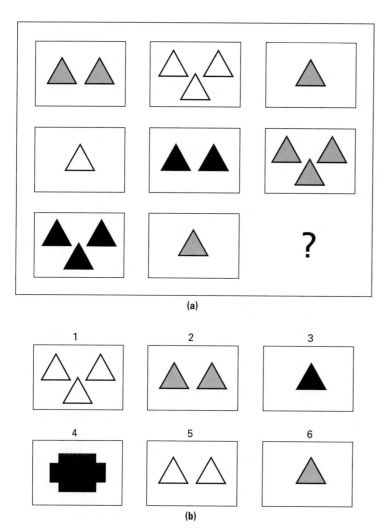

(a)

(b)

Figure 9.10 Raven Progressive Matrix Test of Nonverbal Intelligence Subjects are shown a three-by-three array of eight geometric figures and a space, in the lower-right-hand corner, where the ninth figure belongs. They must pick which of the six alternatives shown at the bottom best fits the pattern. (The correct answer is #5.)

The possibility that working memory and general intelligence are closely coupled suggests that if working memory can be improved through training and practice, a person's general intelligence might increase at the same time. A recent study showed this might indeed be possible. Participants in a training group went through extensive daily training on the N-back task, described earlier as a test that challenges manipulation, maintenance, and updating of working memory (Jaeggi et al., 2008, 2010). The more they were trained on this task, the better they performed on it. More important, however, the improved performance on the N-back task was accompanied by an increase in their general intelligence as measured by other tests, including tests like the Raven Matrix in Figure 9.10. Perhaps, then, what these intelligence tests measure is not fixed and innate but modifiable through selective training that strengthens the ability to put working memory to work.

Interim Summary

- Transient memories are temporary representations of information. They are found in the first two stages—sensory memory and short-term, or working, memory—of the Atkinson-Shiffrin model of the stages of memory storage.

Short-term memories can be maintained by active rehearsal but are easily displaced by new information or distractions.

- Alan Baddeley characterized working memory as consisting of two independent short-term memory buffers—the visuospatial sketchpad, which holds visual and spatial images, and the phonological loop, an auditory memory that uses internal speech rehearsal—along with a central executive.

- In Baddeley's model, the central executive is responsible for manipulating memories in the two buffers by, for example, adding and deleting items, selecting items to guide behavior, and retrieving information from and storing it in long-term memory.

- The manipulation and use of working memory for cognitive control can be measured through neuropsychological tests that assess such functions as controlled updating of short-term memory, setting goals and planning, task switching, and stimulus attention and response inhibition.

9.2 Brain Substrates

Could the frontal lobes contain the brain's chief executive, in charge of working memory, reasoning, and other cognitive functions? There is a growing consensus that the prefrontal cortex, with its extensive connections to more posterior regions of the brain, is critical for initiating executive functions and cognitive control and does so by synthesizing external and internal information needed to guide complex behaviors (Miller & Wallis, 2008). If this is the case, how do the frontal lobes mediate working memory and cognitive control? How does working memory work in the brain? These questions drive current research as scientists seek to understand to what extent psychological theories, such as Baddeley's model, correspond to how working memory is organized in the brain. Does the brain in fact possess a distinct, recognizable working memory system, or is working memory simply the transient and current activity of the brain's memory system in general? What about the hippocampus and medial temporal lobes: are they relevant to working memory, or are they only involved in storing new facts and events in long-term memory as described in Chapter 7?

The Frontal Lobes and Consequences of Frontal-Lobe Damage

Studies of animals and humans implicate the frontal lobes—especially the **prefrontal cortex (PFC),** the most anterior (farthest forward) section of the frontal lobes—as being critical for working memory and executive control. Since the beginning of modern brain research in the mid-1800s, the intellectual functions of planning, foresight, decision making, and related behaviors have been associated with this brain region (Markowitsch, 1992).

In humans, the prefrontal cortex encompasses approximately one-third of the cerebral cortex (Goldman-Rakic, 1987). Cats and many other mammals, on the other hand, get by with frontal lobes that occupy less than 4% of their cerebral cortex. Figure 9.11 compares the relative sizes of the prefrontal cortex in several mammalian species, showing how much larger, proportionally, our prefrontal cortex is compared with the prefrontal cortex in the cat, rhesus monkey, and chimpanzee. Because the prefrontal cortex occupies a markedly larger proportion of the cerebral cortex in humans than in many other mammals, many people have suggested that it is what makes us human. More recent studies, however, have

(a)

Cat

(c)

Rhesus
monkey

(b)

Chimpanzee

(d)

Human

Anterior
(front) ←——————————→ Posterior
(back)

Figure 9.11 Comparative frontal-lobe anatomy These drawings show the relative sizes of the prefrontal cortex in different mammals.
Adapted from Fuster, 1995.

shown that human frontal cortices are not disproportionally larger than those seen in great apes such as gorillas and orangutans. This suggests that the special human cognitive abilities attributed to large frontal lobes may also reflect characteristics other than size, such as more complex interconnections or specialized subregions found within the frontal cortex of humans (Semendeferi, Lu, Schenker, & Damasio., 2002).

Other insights into the role of the prefrontal cortex came from observing the behaviors of people with frontal-lobe damage. During World War I, for example, the many soldiers returning from battle with head wounds provided corroboration of the links between frontal lobes and intellect. A study of 300 veterans returning from World War I with head wounds showed that those veterans with frontal-lobe damage were the most impaired in higher intellectual abilities (Pfeifer, 1922).

One noted characteristic of frontal-lobe damage is a loss of ability to plan and to organize. You may recall Wilder Penfield, the famous neurosurgeon from the mid-twentieth century, whose work on brain mapping was reviewed in Chapter 7. One case described by Penfield was his own sister, who had a large tumor removed from her frontal regions. She had been an accomplished cook, but after the surgery she lost all ability to organize her cooking; she would move haphazardly from dish to dish, leaving some uncooked while others burned (Miller & Wallis, 2003). Or consider Elliot, a successful and happily married accountant, who had always been viewed by others as reliable and responsible. Then, in his late thirties, he developed a large tumor in his frontal lobes. Surgeons were able to remove the tumor and save his life. However, the operation severely damaged his frontal lobes (Eslinger & Damasio, 1985; Damasio, 1994; Miller & Wallis, 2008). Soon after the surgery, he divorced his wife, remarried and divorced again, lost touch with most of his friends and family, got involved in corrupt business deals, and was soon bankrupt. The formerly responsible and cautious Elliot became impulsive and easily swayed by momentary whims, retaining little of his previous ability to organize and plan.

Penfield's sister and Elliot were both behaving as we might expect in the absence of a cognitive-control system. They were no longer guided by long-term goals or task-specific constraints. Rather, they appeared to be ruled by their reflexive and automatic impulses and to have little capacity for foresight and planning. For this reason, people like Penfield's sister and Elliot are described as having **dysexecutive syndrome,** a disrupted ability to think and plan (Duncan, Emslie, Williams, Johnson, & Freer, 1996). As you will read below, patients with frontal-lobe damage routinely exhibit deficits in both executive function and working memory despite normal long-term memory and skill-learning abilities.

In addition to tumors and surgery, frontal lobes can be damaged by strokes or blunt trauma to the front of the head—or, as often happens, from a rapid deceleration (as in a car crash) in which the frontal lobes compress against the front of the skull. Professional (and even some high school) football players, who routinely head-butt other players and experience rapid deceleration, also show a pattern of frontal-lobe damage and associated cognitive problems (Amen et al., 2011).

People with damage to the frontal lobes show deficits on all of the working-memory and cognitive-control tasks described in Section 9.1. For example, they have great difficulty updating working memory in the N-back task as well as performing self-ordered tasks that require frequent updating to recollect items that have been previously chosen (Petrides, 2000). Patients with frontal-lobe damage are also often impaired at tasks that tap short-term memory span, including digit-span tasks, in which they may fail to recall even a short series of numbers (Janowsky, Shimamura, Kritchevsky, & Squire, 1989). Other studies of these patients have shown similar impairments in short-term memory for colors, shapes, and object locations (Baldo & Shimamura, 2000; Ptito, Crane, Leonard, Amsel, & Caramanos, 1995). Additionally, as you might expect, patients with frontal-lobe damage show deficits in neuropsychological tests such as the Tower of Hanoi, which assesses planning abilities and requires maintaining and linking multiple subgoals to achieve the final desired goal. On the Tower of Hanoi task, patients like Elliot or Penfield's sister move the disks around aimlessly, without a clear plan for getting the disks from the first peg to the last.

The ability to shift appropriately from one task to another is a central feature of executive control. Thus, the task-switching test procedures described in Section 9.1 provide another means of assessing frontal-lobe function. One study had participants monitor two streams of simultaneously presented stimuli, a series of letters on the left and a stream of digits on the right (Duncan, Emslie, Williams, Johnson, & Freer, 1996). At the beginning of the experiment, the participant was to read aloud the letters on the left. Later, when a signal cue was sounded, the person was supposed to switch to the other stream and begin reporting the digits. Later still, the signal would sound again as a sign that the participant should switch back to the letters. Although patients with frontal lesions had no trouble complying with the first part of the experiment, they had great difficulty switching between the left and right streams on cue.

The Wisconsin Card Sort Test (see Figure 9.8) is frequently used in clinical settings for assessment of frontal-lobe function. Frontal-lobe patients have no problem learning an initial sorting rule, such as to sort by color. Later, however, when the person must learn a new rule for sorting—say, by shape—frontal-lobe patients are severely impaired at making the transition. They show **perseveration,** which means they fail to learn a new rule but instead persist in using an old rule despite repeated feedback indicating that the old rule is no longer correct. The severe deficits in task shifting associated with frontal-lobe damage suggest that purposeful shifts in processing may be especially demanding of executive-control processes mediated by the frontal lobes (Delis, Squire, Bihrle, & Massman, 1992; Owen et al., 1993).

Carlyle Jacobsen, an early and important researcher in this area, conducted animal studies in the early 1930s that implicated the frontal cortex in working memory (Jacobsen, 1936). Specifically, he looked at the effects of lesions in different parts of the brain on delayed spatial-response learning in monkeys. In these studies, monkeys were permitted to observe food being placed either in a location on the left or on the right of a surface outside their cages. After a delay during which the monkeys were not able to see the food, the monkeys were required to point to where the food had been placed. Jacobsen demonstrated that only monkeys with prefrontal lesions were impaired at responding correctly, exhibiting a selective and delay-dependent deficit in the tasks. Based on these results, he argued that an animal's frontal lobes are critical for maintaining an internal representation of information in working memory over a delay prior to making some response.

One limitation of this early work was the relative crudity of Jacobsen's surgical techniques by modern standards: he removed a rather large part of the prefrontal cortex. More recent research has shown that different subregions of the prefrontal cortex participate in different aspects of working-memory function.

For example, the primate prefrontal cortex can be divided into three main regions: the *orbital prefrontal cortex,* the *medial prefrontal cortex,* and the *lateral prefrontal cortex.* The lateral prefrontal cortex can be further subdivided into two components: the **dorsolateral prefrontal cortex (DLPFC)** on the top and the **ventrolateral prefrontal cortex (VLPFC)** below it, as shown in Figure 9.12. In these images, the orbital frontal cortex is not visible because it lies ventral to (below) the regions shown, and the medial prefrontal cortex is also not visible

Anterior (front) ←→ Posterior (back)

Dorsolateral PFC

Ventrolateral PFC

Human

(a)

Anterior (front) ←→ Posterior (back)

Dorsolateral PFC

Ventrolateral PFC

Macaque monkey

(b)

Figure 9.12 Primate frontal lobes These drawings show subdivisions of the frontal lobes in humans and in macaque monkeys, identifying the dorsolateral prefrontal cortex (PFC) in green and the ventrolateral prefrontal cortex in purple. Note that the very tip of the dorsolateral PFC is sometimes also referred to as the frontal polar cortex.

because it is inside the regions shown, tucked away above and behind the orbital region. The orbital and medial prefrontal cortexes are both implicated in many memory and cognitive-control functions (especially goal-driven behavior and planning), but they are less involved in working memory than the lateral regions of the prefrontal cortex and so will not be discussed further in this chapter. Much of what we know about the role of the DLPFC and VLPFC in working memory comes from recordings of brain activity in humans and monkeys. Data from such studies will be discussed next.

Frontal Brain Activity during Working-Memory Tasks

Guided by lesion studies suggesting that the prefrontal cortex plays a role in working memory, researchers in the early 1970s began to record prefrontal-cortex neural activity during working-memory tasks (Fuster & Alexander, 1971; Kubota & Niki, 1971). In one such study, using a delayed-response task similar to the one used in the Jacobsen studies described above, rhesus macaque monkeys were required to remember either where they had seen a target object or what object they had previously seen (Fuster & Alexander, 1971). The researchers found that some prefrontal-cortex neurons fired only during a delay period and only when the animals were required to maintain information about a spatial location of a particular object. This suggested that the prefrontal cortex was "holding in mind" information needed to make a later response and that the neural activity in the prefrontal cortex was acting as a temporal bridge between stimulus cues and a contingent response concerning object location, linking events across time. Such activity appears to be a key component of sensory-motor behaviors that span delays (Fuster, 2001, 2003). Persistent activity of this type in the DLPFC during blank memory intervals (delays, when no external stimulation is present) is a strong argument implicating the DLPFC as a critical brain region supporting the maintenance of items in working memory (Curtis & D'Esposito, 2006).

Instead of requiring an animal to pick up an object or point to a location, some experiments simply track the animal's gaze. Eye-tracking technology offers well-controlled methods for testing spatial and object working memory in animals. Patricia Goldman-Rakic of Yale University Medical School, one of the pioneers in working-memory research, used this technology in a series of highly influential studies of primate working memory.

In her studies, Goldman-Rakic trained monkeys to fixate on a central spot on a display as shown in Figure 9.13a (top row). The monkeys maintained their fixation on the central spot while a square cue was presented at one of eight locations around the edge of the display (e.g., the upper-right corner, as in Figure 9.13a). After the cue was removed, the monkeys waited during a delay period of several seconds (Figure 9.13b) and then, at a certain signal, responded by moving their gaze to the cue's former location (Figure 9.13c). Moving the gaze to the correct location resulted in a reward.

In electrophysiological recordings of these tasks, Goldman-Rakic and colleagues found that some of the neurons in the dorsolateral prefrontal cortex fired only while the animal was remembering the stimulus location (Funahashi, Bruce, & Goldman-Rakic, 1989). As shown in the electrical recordings in the middle row of Figure 9.13, certain neurons in the prefrontal cortex fire during presentation of the cue itself (Figure 9.13a; note the increase in firing during presentation of the cue in the area between the two red lines on the left), others fire only during the delay period (Figure 9.13b; note the increase in firing during the delay period), while others fire during the response (Figure 9.13c; note the increase in firing to the right of the right-most red line). Each of these three recordings in Figure 9.13 shows a different neuron.

(a) Cue   **(b)** Delay   **(c)** Response

Cue Delay Response   Cue Delay Response   Cue Delay Response

Figure 9.13 **The spatial delayed-response eye-gaze task** (a) The monkey fixates on a central spot on the screen while a cue flashes in the upper-right corner. (b) During a delay period, the cue disappears and the monkey remains fixated on the central point. (c) Finally, when the central spot turns off, the monkey looks where the cue previously appeared. (For clarity, the monkey is shown in mirror image in the figure so we can see it gaze in the direction of the stimulus shown above).

Data from Funahashi, Bruce, & Goldman-Rakic, 1989.

Most interesting of all is that the "delay" neurons were individually tuned to different directional movements. For example, one neuron might code for a movement to the right, while another neuron might code for a downward movement, and so on. Figure 9.14 shows the strong response of a particular neuron when the cue was located at the bottom center of the screen, that is, at 270 degrees (bottom-center graph), compared with the inhibition of its electrical activity when the cue was in the opposite location, namely, at 90 degrees, and to the moderate activity when the cue was at other locations.

Figure 9.14 **Response of one prefrontal cortex neuron during the eye-gaze delayed-response task** Electrophysiological activity of the neuron during the cue, delay, and response periods of the task when the cue was presented at different locations. Note the strong response when the cue was at the bottom location (indicated by the blue outline) compared with the inhibited activity when the cue was presented at the top-center location. From Funahashi et al., 1989. (For clarity, the monkey is shown in mirror image in the figure so that we see it gaze in the same direction as the stimulus being shown to it.)

The strong firing seen in Figure 9.14 during the delay for the trial in which the cue was at 270 degrees could represent one of two things: it could be a memory for where the cue had appeared or it could be an anticipatory coding for the later movement of the eye gaze to that location. To distinguish between these alternatives, the researchers conducted an experiment in which the monkeys were trained to move their eyes to the location opposite to the cue. In that study, about 80% of the delay cells seemed to encode where the target had been (regardless of the eye-gaze response), while the other 20% seemed to encode the intended movement. These results suggest that the neurons of the dorsolateral prefrontal cortex that fire during the delay are encoding a combination of sensory and movement-response information.

The monkeys did quite well at this delayed-response task, but they never performed it with 100% accuracy. Occasionally, they would make an error and move their eyes to the wrong position. Was it just a motor mistake, or was the prefrontal cortex itself confused as to the correct answer? The researchers found the latter to be true: the electrophysiological recordings predicted when a monkey was going to make an error because the "wrong" neurons fired in the dorsolateral prefrontal cortex.

Sustained neuronal activity during the delay period is not limited, however, to the dorsolateral prefrontal cortex. Similar sustained activity can also be seen in the relevant primary and secondary sensory and motor regions in the temporal and parietal lobes of the brain. These regions are reciprocally connected to the prefrontal cortex.

If the sensory and motor cortexes can sustain activity, assuming that sustained activity is indeed critical for working memory, why should the prefrontal cortex be necessary for working memory to function? Earl Miller argued that the key "cognitive" contribution of the prefrontal cortex to working memory is the ability of the prefrontal cortex to sustain activity *despite distractions* (Miller, 2000). To test his hypothesis, Miller and colleagues trained monkeys to maintain the visual memory of an object throughout a delay period filled with visually distracting events (Miller, Erickson, & Desimone, 1996). They found that activity in the posterior visual cortical areas was easily disrupted by the distractors. In contrast, the corresponding dorsolateral prefrontal-cortex activity remained robust despite distractions. The ability of the prefrontal cortex to provide focused control over working memory is consistent with lesion data demonstrating that one salient consequence of prefrontal-cortex damage, both in humans and in monkeys, is a high degree of distractibility. In particular, studies in monkeys have argued that prefrontal cortex neurons, by robustly sustaining their activity, keep behaviorally relevant information at hand, so to speak, and available to guide behaviors (Asaad, Rainer, & Miller, 1998), consistent with the data from monkeys and humans showing the prefrontal cortex to have a key role in guiding goal-directed behaviors.

Studies in humans, too, have shown persistent activity in the DLPFC during the retention interval of delayed-response tasks. Event-related fMRI studies of humans have recorded persistent activity in the DLPFC during retention intervals of delayed-response tasks. This is illustrated in Figure 9.15, which shows similar patterns of activity from both monkey and human DLPFC during the delay period in a task in which subjects were required to withhold responding to a cue during a delay period, as in the studies of Goldman-Rakic and others described above.

Why is this persistent activity in the DLPFC critical for executive-control processes? One view is that top-down signals from the DLPFC have a diverse range of roles in controlling behavior, depending on which brain region is the

Figure 9.15 Activity in monkey and human DLPFC during the retention interval of a delayed-response task (a) Average of single-unit recordings of neurons with delay-period activity from monkey DLPFC (data adapted from Funahashi et al., 1989). (b) Significant maintenance-related activity (left) and average fMRI signal (right) from right DLPFC in a human performing a delayed-response task. The gray bar represents the length of the delay interval. In both examples, the level of DLPFC activity persists throughout the delay, seconds after the stimulus cue has disappeared.
From C. E. Curtis & M. D'Esposito, 2003.

recipient of the signal (Curtis & D'Esposito, 2003). That is, the DLPFC may always be performing the same general function—control—but in controlling different regions, its effects on different behaviors may be quite varied. Thus, top-down signals from the DLPFC might enhance and maintain internal representations of relevant sensory stimuli in different posterior sensory and motor centers until those representations are required for subsequent actions and decisions.

Mapping Executive Processing and Working Memory onto PFC Anatomy

The lesion, electrophysiological, and imaging studies reviewed above leave two critical questions unanswered: (1) how are the frontal lobes organized, and (2) how does working memory actually work? In particular, are there different physical systems (or anatomical regions) in the brain for executive processes (memory manipulation) and rehearsal processes (memory maintenance), as suggested by Baddeley's model? That is, does the *functional* distinction between manipulation and rehearsal proposed by Baddeley correspond to an actual *anatomical* distinction between distinguishable brain regions? Also, are there anatomical distinctions associated with the two material-specific rehearsal stores, namely, the visuospatial sketchpad and the phonological loop? These questions concerning organization and function have dominated research in the neurobiology of working memory, and we turn next to discussing them in more detail.

Maintenance (Rehearsal) versus Manipulation (Cognitive Control)

The manipulation-versus-maintenance distinction suggested by Baddeley's model has been explored extensively by Michael Petrides and colleagues, who have concluded that the dorsal and ventral regions of the prefrontal cortex perform qualitatively different processes (Owen, Evans, & Petrides, 1996; Petrides, 1994, 1996). Their findings, summarized in Figure 9.16, indicate that the ventrolateral prefrontal cortex supports the active controlled

Figure 9.16 Brain substrates of working memory The dorsolateral prefrontal cortex supports higher-order cognitive-control functions, such as monitoring and manipulating of stored information, and acts much like Baddeley's central executive. The ventrolateral prefrontal cortex supports encoding and retrieval of information, performing the functions of the visuospatial sketchpad (right) and phonological rehearsal loops (left). Other brain regions named at bottom are connected to the VLPFC for maintenance of verbal and object and location information.

encoding and retrieval of information. This ventrolateral prefrontal region, in interaction with posterior cortical regions, may be contributing to the roles of the visuospatial sketchpad and phonological rehearsal loop (more recently described as two separate loops, as we observe at the end of the Brain Substrates section) proposed by Baddeley. In contrast, the dorsolateral prefrontal cortex supports higher-order cognitive-control functions, such as monitoring and manipulating of stored information, functioning much like Baddeley's central executive.

To test this mapping of processes to brain regions, as portrayed in Figure 9.16, Petrides and colleagues developed the self-ordered delayed-response tasks described in Section 9.1. You'll recall that in the monkey version of this task (see Figure 9.7), the monkey obtains the most treats by remembering which of three containers it has already chosen. A 10-second delay, during which the containers are hidden, occurs between each opportunity to choose. Monkeys with lesions to parts of the DLPFC were severely impaired at this task and could not determine which containers had already been emptied and which still contained a reward. The spatial component of the information was made irrelevant in this task because the containers were moved randomly during the delays. In contrast, these same monkeys were able to *maintain* object memories over varying delays (as opposed to manipulating those memories) and showed no problems solving basic delayed-*recognition* tasks (Petrides, 1995). In another study, Petrides (2000) showed that increasing the number of items to be monitored in these tasks exacerbated the impairments due to DLPFC lesions, whereas simply extending the delay time did not. Again, this finding implicates the DLPFC in monitoring but not in the maintenance of information in working memory. Thus, basic mnemonic judgments about recently seen objects, which require only maintenance of information during a delay, are not affected by DLPFC lesions. These maintenance functions are instead thought to be controlled by loops between the frontal lobes and more posterior regions of the brain, such as the posterior cortical speech and language areas (for verbal information) and the posterior cortical visual areas (for object and location information), as shown in Figure 9.16.

Several recent studies have attempted to differentiate between the brain substrates for passive rehearsal of information in working memory and those for the more active process of updating information in working memory. Rehearsal supports working memory by reactivating or refreshing briefly stored representations, whereas the updating of information consists of adding information to or removing it from working memory. Imaging studies indicate that there is brain activity in the premotor cortex during rehearsal of visuospatial information (Awh & Jonides, 1998). Other fMRI studies suggest that the ventrolateral prefrontal cortex is activated by simple rehearsal, especially internal rehearsal (Awh et al., 1996). In contrast, more posterior regions of the brain appear to be involved only in the temporary maintenance of spatial working memory, not in its rehearsal. Many other neuroimaging studies have also confirmed a general distinction between storage mechanisms in the posterior regions of the brain and rehearsal mechanisms in the anterior regions (Smith & Jonides, 2004), including the prefrontal cortex, as schematized in Figure 9.16.

The Visuospatial and Phonological-Verbal Buffers

As you learned in the Behavioral Processes section, Baddeley's model of working memory assumed the existence of two main memory buffers, one for visuospatial memory and the other for phonological-verbal memory. Studies of working memory in monkeys have, of course, been limited to studies of visuospatial memory because of the lack of verbal language in these nonhuman primates. All studies of phonological and verbal working memory have thus relied on the use of human participants. In spite of such limitations, there is evidence to support the idea that these two forms of working memory are produced in different parts of the brain. Studies of patients with selective brain damage to different parts of their frontal lobe suggest that the neural substrates of verbal working memory are localized more on the left side of the brain, while spatial working memory is more dependent on the right side of the brain.

Consistent with this finding of right-side dominance in spatial working memory from patient studies, Petrides and colleagues (Petrides, Alivisatos, Evans, & Meyer, 1993a, 1993b) have conducted functional brain imaging studies of healthy individuals performing self-ordered tasks and found that when the items to be monitored were abstract designs, the self-ordered tasks produced significant activity in the DLPFC, predominantly in the right hemisphere (Figure 9.17a). When the items consisted of verbal material, the activity was more intense in the left hemisphere, although strong activity occurred in both the left and right sides of the DLPFC (Figure 9.17b). From these results, the researchers concluded that while the right DLPFC has a dominant role in all monitoring processes, the left DLPFC is specialized for verbal materials.

Behavioral studies reviewed earlier in this chapter have indicated that verbal working memory retains items in a phonological code based on the sounds of the words and that these items are retained through a rehearsal process similar to internally rehearsed speech (Baddeley, 1986). Consistent with the general tendency for language to be left-lateralized in the brain, frontal-lobe patients with damage to the left side are most likely to show specialized deficits in verbal (as opposed to visuospatial) working memory (Shallice, 1988).

Figure 9.17 Brain imaging during self-ordered tasks (a) Imaging data from a self-ordered task in which subjects had to remember previous selections made from a set of abstract designs show predominantly right-hemisphere activity in the prefrontal cortex. (b) Imaging data from a self-ordered task in which the items to be remembered were a set of verbal stimuli show both left- and right-hemisphere activity in the prefrontal cortex (although only the left activity is shown here). Adapted from Petrides, 2000, *Brain Mapping*, with permission from Elsevier.

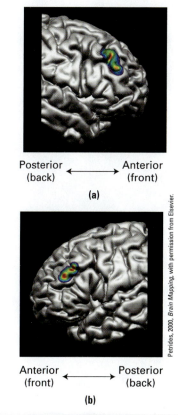

Posterior (back) ←→ Anterior (front)

(a)

Anterior (front) ←→ Posterior (back)

(b)

Petrides, 2000, *Brain Mapping*, with permission from Elsevier.

Improving Your Working Memory

Because working memory and executive control are fundamental to our higher cognitive abilities, it is natural to ask, what can I do to improve mine? A key finding from research on working memory is that our visuospatial and verbal working memories are independent, each with a limited capacity. You can probably keep only about 3 to 5 items in either store at any one time, which makes remembering a 10-digit phone number a bit tricky. One possible solution when you need to remember a long list of items is to make the independence of visuospatial and verbal memory stores work *for* you rather than against you. For example, if you need to remember several words at once, such as people's names, consider converting some of the words into pictures so that both memory buffers can share the daunting task.

The biggest drain on our working memory comes from multi-tasking, or attempting to accomplish several goals at once. How often do you talk on the phone, listen to music, and surf the Internet all at the same time? You can bet that your dorsolateral PFC is working overtime when you do. Of more concern is multi-tasking during dangerous tasks, such as driving in traffic. Have you ever seen someone try to read the newspaper, apply nail polish, or talk on a cell phone while behind the wheel? Unfortunately, traffic accidents often result from people's attempts to multi-task while driving their cars. For this reason, many states have banned cell-phone use while driving, especially the use of handheld phones.

An overloaded working memory impairs the ability to accurately monitor and evaluate our cognitive functioning. You may think your driving is just fine or that you can absorb the main ideas in your professor's lecture while you work on other projects (like Roberta, who studies chemistry during French class), but research has shown that you are probably not operating at as high a level as you think. Focusing on one task at a time greatly improves the ability to use working memory effectively. In contrast, high levels of stress reduce the working-memory span and the ability to concentrate and focus cognitive control. Some research has suggested that stress elevates dopamine levels in the prefrontal cortex, impairing its ability to efficiently monitor and update information.

Why tax your working memory if you don't need to? Maybe it's time to shut off that cell phone, grab a pad of paper (think of it as a third working-memory buffer), and start writing things down.

Given how critical an optimally functioning working memory is to our daily lives, many people wish they could improve theirs. For tips on how this might be possible, see the "Learning and Memory in Everyday Life" box above.

The Functional Significance of Frontal-Posterior Connections

The influence of contemporaneous technologies on the theories and models developed for explaining the workings of the mind was a recurring theme in Chapter 1 (see Table 1.2). You read, for example, that the hydraulic mechanisms of the royal gardens outside Paris in the early 1600s inspired Descartes' view of reflexes in the body, while almost two centuries later, the newly invented telephone exchanges informed Pavlov's view of direct versus indirect (learned) pathways in the brain. The rapid development of digital computers in the 1960s and 1970s had a similarly strong impact on theories of mind in psychology. The computers were equipped with active memory buffers that could be used for running programs on the computer. These active memory buffers were built into circuit boards that were physically distinct from the computer's long-term memory storage, which at the time, in contrast, used magnetic tapes or paper cards with punched holes. For a computer program to access information from the long-term memory devices, the desired information had to be physically transferred from the long-term data-storage systems to the active-memory circuits, the latter being a limited temporary buffer for active use and manipulation by programs currently running on the computer.

It is not surprising that early psychological models of working memory, such as those of Baddeley, Shiffrin, Shallice, and their colleagues, which were being developed in the 1960s and early 1970s, drew on these digital computers as metaphors for understanding the relationships between working memory and long-term memory in the human brain. It was popular then to view the human brain as a biological variant exhibiting the same principles of computing found in digital computers. That is, the idea that working memory was a physical system quite distinct from long-term memory was completely consistent with how digital computers of the era were designed.

Anterior (front)   Posterior (back)

Figure 9.18 **Maintenance in working memory through frontal-posterior circuits** This schematic representation of frontal-posterior connections illustrates two sample loops, one dorsal and the other ventral. For each, the frontal activity projects back to the posterior areas (along red arrows), which in turn project back to the frontal lobes (along green arrows). The net result is that frontal activity induces sustained activation of posterior regions.

The standard psychological model of working memory as popularized by Baddeley and colleagues was hugely influential and extremely valuable for guiding the first few decades of research on working memory and the brain. The core of this standard model was that the functions of working memory arise from operation of specialized brain systems that act as buffers for the temporary storage and manipulation of information (as seen in digital computers of that era) and that frontal cortex (particularly prefrontal cortex) was the critical neural substrate for these buffers. More recently, some researchers have argued that while the prefrontal cortex is essential for most aspects of working memory, we should not jump to the conclusion that the physical substrates of working memory, especially the rehearsal and storage of sensory information, reside completely within the frontal lobes (Postle, 2006). Rather, a novel theory has developed in recent years in which working-memory functions are viewed as arising through coordinated recruitment and sustained activation by the frontal lobes of more posterior brain systems that store sensory representations and perform action-related functions. This new perspective argues that the information in working memory resides in the same place as long-term memory, namely in the posterior sensory, perceptual, and motor brain regions of the cerebral cortex. The role of the frontal cortex in working memory is thus reconceptualized as a system for manipulating and altering whatever parts of the long-term memory regions are to be transiently active and for deciding when they are to be activated and how long the activation should persist.

In summary, this view of working memory sees working memory as emerging from a network of brain regions, all of which send and receive controlling information to and from the prefrontal cortex. Together these networks accomplish the active maintenance of internal representations necessary for goal-directed behavior (D'Esposito, 2007; Postle, 2006), as illustrated in Figure 9.18.

Goal Abstraction and Frontal-Lobe Organization

"What are you doing?" asks your roommate. Any of several answers would be equally correct: "Making a sandwich," "Spreading peanut butter on bread," or "Moving this knife from left to right." These three answers all accurately describe what you are doing at the moment, but they do so at different levels of abstraction. "Making a sandwich" is the most abstract description of your current activity, and it also describes your ultimate goal. There are of course many different ways to make a sandwich, as well as a wide variety of ingredients. "Spreading peanut butter on bread" is thus a more specific description of what

Figure 9.19 The anterior-posterior gradient of goal abstraction within the frontal cortex Three levels of abstraction of goals are shown for two examples—the making of a sandwich (top text in each balloon) and the Tower of Hanoi task (lower text)—illustrating approximate locations in the frontal cortex for control of each level of abstraction.

you are doing and also defines a more specific goal (it begins to identify what type of sandwich you are making). To spread the peanut butter on the bread, however, requires a specific action, the movement of the knife across the bread from left to right (and afterward, back from right to left).

Keeping goals of various degrees of abstraction in working memory as you proceed with a task has long been known to involve the frontal lobes. This is why people like Penfield's sister, with frontal-lobe damage, have so much trouble cooking (including, most likely, preparing peanut butter sandwiches). The Tower of Hanoi, introduced in Chapter 8 (see Figure 8.1), also requires keeping a wide range of goals in mind, from the most abstract ("Move all disks to the right-hand peg") to the most specific level ("Move the yellow disk to the middle peg). Impairments in solving the Tower of Hanoi puzzle have long been recognized as a sign of frontal-lobe dysfunction.

Although neuroscientists have long known that keeping goals in working memory while working on complex tasks depends heavily on the frontal lobes, recent research has suggested that the gradient of abstraction from general plans and goals to more specific action plans follows a physical gradient beginning at the front of the frontal lobes and moving back (Badre, 2008; Badre & D'Esposito, 2007). As illustrated in Figure 9.19, the most abstract plans (make sandwich, move all disks to right peg) depend on the most anterior (front) part of the frontal lobes. The more concrete and specific the goals or plans that must be maintained in working memory, the more posterior the localization of their function within the frontal lobes.

Some of the evidence for this gradient of abstraction comes from people with brain damage due to stroke: people with damage toward the front of their frontal lobes are most impaired at tasks requiring cognitive control at a high level of abstraction. Converging data comes from lesion studies in monkeys that show a double dissociation between the effects of posterior frontal-lobe lesions and the effects of mid-frontal-lobe lesions. Lesions to the more posterior regions of the frontal lobes disrupt performance in domain-specific motor learning tasks but not in domain-general monitoring; in contrast, lesions to the middle part of the

DLPFC impair performance in general monitoring tasks but not in domain-specific tasks (Fuster, 2004; Petrides, 2006).

Human functional imaging studies provide converging evidence for this abstract-specific gradient: tasks that require maintaining more abstract, high-level goals activate a wider part of the frontal lobes, including the more anterior regions toward the frontal pole of the brain (Koechlin, Ody, & Kouneiher, 2003; Badre & D'Esposito, 2007). Imaging studies have also suggested that the flow of control within the frontal cortex goes from the most anterior regions (for the highest levels of abstract goals) toward the back of the frontal lobes (for the more specific subgoals), consistent with the idea that it is the desire to make a sandwich that drives you to butter the bread, not vice versa (Koechlin et al., 2003).

What if it was not your roommate who asked what you were doing but your kid brother? And what if he wanted to help? If your kid brother is 15, you might point him to the cabinets and say, "Make a sandwich for yourself." But if he were only 6, you might hand him a piece of bread with peanut butter on it along with a (plastic) knife and instruct him to spread it back and forth. In other words, the older the child, the more likely you are to assign him a higher-level abstract goal. Younger children need more specific, concrete goals and plans. Might the difference in their abilities be due to differences in the maturity of the circuits in the more anterior parts of their frontal lobes? Indeed, longitudinal data show that maturation of the circuit wiring in the frontal lobes progresses throughout childhood from the more posterior regions that support concrete plans toward the anterior regions that support more abstract planning, with the latter not becoming fully mature until late adolescence (Shaw et al., 2008). Chapter 12 provides more information about critical periods in brain maturation and their impact on cognition across the life-span.

Prefrontal Control of Long-Term Declarative Memory

What was the last movie you saw? To answer this question, you may have to perform a number of mental operations. For example, you might search your memory by calling to mind every movie that you know to be currently playing, noting which ones you have seen and then trying to recall which of them you saw most recently. Alternatively, you could search your memory by thinking back over your recent activities in reverse chronological order. Knowing that you go out to movies on the weekends, you might first think back to last weekend. Did you see a movie? If not, think back to the previous weekend. However you choose to set about answering this question, the process of searching your memory requires considerable strategic manipulation and control of memory processes as well as maintaining, throughout this search, an awareness of your ultimate goal: the name of the last movie you saw. This is exactly the kind of task that uses the prefrontal cortex in multiple capacities. Some patients with prefrontal-cortex damage exhibit significant deficits in retrieval of long-term memories (Shimamura et al., 1995; Mangels, Gershberg, Shimamura, & Knight, 1996).

In the beginning of this chapter, we defined short-term memory as an active, temporary representation of information that either was just perceived or was just retrieved from long-term memory. Most of this chapter has focused on the former class of information—information that was recently experienced. In this section, we briefly discuss how working memory (and hence short-term memory) interacts with long-term memory. We focus especially on long-term memories of previously stored episodes or facts.

Neuroimaging has been particularly useful in furthering our understanding of how the frontal lobes and working memory guide the controlled search of long-term memory. Recall that Petrides and colleagues argued that the ventrolateral prefrontal cortex supports active rehearsal and maintenance functions, while the dorsolateral prefrontal cortex supports higher-order executive-control functions, such as monitoring and manipulation of stored information (Petrides, 2002). Thus, the kinds of executive control and manipulation of memory needed for retrieval of specific episodic memories, such as the last movie you saw, should be subserved by the dorsolateral prefrontal cortex. In fact, this is exactly what functional neuroimaging has shown: the dorsolateral prefrontal cortex is activated during people's attempts to remember past events (Nyberg, Cabeza, & Tulving, 1996; Wagner, Desmond, Glover, & Gabrieli, 1998).

Have you ever met someone at a party who seems familiar and yet you can't remember how you know her? (Is she an elementary school classmate or did you meet on that summer trip to Israel?) You just can't recall, but you do know you met before. On the other hand, very often you will see a person and not only realize that he is familiar but immediately remember how and where you met. (The former phenomenon, known as source amnesia, is introduced in Chapter 7.) According to a study by Anthony Wagner, Daniel Schacter, and colleagues, you probably used your dorsolateral prefrontal cortex in the latter situation, in which you recollected the source of your memory, but not in the former situation, in which you knew that the person was familiar but could not remember why (Dobbins, Foley, Schacter, & Wagner, 2002). In their study, people were shown various words and asked one of two questions: "Is it abstract or concrete?" or "Is it pleasant or unpleasant?" Later, they were shown the words again and were asked either if they remembered seeing the word during the first part of the experiment (that is, did they recall whether the word was considered at all) or if they remembered which task the word appeared in (did they recall judging it on the concrete/abstract dimension or on the pleasant/unpleasant dimension). As shown in Figure 9.20, the dorsolateral prefrontal cortex was more active when people were asked to recall the source of the word (that is, which task it was used in) than when they were asked whether or not the word had appeared at all (regardless of task).

Figure 9.20 Dorsolateral prefrontal activity during recollection of source Comparing trials in which participants were asked to recall the source of a word to trials where they were only asked if the word were familiar, fMRI studies show that multiple left prefrontal, as well as lateral and medial parietal, regions were more active during source recollection than during mere familiarity judgments. (a) The view from the front of the brain; (b) the brain's left side.

Data from Dobbins, Foley, Schacter, & Wagner, 2002.

Anterior (front) → Posterior (back)

Dobbins, I.G., Foley, H., Schacter, D.L., & Wagner, A.D. (2002). Executive control during episodic retrieval: Multiple prefrontal processes subserve source memory. Neuron, 35, 989–996, with permission from Elsevier.

(a) (b)

Of course, long-term memories can only be retrieved after having been encoded and stored. This encoding and storing of new information can be either incidental or intentional. *Incidental storage* occurs when information is learned as an accidental by-product of some other task. For example, if asked when the pot on the stove began boiling, you might recall that the pot was copper colored, even if there was no particular reason for you to have noticed that detail. The alternative, *intentional storage*, occurs when information is learned as the result of an explicit effort to remember a particular fact or event for later retrieval. Much of your studying for exams is an effort to intentionally store new information to be recalled later, whereas recalling that the professor was wearing a hideous red plaid shirt during the lecture is more likely to be a result of incidental storage. (See also the discussion of the explicit vs. implicit distinction in memory in Chapter 7.)

If, as Petrides argued, the ventrolateral prefrontal cortex supports active rehearsal and maintenance functions, then we might expect to see more VLPFC activity during intentional active encoding in contrast to the DLPFC activity seen in retrieval (Petrides, 2002). Functional imaging studies using fMRI and PET have indeed reliably shown that intentional encoding of new memories activates the ventrolateral prefrontal cortex. Because most of these studies used meaningful stimuli, such as images of nameable real-word objects, the *left* VLPFC is primarily activated, consistent with the general tendency of the left prefrontal cortex to be specialized for verbal processing (Nyberg et al., 1996).

The functional role of the left ventrolateral prefrontal cortex during encoding of new semantic information can be further subdivided into the contributions of its anterior (front) and posterior (back) regions, as illustrated in Figure 9.16. Anterior regions are activated during tasks that involve semantic processing (Thompson-Schill, D'Esposito, Aquirre, & Farah, 1997), while posterior regions are activated during phonological processing (Buckner, Raichle, Miezin, & Petersen, 1996). Thus, remembering the name of a wealthy new acquaintance, Bill, by noting that he probably has lots of bills in his wallet (a *semantic* elaboration of a meaning of the word "bill") would likely involve processing by your *anterior* ventrolateral prefrontal cortex. In contrast, rehearsing a complex foreign-sounding name over and over likely involves *phonological* processing in the *posterior* ventrolateral prefrontal cortex.

Further support for this anterior-posterior differentiation comes from a study that compared brain activity of people making either a semantic analysis of words ("Is it abstract or concrete?") or a phonological analysis ("How many syllables does it contain?"). Although the posterior region of the left ventrolateral prefrontal cortex was activated during both tasks—reflecting a common phonological component—only the semantic task resulted in activation of the anterior left ventrolateral prefrontal cortex (Poldrack et al., 1999). In contrast, other researchers subsequently demonstrated that nonsemantic tasks that involved only phonological processing activated the posterior, but not the anterior, regions of the left ventrolateral prefrontal cortex (Wagner, Koutstaal, Maril, Schachter, & Buckner, 2000). Refer again to Figure 9.16 for a schematic map of which type of working memory tasks involve which brain regions.

Overall, there are numerous parallels between the role of the prefrontal cortex in working memory (along with the precise location of its activity) and its role in episodic memory. Thus, the control processes and rehearsal mechanisms implicated in working memory appear to also play crucial roles in the encoding and retrieval of long-term memories for episodic and semantic information (Wagner, 2002).

Test Your Knowledge

Functional Neuroanatomy of the Prefrontal Cortex

For each of the following four activities, identify the region in the prefrontal cortex whose activity is most critical. (Answers appear in the Answers section in the back of the book.)

1. Deciding who should sit where around a dinner table set for eight to avoid seating ex-spouses and feuding ex-business partners next to each other.
2. Rehearsing the toast you will make at your brother's wedding.
3. Learning the definitions of "distributor," "ignition coil," and "carburetor" from reading a car-repair manual.
4. Remembering how to pronounce the name of the French exchange student you just met.
5. Remembering where you parked and deciding which way to walk to your parking spot as you exit the department store at the mall.

Interim Summary

- Studies with both animals and humans implicate the frontal lobes of the brain—especially the prefrontal cortex (PFC), the most anterior section of the frontal lobes—as critical for working memory and cognitive control.

- The ventrolateral prefrontal cortex supports encoding and retrieval of information (including rehearsal for maintenance), performing as the visuospatial sketchpad and phonological rehearsal loop proposed by Baddeley, while the dorsolateral prefrontal cortex supports higher-order executive-control functions such as monitoring and manipulating of stored information, thus doing the job of Baddeley's central executive.

- Working memory is now believed to result from functional interactions between the prefrontal cortex and the rest of the brain.

- During encoding of new verbal information, the *anterior* prefrontal cortex is activated for tasks that involve *semantic* processing, while the *posterior* prefrontal cortex is activated for *phonological* processing.

- The more concrete and specific the goals or plans that must be maintained in working memory, the more posterior the localization of their function within the frontal lobes, forming an anterior-to-posterior gradient that follows the functional gradient from abstract to specific.

9.3 Clinical Perspectives

Research on the role of the prefrontal cortex in working memory and cognitive control has provided clues for improving the diagnosis and treatment of several common neurological and psychiatric disorders. Two of the most common disorders involving dysfunctional prefrontal circuits are schizophrenia and attention deficit/hyperactivity disorder (ADHD).

Schizophrenia

Chapter 6 describes some of the memory deficits associated with hippocampal dysfunction in schizophrenia. In the current chapter, our discussion of schizophrenia focuses instead on the ways in which frontal lobe dysfunction contributes to symptoms of the disorder. People suffering from schizophrenia display disturbances in both cognition and memory, especially in working memory and executive control (Forbes, Carrick, McIntosh, & Lawrie, 2009). This finding is consistent with a wide range of other data suggesting that the dorsolateral prefrontal cortex is dysfunctional in schizophrenia. In contrast, functions attributed to the ventrolateral prefrontal cortex seem relatively unimpaired in patients with schizophrenia. For example, people with schizophrenia have close to normal performance on phonological or visuospatial memory tasks (Barch, Csernansky, Conturo, Snyder, & Ollinger, 2002) and on memory tasks involving only minimal delays or few items to keep track of (Park & Holzman, 1992). However, patients with schizophrenia are especially impaired at visuospatial working-memory tasks when these tasks involve the manipulation or updating of information in working memory (Park & Holzman, 1992). Similar cognitive-control deficits are also seen in close relatives of schizophrenic patients (Park, Holzman, & Goldman-Rakic, 1992).

Neuroimaging provides further insights into prefrontal-cortex dysfunction in schizophrenia. Daniel Weinberger and colleagues presented the first neuroimaging evidence for dorsolateral prefrontal-cortex dysfunction in schizophrenia by measuring blood flow in different cerebral regions (Weinberger, Berman, & Zec, 1986). They found that when patients with schizophrenia tried to solve the Wisconsin Card Sorting Test (see Figure 9.8), their dorsolateral prefrontal cortex showed no evidence of increased blood flow as it would in healthy normal individuals. Thus, in Figure 9.21, the healthy controls—but not the schizophrenic patients—show elevated frontal-lobe activation during the Wisconsin Card Sorting Test (WCS) as compared with a control task that involved only simple counting ("Number"). Moreover, there was a correlation among the schizophrenia subjects between the amount of blood flow in this region and performance: the greater the blood flow in the dorsolateral prefrontal cortex, the better the patients performed on the Wisconsin Card Sorting Test.

More recent studies provide further evidence for a cognitive-control deficit in schizophrenia, localized within the dorsolateral prefrontal cortex. For example, researchers found that schizophrenia correlates with depressed dorsolateral prefrontal-cortex activity during the N-back task, which, as you learned in Section 9.1, is a standard test of the manipulation of working memory. Ventral and posterior prefrontal-cortex activity, however, is normal in these patients, suggesting that rehearsal mechanisms, associated with these ventral and posterior areas, are less affected by schizophrenia (Barch et al., 2002). These neuroimaging results are consistent with postmortem studies of schizophrenic patients that reveal neural pathologies in the dorsolateral prefrontal cortex but not in more ventral regions.

Inefficient Prefrontal Cortical Systems in Schizophrenia

Recent functional-brain-imaging studies of patients with schizophrenia suggest that their reduced capacity for executive aspects of working memory is accompanied by engagement of a larger network of other cortical regions, consistent with the idea that they are recruiting compensatory networks that

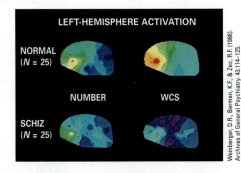

Weinberger, D.R., Berman, K.F., & Zec, R.F. (1986). Archives of General Psychiatry, 43.114–125.

Figure 9.21 Cerebral blood flow during the Wisconsin Card Sorting Test Healthy controls ("NORMAL"), but not the schizophrenic patients ("SCHIZ"), have elevated frontal-lobe activation (shown as more yellow and red areas) during the Wisconsin Card Sorting Test ("WCS") as compared with a control task ("Number").
From Weinberger et al., 1986.

utilize other, less impaired brain regions (Tan et al., 2007). In fact, even when patients are able to keep up with the processing demands of tasks that require cognitive control and do exhibit normal working-memory behaviors, brain imaging shows that these patients are meeting the demands less efficiently by employing greater posterior cerebral metabolic brain activity with less focused cortical activity. Recall from earlier in this chapter the data indicating that higher-order processes in the dorsolateral prefrontal cortex exert control over more ventrolateral regions responsible for less complex processes, such as rehearsal of information within working memory (D'Esposito et al., 1995; Koechlin et al., 2003). In comparison, brain imaging in schizophrenia patients shows increased patterns of activity in their ventrolateral prefrontal cortex, even during tasks where the patients show near-normal working-memory performance (Tan, Choo, Fones, & Chee, 2005, 2006). Evidently, while healthy controls use the dorsolateral prefrontal cortex in executive working-memory tasks, schizophrenia patients are often unable to do so; rather, they engage greater ventrolateral prefrontal cortex involvement, possibly as a form of compensation for the dysfunctional dorsolateral prefrontal response.

Dopamine and the Genetics of Schizophrenia

What is wrong with the dorsolateral prefrontal cortex in schizophrenia patients? One view is that the deficits in working memory and executive control found in schizophrenia may be linked to deficiencies in cortical dopamine processing. **Dopamine** is a neuromodulator that alters neuron-to-neuron communication, and most pharmacological treatments for schizophrenia work by altering the transmission of dopamine.

Genetic research into the causes of schizophrenia includes a search for genes that convey a heightened susceptibility for the disease. For example, Daniel Weinberger and colleagues have shown that mutation in the COMT gene affects dopamine metabolism in the frontal lobes (Egan et al., 2001). COMT is one of several enzymes that are critical for degrading dopamine (and other related neuromodulators). Several pharmaceutical treatments target the COMT enzyme to alter its activity, thereby affecting the availability of dopamine and related neuromodulators. For example, COMT inhibitors prevent the breakdown of dopamine and are used as a treatment in Parkinson's disease to increase levels of dopamine in the brain.

In healthy, normal individuals, the status of the COMT gene was seen to predict 4% of the variance in performance on the Wisconsin Card Sorting Test. As shown in Figure 9.22, having 2, 1, or 0 copies of the less effective

Figure 9.22 Effect of a gene mutation on frontal-lobe function The number of copies of a less effective COMT allele correlates with the relative numbers of perseverative errors on the Wisconsin Card Sorting Test in schizophrenic patients, their siblings, and healthy normal controls. The errors are given as "*t* scores," in which lower values indicate worse performance. Adapted from Egan et al., 2001.

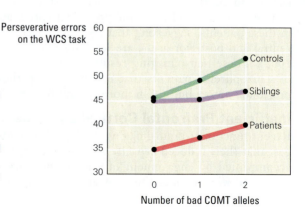

allele for the COMT gene predicted the number of perseverative errors a person would make on the Wisconsin Card Sorting Test. Patients with schizophrenia who had two copies of the less effective allele showed worse performance (lower error *t* scores) on this task than patients with none or one—and the same was true for healthy siblings of schizophrenic patients and for healthy controls drawn from the general population. This finding suggests that a mutation in one kind of gene causes only a small change in cognitive performance but that a combination of mutations in many different genes could push a person past a tipping point into a high-risk category for schizophrenia.

Weinberger and colleagues also used the 2-back task, with its heavy dependence on working memory and executive control, to do brain-imaging studies of the effects of the COMT gene. They looked at the brains of healthy individuals with 0, 1, or 2 copies of the less effective COMT allele to see which brain regions showed activity during the 2-back task. The region that was most highly correlated with this allele was the prefrontal cortex. The more copies of the less effective COMT allele (and hence the worse the dopamine functioning), the less prefrontal-cortex activity was seen during the 2-back task. This suggests that having 1 or 2 copies of the less effective allele (as is most common in those with schizophrenia) impairs activation of the prefrontal cortex during working-memory and executive-function tasks. These studies provide evidence that genetic mutations affecting dopamine activity in the prefrontal cortex are related to the emergence of the cognitive deficits seen in schizophrenia.

As noted earlier, increased prefrontal activation is thought to reflect inefficient function in the prefrontal areas because the increased activity is necessary to support a given level of performance. Several groups have now shown that this prefrontal inefficiency is also present in certain unaffected siblings of schizophrenia patients. The siblings show greater activation than controls even though their task performance does not differ from that of matched controls (Figure 9.23). These results suggest that physiological indices derived

Figure 9.23 Regions of increased, inefficient fMRI activation in unaffected siblings of schizophrenia patients relative to demographically matched control participants during performance of a working-memory paradigm This brain image shows the difference between two groups of subjects: (a) healthy siblings of people with schizophrenia and (b) healthy matched controls. Regions of increased activation in the siblings as compared with the controls include right-dorsolateral and ventrolateral prefrontal cortices. In contrast, behavioral performance did not discriminate between the groups.

Adapted from Figure 2 of Callicott et al. (2003).

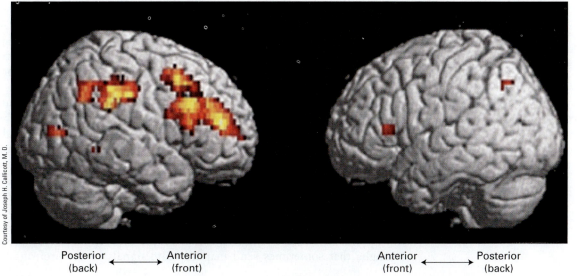

Courtesy of Joseph H. Callicott, M. D.

Posterior (back) ← → Anterior (front)

(a)

Anterior (front) ← → Posterior (back)

(b)

from neuroimaging may provide a more direct reflection of the effects of genes (e.g., increased metabolism of dopamine) than do behavioral changes.

Attention Deficit/Hyperactivity Disorder

Attention deficit/hyperactivity disorder (ADHD) is one of the most commonly diagnosed psychiatric problems in children. About 5% of children are diagnosed with ADHD, although its true prevalence is hard to estimate given that the diagnostic definition of ADHD is under constant refinement. Children and adults with this disorder have great difficulty with cognitive-control processes such as planning, organizing their time, keeping attention focused on a task, and inhibiting responses to distracting stimuli. ADHD symptoms are especially evident in settings that require the exercise of self-control. For example, ADHD children can sit still for hours when they are actively engaged in playing interactive video games, but they have trouble paying attention in school, where they must sit for long periods and pay attention to less captivating information. Given these problems, it is not surprising that students with ADHD are at elevated risk for academic under-achievement (Martinussen & Major, 2011).

Most researchers and clinicians believe that ADHD involves dysfunction in the prefrontal cortex and its cortical and subcortical connections (Solanto, Arnsten, & Castellanos, 2000), including connections to the cerebellum and the basal ganglia. The fact that ADHD patients have difficulty sustaining a behavior or thought over a delay is consistent with the data reviewed earlier showing that prefrontal cortical cells play a critical role in regulating thought and behavioral output through their sustained firing over delays, in the absence of external input. Structural neuroimaging of children with ADHD shows that they have a smaller right prefrontal cortex, the region associated with spatial attention and working memory. Functional-brain-imaging studies have shown evidence of decreased prefrontal activity in ADHD, while diffusion tensor imaging has indicated weaker prefrontal white matter connections (Arnsten, 2006; Castellanos & Tannock, 2002).

Behavioral research suggests that working memory in particular is impaired in patients with ADHD. People with ADHD show marked deficits in mental calculations that require use of working memory (Schweitzer et al., 2000). As with schizophrenia, current medications for ADHD act in part by altering dopamine function in the cortex. The most common treatments for ADHD, such as Ritalin (also known as methylphenidate), are stimulants that either increase dopamine release or block its reuptake at synapses. Unfortunately, the effects of these medications are temporary, and the behavioral problems often reappear after 3 or 4 hours.

There is strong evidence for frontal dysfunction in ADHD, but is the frontal cortex the *origin* of the attentional and cognitive control problems in people with ADHD? Some investigators have suggested that frontal-cortex dysfunction, and the associated working-memory and attentional problems, are actually the consequence of deficits in other subcortical structures, especially the basal ganglia (Volkow, Wang, Fowler, & Ding, 2005, 2007). The basal ganglia, as described in Chapters 5 and 8, are critically involved in skill learning and action selection. If the origins of ADHD are in the basal ganglia, not the frontal lobes, why do stimulants improve working memory and reduce symptoms of ADHD? One view is that people with ADHD have "noisy" basal ganglia that sometimes send inappropriate signals to the prefrontal cortex, resulting in distractible behavior, while at other times the basal ganglia do not signal the prefrontal cortex when appropriate, resulting in perseveration or inattention (Volkow et al., 2005).

How and why do stimulant medications remediate the attentional problems in people with ADHD? One possibility is that stimulant medications increase the saliency of the basal ganglia signal to the prefrontal cortex by increasing extracellular dopamine in the striatal region of the basal ganglia (Volkow et al., 2004, 2005). This hypothesis is consistent with studies (reviewed in Chapter 5) describing a key role for dopamine in the basal ganglia (as well as in the frontal lobes). Recent brain-imaging studies have argued that increased but inefficient activity in the prefrontal cortex, found during certain task conditions in children with ADHD, may serve a compensatory function for dealing with noisy input from the basal ganglia (Sheridan, Hinshaw, & D'Esposito, 2010).

Medications are not the only treatment for ADHD. Behavioral training methods may also offer some relief. Several studies have shown that training children with ADHD over the course of several weeks to improve their working memory during certain tasks results not only in an improvement on the tasks but also in a reduction in core symptoms of inattention and hyperactivity (Klingberg et al. 2005; Beck, Hanson, Puffenberger, Benninger, & Benninger, 2010). Thus, working-memory training appears promising as an intervention for improving cognitive functioning and ADHD symptoms.

Like schizophrenia, ADHD is a heritable psychiatric disorder (which therefore tends to run in families), and scientists are hot on the trail of the genetic bases for this heritability. Recent research has identified some of the genes believed to be linked to ADHD. Like some of the genes associated with schizophrenia, these ADHD genes regulate the function of dopamine in the brain (Durston, 2010). Future research will hopefully identify the genes more clearly, discover how they relate to the behavioral problems of ADHD, and thus provide us with clues for developing more effective treatments. Advances in diagnosis are also sorely needed: studying mental illnesses like schizophrenia and ADHD is difficult because of the lack of clear disease markers, lack of uniformly applied diagnostic criteria, and the growing realization that these disorders are highly heterogeneous, with each patient sharing some but not all symptoms with others in the same diagnostic category.

Interim Summary

- Working-memory impairments become apparent in people with schizophrenia during attempts to maintain a large number of items over a temporal delay, an activity that requires functions associated with the dorsolateral prefrontal cortex. In contrast, functions attributed to the ventrolateral prefrontal cortex seem relatively unimpaired; thus, performance on phonological or visuospatial memory tasks, and on memory tasks involving only minimal delays or few items, appears normal.

- People with ADHD show deficits in mental calculations that require use of working memory.

- Neuroimaging of people with ADHD indicates that they have a smaller prefrontal cortex as well as noisy input signals from the basal ganglia that prevent the basal ganglia from accurately indicating what is or is not important to attend to.

▶ **SYNTHESIS**

Let's return for the last time to Roberta, to see what insights we have gained into the cognitive and other brain processes that she calls on throughout the day. Early that morning, a Tuesday, Roberta checks her class schedule. Her dorsolateral prefrontal cortex is heavily activated while she sorts through her list of courses, paying most attention to the classes she has on Tuesday. This attention helps her plan and organize for that particular day, triggering her memory to recall the items she will need to bring along with her. As she considers them, the various objects are briefly represented in her ventrolateral prefrontal cortex. As she then arranges the items in her backpack, the order and location of each activate the spatial working-memory capabilities of her dorsolateral prefrontal cortex.

When she stops at the bank to get some cash, Roberta relies on her DLPFC to help retrieve her PIN from long-term memory, after which she rehearses it through her phonological loop, activating her VLPFC. With cash in hand, she dashes straight to class, or would have done so had not her DLPFC been maintaining a reminder that tells her she has to switch from her normal routine, suppress her automatic tendency to go directly to French class, and instead make a side trip to the biology department to drop off her homework.

Finally, Roberta arrives at French class. While she listens to the lecture, she also discretely reads bits and pieces of chemistry, relying on activity in her DLPFC to alert her whenever the professor is discussing something especially new or important, at which times she tries to pay more attention to the lecture. What really grabs her attention, however, is his announcement of a surprise vocabulary quiz. If Roberta had not been playing guitar and singing at the local pub until 2 a.m, she might have had the time to study French verbs. This would have kept her left ventrolateral prefrontal cortex quite busy, with the anterior part helping her distinguish the various tenses (semantic information) and the posterior part capturing the subtle differences in pronunciation (phonological information). Unfortunately, she didn't do any such studying (although she had certainly been exercising her VLPFC recalling song lyrics). During the pop quiz, Roberta realizes she has far less knowledge in her long-term memory to draw on than she needs. She engages her DLPFC as she desperately tries to find the answers to the quiz questions in her long-term memory, but alas, she never learned the material in the first place.

All in all, a busy morning for Roberta as her prefrontal cortex, working closely with long-term memory storage areas in the posterior parts of her brain, assists her in controlling her memory, mind, and life.

Key Terms

Concept Check

1. Juan chats with a pretty girl at a party. She tells him her phone number is (617) 555-1812, extension 2001, but he has no way to write it down. How can Juan remember the 14 numbers of her phone number until he can find a pencil and paper?

2. Describe two aspects of executive control that are used both in driving a car and in talking on a cell phone.

3. If you viewed the human brain from behind and a little to the left, which areas of the frontal lobes would be visible? Which would be obscured or hidden?

4. If you could see an image of someone's frontal lobes while they were rehearsing a list of words, would you see more activity on the left side or the right side? What if they were rehearsing visual images?

5. Tanya is trying to concentrate during a neuro-anatomy lecture because she really wants to get into medical school, but she keeps noticing Peter's adorable dimples. Which part of her brain is showing sustained attention to the neuroanatomy images and which part is being distracted by Peter's dimples?

6. In an episode of the old TV show *Seinfeld*, Jerry is trying to remember the name of a woman he met, but all he can recall is that her name is similar to the word for a part of a woman's anatomy. As Jerry struggles to recall her name, is he more likely to be activating his anterior or his posterior left ventrolateral prefrontal cortex?

7. Would a person with ADHD be more likely to take up bird watching or duck hunting?

Emotional Influences on Learning and Memory

DO YOU REMEMBER WHERE you were on the morning of September 11, 2001, at the time of the terrorist attacks on New York City and Washington, D.C.? Most Americans who are old enough to remember that day report that the events are etched into their memory in crisp detail, even if they lived far from the sites and even if they did not personally know anyone who died in the attacks. Some remember hearing the news on TV or radio or from a friend; some remember what they were doing at that moment, what emotions they felt, and how they spent the rest of the day.

But do you remember where you were on, say, the morning of September 10, 2001? Unless something significant happened to you on that day, the odds are that you don't. The reason for this contrast is emotion: the events of September 11 aroused intense emotions, but, for most Americans, September 10 was just another ordinary day. Memories laid down during times of heightened emotion are more likely to be remembered longer, and in greater detail, than memories that are not connected with strong emotions.

This chapter explores the relationship between memory and emotion. Most of the time, this is a positive relationship, with emotion promoting faster learning and more enduring memories. But the darker side is that too much emotion can *interfere* with memory and even cause or contribute to clinical

Peter C. Brandt/Getty Images

disorders—such as depression, stress disorders, and phobias. One of the chief reasons for studying emotion is to understand these linkages— and to help those who suffer from emotions gone awry.

Highly emotional events such as the 9/11 terrorist attacks can produce exceptionally strong and long-lasting memories.

10.1 Behavioral Processes

Suppose a young man, Sammy, is walking home alone late at night and takes a shortcut through a dark alley. He is aware that he's not in the safest of neighborhoods, and he is feeling a little nervous. Suddenly he hears a noise behind him—possibly an attacker—and jumps out of his skin. His heart skips a beat, his hands grow clammy, and his face pales. Breathing heavily, he turns to look behind him for the source of the threat. All of these responses are part of the emotional experience of fear. Some emotional responses—like the reaction to a loud noise in a dark alley—are innate, and others—like Sammy's general anxiety as he walks through what he knows is a dangerous neighborhood—are learned through experience or cultural transmission.

What Is Emotion?

We all know an emotion when we feel one, yet emotion, like attention and consciousness, is one of those psychological concepts that are maddeningly difficult to define. In scientific terms, **emotion** is a cluster of three distinct but interrelated phenomena: physiological responses, overt behaviors, and conscious feelings. Physiological responses associated with emotion may include changes in heart rate, perspiration levels, respiration, and other body functions. Overt (or observable) behaviors associated with emotion include facial expression, vocal tone, and posture. Conscious feelings associated with emotion are the subjective experiences of sadness, happiness, and so on.

Sammy's physiological responses to walking in the dark alley include an increase in heart rate, an increase in perspiration, and a diversion of blood away from the capillaries in his face (making him appear pale). His overt behaviors include jumping and looking around. The conscious feeling is the fear that accompanies his understanding that he is potentially in danger. This cluster of physiological, motor, and conscious reactions constitutes a **fear response**. Other emotions produce different combinations of physiology, behavior, and conscious feelings. For example, a 6-year-old, asked to eat broccoli, may experience a conscious feeling of disgust; her overt behaviors may include sticking out her tongue and poking at her food, and her physiological responses may include a decrease in heart rate.

Emotion researcher Paul Ekman suggests there is a small set of universal emotions, hardwired in humans from birth. This set includes happiness, sadness, anger, fear, disgust, and surprise (Figure 10.1; Ekman & Friesen, 1984; McNally, Bryant, & Ehlers, 2003). (Other researchers would enlarge the basic set slightly to include other emotions, such as interest and shame.) All humans, from all cultures, feel these emotions and can recognize the markers of these emotions in others. For example, Ekman and his colleague Wallace Friesen showed pictures like those in Figure 10.1 to people of an isolated tribe in New Guinea. Although these New Guineans lived in a culture very different from that of industrialized North America, they had no difficulty in recognizing the emotions connoted by the facial expressions of North American college students—and the New Guineans' facial expressions were equally well understood by North Americans (Ekman & Friesen, 1971).

This is not to say that all humans manifest emotion identically. Different cultures may teach their members different rules about the appropriate ways to display emotions in various social contexts. For example, traditional Japanese culture (which places a premium on respect and orderly behavior) encourages suppression of emotional display to a greater degree than American culture (which tends to value individualism more than social order). Thus, while watching a film containing unpleasant scenes, both American and Japanese students display similar overt behaviors (such as grimacing at the nastiest parts), but if an authority figure, such as an experimenter, is present, the Japanese students tend to mask their negative expressions more than American students do (Ekman, 1992). Similarly, in many cultures around the world, men and women show more or less the same physiological measures of emotion, but women are much more likely to express happiness and sadness overtly, perhaps because of cultural rules dictating that "men don't cry" (Eisenberg & Lennon, 1983; Kring & Gordon, 1998). In short, human emotion seems to be innate and universal, but its outward expression may be modified by cultural learning.

Matsumoto & Ekman, Japanese and Caucasian Facial Expressions of Emotion

Figure 10.1 **Faces illustrating "universal" human emotions** Humans of every race and culture seem to experience happiness, surprise, fear, sadness, anger, and disgust and can recognize the expression of these emotions in others.
From Matsumoto and Ekman, 1989.

Autonomic Arousal and the Fight-or-Flight Response

Imagine you are walking through the forest, and you come face-to-face with a bear. First, you probably freeze (an overt behavior). But what physiological responses do you experience? Most likely, your heartbeat speeds up, and your respiration rate increases. Fine hairs on your arms and neck may stand on end, and your hands may sweat. Hormones flood your body, causing you to feel a "rush" of energy and excitement. Other bodily responses may be less noticeable to you: digestion halts, your pupils dilate, and extra blood is directed to the muscles in your legs in case you have to run away.

This collection of bodily responses, called **arousal** or (more colorfully) the **fight-or-flight response**, is the body's way of preparing you to face a challenge or threat: either by fighting or by running away. Blood pressure and heart rate increase, and blood flow—with its cargo of glucose that provides energy—is

Table 10.1

Some components of the fight-or-flight response

Increases in	Decreases in
Blood pressure and heart rate	Digestion
Respiration	Immune system function
Blood glucose level	Sexual arousal
Blood flow to large muscles in legs and arms	Growth
Pain suppression	Touch sensitivity
Perception and awareness	Peripheral vision

diverted toward the body systems that are most likely to help you in this effort, including your brain, your lungs, and the muscles in your legs (Table 10.1). Other systems such as digestion and the immune system are temporarily deprived of energy. These latter systems are important for proper functioning under normal circumstances—but if you don't survive the immediate threat, it doesn't really matter whether you digested that last meal or fought off that cold.

These body changes are mediated by the **autonomic nervous system (ANS)**, the collection of nerves and structures that control internal organs and glands. The word "autonomic" is related to "autonomous," meaning that the ANS can operate autonomously, without conscious control. When the brain senses a challenge or threat, the ANS sends a signal to the adrenal glands, which release **stress hormones**, hormones that act throughout the body to turn the fight-or-flight response on and off. One formal definition of **stress** is any event or stimulus that causes bodily arousal and the release of stress hormones. Major stress hormones include **epinephrine** (also called *adrenaline*) and **glucocorticoids**. The chief glucocorticoid in humans is **cortisol**. In the short term, our reactions to stress through arousal and release of stress hormones prepare us to deal with the challenge before us; normally, once the challenge is past, the ANS turns off the fight-or-flight response, and stress hormone levels drop back to normal.

Strong, pleasant emotions, such as happiness and surprise, can cause physiological arousal that is very similar to the components of the fight-or-flight response. Thus, a young man in the throes of sexual arousal may experience many of the same physiological responses (dilated pupils, increased heart rate and blood pressure, sweating, and so on) as one who is suddenly attacked by a masked gunman. Many of the same features of arousal occur in a range of emotions, although there are differences. For example, heart rate increases during many emotions but falls during disgust (Levenson, 1992). So, why do we experience increased heart rate and blood pressure as components of a pleasant emotion in one situation and as part of a negative emotion in another? Several theories have been proposed.

Theories of Emotion

An early and influential theory of emotion was independently proposed by William James and by the Danish physiologist Carl Lange and so is often called the **James-Lange theory of emotion** (LaBar & LeDoux, 2003). The James-Lange theory states that conscious feelings of emotion occur when the mind senses the physiological responses associated with fear or some other kind of arousal. Figure 10.2a illustrates this idea: first, our bodies respond to an emotional situation with physiological changes; conscious feelings follow as our

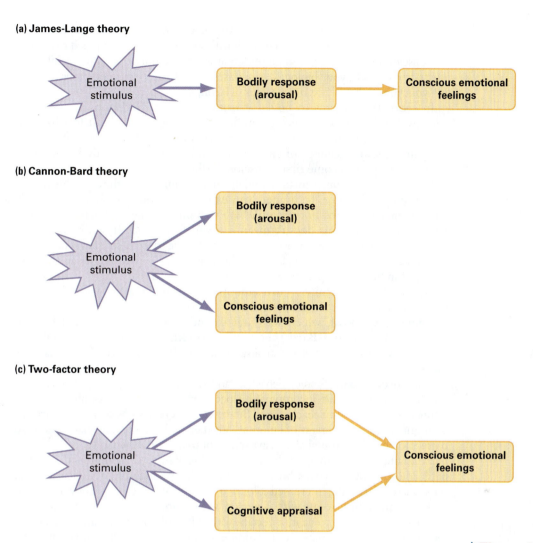

(a) James-Lange theory

Emotional stimulus → Bodily response (arousal) → Conscious emotional feelings

(b) Cannon-Bard theory

Emotional stimulus → Bodily response (arousal)

Emotional stimulus → Conscious emotional feelings

(c) Two-factor theory

Emotional stimulus → Bodily response (arousal) → Conscious emotional feelings

Emotional stimulus → Cognitive appraisal → Conscious emotional feelings

Figure 10.2 **Theories of emotion** (a) The James-Lange theory posits that physiological responses come first and cause our conscious feelings of emotion. (b) The Cannon-Bard theory posits that stimuli simultaneously evoke both emotions and physiological responses. (c) The two-factor theory of emotion posits that emotions are produced through interaction between our cognitive appraisal of the situation and our physiological responses.

mind interprets this physiological response. Several modern researchers have developed related theories, often called **somatic theories of emotion**, all based on the central premise that physiological responses to stimuli come first, and these determine or induce emotions (Damasio, 1996, 1999; Zajonc, 1980, 1984).

One prediction of somatic theories of emotion is that researchers should be able to evoke a given emotion in a person just by inducing the corresponding bodily responses. For example, experimenters can often produce moods in volunteers just by asking the volunteers to move various facial muscles (without telling them what mood this is intended to produce). For example, one instruction went as follows: "Pull your eyebrows down and together; raise your upper eyelids and tighten your lower eyelids; narrow your lips and press them together." How do you feel when you make this expression and hold it for a few seconds? In case you couldn't guess, these facial contortions were meant to simulate anger. Volunteers who made such a face generally showed physiological responses corresponding to the emotion of anger, including increased heart rate and blood pressure. Most of them also reported feelings of mild anger or annoyance (Ekman, 1992).

This process works for positive emotions too. When volunteers were told to turn up the corners of their mouths and crinkle their eyes, they reported a mild overall increase in feelings of happiness (Ekman, 1992). Another way to "induce" happiness is by holding a pencil between your teeth without letting your lips touch the wood; the muscles involved are the same ones that are active during a natural smile, and after a few seconds, your biological responses should affect your conscious feelings, and your mood should improve (Strack, Martin, & Stepper, 1988).

In short, there seems to be some truth behind the old notion of "put on a happy face"—the simple act of smiling can actually make you feel happier. More generally, these results support somatic theories of emotion, which posit that our conscious feelings of emotion depend on what our body is telling us; biological responses come first, conscious feelings second.

But Walter Cannon, a former student of William James, thought this theory was backwards. People, he argued, can experience arousal without necessarily experiencing emotion. For example, after running, a person may experience a racing heart, but this doesn't mean she will feel afraid. In addition, as you read above, many emotion-provoking stimuli give rise to similar sets of biological responses: fight (anger), flight (fear), and sexual excitement can all cause increases in heart rate, perspiration, and hormone release. How, then, does your conscious mind determine which emotion is being signaled by the increased heart rate and other biological responses?

Cannon's proposal, which was later extended by Philip Bard and became known as the **Cannon-Bard theory of emotion**, was that stimuli simultaneously evoke both emotions and arousal (Cannon, 1927). Figure 10.2b illustrates this idea.

A few decades later, Stanley Schachter and Jerome Singer came up with another theory of emotion that incorporated aspects of both the James-Lange and the Cannon-Bard theories. Schachter and Singer claimed James was correct that arousal is an important determinant of emotion, but they said Cannon and Bard were also correct to note that arousal alone isn't sufficient to determine what we feel.

In a famous experiment, Schachter and Singer injected volunteers with epinephrine, one of the stress hormones that help produce physiological arousal (increased heart rate, increased blood pressure, and so on). They then put each volunteer in a room with a person who (unbeknownst to the volunteer) had been instructed to act in a certain way. The volunteers began to catch the mood of their companions. Some volunteers were paired with companions who were acting joyful, and they began to act happy too, whereas volunteers who had been paired with companions who were acting angry began to act annoyed themselves. In other words, epinephrine injections caused bodily arousal, which each volunteer's brain interpreted according to the context in which that individual had been placed (Schachter & Singer, 1962). This suggests that the same ambiguous bodily responses can occur in different emotions, and the label we apply to the responses (e.g., "joy" or "anger") depends on the situation we are in.

This result led Schachter and Singer to propose a **two-factor theory of emotion**, which posits that a combination of cognitive appraisal and perception of biological changes together determine our experience of emotion (Figure 10.2c). In other words, if we are alone in the woods and see a bear, cognitive appraisal warns us of the danger, and this appraisal interacts with our experience of a fight-or-flight response to produce the emotional experience of fear. In contrast, a young man meeting his girlfriend after a long absence may have a similar pattern of physiological arousal, but his cognitive appraisal of the situation will lead to a very different emotional experience. On the one hand, as James proposed, the particular pattern of physiological responses contributes to our conscious feelings of emotion; on the other hand, our cognitive awareness helps us to interpret that arousal in accordance with our current context.

In sum, emotion is a complex phenomenon arising from the interplay of conscious feelings, cognitive assessments, and bodily responses.

A famous experiment supporting the two-factor theory of emotion was the "High Bridge" study (Dutton & Aron, 1974). In this study, an attractive female, stationed on a footbridge, asked male passersby to complete a brief survey. In some cases the footbridge was a low, safe-looking structure; in others it was a swaying cable bridge that spanned a deep ravine (the Capilano Suspension Bridge in Vancouver). After each participant completed the survey, the female would give him her phone number "in case you have further questions." The researchers predicted that men on the dangerous-looking bridge would be highly aroused, likely to misinterpret this feeling as sexual arousal, and therefore more likely to call the woman back looking for a date compared with men who took the survey while on the safe-looking bridge. The results? A few of the men who'd been tested on the low bridge called the experimenter back, but fully 50% of the men tested on the high bridge phoned. In contrast, when the study was repeated with a male survey taker, there were hardly any follow-up phone calls from males tested on either bridge, allowing the researchers to rule out the possibility that participants tested on the high bridge were simply more interested in the scientific details of the experiment.

These moviegoers seem to be enjoying the experience of biological responses normally associated with fear and excitement.

The two-factor theory may also help explain the popularity of horror movies, at which viewers expect to be made to scream in terror. Given that fear is a "negative" emotion, why would otherwise rational people stand in line and pay good money to experience it? Part of the answer is that the strong biological responses caused by a terrifying movie are not so different from the strong biological responses caused by intense joy or sexual pleasure. Viewers know they are relatively safe in the context of the movie theater, and this cognitive assessment allows them to interpret the strong arousal as pleasurable rather than threatening.

Test Your Knowledge

Theories of Emotion

Janet is at a music concert featuring her favorite band. As the lights dim and the band walks onstage to a crashing opening chord, she jumps to her feet and cheers along with the rest of the crowd, her heart racing with excitement. How would each of the following theories of emotion describe this situation? (Answers appear in the Answers section in the back of the book.)

1. James-Lange theory
2. Cannon-Bard theory
3. Two-factor (cognitive appraisal) theory

Assessing Emotion in Nonhuman Animals

So far, we've discussed emotions as defined in and by humans. What about other animals? Can nonhuman animals experience emotion? Many researchers believe that they can.

The literature on animal behavior is rich with examples that seem to describe animal emotions. Poachers shoot an elephant nicknamed Tina; the other elephants in her tribe try to revive her by propping her up and sticking grass in her mouth. When Tina dies despite their efforts, they sprinkle earth and branches over the body; Tina's daughter returns to the site periodically thereafter and strokes the bones with her trunk (Moss, 1988). A female chimpanzee gives birth; as the baby is delivered, the chimpanzee who is the mother's best friend shrieks and embraces nearby chimpanzees, then spends the next few days caring for mother and baby (de Waal, 1996). A killer whale grows sick; his podmates flank him and protect him, helping him stay near the surface, where he can breathe, even guiding him into shallow waters at the risk of beaching themselves, refusing to abandon him until he finally dies (Porter, 1977).

Can elephants feel sadness, monkeys feel empathy, and killer whales feel sympathy? Or are the animals described above simply acting on blind instinct, without any of the emotional overtones we would attribute to humans? Although these animals often *seem* to behave as if they feel emotions, the fact is that we may never know if they experience subjective feelings or, if they do, what those feelings are like. But remember that subjective feelings are only one component of emotions. The other two components, biological responses and overt behaviors, are certainly apparent and can be studied in nonhuman animals.

Fear Responses across Species

As early as the mid-nineteenth century, Charles Darwin noted that many species of animals react to arousing stimuli in similar ways (Darwin, 1872). For example, when a gorilla encounters a frightening stimulus, its first reactions may include a sudden jump ("startle") followed by a period of alert immobility ("freezing"). It may display **piloerection**, meaning that its body hair stands on end; this makes the animal look bigger and more threatening. In extreme situations, the gorilla may defecate or urinate. These responses are remarkably similar to Sammy's physiological reactions in the dark alley: hearing a suspicious noise makes him "jump out of his skin" and then freeze (his heart skipping a beat) while he assesses the situation. Tiny hairs on the back of Sammy's neck and arms may stand on end, and he may develop goose bumps, which Darwin suggested are the remnants of our hairy ancestors' piloerection response. In extreme circumstances, Sammy may even be terrified enough to lose bladder or sphincter control. All of these fear reactions in humans seem to have direct analogues in other primates.

(b)

Photographs by Frans de Waal

(a)

Emotional displays in animals often have striking similarities to displays of human emotion. (a) A capuchin monkey reacts with wide-eyed surprise when it receives an unexpected rebuff from its mother. (b) Primates often hoot with apparent joy in anticipation of food or when meeting companions they haven't seen for a while. From de Waal, 1996.

To some degree, we can see the same reactions in other mammals. A startled rat shows changes in blood pressure, heart rate, and hormonal release that are broadly similar to the changes seen in cats, rabbits, monkeys, and humans. Even fish, reptiles, and birds show some of these responses. For example, many birds fluff their feathers when alarmed, and some fish spread their fins wide or puff up their bodies, which makes them look larger, in a defensive adaptation analogous to piloerection in mammals. When such reactions appear, researchers report that the animal is expressing physiological and behavioral components of a fear response even if we can't be sure whether the animal is actually feeling emotion.

It's important to keep in mind that physiological responses don't automatically equate with emotions in humans either. Remember the woman whose heart races after running but who doesn't feel fear. Similarly, in human "fear-conditioning" experiments using electrical stimulation, ethical concerns typically dictate that subjects are allowed to self-select the intensity of the shock to be "unpleasant but not painful." Under these conditions, humans may produce physiological responses to the shock, but they typically don't report conscious feelings of fear while anticipating upcoming shock (LaBar, 2009). So in humans, just as in rats and other animals, researchers evoking and studying emotional responses need to be clear that physiological responses are consistent with—but not necessarily proof of—emotions.

Beyond Fear

Because fear responses are relatively easy to induce, detect, and record, the vast majority of animal studies on emotion and its effects on learning and memory have focused on the learning of fear responses. But in recent years, there has been increasing attention paid to the other emotions as well. Back in Chapter 5, you read about "yum" and "ugh" responses (Berridge & Robinson, 1998). In particular, rats given a taste of sweetness show rhythmic movements of the mouth and protrusion of the tongue—just like humans tasting something pleasant ("yum!"); rats given a bitter taste show mouth gapes, shakes of the head, and wiping of the face with the paws—just like humans shuddering at a disgusting taste ("ugh!"). Again, while we can't be sure that the rat is experiencing conscious feelings of pleasure or disgust, these physiological responses seem consistent across mammalian species.

One way that humans express the emotion of joy, particularly within a social context, is through laughter. There is now accumulating evidence of laughter-like responses in other mammals too. For instance, tickling is rewarding to young rats, in the sense that they will perform behaviors such as running mazes and pressing levers in order to obtain tickle reinforcement (Burgdorf & Panskepp, 2001). During tickle, rats tend to emit ultrasonic vocalizations that share many acoustic features with the sounds of human laughter (Panksepp & Burgdorf, 2003). Tickle-induced vocalizations can also be elicited in chimpanzees and gorillas (Davila-Ross, Owren, & Zimmerman, 2009). Even dogs emit a characteristic "laugh" vocalization during play, and one study has suggested that dogs in a kennel experience reduced stress if exposed to recordings of dog-laugh vocalizations (Simonet, Versteeg, & Storie, 2005).

The presence of laughter-like vocalizations in rats, dogs, and apes doesn't necessarily mean that these animals have a sense of humor; rather, it appears to be a social expression of joy. Thus, young rats emit laughter-like vocalizations during play behavior, and they prefer to spend time with older animals that "laugh" frequently (Panksepp & Burgdorf, 2003). Although the study of nonhuman laughter is still relatively young, there is already some evidence that the same brain regions that are active during social laughter in humans are also active in these other animals during laughter-like responses (Meyer, Baumann, Wildgruber, & Alter, 2007). Thus, recording laughter-like vocalizations may be one way researchers can measure joy responses in nonhuman animals. Again, we can't be sure that "laughing" animals are experiencing the emotion of joy, only that their physiological and behavioral responses are similar to those exhibited by happy humans.

Learning Emotional Responses: Focus on Fear

Further research into joy responses in animals may produce insights into how nonhuman animals learn joy responses and whether this differs from how they learn fear responses. In the meantime, however, the vast majority of studies on emotional learning in nonhuman animals have focused on learning responses consisting of negative emotions, particularly fear. This is not because fear is inherently more important or interesting than the other emotions but simply because a long tradition exists of how to elicit and recognize fear responses in nonhuman animals. The learning of these emotional responses, including both overt behavior and physiological changes, can be particularly fast, strong, and long lasting.

Conditioned Emotional Responses: Learning to Predict Danger

When a rat is given an unpleasant surprising stimulus, such as an unexpected electric shock, it typically displays a short period of alert immobility (the freezing response). Responding to potential threat by staying very still may help a small animal avoid predators, which often have visual systems tuned to detect movement. It may also allow the animal to allocate full attention to sensory inputs to help it determine what and where the threat is. (Even large animals, including humans, often respond to potential threat with a short period of watchful immobility.) But, after a moment, if nothing further happens, the rat relaxes and goes back to what it was doing before.

The freezing response is not learned; rather, it is an innate fear response to a threatening situation. In this example, the freezing behavior is an unconditioned response (UR) evoked by the shock US. (See Chapter 4 if you need to review classical conditioning and the concepts of CS, US, CR, and UR.) In addition to freezing behavior, the shock US also evokes autonomic unconditioned responses (URs), such as increases in blood pressure and heart rate. However, if the shock US is repeatedly preceded by a neutral conditioned stimulus (CS)—say, a tone or a light—the animal will learn the CS-US association and may then produce conditioned responses (CRs) to the CS. Such CRs are *conditioned emotional responses*, which you read about in Chapter 4. Figure 10.3 shows an example of conditioned emotional responding in rats. In this example, researchers play a 10-second tone, and the rats respond with a brief freezing response (Figure 10.3a). Next, the tone is paired with a foot shock. Later, the tone is presented alone; now the rat expects the foot shock and manifests this learning through a behavioral CR: increased freezing in anticipation of the upcoming shock (Figure 10.3a).

At the same time as the animal learns a freezing CR, other fear responses are conditioned too. Thus, the first time the tone is presented, it evokes a mild, temporary increase in blood pressure (Figure 10.3b); after tone-shock pairing, when the tone is played again there is a sharp rise in blood pressure that persists through the duration of the tone. If the experimenters had chosen to measure other variables indicative of a fight-or-flight response—such as increased heart rate, stress hormone release, or defecation—they would probably have found that the tone elicited many of these responses as well, as further proof of the conditioned emotional response. These learned fear responses are similar to

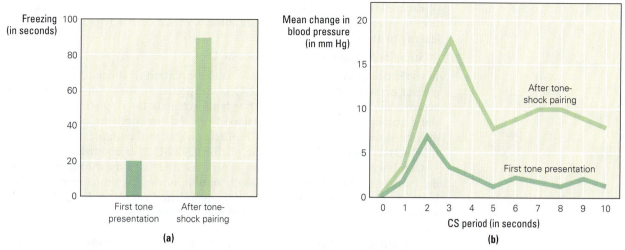

(a)

(b)

Figure 10.3 **Two types of conditioned emotional responding in rats** (a) On first presentation, a tone CS may cause a brief freezing response, but after the CS has been paired with a foot-shock US, it evokes a strong freezing response (the fear CR). (b) Similarly, the first CS presentation evokes only a mild and transient increase in blood pressure, but after CS-US pairing, there is a strong increase in blood pressure that persists through the CS period. Blood pressure changes and freezing are conditioned emotional responses, indicating that the rat has learned the CS-US association. Adapted from LeDoux, 1993.

the behaviors a rat would exhibit on being confronted with a natural fear-provoking stimulus, such as a cat (Fendt & Fanselow, 1999).

The same basic rules of conditioned emotional responding apply in other species too. For example, recall from Chapter 4 that the sea snail *Aplysia* can learn to withdraw its gill (CR) in response to a gentle touch (CS) that predicts a tail shock (US). Is the sea snail "feeling" fear in the same way as a rat huddling in a corner of its cage or as a New Yorker trying to flee the scene of the terrorist attacks on 9/11? We can't be sure. All we can know is that the overt behavior of *Aplysia* is a conditioned emotional response not so different from the overt behavior shown by a freezing rat or a fleeing human.

Conditioned freezing in rats may occur after only a single CS-US pairing, and even lowly *Aplysia* can learn a conditioned gill withdrawal in about four trials. Compare that with the eyeblink conditioning you read about in Chapter 4—which may require several hundred trials in rats and rabbits and dozens of trials in humans—and the inescapable conclusion is that emotional learning is fast.

Another characteristic of conditioned emotional responses is that they can be very long lasting and hard to extinguish. It may take many extinction trials, in which the animal receives presentations of the CS alone with no US, before the animal stops giving a conditioned emotional response. Even then, extinction does not eliminate the learned response; it only reduces the chance that the CS will elicit it. For this reason, conditioned emotional responses are very easily reinstated after extinction: sometimes, merely placing the animal back in the experimental chamber where it experienced the US is enough to restore conditioned emotional responding (Bouton & Peck, 1989).

Conditioned Escape: Learning to Get Away from Danger

Learning to recognize which stimuli signal upcoming danger is a good thing, but getting away from the danger altogether is even better. In **conditioned escape**, animals learn to make particular responses in order to escape from or terminate an aversive stimulus. For example, a rat might receive a series of foot shocks that are terminated if the rat presses a lever, or a rat might be placed in a pool of water and learn to locate and climb onto a submerged platform in order to escape from the water. (Rats are quite competent swimmers, but just like humans at the beach, if the water is chilly, they prefer to get out of it.)

Escape learning is a form of operant conditioning. Remember from Chapter 5 that in operant conditioning, a stimulus S evokes a behavioral response R, leading to an outcome O:

Stimulus S → Response R → Outcome O

In the shock example, the stimulus S is the initiation of shock, the response R is lever pressing, and the outcome O is escape from shock. Since the shock is aversive, this is an example of negative reinforcement: the response causes something aversive (shock) to be subtracted from the environment, and so the frequency of the response increases. Similarly, in the pool example, S is the water, R is locating and climbing onto the platform, and O is escape from the water.

Conditioned escape learning can be very fast; the first time the rat is placed in the pool, it may swim around randomly until it locates the submerged platform, but once it has learned the location of the platform, a rat placed back in the pool will typically swim straight to the platform and climb out of the water.

Conditioned Avoidance: Learning to Avoid Danger Altogether

Even better than escaping from danger is learning to avoid it altogether. In **conditioned avoidance**, animals learn to make particular responses to avoid or prevent arrival of an aversive stimulus. For example, a rat may be placed in a chamber with a response lever. From time to time, a series of foot shocks is delivered, and if the rat presses the lever during this time, it can terminate (escape from) the shock. In addition, a warning signal, such as a tone, is played just before the foot shock starts; if the rat presses the lever before the tone is finished, the foot shock is avoided altogether. Typically, a rat first learns to escape the shock and eventually learns to avoid it altogether by pressing the lever when the warning signal plays.

At first glance, it may appear that avoidance learning also is simple operant conditioning: the warning signal (S) triggers the response (R), which causes avoidance of the shock (O). Since shock is aversive, avoidance of the shock reinforces the response, making the organism more likely to repeat the response in future.

But this simple explanation doesn't quite hold up. As the animal learns the avoidance response, the shock no longer occurs. Therefore, there is no explicit reinforcement for making the avoidance response (since the shock is not presented in the first place, it cannot be subtracted from the environment!). Therefore, the response should extinguish. But it does not. In fact, avoidance behaviors can be incredibly persistent: animals may keep making the avoidance response long after the US is no longer delivered. This is a paradox that requires further explanation.

Some researchers have proposed a *two-factor theory* of avoidance learning, which states that avoidance learning involves an interaction between classical and operant conditioning (Dinsmoor, 1954; Mowrer, 1960). According to this view, the first stage of avoidance learning is actually classical conditioning: as the tone is paired with the shock, it comes to function as a warning signal and becomes a conditioned stimulus (CS) that evokes a conditioned emotional response (fear CR) in anticipation of the upcoming shock (US). Then operant conditioning occurs: the avoidance response (lever pressing) is reinforced because it causes cessation of the warning signal and therefore a reduction in fear (Figure 10.4a). In effect, animals don't learn to lever press in order to avoid the shock; rather, they learn to lever press in order to escape from the warning signal (or, more specifically, from the fear response it produces).

But there are several problems with two-factor theories of avoidance learning (Dymond & Roche, 2009). One major difficulty is that these theories assume that avoidance learning is based on conditioned fear of the warning signal. But, in fact, as the avoidance response is learned, the organism's fear response to the

(a) Two-factor theory

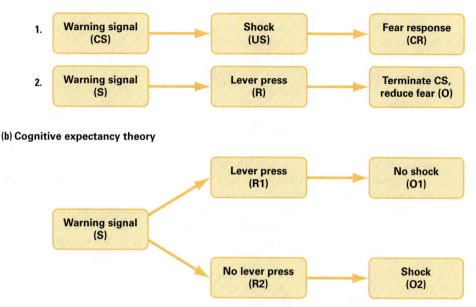

(b) Cognitive expectancy theory

Figure 10.4 Theories of avoidance learning (a) In the two-factor theory of avoidance learning, (1) rats learn a classically conditioned fear response to a warning signal (CS) paired with shock (US); (2) then rats learn an operant response to terminate the warning signal and the fear it evokes. (b) In the cognitive expectancy theory of avoidance learning, rats learn that different responses predict different outcomes and use this cognitive expectancy to guide their decision of which response to make.

warning signal decreases. In this case, the avoidance response should extinguish, just like any other operant response, once the outcome is no longer presented. Yet avoidance learning is often extremely resistant to extinction.

Various researchers have proposed modifications to the basic two-factor theory, to address this and other limitations (B. A. Williams, 2001). For example, cognitive theorists have proposed that animals form *cognitive expectancies* and decide between competing possible behaviors based on those expectancies. According to this view, animals learn the expected outcomes of responding and of not responding and then make a decision to respond or not based on a comparison between the two expected outcomes (Figure 10.4b; Dickinson & Balleine, 2000; Seligman & Johnston, 1973).

More recently, some have argued for integrated theories that combine aspects both of two-factor theory and of cognitive expectancy (Lovibond, Saunders, Weidemann, & Mitchell, 2008). Avoidance learning may therefore be a useful test bed for studying the potentially complex interactions between classical conditioning, operant conditioning, and cognitive processing—and a reminder that many seemingly "simple" behaviors may actually reflect more than one type of learning.

Learned Helplessness

Back in the 1960s, psychologist Martin Seligman and his colleagues studied an avoidance task involving a large box with a low wall that divided the box into two chambers (Overmier & Seligman, 1967; Seligman & Maier, 1967). They placed a dog in one chamber, called the "avoidance" chamber, where the dog periodically received an electric shock. At first, dogs reacted to the shock by running around the chamber; eventually, they learned that they could jump over the wall into the "safe" chamber to escape the shock. If the shock was always preceded by a warning signal, such as a tone, the dogs also learned to jump over the wall as soon as the tone sounded, thus avoiding the shock altogether.

Seligman and his colleagues wondered what would happen if, before a dog was first put in the avoidance chamber, the tone stimulus had already been explicitly paired with a shock in a classical fear-conditioning paradigm:

CS (tone) → US (shock)

If the dog had already learned this CS-US association and knew that the tone signaled shock, would the dog be able to transfer this learning to the avoidance learning paradigm? Might the dog jump over the wall the first time it heard the tone in the avoidance chamber to avoid being shocked?

What the dogs actually did surprised everyone. The first time they heard the tone in the avoidance chamber, the dogs ran around for a few seconds—and then they lay down in the corner and whined. Even after repeated trials, the dogs never learned to jump over the wall and escape the shock. Intrigued, the experimenters tried to encourage the animals to escape: removing the barrier wall, baiting the safe chamber with food, even climbing into the safe chamber themselves and calling to the dogs to cross over. Still, the dogs continued to lie in the corner, miserably enduring the shock.

Seligman concluded that the prior exposure to an inescapable shock (during the classical-conditioning phase) had taught the animals that they were helpless to escape *any* shock—even in the operant-learning phase. Seligman named this phenomenon **learned helplessness**, meaning that exposure to an uncontrollable punisher teaches an expectation that responses are ineffectual, which in turn reduces the motivation to attempt new avoidance responses. Learned helplessness has since been demonstrated in a variety of species, from cockroaches (G. Brown & Stroup, 1988) to rats (Besson, Privat, Eschalier, & Fialip, 1999) to humans (Hiroto, 1974; Hiroto & Seligman, 1974). Rather than being a laboratory oddity, learned helplessness may be a relatively common phenomenon. Understanding this phenomenon may provide clues for how to promote resilience or resistance to negative emotions and even to **depression**, a psychiatric condition characterized by sadness and a general loss of initiative and activity (see "Learning and Memory in Everyday Life" on page 399). Seligman himself has gone on to study what he calls "positive psychology," arguing that just as negative emotional responses such as fear and unhappiness can be learned, so can positive emotional responses such as happiness and hope for the future (Seligman, 1991; Seligman, Steen, Park, & Peterson, 2005).

Effect of Emotions on Memory Storage and Retrieval

The previous section described the learning of emotional responses to stimuli that predict upcoming emotion-evoking events (such as conditioned learning of fear in response to a stimulus that predicts incipient shock) and also described how animals can learn to escape or avoid such events. But there is another important way emotion interacts with learning and memory: strong emotions, in particular, can affect the storage and retrieval of episodic memories.

For example, let's turn again to the morning of September 11, 2001. Most Americans who were old enough to understand what was happening felt strong emotional responses that day, ranging from sadness at the deaths, to anger at the terrorists, to fear that further attacks would follow. And most report that they still have vivid, detailed memories of that day. This phenomenon isn't limited to negative emotions; think back to the happiest day of your life. You can probably describe that day in a comparable level of detail.

One reason we usually have strong memories for episodes of intense emotion (fear and anger, but also happiness and surprise) is that these tend to be memories that we rehearse frequently, reviewing them mentally and talking about them with others (Heuer & Reisberg, 1992). So, for example, in the days following the 9/11 attacks, people discussed the situation with friends

---

"Immunizing" against Learned Helplessness

Although learned helplessness was originally discovered, and studied, under highly controlled laboratory conditions, there is evidence that it also occurs in natural environments—and the consequences can be devastating. For example, Martin Seligman suggested that learned helplessness may be an important component of human depression (Seligman, 1975). People suffering from depression spend a lot of time sitting around or sleeping, sometimes skipping work or school because they lack the energy to leave home. Some depression appears to be triggered by external problems, but affected individuals often feel unable to do anything to change the conditions that are making them feel depressed. Like Seligman's dogs, they seem to sit and endure their pain rather than explore ways to escape or avoid it. The idea that learned helplessness may at least partially underlie human depression is supported by the finding that antidepressant drugs, which alleviate depression in humans, can also eliminate learned helplessness in rats previously exposed to inescapable shock (Besson, Privat, Eschalier, & Fialip, 1999).

If learned helplessness does play a role in human depression, then perhaps the same behavioral techniques that help animals overcome learned helplessness could also benefit depressed patients. For example, Seligman found that if he first trained his animals to escape the shock, then exposed them to inescapable shock, and then tested them again, the animals continued to make escape responses (Seligman, Rosellini, & Kozak, 1975). Apparently, the earlier learning that they could escape shocks "immunized" the animals against learned helplessness when they were later exposed to inescapable shock. Perhaps some humans could be "immunized" against depression in the same way: if humans are exposed early in life to adversities that they can overcome, perhaps this early training could protect them against learned helplessness when confronted with more difficult challenges later in life.

The same insight could apply to educational methods. Some children attribute their academic failures to inescapable conditions: "I'm bad at math" or "I'm not as smart as the other children." Confronted with a new math problem, such a child might not bother to try—just like Seligman's helpless dogs. Maybe this attitude could be reversed or lessened by a training procedure that mixes hard problems with problems the child can solve, gradually teaching the child a way to "escape" from the cycle of failure by exposure to challenges that he can master (Dweck, 1975).

and families and watched intensive TV coverage—and each time, their memories for the original event were retrieved, rehearsed, and strengthened. Since (as you read in Chapter 7) rehearsal strengthens memory, this is one reason most Americans remember September 11 better than September 10. However, the effect of emotion goes beyond rehearsal: strong emotions can actually affect the probability that an episodic memory is encoded in the first place.

Emotion and Encoding of Memories

Researchers can study the effect of emotional content on memory by "creating" emotional experiences in the laboratory and then testing for memories of those events. In a classic set of experiments, one group of participants saw a series of pictures accompanied by a highly emotional story about a boy who goes on an outing with his mother, is involved in a traumatic accident, and must be rushed to surgery, after which his mother arranges to take him home (Cahill, Babinsky, Markowitsch, & McGaugh, 1995; Cahill & McGaugh, 1995; Heuer & Reisberg, 1990). A second group of subjects saw the same pictures, but for them the critical middle part of the narrative was changed to a description of the boy's visiting the hospital during a disaster drill, with hospital workers practicing on volunteers made up to look like trauma victims. Both stories had the same beginning and end; only the critical middle part distinguished the "emotional" story from the "neutral" one (Figure 10.5).

1. A mother and her son are leaving home in the morning.

2. She is taking him to visit his father's workplace.

3. The father is the chief laboratory technician at a nearby hospital.

4. They check before crossing a busy road.

5. While crossing the road, the boy is struck by a runaway car, which critically injures him.

5. While walking along, they pass the scene of a minor accident, which the boy finds interesting.

6. At the hospital, the staff prepares the emergency room, to which the boy is rushed.

6. At the hospital, the staff are preparing for a practice disaster drill, which the boy will watch.

7. All morning long, surgeons struggled to save the boy's life.

7. All morning long, surgeons practiced the standard disaster drill procedures.

8. Specialized surgeons were able to successfully reattach the boy's severed feet.

8. Special make-up artists were able to create realistic-looking injuries on actors for the drill.

9. Afterward, while the father stayed with the boy, the mother left to phone her other child's preschool.

10. She phones the preschool to tell them she will soon pick up her child.

11. Heading to pick up her child, she hails a taxi at the number 9 bus stop.

Figure 10.5 The effect of emotional arousal on memory In this experiment, all participants saw pictures 1 through 4 (as a slide show) with an accompanying narration played on tape. Half of the participants then saw pictures 5 through 8 accompanied by narration of an "emotional" story (shown here in red) describing a serious accident; the remaining participants saw the same pictures but with narration that told a "neutral" story (shown here in black) describing a disaster drill. Finally, both groups saw pictures 9 through 11 with an accompanying narration describing how the mother made arrangements to take her child home. Photos courtesy of Larry Cahill, based on an original design from Heuer and Reisberg, 1990.

Two weeks later, participants were shown the pictures again and asked to recall the accompanying narrative. Those who had heard the emotional accident story remembered the dramatic middle events very well; their memories for the comparatively unemotional beginning and end parts were somewhat worse (Figure 10.6). In contrast, participants who had heard the less exciting story about a disaster drill recalled fewer events, particularly from the middle (Cahill, Uncapher, Kilpatrick, Alkire, & Turner, 2004). Apparently, even though both groups of participants saw the same pictures, those for whom the story was emotionally arousing were better able to encode the details and remember them later (Cahill, Babinsky, Markowitsch, & McGaugh, 1995). The strong encoding and persistence of emotionally charged memories is one reason advertisers often use sexual or otherwise exciting elements in commercials, hoping we'll remember the ad and buy the product later (see "Learning and Memory in Everyday Life" below).

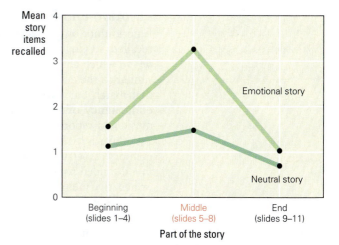

Figure 10.6 **Memory for emotionally arousing material** Participants who heard the emotional story from Figure 10.5 were later able to recall more details of the middle part than participants who saw the same pictures accompanied by the emotionally neutral story.

► **LEARNING AND MEMORY IN EVERYDAY LIFE**

Sex Sells. Sometimes.

In November 2010, British TV aired a perfume commercial that started off by showing the singer Beyoncé seemingly naked. The ad was subsequently banned from daytime television in the United Kingdom as too sexually provocative. In 2008, TV networks in the United States banned a similarly steamy perfume ad featuring Eva Mendes. A few years earlier, in 2005, Paris Hilton made headlines with her commercial in which she soaped down a car while wearing a skimpy bikini—as part of a campaign promoting a hamburger chain. In fact, seldom does a year go by without some advertiser pushing the boundaries with a sexually explicit ad, usually featuring a noted celebrity and often promoting a comparatively nonerotic product such as fast food. Why?

One reason is that viewers who watch a sexually explicit commercial and experience arousal may misinterpret that arousal as an attraction to the product, just like research participants in the "High Bridge"

study who misinterpreted their arousal as attraction to the experimenter.

Another reason is that emotional arousal can increase the strength of memory formation. If a commercial can evoke a strong emotion (for example, sexual interest, excitement, or humor), there is a better chance that viewers will remember the commercial and the product it showcases. In fact, the mere creation of an outrageous ad, and the controversy it engenders, can increase name-brand recognition.

But commercials aren't the only fare on television that provokes emotional arousal. Many TV programs contain violent or sexually explicit material that can be highly arousing. This arousal can impair memory for nonemotional material presented during the commercial break. For example, in one study, participants watched a TV program that was either violent (e.g., *World Wrestling Federation Monday Night Nitro*), sexually explicit (e.g., *Strip Poker*), or neutral (e.g., *Candid Camera*). Each program had

been modified from its original format so that it now contained nine ads for various products such as soda pop, cereal, or laundry detergent. Afterward, participants were asked to recall the advertised brands. Memory was better in participants who saw the ads during the neutral program than in those who had been watching the violent or sexually explicit programs (Bushman & Bonacci, 2002). The violent and sexually explicit programs impaired memory of the commercials in male and female viewers equally, and regardless of whether the individual reported liking the program or not.

Emotion and arousal help direct our attention to potentially important stimuli; violent and sexually explicit TV material captures our attention (whether we enjoy it or not), potentially leaving less attention available for processing other information, such as intervening commercials. Under these circumstances, sex and violence don't sell—and may even work against the effectiveness of the commercial.

Emotion and Retrieval of Memories

Emotion not only affects how memories are stored; it also affects how they are recalled. In Chapter 7 you read about the concept of *transfer-appropriate processing*, in which chances of recall are increased if the cues available at retrieval are similar to the cues available at testing. It is likewise easier to retrieve memories that match our current mood or emotional state; this effect is termed **mood congruency of memory.** For example, in one study, students first listened to music and reported whether it made them feel happy or sad. They then saw a list of words (SHIP, STREET, etc.) and were asked to recall an autobiographical memory associated with each word. Students who had reported being in a happy mood tended to generate mostly positive memories, and relatively few neutral or negative memories, as shown in Figure 10.7 (Eich, Macaulay, & Ryan, 1994). Students in a sad mood recalled fewer positive and more negative memories. Few students in either mood generated many neutral memories—consistent with the general principle that our strongest memories tend to be associated with strong emotions, whether those emotions are positive or negative.

Mood-congruent memory effects occur in real-life contexts too. For example, patients suffering with clinical depression are more likely to recall sad or unpleasant events than pleasant memories (Clark & Teasdale, 1982; Fogarty & Hemsley, 1983). This can lead to a vicious cycle in which the recollection of sad memories makes the patient feel even more depressed and hopeless.

Why might mood influence recall? A strong mood or emotion causes biological responses and subjective feelings, and these can be incorporated into the memory just like other contextual cues. As you learned in Chapter 7, one of the factors influencing our ability to retrieve a memory is the number of cues available to guide retrieval. From this perspective, a strong mood or emotion is simply one kind of memory cue, and as the number of cues available at the time of recall increases, the more likely we are to successfully retrieve the original information.

Flashbulb Memories You've just read how everyday emotions can strengthen memories. Extreme emotions can result in memories that appear to have exceptional strength and durability. Such memories are called **flashbulb memories** because they form quickly, as if the brain were taking "flash photographs" to preserve the incident forever in vivid detail, while other, less arousing memories fade with time (R. Brown & Kulik, 1977). Some of us have flashbulb memories for important personal events, like the death of a parent, a car accident, or a first kiss. We may remember these events vividly, recollecting not just the place and time of day where, say, that first kiss occurred but even things like the smell

Figure 10.7 Mood-congruency of memory People in a happy mood tend to recall more positive than negative or neutral autobiographical memories; by contrast, people in a sad mood recall significantly fewer positive and more negative memories.

Data from Eich et al., 1994. Adapted from Cahill and McGaugh, 1995.

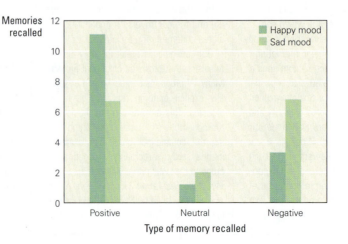

of the room, the sound of a clock ticking in the background, and the color and texture of the clothes we were wearing.

Every so often an event (usually a tragedy) occurs that causes an entire society to form flashbulb memories. September 11 is one example. Other examples include the assassination of public figures—such as President John F. Kennedy or Martin Luther King, Jr.—and disasters such as hurricanes, earthquakes, floods, or spaceship explosions. The assassination of President Kennedy is perhaps the best studied such event. Five decades later, many older Americans still maintain vivid memories of when and how they heard that the president had been shot. For example, 10 years after the event, one man recalled,

> **I was seated in a sixth-grade music class, and over the intercom I was told that the president had been shot. At first, everyone just looked at each other. Then the class started yelling, and the music teacher tried to calm everyone down. About ten minutes later I heard over the intercom that Kennedy had died and that everyone should return to their homeroom. I remember that when I got to my homeroom my teacher was crying and everyone was standing in a state of shock. They told us to go home. (R. Brown & Kulik, 1982 [1977], pp. 23–24)**

Other Americans recalled the moment in similar detail:

> **". . . I was having dinner in a French restaurant . . ."**
> **". . . talking to a woman friend on the telephone . . ."**
> **"The weather was cloudy and gray . . ."**
> **". . . I was carrying a carton of Viceroy cigarettes which I dropped . . ."**
> **(R. Brown & Kulik, 1982 [1977], p. 30)**

Flashbulb memories for the events of September 11, 2001, seem to be similarly vivid. Several years after the event, many people can still remember where they were, what they were doing, and whom they were with when they heard the news. By contrast, memory for other, ordinary days (such as September 10, 2001) is generally much less detailed (Paradis, Solomon, Florer, & Thompson, 2004).

Can Flashbulb Memories Be Trusted? People generally report being very confident of the accuracy of their flashbulb memories. In fact, however, it appears that what distinguishes flashbulb memories from other episodic memories is not that they are more objectively accurate than other memories but rather that we strongly "feel" that they are accurate (Phelps & Sharot, 2008). Viewed this way, flashbulb memories are merely episodic memories that are experienced with great vividness and confidence (Sharot, Martorella, Delgado, & Phelps, 2007). Ulrich Neisser, one of the foremost memory researchers of the twentieth century, recounted a memory of his boyhood as follows:

> **For many years I have remembered how I heard the news of the Japanese attack on Pearl Harbor, which occurred on [December 7, 1941,] the day before my thirteenth birthday. I recall sitting in the living room of our house . . . listening to a baseball game on the radio. The game was interrupted by an announcement of the attack, and I rushed upstairs to tell my mother. This memory has been so clear for so long that I never confronted its inherent absurdity until last year: no one broadcasts baseball games in December! (Neisser, 1982, p. 45)**

Some details of Neisser's flashbulb memory are obviously inconsistent with common sense, and so we (like he) can conclude that his memory is almost certainly wrong in some of its details. However, although baseball is not played in December, football is: the New York Dodgers and Giants (two football teams with the same names as New York baseball teams of the day) were in fact playing on December 7, 1941, when the radio broadcast was interrupted with news of the Pearl Harbor bombing. Neisser's flashbulb memory was probably reasonably accurate—except for the minor detail that he misremembered the type of game he'd been listening to on the radio (Thompson & Cowan, 1986).

Unfortunately, it is not always so easy to determine whether the details of a flashbulb memory are correct or not. For example, when someone remembers dropping a carton of Viceroy cigarettes after hearing of the Kennedy assassination, how can we tell whether that detail is correct? In general, unless the detail is obviously inconsistent with known facts, we cannot be sure of its accuracy.

Several studies have attempted to address this issue by judging flashbulb memories immediately after the arousing event and again sometime later. For example, on September 12, 2001, researchers Jennifer Talarico and David Rubin contacted 54 Duke University students and asked a series of open-ended questions about how the students had heard of the terrorist attacks (Talarico & Rubin, 2003). On average, students remembered about 12 details, such as where they heard the news, who was with them at the time, and so on. The researchers then contacted the same students again later. Talarico and Rubin found that the memories decayed over time, with students remembering fewer details as the weeks and months passed. Students contacted a week after the event might remember only about 10 of the details they'd previously reported, and students contacted 8 months after the event might remember only about 7 details. At the same time, inconsistent details crept into the reports. For example, on September 12, a student might have reported hearing the news from a friend; by May 2002, that same student might "remember" hearing the news on television.

A similar pattern of distortion over time has been demonstrated for memories of other notable events (Neisser & Harsch, 1992; Schmolck, Buffalo, & Squire, 2000). The bottom line on all these studies is that flashbulb memories are long lasting, vivid, and largely accurate—but they are not perfect photographic records of the event: they can be incomplete and can contain inaccurate details.

Why should such errors creep into our memories? Many errors consist of memory misattribution, such as forgetting that a friend told you the news and instead "remembering" that you first heard it on the television or radio (Greenberg, 2004). This is perhaps an understandable mistake, given our cultural tendency to become glued to the TV following a national tragedy; the repetition and visual impact of news coverage may swamp our memories of how we really heard the news. Another possibility is that memories of particularly important events are continuously pondered, rehearsed, and discussed. Each time, we are liable, quite unconsciously, to fill any little gaps in our memory with details that seem to fit the context. Later, we remember those inserted details as part of the original event. As you read in Chapter 7, this is one way that false memories can form. The result is that although

THE FAR SIDE® BY GARY LARSON

© 1993 FarWorks, Inc. All Rights Reserved/Dist. by Creators Syndicate

I was just getting ready to cross the interstate.

I was down by the edge of the lake at the time.

I was in the glen, just finishing a new burrow when I got the news.

I was looking for crawdads in my favorite creek.

I was under a rock, getting ready to shed.

More facts of nature: All forest animals, to this very day, remember exactly where they were and what they were doing when they heard that Bambi's mother had been shot.

many remembered details may be quite correct, others—that seem equally vivid—may be entirely wrong.

So, think back to the morning of September 11, 2001—or another occasion on which you heard important, emotionally arousing news, such as the death of a family member. Where were you when you got the news? What were you doing at the time? Who was with you? It may be instructive to ask those people what they remember about the day and to see whether their memories match yours. Chances are, you will be right about many of the details—after all, strong emotions do encourage strong memories—but at least some of the details that you remember quite vividly, when you can check them against the facts, may turn out to be false memories.

Interim Summary

- Emotions have three components: physiological responses, overt behavioral responses, and conscious feelings. Each component influences the others.

- The major emotions, such as happiness, fear, and anger, seem to be universal, although the overt display of these emotions may be influenced by culture.

- Although we cannot be sure whether nonhuman animals have conscious emotional feelings, their physiological and behavioral responses to emotional stimuli are often very similar to those in humans.

- Conditioned emotional learning is a form of classical conditioning in which a CS (such as a tone) that has been paired with an emotion-evoking US (such as an electric shock) evokes a CR (such as a freezing response or an increased heartbeat). Conditioned escape learning involves operant conditioning: a stimulus S (such as an electric shock) can evoke a motor response R to produce an outcome O (escape from shock).

- Avoidance learning, learning that a particular response results in avoidance of an aversive event, may involve both classical and operant conditioning; in addition, cognitive expectancies may allow the organism to choose between various possible responses.

- Learned helplessness occurs when exposure to an inescapable punisher impairs learning to escape or avoid future punishment.

- Powerful emotions can increase the strength and duration of memory storage. Emotion can also affect retrieval: we are more likely to retrieve memories that fit our current mood.

- Flashbulb memories are vivid and long lasting, but they are not always completely accurate.

10.2 Brain Substrates

From the earliest days of brain science, scientists have tried to understand how the brain gives rise to emotion. One of the most influential attempts to locate the brain substrates of emotion was made by Cornell University anatomist James Papez in 1937. (Papez is pronounced "papes," to rhyme with "grapes.") Papez reviewed literature showing that lesions to various parts of the brain caused different kinds of emotional impairments. For example, human patients with rabies, which causes damage to the hippocampus, can be overly aggressive, and patients with damage to the cingulate cortex often display apathy and depression. Therefore, Papez reasoned, the hippocampus and cingulate cortex must play major roles in emotions—along with other regions such as the thalamus, by which sensory information enters the brain, and the hypothalamus, which helps regulate

Figure 10.8 **Results of functional neuroimaging studies of emotion** The emotions happiness, sadness, disgust, fear, and anger each activated many different brain regions, and no one brain region was activated by all the emotions.

Phan, Wagner, Taylor, & Liberzon, 2002, Figure 1A.

Figure 10.9 **Key brain structures involved in processing emotion** Brain structures that have special roles in emotional learning include the amygdala, hippocampus, thalamus, hypothalamus, and cingulate cortex. The frontal cortex also plays a key role in interpreting the context and monitoring the display of emotion.

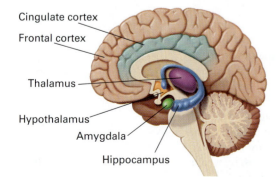

Cingulate cortex
Frontal cortex
Thalamus
Hypothalamus
Amygdala
Hippocampus

the body's response to emotion. Papez proposed that these brain regions operate in a loop, later named the *Papez circuit*, that he described as the central processing pathway for emotion.

The Papez circuit is important historically because it represents one of the first systematic attempts to understand the brain substrates of emotion by combining information about lesion studies with what was then known about anatomical structures. Remarkably, many of the presumed pathways connecting the structures in the Papez circuit were not yet known to exist; Papez merely deduced they must be there. Almost all of them have since been discovered in the brain.

Despite his brilliant reasoning, Papez wasn't exactly right. Some of the structures he included—such as the hippocampus and hypothalamus—are indeed important for emotion, but they are not restricted to processing emotional information. Furthermore, Papez left out some structures, such as the amygdala, that we now know are critical for emotional learning.

We now know that there is no specialized "emotion circuit." Each emotion activates many different brain regions (Phan, Wagner, Taylor, & Liberzon, 2002). One report, which combined data across 55 functional neuroimaging (fMRI and PET) studies of emotion, produced the summary shown in Figure 10.8, which marks the parts of the brain that are activated by the emotions of happiness, sadness, disgust, fear, and anger (Phan, Wagner, Taylor, & Liberzon, 2002). The important things to notice are (1) each emotion activated many different brain regions, and (2) no single brain region was activated by all the different emotions. Thus, emotion appears to be a function of the brain as a whole rather than arising from special circuits dedicated to individual emotions. All the same, some parts of the brain appear to be particularly important for emotion. First and foremost among these is the amygdala.

The Amygdala: A Central Processing Station for Emotions

As shown in Figure 10.9, the **amygdala** is a small almond-shaped structure that lies at the anterior tip of the hippocampus. (The word "amygdala" is taken from the Greek word for "almond.") Just as the brain has one hippocampus in each hemisphere, it also has one amygdala in each hemisphere, at the tip of each hippocampus, but for convenience, most researchers refer to "the amygdala," just as they refer to "the hippocampus."

The amygdala is a collection of more than 10 separate subregions, or *nuclei*, all of which have different input and output pathways. Figure 10.10 depicts some key nuclei and connections within the amygdala. (Many other nuclei and pathways exist but are not shown in Figure 10.10 for simplicity.) The *lateral nucleus* is a primary entry point for sensory information into the amygdala; this sensory information arrives directly from the thalamus and also indirectly from the thalamus by way of the cortex. The *central nucleus* receives inputs from other amygdala nuclei and projects out of the amygdala to the autonomic nervous system (ANS),

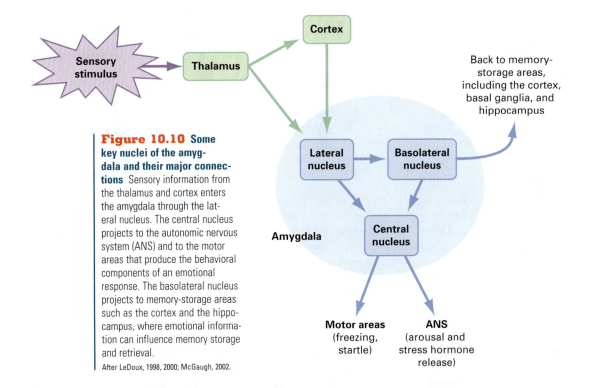

Figure 10.10 Some key nuclei of the amygdala and their major connections Sensory information from the thalamus and cortex enters the amygdala through the lateral nucleus. The central nucleus projects to the autonomic nervous system (ANS) and to the motor areas that produce the behavioral components of an emotional response. The basolateral nucleus projects to memory-storage areas such as the cortex and the hippocampus, where emotional information can influence memory storage and retrieval.

After LeDoux, 1998, 2000; McGaugh, 2002.

driving expression of physiological responses such as arousal and release of stress hormones, and also to motor centers, driving expression of behavioral responses such as freezing and startle. The *basolateral nucleus* receives input from the lateral nucleus and projects to the cerebral cortex, basal ganglia, and hippocampus, providing a pathway by which the amygdala can modulate memory storage and retrieval in those structures. The amygdala is thus critical both in learned emotional responses and in the emotional modulation of memory storage and retrieval.

The Central Nucleus: Expressing Emotional Responses

In the research lab, electrical stimulation of the amygdala can produce dramatic emotional displays. For example, stimulating the amygdala of a predator, such as a cat, can cause a species-typical defensive reaction, including lowering of the head, flattening of the ears, piloerection, and growling or hissing (Roldan, Alvarez-Pelaez, & Fernandez de Molina, 1974). In a prey animal, such as a rabbit, stimulation of the amygdala causes a different species-typical defensive reaction, including freezing and a lowered heart rate (Kapp, Gallagher, Underwood, McNall, & Whitehorn, 1981). Stimulating the amygdala in humans doesn't produce such dramatic results. Humans given amygdala stimulation may report subjective feelings of mild positive or negative emotion, but they are not likely to exhibit an all-out emotional response such as occurs in cats and rabbits (Bancaud, Brunet-Bourgin, Chauvel, & Halgren, 1994; Halgren, 1982).

Why might stimulation of the amygdala cause such a dramatic fear response in some animals but only mild feelings of foreboding in humans? According to a two-factor theory of emotion (see Figure 10.2c), our conscious emotional feelings depend not only on our biological responses but also on how we interpret the situation. In the relatively "safe" context of a lab environment, human participants receiving amygdala stimulation know they are in a controlled situation and that a full panic response is not warranted. On the other hand, in a truly menacing situation—such as a walk through a dark alley at night—outputs from

Figure 10.11
Conditioned emotional responses (a) In humans, a loud boat horn (US) produces a skin conductance response (SCR). If a colored shape (CS) is paired with the US, then healthy humans (controls) produce a strong SCR to the CS. A patient with selective damage to the amygdala (AL) does not show this conditioned emotional response, although a patient with damage to the nearby hippocampus (HL) does. (b) In rats, conditioned emotional responding (freezing) is similarly abolished by AL but not HL.

(a) Adapted from Bechara et al., 1995, Figure 2; (b) adapted from Phillips & LeDoux, 1992.

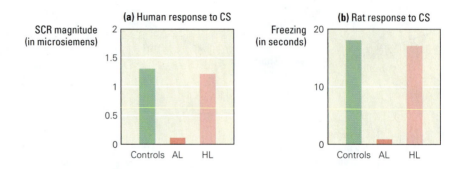

the amygdala would initiate a biological fear response—a speeded heart rate, sweaty palms, and other components of the fight-or-flight response.

Given that the amygdala helps initiate the body's emotional responses, it is not too surprising that lesions of the central nucleus of the amygdala disrupt the ability to learn, as well as display, new emotional responses. Bilateral damage limited to the amygdala is rare in humans (Markowitsch et al., 1994), although a few such cases have been identified and studied. These patients often show deficits in learning emotional responses. For example, Chapter 3 introduced the *skin conductance response* (SCR), a tiny but measurable change in the electrical conductivity of the human skin that occurs when people feel arousal. In healthy people, a loud sound, such as a 100-decibel boat horn (the US), produces a sharp increase in skin conductance (the UR). If this US is always preceded by a neutral stimulus, such as the appearance of a colored shape, healthy participants learn that the visual CS predicts the US, and they therefore produce an SCR to the CS alone (Figure 10.11a). This is an example of classical conditioning.

The SCR is mediated by outputs from the central amygdala to the ANS that cause the skin conductance to change. As a result, conditioning of the SCR can be disrupted by damage to the amygdala. Figure 10.11a shows the responses of a patient with bilateral amygdala damage. Although the US evoked a strong SCR in this patient, the CS did not. This patient could exhibit arousal when startled but could not learn a conditioned emotional response (Bechara et al., 1995). In contrast, a different patient with damage that included the nearby hippocampus (but not the amygdala) could learn a conditioned emotional response as well as controls could. Thus, the amygdala is important for learning and expressing conditioned emotional responses.

Nonhuman animals with lesions of the amygdala central nucleus show similar disruptions in conditioned emotional responding. For example, after three days of CS-US training with a shock US, a normal rat will give an emotional response to the CS that can include physiological changes (such as increased blood pressure) and overt behavioral responses (such as freezing, shown in Figure 10.11b). Lesions that damage the central nucleus of the amygdala abolish this learned fear response, so there is no freezing to the CS alone; just like in humans, damage to the nearby hippocampus that spares the amygdala does not affect the learned freezing response (Phillips & LeDoux, 1992).

These disruptions in conditioned emotional responses occur because the central nucleus provides the major outputs from the amygdala to the ANS and to motor centers that drive the freezing response. (These pathways are shown in Figure 10.10.) Lesion of the central nucleus therefore disrupts the ability to express a learned fear response. Some researchers believe that the conditioned emotional response is learned and stored in the lateral nucleus, with the central nucleus behaving more like a simple way station that signals other brain stations to turn on the fear responses (Cahill, Weinberger, Roozendaal, & McGaugh,

1999; Fanselow & LeDoux, 1999; Maren, 1999; McGaugh & Cahill, 2003). Thus, animals with lesions of the central nucleus might still be able to learn about a fear-evoking CS; they would simply be unable to express this learning by freezing or by activating the ANS. Other researchers suggest that the central nucleus is not only a passive way station but encodes other aspects of emotional learning, particularly when appetitive, or pleasant, rather than aversive, or unpleasant, stimuli are involved (Balleine & Kilcross, 2006; Everitt, Cardinal, Parkinson, & Robbins, 2003).

Two Pathways for Emotional Learning in the Amygdala

As you saw in Figure 10.10, the amygdala receives sensory input from two separate pathways. The thalamus is the first site in the brain where most kinds of sensory input converge and are processed; for this reason, the thalamus is sometimes called the "sensory gateway to the brain." From the thalamus, stimulus information travels directly to the amygdala and also up to the cortex. As you read in Chapter 3, the cortex processes sensory information more fully, discriminating fine details and so on. Information from the cortex also travels down to the amygdala. Emotion researcher Joseph LeDoux proposes that each of these pathways—the direct path from the thalamus to the amygdala and the indirect path from the thalamus to the cortex to the amygdala—plays an important role in responding to fear-evoking stimuli (LeDoux, 1993, 1994). The direct path is faster—carrying information from the thalamus to the amygdala in about 12 milliseconds in rats—but it also conveys less detail, just the bare outlines of stimulus information. The indirect pathway is slower—taking about 19 milliseconds for information from the thalamus to reach the amygdala in rats—but the involvement of the cortex allows much finer discrimination of stimulus details. In LeDoux's terms, the direct path is "fast and rough" and the indirect path is "slow but accurate." The faster, direct path allows us to react quickly in a life-and-death situation, activating the fight-or-flight response; the slower, more accurate path then provides extra information, allowing us to terminate the fear response if the stimulus is not dangerous after all.

Here's a simple example of how this dual pathway might work. Suppose you're walking home alone at night, feeling a little nervous. A big, dark shape approaches. This visual stimulus activates your thalamus, which shoots this information directly to the amygdala. The amygdala interprets this stimulus as possibly signaling danger and activates an immediate fear response ("yikes!"), preparing you to fight or run away. A few milliseconds later, the signals from the thalamus reach your visual cortex, which processes the stimulus more fully and allows you to recognize the stimulus as nonthreatening: it's only a friend walking toward you. The cortex sends this information ("no danger here") down to the amygdala, shutting off the fear response. (It may take a few moments for stress hormone levels to decline enough so that your heart rate returns to normal and your goose bumps fade away.)

The cost of using the "fast-and-rough" pathway from thalamus to amygdala is that you have gotten yourself all worked up over nothing. On the other hand, the cost of overreacting to a harmless stimulus is much less, in general, than the cost of failing to respond to a truly dangerous stimulus (LeDoux, 2000; LeDoux, Iwata, Cicchetti, & Reis, 1988). If the approaching shape really had been a threat, the cost of waiting for your cortex to make a definitive identification could have been the difference between escape and injury. From an evolutionary perspective, animals with a genetic predisposition to freeze or dart for cover when they see movement in the bush ("Was that rustling in the bushes caused by a predator or just the wind? Better to play it safe and survive another day . . .")

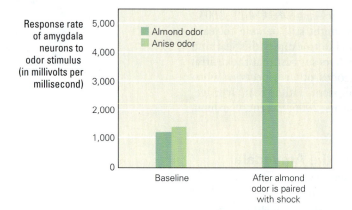

Response rate of amygdala neurons to odor stimulus (in millivolts per millisecond)

Figure 10.12 The lateral amygdala and conditioning Baseline responding of lateral amygdala neurons of a rat is similar for two odors. If one of the odors (almond) is subsequently paired with a tail shock, the response to that odor increases strongly from the baseline value. This is exactly the pattern of responding that would be expected if the lateral amygdala neurons were encoding the associations between odor CS and shock US.

Data from Rosenkranz and Grace, 2002.

are more likely to live long enough to produce offspring that share the same cautious instincts.

Once having survived a brush with danger, the next challenge is to learn from it. Some of this learning probably takes place in the lateral nucleus of the amygdala, where neural connections change as a result of experiencing a neutral CS paired with a fear-evoking US. For example, in one study, researchers implanted recording electrodes into the lateral amygdala of rats so as to simultaneously monitor the activity of about 100 neurons (Rosenkranz & Grace, 2002). When the rats were presented with various odors—say, almond and anise—the neurons showed a low baseline level of response to each (Figure 10.12). The researchers then trained the rats that one odor—say, almond—always preceded a tail-shock US. Not surprisingly, the rats quickly learned to freeze in anticipation of a shock whenever they encountered almond odor, although they showed no such fear response to the anise odor, which had not been paired with shock. Figure 10.12 shows that, after training, neurons in the lateral amygdala responded strongly to the almond odor that had been paired with the US.

This is exactly the pattern you would expect to see if *long-term potentiation* (LTP) were occurring in the lateral amygdala. (To review LTP, see Chapter 2.) Assume that the almond odor activates sensory neurons in the rat's nose, and these in turn project (directly and by way of sensory cortex) to neurons in the lateral nucleus of the amygdala. Initially, presentation of either odor causes little activity in these neurons (the baseline condition in Figure 10.12), but a shock stimulus strongly activates them. If the almond odor is paired with the shock, the almond odor arrives just as the neurons are activated by shock, and since "neurons that fire together, wire together," the synapse between them is strengthened. The end result of these events is that when the almond odor is presented again, it will cause more activity in the lateral amygdala (as shown in Figure 10.12). No such strengthening occurs in pathways carrying information about anise or other odors because they have not been paired with shock.

Does this prove that the lateral amygdala is the site where conditioned emotional responses are stored? Unfortunately, this is not yet completely clear. Some researchers do believe that CS-US associations are stored in some subregions of the amygdala (LeDoux, 2000). Other researchers think the amygdala may merely guide storage in other brain areas such as the cortex (McGaugh, 2000; McIntyre, Power, Roozendaal, & McGaugh, 2003; Paré, 2002). However, these are not necessarily contradictory ideas (Fanselow & LeDoux, 1999). Perhaps the amygdala specializes in learning the CS-US association and producing emotional CRs but also modulates memory storage elsewhere that represents other aspects of the experience—such as the episodic memory of an emotional event. So, let's turn next to consider the ways in which emotion can modulate storage and recall of episodic memory.

The Amygdala and Episodic Memory Storage

Recall the experiment in which a slide show accompanied narration of either an emotionally arousing story or a neutral story (Figure 10.5). Healthy people remembered more details of the emotionally arousing story, particularly from the dramatic middle part, than of the neutral story (Figure 10.6). By contrast, a patient with amygdala damage recalled the beginning and end of the story about as well as did healthy control patients but showed no physiological arousal during the emotional middle section and no tendency, later, to recall that material better (Cahill, Babinsky, Markowitsch, & McGaugh, 1995). It wasn't that the patient couldn't remember the story but that the memory of the middle part didn't get an emotional "boost." This finding implies that the amygdala may provide a signal to strengthen the storage of emotional information in declarative memory.

Even in healthy brains, the degree of amygdala activation may reflect how effectively emotional information is processed and stored in memory. If healthy people are shown emotionally arousing short films while their brain activity is recorded using PET, those individuals with the highest level of amygdala activation during viewing tend to remember more details later than individuals with lower levels of amygdala activity (Cahill et al., 1996). Other studies have documented that the amygdala is also activated while participants view pleasant pictures, and greater amygdala activity during encoding of specific pictures is correlated with better recognition of those pictures later (Canli, Zhao, Brewer, Gabrieli, & Cahill, 2000; Hamann, Ely, Grafton, & Kilts, 1999).

Degree of amygdala activity may therefore help determine whether new information gets stored as an episodic or a semantic memory. Recall from Chapter 7 that episodic memory is information we "remember" and semantic memory is information we "know." The key difference is that episodic memory has supporting contextual information—we remember the time and place where the event that produced the memory happened to us. Healthy adults, shown a series of emotional photographs and asked to recognize them later, can be asked whether they "remember" previously studying that picture or merely "know" that the picture is familiar (but don't actually remember the study episode). Amygdala activity is higher both at encoding (Dolcos, LaBar, & Cabeza, 2004) and recognition (Sharot, Delgado, & Phelps, 2004) of emotionally arousing photographs that are subsequently judged as "remembered" than for those that are merely "known." Thus, emotional arousal (and amygdala activation) may promote encoding of contextual details, creating a subjective sense of "remembering" and causing the information to be stored as an episodic rather than semantic memory (LaBar, 2007). This in turn could be why we often have such a vivid sense of recollection for highly emotional events—flashbulb memories are formed when episodic memories are tagged with a particularly strong feeling of "remembering."

There are also intriguing sex differences in amygdala responses during memory formation: in women, left amygdala activation during encoding predicts better memory later; in men, right amygdala activation predicts better memory later (Cahill et al., 2001; Cahill et al., 2004; Canli, Desmond, Zhao, & Gabrieli, 2002). No one is quite sure yet why these left-right sex differences occur or how they might relate to observed sex differences in memory and behavior (Haman, 2005).

The Role of Stress Hormones

Given the association between amygdala activation and the strength of episodic memory, the next question is, exactly how might the amygdala influence memory storage? One possible pathway is schematized in Figure 10.13. Outputs from the central nucleus of the amygdala travel to the ANS, which in turn signals the adrenal glands to release the stress hormone epinephrine. Epinephrine, along with other stress hormones, helps mediate the various components of the fight-or-flight response, including increased heart rate and dilation of blood vessels, to facilitate blood flow to brain and muscles.

But epinephrine can't affect the brain directly. The brain has a defense called the *blood-brain barrier*, a membrane that controls passage of substances from the blood into the central nervous system, including the brain. This protects the

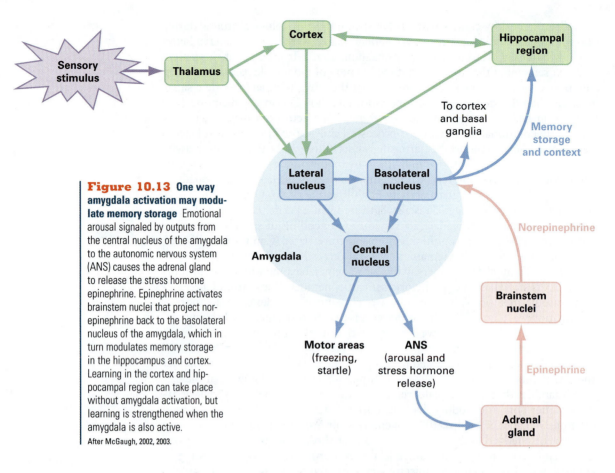

Figure 10.13 **One way amygdala activation may modulate memory storage** Emotional arousal signaled by outputs from the central nucleus of the amygdala to the autonomic nervous system (ANS) causes the adrenal gland to release the stress hormone epinephrine. Epinephrine activates brainstem nuclei that project norepinephrine back to the basolateral nucleus of the amygdala, which in turn modulates memory storage in the hippocampus and cortex. Learning in the cortex and hippocampal region can take place without amygdala activation, but learning is strengthened when the amygdala is also active.
After McGaugh, 2002, 2003.

brain from many chemicals that might otherwise enter and harm it. Epinephrine cannot cross the blood-brain barrier, but it can activate brainstem nuclei that produce the chemically related neurotransmitter norepinephrine, and these nuclei project to the basolateral amygdala, as shown in Figure 10.13 (McGaugh, 2002, 2003). From there, outputs from the basolateral amygdala travel to brain regions including the hippocampus and cortex. Emotional stimuli such as foot shocks do indeed cause increased levels of norepinephrine in the basolateral amygdala—and the precise amount of norepinephrine in an individual rat's amygdala is a good predictor of how well that rat will remember the learning experience (McIntyre, Hatfield, & McGaugh, 2000).

Back in Chapter 7, you read that the cerebral cortex is the primary storage site of episodic memories, with this storage mediated by the hippocampus and other medial temporal lobe structures. So how might release of norepinephrine into the basolateral amygdala affect episodic memory storage in these other brain areas? Let's assume that a rat (or human) experiences an emotional event that causes norepinephrine to activate the basolateral amygdala. The neurons of the basolateral amygdala tend to fire in rhythmic waves (Paré, 2003), and they project out to the cortex, hippocampal region, and other memory-storage sites, where they may cause similarly rhythmic activation in large groups of neurons. Such rhythmic activation of many neurons facilitates LTP between the coactive neurons (again, "neurons that fire together, wire together"). In this way, the basolateral amygdala may facilitate learning in the cortex and hippocampal region.

Just as increasing the levels of norepinephrine in the basolateral amygdala can improve emotional memory, disruptions in norepinephrine transmission can impair emotional memory. Once again, let's consider the study in which Larry Cahill and colleagues showed participants a series of slides accompanied by an emotional story (Figure 10.5). In one variant, before starting the slides and story, Cahill gave some volunteers the drug propranolol, which blocks norepinephrine; the control group received an inactive placebo (Cahill, Prins, Weber, & McGaugh, 1994). Later, those people who'd received the placebo showed the normal pattern of remembering the emotionally charged middle part best (just like the participants in Figure 10.6). In contrast, people who had been given propranolol remembered the middle part no better (and no worse) than the emotionally neutral beginning and end parts. In general, blocking stress hormones (by administering drugs that interfere with epinephrine, norepinephrine, or glucocorticoids) reduces the ability of emotions to enhance memory.

These results help explain why the patient with amygdala damage had poor memory for the emotional middle part of the story. Without input from the amygdala, the other memory-storage areas may not be encouraged to form a strong memory of the emotionally arousing material, so the material is stored no more (or less) strongly than any other information. On the other hand, increasing stress hormones (by injecting epinephrine, norepinephrine, or glucocorticoids) can improve memory for emotional material (Buchanan & Lovallo, 2001; Cahill & Alkire, 2003)—to a point (see "Learning and Memory in Everyday Life" below).

▶ **LEARNING AND MEMORY IN EVERYDAY LIFE**

A Little Stress Is a Good Thing

Three high school students, Larry, Moe, and Curly, are facing a stressful experience: taking their SATs. But they are reacting in different ways. Larry has gained early acceptance to Princeton, so he is relatively relaxed about the exam. Moe is nervous; he needs strong SAT scores to get into the college of his choice. Curly dreads tests of all sorts, and he's downright panicked now. On the (admittedly fictitious) assumption that all three students have equal knowledge going into the exam, who is likely to perform best?

Of course, Curly is at a disadvantage; he is so stressed out that he may well forget everything he ever knew as soon as he looks at the first question. But Larry may also be at a disadvantage if he's too relaxed. A little stress is good for memory, and this applies to recall (taking a test) as well as encoding (initial learning). Mild stress causes the release of stress hormones, including glucocorticoids. The hippocampus has a particularly high concentration

of glucocorticoid receptors (McEwen & Sapolsky, 1995), and low levels of stress hormones facilitate LTP and encourage dendritic growth, improving memory formation and recall (McEwen, 1999). Thus, Moe may actually benefit from his mild anxiety during the SATs.

Unfortunately, although low levels of stress can improve recall, chronic high levels of stress often impair recall (de Quervain, Roozendaal, & McGaugh, 1998; de Quervain, Roozendaal, Nitsch, McGaugh, & Hock, 2000). This may be because, although low levels of stress hormones facilitate hippocampal learning, higher levels can overexcite the hippocampus, interfering with both learning and recall (Benjamin, McKeachie, Lin, & Holinger, 1981). Long-term exposure to high levels of stress may even cause neuronal death in the hippocampus (McEwen, 1997; Sapolsky, 1996).

How much stress is too much? Unfortunately, there is no easy answer: each individual seems to have a

different breaking point (Kemeny, 2003). Furthermore, an individual's response to stress depends partly on whether he or she feels helpless to control it (see "Learning and Memory in Everyday Life" on page 399). If you are constantly feeling stressed, try making a list of the things that bother you and then look for ways of changing (controlling) one or two of them. You can also try methods of reducing stress, such as meditation, yoga, prayer, or exercise, that may help you calm down and may help get your hippocampus back into its normal operating range (Davidson et al., 2003).

As for Curly . . . the best thing he can do is try to calm himself during the test—perhaps by taking deep breaths and thinking positive thoughts (Naveh-Benjamin, 1991). Once his stress hormones drop back to normal levels, his hippocampus can again function normally. This is one reason why, after the SATs are over, Curly will probably remember all those answers that he "forgot" under pressure during the test.

Retrieval and Reconsolidation

The influence of the amygdala isn't limited to the initial learning experience. As you learned in Chapter 7, memories are not formed instantaneously but remain malleable throughout a *consolidation period*, during which time they are vulnerable to such interventions as electroconvulsive shock or head injury. You also read about *reconsolidation*, in which—under some circumstances—reactivation of an old memory makes it vulnerable all over again (Nader, 2003). The reactivation of a memory for an emotional event provides a window of opportunity during which a fresh dose of stress hormones could strengthen the neural circuits encoding that memory. Thus, while the principles of reconsolidation may apply to all types of memory, emotional memories may be particularly susceptible. This in turn suggests one way in which small distortions could creep into flashbulb memories: the memory might initially be accurate, but each time it is recalled, tiny details might be forgotten or altered, and over time, the memory could become quite different from its original form.

Reconsolidation can be demonstrated in rats using a conditioned avoidance procedure. Control rats, after having received a shock in a dark chamber, will hesitate about 60 seconds before daring to enter the dark chamber again (Figure 10.14a). But if the rats are given injections of epinephrine immediately (0 minutes) after the foot shock, this delay skyrockets, so that the rats now hesitate for more than 200 seconds before reentering the dark chamber (Figure 10.14b). As you saw in Figure 10.13, epinephrine stimulates norepinephrine release to the basolateral amygdala, which in turn stimulates learning in the cortex and hippocampus—making the rats remember more strongly that the dark chamber is a dangerous place. The effects of epinephrine are greatest if injection occurs immediately after the foot shock, but epinephrine can still boost memory if administered 10 or 30 minutes after the training session (Gold & van Buskirk, 1975). By 120 minutes, though, the memory seems to have stabilized, and epinephrine injections have no effect.

Figure 10.14 Stress hormones can increase memory If control rats are given a shock the first time they enter a dark chamber, they will delay an average of about a minute before reentering that chamber. Rats given an injection of epinephrine after the training session will delay much longer, indicating that the post-training epinephrine increased their memory for the episode. The effects are time sensitive, so an injection given immediately (0 minutes) after training has more effect than one given after a longer delay.

Adapted from McGaugh, 2003; data from Gold and van Buskirk, 1975.

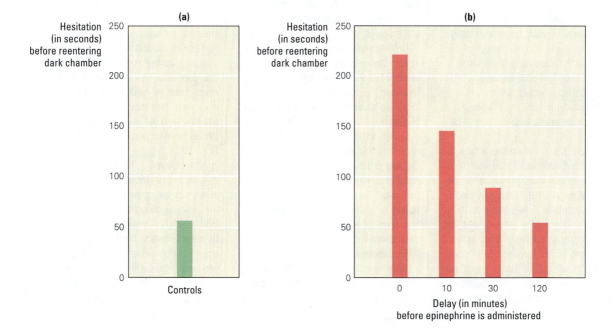

Emotion researcher James McGaugh has suggested that there is an important reason why animals might have evolved so as to allow the emotional system to modulate memory after the fact. In many cases, the importance of a particular event might not be immediately apparent. If a pigeon drinks colored water that contains a nausea-inducing agent, the symptoms of sickness may not appear for some time—but once those symptoms do appear, it is very important for the sick pigeon to be able to encode a strong memory of the colored water. Similarly, a child who scribbles on the wall but isn't punished until hours later, when Mother finds out, must be able to reach back in time and strongly associate the earlier action with the later consequence. In such cases, the ability of stress hormones to affect previously acquired memories allows the amygdala to tinker with the strength of the memory later, when the delayed consequences become apparent (McGaugh, 2003).

Encoding Emotional Contexts in the Hippocampus

In discussing how the amygdala might modulate learning about emotional events, we have already mentioned the hippocampal region, which is critical for new episodic (event) memory formation. But the hippocampal region also plays a role in many other kinds of memory, especially those that require learning about context and other stimulus-stimulus relationships (see Chapter 6). Remember that simple association of a conditioned stimulus (CS) and unconditioned stimulus (US) is not dependent on the hippocampus. For example, consider the rat conditioned-emotional-learning experiments described earlier in which a tone CS is associated with a fear-evoking shock US. Figure 10.11b showed that such CS-US learning is not disrupted in rats with hippocampal lesions, but it is devastated in rats with amygdala lesions (LeDoux, 1994).

During conditioning, a normal rat learns not only about the CS and the US but also about the context in which the US is presented. Thus, after CS-US training in a particular chamber, the rat may show a conditioned emotional response (freezing) as soon as it is placed back into that chamber—before any CS (or US) is presented. In fact, a healthy animal's response to the context may be almost as strong as its response to the CS! This contextual freezing response is greatly reduced in animals with hippocampal lesions (Figure 10.15a). Amygdala lesions also abolish the contextual fear response, possibly because the lesion damages the output pathway from the central nucleus to the motor areas that produce the freezing response (Phillips & LeDoux, 1992).

A similar interplay occurs between hippocampus and amygdala in humans monitored for the skin conductance response. Figure 10.11a showed that healthy humans give an SCR to a CS that has been paired with a US (loud boat horn). A patient with bilateral amygdala damage could not learn this conditioned

Figure 10.15 Conditioned contextual learning (a) During conditioning of an emotional response such as freezing in response to a CS that signals shock, control rats also learn a response (freezing) to the context where shock was experienced; this contextual learning is impaired by both amygdala lesion (AL) and hippocampal lesion (HL). (b) Healthy humans can also report contextual information during a skin conductance conditioning experiment; AL spares this contextual memory, but HL greatly impairs it. These data suggest a dissociation between conditioned emotional responding (which depends on the amygdala) and contextual or episodic learning (which depends on the hippocampus).

(a) Adapted from Phillips and LeDoux, 1992;
(b) adapted from Bechara et al., 1995.

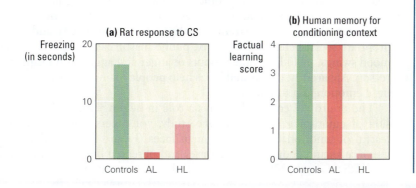

response, but one with bilateral hippocampal damage could (Bechara et al., 1995). After conditioning, participants were asked what they remembered about the experiment. Healthy individuals could report that the CS predicted that the US was coming (Figure 10.15b). The patient with hippocampal damage, who had learned to produce the SCR, could not report any details of the conditioning experiment. This is consistent with the general expectation that a hippocampal lesion abolishes the ability to form new episodic memories but does not prevent simple classical conditioning. The patient with amygdala damage showed the opposite pattern: she could report the details of the conditioning experiment quite well—specifically, that the CS predicted the US—even though she did not generate an SCR to the CS. Thus, amygdala damage in humans seems to spare hippocampal-dependent context learning but to disrupt the learning and expression of an emotional response.

How might the hippocampal region mediate the effect of context on fear learning in the amygdala? The path from amygdala to hippocampal region is a two-way street, as illustrated in Figure 10.13. Signals from the amygdala travel to the hippocampal region. But signals from the hippocampal region containing information about the learning context also travel back to the amygdala, where they can be incorporated into ongoing emotional processing. This is part of the reason why returning to the place (or context) where an emotional experience occurred is often enough to evoke arousal. For example, when individuals return to a place where they experienced intense sadness or fear, they are sometimes struck with a fresh wave of grief or terror. Similarly (and more happily), couples celebrating an anniversary sometimes choose the restaurant where they had their first date because returning to the context where they once experienced strong feelings of romance can help evoke those same emotions again.

Feelings and the Frontal Lobes

The amygdala interacts with the hippocampus during emotional learning and memory, and it also interacts with the cortex. As you read in Chapter 9, the *frontal lobes* of the cortex are often considered the seat of executive function, where we do most of our planning and decision making. The frontal lobes are also intensively involved in social behavior, and appropriate social behavior demands the ability to express emotion and to read it in others.

Patients with damage to the frontal lobes often exhibit fewer and less intense facial expressions (Kolb & Taylor, 1981) and are impaired in their ability to recognize negative facial expressions (such as fear and disgust) in others (Kolb & Taylor, 2000). These patients may show a general disruption of emotion and mood, which can be manifested as social withdrawal and loss of normal emotional display. (The old medical procedure of prefrontal lobotomy was a way of making chronically agitated people "calmer" by destroying parts of the frontal lobes so as to reduce emotional expression.) Other patients with frontal lesions experience the opposite extreme of heightened emotionality and exhibit inappropriate social behavior (profanity, public masturbation, and so on) and rapid mood swings, including violent bouts of anger and aggression for no discernible reason. Apparently, the frontal lobes help people maintain a balance between too little emotion and too much.

The prefrontal cortex also plays a role in helping people "read" the expression of emotion in others. In one study, volunteers were shown pictures of fearful or emotionally neutral human faces (Figure 10.16a) while researchers measured skin conductance responses and observed brain activation with fMRI (L. Williams et al., 2001). By now, you should be completely unsurprised to hear

(a) Fearful face

Neutral face

(b) Amygdala

(c) Medial prefrontal cortex

Figure 10.16 The prefrontal cortex and emotional processing (a) Volunteers were shown pictures of fearful and emotionally neutral faces while brain activity was recorded by fMRI. (b, c) Difference images show that the amygdala was more active during the viewing of fearful faces—and so was the medial prefrontal cortex. The prefrontal cortex may help individuals to interpret the emotional displays they see in others. Adapted from Williams et al., 2001.

that amygdala activation was greater while participants viewed the fearful faces than they viewed the emotionally neutral faces (Figure 10.16b). The novel finding was that fearful faces also caused more activity than emotionally neutral faces in the medial prefrontal cortex (Figure 10.16c). These data are consistent with the idea that this area of the prefrontal cortex is active during emotional processing, helping to interpret the meaning of emotional stimuli, such as other people's facial displays of emotion.

Several researchers have further proposed that the medial prefrontal cortex allows us to process emotional stimuli in a manner appropriate to the context in which the stimuli occur (Hornak et al., 2003; Kolb & Taylor, 1990; Rolls, 1999). For example, your emotional reaction to seeing a bear should be very different depending on whether you encounter the bear as you walk through the woods or through the zoo. The prefrontal cortex may be the brain region that exerts this control on our emotional reactions, modulating the degree to which amygdala outputs produce emotional responses in different contexts. Remember the finding—described at the start of this chapter—that Japanese students tended to mask their emotional reactions in the presence of an authority figure? Most likely, the students were successfully using their frontal cortex to inhibit facial expressions. Similarly, if the big, dark shape you see approaching really is a bear and yet you are not really in danger because you are viewing the bear in the zoo, the amygdala will attempt to turn on the emotional response at the sight of the bear, but the medial prefrontal cortex will dampen this response. In effect, the medial prefrontal cortex tells the amygdala not to bother because the bear *in this particular context* is no threat. Consistent with this idea, experiments show that stimulating the medial prefrontal cortex in rats "turns off" or inhibits the normal emotional response provoked by amygdala stimulation (al Maskati & Zbrozyna, 1989; Quirk, Likhtik, Pelletier, & Paré, 2003).

Back in Chapter 9, you read about the Wisconsin Card Sort task, which requires the sorting of cards first by color, then by shape, and so on. This task is especially disrupted in patients with frontal lobe damage; such patients *perseverate*, clinging to the old sorting rules even though the old responses are no longer reinforced. This type of failure to extinguish seems to reflect a failure to learn that a response that was appropriate in a previous context is no longer appropriate in the current context. Emotional responses are affected the same way. Frontal lobe lesions, particularly lesions of the medial prefrontal cortex, interfere with the ability to learn to make an emotional response under some conditions but to withhold it under other conditions. For example, you saw in Figure 10.3 that normal rats trained to expect that a tone CS predicts a foot shock US will generate various conditioned emotional responses to the CS, such as freezing and changes in heart rate. After a few sessions in which the CS appears without the US, these responses will extinguish. But rats with medial prefrontal lesions continue responding to the CS long after normal rats have learned to ignore it (LeDoux, 1998). Thus, the prefrontal cortex appears to play a general role in helping us decide which of several potential responses, including emotional responses, is appropriate under the current circumstances.

Test Your Knowledge

Brain Substrates of Emotion

Emotional responses depend on a complex interplay between many brain areas, including the amygdala, hippocampus, and prefrontal cortex. Read the story below and identify some ways these brain areas could be contributing at each step identified by a number in parentheses. (Answers appear in the Answers section in the back of the book.)

Jared is afraid of heights. However, on a visit to Washington, DC, his friends say he should go to the top of the Washington Monument for the best view of the city. On the elevator up, Jared feels the beginnings of a nervous reaction (1): his heart beats faster, his mouth feels dry, and his stomach tightens. He remembers when he was similarly terrified standing on the high diving board at school (2).

When he arrives at the observation area, Jared's first impulse is to flatten himself against the wall and stay as far away from the edge as possible. But having come this far, he takes a few deep breaths, walks up to the window, and looks out over the city (3). In spite of everything, he is able to appreciate the beautiful view (4).

Interim Summary

- Emotion depends on many brain areas, and each brain area may contribute to more than one emotion.

- Part of the body's response to strong emotion is to activate the amygdala; outputs from the central nucleus of the amygdala drive many of the behavioral and physiological components of emotional responses. Animals (including people) with amygdala damage show reduced emotionality and a reduced ability to learn conditioned emotional responses.

- The amygdala also modulates storage of emotional memories by means of outputs from the basolateral nucleus projecting to the cortex and the hippocampal region. Memories can be formed in the cortex and hippocampus without amygdala input, but if the emotional system is triggered, then memory formation will be stronger.

- The hippocampal region can, in turn, influence emotional learning by providing information about the context in which the learning occurs. Animals and people with hippocampal damage can still learn an emotional response to a stimulus, but they will fail to learn about the context in which they encountered the stimulus.

- The frontal lobes seem to play an important role in humans' ability to display emotions appropriately and to read emotional expressions in others and also in the ability to process emotional stimuli in a manner appropriate to the context in which they are experienced.

10.3 Clinical Perspectives

Much of the research covered in this chapter has focused on negative emotions—particularly fear—in part because negative emotions have a tremendous impact on our health and well-being. The stress associated with long-term unremitting fear and anger can lead to physiological problems such as high blood pressure and immune system suppression. Negative emotions can also cause psychological problems. Two of these in particular—phobias and posttraumatic stress disorder—may involve learning and memory processes in their development and in their successful treatment.

Phobias

A **phobia** is an excessive and irrational fear of an object, place, or situation. Examples of common phobias include fear of closed spaces (claustrophobia), fear of open spaces (agoraphobia), fear of heights (acrophobia), fear of public speaking (a form of social phobia), fear of snakes (ophidiophobia), and fear of spiders (arachnophobia). In many (not all) cases, the phobia centers on an object or situation in which a fear reaction might be justified. For example, it is appropriate to be alarmed by the sight of a snake since snake venom can be deadly. Similarly, a healthy fear of heights may keep you from falling off cliffs. But when a fear has reached a point where it interferes with daily life, it is classified as a phobia. For example, if a person were so afraid of open spaces that she seldom left her house or so afraid of dogs that she panicked whenever the neighbor's pet barked, these fears would be classified as phobias.

Ophidiophobia, or fear of snakes, is a common phobia.

One theory about the formation of phobias is that they arise through classical conditioning. Back in Chapter 1, you read about John Watson, the "father" of behaviorism. In one famous series of studies, Watson and his research assistant Rosalie Rayner studied fear conditioning in an 11-month-old boy known as Little Albert (possibly a pseudonym). Two months before the experiment began, they'd exposed Albert briefly to a white rat, a rabbit, a bearded Santa Claus mask, a burning newspaper, and various other items. Albert had showed no fear responses when presented with any of these objects although he did react with fear to a loud clanging noise. To study fear conditioning, Watson and Rayner placed a white rat near Albert, allowing him to reach out toward it. As he did, Watson and Rayner startled Albert with the loud clanging noise, and he began to cry. After several pairings of the rat and the noise and a few more pairings a week later, the researchers presented Albert with the rat (and no noise); Albert cried at the sight of the rat and tried to crawl away. The researchers concluded that Little Albert had been classically conditioned to associate the rat (a CS) with a fear-provoking loud noise (the US) (Watson & Rayner, 2000 [1920]). This learning appeared to generalize to other, similar objects: Albert now reacted with fear and avoidance to other objects, including white, furry objects such as the rabbit and the Santa Claus mask, but not to wooden blocks.

While Little Albert was playing with a pet rat, John Watson and Rosalie Rayner paired the rat with a loud, frightening noise. Albert developed a conditioned fear response to the rat. Watson and Rayner (visible in the photo) claimed that they had induced a phobia in Albert and that such classical conditioning could underlie the formation of real-world phobias.

Shortly after, Little Albert and his mother moved away. There is no record of how severe Albert's fear of rats was, how long it persisted, or whether it generalized to rats encountered outside of Watson's lab (Beck, Levinson, & Irons, 2009; Harris, 1979). Today, of course, ethical guidelines would preclude experiments like the one conducted on Little Albert. (At a bare minimum, Watson and Rayner, who knew in advance when Albert would leave the study, should have made an effort to extinguish Albert's conditioned fear before he went.) But the experiment did raise some interesting questions about classical conditioning and phobias. Maybe some naturally arising phobias also reflect classical conditioning; perhaps some people develop claustrophobia after a traumatic experience such as being locked in a closet and others develop a fear of dogs after being attacked by an out-of-control pet.

On the other hand, not everyone who has a fear-evoking experience develops a phobia. One study reported that two-thirds of people with a dog-related phobia can recall a dog-related trauma (such as being bitten), but so can the same percentage of people with no fear of dogs (DiNardo, Guzy, & Bak, 1988). Conversely, some people have a terror of snakes despite never having come into contact with a living snake, and others are morbidly afraid of flying without ever having been in an airplane.

One possible explanation is that some phobias may be conditioned through social transmission. For example, a person can develop a fear of flying after seeing televised reports of an airplane crash or a fear of snakes after seeing other people panic at the sight of snakes. Monkeys show socially transmitted fear too. A monkey raised in the lab will not react with fear the first time it sees a snake. But if the lab-reared monkey is caged next to another monkey and if that neighboring monkey reacts with fear at the sight of a snake, the lab-reared monkey will begin to show the same fear response (Mineka & Cook, 1988). Possibly, the sight of a frightened neighbor is itself a fear-evoking US, and the object that evokes that fear becomes a CS in the observer monkey.

If some phobias arise through conditioning, can they be extinguished in the same way as ordinary conditioned responses—by repeated exposure to the CS with no US? In many cases they can. In **systematic desensitization** therapy for phobias, successive approximations of the CS are presented while the patient learns to remain relaxed; eventually, even the CS itself does not elicit a fear response (Kazdin & Wilcoxon, 1976; Linden, 1981). For example, a person who is afraid of snakes may first be presented with some snake-shaped item (like a hose or rope) different enough from a real snake that no fear reaction is evoked. In successive sessions, the patient is progressively exposed to, say, a toy rubber snake, then a photograph of a real snake, then a person holding a live snake; the steps are taken so gradually that they don't evoke a fear reaction. Eventually, the patient may be asked to touch a live snake, then to hold it himself. As you might imagine, systematic desensitization therapy can be a slow and painstaking process, but it is often successful and long lasting.

Sometimes it is dangerous, inconvenient, or very expensive to expose the patient (and the therapist!) to the object of the phobia. For example, if the patient is afraid of flying over the ocean, systematic desensitization would require her to practice approaching an airport, then practice sitting on a grounded plane, then start taking short overland trips, and finally work up to longer transatlantic flights. This would be prohibitively expensive for most people. Instead, the therapist may recommend virtual-reality therapy using computer-generated virtual environments. The patient can "experience" sitting in an airplane seat, gradually getting used to the sights and sounds of an aircraft and even taking simulated flights before spending the energy and money to board a real plane. Virtual-reality therapy, particularly in combination with other relaxation training and cognitive therapy, can be very effective in treating phobias (Emmelkamp et al., 2002; Muhlberger, Herrmann, Wiedeman, Ellgring, & Pauli, 2001).

Posttraumatic Stress Disorder

Following the terrorist attacks on the World Trade Center on September 11, 2001, thousands of counselors traveled to New York City to offer their services to survivors, families, and rescue workers. In addition to these volunteers, $23 million in federal funds was allocated to Project Liberty, a program that provided free counseling to New Yorkers.

The rationale for this convergence of mental health professionals and funding was the expectation that in the wake of the attacks, many New Yorkers would develop **posttraumatic stress disorder (PTSD)**. PTSD is a psychological syndrome that can develop after a traumatic event (such as combat, rape, or natural disaster); the symptoms include re-experiencing the event (through intrusive recollections, flashbacks, or nightmares), avoidance of reminders of the trauma, and heightened anxiety (McNally, Bryant, & Ehlers, 2003). Such fear reactions are a perfectly normal human response to distressing events, but for most people exposed to trauma, the fear reactions subside with time (Figure 10.17). For individuals with PTSD, the fear reactions may persist for months or years. PTSD may be particularly likely in individuals who experience intentional acts of personal violence: some studies estimate the rates to be as high as 30% for veterans of combat in Iraq but as high as 50 to 80% for female rape victims.

Why might PTSD occur? One prominent theory assigns a role to classical conditioning. By definition, PTSD involves an experience that causes a strong fear response, including feelings of helplessness or terror. This event may function as a US, and it may be such a strong and effective US that any other stimuli that occurred along with it become strongly associated with that US. Thus, sights, sounds, and smells may all become conditioned stimuli. When any such CS is experienced again, it may evoke the memory of the US—and a conditioned fear response. This is one way in which PTSD is hypothesized to differ from phobias: in phobias, a fear reaction is triggered by a particular stimulus (such as a snake or a spider); in PTSD, fear reactions can be triggered by a wide variety of stimuli reminiscent of the original trauma. These fear reactions are not necessarily abnormal, but for most people, re-experiencing these CSs without recurrence of the traumatic US should gradually lead to extinction of the fear response in the weeks and months after the trauma. Individuals with PTSD may simply fail to extinguish the normal fear response to stimuli associated with the traumatic event (Rothbaum & Davis, 2003). In fact, in the laboratory, individuals with PTSD do typically show faster learning but impaired extinction of conditioned emotional responses (Orr et al., 2000; Peri, Ben-Shakhar, Orr, & Shalev, 2000).

Consistent with the theory that PTSD involves a failure of extinction, some of the most widely used treatments for PTSD include exposing the patient to cues that trigger his anxiety but doing so in the absence of danger. The purpose is to encourage extinction of the abnormally strong fear response (Rothbaum & Davis, 2003). Such *extinction therapy* for PTSD may require the patient to repeatedly imagine and describe the feared situations under the guidance of a therapist. Virtual-reality techniques also prove useful—for example, allowing

Figure 10.17 **Patterns of psychological recovery after a traumatic event** Immediately after experiencing a traumatic event, such as rape, combat exposure, or a terrorist attack, most people show a disruption in normal functioning due to fear reactions; these may include heightened anxiety, nightmares, flashbacks, and avoidance of reminders of the trauma. As time passes, most people either bounce back quickly (a pattern described as "resilience") or show initial fear reactions that dissipate with time ("recovery"). But some individuals develop posttraumatic stress disorder (PTSD), with symptoms that persist for months or years after the event. Adapted from Bonanno, 2005.

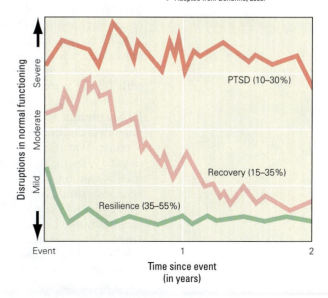

veterans to navigate through a simulated version of the region where they had their most stressful combat-related experiences, undergoing repeated exposure to the fear-evoking stimuli within the safe context of a therapist's office. Under these conditions, many individuals experience gradual reduction of PTSD symptoms.

Researchers are also investigating whether it is possible to reduce the likelihood of an individual developing PTSD by administering drugs such as propranolol that interfere with epinephrine and thereby reduce the body's stress reactions. Some intriguing studies suggest that individuals who have experienced a traumatic episode, such as a car crash, and who then receive a series of propranolol injections may be somewhat less likely to develop PTSD than individuals who do not receive the injections (Pitman et al., 2002; Vaiva et al., 2003). These patients do not forget the traumatic episode, but they stop having such damaging emotional reactions to the memory. An important question is whether such brain-altering treatments should routinely be prescribed for individuals who experience a traumatic event to reduce the risk of PTSD. The question is a complicated one given that the majority of people will never develop PTSD if simply left alone.

In fact, as illustrated in Figure 10.17, PTSD is the exception, not the rule, in individuals exposed to traumatic events. For example, one study estimated that about 10 to 20% of New Yorkers living within a few miles of the World Trade Center displayed fear symptoms two months after 9/11, but six months later, fewer than 2% had PTSD related to the attacks (Galea et al., 2003). Even among a small sample of New Yorkers who had actually been inside the World Trade Center at the time of the attacks, only about 25% had PTSD six months later; another 20% had some PTSD-like symptoms, but more than 50% were maintaining healthy, symptom-free function despite their experiences (Bonanno, Galea, Bucciarelli, & Vlahov, 2006). Apparently, there are some preexisting vulnerability factors that help determine an individual's risk to develop PTSD, which is why one person will develop the disorder but another will prove resilient when exposed to the same traumatic event. Understanding these vulnerability factors is of critical importance because there is some evidence that widespread intervention to prevent PTSD among individuals exposed to traumatic events can actually increase rates of the disorder—presumably by inducing symptoms in individuals who would most likely have been resilient if simply left alone to deal with the trauma in their own way (Bonanno, 2004).

A better approach might be to give the preventive therapy only to those individuals who are most likely to develop PTSD. But how can we identify such individuals in advance? Structural MRI suggests some answers. Individuals with PTSD typically have hippocampal volumes that are somewhat smaller than those of individuals who experienced similar trauma but did not develop PTSD (Smith, 2005). For example, a study by Mark Gilbertson and colleagues examined the brains of a group of combat veterans who had fought in the Vietnam War (Gilbertson et al., 2002). Even though the war officially ended in the 1970s, many veterans of that war still have trouble with combat-related PTSD symptoms. Using MRI, Gilbertson and colleagues showed that those veterans with PTSD typically had a smaller hippocampal volume than veterans who had not developed PTSD (Figure 10.18a, b). One interpretation of these findings would be that PTSD might cause the hippocampus to shrink, since we know that long-term exposure to chronic stress can damage the hippocampus (McEwen, 1997; Sapolsky, 1996). But another possibility was that the veterans who developed PTSD had a smaller hippocampus to start with—and that made them more vulnerable to PTSD.

(a) Veterans with PTSD

(b) Veterans with no PTSD

Hippocampus

(c) Twin brothers of (a)

(d) Twin brothers of (b)

Hippocampus

Figure 10.18 Hippocampal volume and **PTSD** Structural MRI images showing the hippocampus on each side (red and blue). (a) Combat veterans who developed PTSD typically had smaller-than-average hippocampal volume than (b) combat-exposed veterans who did not develop PTSD. (c) The (non-veteran, non-PTSD) twin brothers of PTSD veterans also had smaller-than-average hippocampal volume, but (d) the twin brothers of non-PTSD veterans did not. This suggests that the veterans with PTSD had smaller-than-average hippocampal volume before entering combat and that this may have predisposed them to develop the disorder when exposed to the extreme stress of wartime deployment and combat.

Adapted from Gilbertson et al., 2002.

Gilbertson and colleagues found a clever way to determine the answer: each of the veterans included in the study had an identical twin brother who had not fought in Vietnam and who had never developed PTSD. If the veterans who did develop PTSD (Figure 10.18a) experienced a reduction in hippocampal volume as a result of their trauma, then their unexposed brothers should have a normal hippocampal volume. But if these veterans had a smaller hippocampal volume to start with, then their twins should also have smaller-than-average hippocampal volumes. In fact, the twins of the veterans with PTSD did have smaller-than-average hippocampal volumes too (Figure 10.18c). This suggests that PTSD doesn't *cause* hippocampal shrinkage; instead, it seems that some individuals have a smaller-than-average hippocampal volume, and this may *predispose* them to develop PTSD later (Gilbertson et al., 2002). For example, connections from the hippocampus to the prefrontal cortex are important in extinguishing learned associations; individuals with a slightly smaller hippocampus might be less able to extinguish fear responses than their peers. If an individual leads a relatively quiet life (like the twin brothers who weren't sent to Vietnam), this may not be a problem, but if that same individual is exposed to trauma (like the brothers who did serve in the war), there could be heightened risk for PTSD.

In addition to decreased hippocampal volume, other factors that make individuals vulnerable to PTSD may include genetic factors (Norrholm & Ressler, 2009); increased startle responses to sudden, loud noises (Orr et al., 2003; Pitman et al., 2006); and personality traits such as neuroticism, harm avoidance, and a tendency to withdraw from or avoid novel situations (Aidman & Kollaras-Mitsinikos, 2006; Gil & Caspi, 2006; Hatcher, Whitaker, & Karl, 2009). On the other hand, individuals with strong social support from family and friends are *less* likely to develop PTSD after a traumatic event (Pietrzak, Johnson, Goldstein, Malley, & Southwick, 2009; Polusny et al., 2010). Understanding the factors that make an individual vulnerable to, or resilient against, PTSD could be

Studies suggest that about 30% of combat veterans in Iraq will develop PTSD, which means that two or three of the soldiers in this picture are statistically likely to develop the disorder. Understanding the specific risk factors that make one individual more vulnerable to PTSD than another may help us identify candidates for intervention (such as therapy or increased social support) that might someday help us prevent PTSD from developing in the first place.

Reuters/Ceerwan Aziz RCS/JJ

REUTERS/Ceerwan Aziz RCS/JJ

very useful in screening people for wartime service as well as for jobs such as firefighting, disaster recovery, and foreign aid work, where traumatic situations are especially likely to occur. Not all trauma is avoidable, of course; most people experience one or more traumatic events during the course of a lifetime. But if we knew in advance which individuals are more vulnerable to PTSD, there would be the opportunity to provide those individuals with aggressive care and counseling if and when exposure to trauma occurs.

Interim Summary

- Certain psychological problems may be fear responses gone awry.
- Phobias are excessive fears that interfere with daily life. Some phobias may arise through classical conditioning.
- In posttraumatic stress disorder (PTSD), a natural fear reaction does not subside with time, possibly reflecting a failure of extinction.

▶ SYNTHESIS

If you've ever tried to list the similarities between yourself and a rat, chances are that emotions did not top the list. But humans, chimpanzees, elephants, dogs, rats, and even the lowly *Aplysia* all show emotional responses in the form of overt behaviors and physiological changes. Confronted with the prospect of an electric shock, a rat may freeze and defecate, a sea snail may retract its siphon, and a dog may whine and put its tail between its legs. Each animal is demonstrating a learned fear response, and these responses can be induced and measured by experimenters. The same goes for physiological variables, such as heart rate, respiration, and other components of the fight-or-flight response—many of which are shared by several species. Additionally, emotional learning depends on similar brain substrates in many species, especially mammals, including the amygdala, the hippocampus, and the frontal cortex. This commonality allows the use of insights gained in rats, and even *Aplysia*, to help elucidate the neural bases of human emotional responses.

As you saw in this chapter, the vast majority of research on emotions and learning has focused on a single emotion, fear. One reason is that the critical brain substrates for fear are at least partially understood, whereas the brain substrates for happiness and other positive emotions are only now being discovered. And while we can reasonably assume that anticipating shock leads to fear in animals because we can observe and measure fear responses, it has been less clear whether animals feel "happiness" and, if so, how we could induce and measure this emotion. But newer research is focusing on animal models of emotions such as joy and disgust and may lead to new breakthroughs in understanding the human versions of these emotions too.

Another reason for the historical emphasis on fear is its association with clinical syndromes such as phobias, PTSD, and depression. This link to real-world medicine drives many researchers to study fear in the hope that their findings will have clinical relevance. Indeed, as the propranolol PTSD studies show, we are on the verge of being able to manipulate the way emotion modulates our memory and our physiological responses. These studies suggest that we can dampen the emotional content of memories without erasing the episodic content. For patients whose lives have been devastated by trauma, there may be a moral responsibility to administer such treatment if it will help them recover.

But what do these findings mean for those who do not suffer from disabling emotional disorders? If off-the-shelf, emotion-modifying drugs were available, would people routinely want to lose the emotional content of their "negative" episodic memories? Would the result be happier lives for all or a kind of gray existence in which nothing really matters because nothing causes lasting emotional scars? And without lasting emotional scars, would humans lose some of the ability to learn from mistakes—the very reason emotions may have evolved in the first place?

Key Terms

amygdala, *p. 406*

arousal, *p. 387*

autonomic nervous system (ANS), *p. 388*

Cannon-Bard theory of emotion, *p. 390*

conditioned avoidance, *p. 396*

conditioned escape, *p. 395*

cortisol, *p. 388*

depression, *p. 398*

emotion, *p. 386*

epinephrine, *p. 388*

fear response, *p. 386*

fight-or-flight response, *p. 387*

flashbulb memory, *p. 402*

glucocorticoids, *p. 388*

James-Lange theory of emotion, *p. 388*

learned helplessness, *p. 398*

mood congruency of memory, *p. 402*

phobia, *p. 419*

piloerection, *p. 392*

posttraumatic stress disorder (PTSD), *p. 421*

somatic theories of emotion, *p. 389*

stress, *p. 388*

stress hormone, *p. 388*

systematic desensitization, *p. 420*

two-factor theory of emotion, *p. 390*

Concept Check

1. In earlier chapters, you read about habituation (decreased responding to a repeatedly presented stimulus). Do you think habituation is an example of emotional learning? Why or why not?

2. After losing a game by a lopsided score, professional football teams are statistically more likely to perform worse than usual in their next game, and this tendency is particularly pronounced if the upcoming opponent is considered hard to beat (Reisel & Kopelman, 1995). How might this phenomenon be explained in terms of the principles of emotional learning?

3. Decorticate animals (animals with their cortex surgically removed) often show "sham rage," overreacting to seemingly trivial stimuli as though they were being seriously threatened. Why might this happen?

4. Suppose you have a roommate who is terrified of spiders, to the point of being unable to take a shower if there is a spider in the bathroom unless you're there to kill the spider or remove it. Based on what you read in this chapter, speculate about why your roommate has this fear.

5. Continuing the example in question 4, what might you suggest to help your roommate overcome this fear?

CHAPTER 11

Social Learning and Memory

Observing, Interacting, and Reenacting

DOLPHINS ARE THE ONLY KNOWN animals other than humans that can imitate both actions and sounds on request. Specifically, scientists have trained dolphins to imitate human actors and computer-generated sounds when instructed to do so. Chimpanzees and orangutans can imitate other animals' actions when humans ask them, but they seem to be unable to imitate sounds. Parrots can imitate sounds, but they have little ability to imitate novel sounds on request. Most other animals show no ability to imitate actions or sounds when instructed to do so by humans. This could be because they don't know how to imitate, or don't have the right vocal control mechanisms, or have not been properly trained to imitate, or possibly because, unlike dolphins and apes, they don't understand human instructions.

Yes, you read that last paragraph correctly. Scientists can communicate with dolphins and apes, and these newly discovered communication channels have revealed unsuspected learning and memory abilities in those animals. One dolphin named Akeakamai (pronounced "uh-KAY-uh–ka-MY," Hawaiian for "lover of wisdom") learned to interpret hand signals asking her to imitate the actions of dolphins and humans. She learned this through one-on-one interactions with her human instructors. She would watch intently as a hairless ape stood in front of her, gesticulating rapidly with its oddly shaped "flippers." Over time, she learned that one of those gestures meant she was supposed to imitate a recently demonstrated action, such as a human spinning around or a dolphin shooting a basketball through a hoop. When Akeakamai interpreted this gesture correctly, the instructor rewarded her with shouts of approval. Occasionally, the instructor's vocal accolades proved infectious, and Akeakamai joined in the celebration with her own loud vocalizations. Akeakamai observed the actions of those around her and reacted based on her past training, her recent experiences, and her emotional state.

Observations can contribute to learning and memory in many ways. You can watch television to learn about exotic vacation destinations, listen to the radio to learn about an approaching storm, or read a textbook to learn about how your brain enables you to learn and remember. People generally assume that humans learn much of what they know by interacting socially with others and observing how things work in society. Many believe that this makes human learning and memory different from that of all other animals. However, this view may be based more on presupposition than on experimental evidence. Here we explore what psychologists have discovered about how humans and other animals learn through social observations and interactions.

11.1 Behavioral Processes

Psychologists use the term **social learning** to identify situations in which the learner actively monitors events involving other individuals and then chooses later actions based on their observations. The term **observational learning** is often used as a synonym for social learning. You are currently observing the outcome of intensive textbook-writing efforts and may use your observations (reading) of this text to guide your later actions when you are studying for and taking tests in your classes. If your test includes short-answer questions on learning and memory, you might even answer those questions with sentences very similar to the ones you are reading in these chapters. In fact, the more precisely you replicate what you have read (or heard during lectures) when answering such questions, the more likely it is that your professor will judge your answers to be correct.

Social learning differs from classical and instrumental conditioning in that researchers cannot reliably predict what an organism will learn after observing the actions of others. One reason it is difficult to predict how observations will affect future behavior is that there is no way for one observer (the researcher) to detect what another observer (the research subject) actually perceives while observing. For one thing, an organism can observe a wide variety of events without showing any changes in behavior or giving any other indication of what they have observed. If you watch your fellow students during a lecture, do you think you would be able to tell if one of them doesn't understand English well or if another is daydreaming about being on the beach?

Psychologists are frequently faced with this ambiguity. Edward Thorndike, for example, concluded that cats could not imitate other cats that had learned to escape from a puzzle box (Thorndike, 1898). However, there is no way to know what Thorndike's observer cats were focusing on in those experiments. Perhaps the food outside the box or the identity of the cat trapped in the box were more interesting to the feline observer than the specific actions the cat inside the box was performing.

Another reason it is difficult to predict how observations will affect future behavior is that nothing compels an observer to copy any given model.

Furthermore, even if the observer does copy a particular model, there is more than one way to copy, as we now discuss.

Copying What Is Seen

Social learning differs from most other forms of learning discussed in this book in that not all species can learn by reproducing what they observe. In fact, many psychologists believe that only humans learn extensively by copying. **Copying** consists of replicating what one observes another doing. Children *can* learn a great deal by copying the actions of adults and other children. However, there is very little experimental data showing what children *do* learn through imitation in everyday life.

Much of what we know about the role of imitation in learning stems from influential experimental studies conducted in the early 1960s by Albert Bandura. Bandura (b.1925) grew up in Canada before heading to the University of Iowa for graduate school. Soon after starting his academic career at Stanford University, he became interested in how parents' aggressive behavior might affect the actions of their children. Bandura and his colleagues wanted to see whether preschool children would become more aggressive after observing aggressive adults (Bandura, Ross, & Ross, 1961). They had one group of children observe adults beating up a "Bobo doll" (an inflatable clown doll), while other groups of children (control groups) simply played in an empty room or observed adults playing quietly with toys. Afterward, Bandura used a one-way mirror to spy on the children as they played in a room containing the Bobo doll (Figure 11.1). Children who had observed an adult pummeling the Bobo doll were more likely than children in the control groups to pound on the doll themselves, and most important, their attack styles were often similar to those used by the adults. Bandura and colleagues concluded that the children had learned new aggressive actions by observing the actions of an adult.

Studies like Bandura's Bobo doll experiment seem to suggest that children will copy aggressive acts they have observed. However, the children were tested in a context similar to the one in which they observed the aggression occurring, soon after they viewed the aggressive acts. It is unclear whether they would have behaved similarly if they had encountered a Bobo doll at their neighbor's house. Additionally, the children in Bandura's experiment who showed significant imitation of aggressive acts had first been provoked by being deprived of

Figure 11.1 Scenes from a Bobo doll experiment After viewing an adult acting aggressively toward a Bobo doll, some children imitated what they had seen (Bandura, Ross, & Ross, 1961). The pictures have been paired to emphasize similar actions.

an attractive toy immediately before the test (Bandura, Ross, & Ross, 1961). Specifically, the experimenter told the provoked children that some attractive toys in the room were there for them to play with, but as soon as a child began playing with a toy, she told the child that these were her very best toys and that she had decided to reserve them for some other children. Children who had viewed an aggressive model but who had not been provoked were actually less likely to behave aggressively during the test than children who did not observe any aggressive acts. This finding suggests that viewing aggressive acts can in some cases inhibit aggressive behavior rather than increase it.

One of the main findings from the Bobo doll experiments was that viewing an adult acting aggressively toward an inflatable toy strongly influenced the later behavior of children presented with that same toy, despite the fact that the children were neither reinforced nor punished for their behavior. The absence of reinforcement or punishment would appear to exclude the possibility that the children were learning through instrumental conditioning, which requires that the learners' actions be either reinforced or punished. Bandura proposed that children observed the actions of the adult, formed ideas about what actions could be performed using the doll, and later used memories of those ideas to reproduce the adult's actions (Bandura, 1969). Note that by this account, the formation of memories that changed behavior occurred while the children were observing the adult, *not* when they were imitating the behavior. In other words, what is encoded is information about a specific episode, and the act of imitating is simply a way of recalling the episodic memory. The children's imitative acts simply revealed what they had learned from watching someone demonstrate an action; Bandura called these demonstrations **modeling.** Modeling is a prerequisite for all kinds of copying.

Copying can involve either the replication of actions that have been observed or the performance of novel actions that lead to the observed outcome of a modeler's actions (Morgan, 1896). For example, when Leti was still in elementary school, she happened to see her parents picking berries and putting them in a bucket. She then copied her parents' berry-picking technique but put the berries in her pockets rather than in a bucket. The movements Leti made while picking berries replicated those of her parents. Copying in which motor acts are replicated is called **true imitation.** The movements Leti performed to store the berries that had been picked, however, differed from those of her parents. But Leti and her parents' actions led to a similar outcome—berries were collected in a container. Copying that replicates an outcome without replicating specific motor acts is called **emulation.** We'll discuss both kinds of copying and provide more examples of each in the following sections. We'll also describe several other social-learning mechanisms that look like true imitation but that do not involve copying.

Studies of True Imitation: Copying Actions

Scientists use the term "true imitation" because they often disagree about what behaviors really count as imitation as well as about which organisms possess the ability to imitate (Thorndike, 1898; Thorpe, 1963; Whiten, Horner, Litchfield, & Marshall-Pescini, 2004). One technique that has been developed to investigate imitation abilities is called the **two-action test.** In preparation for this test, two individuals are each trained to perform a different action, but the two actions have the same outcome. For instance, one individual might be trained to dislodge an object that is stuck by hitting at it with a stick, and the other might be trained to pry the object free with a stick. Next, one group of naive observers is allowed to watch a demonstration of one of the techniques, and a second equally naive group is allowed to observe the other technique. If the naive observers later perform the operation in a way that matches the technique they observed, then their behavior is accepted as evidence of true imitation.

The two-action test has enabled researchers to compare imitative capacities across species. For example, a recent experiment compared the imitative tendency of young children (ages 2–4) with that of juvenile chimpanzees (ages 4–5) (Whiten, Custance, Gomez, Teixidor, & Bard, 1996). In this study, children and chimpanzees were shown how to open a plastic box to obtain a food reward (Figure 11.2a). Half of the participants saw an adult human open the box by poking pins out of its latch before lifting the lid. The other half saw an adult human open the box by twisting and pulling the pins out of the latch. After observing their respective models, the participants were given a chance to open the box themselves. Nothing about this task requires precise copying because the box can be opened in many ways that are equally effective. Nevertheless, both children and chimpanzees usually copied the opening technique that they had observed (Figure 11.2b). Children were more likely than chimpanzees to copy the details of the observed actions, including details that were not essential to getting the box open. Two-action tests have been used to study imitation in several species, including birds (Akins & Zentall, 1996; Dawson & Foss, 1965), rodents (Heyes & Dawson, 1990), and primates (Whiten et al., 1996), and in most of these studies, some copying of actions occurred.

Humans can imitate a wide variety of actions, including novel, nonfunctional actions. To assess whether any other animals share the ability to imitate arbitrary actions requires methods that are more flexible than the two-action test or the technique used by Bandura and colleagues. One approach involves teaching animals to imitate on command (often referred to as the "do-as-I-do" task). For example, researchers trained a chimpanzee to imitate a person's actions when the

Precise copying is the hallmark of true imitation.

Figure 11.2 **Two-action test of true imitation in children and chimpanzees** (a) Children and chimpanzees observed an adult human use one of two techniques (poke or twist) to open a plastic box containing a reward. (b) Later, both children and chimpanzees were more likely to use the box-opening technique they had observed than the one they did not observe. This means that both chimps and children can truly imitate.

Adapted from Whiten et al., 1996.

(a)

(b)

person gave the command "Do this!" (Hayes & Hayes, 1952). The researchers would perform an action, such as clapping hands, while telling the chimpanzee to "Do this!" and then would record whether or not the chimpanzee performed the same action. Initially, the chimpanzee was unlikely to imitate the actions the first time they were demonstrated. However, after learning to "Do this!" for about 12 actions, the chimpanzee was able to replicate certain new actions the first time she was asked. In a recent replication of this experiment, two other chimpanzees showed they could replicate 30 actions the first time they saw them (Custance, Whiten, & Bard, 1995). This is the same type of instruction that the dolphin Akeakamai learned to use to imitate actions on request except that she learned to respond to gestures rather that to speech.

One reason psychologists have gone to such great lengths to precisely define true imitation and to develop definitive methods for revealing imitative abilities is because some researchers claim that imitation requires high-level cognitive processes that are unique to humans (Bandura, 1986; Piaget, 1962). For example, imitation by humans is often taken to imply some awareness on the observer's part that he or she is voluntarily copying actions. **Perspective taking**, or imagining oneself in the place of another, is another cognitive ability that some researchers have suggested is a prerequisite for the voluntary imitation of actions. It is an ability that few species other than humans may possess. Perspective taking is thought to facilitate imitation because it enables people (or animals) to imitate others without watching themselves doing so. For example, you can imitate someone's facial expressions without watching yourself make faces. How do you know that your face matches a face you are observing? Your ability to imagine an outside observer's perspective provides feedback that may help you to perform such a feat, but that doesn't mean that imitation requires perspective taking or vice versa. In fact, consideration of the perspective of the individual performing the action may lead you to adopt a totally different strategy that is more effective than imitating what you observed.

Studies of Emulation: Copying Goals

Emulation was defined on page 430 as the attempt to replicate an observed outcome without reproducing the actions the model used to achieve that outcome. Chimpanzees and adult humans often perform actions that replicate the outcome of another's actions rather than copying the specific motor acts observed. For example, chimpanzees that saw people using a rake to collect food outside their cage were more likely to use a rake for this purpose than other chimpanzees, but they did not reliably copy the specific raking actions they observed (Nagell, Olguin, & Tomasello, 1993). A chimpanzee might hold the metal end of the rake and use the wooden end to knock the food closer to the cage. This type of copying has been distinguished from more exact copying, with some theorists claiming that when specific actions are not replicated, the copying does not qualify as true imitation (Tomasello, Davis-Dasilva, Carnak, & Bard, 1987; Wood, 1989).

Most evidence of emulation in chimpanzees and adult humans comes from studies intended to show true imitation. For example, in the plastic-box study described on page 431, the human children were more likely to truly imitate the precise box-opening actions of the model (such as poking the pegs with an index finger), whereas the chimpanzees were more likely to emulate the behavior of the model while using their own methods for opening the plastic box (for example, pushing the pegs with their palms). One interpretation of this difference is that the chimpanzees learned some features of the task by observing the model's behavior but then chose actions different from the ones they had observed in order to perform the task. Matching the outcomes of a set of motor actions by performing somewhat different actions is one kind of emulation. Interestingly, when adult humans were tested on the plastic-box task, their matching behavior was more similar to that of the chimpanzees than to that of the children, in that adults were more likely to emulate than to imitate the model's actions (Horowitz, 2003).

Reproducing Actions without Copying

Although much of social-learning research has focused on organisms imitating the actions of others, there are a number of ways that humans and other animals can replicate the actions of others without employing imitation or emulation. Carefully executed experiments must be conducted to determine which instances of similar behavior involve true imitation, because many of these other phenomena look just like imitation to the casual observer. Below, we describe three phenomena that closely resemble imitation: contagion, observational conditioning, and stimulus enhancement.

When you hear laughter, you too may feel the urge to laugh (which is why laugh tracks are a common feature of sitcoms). When you see someone yawn, you are more likely to yawn. When one baby starts crying on a plane, the other babies who are there will likely join in. The inborn tendency to react emotionally to sights or sounds of emotion in other members of one's species is called **contagion** (Byrne, 1994). Contagion is a relatively common phenomenon in which the observation of a given response increases the likelihood that the observer will produce a similar response. Typically, the kinds of motor acts that lead to contagion are not actions that an animal or person has learned. Babies yawn and cry in utero. Actions that result from contagion usually match the observed actions, but *not* as a result of imitation; the matching reaction is instead often an unconditioned response (UR).

We described a situation in Chapter 10 in which naive lab monkeys learned to fear snakes after watching wild monkeys react fearfully to them (Mineka & Cook, 1988). In this case, observer monkeys experience contagion when they see the fearful responses of wild monkeys. They associate their unconditioned fear (sparked by the wild monkeys) with the snake (a conditioned stimulus). Recall from Chapter 4 that this is exactly the sort of association that is learning during classical conditioning. Instances such as these, in which an individual learns an emotional response after observing it in others, have been described as **observational conditioning** (Heyes, 1994). This is one way that phobias can develop. Observational conditioning need not always lead to panic, however. Observing individuals who respond fearlessly to "dangerous" situations can help a person to learn to overcome a fear of those situations. For instance, watching videotapes of sexual activity can reduce sexual anxiety and increase sexual activity in people with sexual dysfunctions (Nemetz, Craig, & Reith, 1978).

Some instances of observational conditioning are almost indistinguishable from situations that have been described as learning through imitation. In fact, psychologists once used this similarity to argue that all social-learning experiments involve nothing more than classical or instrumental conditioning. Consider the following example. In the wild, blackbirds automatically attack predators when they observe other blackbirds attacking those predators. Once a blackbird has learned from other birds that a particular object is worthy of attack, it will continue to attack this object on sight for quite a while. In lab studies of this phenomenon, one blackbird can "teach" a second bird to attack something as harmless as a plastic bottle (Curio, Ernst, & Vieth, 1978). Researchers get the birds to do this by showing the "model" bird a stuffed owl,

Figure 11.3 Observational conditioning in blackbirds Blackbirds can learn to attack harmless objects such as bottles if they observe other blackbirds doing so—or are tricked into thinking that is what they are observing, as is shown here.
Adapted from Shettleworth, 1998.

a predator that blackbirds naturally attack. Meanwhile, the second bird observes the model's attacks, but a clever optical illusion causes the second bird to think the model is attacking a bottle rather than an owl (Figure 11.3). Consequently, the second blackbird learns to attack bottles.

This might seem like a clear case of imitation: one bird sees another bird attacking a bottle and then does the same thing. Moreover, this experiment is a lot like the Bobo doll experiment described above, which is considered to be a definitive demonstration of imitation by children. The key difference is that in the case of the blackbirds, attacking possible predators is a species-specific behavior (an unconditioned response) that almost always occurs when a blackbird detects either a predator or sees a blackbird attacking something. A simpler explanation of this example of social learning is thus that the observing blackbird is being classically conditioned: the "model" is an unconditioned stimulus, the initial attacks lead to an unconditioned attack response, and the bottle is the conditioned stimulus. This example doesn't show that birds are incapable of social learning or imitation. Researchers have conducted numerous studies of social learning in ravens and crows (Bugnyar & Kotrschal, 2002; Holzhaider, Hunt, & Gray, 2010). This study simply illustrates the difficulties associated with identifying the mechanisms that contribute to social learning in natural situations.

Observational conditioning and contagion are two phenomena in which an observer seems to be imitating the actions of others but is not. A third phenomenon that bears a deceptive resemblance to imitation is when an observer's attention is drawn to stimuli by the actions of others. Redirecting an individual's attention can lead to matching actions that may be mistaken for imitation (Roberts, 1941; Thorpe, 1963). For example, you may have seen a group of people (typically younger people) collectively directing their attention to try and trick other people into looking up at the sky. The way this trick generally works is that the group will start looking up at the sky and pointing as if there were something interesting (or frightening) happening up there. Inevitably, a passerby will look up to where the group is looking to see what all the excitement is about. The passerby then experiences confusion because there is nothing to see.

Because the passerby replicates the looking actions of the tricksters, one might think that the passerby is imitating them. In this case, however, the similarity in actions is a by-product of a similar focus of attention. Just because people watching a movie in a movie theater behave similarly does not mean that they are all imitating one another. Direction of one organism's attention toward specific objects, events, or locations within an environment as a result of another organism's action is called **stimulus enhancement** (Spence, 1937).

Stimulus enhancement can powerfully affect what an individual learns (Heyes, 1994). Essentially, the individual's focus is drawn to a subset of features of the environment that might provide more useful information than other features present. In general, stimulus enhancement increases the likelihood that an animal will be exposed to particular stimuli and their associated consequences. The animal may learn things after being attracted to locations and objects that other animals have been near, but it does so without ever needing to replicate any actions that it may have observed. In the following section, we will describe a somewhat different scenario in which individuals can replicate actions without ever observing them.

Pointing to produce stimulus enhancement Stimulus enhancement consists of directing attention to a particular part of the environment; this can lead to actions that appear similar to imitation.

Getty Images/Imageworks

Test Your Knowledge

What Is Imitation?

Much of what people describe as imitation may not be what scientists consider to be true imitation and in fact might not even involve copying. Below are some scenarios that may seem to, and possibly do, involve imitation. Your job is to try to provide alternative explanations for what is happening. (Answers appear in the Answers section in the back of the book.)

1. You smile at your friend's baby. The baby smiles back. Is your friend's baby imitating you?

2. You discover that almost anything you do makes the baby smile (apparently, you are a talented clown). But when you stick out your tongue at the baby, the baby sticks out her tongue at you. Is she imitating you?

3. Leti sees her father make a face when he is eating asparagus, and his expression seems to indicate that he thinks asparagus is disgusting. Later in the week, Leti's grandmother serves asparagus and notices that Leti is making a similar face while eating. Is Leti imitating her father?

4. While watching *America's Funniest Home Videos*, you see a video of a cat jumping up to turn a doorknob so that it can open the door and go outside. Is the cat imitating people?

5. Leti has stumbled into one of the oldest conundrums of childhood. She tells her friend, "Stop repeating whatever I say!" Her friend replies, "Stop repeating whatever I say!" Leti counters, "I mean it, you better stop!" To which her friend replies, "I mean it, you better stop!" And so on. Is Leti's friend imitating her?

Copying What Is Heard

Much of the research on imitation focuses on identifying when an individual is actually imitating. This emphasis reflects a historical debate initiated by Charles Darwin. He used reports of imitation in animals to argue that animals could reason like humans. Darwin believed that just as anatomical similarities across species provided support for his theory of natural selection, mental similarities across species did too. Edward Thorndike thought that Darwin's claims about imitating animals were nonsense and attempted to show experimentally that animals could not imitate. Ever since, researchers have been battling on both sides of the argument.

As illustrated in the last section, it can be quite tricky to ascertain that an animal is really imitating what it sees or hears. Of course, neither Darwin nor Thorndike had the opportunity to watch home videos of parrots swearing on YouTube. You really only have to see one parrot telling someone to "f*** off" to become convinced that birds can imitate vocalizations.

Vocal Imitation

You vocalize by pushing air through a pair of membranes in your throat so that the membranes vibrate. **Vocal imitation** is a vocal action that re-creates some properties of a sound experienced in the recent past—this action may be either voluntary or involuntary. In many ways, it is like imitating an action you've never seen. For example, when you imitate someone's speech, you don't need to see the motor actions the person used to produce that speech. You only need to hear the outcomes of those actions. Nevertheless, to reproduce features of the speech you heard, you need to produce motor acts similar to the ones the model used when speaking. When you are trying to imitate a sound that you've heard, you can directly compare the sounds you make with memories of the sound you originally heard. Copying of this type, in which stimuli are generated that can be directly compared with the originally observed event, is called **stimulus matching.** Because this is an indirect way of copying actions, vocal imitation and other forms of stimulus matching are often distinguished from true imitation.

When infants are learning to talk, they sometimes imitate speech produced by others around them (Kuhl & Meltzoff, 1996). For example, hearing infants raised in different locales produce speech sounds similar to the ones they hear, whereas deaf infants do not. Infants 12 to 20 weeks old who listened to an adult making vowel sounds immediately produced sounds similar to those they heard (Kuhl & Meltzoff, 1996). This implies that vocal imitation abilities are present very early in development.

Surprisingly, no mammals other than humans are able to imitate speech as well as birds can. In fact, most mammals, including our closest ape relatives, show no ability to imitate sounds and rarely learn to produce vocalizations through experience. Dolphins are the only mammals other than humans that are known to be able to flexibly imitate sounds (Janik & Slater, 1997). Some dolphins, like Akeakamai, have been trained to imitate computer-generated sounds on command (Richards, Wolz, & Herman, 1984) and may also spontaneously imitate sounds (Reiss & McCowan, 1993). Sometimes when Akeakamai was instructed to imitate a sound that she could not easily reproduce, she would produce a transposed copy of the sound (Richards et al., 1984), much as a singer might transpose a song to a higher- or lower-pitch range to make it easier to sing. Several other marine mammal species also show some ability to imitate vocally, including large whales such as the humpback whale as well as some seals (Janik & Slater, 1997). In contrast to mammals, numerous species of birds have the ability to vocally imitate. Some, such as the superb lyrebird, can precisely

Bob Krist/Corbis

Imitating sounds Parrots precisely copy sounds produced by other animals despite being unable to directly observe the actions that generated those sounds.

replicate a wide variety of man-made sounds (including car alarms and hammering carpenters) with astonishing precision.

Animals that do not naturally imitate vocalizations appear to be unable to learn this skill. Early in the twentieth century, researchers made great efforts to teach chimpanzees to speak, without much progress. Catherine Hayes described the most successful effort of the time, in which a chimpanzee named Viki learned to garble "cup," "mama," and "papa." (Hayes, 1951). This achievement provides no evidence of vocal imitation abilities because Viki was explicitly trained to produce words through instrumental conditioning and physical molding of her lip positions. You have probably seen videos of dogs and cats that seem to say "I love you" or "I want my mama." Many animals can be trained to produce speechlike sounds, but this again is an example of instrumental conditioning, not vocal imitation.

The ability to imitate vocalizations of adults may help an infant to learn new communication skills. But to a certain extent the imitating is separate from the learning. For instance, it is relatively easy to construct an electronic toy parrot that can imitate sounds or a robot that can imitate actions (Breazeal & Scassellati, 2002), yet such mimicking machines show little if any capacity to learn social skills. It is only when imitation guides skill learning that the advantages of the imitative ability are revealed. In the following section, we describe situations in which individuals use a combination of perceptual-motor-skill learning and vocal imitation to learn to sing.

Vocal Learning

One form of stimulus matching that researchers have studied extensively is song learning by birds. Song learning is also an example of **vocal learning,** which consists of using memories of sounds to guide one's own attempts at producing similar sounds. Song learning is the most extensively studied form of vocal learning in any species (including humans). The term "vocal learning" is often used to refer to vocal imitation. Although vocal imitation can contribute to vocal learning, it is possible for an individual to vocally learn without needing to imitate, so these two phenomena are not identical. For example, Viki, the "speaking" chimpanzee mentioned above, learned to make a sound like "cup" after extensive training. In that case, she vocally learned without being able to vocally imitate. All animals that can vocalize can vocally learn to some extent, but only a few (mainly birds) learn through vocal imitation.

Birdsongs typically consist of sounds lasting from 1 to 10 seconds separated by regular silent intervals. The timing, order, and qualities of individual sounds in the songs are all components that can be controlled by actions of the singer. Birds that learn their songs do so in part by listening to other birds. Young songbirds in the wild use their memories of the songs produced by mature birds to guide their own song production. Young birds can form memories of adult songs that can last the rest of their lives. Once a bird forms memories of what a "proper" song is like, it can improve its ability to produce songs by comparing its own song with its memories of other songs it has heard. Behavioral experiments show that in order to learn to produce normal adult songs, birds must have heard the songs when they were young and must be able to hear themselves sing.

Scientists can tell that songbirds learn songs socially by isolating the animals at a very young age (even prior to birth) so that they never hear another bird singing. Singing insects, frogs, and monkeys that are isolated early in life will develop relatively normal songs even if they never come into contact with another member of their species (Bradbury & Vehrencamp, 1998). In contrast, many songbirds never produce normal songs if they are isolated during early stages of development (Hinde, 1969).

Like human speech, the songs that birds sing may show differences in dialect, the locale-specific idiosyncrasies of a given language (Baptista & King, 1980; Marler, 1970; Thorpe, 1958). Just as your accent can reveal to others where you grew up and learned to speak, a bird's "accent" can reveal where the bird grew up and learned to sing. Baby birds raised by an adult of another species can sometimes even learn the foreigner's song (Immelman, 1969). This would be the equivalent of an infant being raised by chimpanzees and learning how to produce chimpanzee vocalizations (à la Tarzan). Interestingly, learning to sing foreign songs seems to require that the adult interact with the young bird. If young birds are simply exposed to recordings of foreign songs, they do not learn to sing them (Pepperberg, 1994). By analogy, you would probably be more likely to learn a foreign language spoken by neighbors if you regularly interacted with them than if you simply heard them speaking to one another from a distance.

Song learning seems to occur in three basic phases. To begin with, most songbirds seem to be born with a crude inherited "template" that biases their brain toward storing certain sound patterns. In the first phase of song learning, young birds memorize the songs they hear that best fit their template, and these memorized songs provide a model against which later performance is judged. The second phase ensues when the young bird begins attempting to sing songs. While the bird is singing, it hears itself singing and can compare its own song with memories of songs it has heard in the past (a type of stimulus matching). With practice, the young bird increases the match between its own performance and the songs it remembers hearing. In the third stage of song learning, the bird learns when to sing. For example, a territorial songbird might sing primarily when it hears a song it has never heard before or when it hears a familiar song sung by an unfamiliar bird. The actions and reactions of a nearby female may influence a male songbird's singing. These three phases of song learning are described in, and collectively make up, the **template model of song learning** (Figure 11.4).

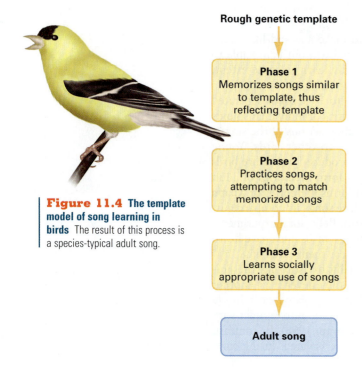

Rough genetic template

Phase 1
Memorizes songs similar to template, thus reflecting template

Phase 2
Practices songs, attempting to match memorized songs

Phase 3
Learns socially appropriate use of songs

Adult song

Figure 11.4 The template model of song learning in birds The result of this process is a species-typical adult song.

Certain species-specific features of bird songs are genetically controlled, constraining what a learning bird is likely to copy. For example, young birds exposed to both the songs of their own species and the songs of other species will typically learn the song associated with their species (Marler, 1997). Similar constraints seem to operate in human infants as well. Infants are exposed to a wide range of sounds, possibly including the sounds of birds, dogs, and musical instruments, yet the sounds they learn to produce themselves are invariably the spoken sounds produced by their own species. This could be because sounds produced by members of the same species are inherently the easiest to replicate (because they were made using similar vocal organs), or perhaps it is because individuals are genetically predisposed to recognize species-specific sounds.

As noted earlier, most mammals do not imitate vocalizations, and even fewer learn to sing through imitation. (See "Learning and Memory in Everyday Life" on page 439 for a brief discussion of how vocal learning can affect people's prowess at karaoke.) In fact, the only mammals other than humans known to do this naturally are some of the larger whales. For instance, humpback whales learn to sing new songs throughout their lives by listening to other whales' songs (Guinee, Chu, & Dorsey, 1983). Intriguingly, they continuously change the properties of their songs throughout their lives (Payne & Payne, 1985), so that in any given year, whales are singing a song that no humpback whale has ever sung before (there are no "golden oldies" in the world of humpback whales). Researchers can tell that whales are learning their songs because when a whale introduces a new song into a particular region, many other whales will then begin to sing that song (Noad, Cato, Bryden, Jenner, & Jenner, 2000). This means the whales are copying the songs they hear other whales singing. Why humpbacks and humans have such flexible vocal-learning capacities remains a mystery. Perhaps this ability provided the advantage of enhanced communication over long distances or maintained the cohesion of social groups (Tyack, 2008). Learning to sing or speak like your parents or peers may make it easier to "fit in" or participate in social activities, which in turn may increase opportunities for learning new things from others. The next section examines how such interactions can contribute to social learning.

Kelvin Aitken/Peter Arnold, Inc.

Singing humpback whale
Humpbacks are the only mammals other than humans that naturally learn to sing songs by hearing them—a unique case of vocal learning.

Social Transmission of Information

Imagine you are waiting to purchase a soda from a vending machine, and you notice that the person ahead of you just lost money in the machine. On the basis of observing the person's misfortune, you might decide not to put your money into that particular machine. This is an example of **social transmission of information,** a process in which an observer learns something new through experiences involving other agents. Social transmission of information is seen

---

◄ **LEARNING AND MEMORY IN EVERYDAY LIFE**

Karaoke

Karaoke is a relatively recent form of musical entertainment in which amateurs attempt to sing popular songs while being accompanied by instrumental music. Such performances have been compared with singing in the shower, but with an audience and less soap. Unlike sing-alongs, in which singing is typically led by someone with at least moderate musical talent, karaoke is pretty much a free-for-all in which singing ability is optional. Some participants in karaoke produce sounds so awful and out of tune that it is hard to believe they actually think their performance counts as singing.

Surprisingly, little is known about what it takes for someone to produce a good karaoke performance. Obviously, you have to be familiar with the song you are attempting to sing, so memory for the tune and the way the words correspond to the notes is a crucial ingredient. This is not sufficient, though, because plenty of people are familiar with songs such as "Happy Birthday" and yet still sound like a broken robot when they attempt to sing them. Recent experiments suggest that the secret ingredient to singing pop songs like a star may be good vocal imitation abilities (Pfordersher & Brown, 2007). A person might have a near-perfect memory of what the original song sounds like, but without the ability to

translate that memory into vocal actions that re-create those sounds, this memory will be of little help.

The good news is that people tend to underestimate their ability to vocally imitate songs. Only about 15% of college students are actually hopeless at karaoke, even though many college students (around 60%) believe their ability to sing melodies familiar to them is quite poor (Pfordresher & Brown, 2007). Perhaps as more is learned about how vocal imitation works, even those who sound like dying cows can be transformed into songbirds.

"That's not my political opinion. That's just stuff I hear on the radio."

in all human cultures. It is historically evident in the development of spoken and written language, and more recently in the development of libraries, television, telephones, and the Internet. Through these various channels, information can be transmitted rapidly to vast numbers of individuals.

The many ways in which humans are able to transmit information enables them to learn more rapidly than all other animals in an almost unlimited range of contexts. Unfortunately, this phenomenon has seldom been studied in the laboratory, except in relation to skill learning. You may recall from Chapter 8 the experiment in which a person was asked to kick a target as rapidly as possible. His performance changed incrementally in keeping with the power law of learning: improving quickly at first and then more slowly. However, when he was shown a film of someone kicking the target in a more effective way, his performance improved dramatically. In this particular example, information about better ways to kick was socially transferred by means of a film. (The person in this experiment probably improved by imitating the model he visually observed, but because the experiment focused on skill learning rather than imitation, the exact mechanism of learning was not closely assessed.)

Because so much transfer of information between humans occurs in highly sophisticated ways, it is easy to overlook examples of socially transferred information in other species. However, the very complexity of social transmission of information in humans causes difficulty for researchers when they try to isolate the basic mechanisms through which it occurs. This is why studies of the simpler forms of information transfer that can be measured in other species are important for understanding the processes underlying this ability.

Learning Through Social Conformity

If you've ever looked through your parents' or grandparents' photo albums, you've probably come across one or more pictures that made you wonder how they could have ever gotten it into their heads to wear clothes that were so ugly or uncomfortable. You may have even found a picture of the younger you wearing clothes and a hairstyle that you would be humiliated to be seen in today. In contrast, if you've seen photos of tigers taken in the 1920s, you would be hard-pressed to tell them apart from photos of tigers that were taken yesterday. Why is it that humans do things to collectively change their appearance over time? Why do you even cut your hair or shave at all? A major reason you do any of these things is because you've learned to do them.

Here's how you can know when learning, and not some other force of nature, is guiding your actions and preferences. If you go to a city in China or Africa that has a climate similar to the one you are used to and compare your hair, clothes, and speech to those of the native inhabitants, you will find that most of the inhabitants are more similar to one another in how they dress and speak than they are to you. This would not be the case if you yourself had lived in that city your whole life. If you were raised in the foreign city, you would probably dress and speak like everyone else there. Cultural differences in dress and language are easily apparent. What is not so apparent is how you learn to choose jeans over a kilt or how you learn to say, "I would choose jeans over a kilt."

Studies of the social transmission of food preferences in rats may shed some light on such questions (Galef & Wigmore, 1983). Infant rats begin life preferring foods their mother has eaten because they can taste those foods in her milk. However, rats naturally pay attention to the food consumption of other rats and can learn to eat novel foods after observing that another rat has eaten them. In studies of this phenomenon, rats are typically housed together in pairs for a few days, during which they are fed rat chow (Figure 11.5a). One rat from each pair—chosen to be the "demonstrator" rat—is moved to another cage. *Both* rats are deprived of food for one day, and then *the demonstrator rat* is fed cinnamon- or cocoa-flavored food (half of the demonstrator rats are given one flavor and half the other), after which the demonstrator rats are returned to their original cages and allowed to interact with the "observer" rat for 15 minutes. On the subsequent day, the observer rat is given access to two food bowls, one containing cocoa-flavored food and the other cinnamon-flavored food. Observer rats typically eat more food of the flavor they smelled on the demonstrator's breath (Figure 11.5b). This shows that the observer rats acquired information about foods from the demonstrator rat and later used this information when choosing food.

Figure 11.5 **Social transmission of food preferences by rats** Given a choice of two novel foods, observer rats are more likely to eat the food they smelled on a demonstrator rat's breath. This means that information about food has been transmitted between the rats.
Adapted from Shettleworth, 1998.

(a)

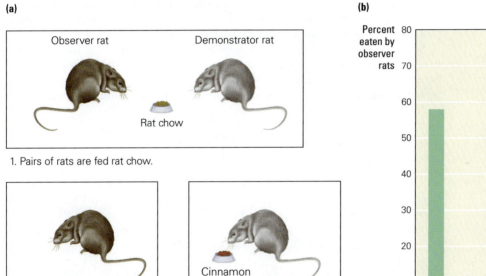

1. Pairs of rats are fed rat chow.

2. The observer rat is removed to another cage: both rats are deprived of food.

3. The demonstrator is given a novel food (cinnamon!).

(b)

Percent eaten by observer rats

4. Briefly together again; the observer rat smells the novel food on the demonstrator rat's breath.

5. Later, the observer rat chooses the food that the demonstrator rat ate.

Observer rats need to smell food in the context of another rat's breath to acquire a new food preference (Galef, 1996). Once a food becomes preferred, that preference may be transmitted to successive generations. Several factors affect how easily food preferences are transmitted to others (Galef & Whiskin, 1997). For example, larger numbers of demonstrations and demonstrating rats increase the likelihood of transfer. Isolated (one-time) observations produce only a short-term effect, but repeated exposures lead to long-term retention.

Rats tend to follow what the majority of colony members do; this tendency to adopt the behavior of the group is called **social conformity.** Social conformity has many protective functions, but it can also hinder the development of novel behavior patterns that might be advantageous. In one experiment, guppies (a kind of fish) were trained to follow specific escape paths in order to evade an artificial predator (Brown & Laland, 2002). The artificial predator consisted of a net being moved across a tank to trap the guppies, and the escape paths were holes at different positions in the net (Figure 11.6). One of two holes was closed during training, and demonstrator guppies quickly learned where the one open hole in the net was located. After training, the demonstrator fish continued to use only the escape path they had learned even after the second hole was opened. When naive fish were introduced into this situation, with both holes open, they typically chose to escape through the hole that they observed the trained fish using. If the demonstrator guppies were then removed from the tank, the observer guppies continued to use the hole they had seen the demonstrator guppies using, even when the alternate path led to a quicker escape.

Social conformity allows rapid acquisition of information that may be adaptive for a particular situation, but it can lead to traditions that may provide no general benefit. Interestingly, a reduction in the number of trained guppies (that is, a decrease in the number of demonstrators during training) increased the

Figure 11.6 Social transmission of escape routes by guppies After demonstrator guppies were trained to escape from a net by swimming through a particular hole (with a second escape hole closed), observer guppies tended to use the same escape path as the demonstrator guppies when both holes were open.

Adapted from Brown & Laland, 2002.

likelihood that new escape solutions would emerge (Brown & Laland, 2002). Apparently, even guppies can be affected by peer pressure.

Effects of Media on Behavior

Eventually, Leti entered elementary school, and her parents (like most) began worrying about how much time she spent watching television and about what she would learn if she watched programs they considered inappropriate. She didn't watch any more TV than the average child (about 24 hours per week), but this still seemed like a lot to Leti's parents. In particular, they worried that commercials might be making their daughter overly materialistic and that trailers for action movies glamorized violent behavior. Their worries intensified when Leti reached adolescence and began copying what they considered to be the "bizarre" behaviors of her YouTube idols (such as wearing a nose ring). Like most parents, Leti's parents worried about what Leti would learn from observing and copying behaviors she encounters through the mass media.

Much public transfer of information in the United States occurs through the mass distribution of moving images and audio signals in the form of television, movies, the Internet, and recorded music. Most of the content transmitted by these media outlets is designed to entertain paying customers. Even news programs focus on the news stories that will attract the most viewers. Over the last few decades, however, there has been increasing concern that the entertaining images and words broadcast by the media are having negative effects on the population. In particular, numerous organizations have concluded that excessive depiction of violence in the mass media is a public health risk because it stimulates violent behavior (Anderson et al., 2003). The basic assumption driving this concern is "monkey see, monkey do"—that people will imitate what they see.

Researchers have collected strong evidence of a general association between violent behavior and increased exposure to violent media (Anderson et al., 2003). For example, the amount of violent TV watched by children in elementary school is correlated with their aggressiveness as teenagers and with their criminal behavior as adults (Anderson et al., 2003). Similarly, statistics show the rate of homicides to have increased dramatically soon after television was introduced in the United States, whereas no such increases were observed in regions where television was banned during the same time period (Centerwall, 1992; see Figure 11.7). Given that such correlations exist, the main questions relevant to this discussion are (1) do violent media increase aggressive behavior or do aggressive individuals find

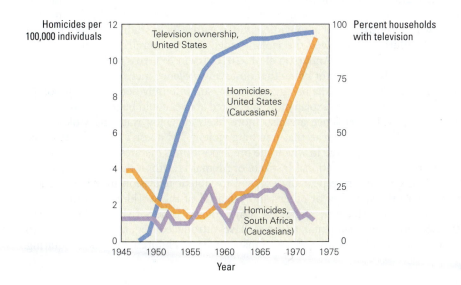

Figure 11.7 Correlation between television and homicides in the United States The rate of homicides increased dramatically among Caucasians in the United States soon after television was introduced, whereas no such increases were observed among Caucasians in South Africa, where television was banned during the same time period.
Adapted from Centerwall, 1992.

violent media more entertaining, and (2) does exposure to violent media lead to social learning and the performance of imitative actions?

Most research addressing these questions has focused on the effects of viewing violent images. In the typical experiment, researchers randomly assign young participants to watch either a short violent film or a short nonviolent film. Later, the researchers observe the participants' behavior. Usually these observations are made a few minutes or days after the participants view the film, in contexts where aggression might normally occur. Such experiments show that children exposed to the violent film are more likely to behave aggressively in play sessions immediately after viewing the film (Cornstock, 1980; Geen, 1990). For example, 7- to 9-year-old boys who scored high on measures of aggressiveness were more likely to physically assault other boys in a hockey game after watching a violent video (Josephson, 1987). As was seen in the Bobo doll experiment, aroused participants are generally more likely than nonaroused participants to behave aggressively after viewing violent images. Researchers produced the arousal by some kind of provocation. Thus, college men who viewed a violent sex film were more willing to deliver electric shocks to a woman who had previously provoked them (by giving them a mild electrical shock in a laboratory experiment) than were men who viewed a violent film containing no sex (Donnerstein & Berkowitz, 1981).

Such short-term experiments generally do not prove that children have learned to be aggressive from watching the violent performances, because a general increase in arousal levels (brought on by watching violent behavior) might be what is leading to the children's increased aggressiveness rather than anything they specifically learned from watching the videos (Anderson et al., 2003). In addition, this research does not provide evidence that exposure to violence in movies and songs increases aggressive behavior any more than violence depicted in other sources of entertainment such as books, plays, and puppet shows. Lastly, researchers have seldom studied the possibility that exposure to violent television shows might be correlated with positive outcomes, such as an increased likelihood that a person will pursue a career as a medical professional, firefighter, soldier, or police officer. Many violent shows depict both heroes and villains, and nothing about watching a video compels children to choose the villains as their models.

Recently, interactive media such as video games and the Internet have become the subjects of similar research. Part of this interest stems from the fact that students who gunned down other students in certain school shootings were avid video game players (Anderson, 2004). Experiments designed to test the negative effects of violent video games compare aggressive behavior in children who have recently played a violent video game with aggressive behavior in children who recently played a nonviolent video game. As in studies of more passive media, children who played the violent video game generally were more likely to behave aggressively (Anderson et al., 2010; Irwin & Gross, 1995).

Such correlations do not prove that observing violence increases violent behavior, and the effects of media on aggression are still intensely debated (Ferguson & Kilburn, 2010). Another explanation, suggested above, could be that children who are predisposed to violence are also more likely to enjoy watching violence on television. This would mean that watching violent TV doesn't cause the violence but is merely another way in which the predisposition is manifested. Nevertheless, a report issued by the National Institute of Mental Health in the 1980s concluded that children who are repeatedly exposed to violent television may become less sensitive to the suffering of others, more fearful of the world around them, and more likely to behave in aggressive ways toward others (APA Online, 2004). Consequently, governmental agencies have introduced regulatory measures to reduce the possible negative effects of mass media on children, including requiring warnings to be displayed on CDs, placing ratings and age restrictions on movie viewing and video games, and requiring televisions for U.S. sale to contain V-chips (V for "violence") that enable parents to restrict what their children watch.

Although researchers have proposed that social learning involving imitation underlies the association between exposure to violent media and aggressive behavior (Anderson et al., 2003), most studies of exposure to violent media do not report instances of emulation or true imitation after exposure. In general, it remains unclear what it is that individuals learn from watching movies or listening to songs.

In addition to the mere presence or absence of violence in mass media, researchers and public officials have voiced concern about the total amount of violence being depicted. Their fear is that greater exposure to violent scenes leads to a higher incidence of aggressive behavior. This may be true, but there are no experiments showing that children who are repeatedly exposed either to the same violent movie or to multiple violent movies are more likely to behave more aggressively than children who have seen such a movie only once. Just as it is difficult to identify the effects of a single entertaining event on future behavior, it is also difficult to predict the effects of multiple exposures to depictions of violence. That being said, the general consensus is that massive amounts of viewing or listening to violence is more likely to do harm than good, whether or not social learning plays a role.

Social-Learning Theory

From the 1940s through the 1960s, experimental and theoretical studies of social learning took an alternative or supplementary approach to more traditional behaviorist interpretations. Much of this research focused on understanding how young children learned to behave appropriately and why they sometimes did not. Based on studies such as Bandura's Bobo doll experiment, psychologists developed a broad theory of human behavioral development called **social-learning theory.** A key feature of social-learning theory is the idea that the kinds of reinforcements an individual has experienced in the past will determine how that individual will act in any given situation. Social-learning theorists proposed that reinforcement determines personality traits (Rotter, 1954) and that social learning is a special case of instrumental conditioning in which actions that replicate observed acts are either directly or indirectly reinforced (Bandura, 1969; Miller & Dollard, 1941).

According to Bandura, observers can gain information about whether a particular action will be rewarded or punished by witnessing the outcomes of a model's actions. A person who imitates actions that have been seen to lead to positive outcomes may in turn experience positive outcomes. If so, the person has a greater likelihood of again copying such actions in the future (consistent with Thorndike's law of effect). For example, if Leti sees a child on TV being given ice cream after cleaning her room, it could inspire her to imitate the child's reward-producing behavior. If she does clean her room, her parents are likely to reinforce her for it, which should increase the chances that Leti will clean her room again in the future and also that she will continue to copy models that she sees getting reinforcers.

Social-learning theory originally focused on instrumental conditioning and the successive approximation of target actions in response to reward and punishment (Miller & Dollard, 1941; Skinner, 1953). Modern social-learning theory places less emphasis on conditioning and instead explains behavior in terms of more cognitive processes, such as thinking and evaluating possible future outcomes and learning social-cognition skills. A basic premise of contemporary social-learning theory is that any behavior can be learned without direct reinforcement or punishment (Bandura, 1986; Ladd & Mize, 1983). Expectations of reinforcers and punishments will influence the likelihood that a learned action will be performed, but the learning itself (the knowledge gained about an action and its outcome) is taken to be the result of observation rather than the result of conditioning. In other words, a relationship between an action and an outcome only needs to be observed, not performed, in order to be learned. Within this framework, an imitated action is simply a performance that reveals what has been learned. For example, Leti doesn't have to clean her room and be rewarded in order to learn that cleaning her room brings rewards; she only needs to be able to observe an appropriate model being rewarded for cleaning.

Bandura cited four basic processes to explain how people learn by copying. First, the *presence of a model* is thought to increase an observer's attention to the situation. The actions of others can be especially salient cues that act as a magnet for attention (Bandura, 1986). Second, memories for the observed situation must be stored in an *accessible format* so that they can guide later actions. If the observer forgets how an action was performed, it will be difficult for that person to imitate the action. Third, the observer must have the *ability to reproduce the action*. You might remember quite well what it looks like when someone dunks a basketball, but unless you can jump quite high, you won't be able to imitate this action. Finally, the observer must have some *motivation for reproducing* the observed actions. You probably wouldn't burn your money just because you saw someone else doing it, even though it would be easy to do.

In some cases, the status or identity of the model can provide the motivation for an observer to imitate an action. For example, individuals are more likely to imitate the actions of someone they admire. Similarity between a model and the observer also increases the likelihood of copying, especially if the outcome is desirable. Leti would be more likely to beat up a Bobo doll if she sees a young girl her age doing it than if she sees an old woman attacking the doll, but not if she sees the girl spanked for her actions. (See "Learning and Memory in Everyday Life" below for more insight into how television characters might serve as models for children.) In other cases, the desirability of the observed outcome in itself is enough to provide motivation for an imitative act. For example,

---

What Can a Child Learn from a Teletubby?

Studies such as Bandura's Bobo doll experiment have convinced many people that violence in movies, video games, television programs, and songs can have detrimental effects on children by causing them to imitate or emulate the violent behaviors they observe. By the same token, some parents worry that their children's personalities and behaviors might be adversely affected by any number of things they might see on television. Leti's parents were concerned about exposing Leti to a children's show called *Teletubbies*, in which baby-faced creatures spoke a nonsense language and sported televisions on their tummies, thereby enabling young kids to watch two TV screens simultaneously!

Leti's parents weren't sure exactly what she might learn from watching this show, but they were positive they didn't want her to adopt the behaviors of a Teletubby, so they made sure she never had a chance to see the program at home.

What might Leti have learned from watching *Teletubbies*? Some parents and educators worried that the show overly promoted television watching by kids (because of the TVs in the characters' tummies). Others worried that the nonsense speech used by Teletubbies might disrupt language development and that the bizarre environment where the Teletubbies roamed might confuse young children. Pro-Teletubby parents reasoned that if

watching violent shows can make a child more violent, then maybe watching peaceful, happy creatures like Teletubbies can make a child more peaceful and happy.

Although we cannot as yet predict how Leti's exposure to *Teletubbies* or other shows would have affected her behavior, we can expect that she would have been more likely to copy models that she perceived as similar to herself. If she identified with a hugging Teletubby, she might have copied its hugging behavior. If she instead identified with an aggressive character on a show, she might have copied its actions. For this reason, to a certain extent, Leti's behavioral history prior to watching a show is the best predictor of what the show might have taught her.

you might be more likely to burn your money if you observe that other people who burn their money are invited to parties with celebrities.

Recently, there has been an explosion of interest in modeling social-learning processes (Galef & Laland, 2005; Kendal, Galef, & von Schaik, 2010). Some of this work continues to focus on children's social development (Crick & Dodge, 1994; Dodge, 2011), but much of it is now concerned with understanding social learning in animals (Laland & Galef, 2009; Margoliash, 2002). Also, emphasis has shifted from describing the mechanisms of social learning within individuals to exploring the social dynamics that determine when an individual will copy others (Jones et al., 2007; Laland, 2004; Rendell et al., 2010). Studies of social learning in animals have also opened up new opportunities for identifying the neural mechanisms of imitation and the social transmission of information, as described in the next section.

Interim Summary

- Psychologists use the term "social learning" to identify situations in which a learner actively monitors the acts of others and later chooses actions based on those observations.

- Copying that involves reproducing motor acts is called true imitation. Copying that involves replicating an outcome without replicating specific motor acts is called emulation.

- In contagion, the observation of a response reflexively evokes that same response. Stimulus enhancement increases the likelihood that an animal will be exposed to particular stimuli and their associated consequences.

- In both action imitation and vocal imitation, sensory representations are translated into the motor acts necessary to replicate the observed events.

- The ability to either imitate or emulate ultimately depends on the availability of memories for facts or events.

- Many bird species learn songs, but among mammals, only humans and a few species of whales show similar vocal-learning abilities.

- Social-learning theorists sometimes describe imitative learning as a special case of instrumental conditioning in which the act of copying is either directly or indirectly reinforced.

11.2 Brain Substrates

The Behavioral Processes section discussed how social learning often seems to depend both on memories for facts and on events (such as memories of actions or their outcomes only experienced once) and skill memories (learning how to perform an action observed in the past). So, you might expect that the neural substrates of social learning would be similar to those previously described in the chapters on memories for facts, events, and skills. But the fact that only a few species seem to be capable of certain kinds of social learning suggests that something beyond these basic neural systems is needed. In the following discussion, we describe neuroscience research on social learning in mammals and birds that provides some clues about how brains make either imitation or the social transmission of information possible.

The basic problem faced by the brain of an imitating animal is how to map observed events onto the motor commands that are needed to generate those same events. In action imitation, the model's observed actions are the events to be replicated. In vocal imitation, the outcomes of the model's actions (the produced sounds) are the events to be replicated.

One proposed explanation for how cortical networks store memories of actions is the **direct-matching hypothesis.** The direct-matching hypothesis proposes that memories for actions are stored in specialized cortical regions that map observed actions onto the motor representations of the acts (Buccino, Binkofski, & Riggio, 2004). In other words, visually observing an action automatically activates the same neural systems required to perform the action, and memories for the action are stored as part of this process. The following section describes recently identified cortical networks that appear to link visual inputs to motor outputs in exactly this way.

Mirror Neurons

The fact that humans can imitate actions implies that the human brain can translate visual inputs into corresponding motor patterns. Neurons that fire both during performance of an action and during visual observations of that same action were first identified in a monkey's cortex (di Pellegrino, Fadiga, Fogassi, Gallese, & Rizzolatti, 1992; Gallese, Fadiga, Fogassi, & Rizzolatti, 1996). Such neurons are called **mirror neurons** because they fire the same way when the monkey performs an action as they do when the monkey sees another monkey or person performing that action (Rizzolatti & Craighero, 2004). Mirror neurons that respond to actions of the hands or the mouth are the most common (Ferrari, Gallese, Rizzolatti, & Fogassi, 2003). For example, some mirror neurons fire most strongly when a monkey either grasps an object or observes a monkey grasping an object. Mirror neurons provide a neural link between seeing an action and doing that action. A monkey could potentially use this link to imitate an observed action because all the monkey would need to do is reactivate neural circuits that had recently been activated.

Some mirror neurons seem to fire most strongly during observation of the outcome of an action rather than in response to observations of the action itself (Gallese et al., 1996). This means that the neurons fire the same way when a monkey is seeing a particular outcome (which could be the result of various actions) as when the monkey is achieving that same outcome. So, mirror neurons provide the kinds of neural links necessary for emulation (copying a goal) as well as imitation (copying an action).

It is difficult to directly observe mirror neurons in humans because invasive surgery is necessary to record from individual neurons. However, indirect measures of cortical activity, such as electroencephalographs (EEGs) (Raymaekers, Wiersema, & Roeyers, 2009), transcranial magnetic stimulation (Gangitano, Mottaghy, & Pascual-Leone, 2001), and cerebral blood flow (Martineau et al., 2010) indicate that regions of the human cortex behave as if they contain mirror neurons. The basic procedure for such studies in humans generally involves an "observation-only" condition, an "imitation" condition, and an "instructed action" condition. For example, researchers might ask participants to (1) observe an image of someone moving a certain finger, (2) imitate someone moving a certain finger, and (3) move a certain finger in response to a specific command (Figure 11.8). Neuroimaging experiments of this kind show overlap between cortical regions that are activated by the performance of an action and cortical regions that are activated by observing that action being performed (Iacoboni et al., 1999; Rizzolatti & Craighero, 2004). The areas of the human brain that become active during both the observation and performance of actions are located in cortical regions similar to those examined in monkeys. This suggests that monkeys and humans may use similar circuits to match observations to actions.

Researchers hypothesize that mirror neurons provide a basic mechanism for simple imitation (Rizzolatti & Sinigaglia, 2010). In fact, some researchers suggest

Figure 11.8 **Mirror neurons in a human cortex?** The red areas indicate regions in cortex that become more active when humans either watched a video of someone moving their finger or when they performed the same finger movements either by imitating the video or following instructions. The line graph on the right shows changes in cortical activation over time when participants were executing movements or observing them.

Adapted from Iacoboni et al., 1999.

that deficits in mirror neurons may contribute to developmental disorders (we discuss this idea in more detail later, in the Clinical Perspectives section). This idea is significant because in the past, researchers assumed that imitation involved higher-level cognitive processes that would be difficult to trace to specific brain activity in humans and impossible to trace to specific brain activity in other animals. If mirror neurons are involved in imitation, then researchers should be able to directly examine the mechanisms of imitation in animal models.

Test Your Knowledge

Who Has Mirror Neurons and What Do They Do?

Mirror neurons in monkeys respond the same to observed actions and performed actions. Which of the following statements are also true of mirror neurons? (Answers appear in the Answers section in the back of the book.)

1. Mirror neurons are important for imitative abilities.

2. Mirror neurons in humans respond like those in monkeys.

3. An animal without mirror neurons cannot imitate actions.

4. Only primates have mirror neurons.

Song Learning in Bird Brains

You might suppose that the neural mechanisms you use to imitate actions would be very different from the brain circuits used by young birds learning to sing. However, they are actually quite similar.

The neural circuits that birds use for learning and producing songs are complex (Figure 11.9). Birds use specific brain regions to store memories of songs and use other regions to learn the perceptual-motor skills for singing. Lesion studies and electrophysiological recordings have identified two main neural regions that birds use for producing songs: the high vocal center (HVC) and the robust nucleus of the archistriatum (RA). The HVC controls the timing of song production—for example, when a bird will start or stop singing and the rate at which notes are produced. The RA controls more detailed features of

Figure 11.9 Neural circuits for song learning by birds Circuits for producing songs are shown in purple, and circuits for storing skill memories used to produce songs are shown in red. The regions involved in song production include the high vocal center (HVC) and the robust nucleus of the archistriatum (RA). Area X and the lateral magnocellular nucleus of the anterior neostriatum (LMAN) are involved in forming memories. The two circuits are interconnected, permitting memories to affect how songs are produced.
Adapted from Brainard & Doupe, 2000.

the individual sounds within a song (Mooney, 2009). Neurons in the RA that fire strongly when a bird hears a song are also seen to become active just before the bird begins to sing. This means that the RA neurons fire similarly when the bird hears particular songs and when the bird sings those same songs. This description should sound familiar to you because it is very similar to the depiction of mirror neuron activity presented above. Neurons in HVC also respond both when birds sing and when they are listening to their own song (Prather et al., 2008). These findings suggest that bird brains contain neurons that map observed events onto vocal acts in a manner comparable with that of the mirror neurons seen in primates.

Birds also possess a neural region called Area X that is thought to be analogous to the mammalian basal ganglia. Lesions to Area X disrupt song learning just as lesions to the basal ganglia of mammals impair perceptual-motor learning (as you may recall from the discussion in Chapter 8 on skill memories). Area X receives inputs from a region called the lateral magnocellular nucleus of the anterior neostriatum (LMAN). The LMAN is thought to function like the frontal cortex in mammals. Disrupting activity in LMAN neurons when a songbird is first hearing other birds' songs impairs, but does not prevent, song learning (Basham, Nordeen, & Nordeen, 1996). Similarly, frontal damage in humans can interfere with a person's ability to learn from social interactions, a topic we discuss in greater detail in the Clinical Perspectives section of this chapter.

Imitation invariably requires a circuit that maps sensory representations onto motor systems, so different species are likely to exhibit similar neural solutions to this problem. Future clarification of the neural processes underlying vocal learning by birds will enable scientists to meaningfully compare the mechanisms underlying imitation of both sounds and sights in the brains of many organisms.

Hippocampal Encoding of Socially Transmitted Food Preferences

When rats learn a food preference from smelling the odor of the food on another rat's breath, they create memories of the experience that can influence their behavior for a lifetime. As little as 10 minutes of exposure to a novel food odor on another rat's breath, with no repetition of exposure, can influence eating behavior at least 3 months later (Clark, Broadbent, Zola, & Squire, 2002).

You may recall from Chapter 7, on memories for facts and events, that when humans experience a unique event and are then able to remember it several months later, an episodic memory has been created. Could it be that rats form episodic memories of experiences involving unique odors coming from another rat's mouth? Based on the studies of human episodic memory described in Chapter 7, you might expect that if a rat were forming memories for such events, then damage to the rat's hippocampus should disrupt its ability to acquire preferences for specific foods from interactions with other rats. Specifically, you might expect that hippocampal damage could disrupt the rat's old memories for past interactions (retrograde amnesia) or disrupt its ability to acquire new memories (anterograde amnesia).

This prediction has received some experimental support. Observer rats were exposed to a food odor on a demonstrator rat's breath and then were given hippocampal lesions 1, 10, or 30 days later. In each case, the lesions reduced the observer rat's preference for the food, but the disruption was worst when the lesion was produced right after the observation period (Bunsey & Eichenbaum, 1995; Clark et al., 2002). In other words, the rats appeared to show retrograde amnesia following hippocampal damage, and the "amnesia" was worse for newly acquired memories than for older ones. This effect is consistent with the results of human studies showing that hippocampal-region damage affected newer episodic memories more than older ones. In short, hippocampal damage disrupts the ability of animals to learn from social interactions in ways that parallel episodic memory deficits in humans suffering from amnesia.

Chapter 7 also described how lesions of the basal forebrain in human patients can lead to amnesia similar to the amnesia caused by hippocampal damage. Recall that this deficit resulted from the loss of neuromodulatory neurons in the basal forebrain that modulated activity in the hippocampus. It turns out that basal forebrain circuits that modulate activity in a rat's hippocampus are similarly critical for social transmission of food preferences. If a rat's basal forebrain is damaged, its memories of previously acquired food preferences will be drastically impaired. Its future ability to learn about novel foods from other rats will not be affected, however—a case of retrograde amnesia without anterograde amnesia (Berger-Sweeney, Stearns, Frick, Beard, & Baxter, 2000; Vale-Martinez, Baxter, & Eichenbaum, 2002). Just as in humans with amnesia, basal forebrain lesions in rats produce patterns of memory loss for socially transmitted information that are comparable with, but distinguishable from, those associated with hippocampal damage.

It seems that in rats, memory for socially transmitted information depends on the hippocampus and basal forebrain. This doesn't necessarily mean that food preferences are based on episodic memories, but it does mean that hippocampal processing is relevant to the mechanisms that enable both rats and humans to learn from socially transmitted information. Memories for facts and events are rarely described by psychologists as resulting from social learning—more often, these memories are described as outcomes of an unspecified process of "storage" or "encoding"—but the similarities between memory loss in humans and impaired social transmission of information in rats suggest that researchers may be using different terminology to describe comparable phenomena.

Interim Summary

- Before any action can be imitated, it must be recognized. Mirror neurons fire in the same way when the monkey performs an action as they do when the monkey sees another monkey performing that action.

- Neuroimaging studies of humans have correlated activation in cortical areas where mirror neurons are likely to be found with the performance or observation of particular actions.

- The song-learning circuits of birds share many features in common with mammalian brain circuits for learning perceptual-motor skills.

- The memories that rats form based on socially transmitted information about foods depend on the hippocampus and basal forebrain.

11.3 Clinical Perspectives

Most of the disorders known to affect social learning have an impact on imitation, often in two seemingly paradoxical ways. Patients with imitative deficits cannot seem to prevent themselves from involuntarily imitating the actions of individuals with whom they are interacting, and yet they have difficulties imitating specific actions when asked to do so. This pattern, which is seen both in individuals with autism and in some stroke patients, is consistent with current theories about the cortical substrates of imitation.

Autism Spectrum Disorders

For centuries, children who would today be diagnosed as having autism were grouped with the insane or mentally retarded. It was only in the last century that researchers began to identify autism as a distinctive pattern of symptoms (Kanner, 1943). **Asperger's syndrome,** a condition marked by many of the same features as autism, was identified around the same time. In Asperger's syndrome, individuals have normal intellectual abilities but a reduced capacity for social skills. A major difference between Asperger's syndrome and autism is that individuals with Asperger's are more likely to speak fluently. In the old days, because children with autism often did not learn speech, they sometimes were misdiagnosed as being deaf! Because of their similarities, Asperger's syndrome and autism are often grouped together and clinically designated as **autism spectrum disorders** (ASD). Studies of autism spectrum disorders provide insight into how social learning contributes to much of what humans learn throughout their lives and into the neural systems that make possible social learning.

Autism spectrum disorders are complex, with many different symptoms. These were not widely familiar to the general public until the 1980s, when a major motion picture called *Rain Man* appeared in theaters. In *Rain Man*, Dustin Hoffman portrays an adult with a rare form of autism associated with amazing calculation and memorizing abilities. The character with autism in *Rain Man*, while not prototypical, does show some of the common signs of autism. In particular, he has difficulties interacting socially, requires highly consistent routines, is susceptible to sensory overload, uses language abnormally when communicating with others, and repeatedly produces certain stereotyped movement patterns. The typical time of onset of autism is within three years after birth (Waterhouse, Fein, & Modahl, 1996).

In addition to engaging in repetitive and stereotyped actions, individuals with autism may repeat words or phrases immediately after hearing them spoken, a phenomenon called **echolalia.** Echolalia requires vocal imitation abilities, which might seem to suggest that individuals with autism would be good imitators. However, these children actually turn out to be worse at imitating actions than other children.

Some of the earliest evidence that children with autism are impaired at imitating actions came from the reports of mothers. For example, one mother reported that she was unable to teach her child to play the "patty-cake" game until she physically moved the child's arms in the correct patterns (Ritvo & Provence, 1953). The fact that the child did eventually learn to play this game shows that the earlier learning deficit was not the result of impaired visual-motor coordination abilities. Instead, the child's impaired ability to imitate most probably prevented him from successfully copying his mother. Another possible explanation for this difficulty, however, is that copying adults may be less reinforcing for children with autism than for other children, and so they may be less motivated to do it, whatever their imitative ability. A popular theory of autism called the *mind-blindness theory* suggests that children with autism have problems with perspective taking that prevent them from imagining themselves in someone else's shoes (Baron-Cohen, 2009).

This theory would explain the boy's deficits in imitation as a side effect of a more general deficit in understanding his mother's intentions.

If children with autism suffer from impaired imitation abilities early on, perhaps this deficit is actually a source of their other behavioral and social impairments (Rogers & Pennington, 1991). Different studies have reported different levels of imitative deficits, however, so it remains unclear exactly which aspects of imitative abilities are affected by autism (Beadle-Brown & Whiten, 2004; Hamilton, 2008). People with autism can recognize when they are being imitated, but they do not reliably imitate the actions of others (Smith & Bryson, 1994; Leighton et al., 2008). Children with autism tested in a do-as-I-do task could imitate simple actions, like drinking, but had problems imitating sequences of actions (Beadle-Brown & Whiten, 2004). When tested in the two-action task portrayed in Figure 11.2 (the task with a plastic box containing a food reward), older children with autism imitated the model's actions normally, but younger children with autism did not (Smith & Bryson, 1998; Whiten & Brown, 1999). Interestingly, imitations of meaningless gestures (like those used in the patty-cake game) and "nonsense" actions performed with a common object seem more likely to be impaired than meaningful actions (DeMeyer et al., 1972; Smith & Bryson, 1994; Williams, Whiten, & Singh, 2004). These findings suggest that there is not an overarching imitative capacity that is "broken" in individuals with autism, but that certain tasks requiring imitation are difficult for them.

As mentioned earlier, spontaneous inappropriate copying of observed speech and actions is actually typical of autism, so why might children with autism have difficulty voluntarily imitating meaningless actions? Neural abnormalities associated with autism provide some clues. Several areas in the brains of individuals with autism are anatomically abnormal, including the sensory cortex, prefrontal cortex, hippocampus, cerebellum, amygdala, and basal ganglia (Brambilla et al., 2003; Minshew & Williams, 2007; Waterhouse et al., 1996). Structural MRI studies show the cerebellum, temporal lobes (including the hippocampus), amygdala, and corpus callosum of individuals with autism are often abnormal in size. In addition, functional MRI experiments show less overall activity-related circulation of blood within the temporal lobes as well as abnormal patterns of cortical activation. Many of these differences in brain structure and function seem to result from abnormal development early in life. One or more of these affected brain regions may contribute to the imitative abnormalities associated with autism.

Recently, researchers began exploring whether the mirror neuron system in the cortex might be contributing to the imitation deficits seen in individuals with autism and in those with Asperger's syndrome (Ramachandran & Oberman, 2006; Rizzolatti & Fabbri-Destro, 2010; Southgate & Hamilton, 2008; Williams, Whiten, Suddendorf, & Perrett, 2001). Neuroimaging studies show that circuits within and around the mirror neuron system in these individuals, and patterns of activation within these circuits, differ systematically from those in typical brains (Martineau et al., 2010; Nishitani, Avikainen, & Hari, 2004; Waiter et al., 2004). For example, Asperger's patients showed slower activation of cortical regions when asked to imitate facial expressions (Figure 11.10). In these studies, measures of cortical activity were recorded using a magnetoencephalograph (MEG) while participants were imitating facial expressions. MEGs are similar to EEGs except that instead of recording changes in electrical activity in a person's brain over time, MEGs record changes in magnetic fields generated by the brain that are measured with highly sensitive magnetometers. Asperger's patients' imitations started later and took longer to complete than those of a control group. Measurements using MEG showed that when participants were imitating the expressions (control participants and Asperger's patients alike), different cortical regions became active at different times, in the following sequence: (1) visual cortex, (2) auditory cortex, (3) parietal

(a)

Nishitani, N., Avikainen, S., & Hari, R. (2004). Abnormal imitation-related cortical activation sequences in Asperger's syndrome. *Annals of Neurology, 55*(4), 558–562.

(b)

Figure 11.10 Asperger's patients show slower responses when imitating facial expressions (a) Participants were asked to imitate facial expressions while activity in their cortex was recorded using MEG. (b) Several different cortical regions became active more slowly in Asperger's patients, including visual cortex (black), auditory cortex (blue), parietal cortex (green), Broca's area (yellow), and motor cortex (red).

Adapted from Nishitani et al., 2004.

cortex, (4) frontal cortex, and (5) motor cortex. Each of these regions was slower to become active in Asperger's patients, suggesting that in those patients, the cortical processes contributing to action imitation were impaired.

Mirror neurons vary in their responsiveness to specific observed and performed actions (Rizzolatti & Sinigaglia, 2010). Some respond only to observed actions, whereas others respond to a wider range of stimuli. If some networks of mirror neurons in a person's brain are dysfunctional, the person could suffer deficits in particular imitative abilities, such as the ability to imitate nonfunctional actions (Williams et al., 2001; Ramachandran & Oberman, 2006). Because individuals with autism have difficulty imitating only certain actions, their deficit might be related to abnormal function in a subset of mirror neurons rather than to a general dysfunction of cortical neural circuits involved in imitation. Alternatively, their deficit might reflect weaknesses in several interacting neural systems, with mirror neurons playing a less critical role (Leighton et al., 2008; Southgate & Hamilton, 2008).

At the moment, it is not clear whether the deficit seen in individuals with autism is truly an imitative deficit or whether it might instead be a deficit in mechanisms underlying stimulus enhancement, emulation, reinforcement mechanisms, emotional processes, or generalization from past experience. Just as many nonimitative actions can look like imitation, many apparent deficits in imitative abilities may actually be deficits in mechanisms other than those directly involved in imitation. As our understanding of observational learning increases, so will our understanding of the roles different brain regions and learning mechanisms play in autism spectrum disorders.

Test Your Knowledge

Imitative Deficits in Individuals with ASD

Individuals with autism spectrum disorders show several differences in their ability to imitate actions. Try to identify which of the below are consistent with imitative deficits observed in these individuals. (Answers appear in the Answers section in the back of the book.)

1. A loud sound leads to a panic response.
2. One specific phrase is repeated incessantly.
3. The individual has problems when trying to keep up with a fitness video.
4. On the phone, the individual often repeats the last phrase she heard.

Imitative Deficits after Stroke

Individuals with autism have atypical imitative capacities because of abnormal brain development. Similar deficits can also occur, however, after brain injuries. As noted in Chapter 8, a common source of brain damage is stroke, which causes neurons in the affected region to die, effectively creating a brain lesion. Stroke-related damage in any of several brain regions is known to disrupt imitative abilities.

You may recall from Chapter 8 on skill memory that damage to the parietal cortex leads to a condition called apraxia, which dramatically impairs purposeful movement. As you might guess, patients with apraxia have great difficulty imitating actions. In fact, one of the tests physicians use to diagnose whether a stroke has produced apraxia is to ask the patient to imitate specific gestures.

Frontal-lobe damage can also affect imitation abilities. Alexander Luria discovered that patients with frontal-lobe damage tend to produce involuntary imitative responses (Luria, 1966). This tendency included echolalia, which you may recall is also common in individuals with autism. Luria examined unintentional imitative responses in his patients by having them perform an action at the same time that he performed a related but incompatible action. For example, Luria might show his fist immediately after asking a patient to hold up his palm. Often, seeing Luria make a fist would interfere with a frontal-lobe patient's ability to show his palm when instructed to do so. The patient would tend instead to involuntarily imitate Luria. Patients with reduced activity in the frontal lobes (such as occurs during major depressive episodes) also show this tendency to automatically imitate observed actions (Archibald, Mateer, & Kerns, 2001). Luria's finding suggests that activity in frontal-lobe circuits normally inhibits such imitation.

To further explore this tendency, Brass and colleagues measured the degree to which observations of finger movements interfered with the ability of patients with brain damage to move their fingers in response to commands (Brass, Derrfuss, Matthes-von Cramon, & von Cramon, 2003). Patients were asked to lift their index finger from a key when they saw the numeral 1 and to lift their middle finger when they saw the numeral 2 (Figure 11.11a). While they performed this task, they watched either a video image of a stationary hand, a video image of a hand producing finger movements consistent with the presented numeral, or a video of a hand producing movements inconsistent with the presented numeral. Frontal-lobe patients made more mistakes than patients with nonfrontal lesions when the movement on the video was inconsistent with the instruction (Figure 11.11b) because they were less able to stop themselves from imitating observed finger movements.

As in autism spectrum disorders, increases in automatic imitation after a stroke are often correlated with deficits in the ability to voluntarily imitate actions. Note that both conditions suggest a loss of autonomy, specifically a lost ability to decide or control which observed acts to copy. Cortical circuits in the frontal and parietal lobes may enable people to control when observations (or memories of observations) guide their actions.

Figure 11.11

Spontaneous imitation induced by frontal-lobe damage Patients with lesions in the frontal cortex or posterior cortex and control participants with no lesions were asked to perform specific finger movements in response to numerals displayed on a screen while ignoring the movements of a hand shown on the screen. (a) The finger movements shown on the screen were either consistent with the instructions or inconsistent with the instructions. (b) Patients with frontal-lobe lesions were more likely (5% versus 2%) to make a mistake when the finger movement shown was inconsistent with the movement corresponding to the displayed numeral.

Adapted from Brass, Derrfuss, Matthes-von Cramon, & von Cramon, 2003.

Brass, M. Derrfuss, J., Matthes-von Cramon, G., & von Cramon, D. Y. (2003). Imitative response tendencies in patients with frontal brain lesions. *Neuropsychology, 17*(2), 265–271.

Consistent   Motionless   Inconsistent

(a)

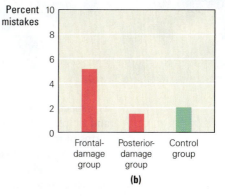

(b)

Interim Summary

- Individuals with autism may repeat words or phrases immediately after hearing them spoken. This phenomenon, called echolalia, requires vocal imitation abilities. However, children with autism actually seem less able to learn from imitation than children without autism.

- Like individuals with autism, patients with frontal-lobe lesions tend to imitate observed actions automatically but have difficulty imitating actions when instructed to do so.

▶ SYNTHESIS

Sticking out your tongue at people to indicate you dislike them is probably not an innate response (although as noted in Chapter 10 on emotional learning, tongue protrusion is an unconditioned response to bad tastes). When Leti's mother sees Leti sticking out her tongue at a neighbor's child, she is likely to conclude that Leti learned this gesture by imitating someone else. Perhaps Leti did learn to stick out her tongue through imitation, as her mother suspects, but many other mechanisms could also account for her learning to do this that do not require copying. Imitation, observational conditioning, stimulus enhancement, and social transmission of information are some of the mechanisms that make social learning—learning through the observation of others—possible in humans and certain other animals. Determining which social-learning mechanisms contribute to specific changes in an individual's behavior is a major challenge that psychologists are still grappling with.

Perhaps Leti's older sister told her to go stick out her tongue at the neighbor. This kind of active instruction through social transmission of information seems to be limited to humans and is closely tied to language abilities. You're receiving socially transmitted information at this very moment. Social transmission of information through lectures and textbooks forms the basis for learning in almost all courses taught in universities and colleges.

College instructors rely on social learning Professors lecture in the hope that students will learn through listening.

Learning theorists have traditionally assumed that learning results from the conditioning of passive reflexive reactions (classical conditioning) or from the reinforcement of voluntary responses (instrumental conditioning). Is social learning anything more than a mixture of classical and instrumental conditioning? Research into how different cortical and subcortical brain regions mediate social learning is already providing some insights into this issue. As you might expect, some social-learning processes, such as observational conditioning, can be explained as a special case of classical conditioning. Other abilities—as when humans, apes, and dolphins imitate actions on command—are more difficult to account for in terms of incremental-learning models and instead seem to require unique cortical-processing mechanisms.

Understanding what happens when social-learning mechanisms go awry can also lead to new ideas about how social learning works. Correlating the imitative deficits in individuals with autism with those of stroke patients may provide clues about the relationship between automatic imitation and voluntary imitation. The fact that in both conditions echolalia tends to co-occur with involuntary imitation of actions and with an inability to imitate certain actions on command suggests that vocal and action imitation may rely on overlapping neural systems. At the same time, many current psychological models of imitative learning assume that action imitation requires processes that are fundamentally different from those involved in vocal imitation.

Albert Bandura has suggested that social learning is a process that permits the rapid, errorless acquisition of cognitive and perceptual-motor skills and that humans who take full advantage of this process have "learned to learn." From this perspective, social learning is itself a cognitive skill of the sort described in Chapter 8, and understanding how individuals learn to learn from others is simply an extension of understanding how organisms learn cognitive skills. With luck, future behavioral and physiological studies of social-learning processes will one day enable scientists to learn how it is that brains learn to learn.

Key Terms

Asperger's syndrome, *p. 452*

autism spectrum disorder, *p. 452*

contagion, *p. 433*

copying, *p. 429*

direct-matching hypothesis, *p. 448*

echolalia, *p. 452*

emulation, *p. 430*

mirror neurons, *p. 448*

modeling, *p. 430*

observational conditioning, *p. 433*

observational learning, *p. 428*

perspective taking, *p. 432*

social conformity, *p. 442*

social learning, *p. 428*

social-learning theory, *p. 445*

social transmission of information, *p. 439*

stimulus enhancement, *p. 435*

stimulus matching, *p. 436*

template model of song learning, *p. 438*

true imitation, *p. 430*

two-action test, *p. 430*

vocal imitation, *p. 436*

vocal learning, *p. 437*

Concept Check

1. Some researchers have suggested that the only way you can be sure that you are observing imitation is if the actions or sounds being copied are so bizarre that there is no other plausible explanation for why they might occur (Thorpe, 1963). What are some other ways researchers can tell when an animal is truly imitating?

2. Descartes and some religious belief systems have championed the idea that, whereas humans learn through effort and insight, other animals learn only by accident. By describing examples of pets performing advanced intellectual feats (such as imitating the actions of their owners), Charles Darwin and his student George Romanes challenged this assumption and attempted to establish that a continuum of mental abilities exists across species (Darwin, 1883; Romanes, 1898). What do such examples tell us about imitation in humans and other animals?

3. Edward Thorndike (1898) defined imitation as learning to do an act from seeing it done, but visual observations are not the only way to get the information needed to imitate or emulate. What are some examples of imitative actions described in this chapter that would not count as imitation under Thorndike's definition?

4. In the wild, animals may gain an advantage from spending more effort investigating areas that have been occupied by other members of the same species. Such behavior could increase the chances of finding food, mates, or a safe place to hide. What forms of social learning might provide animals with these advantages?

5. Children may (a) be born with an ability to copy that depends on specialized mechanisms for matching visual perceptions to motor responses (Meltzoff, 1996; Piaget, 1955), (b) learn to copy through experience, and (c) consciously consider the perspective or social status of other individuals (Guillaume, 1971). For which of these types of learning have neural substrates been identified?

6. Albert Bandura argued that instrumental conditioning without imitation is an inefficient way of learning new actions and that only humans learn by copying because learning from models requires abstracting rules and forming memories based on verbal codes and imagery (Bandura, 1986). List examples in this chapter that either support or refute these ideas.

CHAPTER 12

Development and Aging

Learning and Memory across the Lifespan

TWENTY-YEAR-OLD DENISE is entering the prime of her life. As a state champion on the basketball court, she understands that her body is at the peak of its physical strength and stamina. As a college student, she challenges her brain every day to learn new skills, organize and retrieve information for exams, and integrate new knowledge into her broadening understanding of the adult world.

At Thanksgiving, Denise goes home to visit her family and plays with her young nieces and nephews. The youngest, Kelly, is a 10-month-old busily soaking up information about the world. Kelly is just beginning to stand and start walking, to recognize and respond to spoken words, and to produce babbling sounds that will someday lead to fluent language.

At the other end of the lifespan are Denise's grandparents. Her grandmother, a wise, funny woman, is a walking library of family history and special recipes. But Denise's grandfather has gone downhill since last Thanksgiving. He repeats the same stories over and over again and has trouble remembering Kelly's name. The family worries that this is not just normal old age but a sign of something more serious, such as Alzheimer's disease. The specter of this worry hangs over the family's holiday celebration.

In this chapter, we'll trace the development of learning and memory abilities across the lifespan, starting with infants like Kelly and culminating with elderly individuals like Denise's grandparents. You'll recognize many types of memory that were introduced in earlier chapters, but here we'll view them from the standpoint of how a person's memory changes over the lifespan and how this reflects underlying age-related changes in the brain. You'll also encounter topics that may be new to

Behavioral Processes

The Developing Memory: Infancy through Childhood

Sensitive Periods for Early Learning

Learning and Memory in Everyday Life: Teaching Babies Signs before Speech

Adolescence: Crossing from Childhood into Adulthood

The Aging Memory: Adulthood through Old Age

Brain Substrates

The Genetic Basis of Learning and Memory

Learning and Memory in Everyday Life: Can Exposure to Classical Music Make Babies Smarter?

Neurons and Synapses in the Developing Brain

Brain Changes in Adolescence

The Brain from Adulthood to Old Age

Clinical Perspectives

Down Syndrome

Alzheimer's Disease

Learning and Memory in Everyday Life: Can Mental Exercise Protect against Alzheimer's Disease?

A Connection between Down Syndrome and Alzheimer's Disease

you, such as the ability of adult brains to grow new neurons, the effects of sex hormones on developing and mature memories, and the concept of sensitive periods—"windows of opportunity"—for specific kinds of learning, after which such learning may never again be so easy or effective.

12.1 Behavioral Processes

One reason to study learning and memory across the lifespan is to understand the different capabilities of children compared with young adults and of young adults compared with older adults. Understanding the kinds of learning and memory that are comparatively strong or weak at each age can help us make the most of our potential at every stage of life and can also help educators tailor their teaching methods to different age groups.

As you read, though, be sure to keep in mind that we're talking about the *average* learning and memory abilities of groups at various ages. Within any age group, there is wide variation in the abilities of individuals. For one thing, certain kinds of memory can mature at different rates, so that there are always some youngsters who show a different pattern of development, acquiring new abilities faster or slower than their peers. Similarly, at the other end of the lifespan, certain kinds of learning and memory tend to decline, but others keep going strong—while in some unfortunate individuals, cognitive abilities decline at an accelerated rate, due to injury or disease such as Alzheimer's disease.

With these thoughts in mind, let's begin at the beginning: with the learning and memory of individuals at the earliest stages of life.

The Developing Memory: Infancy through Childhood

If you've spent any time with a young child, you've witnessed the immense surge of learning that takes place in the first few years of life. In those years, a child acquires abilities ranging from the motor skills needed to grasp and walk, to the ability to produce and understand language, to a fund of semantic knowledge about the world. Learning continues across the lifespan, of course, but its progress is especially dramatic in young children. More recently, it's become apparent that some learning occurs even before birth.

Learning before Birth

The human uterus is a surprisingly noisy place. A human fetus is exposed to the sounds of maternal speech and heartbeats as well as noises from the outside world. By about 25 weeks of **gestational age,** or time since conception, a fetus's brain and sense organs are sufficiently developed for the fetus to start perceiving and learning about these sounds.

For example, remember from Chapter 3 that *habituation* is the phenomenon of reduced responding to a repeated stimulus. Habituation can be used to test fetal learning about sounds. Researchers place a speaker against the mother's abdomen and play sounds that the fetus can hear. The first time a sound plays, most human fetuses with gestational ages of 34 to 36 weeks will respond by moving (Figure 12.1). If the same sound is played several times, the fetuses gradually stop responding (Hepper & Shahidullah, 1992). When a different sound is played, the responses reappear—indicating that the loss of response to the first stimulus was due to habituation, not fatigue. Eventually, responses

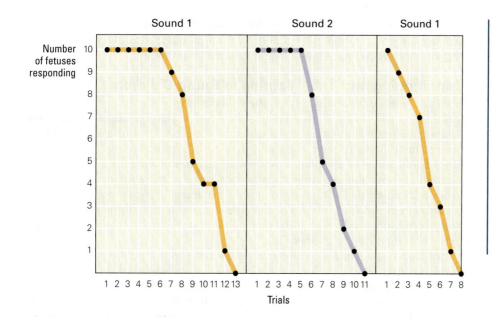

Sound 1   Sound 2   Sound 1

Number of fetuses responding

Trials

Figure 12.1 Habituation to sound in 10 human fetuses When sound 1 is presented, all 10 human fetuses initially respond with movement; as the sound is repeated, the number of fetuses responding decreases. By trial 13, all have habituated. When a new stimulus (sound 2) is presented, all the fetuses again respond; this response also habituates over about a dozen trials. Finally, the original stimulus (sound 1) is presented again. The fetuses show spontaneous recovery of responding followed by fast habituation (only 8 trials). Adapted from Hepper & Shahidullah, 1992.

to the second stimulus habituate too. When the first sound is played again, the fetuses respond but habituate almost immediately, indicating that they "remember" having experienced that sound before. Fetal habituation can be observed in nonhuman species too, including rats (Smotherman & Robinson, 1992).

Such prenatal learning can persist after birth. Researchers Anthony DeCasper and Melanie Spence constructed a set of short stories with strong, simple rhyming patterns, such as excerpts from Dr. Seuss's *The Cat in the Hat* (DeCasper & Spence, 1986). The researchers then asked mothers in the last six weeks of pregnancy to read one of these stories aloud to their unborn babies, twice a day. Two or three days after birth, each newborn was placed in a crib with an artificial nipple positioned where the infant could suck at it. Under these conditions, infants usually suck in bursts: giving a series of brisk individual sucks, pausing a few seconds, and then giving another burst of sucks. For this experiment, the nipple was rigged so that each burst of sucking caused a tape recorder to turn on and play a story recorded in the mother's voice. But it wasn't always the same story. For one set of babies, if a sucking burst followed a longer-than-average pause, then the familiar story played, but if a sucking burst followed a shorter-than-average pause, then an unfamiliar story played:

S (artificial nipple) → R (long pause before sucking burst) → O (familiar story)
S (artificial nipple) → R (short pause before sucking burst) → O (novel story)

For other babies, the contingencies were reversed so that short pauses triggered the familiar story and long pauses triggered the novel story. Over a period of 20 minutes, the infants changed their sucking behavior, timing their pauses in such a way as to result in the familiar story being played more often. In short, the familiar story reinforced a particular pattern of sucking behavior. This learning is an example of *operant conditioning*, which you read about in Chapter 5. Obviously, the babies did not understand the meaning of the words in either story; the difference in their responses probably reflected an ability to discriminate the cadence and rhythm of the two stories. Still, studies like this one demonstrate that prenatal infants are capable of learning and that the learned information persists and can affect behavior after birth. DeCasper and colleagues suggest that fetal exposure to the mother's language patterns may help the brain start to encode language-relevant speech sounds, giving them a head start on acquiring language after birth (DeCasper, Lecanuet, Busnel, Granier-Deferre, & Maugeais, 1994). Newborns come into the world having already experienced stimuli and begun to learn about them.

Conditioning and Skill Learning in Young Children

Despite evidence for fetal learning, the really impressive learning machines are infants. An explosion in learning marks the first few years of life in humans and comparable periods in other species. Just about every kind of learning that is present in adults is present in infants, at least in a rudimentary form. On the other hand, some of an infant's perceptual and motor systems are immature. Until these input and output systems develop more fully, an infant cannot begin to learn about certain stimuli or to express her learning using motor responses (Gerhardstein & West, 2003). For example, cats are born with their eyes sealed shut, so they obviously can't learn much about visual stimuli that are presented to them in the first few hours of life.

For humans, acquisition of *complex motor skills* comes gradually, as physical development produces gradual improvements in muscle strength and perceptual-motor coordination. Newborn humans cannot even hold their heads up unsupported, but most babies can roll over by the time they are 5.5 months old; by 7 months, most can sit up; by a year, most have learned to stand alone or even walk. As coordination improves, babies develop the fine motor skills needed for accurate eye tracking, babbling, and reaching to pick up objects. Skill acquisition is not limited to motor skills either; between 1 and 2 years of age, children begin to master the rudiments of language, and complex grammar and reading are usually evident by 4 to 5 years.

You read above that infants can show operant conditioning, learning particular sucking responses that produce outcomes such as tape recordings turning on and off. In another operant conditioning procedure, researchers hang a mobile over an infant's crib, then tie one end of a ribbon to the baby's leg and the other end to the mobile. When the baby kicks her leg, the mobile moves:

S (crib with mobile) → O (kick) → C (mobile moves)

Just like a rat in a Skinner box, the baby makes her first response by chance. The resulting movement of the mobile, which babies find highly entertaining, reinforces this kicking response. Babies as young as 2 months of age quickly learn to kick vigorously to produce mobile movement (Rovee-Collier, 1993, 1997, 1999). The babies can maintain memory of this learned response for a few days with no reminders—or for up to 21 weeks if they receive periodic reminders in which they see the mobile move when an out-of-sight experimenter pulls the ribbon (Hayne, 1996).

One of the most interesting features of this operant learning in babies is that it is context-dependent, just like the adult learning you read about in Chapter 6. For example, in one variant of the mobile experiment, learning takes place in a crib with a striped crib liner. If this liner is replaced with one having a different pattern, the babies gape passively at the mobile—but don't kick (Borovsky & Rovee-Collier, 1990). Apparently, the change in crib liners represents a new context in which the old rules might not continue to hold. Infants, just like adults, incorporate details of the context during ongoing learning.

Classical conditioning takes place in infants, too. In Chapter 4, you read about eye-blink conditioning, in which a human or rabbit learns that a tone or light (the conditioned stimulus, or CS) predicts an airpuff (the unconditioned stimulus, or US).

Operant learning in infants
Movement of the mobile reinforces kicks.

Courtesy of Carolyn Rovee-Collier

In the *delay-conditioning* paradigm, the CS and US overlap and co-terminate. With repeated CS-US pairings, the human or rabbit learns to respond to the CS by producing an eyeblink (the conditioned response, or CR) so that the eye is protected when the US arrives.

Infant humans can learn eyeblink CRs in the delay-conditioning paradigm, and so can infant rats, although in both species the infants learn more slowly than adults do (Ivkovich, Collins, Eckerman, Krasnegor, & Stanton, 1999; Ivkovich, Paczkowski, & Stanton, 2000; Little, Lipsett, & Rovee-Collier, 1984). By contrast, in the more difficult *trace-conditioning* paradigm, where there is a gap between the end of the CS and the arrival of the US, 2-month-old infants can't learn the eyeblink CR. By 4 years of age, children can learn the CR, but they learn it much more slowly than in the delay-conditioning paradigm; in contrast, young adult humans learn both paradigms about equally quickly (Herbert, Eckerman, & Stanton, 2003). In summary, the basic components of classical conditioning are available in very young individuals, but the capacity continues to develop as the organism matures, allowing the organism to learn more efficiently and under increasingly difficult conditions.

Development of Episodic and Semantic Memory

As you read back in Chapter 7, *semantic memory* involves factual knowledge, whereas *episodic memory* is memory for specific autobiographical events, including the spatial and temporal context in which that event occurred. Both episodic and semantic memory are most often tested through recall and recognition tests. This makes it challenging to assess episodic and semantic memory in pre-verbal infants, and researchers have devised creative techniques to allow infants to express their knowledge even if they can't yet speak about it.

One such technique for assessing memories in human infants is **elicited imitation,** in which infants are shown an action and tested for their ability to mimic this action later (Bauer, 1996). For example, researchers showed a group of 10-month-old children how to operate a toy puppet. Four months later, they presented the children with the same toy puppet. These children showed more interest and ability in operating the puppet than did a second group of same-age children who had never seen the puppet used (N. Myers, Perris, & Speaker, 1994). This difference suggests that the very young children had a memory of the earlier events even if they couldn't verbalize it (Rovee-Collier, 1999).

Imitation is an important way in which youngsters learn about their world. For example, human infants and children learn many motor and cognitive skills by watching and imitating the actions of adults or older siblings, as discussed in Chapter 11. Juveniles of some primate species learn skills, such as cracking nuts, by watching and imitating what their elders do. Young humpback whales learn the route to breeding grounds by following their mothers on an initial migration, and adult orcas appear to teach their offspring how to beach themselves intentionally in order to prey on seals lying on the beach (Rendell & Whitehead, 2001).

Once children grow a little older and master language, it becomes much easier to investigate episodic and semantic memory. During the first few months of age, children begin to imitate the speech sounds they hear around them, and by about 1 to 2 years of age, babies learn and use individual words, usually acquiring a vocabulary of several hundred words (mostly nouns and verbs). Over the next few years, vocabulary continues to develop and children also begin to acquire a knowledge of *syntax*, or the rules governing how words are arranged into sentences. In addition, children learn about physical objects and events; a toddler's incessant "Why?" questions reflect how she is soaking up semantic information about the world. Much of this information, acquired in early childhood, remains with us for life.

Infant imitation From an early age, young-sters learn many motor and cognitive skills from watching and imitating the actions of adults and older siblings. Here 2- to 3-week-old infants imitate facial gestures demonstrated by an adult experimenter.
Adapted from Meltzoff & Moore, 1977.

Meltzoff & Moore, 1977, Figure 1

By contrast, episodic memory in young children appears to develop more slowly. For example, Anna Drummey and Nora Newcombe provided children with 10 questions to which the children didn't already know the answers (such as, "What animal can't make any sounds?" Answer: "A giraffe."). Five of these new facts were presented by a human experimenter, and five were presented by a puppet. A week later, the children returned to the lab and were quizzed on those 10 questions. Factual recall increased with age: 4-year-olds recalled about 23% of the answers they'd been given, 6-year-olds recalled about 32% of the answers, and 8-year-olds recalled about 50% of the answers (Drummey & Newcombe, 2002). Thus, the capacity to encode and verbally express semantic information appears to increase with age across childhood.

The same experimenters next tested whether the children had episodic memo-ries: when a child correctly remembered a fact, the researchers asked the child where the fact had been learned. The oldest children (8-year-olds) could remem-ber the source correctly on about 40% of trials (Figure 12.2). When the 8-year-olds did make a source error, it was usually an *intra-experimental error*, meaning

Figure 12.2 Episodic memory in children Children were taught 10 new facts, some presented by a human and some by a puppet. A week later, the children were quizzed on these facts, and for each fact they remembered, they were asked who had presented it. Older children remembered the correct source about half the time; their mistakes tended to be "intra-experimental" errors: they remembered learning the fact in the context of the experiment but not who had presented it. In contrast, 4-year-olds tended to make many "extra-experimental" errors: falsely "remembering" that they'd learned the facts somewhere outside the experiment. This suggests that children as young as 4 can acquire new semantic memory, but it is only after about age 6 or 8 that they can reliably remember the episodic context in which that new learning occurred.
Data from Drummey & Newcombe, 2002.

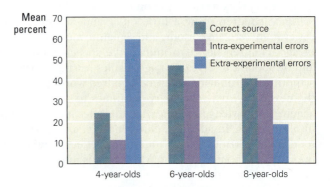

that they correctly recalled having learned the fact during the experiment but simply confused whether they'd heard it from the human or the puppet. Very seldom did the 8-year-olds make *extra-experimental errors*, meaning that they mistakenly recalled having learned the fact somewhere outside the experiment (for example, at school). In other words, if the older children had a semantic memory for the fact, they generally also had at least some memory of the spatial and temporal context in which they'd learned that fact (Drummey & Newcombe, 2002).

Six-year-old children performed very much like 8-year-olds. But the pattern was different in 4-year-old children. First of all, 4-year-olds remembered the correct source much less often than the older children. And when the young children made a source error, they were especially prone to extra-experimental errors, meaning that they tended to misattribute their learning to some context outside the experiment. These results suggest that children as young as 4 can learn semantic information, but it is only by about age 6 or 8 that they can reliably recall not just the fact but also the spatial and temporal context in which that learning was acquired.

It's not clear why the capacity for episodic memory matures more slowly than semantic memory. One factor may be that parts of the brain, such as the hippocampus and prefrontal cortex, which are critical for encoding and recall of episodic memories, are immature in humans at birth and continue to develop during the first few years of life (Durston et al., 2001; Serres, 2001). Another factor may be that very young children do not show evidence of a "cognitive self." One test of whether a child has a sense of self is whether she can recognize herself in the mirror. If a researcher surreptitiously marks a child's face with rouge and the child sees herself in the mirror and touches the marked spot, then we may conclude that the child recognizes the image as her own ("Hey, that's me—and what's that red dot doing on my nose?"). Infants younger than 16 months don't show mirror-recognition behavior, but children older than 24 months do (Lewis & Brooks-Gunn, 1979). This implies that 2-year-olds, but not 1-year-olds, have a sense of themselves as individuals. This cognitive milestone is probably a prerequisite for forming autobiographical memories (Howe & Courage, 1993). You can't remember that a particular event happened to you unless you have a sense of yourself and how you exist in time (Fivush & Nelson, 2004).

On the other hand, some infancy researchers, notably Carolyn Rovee-Collier and colleagues, argue that even very young children can and do form episodic

Copyright © 2006 Angela Georges/Getty Images

A test of self-awareness A red dot is placed on a child's face, and the child is placed in front of the mirror. If the child tries to wipe the dot off her face, researchers conclude the child recognizes her own reflection, providing evidence of self-awareness and a sense of self.

memories—they just may not be able to communicate these verbally the way older children can (Rovee-Collier & Cuevas, 2009). In this sense, the "failure" of young children to display episodic memory is really a failure of the researchers' experimental design. As the elicited imitation experiments discussed earlier show, when infants are challenged to display their memory of recent events by actions, rather than by verbal recall, they can often perform very well.

Sensitive Periods for Early Learning

As you've just read, many kinds of learning are functional early in life but become more efficient as the organism matures. Sometimes, the opposite is true. In some species, certain kinds of learning are most effective early in life, during a specific time window known as a **sensitive period.**

Imprinting

Researcher Konrad Lorenz is being followed by goslings that imprinted on him because he was the first moving object they saw after hatching. Thereafter, they responded to him as if he were their mother.

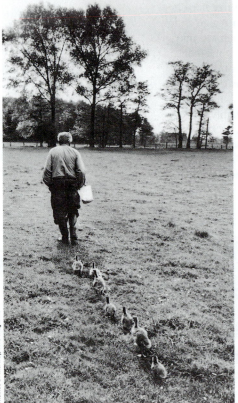

Thomas D. McAvoy/*Time* Magazine

Animals of many species, including birds, are especially likely to form an attachment to the first individual they see after birth. Konrad Lorenz named this phenomenon **imprinting** (Insel & Fernald, 2004; Lorenz, 1935). Normally, the first individual a baby bird sees is its mother or a sibling in the nest, and so the chick appropriately imprints on a member of its own species. But Lorenz found that if he removed a newly hatched goose chick from an incubator, the chick would imprint on him—and would follow him about as if he were its mother. If the gosling were later placed among a brood of goose chicks following a goose mother, it would ignore the members of its own species in preference for following its human "parent." Researchers have shown that chicks can be induced to imprint not only on individuals of the wrong species but even on rotating cylinders and stuffed chickens (Johnson, 1992).

Since Lorenz's time, imprinting has been demonstrated in a variety of other species, including turkeys, sheep, deer, and buffalo (Michel & Tyler, 2005). For example, a sheep that is bottle-fed by humans for the first 10 days of life and is then returned to its flock never develops a natural bond with its mother. As an adult, this animal will care little for other sheep, preferring to be with people—and will itself be a poor mother, allowing its offspring to nurse but not taking any other motherly interest (Scott, 1962). Similarly, Konrad Lorenz's geese not only treated him like a parent but also, on reaching maturity, courted him in preference to seeking mates from their own species!

Imprinting used to be considered an example of learning that had not only a sensitive period but a **critical period**—a limited time window during which learning was possible and irreversible. Now it's known that even imprinting is not as sharply timed or irreversible as was once thought. Clearly, imprinting is fastest and most effective during a particular time window in early life (the sensitive period). But under the right circumstances, the time window for imprinting can be extended, and imprinting can even be reversed (Thomas & Johnson, 2008).

Sensitive Periods for Learning

Many other types of learning show sensitive periods. For example, David Hubel and Torsten Wiesel conducted a classic series of studies in which they sewed shut one eye of newborn cats or monkeys and then after several weeks reopened the eye (Hubel & Wiesel, 1977, 1998). The result? The animals were "blind" in that eye even though they had no physical damage to the visual system. For cats, the period from about 3 weeks to 60 days after birth is a sensitive period for the development of the visual system; for monkeys, the period may last for about the first 6 months of life. Similar effects are seen in human infants born with cataracts that block vision in one eye. If corrective surgery is performed within a few months of birth, vision will develop normally (Maurer & Lewis, 1999), but if surgery is delayed for a few years, normal vision never develops (Vaegan, 1979).

As another example, adult white-crowned sparrows have a repertoire of about seven different sounds that serve various functions, including territory defense and courtship. Six of these sounds are more or less the same in all white-crowned sparrows, but one—the male song—differs by geographical location. In effect, male sparrows from different regions have different "dialects," just as people in different regions may speak the same language but have different accents. Normally, a male white-crowned sparrow spends his first 10 days or so in the nest and then moves out to live independently from, but close to, his parents. During the next few months, he will hear his father and other male neighbors sing, and eventually, he himself will begin to sing, using the same "dialect" as they do.

Male sparrows raised in isolation, with no opportunity to hear other adults, begin to sing too, but their songs are abnormal (Marler, 1970). This suggests that some of the song is innate—perhaps genetically hardwired—but that parts of it are learned through imitation of other adults in the area (Ball & Hulse, 1998). Males raised in isolation but allowed to hear tape recordings of male song can learn normally as long as they hear the song during days 30 through 100 of their life (Marler, 1970). Earlier or later exposure is of no use: once the sensitive period has passed, the males will not learn normal song.

Language Learning

Some researchers have suggested that human language learning also has a sensitive period, which ends by about age 12 (or earlier). Early evidence for this idea came from the famous and tragic case of "Genie," a girl whose psychotic father kept her locked in an isolated room, chained to a potty chair, and who punished her if she made any noise (Curtiss, 1977). The California authorities took Genie away from her parents in 1970, when she was 13 years old. At the time, Genie weighed only 59 pounds and could not straighten her arms or legs nor control her bladder or bowels. She could not speak at all.

Over the next several years, physicians, psychologists, and social workers worked hard to undo the damage that had been done to Genie. Her health improved greatly, and her IQ appeared to be in the low-normal range. But her language never developed beyond that of a 3- to 4-year-old. She could utter simple sentences ("want food"), but not much more. Apparently, Genie's lack of exposure to language during the first decade of life left her unable to acquire the complex grammar and vocabulary that characterizes normal adult speech (Curtiss, 1977; Rymer, 1994). Similarly, her lack of social interactions during development greatly reduced her opportunities to observe and imitate how people use language. As of 2008, Genie, age 51, was living in California as a ward of the state and—according to an anonymous report—had once again reverted to speechlessness.

We don't have to look at cases as extreme as Genie to see evidence of a sensitive period in human language learning. In general, children can learn a second language more easily, and approximate a native accent more closely, than adults can (Newport, 1990). This is partly due to a critical period for the perceptual learning that allows phonetic discrimination.

Human languages have about 25 to 40 speech sounds (called *phonemes*), but not all languages have the same sounds. Adults who speak one language can distinguish between sounds from their own language but often cannot distinguish between pairs of sounds from non-native languages. For example, the phonemes /l/ and /r/ are distinct in English (so that "ray" and "lay" are different words) but not in Japanese; monolingual Japanese adults often cannot distinguish these two phonemes. On the other hand, monolingual English speakers can't hear the difference between a soft "p" and a sharp "p"—two speech sounds that are meaningfully separate in the Thai language. In effect, the phonemes /r/ and /l/ are part of the same sound category for Japanese speakers, while soft "p" and sharp "p" are part of the same sound category for English speakers.

Infants younger than 6 to 8 months can distinguish all these sounds, even when the distinction does not exist in their native language. Infants can express this learning by turning their head for reinforcement to one sound but not the other. Infants get better at distinguishing speech sounds from their own language as they age but become less able to tell non-native sounds apart (Kuhl, 2000). Thus, a 6-month-old "Japanese-speaking" baby will be able to distinguish "lay" and "ray," but an 11-month-old one will not. Similarly, a 6-month-old "English-speaking" infant can distinguish syllables from Hindi that sound alike to adult English speakers (Figure 12.3), but this ability is lost by about 10 to 12 months (Werker & Tees, 1999). Apparently, humans acquiring language—like birds acquiring birdsong—have a window of opportunity to learn to distinguish language sounds; beyond that period, learning is possible, but much less effective. Children who are fortunate enough to live in a bilingual home and be exposed to the sounds of multiple languages during this critical period are much more likely to grow up to be fluent speakers of those languages than children who must try to learn the sounds later. The same principle that early exposure facilitates fluency holds for gestural languages, such as American Sign Language (ASL), as well as for spoken languages. (For more on the possible relationship between learning spoken and gestural languages, see "Learning and Memory in Everyday Life" on page 469).

On the other hand, not everyone agrees with the idea of a sensitive period for language learning. Adults obviously can master second languages, and they often do so more quickly than children, even if their final level of attainment is not as high (Thomas & Johnson, 2008). Apparently, learning a new language is different in children than in adults. In children, the dominant process is social imitation: children learn to mimic the speech around them. By contrast, in adults the dominant process is semantic memory—adopting explicit strategies such as memorization of new vocabulary (Hudson Kam & Newport, 2005), although adults also use perceptual-motor and cognitive skills to produce and understand novel sentences. As a result, given an equivalent amount of time to learn a second language, adults and older children often make much faster progress than younger children (Snow & Hoefnagel-Höhle, 1978).

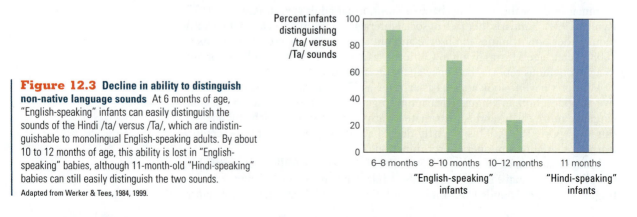

Figure 12.3 Decline in ability to distinguish non-native language sounds At 6 months of age, "English-speaking" infants can easily distinguish the sounds of the Hindi /ta/ versus /Ta/, which are indistinguishable to monolingual English-speaking adults. By about 10 to 12 months of age, this ability is lost in "English-speaking" babies, although 11-month-old "Hindi-speaking" babies can still easily distinguish the two sounds.
Adapted from Werker & Tees, 1984, 1999.

Percent infants distinguishing /ta/ versus /Ta/ sounds

6–8 months 8–10 months 10–12 months "English-speaking" infants

11 months "Hindi-speaking" infants

Teaching Babies Signs before Speech

In the 2004 movie *Meet the Fockers*, the toddler Little Jack uses sign language to inform his grandfather that he'd like a snack and then a nap, after which he'll probably need a diaper change. Just a Hollywood joke about overambitious parenting, right? Well, maybe not. Based on parents' reports, children as young as 6 to 9 months, who haven't yet mastered spoken language, can use gestures to communicate a desire for more food or for a bottle of milk (Acredolo & Goodwyn, 2002). At about 10 to 12 months, children can reach toward an object to indicate that it is wanted or hold an object upward to direct an adult's attention to it (Goodwyn, Acredolo, & Brown, 2000). A few months later, children master representational gestures, such as flapping their arms to represent "bird" or "flight" or spreading and unspreading the index and middle fingers to connote "scissors" or "cutting." Many studies show a positive correlation between gesturing and verbal development: the more gestures children learn between 1 and 2 years of age, the larger their verbal vocabularies at age 2 or 3 (Capone & McGregor, 2004; Goodwyn, Acredolo, & Brown, 2000).

Why might communicating with gestures facilitate the development of verbal language? Susan Goodwyn and colleagues have suggested several possible reasons (Goodwyn, Acredolo, & Brown, 2000). One is simply that infants learn verbal language more quickly if they are exposed to more vocalizations from their parents. A child who points at a bird in a tree can elicit a parental response ("Yes! That's a birdie!"); a child using 20 such gestures may be able to elicit such responses 10 times more often than a child with only two gestures. A second possibility is that babies (like all creatures) learn best about the things they're interested in. Communicating with gestures may allow the child to show the parent what the *child* is interested in, which then cues the parent to introduce language related to that interest. A third possibility is that communicating with gestures provides a "scaffolding" for the development of verbal language. The child learns an "easy" gesture that in turn provides insight into how useful communication can be, which motivates the child to explore other ways to communicate, including spoken language.

In the meantime, gestural language is a way for toddlers to communicate their needs when they do not have the ability to express themselves verbally. Goodwyn and her colleagues report an example in which a 14-month-old boy was able to use his "hot" gesture (blowing hard) to let his mother know when his bathwater was too hot, while another toddler signaled "gentle" (petting the back of one hand) to complain that her parent was holding her legs too tightly during a diaper change (Goodwyn, Acredolo, & Brown, 2000). This isn't quite the sophistication of Hollywood's Little Jack, but it's still impressive for an infant who would otherwise be reduced to frustrated squalling to get her point across.

Adolescence: Crossing from Childhood into Adulthood

Puberty, the process of physical change during which the body transitions to sexual maturity, occurs at different ages in different species. In the United States, girls typically begin the process of puberty around age 10 and have their first menstrual bleeding (menarche) about two years later; first ovulation may occur a year or two after that, at which point girls are capable of sexual reproduction. Boys typically begin puberty around age 12, and full fertility is gained a few years after that. By contrast, elephants reach sexual maturity at about 9 to 12 years of age, and rats reach sexual maturity by the time they're about 14 months old. In some species, puberty does not occur at a predetermined age. For example, a fully grown female prairie vole remains sexually immature until exposed to scent signals from a male outside her kin group; within 24 hours of this exposure, she will become sexually receptive, mate, and form an enduring pair bond with her chosen partner.

Adolescence is defined as the transitional stage between the onset of puberty and entry into adulthood; in humans, this corresponds roughly to the teenage years (ages 13 through 19), although there are wide differences in each individual's physical and social development. Cultural rules also help determine the time frame, and there may be social or religious rites to mark the passage into adulthood. For example, in Western societies, adulthood is associated with the advent of new privileges such as the right to drive, purchase alcohol, and vote;

new responsibilities such as leaving school and seeking full-time employment; and new social roles, such as marriage and parenthood.

Thus, while puberty is a strictly physical process, adolescence is a period of psychological and social change. Adolescence and puberty overlap, but whereas puberty has a defined end point (sexual maturity), the boundaries of adolescence are much less precisely defined.

Maturation of Working Memory

Adolescence is a period of profound psychological changes, including changes in learning and memory abilities. Most prominently, working memory and executive function, which are among the latest learning and memory abilities to mature, continue to develop through adolescence and even early adulthood.

Recall from Chapter 9 that *working memory* is a short-term storage system where information can be held for active processing. In humans, we often measure working memory capacity in terms of *digit span*, the number of digits that a person can hold in memory at the same time. Figure 12.4a shows that young children have a relatively short digit span. On average, they can only remember and repeat three or four digits at a time. But digit span increases through adolescence, so that by age 14 or 15, adolescents can remember approximately seven digits—the same as adults (Engle & Marshall, 1983). Similar results are obtained if the items to be remembered are visual patterns (Gathercole, 1998).

One reason very young children remember fewer numbers and pictures than adults is simply that the children have had less exposure to such things. By adolescence, individuals have accumulated much more experience with numbers, words, and patterns, and this knowledge may give them an advantage at encoding those items into working memory. Consistent with this idea is the finding that, if we use material the children are highly familiar with, their performance improves. In one clever study, adults and children were asked to remember the locations of chess pieces on a chessboard. Ten-year-old chess experts could remember more pieces than non-chess-playing adults, even though the children's digit spans were lower (Chi, 1978). This suggests that the age-related improvement in working memory capacity at least partially reflects exposure to and familiarity with the material to be remembered.

More complex working-memory abilities mature even later. For example, in Chapter 9, you read about the "2-back" task, in which participants are presented with a stream of items; as each new item is presented, participants decide whether it is the same as the one that appeared two items previously. The task can be altered to assess spatial working memory. For example, on each trial, the participant sees an object (such as an "O") at one of several locations on a computer screen; the participant's job is to press a button whenever the location on the current trial is the same as the location two trials back. The 2-back task

Figure 12.4 Working memory in adolescence

(a) Digit span, the number of digits a person can hear and repeat from memory, increases through childhood, reaching normal adult levels (about 7 digits) in late adolescence. (b) Performance on a spatial version of the "2-back" test of working memory improves through adolescence and into young adulthood.

(a) Based on data from Gardner, 1981;
(b) Kwon et al., 2002, Figure 1A.

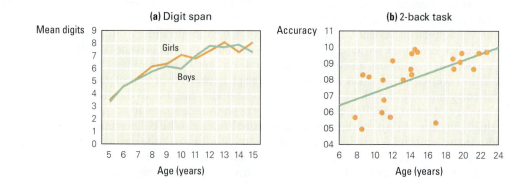

(a) Digit span

(b) 2-back task

requires a great deal of concentration, and even adults don't usually manage to get 100% correct. In one study, the task was administered to children ages 7 to 10 years, adolescents ages 13 to 17 years, and young adults ages 18 to 22 years. Figure 12.4b shows that the improvement of performance with age continued through adolescence and into adulthood (Kwon, Reiss, & Menon, 2002). Other complex working-memory tasks show similar increases throughout adolescence before leveling off, in late adolescence, at adult levels.

Sex Differences in Learning and Memory

Given the dramatic physical changes that occur during adolescence and the fact that most of them are associated with sexual maturation, it's not surprising that many profound sex differences in learning and memory arise during adolescence. For example, young adult women often outperform same-age men on tests of language and verbal memory, such as recalling a list or a story, and on some kinds of spatial learning, such as remembering the locations of objects (Barnfield, 1999). On the other hand, men generally outperform women on other kinds of spatial learning, such as learning the way around a maze (Astur, Ortiz, & Sutherland, 1998). In one study, men and women were asked to study a map of a fictitious town (Galea & Kimura, 1993). On average, men were quicker to learn a route within the town, whereas women were better at remembering the position of landmarks in the town. But these differences don't emerge until puberty. Thus, although adult women outperformed adult men at remembering landmarks in the fictitious town, 8- to 13-year-old girls did no better than same-age boys (Silverman & Eals, 1992).

What could cause such sex differences? One possible cause is cultural influences, such as gender stereotypes in which boys are expected to excel at some kinds of learning while girls are expected to excel at others. But this can't be the whole story. Nonhuman mammals show gender differences too, and these can't easily be attributed to sexual stereotyping. For example, in a radial arm maze, adult male rats are usually better than females at remembering which maze arms never contain any food, and adult female rats are usually better than males at remembering which arms have already been visited on the current day (Bimonte, Hyde, Hoplight, & Denenberg, 2000; Hyde, Sherman, & Denenberg, 2000). And just as in humans, male-female differences in spatial learning appear in sexually mature rats but not in immature ones (Kanit et al., 2000).

Given that male and female rats are unlikely to be subject to cultural stereotypes, some sex differences in learning and memory are more likely to reflect different levels of sex hormones in males and females. Starting in puberty, there is a dramatic increase in the release of sex hormones, primarily **estrogens** in mature females and **androgens,** particularly **testosterone,** in adult males. The increase in sex hormones occurs at about the same time that many sex differences in learning and memory appear, suggesting that the hormones are responsible for many of the behavioral effects. In the Brain Substrates section below, you'll read more about the specific ways these sex hormones influence male and female brains.

The Aging Memory: Adulthood through Old Age

Most of the studies of learning and memory that you've read about in earlier chapters were based on data collected from healthy young adults—whether those adults were humans, rats, chimpanzees, or sea slugs. This is partly because the brain is mature in young adults, so there is less variation among individuals as a result of minor differences in age than there is earlier in life (the difference in performance due to age between a 6-month-old and an 18-month-old human is huge, but the difference due to age between a 20-year-old and a 21-year-old is usually minimal). In fact, most people (barring injury or disease) show relatively stable learning and

Figure 12.5 Human cognition across the lifespan In the Seattle Longitudinal Study, individuals of different ages were tested at 7-year intervals on several types of cognitive ability. Scores have been scaled so that 50 represents the average score expected for that age group; this allows comparisons of data collected from different types of cognitive tests. Most cognitive abilities—including verbal memory—showed little change as subjects aged from 25 to 60 years, but began to decline thereafter.

Adapted from Schaie, 2005, Figure 4. Copyright 2005 Oxford University Press.

memory—and other types of cognitive function—throughout adulthood. For example, the Seattle Longitudinal Study has tested more than 6,000 individuals of different ages (Schaie, 2005). Participants are given tests to evaluate several types of cognitive ability and then re-evaluated at 7-year intervals. As shown in Figure 12.5, the study finds relatively little change in most kinds of cognitive ability—including verbal memory—as participants age from their twenties to their fifties.

Unfortunately, as Figure 12.5 also shows, many cognitive abilities start to decline as humans reach their sixties and beyond. However, while some, such as numeric ability, start to decline in humans as young as the mid-thirties, others, such as verbal ability, tend to remain strong well into old age.

Working Memory

Working memory, one of the last memory systems to fully mature in humans and other animals, is also one of the first to show deficits in the course of healthy aging. For example, as you saw above, healthy young adults have a digit span that averages about 7 digits. However, in elderly adults, the average drops to about 6 to 6.5 digits. This small but significant drop could mean the difference between remembering or forgetting a seven-digit phone number. If the task is made more complicated, such as by presenting different digits simultaneously to each ear, reductions in digit span can be observed as early as age 30 or 40 (Barr, 1980). Why this should be so is not yet entirely clear; but one theory suggests that older adults are more susceptible to proactive interference. As you read back in Chapter 7, proactive interference occurs when previously stored information (such as a prior address or a computer password) interferes with the ability to remember newer information. Possibly, older adults are less able to inhibit irrelevant, older information from entering working memory, where it crowds out the information that is relevant now (Bowles & Salthouse, 2003).

Conditioning and Skill Learning

In general, learning by conditioning declines with age: older adults are less able than younger adults to adapt their behavior in response to reinforcement. For example, classical conditioning of the eyeblink response starts declining at about age 40 or 50 in humans. Older adults take about twice as long to learn an eyeblink response as younger ones do (Solomon, Pomerleau, Bennett, James, & Morse, 1989; Woodruff-Pak & Thompson, 1988). There are similar age-related declines in eyeblink conditioning in rabbits (Solomon & Groccia-Ellison, 1996), rats (Freeman & Nicholson, 2001), and cats (Harrison & Buchwald, 1983). Old age does not prevent such learning, but it makes such learning slower.

Skill learning also declines in old age. In Chapter 8 you read about the *rotary pursuit task*, which requires keeping a stylus positioned over a point on a disk that rotates rapidly. Middle-aged adults can learn this task about as well as young adults, but elderly adults (over age 60) show a precipitous drop-off in performance (Ruch, 1934). Real-world skill learning shows the same age-related decline. For example, one study found that elderly individuals can master the mental and physical skills needed to use computers, but their rate of acquisition is slower than in younger learners, and they make more errors during learning than younger learners do (Czaja, Hammond, Blascovich, & Swede, 1993). In short, you *can* teach an old dog new tricks; it just takes a while longer.

On the other hand, even though the learning of new associations and skills is slowed in healthy aging, highly practiced skills tend to be maintained well. Famous examples are Spanish cellist Pablo Casals, who continued to compose music and conduct orchestras into his nineties, and Jack Nicklaus, who continued to win major golf tournaments in his forties and fifties—besting many younger players. Expert typists in their sixties and seventies can often execute their skill as quickly and accurately as typists in their twenties and thirties (Salthouse, 1984). Many expert chess and bridge players improve, rather than decline, with age, and airline pilots aged 40 to 60 actually have fewer accidents than younger pilots (Birren, 1964), all in support of the axiom that age and experience can often defeat youth and speed.

Episodic and Semantic Memory: Old Memories Fare Better Than New Learning

Existing episodic and semantic memories tend to survive very well, even into extreme old age. Remember from Chapter 7 that semantic memory is normally strengthened by repeated exposure. By the time a person reaches old age, semantic information such as vocabulary and general knowledge about the world have all been encoded, retrieved, and re-encoded many times. Healthy elderly adults generally experience little or no drop-off in the ability to retain and retrieve such semantic memories (Light, 1991). Older individuals also tend to show only a modest drop-off in their ability to recall episodic memories from their distant past (Piolino, Desgranges, Benali, & Eustache, 2002).

But although well-formed memories may survive, elderly adults are generally less effective at forming new episodic and semantic memories. This is reflected in Figure 12.5 by participants' decline in "verbal memory," measured via free-recall tests for a short story and for a list of words. Elderly adults are also much worse than young adults on *paired associate learning*, in which participants first study a list of word pairs and then, given the first word of each pair, are asked to recall the second member of the pair (Canestrari, 1963). The deficit in elderly adults appears to be due to encoding difficulties rather than retrieval difficulties. Thus, for example, elderly adults' performance at paired-associate learning is much improved if items are presented at a slower pace during study, presumably because the elderly adults now have more time to encode the information (Canestrari, 1963). Elderly adults' performance improves too if the studied items have some meaning (Graf, 1990). For example, in one study, college-aged adults outperformed elderly adults on memorizing a list of names of current rock stars, but the elderly adults outperformed the students on memorizing a list of musicians who had been popular with the earlier generation (Hanley-Dunn & McIntosh, 1984).

Aging also affects directed forgetting. As you read back in Chapter 7, directed-forgetting tasks ask participants to study information and then to

Test Your Knowledge

Learning and Memory in Old Age

Learning and memory abilities generally peak in young adulthood and may decline thereafter. Some kinds of learning and memory may begin to decline in middle age, while others may remain relatively robust through healthy old age. See if you can identify the learning and memory processes involved in each of the tasks described below and predict whether or not healthy older people should be able to perform them as well (or nearly as well) as when they were young adults. (Answers appear in the Answers section in the back of the book.)

1. Recalling one's wedding day
2. Remembering the items on this week's shopping list (without writing them down)
3. Remembering how to make coffee
4. Learning the name of a new friend
5. Learning how to program a new DVD player

intentionally forget some of the items. When the participants are given a surprise memory test, they tend to recall fewer of the items they were specifically instructed to forget than items they were supposed to remember or items for which they received no forgetting instructions. Under these conditions, the younger adults can intentionally forget *more* items than elderly adults (Titz & Verhaeghen, 2010). In short, as we age, we seem to have less control over what gets encoded—becoming less able to store the items we do want to keep and simultaneously less able to discard those items we wish to forget.

Emotion may also affect memory differently as we age. In Chapter 10, you read that the emotional content of information can affect how strongly that information gets encoded in memory. Some studies suggest that older adults are more likely than young adults to remember positive information. In one such study, participants viewed a series of 16 positive images, such as smiling children and flowers, and 16 negative images, such as snakes and injured bodies (Charles, Mather, & Carstensen, 2003). Unsurprisingly, on a subsequent free-recall test, young adults recalled significantly more images than elderly adults did. But the nature of the recalled images differed. Whereas the young adults remembered about equal numbers of positive and negative images, the older adults remembered many more positive than negative images. One possible explanation is that younger participants process the negative images more deeply than older participants do—either by conscious choice, or due to age-related changes in the brain structures (such as the amygdala) that mediate emotional processing, or both—and, as you learned in Chapter 7, *depth of processing* at encoding tends to improve memory at recall.

Interim Summary

- An individual's learning and memory abilities vary across the lifespan.
- Some simple learning, such as habituation and recognition, can occur even before birth.
- Most kinds of learning and memory ability are present in at least a rudimentary form from a very early age although they may become more efficient as the individual grows toward adulthood.
- Sensitive periods are windows of time, usually early in life, when particular kinds of learning are easiest or most effective. In humans, there are sensitive

periods for language learning and for social attachment as well as for sensory systems, such as vision.

- During puberty, there is a dramatic increase in release of sex hormones (primarily estrogens in females and androgens, particularly testosterone, in males), which may affect learning and memory and thus contribute to gender differences in learning and memory abilities.

- Learning and memory abilities peak in young adulthood but generally decline in healthy aging. A rule of thumb is that old memories may survive well but new learning may be slowed in aging individuals.

12.2 Brain Substrates

Unsurprisingly, the age-related wax and wane of learning and memory abilities in an individual reflect underlying changes in the brain across the lifespan. In this section, you'll read about those changes. Again, we'll proceed chronologically: starting with the genetic biases laid down before birth, continuing with development in infancy and childhood, looking at the profound changes associated with adolescence and puberty, and finally exploring the changes that occur through adulthood and into old age.

The Genetic Basis of Learning and Memory

Starting at the moment of conception, aspects of an organism's learning and memory abilities are encoded in its genetic structure and begin to guide its future development. The influence of genes on brain function is a relatively new area of study, but researchers are beginning to understand some of the ways genes affect learning and memory.

Genetic Variation and Individual Differences in Learning Abilities

The *BDNF* gene on human chromosome 11 helps regulate production of brain-derived neurotrophic factor (BDNF), a protein that is vital for the health of neurons. Among other functions, BDNF appears to affect learning and memory by enhancing *long-term potentiation*, or LTP (Lu & Gottschalk, 2000; Poo, 2001). Like many genes, the *BDNF* gene comes in several naturally occurring variants, or **alleles.** The most common version of the *BDNF* gene is called the *Val* allele. However, about one-third of people inherit at least one copy of a different version, the *Met* allele, which produces a slightly less effective form of BDNF. People carrying one or two copies of the *Met* allele are slightly worse at learning and memory tasks than people carrying two copies of the *Val* allele. Figure 12.6 shows performance on a test that requires participants to listen to short paragraphs and then repeat them from memory 20 minutes later. People with two copies of the *Val* allele (*Val/Val*) perform better than those with two copies of the *Met* allele (*Met/Met*); people with one copy of each allele (*Val/Met*) are intermediate in performance (Egan et al., 2003).

The *BDNF* gene is only one of many that appear to influence learning and memory behavior. Others include the *5-HT2AR* gene, which encodes the instructions for building a particular kind of receptor for the neurotransmitter serotonin and therefore may help determine the effectiveness of neural transmission (de Quervain et al., 2003); the *WWC1* (or "*KIBRA*") gene, which appears to help

Figure 12.6 Genetic influences on learning and memory in humans BDNF (brain-derived neurotrophic factor) is a protein needed for neuron health and function. People carrying two copies of the *Met* allele (*Met/Met*) of the *BDNF* gene show worse performance on a test of memory recall than people carrying two copies of the *Val* allele (*Val/Val*). People carrying one copy of each allele (*Val/Met*) perform at intermediate levels.
Egan et al., 2003.

BDNF alleles carried

modify synaptic plasticity and may be associated with the rate at which we forget new information (Schneider et al., 2010); and the *SNC1A* gene, which appears to govern how action potentials propagate down the axon, determining whether the message gets passed on to the next neuron (Papassotiropoulos et al., 2009). Like the *BDNF* gene, each of these has several naturally occurring variants, and humans who carry different alleles of these genes have slight but significant differences in their ability to learn and recall new information, such as a list of words.

To date, scientists have identified only a small number of genes that affect memory. There are doubtless many more—and they probably interact with each other in complicated ways. It's also important to remember that genes are only the "recipes" for building and maintaining organisms. The recipe isn't put to any use until the gene is turned on, or *activated*. Similarly, you may have a great recipe for chocolate cake, but it's only when you buy the ingredients, mix the batter, and bake the cake that you actually get to taste the results. We are still far from fully understanding how genes (singly and in combination) affect memory or from understanding the precise mechanisms by which genes are activated to produce these effects, but the advent of new techniques for identifying genes and manipulating their activation promises many new insights in the coming years.

Selective Breeding and Twin Studies

Even without understanding the function of every gene, humans can manipulate genes through selective breeding. Since ancient times, humans have bred animals to obtain particular characteristics: winning racehorses bred together to produce ever-faster offspring, purebred dogs bred together to produce ever-better examples of the breed, and sheep bred together to produce thicker or finer wool. In each case, the idea is that the parent's "desirable" genes may be passed on to its offspring; by mating two animals with desirable characteristics, the breeder maximizes the possibility that the offspring will inherit those characteristics.

An early experiment in the genetics of learning and memory considered whether animals could be bred for learning ability (Tryon, 1940). Psychologist Robert Tryon trained a large group of rats in a complex maze; because of individual differences, some rats (which he called "maze-bright") learned quickly and others ("maze-dull") learned slowly (Figure 12.7a). Tryon then paired off the maze-bright rats and allowed them to breed; he also bred together the maze-dull rats and then trained the resulting offspring in the maze. Again, some offspring from each group learned better than their peers and some learned worse than average (Figure 12.7b).

Tryon repeated the process over and over, breeding together the best of the maze-bright offspring and also breeding together the worst of the maze-dull offspring. By the seventh generation of offspring, there was almost no overlap: those rats from the "maze-bright" line routinely outperformed those rats bred from the "maze-dull" line (Figure 12.7c). Later experiments have shown that many different species, including rats, mice, and fruit flies, can similarly be bred for ability on a variety of learning tasks (Tully, 1996).

Presumably, "maze-bright" and "maze-dull" rats inherited a package of genes from their parents that contributed multiple characteristics that, all together, resulted in good or poor performance in a maze. These genes might be modifying learning indirectly rather than directly. For example, "maze-bright" rats may be less emotional, or more prone to explore, or more active overall—and any of these characteristics could translate into better performance in a maze. In fact, learning ability, like all facets of intelligence, appears to be determined by multiple genes interacting rather than by any single gene.

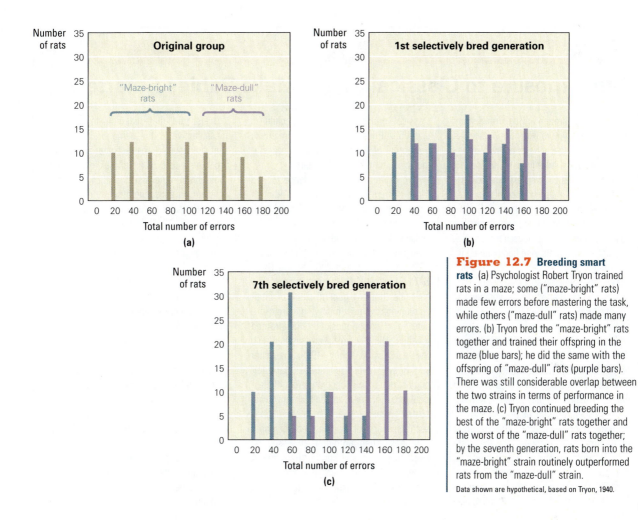

Figure 12.7 Breeding smart rats (a) Psychologist Robert Tryon trained rats in a maze; some ("maze-bright" rats) made few errors before mastering the task, while others ("maze-dull" rats) made many errors. (b) Tryon bred the "maze-bright" rats together and trained their offspring in the maze (blue bars); he did the same with the offspring of "maze-dull" rats (purple bars). There was still considerable overlap between the two strains in terms of performance in the maze. (c) Tryon continued breeding the best of the "maze-bright" rats together and the worst of the "maze-dull" rats together; by the seventh generation, rats born into the "maze-bright" strain routinely outperformed rats from the "maze-dull" strain.

Data shown are hypothetical, based on Tryon, 1940.

And what about inherited learning abilities in humans? Ethical concerns obviously prevent experiments in which pairs of "smart" or "dumb" people are made to breed with each other to see what kinds of offspring result. However, we can get some clues from twin studies. In these studies, researchers compare the mental abilities of identical twins (who have identical genetic makeup) and fraternal twins (who share 50% of their genes on average, just like any other siblings). Identical twins show more similarity than fraternal twins on several kinds of learning and memory measures, including tests of working memory (such as digit span) and memory for verbal and picture information (Finkel, Pedersen, & McGue, 1995; Swan et al., 1999). This suggests that genes play a strong role in determining our learning and memory abilities. Some studies of human twins suggest that more than half of the variation in individuals' memory scores may be accounted for by differences in those individuals' genetic makeup (McClearn et al., 1997; Swan et al., 1999). However, this means that the rest of the variation must be accounted for by nongenetic factors, such as health, stress, living conditions, and social interactions. Genes set up the basic blueprint of an individual's learning and memory abilities, but the final outcome reflects an interaction of heredity and environment. (For more on one way environmental conditions may—or may not—influence cognitive abilities, see "Learning and Memory in Everyday Life" on page 478.)

▶ **LEARNING AND MEMORY IN EVERYDAY LIFE**

Can Exposure to Classical Music Make Babies Smarter?

Walk through any children's store and you're likely to find shelves of music, books, and videos representing an entire industry dedicated to the premise that children exposed to classical music will reap intellectual benefits. It all started in 1993, when physicist Gordon Shaw and developmental psychologist (and concert cellist) Francis Rauscher reported that college students who had listened to 10 minutes of a Mozart sonata before taking an intelligence test scored about 8 or 9 points better than students who had sat quietly during the same interval (Rauscher, Shaw, & Ky, 1993).

The media quickly picked up the story of the "Mozart effect." Entrepreneurs rushed to produce intelligence-enhancing music products for babies, and well-intentioned parents rushed to buy them. Pregnant mothers spent afternoons playing sonatas to their unborn children, the governor of Georgia recommended that the state provide recordings of classical music to the parents of every newborn citizen, and Florida passed a law requiring all state-funded educational programs to play

classical music every day for children under 6. All this effort derived from public perception of the scientific evidence that music could make babies smarter.

But, in fact, scientific evidence for the Mozart effect is mixed at best. Although some studies replicated the original findings (Rideout, Dougherty, & Wernert, 1998; Wilson & Brown, 1997), others did not (Bridgett & Cuevas, 2000; McCutcheon, 2000; McKelvie & Low, 2002; Steele, Bass, & Crook, 1999). Most researchers now conclude that any general claim of intellectual improvement following mere exposure to classical music is unwarranted (Chabris, 1999; Fudin & Lembeissis, 2004; Steele, Bass, & Crook, 1999). Rauscher and Shaw themselves stress that their original paper only found an effect of classical music on very specific tasks involving abstract reasoning and mental imagery, such as imagining how a piece of paper will look when unfolded after several steps of folding and cutting (Rauscher & Shaw, 1998). And there is no evidence that this effect lasts more than 10 to 15 minutes.

It is true that listening to complex music activates the same brain regions that are used in abstract spatial reasoning. The music may "prime" or prepare those brain regions so that they are more efficient on subsequent spatial-reasoning tasks (Rauscher & Shaw, 1998; Rauscher, Shaw, & Ky, 1993). Listening to music can produce changes in mood and arousal that might also affect performance (Chabris, 1999; Steele, 2003; Thompson, Schellenberg, & Husain, 2001). However, such short-term effects would not cause long-term improvements in intelligence or memory ability.

And what about those parents who want a quick way to make their children smarter? Spending large amounts of money on Mozart-for-babies products may not be the answer. At best, such exposure results in a small, temporary increase in a specific kind of spatial ability. On the other hand, listening to Mozart doesn't cause babies any harm, and if early exposure helps foster a lifelong love of music, that may be a worthwhile benefit in and of itself.

Neurons and Synapses in the Developing Brain

As you read above, our genetic inheritance lays down the blueprint for brain function before we're born. From this beginning, the developing brain, in interaction with our surroundings and in response to our experiences, produces the neurons and synapses that then shape our abilities. This process begins before birth and continues throughout childhood and into adolescence.

Early Overproduction of Neurons

Before birth, the brain develops with amazing speed; at certain points in human gestation, up to 250,000 new neurons are added *each minute* (Bornstein & Lamb, 1992). This process of neuronal birth is called **neurogenesis.** By about 25 weeks after conception, the majority of the human fetus's neurons are in place. At this point, the lower-brain centers responsible for such functions as breathing, digestion, and reflexes are almost fully developed.

The process of neurogenesis is not uniform throughout the brain. For example, Purkinje cells in the cerebellum are one class of neuron that form relatively early in gestation (Sidman & Rakic, 1973). This helps explain why classical eyeblink conditioning, which depends on the cerebellum, is already possible in very young infants. But the cerebellum continues to develop after birth too, which may be why older children and adults can condition faster, and under more complicated circumstances, than infants can (Herbert, Eckerman, & Stanton, 2003).

Surprisingly, after a prenatal flurry of neurogenesis, the infant brain undergoes a period of reduction in the number of neurons. Normally, neurons require compounds called *neurotrophic factors* that help them grow and thrive. BDNF, described above, is one example of a neurotrophic factor. Neurons obtain neurotrophic factors from their neighbors. When a neuron is deprived of neurotrophic factors, genes become active that cause the neuron to die. Such natural cell death is called **apoptosis**, to distinguish it from the cell death caused by accident or disease. In a sense, apop-

"*Young man, go to your room and stay there until your cerebral cortex matures.*"

tosis implements the brain's version of Darwinian natural selection: if many neurons are competing for a limited amount of neurotrophic factor, only some can survive. Those neurons that are densely connected to their neighbors, and thus probably play vital roles in brain function, may be more likely to obtain neurotrophic factors and win the competition. Those neurons that have less contact with their neighbors—and thus probably contribute less to overall brain function—may be more likely to die through apoptosis.

During childhood, apoptosis may cull as many as one-third of all the neurons produced prenatally. This may seem like a roundabout way to build a brain: creating billions of neurons and then destroying a large number of them soon after. But the process allows for a great deal of fine-tuning after birth. The brain starts off with plenty of resources, in the form of neurons, and experience determines which of those resources are critical and which are not so necessary.

Pruning of Synapses

In the same way that the brain starts life with an oversupply of neurons, it also begins with a surplus of synapses. The creation of new synapses, called **synaptogenesis,** begins in the human brain as early as 5 months after conception. But after birth, synaptogenesis really gets going, with as many as 40,000 synapses being created *per second* in the infant macaque monkey! Like neurogenesis, synaptogenesis occurs at different rates in different brain areas. For example, in humans, the bulk of synaptogenesis in the visual cortex is completed by about 3 or 4 months of age, but in the prefrontal cortex high rates of synaptogenesis continue until about 6 years of age (Huttenlocher & Dabholkar, 1997).

After this peak in synaptogenesis, the number of synapses begins to decline as the brain begins to prune unnecessary or incorrect connections. Just like neurons, synapses are subjected to a kind of Darwinian natural selection. Those synapses that are frequently used (and therefore presumably important to the neuron's function) are strengthened; those that are seldom used (and therefore presumably less important) may be weakened and may die away altogether. In humans, up to 42% of all synapses in the cortex may be pruned during childhood and adolescence (Bourgeois, 2001). Despite this pruning, there are still plenty of synapses available: the adult human brain, for example, has a staggering

Figure 12.8 Most synapses occur on dendritic spines (a) Left, a reconstruction of a neuron from the cerebral cortex of a monkey; right, a segment of one dendrite studded with spines, small protrusions where the majority of synapses with other neurons are formed.
(b) Spines appear and disappear; over eight sequential days, this dendritic segment showed some spines that survived through the entire experiment (yellow arrowhead), some that lasted a few days then disappeared (red arrowhead), and some that lasted less than a single day (blue arrowhead).

(a) Adapted from Hof & Morrison, 2004;
(b) adapted from Trachtenberg et al., 2002.

(a)

Neuron

(b)

Day 1 Day 2 Day 3 Day 4 Day 5 Day 6 Day 7 Day 8

10^{14} synapses. That's about 1,000 times as many synapses as there are stars in the Milky Way galaxy.

Synaptogenesis continues throughout life, although not at the same furious rate as during infancy. The vast majority of synapses on cortical neurons occur on **spines,** tiny protrusions from dendrites (Figure 12.8a; Ottersen & Helm, 2002). There may be about 100,000 spines per neuron. Throughout life, new spines periodically appear at various locations on the dendrite. If the spines are contacted by another neuron, synapses can be formed and strengthened; otherwise, the unneeded spines disappear to be replaced in due course by new spines elsewhere on the dendrite that may prove more useful (Figure 12.8b; Trachtenberg et al., 2002). Although individual spines come and go, the overall number of spines on a dendrite remains approximately constant; experience and learning determine which individual spines survive.

Sensitive Periods for Neuronal Wiring

Earlier you read about the concept of sensitive periods, time windows during which certain types of learning are particularly efficient or effective. Sensitive periods in learning may reflect sensitive periods in neuronal development, when environmental inputs (such as visual stimulation) can easily alter brain organization by changing local cortical connectivity.

For example, you read above that infant cats and monkeys who have one eye sewn shut during a sensitive period in infancy will be "blind" in that eye when it is opened (Hubel & Wiesel, 1977). Normally, visual stimulation activates sensory neurons in the retina of the eye that project (through several way stations) to neurons in the primary visual cortex (V1). During the first few weeks of life, this visual pathway is very active, and since "neurons that fire together, wire together," connections between neurons in this pathway are strengthened. But if one eye is deprived of sight, there is no activity along the pathway from that eye to V1. The inactive synapses will be weakened or eliminated. At the same time, synapses in the active pathway from the open eye will be strengthened. By the time the deprived eye is reopened, visual activity in that eye will no longer elicit much activity in V1, and this weak activity will not be able to compete for synapses with the strong pathways from the never-closed eye (Majewska & Sur, 2003).

Although sensitive periods restrict our later learning, they are actually beneficial to the developing brain. Early in life, the brain *should* be maximally open to new experiences and be able to change accordingly. But once its basic system is set up, the brain must not change dramatically with each new experience or it would risk overwriting critical older information. Of course the brain remains plastic throughout life, and reorganization can occur (such as the gradual changes in cortical maps that occur with extensive practice of a new motor skill, which you read about in Chapter 8), but the basic organization must remain relatively consistent from day to day. Think of your brain as a canvas on which an artist's early broad strokes define the picture being painted; later, small details can be added or changed, but the overall layout of the picture is fixed.

Brain Changes in Adolescence

As you read above in the Behavioral Processes section, adolescence is a time of profound physical and psychological changes as the child transitions into an adult. The psychological changes, and particularly the changes in learning and memory abilities, reflect changes in the adolescent brain.

Profound Changes in Prefrontal Cortex

Although adolescence causes changes throughout the brain, some of the most profound and obvious changes in the adolescent brain occur in the prefrontal cortex, which appears not to become fully mature until after the teenage years. As you read in Chapter 9, the prefrontal cortex is a seat of many types of cognitive function, including working memory and also judgment and planning. During childhood, the prefrontal cortex undergoes robust synaptogenesis, with the number of synapses peaking around age 11 to 15 years, but during adolescence, large numbers of these synapses are pruned until the number of synapses plateaus at the adult level (Glantz, Gilmore, Hamer, Lieberman, & Jarskog, 2007). At the same time, neurons in the prefrontal cortex begin to show much more complicated branching patterns that probably allow more complex patterns of information flow (Lambe, Krimer, & Goldman-Rakic, 2000).

Another important change during development is that neuronal axons develop *myelin sheaths*, wrappings of a fatty substance called myelin that insulate the electrical signals traveling down the axon, speeding neuronal transmission. The myelin sheaths are produced by *glia*, cells in the brain that provide various support functions to neurons and that are as critical to proper brain function as the neurons themselves. Myelination of neurons in the human cortex doesn't start until after birth, and it continues throughout the first 18 years of life. Some brain areas, such as motor cortex and sensory cortex, are fully myelinated early, but the frontal cortex isn't fully myelinated until late adolescence or early adulthood. Neurons can function before myelination is complete, but transmission will be slow and weak. This could be part of the reason working memory is among the last types of learning and memory to fully mature.

Yet another change in the prefrontal cortex of adolescents is a dramatic increase in the neurotransmitter *dopamine* (Lambe, Krimer, & Goldman-Rakic, 2000). As you read in Chapter 5, dopamine is important for learning about reward and particularly about rewards that will happen in the future. This is probably one reason why, although teenagers tend to be impulsive and risk taking, they mature into adults who show more impulse control and more ability to act based on judgments about the long-term consequences of their behavior.

Effects of Sex Hormones on Brain Organization

In the Behavioral Processes section above, you read about several kinds of learning and memory that are different, on average, in males and females. Since many of the sex differences in learning and memory don't emerge until puberty, a likely explanation is that these kinds of learning and memory are strongly affected by circulating estrogen and testosterone in sexually mature adults.

Not all sex hormone effects occur at puberty, though. In mammals and birds, there is a surge in testosterone near birth. This surge occurs in both sexes, although it is greater in males. Testosterone levels decline during the first year of life in both male and female humans and then remain low until puberty (Overman, Bachevalier, Schuhmann, & Ryan, 1996). But during that critical first year of life, testosterone strongly influences brain development. Curiously, in the brain, "male" hormones such as testosterone are converted to estradiol (a form of the "female" hormone estrogen), and so it may be the high level of estradiol in young males that actually makes their brains develop differently from female brains (Cohen-Bendahan, van de Beck, & Berenbaum, 2005).

And develop differently they do. By adulthood, men's brains are about 100 grams heavier, and contain about 4 billion more neurons, than women's brains (Pakkenberg & Gundersen, 1997). Aside from this difference in overall volume, some brain areas are proportionately larger in one sex than in the other. Figure 12.9 shows some of these areas (Goldstein et al., 2001; Goldstein et al., 2002; Jacobs, Schall, & Schiebel, 1993). One is the lateral frontal cortex, which is important for working memory; this area is usually larger in women than in men, perhaps helping to explain why women often outperform men on working-memory tasks. Other areas that are usually larger in women are the hippocampus and some language areas (such as the area labeled "Supramarginal gyrus" in Figure 12.9). Again, this may help explain why women often outperform men on list learning, which requires both hippocampal-dependent episodic memory and language skill. Conversely, men are often better than women at navigating through space (Astur, Ortiz, & Sutherland, 1998). Such spatial navigation may depend on brain areas that process visual and spatial information, and some of these areas tend to be larger in men than in women, such as the ones labeled "Angular gyrus" and "Visual cortex (V1)" in Figure 12.9. In sum, many of the gender differences in learning and memory may reflect the fact that male and female brains are simply wired differently.

By the time an individual reaches sexual maturity, sex differences in learning and memory reflect both underlying brain organization and the effects of circulating sex hormones. These effects are not always simple to dissect. For example, estrogen reliably stimulates neuronal growth and synaptic plasticity (LTP) in rats (Foy et al., 1999; Woolley, Weiland, McEwen, & Schwartzkroin, 1997). As a result, you'd expect that women should learn better at times in their menstrual cycle when circulating estrogen levels are highest than at other points when estrogen levels are lower. Unfortunately, such a clear pattern has not always been found. For example, although women normally outperform men at learning word pairs, women tested at points in their menstrual cycle when estrogen is high don't outperform women tested when estrogen is low (Phillips & Sherwin, 1992). One reason for this confusing result may be that the fluctuations in women's estrogen levels at different points in the menstrual cycle are very small compared with the difference in estrogen levels between women and men. On the other hand, women taking oral

Figure 12.9 Gender differences in brain volume
Several brain areas (red) are proportionately larger in women than in men, including brain areas important for working memory and language processing, at which women often outperform men. Other brain areas (blue) are proportionately larger in men than in women, including cortical regions important for visual and spatial processing, at which men often outperform women.
Adapted from Goldstein et al., 2002.

Lateral frontal lobe
Supramarginal gyrus
Angular gyrus
Visual cortex (V1)

contraceptives (many of which work by raising levels of estrogen and progesterone) show faster classical conditioning than women not taking oral contraceptives (Figure 12.10; Beck et al., 2008)—and both groups learn faster than males (Holloway, Beck, & Servatius, 2011). Because the women in these studies were not randomly assigned to pill versus placebo groups, the studies can't rule out the possibility that other, pre-existing differences between the groups account for the different levels of performance. Still, the data are consistent with the premise that increasing estrogen (and maybe progesterone) improves learning.

Another way to evaluate the effects of estrogen on learning and memory is to compare learning in transsexuals before and after they have begun hormone therapy. In one study, male-to-female transsexuals using estrogen therapy scored higher on a paired-associate task than a similar group who had not yet started estrogen therapy (Miles, Green, Sanders, & Hines, 1998). Similarly, on a list-learning task, control females recalled the most words, control males recalled the fewest, and male-to-female transsexuals on estrogen scored intermediately—better than control males, though not quite as well as control females (Cohen-Kettenis, van Goozen, Doorn, & Gooren, 1998).

Whereas estrogen may improve verbal learning, there is some evidence that testosterone can improve spatial learning. For example, adult male rats normally outperform females on learning to swim to an escape platform hidden just below the surface in a pool filled with cloudy water. In one study, adult males given additional testosterone performed better than ordinary males (Naghdi, Majlessi, & Bozorgmehr, 2005). But other studies have found that testosterone causes no improvement or even impairs spatial memory (Goudsmit, Van de Poll, & Swaab, 1990). The results are complicated by the fact that testosterone exerts its influence on the brain mainly by affecting estrogen levels: on the one hand, testosterone inhibits estrogen function; on the other hand, when testosterone levels are high, some testosterone may be converted to estrogen, actually increasing estrogen levels in the brain. Perhaps as researchers come to better understand the complicated relationship between estrogen and learning, this will also shed light on the relationship between testosterone and learning.

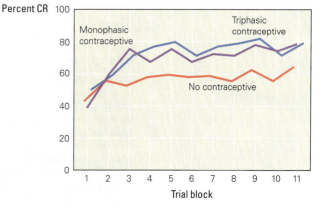

Figure 12.10 **Effects of sex hormones on classical conditioning** Women taking oral contraceptives showed faster acquisition of a conditioned eye-blink response than woman not taking oral contraceptives. This was true both for monophasic contraceptives, which deliver the same dose of estrogen and progesterone every day, and for triphasic contraceptives, which vary the dosages throughout a monthly cycle.

Adapted from Beck et al., 2008, Figure 1.

The Brain from Adulthood to Old Age

Just as the brain grows in volume during development, so does it shrink in old age. This shrinkage begins in adolescence and continues thereafter, so that by age 80, the average human brain has lost about 5% of its weight. Some of this loss may reflect the early stages of degenerative disorders such as Alzheimer's disease. Some may reflect injury; a large-scale MRI study of 3,600 "healthy" individuals aged 65 to 97 years found that more than one-third had brain lesions consistent with small strokes, which had presumably gone unnoticed by the individuals themselves (Bryan et al., 1997). But even in healthy aging, where there is no known disease or injury, some brain shrinkage appears to occur.

Localized Neuron and Synapse Loss

What causes brains to shrink with age? In some areas of the mammalian brain, neurons die off during the course of normal aging. For example, you know that

Test Your Knowledge

Everything Grows Together . . . at Different Rates

All forms of learning and memory available to adults tend to be present in infants, at least in rudimentary form, but some kinds of learning mature faster than others—and this appears to reflect different rates of maturation for the brain substrates on which those types of learning and memory depend. See if you can reorder the types of learning and memory in the table below to produce an accurate, if rough, timetable for reaching maturity. Then reorganize the third column to match them with the corresponding brain area. Bear in mind that this is a rough timetable only, with lots of room for individual differences as well as continued fine-tuning of abilities as the organism reaches adulthood, and that most kinds of learning and memory depend on more than one brain area. (Answers appear in the Answers section in the back of the book.)

Types of Learning and Memory	(Rough) Timetable for Development	Critical Brain Area(s)
Conditioning and skill learning	Present before birth	Frontal lobes
Episodic and semantic memory	Infancy–early childhood	Hippocampus
Sensory processing and habituation	Childhood	Sensory cortex
Social learning and imitation	Late childhood–early adolescence	Mirror neurons in motor cortex
Working memory and executive function	Late adolescence–young adulthood	Cerebellum and basal ganglia

the prefrontal cortex is important for working memory. In a young adult monkey (11 years old) the prefrontal cortex contains numerous, densely packed neurons (Smith, Rapp, McKay, Roberts, & Tuszynski, 2004). In an elderly monkey (25 years old), the same area of prefrontal cortex shows nearly one-third fewer neurons (Figure 12.11a). This age-related loss of neurons in a brain area important for working memory is consistent with the fact that working memory declines sharply with age. Moreover, the degree of impairment shown by an individual aged monkey on working-memory tasks correlates with that individual's degree of neuron loss (Smith, Rapp, McKay, Roberts, & Tuszynski, 2004). Another brain region where neurons are lost with age is the cerebellum (Hall, Miller, & Corsellia, 1975; Woodruff-Pak & Sheffield, 1987). This cell loss is consistent with the finding that classical eyeblink conditioning, which depends on the cerebellum, declines with age (Woodruff-Pak, Logan, & Thompson, 1990).

There may also be age-related decreases in the connectivity between existing neurons. For example, neurons in the cerebral cortex of aged monkeys tend to show fewer dendrites and less complex branching than neurons of young monkeys (Hof & Morrison, 2004). Such reductions in dendritic branching imply a reduction in the ability to receive signals from other neurons (Gallagher & Rapp, 1997). Neurons with fewer dendrites will also take up less space, which could be another reason why some cortical areas shrink with age.

(a) **(b)**

Young adult   Young adult

Aged   Aged

70mm   2 μm

The prefrontal cortex is an area where synapse loss may be particularly marked in aging. Figure 12.8 showed dendritic spines, tiny protrusions on dendrites where the majority of synapses are formed. The number of spines on prefrontal neurons decreases by about 33% overall in aged rhesus monkeys (Figure 12.11b; Dumitriu et al., 2010). But the loss is not universal. There are two kinds of spines: the majority (about 60 to 75%) are small, thin spines that are capable of growing and retracting and are believed to play a role in encoding new information; the minority are large mushroom-shaped spines that tend to stay in place and are believed to be the locus of long-term memories. Although aged monkeys have about 45% fewer thin spines than young monkeys, the number of mushroom spines remains approximately constant (Dumitriu et al., 2010). The age-related reduction in thin spines could be one reason—as you read above—aged individuals often show impairments in their ability to learn new information but little loss of old, well-established memories.

But some brain regions don't appear to lose appreciable numbers of neurons or synapses in old age. One such area is the hippocampus, which doesn't appear to show much age-related neuron loss in humans (West, 1993), monkeys (Peters et al., 1996; Small, Chawla, Buonocore, Rapp, & Barnes, 2004), or rats (Rapp & Gallagher, 1996; Rasmussen, Schliemann, Sorensen, Zimmer, & West, 1996). In fact, many researchers now believe that significant reductions in the number of hippocampal neurons are warning signs of age-related disease, such as early Alzheimer's disease (Gallagher & Rapp, 1997). Similarly, it appears that the aging hippocampus doesn't normally show a decrease in number of synapses (Rosenzweig & Barnes, 2003). Yet, as you read in the Behavioral Processes section, age does cause decline in hippocampal-dependent episodic and semantic memory formation. If not loss of hippocampal neurons, what could cause this decline?

Loss of Synaptic Stability

Carol Barnes and colleagues have suggested that the *total number* of hippocampal neurons and synapses doesn't decline appreciably with aging; what does change is the ability to *maintain changes in synapse strength* (Barnes, Suster,

Figure 12.11 The prefrontal cortex of aging monkeys (a) In young adult monkeys, prefrontal neurons are densely packed. Older monkeys show approximately 32% fewer neurons in the same brain area, and neuron loss in individual monkeys correlates with decline on working-memory tasks.
(b) Prefrontal neurons also show large numbers of spines, the tiny protrusions where synapses can form; in the aged brain, the numbers of spines are greatly reduced.
(a) Adapted from Smith et al., 2004; (b) adapted from Dumitriu et al., 2010, Figure 4.

(a) Young rat session 1

(b) Young rat session 2

(c) Aged rat session 1

(d) Aged rat session 2

Figure 12.12

Hippocampal neurons encoding location in old and young rats (a) While a young rat explored a maze shaped like a figure 8, researchers noted where the rat was when each of several hippocampal neurons (coded as different colors) fired. (b) When the same rat returned to the maze the next day, the pattern of place-dependent neuronal firing is similar. (c) When an aged rat was placed in the maze, hippocampal neurons also fired when the rat was in specific spatial locations. (d) But on the next day, the aged rat's firing pattern changed dramatically. This suggests that spatial learning from the first day does not persist in the aged rat.

Adapted from Barnes et al., 1997.

Shen, & McNaughton, 1997; Rosenzweig & Barnes, 2003). Remember that synapse strength is increased by long-term potentiation (LTP), the process whereby conjoint activity in two neurons strengthens the synaptic connection between them. This is one way that neurons encode new learning. If LTP occurs but then fades away, the new learning will be lost.

To investigate this issue, Barnes and colleagues placed rats in a maze that, viewed from above, had the shape of a squared-off 8. Figure 12.12a shows activity recorded from several neurons in the hippocampus of a young rat during its first session in this maze (Barnes, 1979). In this figure, each neuron is encoded as a different color and each dot represents a location where the neuron fired. One neuron (coded as blue in Figure 12.12a) fired when the rat was near the left end of the center arm. If the rat turned the corner to the right, that neuron would stop firing and another neuron (coded green in Figure 12.12a) would start firing. In this way, just by knowing which neuron was firing at a given moment, the experimenters (and presumably the rat) could deduce the rat's location in the maze.

When this same young rat was returned to the maze later, for a second session, the same hippocampal neurons tended to fire in the same spatial locations as before (Figure 12.12b). For example, the same neuron (coded blue) that had fired when the rat was in the left end of the center arm during session 1 also fired when the rat was in that location during session 2. This consistency of spatial encoding across sessions helps the rat form a reliable mental map of its environment. Obviously, the ability to learn and recognize the environment is a key part of learning and remembering how to navigate around that environment.

Figure 12.12c shows a similar mental map generated by the hippocampal neurons of an older rat on its first session in the 8-shaped maze. It looks a bit different from the session 1 map of the young rat since each individual rat has its own way of encoding space. But when the older rat was returned to the maze for session 2 (Figure 12.12d), the neurons didn't always fire in the same place as before. For example, the neuron (coded blue) that originally fired when the aged rat was in the middle of the maze now fired when the rat was in the top half of the left-hand arm. This differs from the results for the young rat, whose neurons tended to fire in the same places in both sessions. Apparently, both the young rat and the old rat learned about the environment during session 1, but the old rat lost this information much faster than the young rat. One reason this could happen is that LTP in the old rat's hippocampal neurons was unstable and didn't last over the interval between session 1 and session 2. This instability of hippocampal LTP could contribute to age-related deficits in spatial learning as well as in other kinds of learning and memory that depend on the hippocampus, such as episodic memory, which requires remembering the context in which an event occurred.

It's not yet known whether the same instability of hippocampal LTP occurs in aged humans. But there is some evidence that age-related declines in episodic and semantic memory may also be due to reduction in the ability of the hippocampus to encode new information. For example, as you read back in Chapter 7, in the subsequent memory paradigm, researchers record fMRI activity while subjects study new information such as words or pictures; later, subjects are tested with a second set of items and asked whether each is new or familiar.

Typically, young adults show more activity in the medial temporal lobe and frontal lobe while studying items that will later be successfully recalled than while studying items that will later be forgotten (see Figure 7.15). Older adults show the same basic pattern, but the degree of difference in hippocampal and prefrontal activation for subsequently remembered versus subsequently forgotten items is much reduced (Daselaar, Fleck, Dobbins, Madden, & Cabeza, 2006; Dennis & Cabeza, 2011; Dennis et al., 2008).

Together, the results from animals and humans are generally consistent with the idea that age-related declines in new learning result from a general reduction in the ability to encode new information in the hippocampus and prefrontal cortex.

Adult Neurogenesis: New Neurons for Old Brains?

The news isn't all bad. Yes, the aging brain may lose neurons and synapses and LTP may become unstable. But the brain itself may contain some mechanisms to fight this decline, including the ability to grow new neurons. Once it was thought that animals, particularly humans, were born with all the neurons they'd ever have. But we now know that neurogenesis occurs throughout life, although much less prolifically in the adult brain than in the developing brain.

Adult neurogenesis was first reliably observed in birds. Earlier in this chapter, you read how male white-crowned sparrows learn their song during a sensitive period early in life. In contrast, canaries are "lifelong" learners who can alter their song from year to year. Canary song is especially important during the spring, when males sing to defend their territory and to attract mates. This seasonal variation in singing is mirrored in the canaries' brains: one brain area, called the *high vocal center*, or *HVC*, doubles in volume during the spring relative to its size in the fall (Ball & Hulse, 1998).

To investigate this seasonal variation, Fernando Nottebohm and his colleagues injected radioactive *thymidine* into adult canaries. Thymidine is a compound that is taken up by cells undergoing mitotic division, and so it can be used as a marker for newly born cells. The researchers found traces of thymidine in the birds' HVC as well as in the forebrain (Goldman & Nottebohm, 1983), suggesting that new neurons were either being born in these brain areas in the adult bird or migrating there soon after being formed. Nottebohm and his colleagues demonstrated that these newly generated cells developed into functional neurons, making connections with existing neurons and generally appearing anatomically and physiologically indistinguishable from older cells (Burd & Nottebohm, 1985; Paton & Nottebohm, 1984). Similar adult neurogenesis has since also been confirmed in fish, amphibians, and reptiles (Zupanc, 2001).

But what about mammals? In the 1990s, Elizabeth Gould and colleagues injected adult monkeys with a synthetic form of thymidine called *BrdU* (short for "bromodeoxyuridine"). One to three weeks later, the researchers found traces of BrdU in prefrontal, inferior temporal, and parietal cortex, suggesting that these areas contained neurons that had been born in the last few weeks (Gould, Reeves, Graziano, & Gross, 1999). Around the same time, Swedish neuroscientist Peter Eriksson gave BrdU to human cancer patients in an attempt to quantify the progress of their disease by tagging proliferating cancer cells (Eriksson et al., 1998). Unexpectedly, the BrdU labeled not only cancer cells but also neurons in the basal ganglia and in the hippocampus. Neurogenesis has also been observed in the hippocampus of adult rats (Kuhn, Dickinson-Anson, & Gage, 1996) and monkeys (Kornak & Rakic, 1999). Estimates of birthrates vary widely, but one estimate suggested that in the adult macaque monkey, a few thousand new neurons might be born daily in the hippocampus alone (Gould & Gross, 2000).

Neurogenesis in the brain of an adult monkey This radiograph shows a cell labeled with BrdU (arrow) in the dentate gyrus, a subregion of the hippocampus. The cell appears to be in anaphase, the phase of cell division in which the nucleus of the cell has begun to separate but the cell body itself is not yet divided in two.
Adapted from Gould & Gross, 2000.

No one is quite sure what purpose new neurons serve in the adult brain, but one possibility is that they create a constantly renewed pool of "fresh" neurons available to encode new information (Becker, 2005; Kempermann, Wiskott, & Gage, 2004; Wiskott, Rasch, & Kempermann, 2006). If so, then at least some kinds of learning and memory should be improved or impaired by increasing or decreasing the rate of neurogenesis. But so far, there's only indirect evidence for this hypothesis (Aimone, Deng, & Gage, 2010; Shetty, 2010). For example, rats treated with low-dose radiation, which inhibits neurogenesis in the hippocampus, are impaired at new hippocampal-dependent learning (Winocur, Wojtowicz, Sekeres, Snyder, & Wang, 2006). On the other hand, rats undergoing new hippocampal-dependent learning tend to show higher rates of neurogenesis—suggesting that new neurons might be created on demand to encode the new information (Epp, Spritzer, & Galea, 2007). Further, both physical exercise and environmental enrichment increase neurogenesis, which may be why, as you read in Chapter 2, physical exercise and environmental enrichment can improve learning and memory.

Aside from their possible role in normal learning and memory, it would be nice to think that adult-born neurons can be generated to replace old ones that die off in the normal course of aging or even as a result of injury. But it is a long leap from the existing evidence to that conclusion. To date, neurogenesis in the adult primate brain has only been documented unambiguously in a few brain regions, including the hippocampus and the basal ganglia (Eriksson, 2003; Lie, Song, Colamarino, Ming, & Gage, 2004). A few studies have reported evidence of large-scale neurogenesis in the cerebral cortex of adult monkeys (Gould et al., 1999) and human children (Shankle et al., 1998), but other researchers have challenged the methodology of those studies (Korr & Schmitz, 1999; Nowakowski & Hayes, 2000; Rakic, 2002).

Worse, the vast majority of newly born neurons appear to die off within a few weeks after formation (Gould & Gross, 2000). In one study, researchers damaged the basal ganglia in rats and then watched for neurogenesis. The number of newly born neurons that survived longer than two weeks was less than 1% of the number of neurons that had died—meaning there probably weren't enough new cells to make up for the ones that had been damaged (Lie et al., 2004). And even those neurons that do survive may not become functional in the sense of forming viable connections with other neurons.

In sum, so far there's little evidence that adult neurogenesis in mammals is widespread enough—or that the new neurons last long enough—to serve as a general mechanism providing new brainpower. The fact that adult mammals generally can't "regrow" cortical tissue following brain damage suggests that widespread replacement of dead neurons does not normally occur in mammalian brains (Eriksson, 2003). Neurogenesis in adult mammals may be limited to a few cells in a few brain regions (Kempermann et al., 2004). Apparently, in most regions of the human brain, the benefits of new neurons are outweighed by the difficulties of integrating new neurons into old networks without disrupting existing memories.

Interim Summary

- Genes strongly influence learning and memory abilities, although the degree to which they are activated can depend on environment and experience.
- In the developing brain, neurons and synapses are first overproduced, then weeded out in a process similar to Darwinian natural selection: those that make functional connections (and presumably encode important information) survive, while others die off. Growth and pruning occur at

different rates in different brain areas, perhaps helping to explain why some learning and memory abilities mature faster than others.

- Sensitive periods in learning reflect sensitive periods in neuronal development, when specific kinds of environmental input can quickly and easily alter brain organization.

- Gender differences in learning and memory may reflect the effects of sex hormones on the developing brain and also on the activity of the adult brain.

- In the aging brain, some brain areas may lose appreciable numbers of neurons and synapses; changes due to neuronal plasticity (LTP) may also become less stable, meaning that new learning may not survive for long.

- Adult brains can grow new neurons, but many of these new neurons may die off before becoming functional.

12.3 Clinical Perspectives

Finally, let's consider two of the many ways learning and memory can be impaired at different points in the lifespan. Down syndrome strikes individuals at the beginning of their life through a genetic accident that causes a lifelong impairment in learning ability and other aspects of intellectual function. At the other end of the lifespan, Alzheimer's disease afflicts mainly elderly individuals, resulting in a gradual loss of memory and an intellectual decline. As different as these two syndromes may appear, it turns out that there is an intriguing connection between them.

Down Syndrome

Mental retardation is defined as below-normal intellectual function that begins during early development (as opposed to loss of intellectual function that occurs later in life due, for example, to a head injury or stroke). **Down syndrome** is a congenital form of mental retardation that occurs in about 1 of 700 live births (National Down Syndrome Society, 2010). (Although "Down syndrome" is the term currently preferred by medical professionals in the United States and Canada, the older term "Down's syndrome" is still commonly used in the United Kingdom and some other countries.) Down syndrome affects males and females equally and occurs in all ethnic groups—and an apparently analogous syndrome has been observed in our close primate relatives, the chimpanzees (McClure, Belden, Pieper, & Jacobson, 1969).

Children with Down syndrome show retarded development of speech and language. By adulthood, they usually score in the moderately-to-severely retarded range on IQ tests (IQ = 25 to 55), although a few have IQs in the normal range (Pennington, Moon, Edgin, Stedron, & Nadel, 2003). In addition to retarded intellectual development, individuals with Down syndrome have a characteristic facial appearance that includes slanted eyes and a flattened skull and nose. Often, there are also severe medical complications; for example, almost half of all babies born with Down syndrome have congenital heart defects. As recently as 1980, the average life expectancy for individuals with Down syndrome was about 25 years but, largely because of better medical care and treatment, the average lifespan has now almost doubled, to 49 years (Yang, Rasmussen, & Friedman, 2002).

Down syndrome was first described by English physician John Langton Down in the mid-1800s (Down, 1866), but its genetic basis wasn't discovered until a century later (LeJeune, Gautier, & Turpin, 1959). Healthy human beings

Children with Down syndrome have a characteristic facial profile, including a flattened nose and folds of skin over the inner corners of the eyes. Down syndrome affects both genders equally and occurs throughout the world.

carry 23 pairs of chromosomes in almost every cell of the body, with one member of each pair contributed by each parent. Down syndrome nearly always involves a genetic accident in which one parent provides an extra copy of chromosome 21. This means that the embryo inherits three copies of chromosome 21, a condition called **trisomy 21.** In 5 to 10% of cases, the genetic accident occurs in the father, but the bulk of cases originate with the mother, a risk that rises dramatically with maternal age. The likelihood of giving birth to a child with Down syndrome is approximately 1 in 2,000 for a 20-year-old mother but 1 in 1,000 for a 30-year-old and 1 in 10 for a 49-year-old.

Brain Abnormalities and Memory Impairments

Chromosome 21 contains at least 400 genes (Wiseman, Alford, Tybulewicz, & Fisher, 2009). At present, researchers don't know exactly which of those genes cause the mental retardation in Down syndrome; currently, a half-dozen candidate genes have been identified, and any or all of these may contribute (Crnic & Pennington, 2000). We do know that the brains of individuals with Down syndrome appear normal at birth, but by 6 months of age, the brains are visibly smaller than those of other same-age children (Nadel, 2003).

By adolescence, several key brain areas are particularly small in individuals with Down syndrome; these include the hippocampus, frontal cortex, and cerebellum (Wiseman et al., 2009). As a result, we might expect to see particularly severe impairments in memory tasks that depend on these brain areas. To some extent, this seems to be the case. For example, one study considered a group of young adults with Down syndrome (mean age 21 years). On standard intelligence tests, these individuals were found to have an intelligence level slightly above that of 5-year-old children with normal mental abilities (Figure 12.13a; Vicari, Bellucci, & Carlesimo, 2000), but on a hippocampal-dependent task—recalling words from a studied list—the adults with Down syndrome performed significantly worse than the 5-year-olds (Figure 12.13b). By the same token, children with Down syndrome are greatly impaired at recalling recent episodic events, such as what they had for breakfast or what time they went to bed last night (Pennington et al., 2003). In other words, although Down syndrome represents a general mental retardation, the impairments in Down syndrome are particularly profound for memory abilities that depend on the hippocampus (Nadel, 1999, 2003).

Animal Models of Down Syndrome

Since we know that trisomy 21 underlies Down syndrome, researchers have worked to develop animal models with the same genetic abnormality. In mice, for instance, a large region of chromosome 16 appears to serve the same functions as a region on human chromosome 21. Mice born with trisomy 16 (a third copy of their 16th chromosome) generally do not survive birth. (Down syndrome is also a common cause of miscarriage in humans.) So, researchers have bred mice with trisomy of only a segment of chromosome 16 (a condition

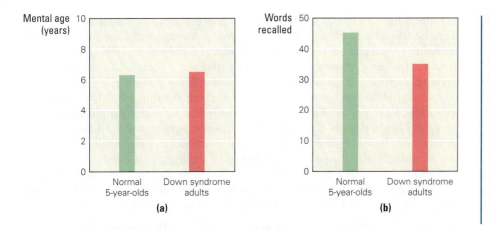

Figure 12.13
Impairments in Down syndrome may be particularly severe for hippocampal-dependent learning (a) A group of young adults (average age 21 years) with Down syndrome had an intelligence level comparable with that of 5-year-olds with normal mental abilities. (b) However, on hippocampal-dependent tests, such as recalling words from a studied list, the young adults with Down syndrome performed much worse than the 5-year-olds.
Data from Vicari et al., 2000.

called *segmental trisomy*). A widely studied example of these mouse strains is called the Ts65Dn mouse (Davisson et al., 1993).

Ts65Dn mice can be contrasted with littermates who share most of the same genes and environment but who do not have the trisomy. Compared with the control littermates, Ts65Dn mice have irregularities in the hippocampus and cortex, just like humans with Down syndrome (Belichenko et al., 2004). The Ts65Dn mice also show memory deficits reminiscent of the memory deficits in humans with Down syndrome. For example, Ts65Dn mice show deficits on hippocampal-dependent tasks, such as remembering the goal location in a maze (Escorihuela et al., 1995).

Ts65Dn mice also have excessive inhibition in the hippocampus and cortex, and this may contribute to their learning and memory deficits. Two genes that have a role in the balance between excitation and inhibition in the brain are the *Olig1* and *Olig2* genes on chromosome 21; three rather than two copies of these genes are present in individuals with Down syndrome and also in Ts65Dn mice, perhaps causing over-inhibition in the hippocampus. When given drugs that reduce neuronal inhibition (by interfering with the inhibitory neurotransmitter GABA), Ts65Dn mice show significant improvement of hippocampal-dependent learning and memory (Fernandez et al., 2007). Moreover, when the number of gene copies is re-normalized (by breeding Ts65Dn females with males that only have one copy of the *Olig1* and *Olig2* genes), hippocampal inhibition is restored to normal levels in the offspring (Chakrabarti et al., 2010). Thus, the mouse models suggest that these two genes may play a key role in the learning and memory deficits in humans with Down syndrome.

Mouse models have also been used to study how behavioral therapy can improve cognitive function in Down syndrome. One intriguing study has shown that being housed in an enriched environment improves spatial memory in Ts65Dn females (though they never do quite as well as control mice). But environmental enrichment actually *exacerbates* the spatial memory impairment in Ts65Dn males (Martínez-Cué et al., 2002). This gender difference is curious, but the overall result is encouraging because it suggests that appropriately enriched postnatal experiences might help remediate the memory deficits associated with Down syndrome in humans.

Alzheimer's Disease

In 1901, German neuropathologist Alois Alzheimer examined a 51-year-old woman named Auguste Deter who could no longer remember her own last name or her husband's name. When Auguste died five years later, Alzheimer examined her brain and found curious abnormalities, including neurons that were bunched up like knotted ropes. Thinking Auguste was a unique case study, Alzheimer published a report on his findings (Alzheimer, 1987 [1907]). The condition became known as **Alzheimer's disease,** a form of *dementia*, or progressive cognitive decline, due to accumulating brain pathology.

Initially, Alzheimer's report raised little interest; at a time when life expectancy was about 50 years, conditions that selectively affected older people appeared to be rare. Now we know that Alzheimer's disease is not rare at all. Recent U.S. government figures estimate that 4.5 million Americans have the disease, including as many as 50% of people over age 85. The disease appears to have similar incidence throughout the world. Famous victims include film star Charlton Heston, civil rights activist Rosa Parks, and Ronald Reagan, who at age 89 no longer remembered having once been president of the United States.

Progressive Memory Loss and Cognitive Deterioration

For many patients, the earliest symptoms of Alzheimer's disease are episodic memory disruptions, such as failures to remember recent conversations or visitors (Collie & Maruff, 2000). As the disease progresses, patients show marked declines in semantic memory, forgetting the names of acquaintances or the layout of familiar locations such as the local supermarket. Patients may ask the same question over and over again, forgetting not only the answer but also the fact that they've asked the question before.

Among the memory processes that survive the longest in Alzheimer's patients are conditioning and skill memory. For example, many patients can execute well-learned skills (Rusted, Ratner, & Sheppard, 1995) and acquire new motor skills such as mirror tracing (Gabrieli, Corkin, Mickel, & Crowden, 1993) and rotary pursuit (Heindel, Salmon, Shults, Walicke, & Butters, 1989) even when they cannot remember verbal information for more than a few minutes. But by the late stages of the disease, memory fails completely, and other cognitive systems begin to fail too. Patients with late-stage Alzheimer's may display personality changes, disorientation, loss of judgment, confusion, loss of speech, and eventually an inability to perform daily activities such as bathing, dressing, and eating. At this point, patients may require round-the-clock supervision and professional care.

Plaques and Tangles in the Brain

Technically, Alzheimer's disease is defined not by its behavioral symptoms, such as memory loss, but rather by the presence of two kinds of pathology in the brain: amyloid plaques and neurofibrillary tangles. **Amyloid plaques** are deposits of *beta-amyloid*, which is an abnormal by-product of a common protein called amyloid precursor protein, or APP (Figure 12.14a). These plaques accumulate in the brain of a patient with Alzheimer's disease, and some researchers believe they are toxic to nearby neurons. In 2000, an experimental vaccine was developed that could clear out amyloid plaques in human brains, but it did not have any significant effect on the cognitive symptoms in Alzheimer's patients, and so it was never approved for use as a treatment (Holmes et al., 2008). More recently, some researchers have suggested that the amyloid plaques are not the true culprit in Alzheimer's disease but rather an innocent by-product or even evidence of the brain's attempt to isolate and protect against damaging types of beta-amyloid (Gandy et al., 2010; Nikolaev, McLaughlin, O'Leary, & Tessier-Lavigne, 2009).

The second hallmark of Alzheimer's disease in the brain is the presence of **neurofibrillary tangles,** the "knotted ropes" Alois Alzheimer described in his original report. Neurofibrillary tangles are the collapsed wreckage of proteins that normally function as scaffolding to hold a neuron in place and that help ferry nutrients around the cell (Figure 12.14b). Some researchers believe that

(a)

(b)

Figure 12.14 **The hallmarks of Alzheimer's disease in the brain** (a) An amyloid plaque (the dark spot in the center of the image), surrounded by a residue of degenerating cells. (b) Neurofibrillary tangles (seen as darkened areas) within neurons.

(a) Cecil Fox/Science Source/Photo Researchers; (b) adapted Hardy & Gwinn-Hardy, 1998, Figure 3.

these tangles, rather than the amyloid plaques, hold the real key to understanding Alzheimer's disease (Johnson & Bailey, 2002).

As plaques and tangles accumulate in the brain, synapse loss and neuron death occur on a large scale. Amyloid plaques tend to be fairly evenly distributed throughout the cerebral cortex, with the hippocampus relatively spared. In contrast, neurofibrillary tangles accumulate first in the hippocampus and nearby areas. The hippocampus and nearby brain areas of patients with early Alzheimer's disease are smaller than normal, as can be seen on structural MRI (de Leon, George, Stylopoulos, Smith, & Miller, 1989). This pattern of hippocampal damage with relative sparing of frontal lobes in early Alzheimer's is the opposite of "healthy" aging, which, as you read earlier, tends to involve shrinkage of the cerebral cortex with relatively little loss of neurons or synapses in the hippocampus (Braak & Braak, 1997; Price & Morris, 1999).

In fact, hippocampal shrinkage may represent an early, presymptomatic stage of Alzheimer's disease. Figure 12.15 shows MRIs of two brains: one of an elderly individual with normal hippocampal volume and one of an individual whose hippocampus shows significant shrinkage. Statistically, the individual shown in Figure 12.15b is at higher risk of developing Alzheimer's disease within the next few years compared with the individual in Figure 12.15a, whose hippocampus appears normal for his age group (Convit et al., 2000; de Leon et al., 1993; Jack et al., 1999). One interpretation is that this hippocampal atrophy represents an early stage of Alzheimer's disease, when brain pathology has not yet advanced to the point where behavioral symptoms begin to appear.

Back in Chapter 6, you read about the role of the hippocampus and associated hippocampal region structures in such tasks as acquired equivalence that require the ability to generalize when familiar information is presented in a new way. Consequently, you might expect that individuals with atrophy of the hippocampus might be selectively impaired at such generalization, experiencing subtle deficits that might appear well before the onset of clinical symptoms of Alzheimer's disease. Some early evidence suggests this is so. Catherine Myers and colleagues gave a test of acquired equivalence to a group of elderly individuals who had each also received MRI to assess hippocampal volume. Those individuals with normal hippocampal volume performed well, but those with mild-to-moderate hippocampal atrophy (equivalent to a volume reduction of about 10 to 15%)

(a) Normal elderly brain

(b) Hippocampel atrophy in elderly brain

Images courtesy of Dr. Mony de Leon NYU School of Medicine

Figure 12.15 **The hippocampus and Alzheimer's disease** Two magnetic resonance images (MRIs) showing horizontal slices through the human brain. In each image, an arrow points to the hippocampus. (a) In this brain, the hippocampal volume appears normal for the person's age group. (b) This brain shows significant atrophy or shrinkage of the hippocampus in both hemispheres. This atrophy indicates risk for cognitive decline and may even represent the earliest stages of Alzheimer's disease, when brain pathology has not yet advanced to the point where behavioral symptoms begin to appear.

Images adapted from de Leon et al., 1993.

were severely impaired at generalization (C. Myers et al., 2002). Further, non-demented elderly individuals who showed poor performance on the acquired equivalence task were more likely to show symptoms of cognitive decline two years later (C. Myers, Kluger, Golomb, Gluck, & Ferris, 2008). Although preliminary, these data suggest that poor performance on acquired equivalence tasks and other tests of hippocampal-dependent generalization might provide very sensitive early-warning signals to help diagnose which elderly individuals are at highest risk of developing Alzheimer's disease within the next few years.

Diagnosing and Treating Alzheimer's Disease

Currently, a diagnosis of Alzheimer's disease is only confirmed if plaques and tangles are seen in the patient's brain at autopsy, when a portion of the brain is removed and examined for these markers. For this reason, living patients with Alzheimer's symptoms are only diagnosed as having "probable Alzheimer's." In making this diagnosis, clinicians may also consider MRI scans of brain structure, PET scans to image beta-amyloid deposits, and tests of cerebrospinal fluid to check for unusually high levels of circulating beta-amyloid and other biomarkers. At present, a diagnosis of Alzheimer's based on a combination of these tests, as well as the individual's symptoms and genetic history, can be made with about 90% accuracy. In the remaining 10% of cases, patients may have some other form of dementia that produces symptoms similar to Alzheimer's.

As of 2011, five medications are approved in the United States to treat patients with Alzheimer's disease. Four of these—donepezil, galantamine, rivastigmine, and tacrine—are *cholinesterase inhibitors*, which work by reducing the breakdown of unused acetylcholine in synapses between neurons. A fifth drug, memantine, was approved in 2003; memantine blocks certain receptors for the excitatory neurotransmitter glutamate, which is produced in overly large amounts in the brains of patients with Alzheimer's. These five drugs aren't effective in all patients, and they only treat symptoms temporarily rather than stopping or reversing the underlying brain damage. Clearly, more effective treatments are needed. As of this writing, more than 500 candidate drugs have been tested, and at least 100 more are currently in various stages of research; however, since 2003, no additional drugs have yet proven both safe enough and effective enough to be approved for use in patients with Alzheimer's.

Genetic Basis of Alzheimer's Disease

To date, several genes have been implicated in Alzheimer's disease. Most progress has been made in understanding the genetic basis of a rare early-onset form of Alzheimer's. Early-onset Alzheimer's represents less than 1% of all cases of the disease, but it is especially heartbreaking because it can strike people as young as 35 to 50 years old. Mutations on three genes are associated with early-onset Alzheimer's: the *APP* gene on chromosome 21, the *presenilin-1* (*PS1*) gene on chromosome 14, and the *presenilin-2* (*PS2*) gene on chromosome 1. A child who inherits just one of these mutated genes from either parent will inevitably develop Alzheimer's (unless she dies of something else first).

Another gene, *APOE* on chromosome 19, has been associated with the more common, late-onset form of Alzheimer's, which appears in individuals age 60 or older. *APOE* comes in several alleles, three of which—called *E2*, *E3*, and *E4*—occur frequently in the general population. The *E3* allele is the most common and is considered the "normal" allele; many people carry two copies of *E3* (one inherited from each parent). People who carry one copy of the *E4* allele are at three times higher risk of developing Alzheimer's, and people carrying two copies of *E4* are at 15 times higher risk (Blennow, de Leon, & Zetterberg, 2006). On the other hand, having one or two copies of the *E2* allele reduces the risk of developing Alzheimer's.

At present, it's unclear why these alleles have such effects. Some studies suggest that *E4* carriers have fewer dendritic spines in the hippocampus than *E3* carriers do, but we don't know whether this is a cause or an effect of developing Alzheimer's disease (Teter & Finch, 2004). Another possibility is that the *APOE* gene may help control how the brain clears out beta-amyloid; some alleles (such as *E2*) may perform this function well, but other alleles (such as *E4*) may be less effective and allow plaques to build up, contributing to the brain pathology in Alzheimer's patients.

Other genes that have been identified as conferring risk for late-onset Alzheimer's disease include the *CLU*, *PICALM*, and *CR1* genes (Jun et al., 2010; Seshadri et al., 2010). And these genes alone don't tell the whole story. For example, some individuals carrying two "good" copies of the *APOE E2* allele still develop late-onset Alzheimer's, and some individuals carrying two "bad" copies of the *APOE E4* allele never do. It seems likely that these genes only predispose a person to develop Alzheimer's, meaning that additional environmental factors (such as exposure to toxins, poor vascular health, or brain inflammation) are needed to actually trigger the disease. The good news is that if environmental factors help trigger the disease, then changing these factors might prevent the disease from developing (see "Learning and Memory in Everyday Life: Can Mental Exercise Protect against Alzheimer's Disease?" below).

▶ **LEARNING AND MEMORY IN EVERYDAY LIFE**

Can Mental Exercise Protect against Alzheimer's Disease?

Many researchers have argued that high levels of cognitive activity ("mental exercise") can help protect against Alzheimer's disease. There is accumulating evidence that older individuals who participate in mentally challenging pastimes—reading, playing chess, or doing crossword puzzles—are less likely to experience cognitive decline than those who engage in more passive pursuits such as watching television (Bennett et al., 2003; Wilson & Bennett, 2003). Individuals with a high educational level or a wide social support network are also at lower risk of Alzheimer's, and when such individuals do develop it, they can often tolerate a greater degree of brain pathology before they begin to show clinical symptoms (Scarmeas & Stern, 2004). In all these cases, the common theme is that mental activity protects against Alzheimer's disease.

One possible interpretation of these findings is the idea of *cognitive reserve*. On average, individuals who have been cognitively active throughout life enter old age at a high level of cognitive function. If Alzheimer's disease strikes, these individuals have further to decline before showing sufficient loss of function to interfere with daily life (Scarmeas & Stern, 2004; Stern, Albert, Tang, & Tsai, 1999). A second, not mutually exclusive possibility is that cognitive activity actually combats Alzheimer's disease. You read in Chapter 2 that *environmental enrichment* can lead to changes in the brains of adult animals, including growth of new neurons and connections. Similar changes in the brains of physically and cognitively active people might help them compensate for the loss of neurons and connections that occur in early Alzheimer's (Nithianantharajah & Hannan, 2009; Wilson & Bennett, 2003).

So far, the studies linking cognitive activity with reduced Alzheimer's risk are *correlational studies*. As you read in Chapter 1, just because two variables are correlated does not permit us to conclude that one causes the other. On the one hand, it is possible that mental exercise indeed helps prevent Alzheimer's and that people who choose to spend their time on mentally challenging pursuits, such as crossword puzzles, are in fact protecting themselves against the risk of developing Alzheimer's. But it is also possible that individuals in the earliest (presymptomatic) stages of Alzheimer's are simply less competent at such mentally challenging pursuits, and so they are unlikely to choose to pass their time this way—just as someone with chronic joint pain might be unlikely to choose to engage in extreme physical sports. Viewed this way, cognitive inactivity would not be a *cause* of Alzheimer's but rather a *symptom*. In 2010, an independent government panel of experts concluded that there simply isn't enough evidence to conclude that mental exercise actually protects against Alzheimer's disease (Daviglus et al., 2010).

One reason for this disappointing finding may be that no *single* lifestyle choice determines whether we will or won't get Alzheimer's disease. Rather, it may be that a number of seemingly minor lifestyle choices—including healthy diet, regular low-level exercise, and mental and social stimulation—all work together to help prevent or at least postpone the onset of cognitive decline in individuals at risk for Alzheimer's.

A Connection between Down Syndrome and Alzheimer's Disease

Did you notice a connection between the genes implicated in Down syndrome and Alzheimer's disease? Chromosome 21, the chromosome that is tripled in Down syndrome, also contains the *APP* gene, which is implicated in one form of Alzheimer's disease. This intriguing fact has led researchers to look for connections between Down syndrome and Alzheimer's. In fact, almost all people with Down syndrome who survive beyond age 40 develop plaques and tangles in their brains—just like Alzheimer's patients (Moncaster et al., 2010). And about 50% of adults with Down syndrome show memory decline and other symptoms similar to the cognitive impairments in Alzheimer's disease (Brugge et al., 1994; Cutler, Hesten, Davies, Haxby, & Schapiro, 1985). Learning and memory in Ts65Dn mice can be improved by drugs that reduce beta-amyloid (Netzer et al., 2010) as well as by the Alzheimer's drug memantine (Rueda et al., 2010), and so there is some hope that these drugs may also improve cognition in humans with Down syndrome.

But the other 50% of adults with Down syndrome do not show age-related cognitive decline—even though they have the same brain pathology! As yet, it's not clear why this should be so. But the explanation might add to our understanding of both Alzheimer's disease and Down syndrome and suggest some possible therapies to help prevent such brain pathology from causing memory decline.

Interim Summary

- Down syndrome is a condition in which babies are born with an extra copy of chromosome 21. Children with Down syndrome have cognitive impairments, including memory impairments, and certain brain areas, including the hippocampus, frontal cortex, and cerebellum, tend to be abnormally small.

- In Alzheimer's disease, plaques and tangles accumulate in the brain. Memory symptoms prominent early in the disease are consistent with the finding that the hippocampus and nearby medial temporal areas suffer pathology early in the disease. Several genes have been identified that may contribute to an individual's risk for the common, late-onset form of the disease.

▶ SYNTHESIS

At the beginning of this chapter, you met Denise, the quintessential "healthy young adult," at the peak of physical health and also of memory ability. Aside from appreciating her own memory abilities, how might Denise apply the lessons of this chapter next time she's home for the holidays?

First, let's think about Denise's young niece Kelly. At 10 months of age, many areas of Kelly's brain are still undergoing intensive neurogenesis, synaptogenesis, and myelination. Yet Kelly is already quite capable of habituation, conditioning, skill learning, and observational learning, and she can express this learning by action and imitation, if not yet by words. On the other hand, her episodic memories may not yet have the same richness of information about spatial and temporal context as adult memories. In addition, Kelly's frontal lobes are also not yet fully operational, which means she may have trouble juggling several pieces of information in memory at the same time. This works to the family's advantage when Kelly cries in frustration: it's still fairly easy to distract her attention from whatever upsets her by waving a shiny, brightly colored toy.

Denise may also be able to apply learning and memory principles to her interactions with her grandparents. Although her grandmother seems to be handling old age well, Denise can expect there will be some deficiencies in the older woman's working memory and in her ability to form new episodic memories, and she can be understanding and supportive when her grandmother misplaces something or tells a favorite story for the tenth time. But Denise should take advantage of her grandmother's fund of semantic and episodic knowledge while it's still available, perhaps encouraging the older woman to create a family cookbook or written history to preserve these memories for future generations.

Denise's grandfather is a more difficult case. Instead of chalking his memory deficits up to old age, Denise should encourage the family to take him for a thorough neuropsychological exam to determine whether his memory lapses reflect early Alzheimer's disease or whether they stem from some other type of dementia that might be treatable. If the diagnosis is "probable Alzheimer's," then the sad fact is that Denise's family is in for a long struggle as they watch her grandfather slowly decline and become more dependent on a caregiver's assistance. Although there is currently no way to reverse or prevent the cognitive decline in Alzheimer's disease, the younger members of the family can hope that by the time they become grandparents themselves, better treatments will be available, increasing their chances of facing old age with their brains and memories intact.

Key Terms

adolescence, *p. 469*	apoptosis, *p. 479*	gestational age, *p. 460*	sensitive period, *p. 466*
allele, *p. 475*	critical period, *p. 466*	imprinting, *p. 466*	spine, *p. 480*
Alzheimer's disease, *p. 492*	Down syndrome, *p. 489*	neurofibrillary tangles, *p. 492*	synaptogenesis, *p. 479*
amyloid plaques, *p. 492*	elicited imitation, *p. 463*	neurogenesis, *p. 478*	testosterone, *p. 471*
androgens, *p. 471*	estrogens, *p. 471*	puberty, *p. 469*	trisomy 21, *p. 490*

Concept Check

1. Kelly is 10 months old and can already say a few words, such as "mama" and "juice." Kelly's older brother, Kyle, didn't speak until he was nearly 20 months old. What factors might have contributed to such a difference in healthy children?

2. A healthy 80-year-old businessman wants to continue working at his job although he admits his memory isn't quite what it used to be. What are some habits he could develop that might help him minimize memory lapses?

3. If one eye is blocked during an organism's sensitive period for vision, there may be no vision in that eye once the blindfold is removed. This sensitive period runs from 3 weeks to 3 months in cats, which are born blind, and from birth to a year or so in humans. Why might the sensitive period for visual development be different in different mammals?

4. Among tree lizards, some males are dominant and defend territories; others are nomadic foragers. Males given testosterone injections during the first 30 days of life are more likely to grow up to be dominant territory holders, while similar injections have no effect on adult nondominant males. Why might this be?

5. "Antagonistic pleiotropy" is a formal name for the idea that processes that are beneficial early in life (while an organism is still capable of reproducing) may have adverse consequences later in life. As long as the organism carrying a gene survives long enough to produce offspring, that gene can propagate through the population. How might this principle apply to the genes associated with Alzheimer's? Can you think of other examples from this chapter where processes that are beneficial early in life would be maladaptive if they continued into later life?

ANSWERS TO TEST YOUR KNOWLEDGE SECTIONS

CHAPTER 1

Ebbinghaus and Galton's Contributions to Scientific Methodology

1. Experimental group; control group
2. Confounds
3. Subject bias/experimenter bias; double-blind

Who's Who in the History of Learning and Memory?

1. Aristotle; Descartes
2. Locke
3. James
4. Erasmus Darwin; Charles (Darwin)
5. Francis Galton
6. Ebbinghaus; Pavlov; Thorndike

CHAPTER 2

Equipotentiality versus Phrenology

Gall proposed that particular mental abilities were associated with specific cortical regions. Lashley proposed that mental abilities were not associated with specific cortical regions but instead could be performed by any sufficiently large region of cortex. Gall used correlations between skull features and individual variations in humans to support his ideas. Lashley used differences in the capacity of rats to learn mazes after undergoing cortical lesion to support his theory.

Synaptic Transmission

All of the statements correctly describe a process of synaptic transmission.

Synaptic Plasticity

1. True. This is what happened in the original LTP studies: the researchers stimulated one neuron and observed LTP in the postsynaptic neuron, indicating that the synapse had been strengthened.
2. False. The best ways to observe synaptic plasticity are to look for physical changes in synapses or for changes in firing patterns as a result of the learning experience.
3. False. A neuron changes its firing pattern when its inputs change, whether or not any synaptic change takes place.
4. True.
5. False. fMRI does not measure neural activity and cannot detect synapses; it measures changes in blood flow, which is an indirect measure of neural activity.
6. False. LTP has only occasionally been observed in animals that are learning. It is commonly measured independent of any observable behavior.

CHAPTER 3

Maximizing Habituation

1. The weaker the stimulus, the faster the habituation. So, one option is to try to make the stimulus—in this case the itch—smaller, perhaps by using lotion or by wearing an undershirt.
2. Sensitization is associated with increased arousal. If you decrease your arousal—say, by going to sleep—you will decrease the likelihood of sensitization. Sleeping, or just meditating, will also make the stimulus weaker, further increasing the rate of habituation. Avoid stimulants such as caffeine.
3. Assuming that you've slathered on the lotion so that the itching is not too intense, wear the shirt all the time. The more you wear it, the more your responses will become habituated to its itchiness. You might also try fabric softener.

Perceptual Learning versus Habituation

1. This dog show judge has learned to perceptually discriminate a dog's quality based in part on its teeth or other features of its mouth. The dog's response has become habituated to strangers sticking their hands and face near its mouth.
2. This man has probably learned to perceive differences among wines based on odors—an example of perceptual learning. He has also presumably gotten used to wearing coats and ties.
3. Repeated experiences have caused the homeless man to be accustomed to being ignored by the general public and has cause the pedestrians to be accustomed to seeing destitute people on the street.

Synaptic Mechanisms of Learning in *Aplysia*

1. The reduction in synaptic connections indicates habituation; less glutamate is being released in the stimulus-response pathway.
2. The increase in glutamate release indicates sensitization; stimulus-response pathways are more likely to become active.
3. The increased number of connections suggests sensitization; the increase in connections should increase the amount of glutamate released in stimulus-response pathways.
4. The number of action potentials generated usually reflects the amount of glutamate released; if this number is reduced, glutamate release is probably reduced, suggesting habituation.

CHAPTER 4

Classical Conditioning in Everyday Life

US = bedbugs, UR = itch due to bedbugs,
CS = commercial for hotel, CR = anticipatory itch.

More Classical Conditioning in Everyday Life

1. US, model; UR, sexual arousal (in men, who are the targeted customers); CS, the car; CR, arousal of pleasurable feelings at the thought and sight of the sports car.
2. US, hot pizza for dinner; UR, anticipation of dinner and salivation; CS, smell of cardboard burning; CR, hunger pangs and salivation.

Computing the Prediction Error

Prediction error = actual US (90) − expected US (30) = 60.

The Learning Rate

1. More
2. We know that the new value w_{Light} is 60, which should equal the old value, 20, plus $\beta(100 − 20)$, so $60 = 20 + \beta(100 − 20)$, or $60 = 20 + \beta 80$. Subtract 20 from both and we get $40 = \beta 80$, for which we can deduce that the only value of β that works would be .5.

The Rescorla-Wagner Model

1. 0
2. decrease

Contrasting the Rescorla-Wagner and Mackintosh Models

1. US, CS
2. (a) Mackintosh; (b) Rescorla-Wagner

Cerebellar Anatomy

1. US; 2. CS; 3. CS; 4. US; 5. CR. Note that the UR pathway does not involve the cerebellum and therefore is not a correct answer for any of these.

Cellular Bases of Invertebrate Conditioning

1. Motor; glutamate; habituation
2. Increase; activity-dependent enhancement
3. CREB-1, CREB-2

CHAPTER 5

Is It Classical or Operant?

1. Whistling is the stimulus, birds arriving is the learned response, eating crumbs is the outcome. The birds don't get the crumbs (O) unless they arrive (R), so this is operant conditioning.
2. Lightning is the stimulus, the learned response is hiding, and the outcome is thunder. Thunder always follows lightning, whether or not the hiding occurs. Therefore, this is classical conditioning (CS = lightning, US = thunder, CR = hiding).
3. Presence of clouds is the stimulus, carrying the umbrella is the learned response, and staying dry is the outcome.

The outcome (O) doesn't occur unless Miguel carries the umbrella (R), so this is operant conditioning.
4. The noise of flushing is the stimulus, the learned response is flinching, and the outcome is scalding water. The scalding water occurs whether or not Carlos flinches. Therefore, this is classical conditioning (CS = noise, US = hot water, CR = flinching).

Reinforcement vs. Punishment

1. (a) Lucy; (b) S is seeing candy (or going shopping with mother); (c) R is tantrum; (d) C is obtaining candy; (e) candy is added—so this is "positive"; (f) response increases—so this is a reinforcement paradigm. *Conclusion:* Lucy learns to throw tantrums to obtain candy. This is positive reinforcement.
2. (a) Susan; (b) S is her child's tantrum; (c) R is giving candy; (d) C is the tantrum stops (or is avoided altogether); (e) the tantrum is taken away—so this is "negative"; (f) response increases—so this is a reinforcement paradigm. *Conclusion:* Susan learns to give her child candy to stop (or avoid) tantrums. This is negative reinforcement.
3. (a) Snoopy; (b) S is being in the yard; (c) R is crossing the boundary; (d) C is the noise; (e) the noise is added—so this is "positive"; (f) response decreases—so this is a punishment paradigm. *Conclusion:* Snoopy learns to stay inside the yard. This is positive punishment.
4. (a) Miguel; (b) S is a rough tackle; (c) R is starting a fistfight; (d) C is playing privileges taken away; (e) playing privileges are taken away—so this is "negative"; (f) response decreases—so this is a punishment paradigm. *Conclusion:* Miguel learns not to fight. This is negative punishment.

CHAPTER 6

Discrete or Distributed Representation Models?

1. A discrete-component model is sufficient because all the tones are predictive of shock and there is no need to discriminate among them.
2. A distributed representation because the model needs to have a way to capture the degree to which green is more or less similar to blue and red.

Configural Representation of Cues

There are six different elemental cues in this example: small, large, black, white, circle, and square. Six cues can be combined into 15 different pairs. However, three of these pairs are not possible because the features are from the same dimension, and something cannot be both big and small (or black and white, or circle and square). So this leaves a total of 12 possible configural cues (note that order within a configural cue is not relevant): small-black, small-white, small-circle, small-square, large-black, large-white, large-circle, large-square, black-circle, black-square, white-circle, white-square.

Discriminating between Generalization Paradigms

1. b (negative patterning). candy → good, flowers → good, candy + flowers → bad.
2. c (sensory preconditioning). Phase 1: deep voice + beard. Phase 2: beards → strong. Phase 3: infer deep voice → strong.
3. a (discrimination training). music1 → Brahms, music2 → Shubert.
4. d (acquired equivalence). Mark → food1, Kaori → food1; Mark → music1; infer Kaori → music1.

Cortical Plasticity and Generalization

1. Increases
2. Fewer

Schizophrenia, the Hippocampus, and Generalization

Faster, because this is an example of latent inhibition, and while healthy people would be slow to learn the tone-shock association after this pretraining, those with schizophrenia fail to tune out a cue, like the tone, that has been shown to be irrelevant.

CHAPTER 7
Episodic versus Semantic Memory

1. It depends. Knowing that coffee is better at Starbucks than at the student center is an example of general knowledge about the world, so it counts as semantic memory. (Knowing how to get to Starbucks from the present location counts as semantic memory too.) But why does the college senior think that the coffee is better at Starbucks? If he can remember a specific episode in which he went to the student center and had terrible coffee and if this is why he believes Starbucks is superior, then that is an episodic memory.
2. The student remembers the meaning of *carpe diem* using semantic memory, and he has no episodic memory of acquiring this information.
3. Here, the student does have an episodic memory, tagged in space and time, of studying the phrase *ne tentes, autperfice*, but no semantic memory for what the phrase means in English (roughly, "either succeed, or don't bother trying").

Don't Forget Your Amnesias

1. *What is lost or disrupted:* the ability to form new episodic and semantic memories. *Common causes:* damage to the medial temporal lobes (or the diencephalon or basal forebrain).
2. *What is lost or disrupted:* all personal (episodic and semantic) memories. *Common causes:* strong psychological trauma but no obvious physiological injury.
3. *What is lost or disrupted:* the ability to retrieve existing episodic (and possibly semantic) memories. *Common causes:* broad damage to the medial temporal lobes and beyond.

4. *What is lost or disrupted:* the context describing where or when an episodic memory was acquired. *Common causes:* possibly, damage to the frontal cortex; can also occur intermittently in healthy people.
5. *What is lost or disrupted:* anterograde (and possibly retrograde) memory, usually for a day or less. *Common causes:* head injury, hypoglycemic episode, or brief interruption of blood flow to the brain.

CHAPTER 8
Open and Closed Skills

1. Mostly open: balancing a ball on one's nose requires continuous feedback.
2. Mostly closed: swimming movements are predefined, and inputs are stable.
3. Mostly open if skilled: kissing requires continuous feedback.
4. Mostly open: fishing requires accurate prediction of changing inputs.
5. Depends on the fish and the insect. Mostly closed if the insect falls into the water; mostly open if the insect lives underwater.
6. Depends on the type of music. Mostly closed if classical; mostly open if jazz.
7. Mostly closed: dart-throwing movements are predefined, and inputs are stable.

Tasks That Test Skill Memory

- The rotary pursuit task is a standard perceptual-motor skill learning task that measures how quickly individuals learn to coordinate their movements with a spinning disk. It has also been used to measure similarities in how twins perform before and after learning.
- The Tower of Hanoi is a classic task for studying cognitive skill learning. It involves moving disks from one peg to another until all are stacked on a new peg.
- The serial reaction time task is a perceptual-motor learning task that requires participants to press a key in response to a light as quickly as possible. It is used to test for unconscious (implicit) skill learning.

Which Cortical Regions Change during Skill Learning?

Behavioral studies (described in the Behavioral Processes section of this chapter) show that chess experts visually scan the chessboard in ways that differ from those of amateur chess players. Experiments with monkeys show that learning to distinguish tactile stimulation leads to changes in somatosensory cortex, the cortical region involved in processing tactile inputs. In combination, these findings suggest that one cortical region where you might see differences between novices and grand masters is in the visual cortex because it is a major source of the information that chess players use to select moves.

CHAPTER 9
Functional Neuroanatomy of the Prefrontal Cortex

1. Monitoring and manipulating information requires the DLPFC.
2. Verbal rehearsal requires the left VLPFC.
3. Semantic encoding is done by the anterior left VLPFC.
4. Phonological encoding is a specialty of the posterior left VLPFC.
5. Visuospatial rehearsal requires the right VLPFC.

CHAPTER 10
Theories of Emotion

1. James-Lange: Janet sees and hears the band; her body experiences arousal, including increased heart rate and pupil dilation; as a result of this arousal, she feels joy and excitement.
2. Cannon-Bard: Janet sees and hears the band. In response to these stimuli, she feels joy and excitement, and at the same time, her body experiences arousal.
3. Two-factor theory: Janet sees and hears the band, which causes arousal; in the context of a music concert, Janet interprets this arousal as signaling joy and excitement.

Brain Substrates of Emotion

1. The elevator ride may be a CS that activates Jared's amygdala; outputs from the central nucleus travel to the ANS and turn on the fight-or-flight response.
2. Jared's current fear response acts as a contextual stimulus and helps the hippocampus and/or cortex trigger memories of earlier events that caused a fear response. If the diving incident was traumatic enough, Jared may even have a flashbulb memory for the event.
3. Rationally, Jared knows he won't fall off the Washington Monument. His prefrontal cortex, the site of higher decision making, helps to overrule the impulse to flee.
4. Appreciation of the beautiful view is itself an emotional response. If Jared is lucky, his amygdala will help process this emotional response and send signals to the prefrontal cortex and elsewhere. Maybe the next time he's at the top of a tall building, Jared will remember his pleasure at the view from the top of the Washington Monument, and this will help counteract some of his fear.

CHAPTER 11
What Is Imitation?

1. Perhaps the baby is imitating you. However, another possibility is that smiling faces are a reinforcing stimulus for the baby. Reinforced babies are more likely to smile, and thus the baby may be responding to you in the same way that she would if you had handed her a cookie (another reinforcing stimulus). No copying is required.
2. This could just be a case of contagion. If a few pigeons in a group start to fly, there is a good chance that you will see other pigeons start to fly, not because they are copying each other but as a reflexive response—the same as when schooling fish move in synchrony. To assess this possibility, you need to know more about what causes babies to stick out their tongues.
3. This could be a case of observational conditioning. Perhaps Leti has seen her father eating asparagus several times. Seeing her father express disgust might induce similar negative emotions in Leti. The asparagus could become a conditioned stimulus that leads to a conditioned response of disgust. Alternatively, maybe this is the first time Leti has tried asparagus and she simply does not like it.
4. Darwin thought so. However, the cat might have been trained to perform these actions through shaping. (Remember the waterskiing squirrels in Chapter 5, on instrumental conditioning?) Alternatively, this could be a case of stimulus enhancement. Humans approaching the door always focus their actions on the doorknob, which might direct the cat's attention to the doorknob as well. Cats often hit the objects of their attention with their paws. A few instances of accidental door opening would likely increase the cat's tendency to swat at the doorknob.
5. Yes. Leti's friend is replicating Leti's actions in a way that cannot be explained as anything other than imitation (unless they are both reading from scripts).

Who Has Mirror Neurons and What Do They Do?

1. There is no direct evidence in monkeys or humans that mirror neurons are necessary for imitative abilities, so whether they are important or not is not yet known.
2. There are currently no measures of recordings from mirror neurons in humans that could be directly compared with those from monkeys, and so this is currently unknown.
3. This is not known because it is extremely difficult to verify that any animal does not have mirror neurons.
4. Primates are the only species in which mirror neurons related to visual observations of actions have been observed, but this does not provide evidence that other animals do not also have mirror neurons.

Imitative Deficits in Individuals with ASD

1. This is a symptom seen in some individuals with ASD but has nothing to do with imitation or social learning.
2. Compulsive repetition of actions is a symptom but is not related to imitation.
3. Fitness videos often require viewers to imitate arbitrary actions, so this difficulty could reflect an imitative deficit.
4. This is an example of echolalia, which is an imitative deficit often seen in individuals with ASD.

CHAPTER 12

Learning and Memory in Old Age

1. This involves recalling an old episodic memory; recall of old, well-formed episodic memories tends *not* to decline much in healthy old age.

2. This involves working memory, which *does* tend to decline with old age.

3. This involves performance of a well-learned skill, which tends *not* to decline with healthy aging.

4. This involves acquiring new semantic information, an ability that *does* tend to decline with old age.

5. This involves learning a new skill, an ability that *does* tend to decline with old age.

Everything Grows Together...at Different Rates

Types of Learning and Memory	Timetable for Development	Critical Brain Area(s)
Sensory processing and habituation	Present before birth (in at least some forms)	Sensory cortex
Conditioning and skill learning	Infancy to early childhood (in at least some forms)	Cerebellum and basal banglia
Social learning and imitation	Childhood (some forms can have critical periods).	Mirror neurons in the motor cortex
Episodic and semantic memory	Late childhood–early adolescence	Hippocampus
Working memory and executive function	Late adolescence–young adulthood	Frontal lobes

acetylcholine (ACh) A neuromodulator that strongly influences hippocampal function.

acoustic startle reflex A defensive response (such as jumping or freezing) to a startling stimulus (such as a loud noise).

acquired equivalence A learning and generalization paradigm in which prior training in stimulus equivalence increases the amount of generalization between two stimuli even if those stimuli are superficially dissimilar.

activity-dependent enhancement Paired training of CS and US that produces an increase in the glutamate vesicles released from sensory to motor neurons.

adolescence The transitional stage between puberty and adulthood, corresponding roughly to the teenage years in humans (ages 13 to 19).

agnosia A relatively selective disruption of the ability to process a particular kind of information, such as difficulty recognizing objects (a form of visual agnosia) or understanding the meaning of spoken words (a form of auditory agnosia).

allele Naturally occurring variant of a gene.

Alzheimer's disease A form of progressive cognitive decline due to accumulating brain pathology (specifically, *amyloid plaques* and *neurofibrillary tangles*).

amnesia Memory loss.

amygdala A collection of brain nuclei lying at the anterior tip of each *hippocampus*, critical for learning and expressing emotional responses as well as mediating the emotional modulation of memory formation.

amyloid plaques Deposits of beta-amyloid protein that accumulate in the brains of patients with *Alzheimer's disease*.

androgens The principal sex hormones present in adult males.

anterograde amnesia A severe loss of the ability to form new episodic and semantic memories.

Aplysia A marine invertebrate (also called sea slug or sea hare) much studied by neuroscientists because of its simple and unvarying nervous system.

apoptosis Natural cell death, as opposed to cell death caused by accident or disease.

appetitive conditioning Conditioning in which the US is a positive event (such as food delivery).

apraxia A condition involving damage to the cerebral hemispheres and consequent difficulties in coordinating purposeful, skilled movements.

arousal A collection of bodily responses (including increased blood flow to muscles, increased respiration, and depressed digestion and immune function) that prepare the body to face a threat; also known as the *fight-or-flight response*.

Asperger's syndrome A developmental disorder in which individuals have normal intellectual abilities but a reduced capacity for social skills.

association cortex Areas of cerebral cortex involved in associating information within and across sensory modalities.

associationism The principle that memory depends on the formation of linkages ("associations") between pairs of events, sensations, and ideas, such that recalling or experiencing one member of the pair elicits a memory or anticipation of the other.

associative stage The second stage in Fitts's model of skill learning; in this stage, learners begin using stereotyped actions when performing a skill and rely less on actively recalled memories of rules.

autism spectrum disorder A set of disorders including Asperger's syndrome and autism associated with deficits in social interactions and social learning.

autonomic nervous system (ANS) A collection of nerves and structures that control internal organs and glands.

autonomous stage The third stage in Fitts's model of skill learning; in this stage, a skill or subcomponents of the skill become motor programs.

aversive conditioning Conditioning in which the US is a negative event (such as a shock or an airpuff to the eye).

axon The output extension of a neuron, specialized for transmitting information to other neurons or to muscles.

basal forebrain A collection of structures that lie at the base of the forebrain and are important in the production of acetylcholine that is distributed throughout the brain.

basal ganglia A group of brain structures, including the dorsal striatum and nucleus accumbens, that are important in learning voluntary responses.

behavioral addiction Addiction to a behavior that produces reinforcement as well as cravings and withdrawal symptoms when the behavior is prevented.

behavioral economics The study of how organisms allocate their time and resources among possible options.

behaviorism A school of thought that argues that psychology should restrict itself to the study of observable behaviors (such as lever presses, salivation, and other measurable actions) and not seek to infer unobservable mental processes.

blind design An experimental design in which the participants do not know the hypothesis being tested or whether they are part of the experimental group or the control group. See also *double-blind design*.

bliss point In behavioral economics, the allocation of resources that maximizes subjective value or satisfaction.

blocking A two-phase training paradigm in which prior training to one cue (CS1 → US) blocks later learning of a second cue when the two are paired together in the second phase of the training (CS1 + CS2 → US).

brainstem A group of structures that connects the rest of the brain to the spinal cord and plays key roles in regulating automatic functions such as breathing and body temperature.

Cannon-Bard theory of emotion The theory that conscious emotions stimulate appropriate behaviors and physiological responses.

category learning The process by which animals and humans learn to classify stimuli into categories.

cell body The central part of the neuron that contains the nucleus and integrates signals from all the dendrites; also known as the soma.

central executive The component of Baddeley's model of working memory that monitors and manipulates the two working memory buffers.

central nervous system (CNS) The part of the vertebrate nervous system consisting of the brain and spinal cord.

cerebellum A brain region lying below the cerebral cortex in the back of the head. It is responsible for the regulation and coordination of complex voluntary muscular movement, including classical conditioning of motor-reflex responses.

cerebral cortex The brain tissue covering the top and sides of the brain in most vertebrates; involved in storage and processing of sensory inputs and motor outputs.

chaining An operant conditioning technique in which organisms are gradually trained to execute complicated sequences of discrete responses.

classical conditioning A type of learning in which the organism learns to respond with a conditioned

response (CR) to a previously neutral stimulus (the CS) that has been repeatedly presented along with an unconditioned stimulus (US); also called Pavlovian conditioning.

closed skill A skill that involves performing predefined movements that, ideally, never vary.

cochlear implant A sensory prosthesis that directly stimulates auditory nerves to produce hearing sensations in deaf individuals.

cognitive control The manipulation and application of working memory for planning, task switching, attention, stimulus selection, and the inhibition of inappropriate reflexive behaviors.

cognitive map An internal psychological representation of the spatial layout of the external world.

cognitive psychology A subfield of psychology that focuses on human abilities—such as thinking, language, and reasoning—that are not easily explained by a strictly behaviorist approach.

cognitive skill A skill that requires problem solving or the application of strategies.

cognitive science The interdisciplinary study of thought, reasoning, and other higher mental functions.

cognitive stage The first stage in Fitts's model of skill learning; in this stage, an individual must exert some effort to encode the skill on the basis of information gained through observation, instruction, and trial and error.

combinatorial explosion The rapid expansion of resources required to encode configurations as the number of component features increases.

comparator model The theory that each time the brain detects a stimulus, it forms a representation of that stimulus to compare against existing representations of previously experienced stimuli; if there is no match, an orienting response is triggered.

computed tomography (CT) A method of structural neuroimaging based on multiple x-rays.

concurrent reinforcement schedule A reinforcement schedule in which the organism can make any

of several possible responses, each of which may lead to a different outcome reinforced according to a different reinforcement schedule.

conditioned avoidance An experimental design in which animals learn to make particular responses to avoid or prevent exposure to an aversive stimulus.

conditioned emotional response In classical conditioning, a behavioral response (such as freezing) or a physiological response (such as change in heart rate) that occurs in response to a conditioned stimulus (CS) that has been paired with an emotion-evoking unconditioned stimulus (US).

conditioned escape An experimental design in which animals learn to make particular responses in order to escape from or terminate an aversive stimulus.

conditioned response (CR) The trained response to a conditioned stimulus (CS) in anticipation of the unconditioned stimulus (US) that it predicts.

conditioned stimulus (CS) A cue that is paired with an unconditioned stimulus (US) and comes to elicit a conditioned response (CR).

conditioned taste aversion A conditioning preparation in which a subject learns to avoid a taste that has been paired with an aversive outcome, usually nausea.

confabulation A condition associated with some forms of amnesia in which individuals, when asked to remember past events, respond with highly detailed but false memories.

configural node A detector for a unique configuration of two cues, such as a certain tone and light.

confound An extraneous variable that happens to co-vary with the variable(s) being examined and could contribute to the observed results.

connectionist models Networks of uniform and unlabeled connections between simple processing units called nodes.

consequential region A set of stimuli in the world that share the same consequence as a stimulus whose consequence is already known.

consolidation period A length of time during which new episodic and semantic memories are vulnerable and easily lost or altered; each time a memory is recalled, it may become vulnerable again until it is "reconsolidated."

constant practice Practice involving a constrained set of materials and skills.

constraint-induced movement therapy A motor rehabilitation technique in which unaffected limbs are restrained to increase usage of dysfunctional limbs.

contagion An inborn tendency to react emotionally to visual or acoustic stimuli that indicate an emotional response by other members of one's species, typically in ways that replicate the observed response.

contiguity Nearness in time (temporal contiguity) or space (spatial contiguity).

continuous reinforcement schedule A reinforcement schedule in which every instance of the response is followed by the consequence.

control group In an experiment, the group of participants that does not get the experimental treatment; contrast *experimental group*.

copying The act of doing what one observes another organism doing.

correlational study A study that examines the degree to which two variables tend to vary together: as one increases (or decreases), does the other increase (or decrease) too?

cortical plasticity The capacity to change cortical organization as a result of experience.

cortisol The chief *glucocorticoid* in humans.

critical period A limited time window during which a certain kind of learning is possible (and irreversible). Compare *sensitive period*.

CS modulation theory Theories of conditioning holding that the stimulus that enters into an association is determined by a change in how the CS is processed.

cued recall A memory test that involves some kind of prompt or cue to aid recall.

cumulative recorder A device that records behavioral responses; the height of the line drawn represents the number of responses that have been made (cumulatively) up to the present time.

data Facts and figures from which conclusions can be inferred.

declarative memory A broad class of memories, both semantic and episodic, that can typically be verbalized ("declared") or explicitly communicated in some other way (contrast *nondeclarative memory*).

deep brain stimulation A procedure that delivers an electrical current into a patient's brain through one or more implanted electrodes; used to alleviate tremors and other motor symptoms associated with Parkinson's disease.

delay conditioning A conditioning procedure in which there is no temporal gap between the end of the CS and the beginning of the US, and in which the CS co-terminates with the US.

delayed nonmatch-to-sample task A test of visual memory in which a subject must indicate which of two novel objects is not the same as one that was recently seen.

dendrite Extension of a neuron that is specialized to receive signals from other neurons.

dependent variable In an experiment, the factor whose change is measured as an effect of changes in the independent variable.

depression A psychiatric condition that involves sadness as well as a general loss of initiative and activity.

depth-of-processing effect The finding that, in general, deeper processing leads to better remembering of that information.

diencephalon A brain area that lies near the core of the brain, just above the brainstem, and includes the thalamus, the hypothalamus, and the mammillary bodies.

difference image An image of differences in brain activity obtained by taking an fMRI or PET image of a person performing a particular task, then subtracting the image of the same individual at baseline (not performing a task).

differentiation theory The theory that the brain develops representations of stimuli over time by incorporating additional details each time the stimulus is presented.

diffusion tensor imaging (DTI) A type of MRI that measures the diffusion of water in brain tissue, permitting bundles of axons throughout the brain to be imaged.

directed forgetting A procedure in which subjects are first asked to learn information and later asked to remember or forget specific items; typically, memory is worse for items a subject was directed to forget.

direct-matching hypothesis The proposal that memories for actions are stored in specialized cortical regions that map observed actions onto the motor representations of the acts.

discrete trial paradigm An operant conditioning paradigm in which the experimenter defines the beginning and end points of each trial.

discrete-component representation A representation in which each individual stimulus (or stimulus feature) corresponds to one element (node) in the model.

discrimination Recognition that two stimuli are different and knowing which to prefer.

discrimination training Behavioral training in which one of a number of different (but similar) stimuli are presented on each trial and only one of the stimuli is a correct choice.

discrimination training Training an individual to respond differently to different stimuli.

discriminative stimuli In operant conditioning, stimuli that signal whether a particular response will lead to a particular outcome.

dishabituation A renewal of a response, previously habituated, that occurs when the organism is presented with a novel stimulus; compare *habituation*.

distributed representation A representation in which information is coded as a pattern of activation distributed across many different nodes.

dopamine A neuromodulator that alters neuron-to-neuron communication.

dorsal striatum A region of the basal ganglia that is important for stimulus-response learning.

dorsolateral prefrontal cortex The left and right sides of the topmost part of the prefrontal cortex (PFC), often abbreviated DLPFC.

double-blind design An experimental design in which neither the experimenters nor the subjects know group assignment.

Down syndrome A congenital form of mental retardation due to *trisomy 21*.

drive reduction theory The theory that organisms have innate drives to obtain primary reinforcers and that learning is driven by the biological need to reduce those drives.

drug A chemical substance that alters the biochemical functioning of the body and in many cases affects the brain.

dual process theory The theory that habituation and sensitization are independent of each other but operate in parallel.

dualism The principle that the mind and body exist as separate entities.

dysexecutive syndrome A disrupted ability to think and plan.

echolalia The automatic repetition of words or phrases immediately after hearing them spoken.

electroconvulsive shock A brief pulse of electricity that is passed through the brain and can severely disrupt newly formed memories; electroconvulsive therapy is sometimes used to alleviate severe depression.

electroencephalography (EEG) A method for measuring electrical activity in the brain by means of electrodes placed on the scalp; the resulting image is an electroencephalogram (also EEG).

elicited imitation A technique for assessing memory in infants by observing their ability to mimic actions they have seen earlier.

emotion A cluster of three distinct but interrelated sets of phenomena—physiological responses, overt behaviors, and conscious feelings—produced in response to an affecting situation.

empiricism A philosophical school of thought that holds that all the ideas we have are the result of experience; contrast *nativism*.

emulation Copying that involves replicating an outcome without replicating specific motor acts.

endogenous opioids Naturally occurring neurotransmitter-like substances that have many of the same effects as opiate drugs such as heroin and morphine; may help signal hedonic value of reinforcers in the brain.

engram A physical change in the brain that forms the basis of a memory.

enriched environment An environment that provides sensory stimulation and opportunities to explore and learn; for a rat, this may mean housing in a large cage with many toys to play with and other rats to socialize with.

epinephrine A stress hormone that helps to mediate the *fight-or-flight response*; also known as *adrenaline*.

episodic memory Memory for specific autobiographical events; it includes information about the spatial and temporal contexts in which the event occurred.

error-correction learning A mathematical specification of the conditions for learning that holds that the degree to which an outcome is surprising modulates the amount of learning that takes place.

estrogens The principal sex hormones present in adult females.

eugenics A program for encouraging marriage and procreation for the healthiest, strongest, and most intelligent members of society, while discouraging childbearing for mentally or physically unfit people.

event-related potential (ERP) Electroencephalograms (EEGs) from a single individual averaged over multiple repetitions of an event (such as a repeated stimulus presentation).

evolution The theory that species change over time, with new traits or characteristics passed from one generation to the next; natural selection is one mechanism by which evolution occurs.

evolutionary psychology A branch of psychology that studies how behavior evolves through natural selection.

executive control The manipulation of working memory through the updating of stored information to facilitate goals, planning, task switching, stimulus selection, and response inhibition.

experiment A test made to examine the validity of a hypothesis, usually by actively manipulating the variable(s) being investigated and measuring the effect on a behavior.

experimental group In an experiment, the group of participants that gets some treatment of manipulation designed to test the experimental hypothesis; contrast *control group*.

experimenter bias The degree to which an experimenter's prior knowledge or expectations can (consciously or unconsciously) influence the outcome of an experiment.

expert A person who performs a skill better than most.

explicit learning A learning process that includes the ability to verbalize about the actions or events being learned.

explicit memory A category of memory that includes semantic memory and episodic memory and consists of memories of which the person is aware: you know that you know the information (contrast *implicit memory*).

extinction The process of reducing a learned response to a stimulus by ceasing to pair that stimulus with a reward or punishment.

eyeblink conditioning A classical conditioning procedure in which the US is an airpuff to the eye and the conditioned and unconditioned responses are eyeblinks.

false memory Memory of an event that never actually happened.

familiarity The perception of similarity that occurs when an event is repeated.

fear response A cluster of physiological, motor, and conscious reactions that accompany the emotion of fear. In the laboratory, these physiological changes and motor behaviors are often taken to imply presence of fear whether or not the accompanying conscious experience of fear can be documented.

fight-or-flight response A collection of bodily responses (including increased blood flow to muscles, increased respiration, and depressed digestion and immune function) that prepares the body to face a threat; also known as *arousal*.

fixed-interval (FI) schedule In operant conditioning, a reinforcement schedule in which the first response after a fixed amount of time is reinforced; thus, FI 1-m means that reinforcement arrives for the first response made after a one-minute interval since the last reinforcement.

fixed-ratio (FR) schedule In operant conditioning, a reinforcement schedule in which a specific number of responses are required before a reinforcer is delivered; for example, FR 5 means that reinforcement arrives after every fifth response.

flashbulb memory A memory formed under conditions of extreme emotions that seems especially vivid and long lasting.

forgetting The loss or deterioration of memory over time.

fornix A fiber bundle that connects portions of the diencephalon and basal forebrain to the hippocampus.

free recall A memory test that involves simply generating requested information from memory.

free-operant paradigm An operant conditioning paradigm in which the animal can operate the apparatus "freely," responding to obtain reinforcement (or avoid punishment) when it chooses.

frontal cortex Those regions of cortex that lie within the frontal lobes and that may play a role in determining which memories are stored.

frontal lobe The part of the cerebral cortex lying at the front of the human brain; enables a person to plan and perform actions.

functional amnesia A sudden massive retrograde memory loss that seems to result from psychological causes rather than physical causes such as brain injury; also called *psychogenic amnesia*.

functional magnetic resonance imaging (fMRI) A method of functional neuroimaging based on comparing an MRI of the brain during performance of a task with an MRI of the brain at rest.

functional neuroimaging Techniques (such as fMRI or PET) for observing the activity or function of a living brain.

generalization The transfer of past learning to novel events and problems.

generalization gradient A graph showing how physical changes in stimuli (plotted on the horizontal axis) correspond to changes in behavioral responses (plotted on the vertical axis).

gestational age Time since conception.

glia A type of cell that provides functional or structural support to neurons.

glucocorticoids A group of *stress hormones* (including *cortisol* in humans)

that help to mediate the *fight-or-flight response*.

habituation A decrease in the strength or occurrence of a behavior after repeated exposure to the stimulus that produces that behavior; compare *dishabituation*.

Hebbian learning The principle that learning involves strengthening the connections of coactive neurons; often stated as, "Neurons that fire together, wire together."

hedonic value of a stimulus The subjective "goodness" or value of that stimulus.

heterosynaptic Occurring in several nearby synapses simultaneously.

hippocampal region The hippocampus and associated brain regions, including the entorhinal cortex and dentate gyrus. In humans, also referred to as the medial temporal lobe.

hippocampus A brain structure located in the medial temporal lobe that is important for new memory formation.

homeostasis The tendency of the body (including the brain) to gravitate toward a state of equilibrium or balance.

homosynaptic Occurring in one synapse without affecting nearby synapses.

Huntington's disease An inherited disorder that causes gradual damage to neurons throughout the brain, especially in the basal ganglia and cerebral cortex. It results in various psychological problems (e.g., mood disorders, hypersexuality, depression, and psychosis) and a gradual loss of motor abilities.

hypothesis A tentative explanation for an observation, phenomenon, or scientific problem that can be tested by further investigation.

identical elements theory Thorndike's proposal that learned abilities transfer to novel situations to an extent that depends on the number of elements in the new situation that are identical to those in the situation in which the skills were encoded.

implicit learning Learning that occurs without the learner's awareness of improvements in performance or, in the case of people with amnesia, awareness that practice has occurred.

implicit memory Memory that occurs without the learner's awareness (contrast *explicit memory*).

imprinting The tendency of young animals of some species to form an attachment to the first individual they see after birth.

incentive salience hypothesis of dopamine function The theory that dopamine helps provide organisms with the motivation to work for reinforcement.

independent variable The factor that is manipulated in an experiment, such as the factor that differentiates the control group and experimental group; contrast *dependent variable*.

inferior olive A nucleus of cells with connections to the thalamus, cerebellum, and spinal cord.

instrumental conditioning The process whereby organisms learn to make responses in order to obtain or avoid important consequences; compare *classical conditioning*.

interference Reduction in the strength of a memory due to overlap with the content of other memories.

interpositus nucleus One of the cerebellar deep nuclei.

interstimulus interval (ISI) The temporal gap between the onset of the CS and the onset of the US.

James-Lange theory of emotion The theory that conscious feelings of emotion occur when the mind senses the physiological responses associated with fear or some other kind of arousal.

knowledge of results Feedback about performance of a skill; critical to the effectiveness of practice.

Korsakoff's disease A condition caused by a deficiency in thiamine (a

B vitamin) that sometimes accompanies chronic alcohol abuse; patients often show severe anterograde amnesia and engage in confabulation.

latent inhibition A conditioning paradigm in which prior exposure to a CS retards later learning of the CS-US association during acquisition training.

latent learning Learning that is undetected (latent) until explicitly demonstrated at a later stage.

law of effect The observation, made by Thorndike, that the probability of a particular behavioral response increases or decreases depending on the consequences that have followed that response in the past.

learned helplessness A phenomenon in which exposure to an uncontrollable punisher teaches an expectation that responses are ineffectual, which in turn reduces the motivation to attempt new avoidance responses.

learned non-use A condition in which an individual gradually stops using a limb that has been affected by stroke or other brain injury and instead relies on the other, unaffected limb.

learning The process by which changes in behavior arise as a result of experiences interacting with the world.

learning curve A graph showing learning performance (the dependent variable, usually plotted along the vertical axis) as a function of training time (the independent variable, usually plotted along the horizontal axis).

learning rate A value that can range from 0 to 1 and controls how much learning takes place after each trial.

learning specificity The degree to which learning about one set of stimuli transfers to another group of stimuli.

lesion Damage caused by injury or illness.

long-term depression (LTD) A process in which synaptic transmission becomes less effective as a result of recent activity; with long-term potentiation, widely believed to represent a

form of synaptic plasticity that could be the neural mechanism for learning.

long-term potentiation (LTP) A process in which synaptic transmission becomes more effective as a result of recent activity; with long-term depression, widely believed to represent a form of synaptic plasticity that could be the neural mechanism for learning.

magnetic resonance imaging (MRI) A method of structural neuroimaging based on recording changes in magnetic fields.

massed practice Concentrated, continuous practice of a skill.

matching law of choice behavior The principle that an organism, given a choice between multiple responses, will make a particular response at a rate proportional to how often that response is reinforced relative to the other choices.

mathematical psychology A subfield of psychology that uses mathematical equations to describe the laws of learning and memory.

medial temporal lobes The medial (or inner) surface of the temporal lobes that contains the hippocampus, the amygdala, and other structures important for memory.

memory The record of past experiences acquired through learning.

mere exposure learning Learning through mere exposure to stimuli, without any explicit prompting and without any outward responding.

mirror neurons Neurons that respond during performance of an action and during visual observations of that same action.

mirror reading An experimental task that requires individuals to read mirror-reversed text; used to test cognitive skill learning.

mirror tracing An experimental task that requires individuals to trace drawings by watching a mirror image of their hand and the figure to be traced, with the hand and figure concealed; used to test perceptual-motor-skill learning.

misattribution Mistaken recall of the source of learned information.

mnemonics Techniques that make information easier to memorize.

modeling Demonstration of actions.

mood congruency of memory The principle that it is easier to retrieve memories that match our current mood or emotional state.

motivational value of a stimulus The degree to which an organism is willing to work to obtain access to that stimulus.

motor program A sequence of movements that an organism can perform automatically (with minimal attention).

multimodal Related to or responding to more than one sensory modality.

multiple memory trace theory The theory that episodic (and possibly semantic) memories are encoded by an ensemble of hippocampal and cortical neurons and that both hippocampus and cortex are normally involved in storing and retrieving even very old memories (contrast *standard consolidation theory*).

nativism A philosophical school of thought that holds that the bulk of knowledge is inborn (or native); contrast *empiricism*.

natural selection A proposed mechanism for evolution, also known as "survival of the fittest," which holds that species evolve when there is some trait that varies naturally across individuals, is inheritable, and increases an individual's "fitness," or chance of survival and reproductive success.

negative patterning A behavioral paradigm in which the response to the individual cues should be positive while the response to the pattern is negative (no response).

negative punishment A type of operant conditioning in which the response causes a reinforcer to be taken away or "subtracted from" the environment; over time, the response becomes less frequent.

negative reinforcement A type of operant conditioning in which the response causes a punisher to be taken away or "subtracted from" the environment; over time, the response becomes more frequent.

nervous system An organism's system of tissues specialized for distributing and processing information.

neurofibrillary tangles Collapsed remains of the proteins that normally hold a neuron in place and help to transport nutrients around the cell; such tangles occur in the brains of patients with *Alzheimer's disease*.

neurogenesis Creation of new *neurons* in the brain.

neuromodulator A neurotransmitter that acts to modulate activity in a large number of neurons rather than in a single synapse.

neuron A type of cell that is specialized for information processing.

neurophysiology The study of the activity and function of neurons.

neuropsychology The branch of psychology that deals with the relation between brain function and behavior.

neuroscience The study of the brain and the rest of the nervous system.

neurotransmitter One of several classes of molecule released by neurons to carry chemical messages to other neurons.

nondeclarative memory A broad class of memory that includes skill memory and other types of learning that do not fall under the heading of episodic or semantic memory and that are not always consciously accessible or easy to verbalize (contrast *declarative memory*).

novel object recognition An organism's detection of and response to unfamiliar objects during exploratory behavior.

nucleus basalis A small group of neurons located in the basal forebrain.

observational conditioning A process in which an individual learns an emotional response after observing similar responses in others.

observational learning A process in which the learner actively monitors events and then chooses later actions based on those observations.

occipital lobe The part of the cerebral cortex lying at the rear of the human brain; important for visual processing.

open skill A skill in which movements are made on the basis of predictions about changing demands of the environment.

operant conditioning The process whereby organisms learn to make responses in order to obtain or avoid important consequences; compare *classical conditioning*.

orbitofrontal cortex An area of the prefrontal cortex that is important for learning to predict the outcomes of particular responses.

orienting response An organism's innate reaction to a novel stimulus.

parietal lobe The part of the cerebral cortex lying at the top of the human brain; important for processing somatosensory (touch) information and motor outputs.

Parkinson's disease A disorder resulting from disruptions in the normal functioning of the basal ganglia and progressive deterioration of motor control and perceptual-motor-skill learning.

partial reinforcement schedule A reinforcement schedule in which only some responses are reinforced.

pathological addiction A strong habit that is maintained despite harmful consequences.

perceptual learning Learning in which experience with a set of stimuli makes it easier to distinguish those stimuli.

perceptual-motor skill Learned movement patterns guided by sensory inputs.

peripheral nervous system (PNS) The part of the nervous system that carries information from sensory receptors to the central nervous system and carries commands from the CNS to muscles.

perseveration A failure to learn a new response, especially as demonstrated by continued adherence to an old, no longer valid response rule.

perspective taking Imagining oneself in the place of another.

phobia An excessive and irrational fear of an object, place, or situation.

phonological loop An auditory memory maintained by internal (subvocal) speech rehearsal.

phrenology A field of study that attempted to determine mental abilities by measuring head shape and size.

piloerection A fear response in mammals in which body hair stands on end, making the animal look bigger and more threatening than it is.

place cell A neuron that fires maximally when the organism enters a particular location within an environment.

place field The spatial location that evokes maximal activity in a place cell.

placebo An inactive substance, such as a sugar pill, that is administered to the control subjects in an experiment to compare against the effects of an active substance, such as a drug.

positive punishment A type of operant conditioning in which the response causes a punisher to be "added" to the environment; over time, the response becomes less frequent.

positive reinforcement A type of operant conditioning in which the response causes a reinforcer to be "added" to the environment; over time, the response becomes more frequent.

positron emission tomography (PET) A method of functional neuroimaging based on injecting a radioactive chemical into the bloodstream and measuring its accumulation in active areas of the brain.

postreinforcement pause In operant conditioning with a fixed-ratio (FR) schedule of reinforcement, a brief pause following a period of fast responding leading to reinforcement.

postsynaptic On the receiving side of a synapse.

posttraumatic stress disorder (PTSD) A psychological syndrome that can develop after exposure to a horrific event (such as combat, rape, or natural disaster); symptoms include reexperiencing the event (through intrusive recollections, flashbacks, or nightmares), avoidance of reminders of the trauma, and heightened anxiety.

power law of learning A law stating that the degree to which a practice trial improves performance diminishes after a certain point, so that additional trials are needed to further improve the skill; learning occurs quickly at first, then slows.

prediction error The difference between what was predicted and what actually occurred.

prefrontal cortex (PFC) The frontmost (anterior) part of the frontal lobe cortex, essential for working memory and executive control.

Premack principle The theory that the opportunity to perform a highly frequent behavior can reinforce a less frequent behavior; later refined as the *response deprivation hypothesis*.

presynaptic On the sending side of a synapse.

primary reinforcers Stimuli such as food, water, sex, and sleep that are innately reinforcing, meaning that organisms have a drive to obtain these things and will tend to repeat behaviors that result in access to them.

priming A phenomenon in which prior exposure to a stimulus can improve the ability to recognize that stimulus later.

proactive interference Disruption of new learning by previously stored information.

psychology The study of mind and behavior.

puberty The process of physical change during which the body transitions to sexual maturity, usually beginning around age 10 in human females and age 12 in human males.

punisher A consequence of behavior that leads to decreased likelihood of that behavior occurring again in the future.

punishment In operant conditioning, the process of providing outcomes for a behavior that decrease the probability of that behavior occurring again in the future.

Purkinje cells Large drop-shaped and densely branching neurons in the cerebellar cortex.

radical behaviorism An extreme form of behaviorism, championed by B. F. Skinner, holding that consciousness and free will are illusions and that even so-called higher cognitive functions (e.g., human language) are merely complex sets of stimulus-response associations.

receptive field The range (or "field") of physical stimuli that activate a single neuron.

receptor A specialized molecule, located on the surface of a neuron, to which one or more particular neurotransmitters can bind; when a neurotransmitter activates a receptor, effects may be initiated in the neuron.

recognition A memory test that involves picking out (or recognizing) a studied item from a set of options.

reflex An involuntary and automatic (unlearned) response; also, a pathway from sensory stimulus to motor response.

reflex arc An automatic pathway from a sensory stimulus to a motor response.

reinforcement In operant conditioning, the process of providing outcomes for a behavior that increase the probability of that behavior occurring again in the future.

reinforcement schedule A schedule or set of rules determining how often reinforcement is delivered in an operant conditioning paradigm. See also *continuous reinforcement schedule, partial reinforcement schedule, fixed-ratio (FR) schedule, fixed-interval (FI) schedule, variable-ratio (VR) schedule, variable-interval (VI) schedule, concurrent reinforcement schedule*.

reinforcer A consequence of behavior that leads to increased likelihood of that behavior occurring again in the future.

response The behavioral consequence of perception of a stimulus.

response deprivation hypothesis A refinement of the Premack principle stating that the opportunity to perform any behavior can be reinforcing if access to that behavior is restricted.

retention curve A graph showing forgetting or relearning as a function of time since initial learning.

retroactive interference Disruption of old (previously stored) information by new learning.

retrograde amnesia Loss of memories for events dating from before a brain injury or disruption; memory loss generally occurs in a time-graded manner so that more recent memories are devastated but older ones may be spared.

Ribot gradient A pattern of retrograde memory loss in which recently acquired memories are more prone to disruption than older memories.

rotary pursuit task An experimental task that requires individuals to keep the end of a pointed stick (stylus) above a fixed point on a rotating disk; used to study perceptual-motor-skill learning.

secondary reinforcers Stimuli that have no intrinsic value but that have been paired with primary reinforcers or that provide access to primary reinforcers.

self-control An organism's willingness to forego a small immediate reinforcement in favor of a large future reinforcement.

semantic memory Memory for facts or general knowledge about the world, including general personal information.

sensitive period A time window, usually early in life, during which a certain kind of learning is most effective.

sensitization A phenomenon in which a salient stimulus (such as an electric shock) temporarily increases the strength of responses to other stimuli.

sensory cortex Areas of cerebral cortex involved in processing sensory information such as sight and sounds.

sensory memory Brief, transient sensations of what has just been perceived when someone sees, hears, or tastes something.

sensory preconditioning Training in which presentation of two stimuli together as a compound results in a later tendency to generalize what is known about one of these stimuli to the other.

sensory prosthesis A mechanical device designed to supplement or substitute for a faulty sensory modality such as vision or hearing; the device's sensory detectors interface with brain areas that normally process those sensory inputs.

serial reaction time task An experimental task that requires individuals to press keys in specific sequences on the basis of cues provided by a computer; used to study implicit learning.

shaping An operant conditioning technique in which successive approximations to a desired response are reinforced.

short-term memory A temporary memory that is maintained through active rehearsal.

single-cell recording Use of an implanted electrode to detect electrical activity (spiking) in a single cell (such as a neuron).

skill An ability that can improve over time through practice.

skill decay Loss of a skill because of non-use.

skin conductance response (SCR) A change in the skin's electrical conductivity associated with emotions such as anxiety, fear, or surprise; also known as the galvanic skin response (GSR).

Skinner box A conditioning chamber in which reinforcement or punishment is delivered automatically whenever an animal makes (or ceases making) a particular response (such as pressing a lever).

social conformity The tendency to adopt the behavior of the group.

social learning Learning from others; often used as a synonym for observational learning.

social transmission of information A process seen in all human cultures in which an observer learns something new through experiences with others.

social-learning theory A theory of human behavior prominent from the 1940s through the 1960s that proposed that the kinds of reinforcements an individual has experienced in past social contexts will determine how that individual will act in any given situation.

soma The central part of the neuron that contains the nucleus and integrates signals from all the dendrites; also known as the cell body.

somatic theories of emotion Theories of emotion based on the central premise that physiological responses to stimuli come first, and these determine or induce emotions.

source amnesia Remembering a fact or event but misattributing the source or context in which this information was acquired.

spaced practice Practice of a skill that is spread out over several sessions.

spatial learning The acquisition of information about one's surroundings.

spine A tiny protrusion on a *dendrite* where *synapses* may form.

spontaneous recovery Reappearance (or increase in strength) of a previously habituated response after a short period of no stimulus presentation.

standard consolidation theory The theory that the hippocampus and related medial temporal lobe structures are required for storage and retrieval of recent episodic memories but not older ones (contrast *multiple memory trace theory*).

stimulus A sensory event that provides information about the outside world.

stimulus enhancement A process in which observation of other individuals causes an organism's attention to be directed toward specific objects or events within an environment.

stimulus matching A type of imitation in which the observer generates stimuli that can be directly compared with the originally observed stimuli.

stimulus representation The form in which information about stimuli is encoded within a model or brain.

stress Any stimulus or event that causes bodily arousal and release of stress hormones.

stress hormone A hormone that is released in response to signals from the *autonomic nervous system* (*ANS*) and helps mediate the *fight-or-flight response*; examples include norepinephrine and the *glucocorticoids*.

stroke When blood flow to some region of the brain stops or when an artery ruptures, causing neurons in the affected region to die.

structural neuroimaging Techniques (such as MRI and CT) for creating images of anatomical structures within the living brain.

subject bias The degree to which a subject's prior knowledge or expectations concerning an experiment can (consciously or unconsciously) influence the outcome.

substantia nigra pars compacta (SNc) A part of the basal ganglia that contains dopamine-producing neurons that project to the striatum.

synapse A narrow gap between two neurons across which chemical messages can be transmitted.

synaptic depression A reduction in synaptic transmission; a possible neural mechanism underlying habituation.

synaptic plasticity The ability of synapses to change as a result of experience.

synaptogenesis Creation of new *synapses*.

systematic desensitization Therapy for *phobias* in which successive approximations of the fear-evoking stimulus are presented while the patient learns to remain relaxed; eventually, even presentation of the stimulus itself does not elicit a fear reaction.

talent A person's genetically endowed ability to perform a skill better than most.

template model of song learning A model of song learning having three basic phases: song memorization, song practice, and song utilization.

temporal lobe The part of the cerebral cortex lying at the sides of the human brain; important for language and auditory processing and for learning new facts and forming new memories of events.

testosterone The most important *androgen* and hence the principal male sex hormone.

theory A set of statements devised to explain a group of facts.

theory of equipotentiality The theory that memories are stored globally, by the brain as a whole, rather than in one particular brain area.

tolerance A decrease in reaction to a drug so that larger doses are required to achieve the same effect.

topographic representation A stimulus representation in which the physical closeness of the representations in the brain (or model) for two stimuli is a reflection of their physical proximity or similarity in the external world.

trace conditioning A conditioning procedure in which there is a temporal gap between the end of the CS and the beginning of the US.

transfer specificity The restricted applicability of learned skills to specific situations.

transfer-appropriate processing effect The finding that, in general, memory retrieval is best when the cues available at testing are similar to those available at encoding.

transient global amnesia (TGA) A transient, or temporary, disruption of memory typically including elements of both anterograde and retrograde amnesia.

transient memories Nonpermanent memories that last seconds or minutes. The Atkinson-Shiffrin model describes two types: sensory and short-term.

trial-level model A theory of learning in which all of the cues that occur during a trial and all of the changes that result are considered a single event.

trisomy 21 A genetic "accident" in which the embryo inherits three (rather than two) copies of chromosome 21, resulting in *Down syndrome*.

true imitation Copying that involves reproducing motor acts.

two-action test A technique developed to demonstrate imitation abilities that involves exposing naive animals to demonstrators trained to achieve the same goal using different actions.

two-factor theory of emotion The theory that a combination of cognitive appraisal and perception of biological changes together determines our experience of emotion.

unconditioned response (UR) The naturally occurring response to an unconditioned stimulus (US).

unconditioned stimulus (US) A cue that has some biological significance and in the absence of prior training naturally evokes a response.

US modulation theory Theories of conditioning that say the stimulus that enters into an association is determined by a change in how the US is processed.

variable practice Practice involving the performance of skills in a wide variety of contexts.

variable-interval (VI) schedule In operant conditioning, a reinforcement schedule in which the first response after a fixed amount of time, on average, is reinforced; thus, VI 1-m means that the first response after one minute, on average, is reinforced.

variable-ratio (VR) schedule In operant conditioning, a reinforcement schedule in which a certain number of responses, on average, are required before a reinforcer is delivered; thus, VR 5 means that, on average, every fifth response is reinforced.

ventral tegmental area (VTA) A region in the midbrain that contains dopamine-producing neurons that project to the frontal cortex and other brain areas.

visual sensory memory The initial temporary storage for information perceived by the visual system.

visuospatial sketchpad The component of Baddeley's model of working memory that holds visual and spatial images for manipulation.

vocal imitation Copying that involves reproducing sounds.

vocal learning Acquiring the ability to produce sounds using memories of those sounds.

word-length effect The tendency for a person to remember fewer words from a list as the length of the words increases.

word-stem completion task A task in which participants are asked to fill in the blanks in a list of word stems (e.g., MOT___) to produce the first word that comes to mind; in a priming experiment, participants are more likely to produce a particular word (e.g., MOTEL) if they have been exposed to that word previously.

working memory The active maintenance and manipulation of short-term memory.

REFERENCES

Ackerman, P. L. (2006). Cognitive sex differences and mathematics and science achievement. *American Psychologist, 61*, 722–723.

Ackerman, P. L. (2007). New developments in understanding skilled performance. *Current Directions in Psychological Science, 16*, 235–239.

Ackerman, P. L., Kanfer, R., & Goff, M. (1995). Cognitive and noncognitive determinants and consequences of complex skill acquisition. *Journal of Experimental Psychology: Applied, 1*, 270–304.

Acredolo, L., & Goodwyn, S. (2002). *Baby signs*. Chicago: Contemporary Books.

Addis, D. R., Moscovitch, M., Crawley, A. P., & McAndrews, M. P. (2004). Recollective qualities modulate hippocampal activation during autobiographical memory retrieval. *Hippocampus, 14*, 752–762.

Aggleton, J., & Mishkin, M. (1983). Visual recognition impairment following medial thalamic lesion in monkeys. *Neuropsychologia, 21*, 189–197.

Aglioti, S. M., Cesari, P., Romani, M., & Urgesi, C. (2008). Action anticipation and motor resonance in elite basketball players. *Nature Neuroscience, 11*, 1109–1116.

Aidman, E. V., & Kollaras-Mitsinikos, L. (2006). Personality dispositions in the prediction of posttraumatic stress reactions. *Psychological Reports, 99*(2), 569–580.

Aimone, J. B., Deng, W., & Gage, F. H. (2010). Adult neurogenesis: integrating theories and separating functions. *Trends in Cognitive Science, 14*(7), 325–337.

Akins, C. K., & Zentall, T. R. (1996). Imitative learning in male Japanese quail (*Coturnix japonica*) using the two-action method. *Journal of Comparative Psychology, 110*(3), 316–320.

al Maskati, H., & Zbrozyna, A. (1989). Cardiovascular and motor components of the defence reaction elicited in rats by electrical and chemical stimulation in amygdala. *Journal of the Autonomic Nervous System, 28*(2), 127–131.

Alberici, E., Pichiecchio, A., Caverzasi, E., Farina, L. M., Persico, A., Cavallini, A., et al. (2008). Transient global amnesia: hippocampal magnetic resonance imaging abnormalities. *Functional Neurology, 23*(3), 149–152.

Allen, M. T., Chelius, L., & Gluck, M. A. (2002). Selective entorhinal lesions and non-selective cortical-hippocampal region lesions, but not selective hippocampal lesions, disrupt learned irrelevance in rabbit eyeblink conditioning. *Cognitive Affective and Behavioral Neuroscience, 2*, 214–226.

Allen, M. T., Padilla, Y., Myers, C. E., & Gluck, M. A. (2002). Blocking in rabbit eyeblink conditioning is not due to learned inattention. *Integrative Physiological and Behavioral Science, 37*(4), 254–264.

Allison, J. (1983). *Behavioral economics*. New York: Praeger.

Allison, J. (1993). Response deprivation, reinforcement, and economics. *Journal of the Experimental Analysis of Behavior, 60*, 129–140.

Allport, G. W. (1954). *The nature of prejudice*. Reading, MA: Addison-Wesley.

Alzheimer, A. (1987 [1907]). Über eine eigenartige Erkrankung der Hirnrinde [About a peculiar disease of the cerebral cortex]. Translated by L. Jarvik and H. Greenson. *Alzheimer's Disease and Associated Disorders, 1*, 3–8.

Amen, D. G., Newberg, W., Thatcher, R., Jin, Y., Wu, J., Keater, D., & Willeumier, K. (2011). Impact of playing American professional football on long-term brain function. *Journal of Neuropsychiatry & Clinical Neurosciences, 23*, 98–106.

Anderson, C. A. (2004). An update on the effects of playing violent video games. *Journal of Adolescence, 27*(1), 113–122.

Anderson, C. A., Berkowitz, L., Donnerstein, E., Huesmann, L. R., Johnson, J. D., Linz, D., et al. (2003). The influence of media violence on youth. *Psychological Science in the Public Interest, 4*, 82–110.

Anderson, C. A., & Bushman, B. J. (2001). Effects of violent video games on aggressive behavior, aggressive cognition, aggressive affect, physiological arousal, and prosocial behavior: a meta-analytic review of the scientific literature. *Psychological Science, 12*, 353–359.

Anderson, C. A., Shibuya, A., Ihori, N., Swing, E. L., Bushman, E. J., Sakamoto, A., et al. (2010). Violent video game effects on aggression, empathy, and prosocial behavior in eastern and western countries: a metanalytic review. *Psychological Bulletin, 136*(2), 151–173.

Anderson, J. R. (1976). *Language, memory, and thought*. Hillsdale, NJ: Erlbaum.

Anderson, J. R. (1981). Interference: the relationship between response latency and response accuracy. *Journal of Experimental Psychology: Human Learning and Memory, 7*, 311–325.

Anderson, J. R. (1982). Acquisition of cognitive skill. *Psychological Review, 89*, 369–406.

Anderson, J. R., Corbett, A. T., Koedinger, K. R., & Pelletier, R. (1995). Cognitive tutors: lessons learned. *Journal of the Learning Sciences, 4*, 167–207.

Anderson, J. R., Fincham, J. M., & Douglass, S. (1997). Practice and retention: A unifying analysis. *Journal of Experimental Psychology: Learning, Memory, and Cognition, 25*, 1120–1136.

Anderson, M., Ochsner, K., Kuhl, B., Cooper, J., Robertson, E., Gabrieli, S., et al. (2004). Neural systems underlying the suppression of unwanted memories. *Science, 303*(5655), 232–235.

APA Online. (2004). Violence in the media—psychologists help protect children from harmful effects. Retrieved from http://www.psychologymatters.org/mediaviolence.html

Archibald, S. J., Mateer, C. A., & Kerns, K. A. (2001). Utilization behavior: clinical manifestations and neurological mechanisms. *Neuropsychology Review, 11*(3), 117–130.

Arkes, H. R., & Tetlock, P. E. (2004). Attributions of implicit prejudice, or "Would Jesse Jackson 'fail' the implicit association test?" *Psychological Inquiry, 15*(4), 257–278.

Arnsten, A. F. (2006). Fundamentals of attention-deficit/hyperactivity disorder: circuits and pathways. *Journal of Clinical Psychiatry, 67*(suppl. 8), 7–12.

Aron, A., Fisher, H., Mashek, D., Strong, G., Li, H., & Brown, L. L. (2005). Reward, motivation, and emotion systems associated with early-stage intense romantic love. *Journal of Neurophysiology, 94*, 327–337.

Arthur, W., Bennett, W., Stanush, P. L., & McNelly, T. L. (1998). Factors that influence skill decay and retention: a quantitative review and analysis. *Human Performance, 11*(1), 57–101.

Arthur, W., Day, E. A., Villado, A. J., Boatman, P. R., Kowollik, V., Bennett, W., & Bhupatkar, A. (2010). The effect of distributed practice on immediate posttraining and long-term performance on a complex command-and-control simulation task. *Human Performance, 23*, 428–445.

Asaad, W. F., Rainer, G., & Miller, E. K. (1998). Neural activity in the primate prefrontal cortex during associative learning. *Neuron, 21*, 1399–1407.

Ash, D., & Holding, D. (1990). Backward versus forward chaining in the acquisition of a keyboard skill. *Human Factors, 32*, 139–146.

Ashby, F. G., & Waldron, E. (2000). The neuropsychological bases of category learning. *Current Directions in Psychological Science, 9*(1), 10–14.

Ashmore, R. D., & Del Boca, F. K. (1981). Conceptual approaches to stereotypes and stereotyping. In D. L. Hamilton (Ed.), *Cognitive processes in stereotyping and intergroup behavior* (pp. 1–35). Hillsdale, NJ: Erlbaum.

Astur, R., Ortiz, M., & Sutherland, R. (1998). A characterization of performance by men and women in a virtual Morris water task: a large and reliable sex difference. *Behavioural Brain Research, 93*, 185–190.

Atkinson, R. C., & Shiffrin, R. M. (1968). Human memory: a proposed system and its control processes. In Spence, K. W., & Spence, J. T. (Eds.), *The psychology of learning and motivation* (Vol. 2, pp. 89–195). New York: Academic Press.

Awh, E., & Jonides, J. (1998). Spatial selective attention and spatial working memory. In R. Parasuraman (Ed.), *The attentive brain*. Cambridge, MA: MIT Press.

Awh, E., Jonides, J., Smith, E. E., Schumacher, E. H., Koeppe, R. A., & Katz, S. (1996). Dissociation of storage and rehearsal in verbal working memory: evidence from PET. *Psychological Science, 7*, 25–31.

Baddeley, A. D. (1986). *Working memory.* New York: Oxford University Press.

Baddeley, A. D., & Hitch G. (1974). Working memory. In G. A. Bower (Ed.), *Recent advances in learning and motivation* (vol. 8, pp. 47–90). New York: Academic Press.

Baddeley, A. D., & Longman, D. (1978). The influence of length and frequency of training session on the rate of learning to type. *Ergonomics, 21*, 627–635.

Baddeley, A. D., Thomson, N., & Buchanan, M. (1975). Word length and the structure of short-term memory. *Journal of Verbal Learning and Verbal Behavior, 14*, 375–589.

Badre, D. (2008). Cognitive control, hierarchy, and the rostro-caudal organization of the frontal lobes. *Trends in Cognitive Sciences, 12*, 193–200.

Badre, D., & D'Esposito, M. (2007). Functional magnetic resonance imaging evidence for a hierarchical organization of the prefrontal cortex. *Journal of Cognitive Neuroscience, 19*, 2082–2099.

Badre, D., Hoffman, J., Cooney, J. W., & D'Esposito, M. (2009). Hierarchical cognitive control deficits following damage to the human frontal lobe. *Nature Neuroscience, 12*, 515–522.

Bahrick, H., Bahrick, P., & Wittlinger, R. (1975). Fifty years of memory for names and faces: a cross-sectional approach. *Journal of Experimental Psychology: General, 104*, 54–75.

Bakin, J. S., & Weinberger, N. M. (1990). Classical conditioning induces CS-specific receptive field plasticity in the auditory cortex of the guinea pig. *Brain Research, 536*, 271–286.

Bakin, J. S., & Weinberger, N. M. (1996). Induction of a physiological memory in the cerebral cortex by stimulation of the nucleus basalis. *Proceedings of the National Academy of Sciences USA, 93*, 11219–11224.

Baldo, J. V., & Shimamura, A. P. (2000). Spatial and color working memory in patients with lateral prefrontal cortex lesions. *Psychobiology, 28*, 156–167.

Ball, G., & Hulse, S. (1998). Birdsong. *American Psychologist, 53*, 37–58.

Balleine, B., Daw, N., & O'Doherty, J. (2008). Multiple forms of value learning and the function of dopamine. In P. W. Glimcher, C. Camerer, E. Fehr & R. A. Poldrack (Eds.), *Neuroeconomics: decision making and the brain* (pp. 367–387). London: Academic Press.

Balleine, B. W., & Kilcross, S. (2006). Parallel incentive processing: an integrated view of amygdala function. *Trends in Neuroscience, 29*(5), 272–279.

Bancaud, J., Brunet-Bourgin, F., Chauvel, P., & Halgren, E. (1994). Anatomical origin of déjà vu and vivid "memories" in human temporal lobe epilepsy. *Brain, 117* (Pt. 1), 71–90.

Bandura, A. (1969). *Principles of behavior modification.* New York: Holt, Reinhart, & Winston.

Bandura, A. (1986). *Social foundations of thought and action: a social cognitive theory.* Englewood Cliffs, NJ: Prentice-Hall.

Bandura, A., Ross, D., & Ross, S. A. (1961). Transmission of aggression through imitation of aggressive models. *Journal of Abnormal and Social Psychology, 63,* 575–582.

Bao, J. X., Kandel, E. R., & Hawkins, R. D. (1998). Involvement of presynaptic and postsynaptic mechanisms in a cellular analog of classical conditioning at *Aplysia* sensory-motor neuron synapses in isolated cell culture. *Journal of Neuroscience 18*(1), 458–466.

Baptista, L. F., & King, J. R. (1980). Geographical variation in song and song dialects of montane white-crowned sparrows. *Condor, 82,* 267–281.

Bar-Hillel, M. (1984). Representativeness and the fallacies of probability. *Acta Psychologica, 55,* 91–107.

Barch, D. M., Csernansky, J., Conturo, T., Snyder, A. Z., & Ollinger, J. (2002). Working and long-term memory deficits in schizophrenia: Is there a common underlying prefrontal mechanism? *Journal of Abnormal Psychology, 111,* 478–494.

Barnes, C. A. (1979). Memory deficits associated with senescence: a neurophysiological and behavioral study in the rat. *Journal of Comparative and Physiological Psychology, 93*(1), 74–104.

Barnes, C. A., Suster, M. S., Shen, J., & McNaughton, B. L. (1997). Multistability of cognitive maps in the hippocampus of old rats. *Nature, 388,* 272–275.

Barnes, T. D., Kubota, Y., Hu, D., Jin, D. Z., & Graybiel, A. M. (2005). Activity of striatal neurons reflects dynamic encoding and recoding of procedural memories. *Nature, 437,* 1158–1161.

Barnfield, A. (1999). Development of sex differences in spatial memory. *Perceptual and Motor Skills, 89*(1), 339–350.

Baron-Cohen, S. (2009). Autism: the Empathizing-Synthesizing (E-S) theory. *Annals of the New York Academy of Sciences, 1156,* 68–80.

Barr, R. (1980). Some remarks on the time-course of aging. In L. Poon, J. Fozard, L. Cermak, D. Arenberg & L. Thompson (Eds.), *New directions in memory and aging* (pp. 143–149). Hillsdale, NJ: Erlbaum.

Bartsch, D., Ghirardi, M., Skehel, P. A., Karl, K. A., Herder, S. P., Chen, M., Bailey, C. H., & Kandel, E. R. (1995). *Aplysia* CREB2 represses long-term facilitation: Relief of repression converts transient facilitation into long-term functional and structural change. *Cell, 83,* 979–992.

Basham, M. E., Nordeen, E. J., & Nordeen, K. W. (1996). Blockade of NMDA receptors in the anterior forebrain impairs sensory acquisition in the zebra finch. *Neurobiology of Learning and Memory, 66,* 295–304.

Bauer, P. (1996). What do infants recall of their lives? Memory for specific events by one- to two-year-olds. *American Psychologist, 51,* 29–41.

Bauer, R., & McDonald, C. (2003). Auditory agnosia and amusia. In T. Feinberg & M. Farah (Eds.), *Behavioral neurology and neuropsychology* (2nd ed., pp. 257–270). New York: McGraw-Hill.

Baum, W. M. (2002). From molecular to molar: a paradigm shift in behavior analysis. *Journal of the Experimental Analysis of Behavior, 78,* 95–116.

Baum, W. M. (2004). Molar and molecular views of choice. *Behavioural Processes, 66,* 349–359.

Baumrind, D. (2002). Ordinary physical punishment: is it harmful? Comment on Gershoff (2002). *Psychological Bulletin, 128,* 580–589.

Bayley, P. J., Gold, J. J., Hopkins, R. O., & Squire, L. R. (2005). The neuroanatomy of remote memory. *Neuron, 46,* 799–810.

Beadle-Brown, J. D., & Whiten, A. (2004). Elicited imitation in children and adults with autism: Is there a deficit? *Journal of Intellectual & Developmental Disability, 292,* 147–163.

Bechara, A., Tranel, D., Damasio, H., Adolphs, R., Rockland, C., & Damasio, A. (1995). Double dissociation of conditioning and declarative knowledge relative to the amygdala and hippocampus in humans. *Science, 269,* 1115–1118.

Beck, B. (1980). *Animal tool behavior: the use and manufacture of tools by animals.* New York: Garland STPM Press.

Beck, H. P., Levinson, S., & Irons, G. (2009). Finding Little Albert: a journey to John B. Watson's infant laboratory. *American Psychologist, 64*(7), 605–614.

Beck, K. D., McLaughlin, J., Bergen, M. T., Cominski, T. P., Moldow, R. L., & Servatius, R. J. (2008). Facilitated acquisition of the classically conditioned eyeblink response in women taking oral contraceptives. *Behavioural Pharmacology, 19*(8), 821–828.

Beck, S. J., Hanson, C. A., Puffenberger, S. S., Benninger, K. L., & Benninger, W. B. (2010). A controlled trial of working memory training for children and adolescents with ADHD. *Journal of Clinical Child & Adolescent Psychology, 39*(6), 825–836.

Becker, S. (2005). A computational principle for hippocampal learning and neurogenesis. *Hippocampus, 15*(6), 722–738.

Bee, M. A. (2001). Habituation and sensitization of aggression in bullfrogs (*Rana catesbeiana*): testing the dual-process theory of habituation. *Journal of Comparative Psychology, 115,* 307–316.

Beglinger, L. J., Gaydos, B. L., Kareken, D. A., Tangphao-Daniels, O., Siemers, E. R., & Mohs, R. C. (2004).

Neuropsychological test performance in healthy volunteers before and after donepezil administration. *Journal of Psychopharmacology, 18*, 102–108.

Bekerian, D., & Baddeley, A. (1980). Saturation advertising and the repetition effect. *Journal of Verbal Learning and Verbal Behavior, 19*(1), 17–25.

Belichenko, P. V., Masliah, E., Kleschevnikov, A. M., Villar, A., Epstein, C. J., Salehi, A., et al. (2004). Synaptic structural abnormalities in the Ts65Dn mouse model of Down Syndrome. *Journal of Comparative Neurology, 480*(3), 281–298.

Bell, C. (1811). *An idea of a new anatomy of the brain.* London: Strahan and Preston.

Benabid, A. L. (2003). Deep brain stimulation for Parkinson's disease. *Current Opinion in Neurobiology, 13*, 696–706.

Benjamin, M., McKeachie, W., Lin, Y.-G., & Holinger, D. (1981). Test anxiety: deficits in information processing. *Journal of Educational Psychology, 73*, 816–824.

Bennett, D., Wilson, R., Schneider, J., Evans, D., Mendes de Leon, C., Arnold, S., et al. (2003). Education modifies the relation of AD pathology to level of cognitive function in older persons. *Neurology, 60*(12), 1909–1915.

Berger-Sweeney, J., Stearns, N. A., Frick, K. M., Beard, B., & Baxter, M. G. (2000). Cholinergic basal forebrain is critical for social transmission of food preferences. *Hippocampus, 10*(6), 729–738.

Bergvall, U. A., Rautio, P., Luotola, T., & Leimar, O. (2007). A test of simultaneous and successive negative contrast in fallow deer foraging behaviour. *Animal Behaviour, 74*, 395–402.

Berke, J. (2003). Learning and memory mechanisms involved in compulsive drug use and relapse. In J. Wang (Ed.), *Methods in molecular medicine, vol. 79: drugs of abuse: neurological reviews and protocols* (pp. 75–101). Totowa, NJ: Humana Press.

Bernard, F. A., Bullmore, E. T., Graham, K. S., Thompson, S. A., Hodges, J. R., & Fletcher, P. C. (2004). The hippocampal region is involved in successful recognition of both remote and recent famous faces. *Neuroimage, 22*, 1704–1714.

Berridge, K. C. (1996). Food reward: brain substrates of wanting and liking. *Neuroscience and Biobehavioral Reviews, 20*(1), 1–25.

Berridge, K. C. (2007). The debate over dopamine's role in reward: the case for incentive salience. *Psychopharmacology, 191*(3), 391–431.

Berridge, K. C., & Robinson, T. (1998). What is the role of dopamine in reward: hedonic impact, reward learning, or incentive salience? *Brain Research Reviews, 28*, 309–369.

Berry, S. D., & Thompson, R. F. (1978). Neuronal plasticity in the limbic system during classical conditioning of the rabbit nictitating membrane response. I. The hippocampus. *Brain Research, 145*, 323–346.

Besson, A., Privat, A., Eschalier, A., & Fialip, J. (1999). Dopaminergic and opioidergic mediations of tricyclic antidepressants in the learned helplessness paradigm. *Pharmacology, Biochemistry and Behavior, 64*, 541–548.

Biederman, I., & Shiffrar, M. (1987). Sexing day-old chicks: a case study and expert systems analysis of a difficult perceptual learning task. *Journal of Experimental Psychology: Learning, Memory, and Cognition, 13*, 640–645.

Bimonte, H., Hyde, L., Hoplight, B., & Denenberg, V. (2000). In two species, females exhibit superior working memory and inferior reference memory on the water radial-arm maze. *Physiology and Behavior, 70*(3–4), 311–317.

Birren, J. (1964). *The psychology of aging.* Englewood Cliffs, NJ: Prentice Hall.

Blennow, K., de Leon, M. J., & Zetterberg, H. (2006). Alzheimer's disease. *Lancet, 368*(9533), 387–403.

Bliss, T. V., & Gardner-Medwin, A. (1973). Long-lasting potentiation of synaptic transmission in the dentate area of the unanaesthetized rabbit following stimulation of the perforant path. *Journal of Physiology (London), 232*, 357–371.

Bliss, T. V., & Lømo, T. (1973). Long-lasting potentiation of synaptic transmission in the dentate area of the anaesthetized rabbit following stimulation of the perforant path. *Journal of Physiology, 232*, 331–356.

Blough, D. S. (1975). Steady-state data and a quantitative model of operant generalization and discrimination. *Journal of Experimental Psychology: Animal Behavior Processes, 104*, 3–21.

Bonanno, G. A. (2004). Loss, trauma, and human resilience: have we underestimated the human capacity to thrive after extremely aversive events? *American Psychologist, 59*(1), 20–28.

Bonanno, G. A. (2005). Resilience in the face of potential trauma. *Current Directions in Psychological Science, 14*(3), 135–138.

Bonanno, G. A., Galea, S., Bucciarelli, A., & Vlahov, D. (2006). Psychological resilience after disaster: New York City in the aftermath of the September 11th terrorist attack. *Current Directions in Psychological Science, 17*(3), 181–186.

Bonardi, C., Rey, V., Richmond, M., & Hall, G. (1993). Acquired equivalence of cues in pigeon autoshaping: effects of training with common consequences and common antecedents. *Animal Learning and Behavior, 21*(4), 369–376.

Bond, A. B., & Kamil, A. C. (1999). Searching image in blue jays: facilitation and interference in sequential priming. *Animal Learning and Behavior, 27*, 461–471.

Bornstein, M., & Lamb, M. (1992). *Development in infancy* (3rd ed.). New York: McGraw-Hill.

Borovsky, D., & Rovee-Collier, C. (1990). Contextual constraints on memory retrieval at six months. *Child Development, 61*, 1569–1583.

Borszcz, G., Cranney, J., & Leaton, R. (1989). Influence of long-term sensitization of the acoustic startle response in rats: central gray lesions, preexposure, and extinction. *Journal of Experimental Psychology: Animal Behavior Processes, 15*, 54–64.

Bourgeois, J.-P. (2001). Synaptogenesis in the neocortex of the newborn: the ultimate frontier for individuation? In C. Nelson & M. Luciana (Eds.), *Handbook of developmental cognitive neuroscience.* Cambridge, MA: MIT Press.

Bourtchuladze, R., Frenguelli, B., Blendy, J., Cioffi, D., Schutz, G., & Silva, A. J. (1994). Deficient long-term memory in mice with a targeted mutation of the CAMP-responsive element-binding protein. *Cell, 79*, 59–68.

Bouton, M. E. (2000). A learning theory perspective on lapse, relapse, and the maintenance of behavioral change. *Health Psychology, 19*(1), 57–63.

Bouton, M. E., & Peck, C. A. (1989). Context effects on conditioning, extinction and reinstatement in an appetitive conditioning paradigm. *Animal Learning and Behavior, 17*, 188–198.

Bower, G. H. (1961). Application of a model to paired-associate learning. *Psychometrika, 26*, 255–280.

Bower, G. H., & Trabasso, T. R. (1964). Concept identification. In R. C. Atkinson (Ed.), *Studies in mathematical psychology* (pp. 32–93). Stanford, CA: Stanford University Press.

Bower, G., & Trabasso, T. (1968). *Attention in learning: theory and research.* New York: Wiley.

Bowles, R. P., & Salthouse, T. A. (2003). Assessing the age-related effects of proactive interference on working memory tasks using the Rasch model. *Psychology and Aging, 18*(3), 608–615.

Braak, H., & Braak, E. (1997). Frequency of stages of Alzheimer-related lesions in different age categories. *Neurobiology of Aging, 18*, 351–357.

Bradbury, J. W., & Vehrencamp, S. L. (1998). *Principles of animal communication.* Sunderland, MA: Sinauer.

Brady, F. (2008). The contextual interference effect and sport skills. *Perceptual and Motor Skills, 106*, 461–472.

Brainard, M. S., & Doupe, A. J. (2000). Auditory feedback in learning and maintenance of vocal behavior. *Nature Reviews Neuroscience, 1*, 31–40.

Brambilla, P., Hardan, A., di Nemi, S. U., Perez, J., Soares, J. C., & Barale, F. (2003). Brain anatomy and development in autism: review of structural MRI studies. *Brain Research Bulletin, 61*(6), 557–569.

Brand, M., & Markowitsch, H. (2004). Amnesia: neuroanatomic and clinical issues. In T. Feinberg & M. Farah (Eds.), *Behavioral neurology and neuropsychology* (2nd ed., pp. 431–443). New York: McGraw-Hill.

Bransford, J., & Johnson, M. (1972). Contextual prerequisites for understanding: some investigations of comprehension and recall. *Journal of Verbal Learning and Verbal Behavior, 11*, 717–727.

Brass, M., Derrfuss, J., Matthes-von Cramon, G., & von Cramon, D. Y. (2003). Imitative response tendencies in patients with frontal brain lesions. *Neuropsychology, 17*(2), 265–271.

Brauer, L., & de Wit, H. (1996). Subjective responses to D-amphetamine alone and after pimozide pretreatment in normal, healthy volunteers. *Biological Psychiatry, 39*, 26–32.

Brauer, L., & de Wit, H. (1997). High dose pimozide does not block amphetamine-induced euphoria in normal volunteers. *Pharmacology, Biochemistry and Behavior, 56*, 265–272.

Breazeal, C., & Scassellati, B. (2002). Robots that imitate humans. *Trends in Cognitive Sciences, 6*(11), 481–487.

Brehmer, Y., Li, S. C., Muller, V., von Oertzen, T., & Lindenberger, U. (2007). Memory plasticity across the life span: uncovering children's latent potential. *Developmental Psychology, 43*, 465–478.

Breiter, H., Aharon, I., Kahneman, D., Dale, A., & Shizgal, P. (2001). Functional imaging of neural responses to expectancy and experience of monetary gains and losses. *Neuron, 30*, 619–639.

Breland, K., & Breland, M. (1951). A field of applied animal psychology. *American Psychologist, 6*, 202–204.

Brembs, B. (2003). Operant reward learning in *Aplysia*. *Current Directions in Psychological Science, 12*(6), 218–221.

Brewer, J., Zhao, Z., Desmond, J., Glover, G., & Gabrieli, J. (1998). Making memories: brain activity that predicts whether visual experiences will be remembered or forgotten. *Science, 281*, 1185–1187.

Bridgett, D., & Cuevas, J. (2000). Effects of listening to Mozart and Bach on the performance of a mathematical test. *Perceptual and Motor Skills, 90*, 1171–1175.

Brooks, L. (1968). Spatial and verbal components of the act of recall. *Canadian Journal of Psychology, 22*, 349–368.

Brown, C., & Laland, K. N. (2002). Social learning of a novel avoidance task in the guppy: conformity and social release. *Animal Behaviour, 64*, 41–47.

Brown, G., & Stroup, K. (1988). Learned helplessness in the cockroach (*Periplaneta Americana*). *Behavioral and Neural Biology, 50*, 246–250.

Brown, J. (1969). Factors affecting self-punitive locomotive behaviors. In B. Campbell & R. Church (Eds.), *Punishment and aversive behavior* (pp. 467–514). New York: Appleton-Century-Crofts.

Brown, J. W. (Ed.). (1988). *Agnosia and apraxia: selected papers of Liepmann, Lange, and Pötzl.* Hillsdale, NJ: Lawrence Erlbaum.

Brown, R., & Kulik, J. (1982 [1977]). Flashbulb memories. *Cognition, 5*, 73–99.

Brugge, K., Nichols, S., Salmon, D., Hill, L., Delis, D., Aaron, L., et al. (1994). Cognitive impairments in adults with Down's syndrome: similarities to early cognitive changes in Alzheimer's disease. *Neurology, 44*(2), 232–238.

Brunelli, M., Castellucci, V., & Kandel, E. R. (1976). Synaptic facilitation and behavioral sensitization in *Aplysia*: possible role of serotonin and cyclic AMP. *Science, 194*, 1178–1181.

Bryan, R., Wells, S., Miller, T., Elster, A., Jungreis, C., Poirier, V., et al. (1997). Infarctlike lesions in the brain: prevalence and anatomic characteristics at MR imaging of the elderly—data from the Cardiovascular Health Study. *Radiology, 202*, 47–54.

Buccino, G., Binkofski, F., & Riggio, L. (2004). The mirror neuron system and action recognition. *Brain and Language, 89*(2), 370–376.

Buchanan, T., & Lovallo, W. (2001). Enhanced memory for emotional material following stress-level cortisol treatment in humans. *Psychoneuroendocrinology, 26*, 307–317.

Buckner, R. L., Raichle, M. E., Miezin, F. M., & Petersen, S. E. (1996). Functional anatomic studies of memory retrieval for auditory words and visual pictures. *Journal of Neuroscience, 16*, 6219–6235.

Bugnyar, T., & Kotrschal, K. (2002). Observational learning and the raiding of food caches in ravens, *Corvus corax*: Is it "tactical" deception? *Animal Behaviour, 64*, 185–195.

Bunsey, M., & Eichenbaum, H. (1995). Selective damage to the hippocampal region blocks long-term retention of a natural and nonspatial stimulus-stimulus association. *Hippocampus, 5*(6), 546–556.

Burd, G., & Nottebohm, F. (1985). Ultrastructural characterization of synaptic terminals formed on newly generated neurons in a song control nucleus of the adult canary forebrain. *Journal of Comparative Neurology, 240*, 143–152.

Burgdorf, J., & Panskepp, J. (2001). Tickling induces reward in adolescent rats. *Physiology and Behavior, 72*, 167–173.

Bushman, B. J., & Bonacci, A. M. (2002). Violence and sex impair memory for television ads. *Journal of Applied Psychology, 87*, 557–564.

Butki, B. D., & Hoffman, S. J. (2003). Effects of reducing frequency of intrinsic knowledge of results on the learning of a motor skill. *Perceptual and Motor Skills, 97*, 569–580.

Butler, A. C., & Roediger, H. L. (2007). Testing improves long-term retention in a simulated classroom setting. *European Journal of Cognitive Psychology, 19*(4/5), 514–527.

Butters, N., Wolfe, J., Martone, M., Granholm, E., & Cermak, L. (1985). Memory disorders associated with Huntington's disease: verbal recall, verbal recognition, and procedural memory. *Neuropsychologia, 23*, 729–743.

Buzsáki, G. (1989). Two-stage model of memory trace formation: a role for "noisy" brain states. *Neuroscience, 31*, 551–557.

Buzsáki, G. (2002). Theta oscillations in the hippocampus. *Neuron, 33*, 324–340.

Buzsáki, G., & Gage, F. (1989). Absence of long-term potentiation in the subcortically deafferented dentate gyrus. *Brain Research, 484*, 94–101.

Byrne, R. W. (1994). The evolution of intelligence. In P. Slater & T. R. Halliday (Eds.), *Behavior and evolution* (pp. 223–264). London: Cambridge University Press.

Cabeza, R., & Nyberg, L. (2000). Imaging cognition II: an empirical review of 275 PET and fMRI studies. *Journal of Cognitive Neurology, 12*, 1–47.

Cabeza, R., Rao, S., Wagner, A., Mayer, A., & Schacter, D. (2001). Can medial temporal lobe regions distinguish true from false? An event-related functional MRI study of veridical and illusory recognition memory. *Proceedings of the National Academy of Sciences USA, 98*(8), 4805–4810.

Cahill, L. R., & Alkire, M. (2003). Epinephrine enhancement of human memory consolidation: interaction with arousal at encoding. *Neurobiology of Learning and Memory, 79*, 194–198.

Cahill, L. R., Babinsky, R., Markowitsch, H., & McGaugh, J. (1995). The amygdala and emotional memory. *Nature, 377*, 295–296.

Cahill, L. R., Haier, R., Fallon, J., Alkire, M., Tang, C., Keator, D., et al. (1996). Amygdala activity at encoding correlated with long-term, free recall of emotional information. *Proceedings of the National Academy of Sciences USA, 93*(15), 8016–8021.

Cahill, L. R., Haier, R., White, N., Fallon, J., Kilpatrick, L., Lawrence, C., et al. (2001). Sex-related difference in amygdala activity during emotionally influenced memory storage. *Neurobiology of Learning and Memory, 75*, 1–9.

Cahill, L. R., & McGaugh, J. (1995). A novel demonstration of enhanced memory associated with emotional arousal. *Consciousness and Cognition, 4*(4), 410–421.

Cahill, L. R., Prins, B., Weber, M., & McGaugh, J. (1994). Beta-adrenergic activation and memory for emotional events. *Nature, 371*(6499), 702–704.

Cahill, L. R., Uncapher, M., Kilpatrick, L., Alkire, M. T., & Turner, J. (2004). Sex-related hemispheric lateralization of amygdala function in emotionally-influenced memory: an FMRI investigation. *Learning & Memory, 11*, 261–266.

Cahill, L. R., Weinberger, N., Roozendaal, B., & McGaugh, J. (1999). Is the amygdala a locus of "conditioned fear"? Some questions and caveats. *Neurons, 23*, 227–228.

Callicott, J. H., Egan, M. F., Mattay, V. S., Bertolini, A., Bone, A. D., Verchinski, B., & Weinbergers, D. R. (2003). Abnormal fMRI response of the dorsolateral prefrontal cortex in cognitively intact siblings of patients with schizophrenia. *American Journal of Psychiatry 160*, 709–719.

Canli, T., Desmond, J. E., Zhao, Z., & Gabrieli, J. D. E. (2002). Sex differences in the neural basis of emotional memories. *Proceedings of the National Academy of Science USA, 99*, 10789–10794.

Canli, T., Zhao, Z., Brewer, J., Gabrieli, J., & Cahill, L. (2000). Event-related activation in the human amygdala associates with later memory for individual emotional experience. *Journal of Neuroscience, 20,* RC99.

Cannon, W. B. (1927). The James-Lange theory of emotion: a critical examination and an alternative theory. *American Journal of Psychology, 39,* 10–124.

Capaldi, E., Robinson, G., & Fahrback, S. (1999). Neuroethology of spatial learning: the birds and the bees. *Annual Review of Psychology, 50,* 651–682.

Capone, N. C., & McGregor, K. K. (2004). Gesture development: a review for clinical and research practices. *Journal of Speech, Language, and Hearing Research, 47,* 173–186.

Carew, T. J., Hawkins, R. D., & Kandel, E. R. (1983). Differential classical conditioning of a defensive gill-withdrawal reflex in *Aplysia californica. Science, 219,* 397–400.

Carroll, K. M. (1999). Behavioral and cognitive behavioral treatments. In B. McCrady & E. S. Epstein (Eds.), *Addictions: a comprehensive guidebook* (pp. 250–267). New York: Oxford University Press.

Caselli, R. (2003). Tactile agnosia and disorders of tactile perception. In T. Feinberg & M. Farah (Eds.), *Behavioral neurology and neuropsychology* (2nd ed., pp. 271–283). New York: McGraw-Hill.

Cassel, J., Cassel, S., Galani, R., Kelche, C., Will, B., & Jarrard, L. (1998). Fimbria-fornix vs. selective hippocampal lesions in rats: effects on locomotor activity and spatial learning and memory. *Neurobiology of Learning and Memory, 69*(1), 22–45.

Castellanos, F. X., & Tannock, R. (2002). Neuroscience of attention-deficit/hyperactivity disorder: the search for endophenotypes. *Nature Reviews Neuroscience, 3,* 617–628.

Castellucci, V. F., & Kandel, E. R. (1974). A quantal analysis of the synaptic depression underlying habituation of the gill-withdrawal reflex in *Aplysia. Proceedings of the National Academy of Sciences USA, 71,* 5004–5008.

Castellucci, V. F., & Kandel, E. R. (1976). Presynaptic facilitation as a mechanism for behavioral sensitization in *Aplysia. Science, 194,* 1176–1178.

Centerwall, B. S. (1992). Television and violence: the scale of the problem and where to go from here. *Journal of the American Medical Association, 22,* 3059–3063.

Chabris, C. (1999). Prelude or requiem for the Mozart effect? *Nature, 400,* 826–827.

Chakrabarti, L., Best, T. K., Cramer, N. P., Carney, R. S., Isaac, J. T., Galdzicki, Z., et al. (2010). Olig1 and Olig2 triplication causes developmental brain defects in Down syndrome. *Nature Neuroscience, 13*(8), 927–934.

Charles, S., Mather, M., & Carstensen, L. (2003). Aging and emotional memory: the forgettable nature of negative images for older adults. *Journal of Experimental Psychology: General, 132*(2), 310–324.

Charness, N., Reingold, E. M., Pomplun, M., & Stampe, D. M. (2001). The perceptual aspect of skilled performance in chess: evidence from eye movements. *Memory and Cognition, 29,* 1146–1152.

Chen, L., Bao, S., Lockard, J. M., Kim, J. K., & Thompson, R. F. (1996). Impaired classical eyeblink conditioning in cerebellar-lesioned and Purkinje cell degeneration (pcd) mutant mice. *Journal of Neuroscience, 16,* 2829–2838.

Chen, L. Y., Rex, C. S., Casale, M. S., Gall, C. M., & Lynch, G. (2007). Changes in synaptic morphology accompany actin signaling during LTP. *Journal of Neuroscience, 27,* 5363–5372.

Chi, M. (1978). Knowledge structures and memory development. In R. Siegler (Ed.), *Children's thinking: What develops?* Hillsdale, NJ: Erlbaum.

Chomsky, N. (1959). A review of B. F. Skinner's verbal behavior. *Language, 35*(1), 26–58.

Clark, D., & Teasdale, J. (1982). Diurnal variation in clinical depression and accessibility of positive and negative experiences. *Journal of Abnormal Psychology, 91,* 87–95.

Clark, R. E., Broadbent, N. J., Zola, S. M., & Squire, L. R. (2002). Anterograde amnesia and temporally graded retrograde amnesia for a nonspatial memory task after lesions of hippocampus and subiculum. *Journal of Neuroscience, 22*(11), 4663–4669.

Clarke, G. (2002). Learning to understand speech with the cochlear implant. In M. Fahle & T. Poggio (Eds.), *Perceptual learning* (pp. 147–160). Cambridge, MA: MIT Press.

Clayton, N., & Dickinson, A. (1999). Scrub jays (*Aphelocoma coerulescens*) remember the relative time of caching as well as the location and content of their caches. *Journal of Comparative Psychology, 113,* 403–417.

Clayton, N., Yu, K., & Dickinson, A. (2001). Scrub jays (*Aphelocoma coerulescens*) form integrated memories of the multiple features of caching episodes. *Journal of Experimental Psychology: Animal Behavior Processes, 27,* 17–29.

Cohen, N. J., Poldrack, R. A., & Eichenbaum, H. (1997). Memory for items and memory for relations in the procedural/declarative memory framework. *Memory, 5,* 131–178.

Cohen, N. J., & Squire, L. R. (1980). Preserved learning and retention of pattern-analyzing skill in amnesia: dissociation of knowing how and knowing that. *Science, 210,* 207–210.

Cohen, T. E., Kaplan, S. W., Kandel, E. R., & Hawkins, R. D. (1997). A simplified preparation for relating cellular events to behavior: mechanisms contributing to habituation, dishabituation, and sensitization of the *Aplysia* gill-withdrawal reflex. *Journal of Neuroscience, 17,* 2886–2899.

Cohen-Bendahan, C., van de Beck, C., & Berenbaum, S. (2005). Prenatal sex hormone effects on child and adult sex-typed behavior. *Neuroscience and Biobehavioral Reviews, 29*(2), 353–384.

Cohen-Kettenis, P., van Goozen, S., Doorn, C., & Gooren, L. (1998). Cognitive ability and cerebral lateralisation in transsexuals. *Psychoneuroendocrinology, 23*(6), 631–641.

Collie, A., & Maruff, P. (2000). The neuropsychology of preclinical Alzheimer's disease and mild cognitive impairment. *Neuroscience and Biobehavioral Reviews, 24*, 365–374.

Collinson, S. L., Meyyappan, A., & Rosenfeld, J. V. (2009). Injury and recovery: severe amnestic syndrome following traumatic brain injury. *Brain Injury, 23*(1), 71–77.

Conder, C., & Finnstrom, K. (December 30, 2009). Are dogs the key to bomb detection at airports? *cnn.com*.

Condon, C. D., & Weinberger, N. M. (1991). Habituation produces frequency-specific plasticity of receptive fields in the auditory cortex. *Behavioral Neuroscience, 105*(3), 416–430.

Conn, P., Battaglia, G., Marino, M., & Nicoletti, F. (2005). Metabotropic glutamate receptors in the basal ganglia motor circuit. *Nature Reviews Neuroscience, 6*, 787–798.

Convit, A., de Asis, J., de Leon, M., Tarshish, C., De Santi, S., & Rusinek, H. (2000). Atrophy of the medial occipitotemporal, inferior, and middle temporal gyri in nondemented elderly predict decline to Alzheimer's Disease. *Neurobiology of Aging, 21*, 19–26.

Conway, M. A. (2009). Episodic memories. *Neuropsychologia, 47*(11), 2305–2313.

Cooper, B. G., & Mizumori, S. J. (2001). Temporary inactivation of the retrosplenial cortex causes a transient reorganization of spatial coding in the hippocampus. *Journal of Neuroscience, 21*, 3986–4001.

Corkin, S. (2002). What's new with the amnesic patient H.M.? *Nature Reviews Neuroscience, 3*, 153–160.

Corkin, S., Amaral, D., Gonzalez, A., Johnson, K., & Hyman, B. (1997). H. M.'s medial temporal lobe lesion: findings from magnetic resonance imaging. *Journal of Neuroscience, 17*, 3964–3979.

Cornstock, G. (1980). New emphases in research on the effects of television and film violence. In E. L. Palmer & A. Dorr (Eds.), *Children and the faces of television: teaching, violence, selling* (pp. 129–148). New York: Academic Press.

Corter, J. E., & Gluck, M. A. (1992). Explaining basic categories: feature predictability and information. *Psychological Bulletin, 111*(2), 291–303.

Coutureau, E., Killcross, A. S., Good, M., Marshall, V. J., Ward-Robinson, J., & Honey, R. C. (2002). Acquired equivalence and distinctiveness of cues: II. neural manipulations and their implications. *Journal of Experimental Psychology: Animal Behavior Processes, 28*(4), 388–396.

Craik, F., & Lockhart, R. (1972). Levels of processing: a framework for memory research. *Journal of Verbal Learning and Verbal Behavior, 11*, 671–684.

Craik, F., & Tulving, E. (1975). Depth of processing and the retention of words in episodic memory. *Journal of Experimental Psychology: General, 104*(3), 268–294.

Crick, N. R., & Dodge, K. A. (1994). A review and reformulation of social information processing mechanisms in children's social adjustment. *Psychological Bulletin, 115*, 74–101.

Crnic, L., & Pennington, B. (2000). Down syndrome: neuropsychology and animal models. In C. Rovee-Collier, L. Lipsitt & H. Hayne (Eds.), *Progress in infancy research* (Vol. I, pp. 69–111). Mahwah, NJ: Erlbaum.

Crystal, J. D. (2010). Episodic-like memory in animals. *Behavioural Brain Research, 215*(2), 235–243.

Cummings, D. M., Milnerwood, A. J., Dallerac, G. M., Vatsavayai, S. C., Hirst, M. C., & Murphy, K. P. S. J. (2007). Abnormal cortical synaptic plasticity in a mouse model of Huntington's disease. *Brain Research Bulletin, 72*, 103–107.

Curio, E., Ernst, U., & Vieth, W. (1978). The adaptive significance of avian mobbing. *Zeitschrift für Tierpsychologie, 48*, 184–202.

Curtis, C. E., & D'Esposito, M. (2003). Persistent activity in the prefrontal cortex during working memory. *Trends in Cognitive Sciences, 7*, 415–423.

Curtis, C. E., & D'Esposito, M. (2006). Working memory. In R. Cabezza & A. Kingstone (Eds.), *Handbook of functional neuroimaging of cognition* (2nd ed.). Cambridge, MA: MIT Press.

Curtiss, S. (1977). *Genie: a psycholinguistic study of a modern-day "wild child."* New York: Academic Press.

Cusato, B., & Domjan, M. (1998). Special efficacy of sexual conditioned stimuli that include species typical cues: test with a CS pre-exposure design. *Learning and Motivation, 29*, 152–167.

Custance, D. M., Whiten, A., & Bard, K. A. (1995). Can young chimpanzees imitate arbitrary actions? Hayes and Hayes revisited. *Behaviour, 132*, 839–858.

Cutler, N., Hesten, L., Davies, P., Haxby, J., & Schapiro, M. (1985). Alzheimer's disease and Down's syndrome: new insights. *Annals of Internal Medicine, 103*, 566–578.

Czaja, S., Hammond, K., Blascovich, J., & Swede, H. (1993). Age-related differences in learning to use a text editing system. *Behavior and Information Technology, 8*, 309–319.

D'Esposito, M. (2007). From cognitive to neural models of working memory. *Philosophical Transactions of the Royal Society London: B, 362*(1481), 761–762.

D'Esposito, M., Detre, J. A., Alsop, D. C., Shin, R. K., Atlas, S., & Grossman, M. (1995). The neural basis of the central executive system of working memory. *Nature 378*, 279–281.

Damasio, A. R. (1994). *Descartes' error: emotion, reason, and the human brain.* New York: Putman.

Damasio, A. R. (1996). The somatic marker hypothesis and the possible functions of the prefrontal cortex. *Philosophical Transactions of the Royal Society of London: B, 351*, 1413–1420.

Damasio, A. R. (1999). *The feeling of what happens: body and emotion in the making of consciousness.* New York: Harcourt Brace.

Damasio, A. R., Graff-Radford, N., Eslinger, P., Damasio, H., & Kassell, N. (1985). Amnesia following basal forebrain lesions. *Archives of Neurology, 42,* 263–271.

Daneman, M., & Carpenter, P. A. (1980). Individual differences in working memory and reading. *Journal of Verbal Learning and Verbal Behavior, 12,* 450–466.

Darwin, C. (1845). *Journal of researches into the natural history and geology of the countries visited during the voyage of H.M.S. Beagle round the world: under the command of Capt. Fitz Roy.* London: John Murray.

Darwin, C. (1859). *On the origin of species by means of natural selection: or the preservation of favoured races in the struggle for life.* London: John Murray.

Darwin, C. (1872). *The expression of emotions in man and animals.* Chicago: Chicago University Press (1965).

Darwin, C. (1883). *The descent of man and selection in relation to sex.* New York: Appleton-Century-Crofts.

Darwin, E. (1794). *Zoönomia, vol. I; or, the laws of organic life.* London.

Daselaar, S. M., Fleck, M. S., Dobbins, I. G., Madden, D. J., & Cabeza, R. (2006). Effects of healthy aging on hippocampal and rhinal memory functions: an event-related fMRI study. *Cerebral Cortex, 16*(12), 1771–1782.

Dash, P. K., Hochner, B., & Kandel, E. R. (1990). Injection of cAMP-responsive element into the nucleus of *Aplysia* sensory neuron blocks long-term facilitation. *Nature, 345,* 718–721.

Daum, I., Schugens, M. M., Ackermann, H., Lutzenberger, W., Dichgans, J., & Birbaumer, N. (1993). *Behavioral Neuroscience, 107*(5), 748–756.

Davachi, L., Mitchell, J., & Wagner, A. (2003). Multiple routes to memory: distinct medial temporal lobe processes build item and source memories. *Proceedings of the National Academy of Sciences USA, 100*(4), 2157–2162.

Davidson, R., Kabat-Zinn, J., Schumacher, J., Rosenkranz, M., Muller, D., Santorelli, S., et al. (2003). Alterations in brain and immune function produced by mindfulness meditation. *Psychosomatic Medicine, 65,* 564–570.

Daviglus, M. L., Bell, C. C., Berrettini, W., Bowen, P. E., Connolly, E. S., Jr., Cox, N. J., et al. (2010). National Institutes of Health State-of-the-Science Conference statement: preventing Alzheimer disease and cognitive decline. *Annals of Internal Medicine, 153*(3), 176–181.

Davila-Ross, M., Owren, M. J., & Zimmerman, E. (2009). Reconstructing the evolution of laughter in great apes and humans. *Current Biology, 19,* 1106–1111.

Davis, H. (1989). Theoretical note on the moral development of rats (*Rattus norvegicus*). *Journal of Comparative Psychology, 103,* 88–90.

Davis, M. (1972). Differential retention of sensitization and habituation of the startle response in the rat. *Journal of Comparative and Physiological Psychology, 78,* 260–267.

Davis, M. (1980). Habituation and sensitization of a startle-like response elicited by electrical stimulation at different points in the acoustic startle circuit. In E. Grastyan & P. Molnar (Eds.), *Advances in physiological science: Vol. 16. Sensory functions* (pp. 67–78). Elmsford, NY: Pergamon Press.

Davis, M. (1989). Sensitization of the acoustic startle reflex by footshock. *Behavioral Neuroscience, 103,* 495–503.

Davisson, M., Schmidt, C., Reeves, R., Irving, N., Akeson, E., Harris, B., et al. (1993). Segmental trisomy as a model for Down syndrome. In C. Epstein (Ed.), *Phenotypic mapping of Down syndrome and other aneuploid conditions* (pp. 117–133). New York: Wiley-Liss.

Dawson, B. V., & Foss, B. M. (1965). Observational learning in budgerigars. *Animal Behaviour, 13,* 470–474.

de Leon, M., George, A., Stylopoulos, L., Smith, G., & Miller, D. (1989). Early marker for Alzheimer's disease: the atrophic hippocampus. *The Lancet, 2*(8664), 672–673.

de Leon, M., Golomb, J., George, A., Convit, A., Tarshish, C., McRae, T., et al. (1993). The radiologic prediction of Alzheimer disease: the atrophic hippocampal formation. *American Journal of Neuroradiology, 14,* 897–906.

de Quervain, D., Henke, K., Aerni, A., Coluccia, D., Wollmer, M., Hock, C., et al. (2003). A functional genetic variation of the 5-HT2a receptor affects human memory. *Nature Neuroscience, 6*(11), 1141–1142.

de Quervain, D., Roozendaal, B., & McGaugh, J. (1998). Stress and glucocorticoids impair retrieval of long-term spatial memory. *Nature, 394,* 787–790.

de Quervain, D., Roozendaal, B., Nitsch, R., McGaugh, J., & Hock, C. (2000). Acute cortisone administration impairs retrieval of long-term declarative memory in humans. *Nature Neuroscience, 3,* 313–314.

de Waal, F. (1996). *Good natured: the origins of right and wrong in humans and other animals.* Cambridge, MA: Harvard University Press.

DeCasper, A., Lecanuet, J.-P., Busnel, M.-C., Granier-Deferre, C., & Maugeais, R. (1994). Fetal reactions to recurrent maternal speech. *Infant Behavior and Development, 17*(2), 159–164.

DeCasper, A., & Spence, M. (1986). Prenatal maternal speech influences newborns' perception of speech sounds. *Infant Behavior and Development, 9*(2), 133–150.

Deese, J. (1959). On the prediction of occurrence of particular verbal intrusions in immediate recall. *Journal of Experimental Psychology, 58,* 17–22.

Delis, D. C., Squire, L. R., Bihrle, A., & Massman, P. (1992). Componential analysis of problem-solving ability: performance of patients with frontal lobe damage and amnesic patients with frontal lobe damage and amnesic patients on a new sorting test. *Neuropsychologia, 30*(8), 683–697.

Della Marca, G., Broccolini, A., Vollono, C., Dittoni, S., Frisullo, G., Pilato, F., et al. (2010). The stolen memory: a case of transient global amnesia. *Biological Psychiatry, 67*(6), e31–e32.

Delong, M. R., & Wichmann, T. (2007). Circuits and circuit disorders of the basal ganglia. *Archives of Neurology, 64*, 20–24.

DeLuca, J. (2000). A cognitive neuroscience perspective on confabulation. *Neuro-Psychoanalysis, 2*, 119–132.

DeLuca, J., & Diamond, B. (1995). Aneurysm of the anterior communicating artery: a review of neuroanatomical and neurophysiological sequelae. *Journal of Clinical and Experimental Neuropsychology, 17*(1), 100–121.

DeMeyer, M. K., Alpern, G. D., Barton, S., DeMyer, W. E., Churchill, D. W., Hingtgen, J. N., et al. (1972). Imitation in autistic, early schizophrenic, and non-psychotic subnormal children. *Journal of Autism and Childhood Schizophrenia, 2*(3), 264–287.

Dennis, N. A., & Cabeza, R. (2011). Age-related dedifferentiation of learning systems: an fMRI study of implicit and explicit learning. *Neurobiology of Aging, 32*(12), 2318. e2317–2318.e2330.

Dennis, N. A., Hayes, S. M., Prince, S. E., Madden, D. J., Huettel, S. A., & Cabeza, R. (2008). Effects of aging on the neural correlates of successful item and source memory encoding. *Journal of Experimental Psychology: Learning, Memory and Cognition, 34*(4), 791–808.

Dere, E., Kart-Tecke, E., Huston, J. P., & De Souza Silva, M. A. (2006). The case for episodic memory in animals. *Neuroscience and Biobehavioral Reviews, 30*(8), 1206–1224.

Descartes, R. (1637). *Discours de la méthode pour bien conduire sa raison, et chercher la verité dans les sciences* [Discourse on the method of rightly conducting the reason in the search for truth in the sciences].

Descartes, R. (1662). *De homine.* Leyden (in Latin.)

Desmurget, M., Grafton, S. T., Vindras, P., Grea, H., & Turner, R. S. (2003). Basal ganglia network mediates the control of movement amplitude. *Experimental Brain Research, 153*, 197–209.

Devlin, J., Russell, R., Davis, M., Price, C., Moss, H., Fadili, M., & Tyler, L. (2002). Is there an anatomical basis for category-specificity? Semantic memory studies in PET and fMRI. *Neuropsychologia, 40*, 54–75.

Dewsbury, D. A. (1981). Effects of novelty on copulatory behavior: the Coolidge effect and related phenomena. *Psychological Bulletin, 89*, 464–482.

Dewsbury, D. A. (1990). Early interactions between animal psychologists and animal activists and the founding of the APA committee on precautions in animal experimentation. *American Psychologist, 45*, 315–327.

di Pellegrino, G., Fadiga, L., Fogassi, L., Gallese, V., & Rizzolatti, G. (1992). Understanding motor events: a neurophysiological study. *Experimental Brain Research, 91*(1), 176–180.

Dickinson, A. (1980). *Contemporary animal learning theory.* Cambridge, England: Cambridge University Press.

Dickinson, A., & Balleine, B. W. (2000). Causal cognition and goal-directed action. In C. Heyes & L. Huber (Eds.), *The evolution of cognition* (pp. 185–204). Cambridge, MA: MIT Press.

DiNardo, P., Guzy, L., & Bak, R. (1988). Anxiety response patterns and etiological factors in dog-fearful and non-fearful subjects. *Behaviour Research and Therapy, 26*, 245–252.

Dinse, H. R., & Merzenich, M. M. (2002). Adaptation of inputs in the somatosensory system. In M. Fahle & T. Poggio (Eds.), *Perceptual learning* (pp. 19–42). Cambridge, MA: MIT Press.

Dinse, H. R., Ragert, P., Pleger, B., Schwenkreis, P., & Tegenthoff, M. (2003). Pharmacological modulation of perceptual learning and associated cortical reorganization. *Science, 301*, 91–94.

Dinsmoor, J. A. (1954). Punishment. I. The avoidance hypothesis. *Psychological Review, 61*(1), 34–46.

Dobbins, I. G., Foley, H., Schacter, D. L., & Wagner, A. D. (2002). Executive control during episodic retrieval: multiple prefrontal processes subserve source memory. *Neuron, 35*, 989–996.

Dodge, K. A. (2011). Social information processing models of aggressive behavior. In M. Mikulncer & P. R. Shaver (Eds.), *Understanding and reducing aggression, violence, and their consequences* (pp. 165–186). Washington, DC: American Psychological Association.

Dolcos, F., LaBar, K. S., & Cabeza, R. (2004). Interaction between the amygdala and the medial temporal lobe memory system predicts better memory for emotional events. *Neuron, 42*, 855–863.

Domjan, M. (1977). Selective suppression of drinking during a limited period following aversive drug treatment in rats. *Journal of Experimental Psychology: Animal Behavior Processes, 8*, 204–210.

Domjan, M., Lyons, R., North, N. C., & Bruell, J. (1986). Sexual Pavlovian conditioned approach behavior in male Japanese quail (*Coturnix coturnix japonica*). *Journal of Comparative Psychology, 100*, 413–421.

Donnerstein, E., & Berkowitz, L. (1981). Victim reactions in aggressive erotic films as a factor in violence against women. *Journal of Personality and Social Psychology, 41*(4), 710–724.

Dougherty, D. M., & Lewis, P. (1991). Stimulus generalization, discrimination learning, and peak shift in horses. *Journal of the Experimental Analysis of Behavior, 56*, 97–104.

Down, J. (1866). Observations on ethnic classification of idiots. *Mental Science, 13*, 121–128.

Dowsey-Limousin, P., & Pollak, P. (2001). Deep brain stimulation in the treatment of Parkinson's disease: a review and update. *Clinical Neuroscience Research, 1*, 521–526.

Doyon, J., Bellec, P., Amsel, R., Penhune, V., Monchi, O., Carrier, J., et al. (2009). Contributions of the basal ganglia and functionally related brain structures to motor learning. *Behavioural Brain Research, 199,* 61–75.

Doyon, J., Penhune, V., & Ungerleider, L. G. (2003). Distinct contribution of the cortico-striatal and cortico-cerebellar systems to motor skill learning. *Neuropsychologia, 41,* 252–262.

Draganski, B., Gaser, C., Busch, V., Schuierer, G., Bogdahn, U., & May, A. (2004). Neuroplasticity: changes in grey matter induced by training. *Nature, 427,* 311–312.

Driemeyer, J., Boyke, J., Gaser, C., Buchel, C., & May, A. (2008). Changes in gray matter induced by learning—revisited. *PLOS One, 3,* e2669.

Drummey, A., & Newcombe, N. (2002). Developmental changes in source memory. *Developmental Science, 5*(4), 502–513.

Dudai, Y. (2004). The neurobiology of consolidations, or, How stable is the engram? *Annual Review of Psychology, 55,* 51–87.

Dudai, Y., Jan, Y. N., Byers, D., Quinn, W. G., & Benzer, S. (1976). Dunce, a mutant of *Drosophila* deficient in learning. *Proceedings of the National Academy of Science USA, 73*(5), 1684–1688.

Dumitriu, D., Hao, J., Hara, Y., Kaufmann, J., Janssen, W. G. M., Lou, W., et al. (2010). Selective changes in thin spine density and morphology in monkey prefrontal cortex correlate with aging-related cognitive impairment. *Journal of Neuroscience, 30*(22), 7507–7515.

Duncan, C. (1949). The retroactive effect of electroshock on learning. *Journal of Comparative and Physiological Psychology, 42,* 32–44.

Duncan, J., Emslie, H., Williams, P., Johnson, R., & Freer, C. (1996). Intelligence and the frontal lobe: the organization of goal-directed behavior. *Cognitive Psychology, 30,* 257–303.

Dunwiddie, T., & Lynch, G. (1978). Long-term potentiation and depression of synaptic responses in the rat hippocampus: localization and frequency dependency. *Journal of Physiology, 276,* 353–367.

Durston, S. (2010). Imaging genetics in ADHD. *NeuroImage, 53,* 832–838.

Durston, S., Hulshoff, E., Hilleke, E., Casey, B., Giedd, J., Buitelaar, J., et al. (2001). Anatomical MRI of the developing human brain: What have we learned? *Journal of the American Academy of Child and Adolescent Psychiatry, 40,* 1012–1020.

Dutton, D. G., & Aron, A. P. (1974). Some evidence for heightened sexual attraction under conditions of high anxiety. *Journal of Personality and Social Psychology, 30*(4), 510–517.

Dweck, C. (1975). The role of expectations and attributions in the alleviation of learned helplessness. *Journal of Personality and Social Psychology, 31,* 674–685.

Dymond, S., & Roche, B. (2009). A contemporary behavioral anaysis of anxiety and avoidance. *The Behavior Analyst, 32,* 7–28.

Eacott, M. J., & Easton, A. (2010). Episodic memory in animals: remembering which occasion. *Neuropsychologia, 48*(8), 2273–2280.

Ebbinghaus, H. (1964). *Memory: a contribution to experimental psychology* (H. Ruger & C. Bussenius, Trans.). New York: Dover. (Original work published 1885.)

Eddy, D. M. (1982a). Clinical policies and the quality of clinical practice. *New England Journal of Medicine, 307*(6), 343–347.

Eddy, D. M. (1982b). Probabilistic reasoning in clinical medicine: problems and opportunities. In D. Kahneman, P. Slovic, & A. Tversky (Eds.). *Judgement under uncertainty: heuristics and biases* (pp. 249–267). Cambridge, UK: Cambridge University Press.

Egan, M. F., Goldberg, T. E., Kolachana, B. S., Callicot, J. H., Mazzanti, C. M., Straub, R. E., et al. (2001). Effect of COMT Val 108/158 Met genotype on frontal lobe function and risk for schizophrenia. *Proceedings of the National Academy of Sciences USA, 98,* 6917–6922.

Egan, M. F., Kojima, M., Callicott, J. H., Goldberg, T. E., Kolachana, B. S., Bertolino, A., et al. (2003). The BDNF val66met polymorphism affects activity-dependent secretion of BDNF and human memory and hippocampal function. *Cell, 112,* 257–269.

Eich, E., Macaulay, D., & Ryan, L. (1994). Mood dependent memory for events of the personal past. *Journal of Experimental Psychology: General, 123,* 201–215.

Eichenbaum, H. (2000). A cortical-hippocampal system for declarative memory. *Nature Reviews Neuroscience, 1,* 41–50.

Eichenbaum, H., Yonelinas, A. P., & Ranganath, C. (2007). The medial temporal lobe and recognition memory. *Annual Review of Neuroscience, 30,* 123–152.

Eisenberg, N., & Lennon, R. (1983). Sex differences in empathy and related capacities. *Psychological Bulletin, 94,* 100–131.

Eisenstein, E. M., Eisenstein, D., & Bonheim, P. (1991). Initial habituation or sensitization of the GSR depends on magnitude of first response. *Physiology and Behavior, 49,* 211–215.

Ekman, P. (1992). Facial expressions of emotion: new findings, new questions. *Psychological Science, 3,* 34–38.

Ekman, P., & Friesen, W. (1971). Constants across cultures in the face and emotion. *Journal of Personality and Social Psychology, 17,* 124–129.

Ekman, P., & Friesen, W. (1984). *Unmasking the face.* Palo Alto, CA: Consulting Psychology Press.

Elbert, T., Pantev, C., Wienbruch, C., Rockstroh, B., & Taub, E. (1995). Increased cortical representation of the fingers of the left hand in string players. *Science, 270,* 305–307.

Emmelkamp, P., Krijn, M., Hulsbosch, A., de Vries, S., Schuemie, M., & van der Mast, C. (2002). Virtual reality treatment versus exposure *in vivo*: a comparative evaluation in acrophobia. *Behavior Research and Therapy, 40*(5), 509–516.

Engle, R., & Marshall, K. (1983). Do developmental changes in digit span result from acquisition strategies? *Journal of Experimental Child Psychology, 36,* 429–436.

Epp, J. R., Spritzer, M. D., & Galea, L. A. (2007). Hippocampus-dependent learning promotes survival of new neurons in the dentate gyrus at a specific time during cell maturation. *Neuroscience, 149*(2), 273–285.

Erickson, K. I., Boot, W. R., Basak, C., Neider, M. B., Prakash, R. S., Voss, M. W., et al. (2010). Striatal volume predicts level of video game skill acquisition. *Cerebral Cortex, 20,* 2522–2530.

Ericsson, K. A. (2003). Exceptional memorizers: made, not born. *Trends in Cognitive Sciences, 7*(6), 233–235.

Ericsson, K. A., Krampe, R., & Tesch-Romer, C. (1993). The role of deliberate practice in the acquisition of expert performance. *Psychological Review, 100,* 363–406.

Ericsson, K. A., & Lehman, A. (1996). Expert and exceptional performance: evidence of maximal adaptation to task constraints. *Annual Review of Psychology, 47,* 273–305.

Eriksson, P. (2003). Neurogenesis and its implications for regeneration in the adult brain. *Journal of Rehabilitation Medicine, 41*(Supplement*),* 17–19.

Eriksson, P., Perfilieva, E., Björk-Eriksson, T., Alborn, A., Nordberg, C., Peterson, D., et al. (1998). Neurogenesis in the adult human hippocampus. *Nature Medicine, 4,* 1313–1317.

Escorihuela, R., Fernandez-Teruel, A., Vallina, I., Baamonde, C., Lumbreras, M., Dierssen, M., et al. (1995). A behavioral assessment of Ts65Dn mice: a putative Down syndrome model. *Neuroscience Letters, 199*(2), 143–146.

Eslinger, P. J., & Damasio, A. R. (1985). Severe disturbance of higher cognition after bilateral frontal lobe ablation: patient EVR. *Neurology, 35*(12), 1731–1741.

Estes, W. K. (1950). Toward a statistical theory of learning. *Psychological Review, 57,* 94–107.

Estes, W. K., & Skinner, B. F. (1941). Some quantitative properties of anxiety. *Journal of Experimental Psychology, 29,* 390–400.

Evans, A. H., & Lees, A. J. (2004). Dopamine dysregulation syndrome in Parkinson's disease. *Current Opinion in Neurology, 17,* 393–398.

Everitt, B. J., Cardinal, R. N., Parkinson, J. A., & Robbins, T. W. (2003). Appetitive behavior: impact of amygdala-dependent mechanisms of emotional learning. *Annals of the New York Academy of Sciences, 985,* 233–250.

Exner, C., Koschack, J., & Irle, E. (2002). The differential role of premotor frontal cortex and basal ganglia in motor sequence learning: evidence from focal basal ganglia lesions. *Learning and Memory, 9,* 376–386.

Fanselow, M., & LeDoux, J. (1999). Why we think plasticity underlying Pavlovian fear conditioning occurs in the basolateral amygdala. *Neuron, 23,* 229–232.

Farah, M. (2003). Visual perception and visual imagery. In T. Feinberg & M. Farah (Eds.), *Behavioral neurology and neuropsychology* (2nd ed., pp. 227–232). New York: McGraw-Hill.

Farkas, M., Polgár, P., Kelemen, O., Réthelvi, J., Bitter, I., Myers, C. E., et al. (2008). Associative learning in deficit and non-deficit schizophrenia. *Neuroreport, 19*(1), 55–58.

Featherstone, R., & McDonald, R. (2004). Dorsal striatum and stimulus-response learning: lesions of the dorsolateral, but not dorsomedial, striatum impair acquisition of a simple discrimination task. *Behavioural Brain Research, 150,* 15–23.

Fendt, M., & Fanselow, M. (1999). The neuroanatomical and neurochemical basis of fear. *Neuroscience and Biobehavioral Reviews, 23,* 743–760.

Ferguson, C. J., & Kilburn, J. (2010). Much ado about nothing: the misestimation and overinterpretation of violent video game effects in eastern and western nations: comment on Anderson et al. (2010). *Psychological Bulletin, 136*(2), 174–178.

Fernandez, F., Morishita, W., Zuniga, E., Nguyen, J., Blank, M., Malenka, R. C., et al. (2007). Pharmacotherapy for cognitive impairment in a mouse model of Down syndrome. *Nature Neuroscience, 10*(4), 411–413.

Ferrari, M. (1999). Influence of expertise on the intentional transfer of motor skill. *Journal of Motor Behavior, 31,* 79–85.

Ferrari, P. F., Gallese, V., Rizzolatti, G., & Fogassi, L. (2003). Mirror neurons responding to the observation of ingestive and communicative mouth actions in the monkey ventral premotor cortex. *European Journal of Neuroscience, 17*(8), 1703–1714.

Finkel, D., Pedersen, N., & McGue, M. (1995). Genetic influences on memory performance in adulthood: comparison of Minnesota and Swedish twin data. *Psychology and Aging, 10*(3), 437–446.

Fiorentini, A., & Berardi, N. (1981). Learning in grating waveform discrimination: specificity for orientation and spatial frequency. *Vision Research, 21,* 1149–1158.

Fiorito, G., Agnisola, C., d'Addio, M., Valanzano, A., & Calamandrei, G. (1998). Scopolamine impairs memory recall in *Octopus vulgaris*. *Neuroscience Letters, 253,* 87–90.

Fisher, A. E. (1962). Effects of stimulus variation on sexual satiation in the male rat. *Journal of Comparative and Physiological Psychology, 55,* 614–620.

Fisher, H., Aron, A., & Brown, L. L. (2005). Romantic love: an fMRI study of a neural mechanism for mate choice. *Journal of Comparative Neurology, 493,* 58–62.

Fitts, P. (1964). Perceptual-motor skill learning. In A. Melton (Ed.), *Categories of human learning* (pp. 243–285). New York: Academic Press.

Fivush, R., & Nelson, K. (2004). Culture and language in the emergence of autobiographical memory. *Psychological Science, 15*(9), 573–577.

Flaherty, C. F. (1982). Incentive contrast: a review of behavioral changes following shifts in reward. *Animal Learning and Behavior, 10*(4), 409–440.

Flourens, P. (1824). Investigations of the properties and the functions of the various parts which compose the cerebral mass. In *Some papers on the cerebral cortex* (G. von Bonin, Trans., pp. 3–21). Springfield, IL: Charles C Thomas.

Flynn, J. (1972). Patterning mechanisms, patterned reflexes, and attack behaviour in cats. In J. Cole & D. Jensen (Eds.), *Nebraska symposium on motivation* (pp. 125–153). Lincoln: University of Nebraska Press.

Fogarty, S., & Hemsley, D. (1983). Depression and the accessibility of memories—a longitudinal study. *British Journal of Psychiatry, 142,* 232–237.

Forbes, N. F., Carrick, L. A., McIntosh, A. M., & Lawrie, S. M. (2009). Working memory in schizophrenia: a meta-analysis. *Psychological Medicine, 39,* 889–905.

Fox, P. W., Hershberger, S. L., & Bouchard, T. J., Jr. (1996). Genetic and environmental contributions to the acquisition of a motor skill. *Nature, 384,* 356–358.

Foy, M., Xu, J., Xie, X., Brinton, R., Thompson, R., & Berger, T. (1999). 17ß-estradiol enhances NMDA receptor-mediated EPSPs and long-term potentiation. *Journal of Neurophysiology, 81,* 925–929.

Francis, P., Palmer, A., Snape, M., & Wilcock, G. (1999). The cholinergic hypothesis of Alzheimer's disease: a review of progress. *Journal of Neurology, Neurosurgery, and Psychiatry, 66,* 137–147.

Frascella, J., Potenza, M. N., Brown, L. L., & Childress, A. R. (2010). Shared brain vulnerabilities open the way for nonsubstance addictions: carving addiction at a new joint? *Annals of the New York Academy of Sciences, 1187,* 294–315.

Freeman, J., & Nicholson, D. (2001). Ontogenetic changes in the neural mechanisms of eyeblink conditioning. *Integrative Physiological and Behavioral Science, 36*(1), 15–25.

Fried, I., MacDonald, K., & Wilson, C. (1997). Single neuron activity in human hippocampus and amygdala during recognition of faces and objects. *Neuron, 18,* 753–765.

Friston, K. J., Frith, C. D., Passingham, R. E., Liddle, P. F., & Frackowiak, R. S. J. (1992). Motor practice and neurophysiological adaptation in the cerebellum: a positron emission tomography study. *Proceedings of the Royal Society London, 244,* 241–246.

Fritz, J. B., David, S. V., Radtke-Schuller, S., Yin, P. B., & Shamma, S. A. (2010). Adaptive, behaviorally gated, persistent encoding of task-relevant auditory information in ferret frontal cortex. *Nature Neuroscience, 13,* 1011–1019.

Fudin, R., & Lembeissis, E. (2004). The Mozart effect: questions about the seminal findings of Rauscher, Shaw & colleagues. *Perceptual and Motor Skills, 98*(2), 389–405.

Funahashi, S., Bruce, C. J., & Goldman-Rakic, P. S. (1989). Mnemonic coding of visual space in the monkey's dorsolateral prefrontal cortex. Journal of *Neurophysiology, 61,* 331–349.

Fuster, J. M. (1995). *Memory in the cerebral cortex.* Cambridge, MA: MIT Press.

Fuster, J. M. (2001). The prefrontal cortex—an update: time is of the essence. *Neuron, 30,* 319–333.

Fuster, J. M. (2003). Functional neuroanatomy of executive process. In P. Holligar (Ed.), *Oxford handbook of clinical neuropsychology* (pp. 753–765). Oxford, UK: Oxford University Press.

Fuster, J. M. (2004). Upper processing stages of the perception-action cycle. *Trends in Cognitive Sciences, 8*(4), 143–145.

Fuster, J. M., & Alexander, G. E. (1971). Neuron activity related to short-term memory. *Science, 173*(997), 652–654.

Gabrieli, J. D. (1998). Cognitive neuroscience of human memory. *Annual Review of Psychology, 49,* 87–115.

Gabrieli, J. D., Corkin, S., Mickel, S. F., & Growdon, J. H. (1993). Intact acquisition and long-term retention of mirror-tracing skill in Alzheimer's disease and in global amnesia. *Behavioral Neuroscience, 107,* 899–910.

Gabrieli, J. D., Stebbins, G. T., Singh, J., Willingham, D. B., & Goetz, C. G. (1997). Intact mirror-tracing and impaired rotary pursuit skill learning in patients with Huntington's disease: evidence for dissociable memory systems in skill learning. *Neuropsychology, 11,* 272–281.

Gadian, D. G., Aicardi, J., Watkins, K. E., Porter, D. A., Mishkin, M., & Vargha-Khadem, F. (2000). Developmental amnesia associated with early hypoxic-ischaemic injury. *Brain, 123*(Pt 3), 499–507.

Gaffan, D., & Hornak, J. (1997). Amnesia and neglect: beyond the Delay-Brion system and the Hebb synapse. *Philosophical Transactions of the Royal Society of London—Series B, 352*(1360), 1481–1488.

Gaffan, D., & Parker, A. (1996). Interaction of perirhinal cortex with the fornix-fimbria: memory for objects and "object-in-place" memory. *Journal of Neuroscience, 16*(18), 5864–5869.

Galbicka, G. (1994). Shaping in the 21st century: moving percentile schedules into applied settings. *Journal of Applied Behavior Analysis, 27*(4), 739–760.

Galea, A., & Kimura, D. (1993). Sex differences in route-learning. *Personality and Individual Differences, 14,* 53–65.

Galea, S., Vlahov, D., Resnick, H., Ahern, J., Susser, E., Gold, J., et al. (2003). Trends of probable post-traumatic stress disorder in New York City after the September 11 terrorist attacks. *American Journal of Epidemiology, 158*(6), 514–524.

Galef, B. G., Jr. (1996). Social enhancement of food preferences in Norway rats: a brief review. In C. M. Heyes & B. G. Galef, Jr. (Eds.), *Social learning in animals: the roots of culture* (pp. 49–64). New York: Academic Press.

Galef, B. G., Jr., & Laland, K. N. (2005). Social learning in animals: empirical studies and theoretical models. *Bioscience, 55*(6), 489–499.

Galef, B. G., Jr., & Whiskin, E. E. (1997). Effects of social and asocial learning on longevity of food-preference traditions. *Animal Behaviour, 53*(6), 1313–1322.

Galef, B. G., Jr., & Wigmore, S. W. (1983). Transfer of information concerning distant foods: a laboratory investigation of the "Information-centre" hypothesis. *Animal Behaviour, 31,* 748–758.

Gall, F., & Spurzheim, J. (1810). *Anatomie et physiologie du système nerveux en général, et du cerveau en particulier, avec des observations sur la possibilité de reconnaître plusieurs dispositions intellectuelles et morales de l'homme et des animaux, par la configuration de leur têtes.* Paris: F. Schoell.

Gallagher, M., & Rapp, P. (1997). The use of animal models to study the effects of aging on cognition. *Annual Review of Psychology, 48,* 339–370.

Gallese, V., Fadiga, L., Fogassi, L., & Rizzolatti, G. (1996). Action recognition in the premotor cortex. *Brain, 119*(Pt 2), 593–609.

Gallistel, C. R., & Gibbon, J. (2000). Time, rate, and conditioning. *Psychological Review 107*(2), 289–344.

Galton, F. (1869). *Heriditary genius.* London: Macmillan.

Galton, F. (1872). Statistical inquiries into the efficacy of prayer. *Fortnightly Review, 12,* 125–135.

Galton, F. (1883). *Inquiries into human faculty and its development.* London: Macmillan.

Galton, F. (1899). The median estimate. *Report of the British Association for the Advancement of Science, 69,* 638–640.

Gandy, S., Simon, A. J., Steele, J. W., Lublin, A. L., Lah, J. J., Walker, L. C., et al. (2010). Days to criterion as an indicator of toxicity associated with human Alzheimer amyloid-beta oligomers. *Annals of Neurology, 68*(2), 220–230.

Gangitano, M., Mottaghy, F. M., & Pascual-Leone, A. (2001). Phase-specific modulation of cortical motor output during movement observation. *Neuroreport, 12*(7), 1489–1492.

Garcia, J., & Koelling, R. A. (1966). Relation of cue to consequence in avoidance learning. *Psychonomic Science, 4,* 123–124.

Gardner, R. (1981). Digits forward and digits backward as two separate tests: normative data on 1567 school children. *Journal of Clinical Child Psychology, summer,* 131–135.

Gatchel, R. (1975). Effect of interstimulus interval length on short- and long-term habituation of autonomic components of the orienting response. *Physiological Psychology, 3,* 133–136.

Gathercole, S. (1998). The development of memory. *Journal of Child Psychology and Psychiatry, 39*(1), 3–27.

Gauthier, L. V., Taub, E., Perkins, C., Ortmann, M., Mark, V. W., & Uswatte, G. (2008). Remodeling the brain: plastic structural brain changes produced by different motor therapies after stroke. *Stroke, 39,* 1520–1525.

Geen, R. G. (1990). *Human aggression.* Pacific Grove, CA: Brooks/Cole.

Georgopoulos, A. P., Taira, M., & Lukashin, A. (1993). Cognitive neurophysiology of the motor cortex. *Science, 260,* 47–52.

Gerhardstein, P., & West, R. (2003). The relation between perceptual input and infant memory. In H. Hayne & J. Fagen (Eds.), *Progress in infancy research* (Vol. 3, pp. 121–158). Mahwah, NJ: Erlbaum.

Gershoff, E. (2002). Child abuse and neglect and the brain: a review. *Journal of Child Psychiatry and Allied Disciplines, 41,* 97–116.

Ghilardi, M. F., Silvestri, G., Feigin, A., Mattis, P., Zgaljardic, D., Moisello, C., et al. (2008). Implicit and explicit aspects of sequence learning in presymptomatic Huntington's disease. *Parkinsonism & Related Disorders, 14,* 457–464.

Gibson, E. (1991). *An odyssey in learning and perception.* Cambridge, MA: MIT Press.

Gibson, E., & Walk, R. (1956). The effect of prolonged exposure to visual patterns on learning to discriminate them. *Journal of Comparative and Physiological Psychology, 49,* 239–242.

Gibson, J. J., & Gibson, E. J. (1955). Perceptual learning: differentiation or enrichment. *Psychological Review, 62,* 32–41.

Gil, S., & Caspi, Y. (2006). Personality traits, coping style, and perceived threat as predictors of posttraumatic stress disorder after exposure to a terrorist attack: a prospective study. *Psychosomatic Medicine, 68*(6), 904–909.

Gilbertson, M., Shenton, M., Ciszewski, A., Kasai, K., Lasko, N., Orr, S., et al. (2002). Smaller hippocampal volume predicts pathologic vulnerability to psychological trauma. *Nature Neuroscience, 5*(11), 1111–1113.

Glantz, L. A., Gilmore, J. H., Hamer, R. M., Lieberman, J. A., & Jarskog, L. F. (2007). Synaptophysin and PSD-95 in the human prefrontal cortex from mid-gestation into early adulthood. *Neuroscience, 149*(3), 582–591.

Glass, R. (2001). Electroconvulsive therapy: time to bring it out of the shadows. *Journal of the American Medical Association, 285,* 1346–1348.

Globus, A., Rosenzweig, R., Bennet, E., & Diamond, M. (1973). Effects of differential experience on dendritic spine counts in rat cerebral cortex. *Journal of Comparative and Physiological Psychology, 82,* 175–181.

Gluck, M. A., Allen, M. T., Myers, C. E., & Thompson, R. F. (2001). Cerebellar substrates for error-correction in motor conditioning. *Neurobiology of Learning and Memory, 76,* 314–341.

Gluck, M. A., & Bower, G. H. (1988a). From conditioning to category learning: an adaptive network model. *Journal of Experimental Psychology: General, 117*(3), 227–247.

Gluck, M. A., & Bower, G. H. (1988b). Evaluating an adaptive network model of human learning. *Journal of Memory and Language, 27,* 166–195.

Gluck, M. A., Bower, G. H., & Hee, M. (1989). A configural-cue network model of animal and human associative learning. In *11th Annual Conference of Cognitive Science Society* (pp. 323–332). Ann Arbor, MI.

Gluck, M. A., & Myers, C. E. (1993). Hippocampal mediation of stimulus representation: a computational theory. *Hippocampus, 3,* 491–516.

Gluck, M. A., & Myers, C. E. (2001). *Gateway to memory: an introduction to neural network models of the hippocampus and learning.* Cambridge, MA: MIT Press.

Gluck, M. A., Reifsnider, E. S., & Thompson, R. F. (1990). Adaptive signal processing and the cerebellum: models of classical conditioning and VOR adaptation. In M. A. Gluck and D. E. Rumelhart (Eds.), *Neuroscience and connectionist theory* (pp. 131–185). Hillsdale, NJ: Lawrence Erlbaum.

Godde, B., Ehrhardt, J., & Braun, C. (2003). Behavioral significance of input-dependent plasticity of human somatosensory cortex. *Neuroreport, 14,* 543–546.

Godden, D., & Baddely, A. (1975). Context-dependent memory in two natural environments: on land and under water. *British Journal of Psychology, 66,* 325–331.

Goff, L., & Roediger, H. (1998). Imagination inflation for action events: repeated imaginings lead to illusory recollections. *Memory and Cognition, 26,* 20–33.

Gold, P., & van Buskirk, R. (1975). Facilitation of time-dependent memory processes with posttrial epinephrine injections. *Behavioral Biology, 13,* 145–153.

Goldman, S., & Nottebohm, F. (1983). Neuronal production, migration, and differentiation in a vocal control nucleus of the adult female canary brain. *Proceedings of the National Academy of Sciences USA, 80,* 2390–2394.

Goldman-Rakic, P. S. (1987). Circuitry of primate prefrontal cortex and regulation of behavior by representational memory. In F. Plum (Ed.), *Handbook of physiology: the nervous system* (pp. 373–417). Bethesda, MD: American Physiological Society.

Goldstein, J., Seidman, L., Horton, N., Makris, N., Kennedy, D., Caviness, V., et al. (2001). Normal sexual dimorphism of the adult human brain assessed by in vivo magnetic resonance imaging. *Cerebral Cortex, 11,* 490–497.

Goldstein, J., Seidman, L., O'Brien, L., Horton, N., Kennedy, D., Makris, N., et al. (2002). Impact of normal sexual dimorphisms on sex differences in structural brain abnormalities in schizophrenia assessed by magnetic resonance imaging. *Archives of General Psychiatry, 59*(2), 154–164.

Goldstone, R. L. (1994). Influences of categorization on perceptual discrimination. *Journal of Experimental Psychology: General, 123,* 178–200.

Gonzalez-Martinez, V., Comte, F., de Verbizier, D., & Carlander, B. (2010). Transient global amnesia: concordant hippocampal abnormalities on positron emission tomography and magnetic resonance imaging. *Archives of Neurology, 67*(4), 510.

Goodwin, J. E., Eckerson, J. M., & Voll, C. A., Jr. (2001). Testing specificity and guidance hypotheses by manipulating relative frequency of KR scheduling in motor skill acquisition. *Perceptual and Motor Skills, 93,* 819–824.

Goodwin, J. E., & Meeuwsen, H. J. (1995). Using bandwidth knowledge of results to alter relative frequencies during motor skill acquisition. *Research Quarterly for Exercise and Sports, 66,* 99–104.

Goodwyn, S. W., Acredolo, L. P., & Brown, C. A. (2000). Impact of symbolic gesturing on early language development. *Journal of Nonverbal Behavior, 24,* 81–103.

Gormezano, I., Kehoe, E. J., & Marshall, B. S. (1983). Twenty years of classical conditioning research with the rabbit. *Progress in Psychobiology and Physiological Psychology, 10,* 197–275.

Goudsmit, E., Van de Poll, N., & Swaab, D. (1990). Testosterone fails to reverse spatial memory decline in aged rats and impairs retention in young and middle-aged animals. *Behavioral and Neural Biology, 53,* 6–20.

Gould, E., & Gross, C. (2000). New neurons: extraordinary evidence or extraordinary conclusion?—authors' response. *Science, 288,* 771a.

Gould, E., Reeves, A., Graziano, M., & Gross, C. (1999). Neurogenesis in the neocortex of adult primates. *Science, 286,* 548–552.

Graf, P. (1990). Life-span changes in implicit and explicit memory. *Bulletin of the Psychonomic Society, 28,* 353–358.

Graf, P., & Schacter, D. (1985). Implicit and explicit memory for new associations in normal and amnesic subjects. *Journal of Experimental Psychology: Learning, Memory, and Cognition, 11*(3), 501–518.

Graf, P., Squire, L. R., & Mandler, G. (1984). The information that amnesic patients do not forget. *Journal of Experimental Psychology: Learning, Memory, and Cognition, 10,* 164–178.

Grant, J. E., Kim, S. W., & Hartman, B. K. (2008). A double-blind, placebo-controlled study of the opiate antagonist naltrexone in the treatment of pathological gambling urges. *Journal of Clinical Psychiatry, 69*(5), 783–389.

Graybiel, A. M. (1995). Building action repertoires: memory and learning functions of the basal ganglia. *Current Opinion in Neurobiology, 5,* 733–741.

Graybiel, A. M. (2005). The basal ganglia: learning new tricks and loving it. *Current Opinion in Neurobiology, 15,* 638–644.

Graybiel, A. M. (2008). Habits, rituals, and the evaluative brain. *Annual Review of Neuroscience, 31,* 359–387.

Green, C. S., & Bavelier, D. (2003). Action video game modifies visual selective attention. *Nature, 423,* 534–537.

Green, L., Fischer, E., Perlow, S., & Sherman, L. (1981). Preference reversal and self control: choice as a function of reward amount and delay. *Behavior Analysis Letters, 1,* 43–51.

Green, L., Fry, A., & Myerson, J. (1994). Discounting of delayed rewards: a life-span comparison. *Psychological Science, 5,* 33–36.

Greenberg, D. L. (2004). President Bush's false 'flashbulb' memory of 9/11/01. *Applied Cognitive Psychology, 18,* 363–370.

Greenberg, D. L., & Verfaellie, M. (2010). Interdependence of episodic and semantic memory: evidence from neuropsychology. *Journal of the International Neuropsychological Society, 16*(5), 748–753.

Greenough, W., West, R., & DeVoogd, T. (1978). Subsynaptic plate perforations: changes with age and experience in the rat. *Science, 202,* 1096–1098.

Greenwald, A. G., McGhee, D. E., & Schwartz, J. L. K. (1998). Measuring individual differences in implicit cognition: the implicit association test. *Journal of Personality and Social Psychology, 74,* 1464–1480.

Griffiths, D., Dickinson, A., & Clayton, N. (1999). Episodic memory: what can animals remember about their past? *Trends in Cognitive Sciences, 3,* 74–80.

Gross, R. G., & Grossman, M. (2008). Update on apraxia. *Current Neurology and Neuroscience Reports, 8,* 490–496.

Groves, P. M., & Thompson, R. F. (1970). Habituation: a dual-process theory. *Psychological Review, 77,* 419–450.

Guillaume, P. (1971). *Imitation in children.* Chicago: University of Chicago Press.

Guinee, L. N., Chu, K., & Dorsey, E. M. (1983). Changes over time in the songs of known individual humpback whales (*Megaptera novaeangliae*). In R. Payne (Ed.), *Communication and behavior of whales.* Boulder, CO: Westview Press.

Guttman, N., & Kalish, H. (1956). Discriminability and stimulus generalization. *Journal of Experimental Psychology, 51,* 79–88.

Hackenberg, T. D. (2009). Token reinforcement: a review and analysis. *Journal of the Experimental Analysis of Behavior, 91*(2), 257–286.

Haglund, K., & Collett, C. (1996). Landmarks interviews. *Journal of NIH Research, 8,* 42–51.

Halgren, E. (1982). Mental phenomena induced by stimulation in the limbic system. *Human Neurobiology, 1*(4), 251–260.

Hall, G. (1991). *Perceptual and associative learning.* Oxford: Oxford University Press.

Hall, G. (2009). Perceptual learning in human and nonhuman animals: A search for common ground. *Learning & Behavior, 37,* 133–140.

Hall, G., & Honey, R. (1989). Contextual effects in conditioning, latent inhibition, and habituation: associative and retrieval functions of contextual cues. *Journal of Experimental Psychology: Animal Behavior Processes, 15*(3), 232–241.

Hall, G., Ray, E., & Bonardi, C. (1993). Acquired equivalence between cues trained with a common antecedent. *Journal of Experimental Psychology: Animal Behavior Processes, 19,* 391–399.

Hall, T., Miller, K., & Corsellia, J. (1975). Variations in the human Purkinje cell population according to age and sex. *Neuropathology and Applied Neurobiology, 1,* 267–292.

Halsband, U., Schmitt, J., Weyers, M., Binkofski, F., Grutzner, G., & Freund, H. J. (2001). Recognition and imitation of pantomimed motor acts after unilateral parietal and premotor lesions: a perspective on apraxia. *Neuropsychologia, 39,* 200–216.

Hamann, S. (2005). Sex differences in the responses of the human amygdala. *Neuroscientist, 11*(4), 288–293.

Hamann, S., Ely, T., Grafton, S., & Kilts, C. (1999). Amygdala activity related to enhanced memory for pleasant and aversive stimuli. *Nature Neuroscience, 2*(3), 289–293.

Hamilton, A. F. D. C. (2008). Emulation and mimicry for social interaction: a theoretical approach to imitation in autism. *Quarterly Journal of Experimental Psychology, 61*(1), 101–115.

Hampstead, B. M., & Koffler, S. P. (2009). Thalamic contributions to anterograde, retrograde, and implicit memory: a case study. *Clinical Neuropsychology, 23*(7), 1232–1249.

Haney, M., Foltin, R., & Fischman, M. (1998). Effects of pergolide on intravenous cocaine self-administration in men and women. *Psychopharmacology, 137,* 15–24.

Hanley-Dunn, P., & McIntosh, J. (1984). Meaningfulness and recall of names by young and old adults. *Journal of Gerontology, 39,* 583–585.

Hannula, D. E., Simons, D. J., & Cohen, N. J. (2005). Imaging implicit perception: promise and pitfalls. *Nature Reviews Neuroscience, 6,* 247–255.

Hanson, H. M. (1959). Effects of discrimination training on stimulus generalization. *Journal of Experimental Psychology, 58,* 321–334.

Hardt, O., Einarsson, E. O., & Nader, K. (2010). A bridge over troubled water: reconsolidation as a link between cognitive and neuroscientific memory traditions. *Annual Review of Psychology, 61*, 141–167.

Hardy, J., & Gwinn-Hardy, K. (1998). Classification of primary degenerative disease. *Science, 282*, 1075–1079.

Harris, B. (1979). Whatever happened to Little Albert? *American Psychologist, 34*(2), 151–160.

Harrison, J., & Buchwald, J. (1983). Eyeblink conditioning deficits in the old cat. *Neurobiology of Aging, 4*, 45–51.

Hart, B. (2001). Cognitive behaviour in Asian elephants: use and modification of branches for fly switching. *Animal Behaviour, 62*, 839–847.

Hart, J., & Gordon, B. (1992). Neural subsystems for object knowledge. *Nature, 359*(6390), 60–64.

Hasselmo, M. (1999). Neuromodulation: acetylcholine and memory consolidation. *Trends in Cognitive Sciences, 3*(9), 351–359.

Hatcher, M. B., Whitaker, C., & Karl, A. (2009). What predicts post-traumatic stress following spinal cord injury? *British Journal of Health Psychology, 14*, 541–561.

Hatze, H. (1976). Biomechanical aspects of a successful motion optimization. In P. V. Komi (Ed.), *Biomechanics V-B* (pp. 5–12). Baltimore: University Park Press.

Hawkins, R. D., Abrams, T. W., Carew, T. J., & Kandel, E. R. (1983). A cellular mechanism of classical conditioning in *Aplysia*: activity-dependent amplification of presynaptic facilitation. *Science, 219*, 400–405.

Hayes, C. (1951). *The ape in our house.* New York: Harper & Bros.

Hayes, K. J., & Hayes, C. (1952). Imitation in a home-reared chimpanzee. *Journal of Comparative and Physiological Psychology, 45*, 450–459.

Hayne, H. (1996). Categorization in infancy. In C. Rovee-Collier & L. Lipsitt (Eds.), *Advances in infancy research* (Vol. 10, pp. 79–120). Norwood, NJ: Ablex Publishing Corporation.

Hays, M., Allen, C., & Hanish, J. (2005). Kissing 101. Retrieved January 2007 from www.virtualkiss.com/kissing-school

Hayward, M. D., Schaich-Borg, A., Pintar, J. E., & Low, M. J. (2006). Differential involvement of endogenous opioids in sucrose consumption and food reinforcement. *Pharmacology, Biochemistry, & Behavior, 85*(3), 601–611.

Hebb, D. (1947). The effects of early experience on problem solving at maturity. *American Psychologist, 2*, 737–745.

Hebb, D. (1949). *The organization of behavior.* New York: Wiley.

Heckers, S. (2001). Neuroimaging studies of the hippocampus in schizophrenia. *Hippocampus 11*, 520–528.

Heckers, S., Rauch, S. L., Goff, D., Savage, C. R., Schacter, D. L, Fischman, A. J., & Alpert, N. M. (1998). Impaired recruitment of the hippocampus during conscious recollection in schizophrenia. *Nature Neuroscience, 1*, 318–323.

Heilman, K. M., Rothi, L. J., & Valenstein, E. (1982). Two forms of ideomotor apraxia. *Neurology, 32*, 342–346.

Heindel, W., Salmon, D., Shults, C., Walicke, P., & Butters, N. (1989). Neuropsychological evidence for multiple implicit memory systems: a comparison of Alzheimer's, Huntington's and Parkinson's disease patients. *Journal of Neuroscience, 9*(2), 582–587.

Hepper, P., & Shahidullah, S. (1992). Habituation in normal and Down's syndrome fetuses. *Quarterly Journal of Experimental Psychology B, 44B*(3–4), 305–317.

Herbert, J., Eckerman, C., & Stanton, M. (2003). The ontogeny of human learning in delay, long-delay, and trace eyeblink conditioning. *Behavioral Neuroscience, 117*(6), 1196–1210.

Herrnstein, R. (1961). Relative and absolute strength of a response as a function of frequency of reinforcement. *Journal of the Experimental Analysis of Behavior, 4*, 267–272.

Heuer, F., & Reisberg, D. (1990). Vivid memories of emotional events: the accuracy of remembered minutiae. *Memory and Cognition, 18*, 496–506.

Heuer, F., & Reisberg, D. (1992). Emotion, arousal, and memory for detail. In S.-A. Christianson (Ed.), *The handbook of emotion and memory* (pp. 151–180). Hillsdale, NJ: Erlbaum.

Hews, D., Knapp, R., & Moore, M. (1994). Early exposure to androgens affects adult expression of alternative male types in tree lizards. *Hormones & Behavior, 28*, 96–115.

Hews, D., & Moore, M. (1996). A critical period for the organization of alternative male phenotypes of tree lizards by exogenous testosterone? *Physiology and Behavior, 60*(2), 425–529.

Heyes, C. M. (1994). Social learning in animals: categories and mechanisms. *Biological Reviews of the Cambridge Philosophical Society, 69*(2), 207–231.

Heyes, C. M., & Dawson, G. R. (1990). A demonstration of observational learning in rats using a bidirectional control. *Quarterly Journal of Experimental Psychology B, 42*(1), 59–71.

Hinde, R. A. (1969). *Bird vocalizations.* Cambridge, England: Cambridge University Press.

Hiroto, D. (1974). Locus of control and learned helplessness. *Journal of Experimental Psychology, 102*, 187–193.

Hiroto, D., & Seligman, M. (1974). Generality of learned helplessness in man. *Journal of Personality and Social Psychology, 31*, 311–327.

Hodzic, A., Veit, R., Karim, A. A., Erb, M., & Godde, B. (2004). Improvement and decline in tactile discrimination behavior after cortical plasticity induced by passive tactile coactivation. *Journal of Neuroscience, 24*, 442–446.

Hof, P., & Morrison, J. (2004). The aging brain: morphomolecular senescence of cortical circuits. *Trends in Neurosciences, 27*(19), 607–613.

Hoffman, K. L., & Logothetis, N. K. (2009). Cortical mechanisms of sensory learning and object recognition. *Philosophical Transactions of the Royal Society B: Biological Sciences, 364*, 321–329.

Holding, D. H. (Ed.). (1981). *Human skills.* Chichester: John Wiley.

Holloway, J. L., Beck, K. D., & Servatius, R. J. (2011). Facilitated acquisition of the classically conditioned eyeblink response in females is augmented in those taking oral contraceptives. *Behavioural Brain Research, 216*(1), 302–407.

Holmes, C., Boche, D., Wilkinson, D., Yadegarfar, G., Hopkins, V., Bayer, A., et al. (2008). Long-term effects of Abeta42 immunisation in Alzheimer's disease: follow-up of a randomised, placebo-controlled phase I trial. *Lancet, 372*(9634), 216–223.

Holzhaider, J. C., Hunt, G. R., & Gray, R. D. (2010). Social learning in New Caledonian crows. *Learning & Behavior, 38*, 206–219.

Honey, R., & Hall, G. (1991). Acquired equivalence and distinctiveness of cues using a sensory-preconditioning procedure. *Quarterly Journal of Experimental Psychology, 43B*, 121–135.

Honey, R., Watt, A., & Good, M. (1998). Hippocampal lesions disrupt an associative mismatch process. *Journal of Neuroscience, 18*(6), 2226–2230.

Hornak, J., Bramham, J., Rolls, E., Morris, R., O'Doherty, J., Bullock, P., et al. (2003). Changes in emotion after circumscribed surgical lesions of the orbitofrontal and cingulate cortices. *Brain, 126* (Pt. 7), 1691–1712.

Horowitz, A. C. (2003). Do humans ape? Or do apes human? Imitation and intention in humans (*Homo sapiens*) and other animals. *Journal of Comparative Psychology, 117*(3), 325–336.

Howard, R. W. (2009). Individual differences in expertise development over decades in a complex intellectual domain. *Memory & Cognition, 37*, 194–209.

Howe, M., & Courage, M. (1993). On resolving the enigma of childhood amnesia. *Psychological Bulletin, 113*, 305–326.

Hubel, D., & Wiesel, T. (1977). The Ferrier Lecture: functional architecture of macaque monkey visual cortex. *Proceedings of the Royal Academy of London: B198*, 1–59.

Hubel, D., & Wiesel, T. (1998). Early exploration of the visual cortex. *Neuron, 20*(3), 401–412.

Hubert, V., Beaunieux, H., Chetelat, G., Platel, H., Landeau, B. Danion, J. M., et al. (2007). The dynamic network subserving the three phases of cognitive procedural learning. *Human Brain Mapping, 28*, 1415–1429.

Hudson Kam, C. L., & Newport, E. L. (2005). Regularizing unpredictable variation: the roles of adult and child learners in language formation and change. *Language Learning and Development, 1*, 151–195.

Hull, C. L. (1943). *Principles of behavior.* New York: Appleton-Century-Crofts.

Hull, C. L. (1952). *A behavior system: an introduction to behavior theory concerning the individual organism.* New Haven: Yale University Press.

Hunt, G. R., Corballis, M. C., & Gray, R. D. (2001). Animal behaviour: laterality in tool manufacture by crows. *Nature, 414*, 707.

Huttenlocher, P., & Dabholkar, A. (1997). Regional differences in synaptogenesis in human cerebral cortex. *Journal of Comparative Neurology, 387*, 167–178.

Hyde, L., Sherman, G., & Denenberg, V. (2000). Nonspatial water radial-arm maze learning in mice. *Brain Research, 863*(1–2), 151–159.

Iacoboni, M., Woods, R. P., Brass, M., Bekkering, H., Mazziotta, J. C., & Rizzolatti, G. (1999). Cortical mechanisms of human imitation. *Science, 286*(5449), 2526–2528.

Immelman, K. (1969). Song development in the zebra finch and other estrildid finches. In R. A. Hinde (Ed.), *Bird vocalizations* (pp. 61–74). Cambridge: Cambridge University Press.

Insel, T., & Fernald, R. (2004). How the brain processes social information: searching for the social brain. *Annual Review of Neuroscience, 27*, 697–722.

Irwin, A. R., & Gross, A. M. (1995). Cognitive tempo, violent video games, and aggressive behavior in young boys. *Journal of Family Violence, 10*, 337–350.

Ivkovich, D., Collins, K., Eckerman, C., Krasnegor, N., & Stanton, M. (1999). Classical delay eyeblink conditioning in 4- and 5-month-old human infants. *Psychological Science, 10*(1), 4–8.

Ivkovich, D., Paczkowski, C., & Stanton, M. (2000). Ontogeny of delay versus trace conditioning in the rat. *Developmental Psychobiology, 36*(2), 148–160.

Izquierdo, A., Suda, R. K., & Murray, E. A. (2004). Bilateral orbito prefrontal cortex lesions in rhesus monkeys disrupt choices guided by both reward value and reward contingency. *Journal of Neuroscience, 24*(34), 7540–7548.

Jack, C., Petersen, R., Xu, Y., O'Brien, P., Smith, G., Ivnik, R., et al. (1999). Prediction of AD with MRI-based hippocampal volume in mild cognitive impairment. *Neurology, 52*, 1397–1403.

Jacobs, B., Schall, M., & Schiebel, A. (1993). A quantitative dendritic analysis of Wernicke's area. II. Gender, hemispheric, and environmental factors. *Journal of Comparative Neurology, 237*, 97–111.

Jacobs, D. H., Adair, J. C., Williamson, D. J., Na, D. L., Gold, M., Foundas, A. L., et al. (1999). Apraxia and motor-skill acquisition in Alzheimer's disease are dissociable. *Neuropsychologia, 37*, 875–880.

Jacobsen, C. F. (1936). Studies of cerebral function in primates. I. The functions of the frontal association areas in monkeys. *Comparative Psychology Monographs, 13*, 1–60.

Jaeggi, S. M., Buschkuehl, M., Jonides, J., & Perrig, W. J. (2008). Improving fluid intelligence with training on working memory, *Proceedings of the National Academy of Sciences USA, 105*(19), 6791–6792.

Jaeggi, S. M., Studer-Luethi, B., Buschkuehl, M., Su, Y., Jonides, J., & Perrig, W. J. (2010). The relationship between n-back performance and matrix reasoning—implications for training and transfer. *Intelligence, 38*(6), 625–635.

James, W. (1890). *The principles of psychology.* New York: Henry Holt.

Janik, V., & Slater, P. (1997). Vocal learning in mammals. *Advances in the Study of Behavior, 26*, 59–99.

Janowsky, J. S., Shimamura, A. P., Kritchevsky, M., & Squire, L. R. (1989). Cognitive impairment following frontal lobe damage and its relevance to human amnesia. *Behavioral Neuroscience, 103*, 548–560.

Jarrard, L., Okaichi, H., Steward, O., & Goldschmidt, R. (1984). On the role of hippocampal connections in the performance of place and cue tasks: comparisons with damage to hippocampus. *Behavioral Neuroscience, 98*(6), 946–954.

Jay, T. M. (2003). Dopamine: a potential substrate for synaptic plasticity and memory mechanisms. *Progress in Neurobiology, 69*, 375–390.

Jenkins, H. M., & Harrison, R. H. (1962). Generalization gradients of inhibition following auditory discrimination training. *Journal of the Experimental Analysis of Behavior, 5*, 435–441.

Jenkins, K. G., Kapur, N., & Kopelman, M. D. (2009). Retrograde amnesia and malingering. *Current Opinion in Neurology, 22*(6), 601–605.

Jog, M. S., Kubota, Y., Connolly, C. I., Hillegaart, V., & Graybiel, A. M. (1999). Building neural representations of habits. *Science, 286*, 1745–1749.

Johnson, G., & Bailey, C. (2002). Tau, where are we now? *Journal of Alzheimer's Disease, 4*, 375–398.

Johnson, M. (1992). Imprinting and the development of face recognition: from chick to man. *Current Directions in Psychological Science, 1*, 52–55.

Jones, B. C., DeBruine, L. M., Little, A. C., Burris, R. P., & Feinberg, D. R. (2007). Social transmission of face preferences among humans. *Proceedings of the Royal Society London: B, 274*, 899–903.

Jones, G. V. (1990). Misremembering a common object: when left is not right. *Memory and Cognition, 18*(2), 174–182.

Josephson, W. L. (1987). Television violence and children's aggression: testing the priming, social script, and disinhibition predictions. *Journal of Personality and Social Psychology, 53*(5), 882–890.

Joslyn, S. L., & Oakes, M. A. (2005). Directed forgetting of autobiographical events. *Memory and Cognition, 33*(4), 577–587.

Jun, G., Naj, A. C., Beecham, G. W., Wang, L. S., Buros, J., Gallins, P. J., et al. (2010). Meta-analysis confirms CR1, CLU, and PICALM as Alzheimer disease risk loci and reveals interactions with APOE genotypes. *Archives of Neurology.*

Jung, R. E., & Haier, R. J. (2007). The parieto-frontal integration theory of intelligence: converging neuroimaging evidence. *Behavioral and Brain Sciences, 30*, 135–154.

Kahn, D. M., & Krubitzer, L. (2002). Massive cross-modal cortical plasticity and the emergence of a new cortical area in developmentally blind mammals. *Proceedings of the National Academy of Sciences USA, 99*, 11429–11434.

Kahneman, D., & Tversky, A. (1973). On the psychology of prediction. *Psychological Review, 80*, 237–251.

Kamin, L. (1969). Predictability, surprise, attention and conditioning. In B. Campbell and R. Church (Eds.), *Punishment and aversive behavior* (pp. 279–296). New York: Appleton-Century-Crofts.

Kanit, L., Taskiran, D., Yilmaz, O., Balkan, B., Demiroeren, S., Furedy, J., et al. (2000). Sexually dimorphic cognitive style in rats emerges after puberty. *Brain Research Bulletin, 52*(4), 243–248.

Kanner, L. (1943). Autistic disturbances of affective contact. *Nervous Child, 2*, 217–250.

Kapp, B., Gallagher, M., Underwood, M., McNall, C., & Whitehorn, D. (1981). Cardiovascular responses elicited by electrical stimulation of the amygdala central nucleus in the rabbit. *Brain Research, 234*, 251–262.

Kapur, N., & Coughlan, A. (1980). Confabulation and frontal lobe dysfunction. *Journal of Neurology, Neurosurgery and Psychiatry, 43*, 461–463.

Kapur, N., Friston, K. J., Young, A., Frith, C. D., & Frackowiak, R. S. (1995). Activation of human hippocampal formation during memory for faces: a PET study. *Cortex, 31*, 99–108.

Kapur, N., Millar, J., Abbott, P., & Carter, M. (1998). Recovery of function processes in human amnesia: evidence from transient global amnesia. *Neuropsychologia, 36*(1), 99–107.

Kapur, N., Thompson, S., Cook, P., Lang, D., & Brice, J. (1996). Anterograde but not retrograde memory loss following combined mammillary body and medial thalamic lesions. *Neuropsychologia, 34*(1), 1–8.

Karlen, S. J., Kahn, D. M., & Krubitzer, L. (2006). Early blindness results in abnormal corticocortical and thalamocortical connections. *Neuroscience, 142*, 843–858.

Karni, A., Meyer, G., Rey-Hipolito, C., Jezzard, P., Adams, M. M., Turner, R., & Ungerleider, L. G. (1998).

The acquisition of skilled motor performance: fast and slow experience-driven changes in primary motor cortex. *Proceedings of the National Academy of Sciences USA, 95,* 861–868.

Kart-Teke, E., De Souza Silva, M. A., Huston, J., & Dere, E. (2006). Wistar rats show episodic-like memory for unique experiences. *Neurobiology of Learning and Memory, 85*(2), 173–182.

Kazdin, A., & Benjet, C. (2003). Spanking children: evidence and issues. *Current Directions in Psychological Science, 12*(3), 99–103.

Kazdin, A., & Wilcoxon, L. (1976). Systematic desensitization and nonspecific treatment effects: a methodological evaluation. *Psychological Bulletin, 83,* 729–758.

Kehoe, E. J. (1988). A layered network model of associative learning. *Psychological Review, 95*(4), 411–433.

Kemeny, M. (2003). The psychobiology of stress. *Current Directions in Psychological Science, 12*(4), 124–129.

Kemler, D. G., & Smith, L. B. (1978). Is there a developmental trend from integrality to separability in perception? *Journal of Experimental Child Psychology, 26,* 498–507.

Kempermann, G., Wiskott, L., & Gage, F. (2004). Functional significance of adult neurogenesis. *Current Opinion in Neurobiology, 14*(2), 186–191.

Kendal, R. L., Galef, B. G., & van Schaik, C. P. (2010). Social learning research outside the laboratory: How and why? *Learning and Behavior, 38,* 187–194.

Kéri, S., Nagy, O., Kelemen, O., Myers, C. E., & Gluck, M. A. (2005). Dissociation between medial temporal and basal ganglia memory systems in schizophrenia. *Schizophrenia Research, 77,* 321–328.

Kikuchi, H., Fujii, T., Abe, N., Suzuki, M., Takagi, M., Mugikura, S., et al. (2010). Memory repression: brain mechanisms underlying dissociative amnesia. *Journal of Cognitive Neuroscience, 22*(3), 602–613.

Kilgard, M., & Merzenich, M. (1998). Cortical map reorganization enabled by nucleus basalis activity. *Science, 279,* 1714–1718.

Kim, J., Krupa, D., & Thompson, R. F. (1998). Inhibitory cerebello-olivary projections and blocking effect in classical conditioning. *Science, 279,* 570–573.

Kirchmayer, U., Davoli, M., Verster, A., Amato, L., Ferri, A., & Perucci, C. (2002). A systematic review on the efficacy of naltrexone maintenance treatment in preventing relapse in opioid addicts after detoxification. *Addiction, 97*(10), 1241–1249.

Kleim, J. A., Hogg, T. M., VandenBerg, P. M., Cooper, N. R., Bruneau, R., & Remple, M. (2004). Cortical synaptogenesis and motor map reorganization occur during late, but not early, phase of motor skill learning. *Journal of Neuroscience, 24,* 628–633.

Kleim, J. A., Swain, R. A., Czerlanis, C. M., Kelly, J. L., Pipitone, M. A., & Greenough, W. T. (1997).

Learning-dependent dendritic hypertrophy of cerebellar stellate cells: plasticity of local circuit neurons. *Neurobiology of Learning and Memory, 67,* 29–33.

Klingberg, T., Fernell, E., Oleson, P. J., Johnson, M., Gustafsson, P., Dahlstrom, K., Gilberg, et al. (2005). Computerized training of working memory in children with ADHAD: a randomized, controlled trial. *Journal of the American Academy of Child and Adolescent Psychiatry, 44*(2), 177–186.

Klinke, R., Kral, A., Heid, S., Tillein, J., & Hartmann, R. (1999). Recruitment of the auditory cortex in congenitally deaf cats by long-term cochlear electrostimulation. *Science, 285,* 1729–1733.

Knapp, H. D., Taub, E., & Berman, A. J. (1963). Movements in monkeys with deafferented forelimbs. *Experimental Neurology, 7,* 305–315.

Knowlton, B. J., Squire, L. R., & Gluck, M. A. (1994). Probabilistic classification learning in amnesia. *Learning & Memory, 1,* 106–120.

Knowlton, B. J., Squire, L. R., Paulsen, J. S., Swerdlow, N. R., Swenson, M., & Butters, N. (1996). Dissociations within nondeclarative memory in Huntington's disease. *Neuropsychology, 10,* 538–548.

Knutson, B., Fong, G., Adams, C., Varner, J., & Hommer, D. (2001). Dissociation of reward anticipation and outcome with event-related fMRI. *Neuroreport, 21,* 3683–3687.

Kobre, K., & Lipsitt, L. (1972). A negative contrast effect in newborns. *Journal of Experimental Child Psychology, 14,* 81–91.

Koechlin, E., Ody, C., & Kouneiher, F. (2003). The architecture of cognitive control in the human prefrontal cortex. *Science 302,* 1181–1185.

Koenig, O., Thomas-Anterion, C., & Laurent, B. (1999). Procedural learning in Parkinson's disease: intact and impaired cognitive components. *Neuropsychologia, 37,* 1103–1109.

Köhler, S., Moscovitch, M., Winocur, G., & McIntosh, A. (2000). Episodic encoding and recognition of pictures and words: role of the human medial temporal lobes. *Acta Psychologica, 105,* 159–179.

Kolb, B., & Taylor, L. (1981). Affective behavior in patients with localized cortical excisions: role of lesion site and side. *Science, 214,* 89–91.

Kolb, B., & Taylor, L. (1990). Neocortical substrates of emotional behavior. In N. Stein, B. Leventhal & T. Trabasso (Eds.), *Psychological and biological approaches to emotion* (pp. 115–144). Hillsdale, NJ: Erlbaum.

Kolb, B., & Taylor, L. (2000). Facial expression, emotion, and hemispheric organization. In R. Lane & L. Nadel (Eds.), *Cognitive neuroscience of emotion* (pp. 62–83). New York: Oxford University Press.

Kopelman, M. D., Thomson, A. D., Guerrini, I., & Marshall, E. J. (2009). The Korsakoff syndrome: clinical aspects, psychology and treatment. *Alcohol, 44*(2), 148–154.

Kornak, D., & Rakic, P. (1999). Continuation of neurogenesis in the hippocampus of the adult macaque monkey. *Proceedings of the National Academy of Sciences USA, 96,* 5768–5773.

Korr, H., & Schmitz, C. (1999). Facts and fictions regarding post-natal neurogenesis in the developing human cerebral cortex. *Journal of Theoretical Biology, 200,* 291–297.

Koukounas, E., & Over, R. (2001). Habituation of male sexual arousal: effects of attentional focus. *Biological Psychology, 58,* 49–64.

Krank, M. D., & Wall, A. M. (1990). Cue exposure during a period of abstinence reduces the resumption of operant behavior for oral ethanol reinforcement. *Behavioral Neuroscience, 104,* 725–733.

Krieman, G., Koch, C., & Fried, I. (2000). Category-specific visual responses of single neurons in the human medial temporal lobe. *Nature Neuroscience, 3*(9), 946–953.

Kring, A., & Gordon, A. (1998). Sex differences in emotion: expression, experience, and physiology. *Journal of Personality and Social Psychology, 74,* 686–803.

Kringelbach, M. L., & Rolls, E. T. (2004). The functional neuroanatomy of the human orbitofrontal cortex: evidence from neuroimaging and neuropsychology. *Progress in Neurobiology, 72,* 341–372.

Kritchevsky, M., Chang, J., & Squire, L. (2004). Functional amnesia: clinical description and neuropsychological profile of 10 cases. *Learning and Memory, 11*(2), 213–227.

Kritchevsky, M., & Squire, L. (1989). Transient global amnesia: evidence for extensive, temporally graded retrograde amnesia. *Neurology, 39,* 213–218.

Kritchevsky, M., Squire, L., & Zouzounis, J. (1988). Transient global amnesia: characterization of anterograde and retrograde amnesia. *Neurology, 38,* 213–219.

Kruschke, J. K., Kappenman, E. S., & Hetrick, W. P. (2005). Eye gaze and individual differences consistent with learned attention in associative blocking and highlighting. *Journal of Experimental Psychology: Learning, Memory, & Cognition, 31*(5), 830–845.

Krutzen, M., Mann, J., Heithaus, M. R., Connor, R. C., Bejder, L., & Sherwin, W. B. (2005). Cultural transmission of tool use in bottlenose dolphins. *Proceedings of the National Academy of Sciences USA, 102,* 8939–8943.

Kubota, K., & Niki, H. (1971). Prefrontal cortical unit activity and delayed alternation performance in monkeys. *Journal of Neurophysiology, 34*(3), 337–347.

Kuhl, P. K. (2000). A new view of language acquisition. *Proceedings of the National Academy of Sciences USA, 97*(22), 11850–11857.

Kuhl, P. K., & Meltzoff, A. N. (1996). Infant vocalizations in response to speech: vocal imitation and developmental change. *Journal of the Acoustical Society of America, 100,* 2425–2438.

Kuhn, H., Dickinson-Anson, H., & Gage, F. (1996). Neurogenesis in the dentate gyrus of the adult rat: age-related decrease of neurongal progenitor proliferation. *Journal of Neuroscience, 16,* 2027–2033.

Kujala, Y., & Naatanen, R. (2010). The adaptive brain: a neurophysiological perspective. *Progress in Neurobiology, 91,* 55–67.

Kwon, H., Reiss, A., & Menon, V. (2002). Neural basis of protracted developmental changes in visuo-spatial working memory. *Proceedings of the National Academy of Sciences USA, 99*(20), 13336–13341.

Laan, E., & Everaerd, W. (1995). Habituation of female sexual arousal to slides and film. *Archives of Sexual Behavior, 24,* 517–541.

LaBar, K. S. (2007). Beyond fear: emotional memory mechanisms in the human brain. *Current Directions in Psychological Science, 16*(4), 173–177.

LaBar, K. S. (2009). Imaging emotional influences on learning and memory. In F. Roesler, C. Ranganath, B. Roeder & R. H. Kluwe (Eds.), *Neuroimaging and psychological theories of human memory* (pp. 331–348). New York: Oxford University Press.

LaBar, K. S., & LeDoux, J. (2003). Emotion and the brain: an overview. In T. Feinberg & M. Farah (Eds.), *Behavioral neurology and neuropsychology* (2nd ed., pp. 711–724). New York: McGraw-Hill.

Ladd, G. W., & Mize, J. (1983). A cognitive social learning model of social skill training. *Psychological Review, 90,* 127–157.

Laforce, R., Jr., & Doyon, J. (2001). Distinct contribution of the striatum and cerebellum to motor learning. *Brain and Cognition, 45,* 189–211.

Laland, K. N. (2004). Social learning strategies. *Learning & Behavior, 32,* 4–14.

Laland, K. N., & Galef, B. G. (2009). *The question of animal culture.* Cambridge, MA: Harvard University Press.

Lalonde, R., & Botez, M. (1990). The cerebellum and learning processes in animals. *Brain Research Reviews, 15,* 325–332.

Lambe, E. K., Krimer, L. S., & Goldman-Rakic, P. (2000). Differential postnatal development of catecholamine and serotonin inputs to identified neurons in the prefrontal cortex of rhesus monkey. *Journal of Neuroscience, 20*(23), 8760–8787.

Lang, P. J., Davis, M., & Ohman, A. (2000). Fear and anxiety: animal models and human cognitive psychophysiology. *Journal of Affective Disorders, 61,* 137–159.

Langston, R. F., & Wood, E. R. (2010). Associative recognition and the hippocampus: differential effects of hippocampal lesions on object-place, object-context, and object-place-context memory. *Hippocampus, 20,* 1139–1153.

Larzelere, R. (2000). Child outcomes of nonabusive and customary physical punishment by parents: an updated literature review. *Clinical Child and Family Psychology Review, 3*, 199–221.

Lashley, K. (1924). Studies of the cerebral function in learning: V. The retention of motor habits after destruction of the so-called motor areas in primates. *Archives of Neurology and Psychiatry, 12*, 249–276.

Lashley, K. S. (1929). *Brain mechanisms and intelligence: a quantitative study of injuries to the brain.* Chicago: University of Chicago Press.

Le Merrer, J., Becker, J. A., Befort, K., & Kieffer, B. L. (2009). Reward processing by the opioid system in the brain. *Physiological Reviews, 89*, 1379–1412.

Lebrecht, S., Pierce, L. J., Tarr, M. J., Tanaka, J. W. (2009). Perceptual other-race training reduces implicit racial bias. *PLOS One, 4*, e4215.

LeDoux, J. (1993). Emotional memory systems in the brain. *Behavioural Brain Research, 58*, 69–79.

LeDoux, J. (1994). Emotion, memory and the brain. *Scientific American, 270*(6), 50–57.

LeDoux, J. (1998). *The emotional brain: the mysterious underpinnings of emotional life.* New York: Touchstone.

LeDoux, J. (2000). Emotion circuits in the brain. *Annual Review of Neuroscience, 23*, 155–184.

LeDoux, J., Iwata, J., Cicchetti, P., & Reis, D. (1988). Different projections of the central amygdaloid nucleus mediate autonomic and behavioral correlates of conditioned fear. *Journal of Neuroscience, 8*(7), 2517–2529.

Legg, E., & Gotestam, K. (1991). The nature and treatment of excessive gambling. *Acta Psychiatrica Scandinavica, 84*(2), 113–120.

Leggio, M. G., Molinari, M., Neri, P., Graziano, A., Mandolesi, L., & Petrosini, L. (2000). Representation of actions in rats: the role of cerebellum in learning spatial performances by observation. *Proceedings of the National Academy of Sciences, 97*(5), 2320–2325.

Leibniz, G. W. (1704). *Nouveaux essais sur l'entendement humain* [New essays on human understanding].

Leighton, J., Bird, G., Charman, T., & Heyes, C. (2008). Weak imitative performance is not due to a functional "mirroring" deficit in adults with autism spectrum disorders. *Neuropsychologica, 46*, 1041–1049.

Leiguarda, R. C., & Marsden, C. D. (2000). Limb apraxias: higher-order disorders of sensorimotor integration. *Brain, 123*(Pt. 5), 860–879.

LeJeune, J., Gautier, M., & Turpin, R. (1959). Etudes des chromosomes somatiques de neuf enfants mongoliens. *Comptes Renus de l'Academic les Sciences, 48*, 1721.

Lenck-Santini, P. P., Save, E., & Poucet, B. (2001). Evidence for a relationship between place-cell spatial firing and spatial memory performance. *Hippocampus, 11*, 377–390.

Leshner, A. (1999). Science-based views of drug addiction and its treatment. *Journal of the American Medical Association, 282*, 1314–1316.

Levenson, R. (1992). Autonomic nervous system differences among emotions. *Psychological Science, 3*(1), 23–27.

Lever, C., Wills, T., Cacucci, F., Burgess, N., & O'Keefe, J. (2002). Long-term plasticity in hippocampal place-cell representation of environmental geometry. *Nature, 416*, 90–94.

Lewis, C. (1981). Skill in algebra. In J. R. Anderson (Ed.), *Cognitive skill learning* (pp. 85–110). Hillsdale, NJ: Lawrence Erlbaum.

Lewis, L. B., Saenz, M., & Fine, I. (2010). Mechanisms of cross-modal plasticity in early-blind subjects. *Journal of Neurophysiology, 104*, 2995–3008.

Lewis, M. C., & Brooks-Gunn, J. (1979). *Social cognition and the acquisition of self.* New York: Plenum.

Lie, C., Song, H., Colamarino, S., Ming, G.-l., & Gage, F. (2004). Neurogenesis in the adult brain: new strategies for central nervous system diseases. *Annual Review of Pharmacology and Toxicology, 44*, 399–421.

Light, L. (1991). Memory and aging: four hypotheses in search of data. *Annual Review of Psychology, 42*, 333–376.

Linden, W. (1981). Exposure treatments for focal phobias. *Archives of General Psychiatry, 38*, 769–775.

Linton, M. (1982). Transformations of memory in everyday life. In U. Neisser (Ed.), *Memory observed: remembering in natural contexts* (pp. 77–91). San Francisco: Freeman.

Little, A., Lipsett, L., & Rovee-Collier, C. (1984). Classical conditioning and retention of the infant's eyelid response: effects of age and interstimulus interval. *Journal of Experimental Child Psychology, 37*, 512–524.

Liu, J., & Wrisberg, C. A. (1997). The effect of knowledge of results delay and the subjective estimation of movement form on the acquisition and retention of a motor skill. *Research Quarterly for Exercise and Sports, 68*, 145–151.

Locke, J. (1690). *An essay concerning human understanding.* London: T. Basset.

Locke, J. (1693). *Some thoughts concerning education.* London: Churchill.

Loftus, E. (1996). *Eyewitness testimony.* Cambridge, MA: Harvard University Press.

Loftus, E. (2003). Our changeable memories: legal and practical implications. *Nature Reviews Neuroscience, 4*, 231–234.

Loftus, E., & Pickrell, J. (1995). The formation of false memories. *Psychiatric Annals, 25*(12), 720–725.

Lømo, T. (1966). Frequency potentiation of excitatory synaptic activity in the dentate area of the hippocampal formation [abstract]. *Acta Physiologica Scandinavica, 68*, 128.

Lorenz, K. (1935). Der Kumpan in der Umwelt des Vogels [Companions as factors in the bird's environment]. *Journal of Ornithology, 83*, 137–215.

Lovaas, O. (1987). Behavioral treatment and normal educational and intellectual functioning in young autistic children. *Journal of Consulting and Clinical Psychology, 55*, 3–9.

Lovibond, P. F., Saunders, J. C., Weidemann, G., & Mitchell, C. J. (2008). Evidence for expectancy as a mediator of avoidance and anxiety in a laboratory model of human avoidance learning. *Quarterly Journal of Experimental Pscyhology, 61*(8), 1199–1216.

Lu, B., & Gottschalk, W. (2000). Modulation of hippocampal synaptic transmission and plasticity by neurotrophins. *Progress in Brain Research, 128*, 231–241.

Lubow, R. E. (1973). Latent inhibition. *Psychological Bulletin, 79*, 398–407.

Lubow, R. E. (1989*). Latent inhibition and conditioned attention theory.* Cambridge, UK: University Press.

Lubow, R. E., & Moore, A. U. (1959). Latent inhibition: the effect of nonreinforced preexposure to the conditioned stimulus. *Journal of Comparative and Physiological Psychology, 52*, 415–419.

Luria, A. R. (1966). *Higher cortical functions in man.* New York: Basic Books.

Luria, A. R. (1982 [1968]). *The mind of a mnemonist* (Lynn Solotaroff, Trans.), New York, Basic Books. In U. Neisser (Ed.), *Memory observed: remembering in natural contexts* (pp. 382–389). San Francisco: Freeman.

Lynn, S. K., Cnaani, J., & Papaj, D. R. (2005). Peak shift discrimination learning as a mechanism of signal evolution. *Evolution, 59*, 1300–1305.

Ma, H. I., Trombly, C. A., & Robinson-Podolski, C. (1999). The effect of context on skill acquisition and transfer. *American Journal of Occupational Therapy, 53*, 138–144.

Mackintosh, N. J. (1975). A theory of attention: variations in the associability of stimuli with reinforcement. *Psychological Review, 82*(4), 276–298.

Magendie, F. (1822). Expériences sur les fonctions des racines des nerfs rachidiens. *Journal de physiologie expérimentale et de pathologie, 2*, 366–371.

Magill, R. (1993). *Motor learning: concepts and applications.* Dubuque, IA: William C. Brown.

Maguire, E. A. (2001). Neuroimaging studies of autobiographical event memory. *Philosophical Transactions of the Royal Society B: Biological Sciences, 356*, 1441–1451.

Maguire, E. A., Gadian, D. G., Johnsrude, I. S., Good, C. D., Ashburner, J., Frackowiak, R. S., & Frith, C. D. (2000). Navigation-related structural change in the hippocampi of taxi drivers. *Proceedings of the National Academy of Science USA, 97*, 4398–4403.

Maguire, E. A., Valentine, E. R., Wilding, J. M., & Kapur, N. (2003). Routes to remembering: the brains behind superior memory. *Nature Neuroscience, 6*, 90–94.

Mair, R., Knoth, R., Rabchenuk, S., & Langlais, P. (1991). Impairment of olfactory, auditory, and spatial serial reversal learning in rats recovered from pyrithiamine-induced thiamine deficiency. *Behavioral Neuroscience, 105*(3), 360–374.

Majewska, A., & Sur, M. (2003). Motility of dendritic spines in visual cortex *in vivo*: changes during the critical period and effects of visual deprivation. *Proceedings of the National Academy of Sciences USA, 100*(26), 16024–16029.

Malcuit, G., Bastien, C., & Pomerleau, A. (1996). Habituation of the orienting response to stimuli of different functional values in 4-month-old infants. *Journal of Experimental Child Psychology, 62*, 272–291.

Malpass, R. S., & Kravitz, L. (1969). Recognition for faces of own and other race. *Journal of Personality and Social Psychology, 13*, 330–334.

Mangels, J. A., Gershberg, F. B., Shimamura, A. P., & Knight, R. T. (1996). Impaired retrieval from remote memory in patients with frontal lobe lesions, *Neuropsychology, 10*, 32–41.

Manns, J., Hopkins, R., & Squire, L. (2003). Semantic memory and the human hippocampus. *Neuron, 38*, 127–133.

Marcus, E. A., Nolen, T. G., Rankin, C. H., & Carew, T. J. (1988). Behavioral dissociation of dishabituation, sensitization, and inhibition in *Aplysia*. *Science, 241*, 210–213.

Maren, S. (1999). Long-term potentiation in the amygdala: a mechanism for emotional learning and memory. *Trends in Neurosciences, 22*, 561–567.

Margoliash, D. (2002). Evaluating theories of bird song learning: implications for future directions. *Journal of Comparative Physiology A—Neuroethology, Sensory, Neural and Behavioral Physiology, 188*, 851–866.

Markowitsch, H. (1983). Transient global amnesia. *Neuroscience and Biobehavioral Reviews, 7*, 35–43.

Markowitsch, H. (1992). *Intellectual functions and the brain—an historical perspective.* Kirkland, WA: Hogrefe and Huber.

Markowitsch, H., Calabrese, P., Wurker, M., Durwen, H., Kessler, J., Babinsky, R., et al. (1994). The amygdala's contribution to memory—a study on two patients with Urbach-Wiethe disease. *Neuroreport, 5*(11), 1349–1352.

Markowitsch, H., Kessler, J., Van der Ven, C., Weber-Luxenburger, G., Albers, M., & Heiss, W. (1998). Psychic trauma causing grossly reduced brain metabolism and cognitive deterioration. *Neuropsychologia, 36*, 77–82.

Marler, P. (1970a). Birdsong and speech development: could there be parallels? *American Scientist, 58*(6), 669–673.

Marler, P. (1970b). A comparative approach to vocal song learning: song development in white-crowned sparrows. *Journal of Comparative and Physiological Psychology, 71*, 1–25.

Marler, P. (1997). Three models of song learning: evidence from behavior. *Journal of Neurobiology, 33*(5), 501–516.

Marsh, R., & Bower, G. (1993). Eliciting cryptomnesia: unconscious plagiarism in a puzzle task. *Journal of Experimental Psychology: Learning, 19*(3), 673–688.

Martin, M., & Jones, G. V. (1995). Danegeld remembered: taxing further the coin head illusion. *Memory 3*(1), 97–104.

Martineau, J., Andersson, F., Barthelemy, C., Cottier, J. P., & Destrieux, C. (2010). Atypical activation of the mirror neuron system during perception of hand motion in autism. *Brain Research, 1320*, 168–175.

Martínez-Cué, C., Baamonde, C., Lumbreras, M., Paz, J., Davisson, M., Schmidt, C., et al. (2002). Differential effects of environmental enrichment on behavior and learning of male and female Ts65Dn mice, a model for Down syndrome. *Behavioural Brain Research, 134*, 185–200.

Martinussen, R., & Major, A. (2011). Working memory weaknesses in students with ADHD: implications for instruction. *Theory into Practice, 50*(1), 68–75.

Mathes, W. F., Nehrenberg, D. L., Gordon, R., Hua, K., Garland, T., & Pomp, D. (2010). Dopaminergic dysregulation in mice selectively bred for excessive exercise or obesity. *Behavioural Brain Research, 210*(2), 155–163.

Matson, J. L., & Boisjoli, J. A. (2009). The token economy for children with intellectual disability and/or autism: a review. *Research in Developmental Disabilities, 30*(2), 240–248.

Matsumoto, D., & Ekman, P. (1989). American-Japanese cultural differences in intensity ratings of facial expressions of emotion. *Motivation and Emotion, 13*, 143–157.

Matsumoto, M., & Hikosaka, O. (2009). Two types of dopamine neuron distinctly convey positive and negative motivational signals. *Nature, 459*(7248), 837–841.

Maurer, D., & Lewis, T. (1999). Rapid improvement in the acuity of infants after visual input. *Science, 286*, 108–110.

Mazarakis, N. K., Cybulska-Klosowicz, A., Grote, H., Pang, T., Van Dellen, A., Kossut, M., et al. (2005). Deficits in experience-dependent cortical plasticity and sensory-discrimination learning in presymptomatic Huntington's disease mice. *Journal of Neuroscience, 25*, 3059–3066.

McAllister, W. R. (1953). Eyelid conditioning as a function of the CS-US interval. *Journal of Experimental Psychology, 45*(6), 417–422.

McBride, W. J., Murphy, J. M., & Ikemoto, S. (1999). Localization of brain reinforcement mechanisms: intracranial self-administration and intracranial place-conditioning studies. *Behavioural Brain Research, 101*(2), 129–152.

McCarthy, R., & Warrington, E. (1985). Category specificity in an agrammatic patient: the relative impairment of verb retrieval and comprehension. *Neuropsychologia, 23*(6), 709–727.

McClearn, G., Johansson, B., Berg, S., Pedersen, N., Ahern, F., Petrill, S., et al. (1997). Substantial genetic influence on cognitive abilities in twins 80 or more years old. *Science, 276*(5318), 1560–1563.

McClure, H. M., Belden, K. H., Pieper, W. A., & Jacobson, C. B. (1969). Autosomal trisomy in a chimpanzee: resemblance to Down's syndrome. *Science, 165*(897), 1010–1012.

McConnell, S. K., & Spitzer, N. C. (Eds.). (2003). *Fundamental neuroscience* (2nd ed., pp. 1353–1376). New York: Academic Press.

McCormick, D. A., & Thompson, R. F. (1984). Neuronal responses of the rabbit cerebellum during acquisition and performance of a classically conditioned nictitating membrane-eyelid response. *Journal of Neuroscience, 4*(11), 2811–2822.

McCutcheon, L. (2000). Another failure to generalize the Mozart effect. *Psychological Reports, 87*(1), 325–330.

McDonald, R. J., & White, N. M. (1994). Parallel information processing in the water maze: evidence for independent memory systems involving dorsal striatum and hippocampus. *Behavioral and Neural Biology, 61*(3), 260–270.

McEwen, B. (1997). Possible mechanism for atrophy of the human hippocampus. *Molecular Psychiatry, 2*, 255–262.

McEwen, B. (1999). Stress and hippocampal plasticity. *Annual Review of Neuroscience, 22*, 105–122.

McEwen, B., & Sapolsky, R. (1995). Stress and cognitive function. *Current Opinion in Neurobiology, 5*, 205–216.

McGaugh, J. L. (2000). Memory—a century of consolidation. *Science, 287*(5451), 248–251.

McGaugh, J. L. (2002). Memory consolidation and the amygdala: a systems perspective. *Trends in Neurosciences, 25*(9), 456–460.

McGaugh, J. L. (2003). *Memory and emotion: the making of lasting memories.* New York: Columbia University Press.

McGaugh, J. L., & Cahill, L. (2003). Emotion and memory: central and peripheral contributions. In R. Davidson, K. Scherer & H. Goldsmith (Eds.), *Handbook of affective sciences* (pp. 93–116). New York: Oxford University Press.

McIntyre, C., Hatfield, T., & McGaugh, J. (2000). Amygdala norepinephrine levels after training predict inhibitory avoidance retention performance in rats. *European Journal of Neuroscience, 16*, 1223–1226.

McIntyre, C., Power, A., Roozendaal, B., & McGaugh, J. (2003). Role of the basolateral amygdala in memory consolidation. *Annuals of the New York Academy of Sciences, 985*, 273–293.

McKelvie, P., & Low, J. (2002). Listening to Mozart does not improve children's spatial ability: final curtains for the Mozart effect. *British Journal of Developmental Psychology, 20*, 241–258.

McLaren, I. P. L., & Mackintosh, N. J. (2002). Associative learning and elemental representation: II. generalization and discrimination. *Animal Learning and Behavior, 30*, 177–200.

McLellan, A., Lewis, D., O'Brien, C., & Kleber, H. (2000). Drug dependence, a chronic medical illness: implications for treatment, insurance, and outcomes evaluation. *Journal of the American Medical Association, 284*, 1689–1695.

McNally, R., Bryant, R., & Ehlers, A. (2003). Does early psychological intervention promote recovery from post-traumatic stress? *Psychological Science in the Public Interest, 4*(2), 45–79.

Mehta, M. A., Owen, A. M., Sahakian, B. J., Mavaddat, N., Pickard, J. D., & Robbins, T. W. (2000). Methylphenidate enhances working memory by modulating discrete frontal and parietal lobe regions in the human brain. *Journal of Neuroscience, 20*, RC65.

Meissner, C. A., & Brigham, J. C. (2001). Thirty years of investigating the own-race bias in memory for faces—a meta-analytic review. *Psychology Public Policy and Law, 7*, 3–35.

Meltzoff, A. N. (1996). The human infant as imitative generalist: a 20-year progress report on infant imitation with implications for comparative psychology. In C. M. Heyes & B. G. Galef (Eds.), *Social learning in animals: the roots of culture* (pp. 347–370). San Diego, CA: Academic Press.

Meltzoff, A. N., & Moore, M. (1977). Imitation of facial and manual gestures by human neonates. *Science, 198*, 75–78.

Mercado, E., III (2008). Neural and cognitive plasticity: from maps to minds. *Psychological Bulletin, 134*, 109–137.

Mercado, E., III, Murray, S., Uyeyama, R., Pack, A., & Herman, L. (1998). Memory for recent actions in the bottlenosed dolphin (*Tursiops truncates*): repetition of arbitrary behaviors using an abstract rule. *Animal Learning and Behavior, 26*(2), 210–218.

Meyer, M., Baumann, S., Wildgruber, D., & Alter, K. (2007). How the brain laughs. Comparative evidence from behavioral, electrophysiological and neuroimaging studies in human and monkey. *Behavioural Brain Research, 182*(2), 245–260.

Michel, G. F., & Tyler, A. N. (2005). Critical period: a history of the transition from questions of when, to what, to how. *Developmental Psychobiology, 46*, 209–221.

Miles, C., Green, R., Sanders, G., & Hines, M. (1998). Estrogen and memory in a transsexual population. *Hormones and Behavior, 34*(2), 199–208.

Miller, E. K. (2000). The prefrontal cortex and cognitive control. *Nature Reviews Neuroscience, 1*, 59–65.

Miller, E. K., Erickson, C. A., & Desimone, R. (1996). Neural mechanisms of visual working memory in prefrontal cortex of the macaque. *Journal of Neuroscience 16*, 5154–5167.

Miller, E. K., & Wallis, J. D. (2008). The prefrontal cortex and executive brain functions. *Fundamental Neuroscience* (3d ed.). New York: Elsevier.

Miller, G. A. (1956). The magical number seven, plus or minus two: some limits on our capacity for processing information. *Psychological Review, 63*, 81–97.

Miller, J. W., Petersen, R. C., Metter, E. J., Millikan, C. H., & Yanagihara, T. (1987). Transient global amnesia: clinical characteristics and prognosis. *Neurology, 37*(5), 733–737.

Miller, N. E., & Dollard, J. (1941). *Social learning and imitation*. New Haven, CT: Yale University Press.

Milner, B. (1966). Amnesia following operation on the temporal lobes. In C. Whitty & O. Zangwill (Eds.), *Amnesia* (pp. 109–133). New York: Appleton-Century-Crofts.

Milner, B., Corkin, S., & Teuber, J. (1968). Further analysis of the hippocampal amnesic syndrome: a 14-year follow-up study of HM. *Neuropsychologia, 6*, 215–234.

Mineka, S., & Cook, M. (1988). Social learning and the acquisition of snake fear in monkeys. In T. R. Zentall & B. G. Galef (Eds.), *Social learning: psychological and biological perspectives* (pp. 51–73). Hillsdale, NJ: Erlbaum.

Minshew, N. J., & Williams, D. L. (2007). The new neurobiology of autism—cortex, connectivity, and neuronal organization. *Archives of Neurology, 64*, 945–950.

Misanin, J. R., Miller, R. R., & Lewis, D. J. (1968). Retrograde amnesia produced by electroconvulsive shock after reactivation of a memory trace. *Science, 160*, 554–555.

Mishkin, M. (1978). Memory in monkeys severely disrupted by combined but not by separate removal of amygdala and hippocampus. *Nature, 273*, 297–299.

Mizumori, S. J., Miya, D. Y., & Ward, K. E. (1994). Reversible inactivation of the lateral dorsal thalamus disrupts hippocampal place representation and impairs spatial learning. *Brain Research, 644*, 168–174.

Mobbs, D., Greicius, M., Abdel-Azim, E., Menon, V., & Reiss, A. (2003). Humor modulates the mesolimbic reward centers. *Neuron, 40*(5), 1041–1048.

Moncaster, J. A., Pineda, R., Moir, R. D., Lu, S., Burton, M. A., Ghosh, J. G., et al. (2010). Alzheimer's disease amyloid-beta links lens and brain pathology in Down syndrome. *PLoS One, 5*(5), e10659.

Mooney, R. (2009). Neurobiology of song learning. *Current Opinion in Neurobiology, 19*, 654–660.

Moore, J. W., & Gormezano, I. (1961). Yoked comparisons of instrumental and classical eyelid conditioning. *Journal of Experimental Psychology, 62*, 552–559.

Moray, N., Bates, A., & Barnett, T. (1965). Experiments on the four-eared man. *Journal of the Acoustical Society of America, 38*(2), 196–201.

Morgan, C. L. (1896). *Habit and instinct*. London: Edward Arnold.

Morishita, H., & Hensch, T. K. (2008). Critical period revisited: impact on vision. *Current Opinion in Neurobiology, 18*, 101–107.

Morris, C., Bransford, J., & Franks, J. (1977). Levels of processing versus transfer appropriate processing. *Journal of Verbal Learning and Verbal Behavior, 16*(5), 519–533.

Moscovitch, M., & Nadel, L. (1998). Consolidation and the hippocampal complex revisited: in defense of the multiple-trace model. *Current Opinion in Neurobiology, 8*, 297–300.

Moss, C. (1988). *Elephant memories: thirteen years in the life of an elephant family.* New York: Fawcett Columbine.

Mowrer, O. H. (1960). *Learning theory and behavior.* New York: Wiley.

Muhlberger, A., Herrmann, M., Wiedeman, G., Ellgring, H., & Pauli, P. (2001). Repeated exposure of flight phobics to flights in virtual reality. *Behavioral Research Therapy, 39*(9), 1033–1050.

Murray, E. A., O'Doherty, J. P., & Schoenbaum, G. (2007). What we know and do not know about the functions of the orbitofrontal cortex after 20 years of cross-species studies. *Journal of Neuroscience, 27*(31), 8166–8169.

Myers, C. E., Ermita, B. R., Hasselmo, M., & Gluck, M. A. (1998). Further implications of a computational model of septohippocampal cholinergic modulation in eyeblink conditioning. *Psychobiology, 26*(1), 1–20.

Myers, C. E., Kluger, A., Golomb, J., Ferris, S., de Leon, M. J., Schnirman, G., et al. (2002). Hippocampal atrophy disrupts transfer generalization in non-demented elderly. *Journal of Geriatric Psychiatry and Neurology, 15*(2), 82–90.

Myers, C. E., Kluger, A., Golomb, J., Gluck, M. A., & Ferris, S. (2008). Learning and generalization tasks predict short-term outcome in non-demented elderly. *Journal of Geriatric Psychiatry and Neurology, 21*, 93–103.

Myers, C. E., Shohamy, D., Gluck, M. A., Grossman, S., Kluger, A., Ferris, S., et al. (2003). Dissociating hippocampal versus basal ganglia contributions to learning and transfer. *Journal of Cognitive Neuroscience, 15*(2), 185–193.

Myers, N., Perris, E., & Speaker, C. (1994). Fifty months of memory: a longitudinal study in early childhood. *Memory, 2*, 383–415.

Nadel, L. (1999). Down syndrome in cognitive neuroscience perspective. In H. Tager-Flusberg (Ed.), *Neurodevelopmental disorders* (pp. 197–221). Cambridge, MA: MIT Press.

Nadel, L. (2003). Down syndrome: a genetic disorder in biobehavioral perspective. *Genes, Brain, and Behavior, 2*(3), 156–166.

Nadel, L., & Land, D. (2000). Memory traces revisited. *Nature Reviews Neuroscience, 1*(3), 209–212.

Nadel, L., & Moscovitch, M. (1997). Memory consolidation, retrograde amnesia and the hippocampal complex. *Current Opinion in Neurobiology, 7*(2), 217–227.

Nadel, L., & Moscovitch, M. (2001). The hippocampal complex and long-term memory revisited. *Trends in Cognitive Science, 5*, 228–230.

Nadel, L., Samsonovich, A., Ryan, L., & Moscovitch, M. (2000). Multiple trace theory of human memory: computational, neuroimaging and neuropsychological results. *Hippocampus, 10*, 352–368.

Nader, K. (2003). Memory traces unbound. *Trends in Neurosciences, 26*(2), 65–72.

Nader, K., & Hardt, O. (2009). A single standard for memory: the case for reconsolidation. *Nature Reviews Neuroscience, 10*(3), 224–234.

Nader, K., Schafe, G. E., & LeDoux, J. E. (2000a). Fear memories require protein synthesis in the amygdala for reconsolidation after retrieval. *Nature, 406*, 722–727.

Nader, K., Schafe, G. E., & LeDoux, J. E. (2000b). The labile nature of consolidation theory. *Nature Reviews Neuroscience, 1*(3), 216–219.

Nagell, K., Olguin, R. S., & Tomasello, M. (1993). Processes of social learning in the tool use of chimpanzees (*Pan troglodytes*) and human children (*Homo sapiens*). *Journal of Comparative Psychology, 107*(2), 174–186.

Naghdi, N., Majlessi, N., & Bozorgmehr, T. (2005). The effect of intrahippocampal injection of testosterone enanthate (an androgen receptor agonist) and anisomycin (protein synthesis inhibitor) on spatial learning and memory in adult, male rats. *Behavioural Brain Research, 156*(2), 263–268.

Nargeot, R., Baxter, D., Patterson, G., & Byrne, J. (1999). Dopaminergic synapses mediate neuronal changes in an analogue of operant conditioning. *Journal of Neurophysiology, 81*, 1983–1987.

Naskar, S., Sood, S. K., Goyal, V., & Dhara, M. (2010). Mechanism(s) of deep brain stimulation and insights into cognitive outcomes of Parkinson's disease. *Brain Research Reviews, 65*, 1–13.

National Down Syndrome Society. (2010). *Fact sheet.*

National Institutes of Health Consensus Conference. (1985). Electroconvulsive therapy. *Journal of the American Medical Association, 254*, 2103–2108.

Naveh-Benjamin, M. (1991). A comparison of training programs intended for different types of test-anxious students: further support for an information processing model. *Journal of Educational Psychology, 83*, 134–139.

Neath, I. (2010). Evidence for similar principles in episodic and semantic memory: the presidential serial position function. *Memory and Cognition, 38*(5), 659–667.

Neisser, U. (1982). Snapshots or benchmarks? In U. Neisser (Ed.), *Memory observed: remembering in natural contexts* (pp. 43–49). San Francisco: Freeman.

Neisser, U., & Harsch, N. (1992). Phantom flashbulbs: false recollections of hearing the news about *Challenger.* In E. Winograd & U. Neisser (Eds.), *Affect and accuracy in recall: studies of "flashbulb" memories* (pp. 9–31). New York: Cambridge University Press.

Nemetz, G. H., Craig, K. D., & Reith, G. (1978). Treatment of sexual dysfunction through symbolic modeling. *Journal for Consulting and Clinical Psychology, 46*, 62–73.

Netzer, W. J., Powell, C., Nong, Y., Blundel, J., Wong, L., Duff, K., et al. (2010). Lowering ß-amyloid levels rescues learning and memory in a Down syndrome mouse model. *PLoS One5*, 6(e10943).

Neufield, P., & Dwyer, J. (2000). *Actual innocence: five days to execution and other dispatches from the wrongly convicted.* New York: Doubleday.

Neuringer, A. (1969). Animals respond for food in the presence of free food. *Science, 166*, 399–401.

Newell, A., & Rosenbaum, P. S. (1981). Mechanism of skill acquisition and the law of practice. In J. R. Anderson (Ed.), *Cognitive skill acquisition* (pp. 1–56). Hillsdale, NJ: Lawrence Erlbaum.

Newell, K. M. (1991). Motor skill acquisition. *Annual Review of Psychology, 42*, 213–237.

Newport, E. (1990). Maturational constraints on language learning. *Cognitive Science, 14*, 11–28.

Nickerson, R. S., & Adams, M. J. (1979). Long-term memory for a common object. *Cognitive Psychology, 11*(3), 287–307.

Nikolaev, A., McLaughlin, T., O'Leary, D. D., & Tessier-Lavigne, M. (2009). APP binds DR6 to trigger axon pruning and neuron death via distinct caspases. *Nature, 457*(7232), 981–989.

Nishimura, Y., Yalgin, C., Akimoto, S., Dourmanis, J., Sasjima, R., Nukina, N., & Miyakawa, H. (2010). Selection of behaviors and segmental coordination during larval locomotion is disrupted by nuclear polyglutamine inclusions in a new *Drosophila* Huntington's disease-like model. *Journal of Neurogenetics, 24*, 194–206.

Nishitani, N., Avikainen, S., & Hari, R. (2004). Abnormal imitation-related cortical activation sequences in Asperger's syndrome. *Annals of Neurology, 55*(4), 558–562.

Nithianantharajah, J., Barkus, C., Vijiaratnam, N., Clement, O., & Hannan, A. J. (2009). Modeling brain reserve: experience-dependent neuronal plasticity in healthy and Huntington's disease transgenic mice. *American Journal of Geriatric Psychiatry, 17*, 196–209.

Nithianantharajah, J., & Hannan, A. J. (2009). The neurobiology of brain and cognitive reserve: mental and physical activity as modulators of brain disorders. *Progress in Neurobiology, 89*(4), 369–382.

Noad, M. J., Cato, D. H., Bryden, M. M., Jenner, M. N., & Jenner, K. C. S. (2000). Cultural revolution in whale songs. *Nature, 408*, 537.

Norman, D. A., & Shallice, T. (1986). Attention to action: willed and automatic control of behavior. In R. J. Davidoson, G. E. Schwartz, & D. Shapiro (Eds.), *Consciousness and self-regulation* (vol. 4, pp. 1–17). New York: Plenum.

Norrholm, S. D., & Ressler, K. J. (2009). Genetics of anxiety and trauma-related disorders. *Neuroscience, 164*(1), 272–287.

Nowakowski, R., & Hayes, N. (2000). New neurons: extraordinary evidence or extraordinary conclusion? *Science, 288*, 771a.

Nudo, R. J., Milliken, G. W., Jenkins, W. M., & Merzenich, M. M. (1996). Use-dependent alterations of movement representations in primary motor cortex of adult squirrel monkeys. *Journal of Neuroscience, 16*, 785–807.

Nyberg, L., Cabeza, R., & Tulving, E. (1996). PET studies of encoding and retrieval: the HERA model. *Psychonomic Bulletin & Review, 3*, 135–148.

O'Keefe, J., & Dostrovsky, J. (1971). The hippocampus as a spatial map: preliminary evidence from unit activity in the freely-moving rat. *Brain Research, 34*, 171–175.

O'Doherty, J., Dayan, P., Schultz, J., Deichmann, R., Fristen, K., & Dolan, R. (2004). Dissociable roles of ventral and dorsal striatum in instrumental conditioning. *Science, 304*(5669), 452–455.

Okado, Y., & Stark, C. (2003). Neural processing associated with true and false memory retrieval. *Cognitive, Affective and Behavioral Neuroscience, 3*, 323–334.

Olds, J. (1955). "Reward" from brain stimulation in the rat. *Science, 122*, 878.

Olds, J. (1958). Self-stimulation of the brain. *Science, 127*, 315–323.

Olton, D. (1983). Memory functions and the hippocampus. In W. Seifert (Ed.), *Neurobiology of the hippocampus* (pp. 335–373). London: Academic Press.

Orr, S. P., Metzger, L. J., Lasko, N. B., Macklin, M. L., Hu, F. B., Shalev, A. Y., et al. (2003). Physiologic responses to sudden, loud tones in monozygotic twins discordant for combat exposure. *Archives of General Psychiatry, 60*, 283–288.

Orr, S. P., Metzger, L. J., Lasko, N. B., Macklin, M. L., Peri, T., & Pitman, R. K. (2000). De novo conditioning in trauma-exposed individuals with and without posttraumatic stress disorder. *Journal of Abnormal Psychology, 109*(2), 290–298.

Orth, M., Schippling, S., Schneider, S. A., Bhatia, K. P., Talelli, P., Tabrizi, S. J., et al. (2010). Abnormal motor cortex plasticity in premanifest and very early manifest Huntington disease. *Journal of Neurology, Neurosurgery, and Psychiatry, 81*, 267–270.

Ottersen, O., & Helm, P. (2002). Neurobiology: how hardwired is the brain? *Nature, 420*, 751–752.

Ouellet, J., Rouleau, I., Labrecque, R., Bernier, G., & Scherzer, P. B. (2008). Two routes to losing one's past life: a brain trauma, an emotional trauma. *Behavioral Neurology, 20*(1–2), 27–38.

Overman, W., Bachevalier, J., Schuhmann, E., & Ryan, P. (1996). Cognitive gender differences in very young children parallel biologically based cognitive gender differences in monkeys. *Behavioral Neuroscience, 110*, 673–684.

Overmier, J., & Seligman, M. (1967). Effects of inescapable shock upon subsequent escape and avoidance learning. *Journal of Comparative and Physiological Psychology, 63*, 23–33.

Owen, A. M., Evans, A. C., & Petrides, M. (1996). Evidence for a two-stage model of spatial working memory processing within the lateral frontal cortex: a positron emission tomography study. *Cerebral Cortex, 6*(1), 31–38.

Owen, A. M., Roberts, A. C., Hodges, J. R., Summers, B. A., Polkey, C. E., & Robbins, T. W. (1993). Contrasting mechanisms of impaired attentional set-shifting in patients with frontal lobe damage or Parkinson's disease. *Brain, 116,* 1159–1179.

Packard, M. G., Hirsh, R., & White, N. M. (1989). Differential effects of fornix and caudate nucleus lesions on two radial maze tasks: evidence for multiple memory systems. *Journal of Neuroscience, 9,* 1465–1472.

Padoa-Schioppa, C., & Assad, J. A. (2006). Neurons in the orbitofrontal cortex encode economic value. *Nature, 441*(7090), 223–226.

Pakkenberg, B., & Gundersen, H. (1997). Neocortical neuron number in humans: effect of sex and age. *Journal of Comparative Neurology, 384,* 312–320.

Panksepp, J., & Burgdorf, J. (2003). "Laughing" rats and the evolutionary antecedents of human joy? *Physiology and Behavior, 79*(3), 533–547.

Papassotiropoulos, A., Henke, K., Stefanova, E., Aerni, A., Muller, A., Demougin, P., et al. (2009). A genome-wide survey of human short-term memory. *Molecular Psychiatry.*

Paradis, C. M., Solomon, L. Z., Florer, F., & Thompson, T. (2004). Flashbulb memories of personal events of 9/11 and the day after for a sample of New York City residents. *Psychological Reports, 95*(1), 304–310.

Paré, D. (2002). Mechanisms of Pavlovian fear conditioning: has the engram been located? *Trends in Neurosciences, 25*(9), 436–437.

Paré, D. (2003). Role of the basolateral amygdala in memory consolidation. *Progress in Neurobiology, 70,* 409–420.

Park, S., & Holzman, P. S. (1992). Schizophrenics show spatial working memory deficits. *Archives of General Psychiatry, 49,* 975–982.

Park, S., Holzman, P. S., & Goldman-Rakic, P. S. (1992). Spatial working memory deficits in the relatives of schizophrenia patients. *Archives of General Psychiatry, 52,* 821–828.

Paton, J., & Nottebohm, F. (1984). Neurons generated in the adult brain are recruited into functional circuits. *Science, 225,* 1046–1048.

Pavlov, I. P. (1927). *Conditioned reflexes: an investigation of the physiological activity of the cerebral cortex.* London: Oxford University Press.

Payne, K., & Payne, R. (1985). Large scale changes over 19 years in songs of humpback whales in Bermuda. *Zeitschrift für Tierpsychologie, 68,* 89–114.

Pearce, A. J., Thickbroom, G. W., Byrnes, M. L., & Mastaglia, F. L. (2000). Functional reorganization of the corticomotor projection to the hand in skilled racquetball players. *Experimental Brain Research, 130,* 238–243.

Pearce, J., & Hall, G. (1980). A model for Pavlovian learning: variations in the effectiveness of conditioned but not of unconditioned stimuli. *Psychological Review, 87,* 532–552.

Pedreira, M., Romano, A., Tomsic, D., Lozada, M., & Maldonado, H. (1998). Massed and spaced training build up different components of long-term habituation in the crab *Chasmagnathus. Animal Learning and Behavior, 26,* 34–45.

Peisner-Feinberg, E., Burchinal, M., & Clifford, R. (2001). The relation of preschool child-care quality to children's cognitive and social developmental trajectories through second grade. *Child Development, 72,* 1534–1553.

Penfield, W., & Boldrey, E. (1937). Somatic motor and sensory representations in cerebral cortex of man as studied by electrical stimulation. *Brain, 60,* 389–443.

Penfield, W., & Rasmussen, T. (1950). *The cerebral cortex of man: a clinical study of the localization of function.* New York: Macmillan.

Pennington, B., Moon, J., Edgin, J., Stedron, J., & Nadel, L. (2003). The neuropsychology of Down syndrome: evidence for hippocampal dysfunction. *Child Development, 74*(1), 75–93.

Pepperberg, I. M. (1994). Vocal learning in gray parrots (*Psittacus erithacus*)—effects of social interaction, reference, and context. *Auk, 111,* 300–313.

Peri, T., Ben-Shakhar, G., Orr, S. P., & Shalev, A. Y. (2000). Psychophysiologic assessment of aversive conditioning in posttraumatic disorder. *Biological Psychiatry, 47*(6), 512–519.

Perret, S. P., Ruiz, B. P., & Mauk, M. D. (1993). Cerebellar cortex lesions disrupt learning-dependent timing of conditioned eyelid responses. *Journal of Neuroscience, 13,* 1708–1718.

Perry, L. K., Samuelson, L. K., Malloy, L. M., & Schiffer, R. N. (2010). Learn locally, think globally: exemplar variability supports higher-order generalization and word learning. *Psychological Science, 1*(12), 1894–1902.

Peters, A., Rosene, D., Moss, M., Kemper, T., Abraham, C., Tigges, J., et al. (1996). Neurobiological bases of age-related cognitive decline in the rhesus monkey. *Journal of Neuropathology and Experimental Neurology, 55,* 861–874.

Petrides, M. (1991). Monitoring of selections of visual stimuli and the primate frontal cortex. *Proceedings of the Royal Society of London B, 246,* 293–298.

Petrides, M. (1994). Frontal lobes and working memory: evidence from investigations of the effects on cortical excisions in nonhuman primates. In F. Boller & J. Grafman (Eds.), *Handbook of neuropsychology* (vol. 9, pp. 59–82). Amsterdam: Elsevier.

Petrides, M. (1995). Impairments on nonspatial self-ordered and externally ordered working memory tasks after lesions of the mid-dorsal part of the lateral frontal cortex in the monkey. *Journal of Neuroscience 15*, 359–375.

Petrides, M. (1996). Specialized systems for the processing of mnemonic information within the primate frontal cortex. *Philosophical Transactions of the Royal Society of London, Series B, 351*, 1455–1461.

Petrides, M. (2000). Frontal lobes and memory. In F. Boller & J. Grafman (Eds.), *Handbook of neuropsychology* (2nd ed., vol. 2, pp. 67–84). Amsterdam: Elsevier.

Petrides, M. (2002). The mid-ventrolateral prefrontal cortex and active mnemonic retrieval. *Neurobiology of Learning and Memory, 78*, 528–538.

Petrides, M. (2006). The rostro-caudal axis of cognitive control processing within lateral frontal cortex. In S. Dehaene (Ed.), *From monkey brain to human brain: a Fyssen Foundation symposium* (pp. 293–314). Cambridge, MA: MIT Press.

Petrides, M., Alivisatos, B., Evans, A. C., & Meyer, E. (1993a). Dissociation of human mid- dorsolateral from posterior dorsolateral frontal cortex in memory processing. *Proceedings of the National Academy of Sciences USA, 90*(3), 873–877.

Petrides, M., Alivisatos, B., Meyer, E., & Evans, A. C. (1993b). Functional activation of the human frontal cortex during the performance of verbal working memory tasks. *Proceedings of the National Academy of Sciences USA, 90*(3), 878–882.

Petrides, M., & Milner, B. (1982). Deficits on subject-ordered tasks after frontal and temporal-lobe lesions in man. *Neuropsychologia, 20*, 249–262.

Pettigrew, T. (1979). The ultimate attribution error: extending Allport's cognitive analysis of prejudice. *Personality & Social Psychology Bulletin, 5*(4), 461–476.

Pfeifer, B. (1922). Die Bedeutung psychologischer Leistungs- und Arbeitsprüfungen für die Topik der Grosshirnrinde [On the role of psychological tests of performance and work for the topical arrangement of the cerebral cortex]. *Zeitschrift für die gesamte Neurologie und Psychiatrie, 30*, 139–142.

Pfordersher, P. Q., & Brown, S. (2007). Poor-pitch singing in the absence of "tone deafness." *Music Perception, 25*, 95–115.

Phan, K., Wagner, T., Taylor, S., & Liberzon, I. (2002). Functional neuroanatomy of emotion: a meta-analysis of emotion activation studies in PET and fMRI. *NeuroImage, 16*, 331–348.

Phelps, E. A., & Sharot, T. (2008). How (and why) emotion enhances the subjective sense of recollection. *Current Directions in Psychological Science, 17*(2), 147–152.

Phillips, R., & LeDoux, J. (1992). Differential contribution of amygdala and hippocampus to cued and contextual fear conditioning. *Behavioral Neuroscience, 106*(2), 274–285.

Phillips, S., & Sherwin, B. (1992). Variations in memory function and sex steroid hormone across the menstrual cycle. *Psychoneuroendocrinology, 17*(5), 497–506.

Piaget, J. (1955). *The child's construction of reality*. London: Routledge.

Piaget, J. (1962). *Play, dreams, and imitation in childhood*. New York: Norton.

Pietrzak, R. H., Johnson, D. C., Goldstein, M. B., Malley, J. C., & Southwick, S. M. (2009). Psychological resilience and postdeployment social support protect against traumatic stress and depressive symptoms in soldiers returning from Operations Enduring Freedom and Iraqi Freedom. *Journal of Special Operations Medicine, 9*(3), 67–73.

Pilz, K., Veit, R., Braun, C., & Godde, B. (2004). Effects of co-activation on cortical organization and discrimination performance. *Neuroreport, 15*, 2669–2672.

Pinsker, H., Kupfermann, I., Castellucci, V., & Kandel, E. (1970). Habituation and dishabituation of the gill-withdrawal reflex in *Aplysia. Science, 167*, 1740–1742.

Piolino, P., Desgranges, B., Benali, K., & Eustache, F. (2002). Episodic and semantic remote autobiographical memory in ageing. *Memory, 10*(4), 239–257.

Pitman, R. K., Gilbertson, M. W., Gurvits, T. V., May, F. S., Lasko, N. B., Metzger, L. J., et al. (2006). Clarifying the origin of biological abnormalities in PTSD through the study of identical twins discordant for combat exposure. *Annals of the New York Academy of Sciences, 1071*, 242–254.

Pitman, R. K., Sanders, K., Zusman, R., Healy, A., Cheema, F., Lasko, N., et al. (2002). Pilot study of secondary prevention of posttraumatic stress disorder with propranolol. *Biological Psychiatry, 51*(2), 189–192.

Plaud, J., Gaither, G., Henderson, S., & Devitt, M. (1997). The long-term habituation of sexual arousal in human males: a crossover design. *Psychological Record, 47*, 385–398.

Pohl, P. S., McDowd, J. M., Filion, D. L., Richards, L. G., & Stiers, W. (2001). Implicit learning of a perceptual-motor skill after stroke. *Physical Therapy, 81*, 1780–1789.

Poldrack, R. A., Clark, J., Pare-Blagoev, E. J., Shohamy, D., Creso-Moyano, J., Myers, C. E., & Gluck, M. A. (2001). Interactive memory systems in the brain. *Nature, 414*, 546–550.

Poldrack, R. A., & Gabrieli, J. D. E. (2001). Characterizing the neural mechanisms of skill learning and repetition priming: evidence from mirror reading. *Brain, 124*(Pt. 1), 67–82.

Poldrack, R. A., Prabhakaran, V., Seger, C. A., & Gabrieli, J. D. E. (1999). Striatal activation during acquisition of a cognitive skill. *Neuropsychology, 13*, 564–574.

Poldrack, R. A., Wagner, A. D., Prull, M. W., Desmond, J. E., Glover, G. H., & Gabrieli, J. D. E. (1999). Functional specialization for semantic and phonological processing in the left inferior frontal cortex. *NeuroImage 10*, 15–35.

Polgár, P., Farkas, M., Nagy, O., Kelemen, O., Réthelvi, J., Bitter, I., et al. (2009). How to find the way out from four rooms? The learning of "chaining" associations may shed light on the neuropsychology of the deficit syndrome in schizophrenia. *Schizophrenia Research, 99*(1–3), 200–207.

Polusny, M. A., Erbes, C. R., Murdoch, M., Arbisi, P. A., Thuras, P., & Rath, M. B. (2010). Prospective risk factors for new-onset post-traumatic stress disorder in National Guard soldiers deployed to Iraq. *Psychological Medicine, 10*, 1–12.

Poo, M. (2001). Neurotrophins as synaptic modulators. *Nature Reviews Neuroscience, 2*, 24–32.

Port, R., & Patterson, M. (1984). Fimbrial lesions and sensory preconditioning. *Behavioral Neuroscience, 98*, 584–589.

Porter, J. (1977). Pseudorca stranding. *Oceans, 4*, 8–14.

Postle, B. R. (2006). Working memory as an emergent property of the mind and brain. *Neuroscience, 139*, 23–38.

Potenza, M., Kosten, T., & Rounsaville, B. (2001). Pathological gambling. *Journal of the American Medical Association, 286*(2), 141–144.

Prather, J. F., Peters, S., Nowicki, S., & Mooney, R. (2008). Precise auditory-vocal mirroring in neurons for learned vocal communication. *Nature, 451*, 305–310.

Premack, D. (1959). Toward empirical behavior laws I: Positive reinforcement. *Psychological Review, 66*, 219–233.

Premack, D. (1961). Predicting instrumental performance from the independent rate of contingent response. *Journal of Experimental Psychology, 61*, 163–171.

Premack, D. (1962). Reversibility of the reinforcement relation. *Science, 136*, 255–257.

Preston, K., Umbricht, A., & Epstein, D. (2000). Methadone dose increase and abstinence reinforcement for treatment of continued heroin use during methadone maintenance. *Archives of General Psychiatry, 57*(4), 395–404.

Price, J., & Morris, J. (1999). Tangles and plaques in nondemented aging and "preclinical" Alzheimer's disease. *Annals of Neurology, 45*, 358–368.

Proteau, L., Marteniuk, R. G., & Levesque, L. (1992). A sensorimotor basis for motor learning: evidence indicating specificity of practice. *Quarterly Journal of Experimental Psychology, 44A*, 557–575.

Pryor, K., Haag, R., & O'Reilly, J. (1969). The creative porpoise: training for novel behavior. *Journal of the Experimental Analysis of Behavior, 12*, 653–661.

Przybyslawsky, J., & Sara, S. J. (1997). Reconsolidation of memory after its reactivation. *Behavioural Brain Research, 84*, 24–27.

Ptito, A., Crane, J., Leonard, G., Amsel, R., & Caramanos, Z. (1995). Visual-spatial localization by patients with frontal lobe lesions invading or sparing area 46. *Neuroreport, 6*(13), 45–48.

Purtle, R. B. (1973). Peak shift: a review. *Psychological Bulletin, 80*, 408–421.

Quirk, G., Likhtik, E., Pelletier, J., & Paré, D. (2003). Stimulation of medial prefrontal cortex decreases the responsiveness of central amygdala output neurons. *Journal of Neuroscience, 23*(25), 8800–8807.

Quiroga, R. Q., Krieman, G., Koch, C., & Fried, I. (2008). Sparse but not "grandmother-cell" coding in the medial temporal lobe. *Trends in Cognitive Sciences 12*(3), 87–91.

Quiroga, R. Q., Reddy, L., Kreiman, G., Koch, C., & Fried, I. (2005). Invariant visual representations by single neurons in the human brain. *Nature, 435*, 1102–1107.

Radelet, M. (2002). Wrongful convictions of the innocent. *Judicature, 86*, 67–68.

Raine, A., Hulme, C., Chadderton, H., & Bailey, P. (1991). Verbal short-term memory span in speech-disordered children: Implications for articulatory coding in short-term memory. *Child Development, 62*, 415–423.

Rakic, P. (2002). Neurogenesis in adult primate neocortex: an evaluation of the evidence. *Nature Reviews Neuroscience, 3*, 65–71.

Ramachandran, V. S., & Oberman, L. M. (2006). Broken mirrors—a theory of autism. *Scientific American, 295*, 62–69.

Ramón y Cajal, S. (1990). *New ideas on the structure of the nervous system in man and vertebrates* (L. Swanson & L. Swanson, Trans.). Cambridge, MA: MIT Press. (Original work, *Les nouvelles ideés sur la structure du système nerveux chez l'homme et chez les vertébrés*, published 1894).

Rankin, C. H. (2004). Invertebrate learning: what can't a worm learn? *Current Biology, 14*, R617–R618.

Rankin, C. H., & Broster, B. S. (1992). Factors affecting habituation and recovery from habituation in the nematode *Caenorhabditis elegans*. *Behavioral Neuroscience, 106*, 239–249.

Rapp, P., & Gallagher, M. (1996). Preserved neuron number in the hippocampus of aged rats with spatial learning deficits. *Proceedings of the National Academy of Sciences USA, 93*, 9926–9930.

Rasmussen, T., Schliemann, T., Sorensen, J., Zimmer, J., & West, M. (1996). Memory impaired aged rats: no loss of principal hippocampal and subicular neurons. *Neurobiology of Aging, 17*(1), 143–147.

Rauscher, F., & Shaw, G. (1998). Key components of the Mozart effect. *Perceptual and Motor Skills, 86*, 835–841.

Rauscher, F., Shaw, G., & Ky, K. (1993). Music and spatial task performance. *Nature, 365*, 611.

Rawson, R., & Tennant, F. (1984). Five-year follow-up of opiate addicts with naltrexone and behavior therapy. *NIDA Research Monographs, 49*, 289–295.

Raymaekers, R., Wiersema, J. R., & Roeyers, H. (2009). EEG study of the mirror neuron system in children with high functioning autism. *Brain Research, 1304*, 113–121.

Recanzone, G. H., Merzenich, M. M., Jenkins, W. M., Grajski, K. A., & Dinse, H. R. (1992). Topographic reorganization of the hand representation in cortical area 3b of owl monkeys trained in a frequency-discrimination task. *Journal of Neurophysiology, 67*, 1031–1056.

Redgrave, P., Rodriguez, M., Smith, Y., Rodriguez-Oroz, M. C., Lehericy, S., Bergman, H., et al. (2010). Goal-directed and habitual control in the basal ganglia: implications for Parkinson's disease. *Nature Reviews Neuroscience, 11*, 760–772.

Reed, J., & Squire, L. (1998). Retrograde amnesia for facts and events: findings from four new cases. *Journal of Neuroscience, 18*(10), 3943–3954.

Reisel, W., & Kopelman, R. (1995). The effects of failure on subsequent group performance in a professional sports setting. *Journal of Psychology: Interdisciplinary and Applied, 129*(1), 103–113.

Reiss, D., & McCowan, B. (1993). Spontaneous vocal mimicry and production by bottlenose dolphins (*Tursiops truncatus*): evidence for vocal learning. *Journal of Comparative Psychology, 107*(3), 301–312.

Remington, B., Roberts, P., & Glauthier, S. (1977). The effect of drink familiarity on tolerance to alcohol. *Addictive Behaviors, 22*, 45–53.

Rendell, L., Boyd, R., Cownden, D., Enquist, M., Eriksson, K., Feldman, M. W., et al. (2010). Why copy others? Insights from the social learning tournament. *Science, 328*, 208–213.

Rendell, L., & Whitehead, H. (2001). Culture in whales and dolphins. *Behavioral and Brain Sciences, 24*, 309–382.

Renner, M., & Rosenzweig, M. (1987). *Enriched and impoverished environments: effects on brain and behavior.* New York: Springer-Verlag.

Rescorla, R. A. (1968). Probability of shock in the presence and absence of CS in fear conditioning. *Journal of Comparative and Physiological Psychology. 66*(1), 1–5.

Rescorla, R. A. (1976). Stimulus generalization: some predictions from a model of Pavlovian conditioning. *Journal of Experimental Psychology: Animal Behavior Processes, 2*(1), 88–96.

Rescorla, R. A., & Wagner, A. R. (1972). A theory of Pavlovian conditioning: variations in the effectiveness of reinforcement and non-reinforcement. In A. Black & W. Prokasy (Eds.), *Classical conditioning II: current research and theory* (pp. 64–99). New York: Appleton-Century-Crofts.

Reynaud, M., Karila, L., Blecha, L., & Benyamina, A. (2010). Is love passion an addictive disorder? *American Journal of Drug and Alcohol Abuse, 36*(5), 261–267.

Ribot, T. (1882). *The diseases of memory.* New York: Appleton.

Richards, D. G., Wolz, J. P., & Herman, L. M. (1984). Vocal mimicry of computer-generated sounds and vocal labeling of objects by a bottlenosed dolphin, *Tursiops truncatus. Journal of Comparative Psychology, 98*(1), 10–28.

Rideout, B., Dougherty, S., & Wernert, L. (1998). Effect of music on spatial performance: a test of generality. *Perceptual and Motor Skills, 86*, 512–514.

Rideout, H., & Parker, L. (1996). Morphine enhancement of sucrose palatability: analysis by the taste reactivity test. *Pharmacology, Biochemistry, and Behavior, 53*, 731–734.

Ritvo, E. R., & Provence, S. (1953). Form perception and imitation in some autistic children: diagnostic findings and their contextual interpretation. *Psychoanalytic Child Study, 8*, 155–161.

Rizzolatti, G., & Craighero, L. (2004). The mirror-neuron system. *Annual Review of Neuroscience, 27*, 169–192.

Rizzolatti, G., & Fabbri-Destro, M. (2010). Mirror neurons: from discovery to autism. *Experimental Brain Research, 200*, 223–237.

Rizzolatti, G., & Sinigaglia, C. (2010). The functional role of the parieto-frontal mirror circuit: interpretations and misinterpretations. *Nature Reviews Neuroscience, 11*, 264–274.

Robbins, T. (1996). Refining the taxonomy of memory. *Science, 273*, 1353–1354.

Roberts, D. (1941). Imitation and suggestion in animals. *Bulletin of Animal Behaviour, 1*, 11–19.

Roberts, W. A. (2002). Are animals stuck in time? *Psychological Bulletin, 128*(3), 473–489.

Roberts, W. A., & Feeney, M. C. (2009). The comparative study of mental time travel. *Trends in Cognitive Science, 13*(6), 271–277.

Robertson, E. M. (2007). The serial reaction time task: Implicit motor skill learning? *Journal of Neuroscience, 27*, 10073–10075.

Roediger, H., & McDermott, K. (1995). Creating false memories: remembering words not presented in lists. *Journal of Experimental Psychology: Learning, Memory and Cognition, 21*(4), 803–814.

Rogers, S. J., & Pennington, B. F. (1991). A theoretical approach to the deficits in infantile autism. *Development and Psychopathology, 3*, 137–162.

Roldan, E., Alvarez-Pelaez, R., & Fernandez de Molina, A. (1974). Electrographic study of the amygdaloid defense response. *Physiology and Behavior, 13*, 779–787.

Rolls, E. (1999). *The brain and emotion.* Oxford, UK: Oxford University Press.

Romanes, G. J. (1898). *Mental evolution in animals.* New York: Appleton-Century-Crofts.

Rosenbaum, D. A., Carlson, R. A., & Gilmore, R. O. (2001). Acquisition of intellectual and perceptual-motor skills. *Annual Review of Psychology, 52*, 453–470.

Rosenkranz, J., & Grace, A. (2002). Dopamine-mediated modulation of odour-evoked amygdala potentials during Pavlovian conditioning. *Nature, 417*, 282–287.

Rosenkranz, K., Butler, K., Williamon, A., & Rothwell, J. C. (2009). Regaining motor control in musician's dystonia by restoring sensorimotor organization. *Journal of Neuroscience, 29*, 14627–14636.

Rosenzweig, E. S., & Barnes, C. A. (2003). Impact of aging on hippocampal function: plasticity, network dynamics, and cognition. *Progress in Neurobiology, 69*(3), 143–179.

Rosenzweig, E. S., Redish, A. D., McNaughton, B. L., & Barnes, C. A. (2003). Hippocampal map realignment and spatial learning. *Nature Neuroscience, 6*, 609–615.

Rosenzweig, M. (1984). Experience, memory and the brain. *American Psychologist, 39*, 365–376.

Rotenberg, A., Abel, T., Hawkins, R. D., Kandel, E. R., & Muller, R. U. (2000). Parallel instabilities of long-term potentiation, place cells, and learning caused by decreased protein kinase A activity. *Journal of Neuroscience, 20*, 8096–8102.

Rothbaum, B. O., & Davis, M. (2003). Applying learning principles to the treatment of post-trauma reactions. *Annals of the New York Academy of Sciences, 1008*, 112–121.

Rothi, L., Ochipa, C., & Heilman, K. (1991). A cognitive neuropsychological model of limb praxis. *Cognitive Neuropsychology, 8*, 443–458.

Rotter, J. B. (1954). *Social learning and clinical psychology*. Englewood Cliffs, NJ: Prentice-Hall.

Routtenberg, A., & Lindy, J. (1965). Effects of the availability of rewarding septal and hypothalamic stimulation on barpressing for food under conditions of deprivation. *Journal of Comparative and Physiological Psychology, 60*, 158–161.

Rovee-Collier, C. (1993). The capacity for long-term memory in infancy. *Current Directions in Psychological Science, 2*, 130–135.

Rovee-Collier, C. (1997). Dissociations in infant memory: rethinking the development of implicit and explicit memory. *Psychological Review, 107*(3), 467–498.

Rovee-Collier, C. (1999). The development of infant memory. *Current Directions in Psychological Science, 8*(3), 80–85.

Rovee-Collier, C., & Cuevas, K. (2009). Multiple memory systems are unnecessary to account for infant memory development: an ecological model. *Developmental Psychology, 45*(1), 160–174.

Ruch, F. (1934). The differentiative effects of age upon human learning. *Journal of General Psychology, 11*, 261–286.

Rueda, N., Llorens-Martín, M., Flórez, J., Valdizán, E., Banerjee, P., Trejo, J. L., et al. (2010). Memantine normalizes several phenotypic features in the Ts65Dn mouse model of Down syndrome. *Journal of Alzheimer's Disease, 21*(1), 277–290.

Rumelhart, D., & McClelland, J. (Eds.). (1986). *Parallel distributed processing: explorations in the microstructure of cognition*. Cambridge, MA: MIT Press.

Rumelhart, D., McClelland, J., & The PDP Research Group. (1986). *Parallel distributed processing: explorations in the microstructure of cognition* (2 vols.). Cambridge, MA: MIT Press.

Rusted, J., Ratner, H., & Sheppard, L. (1995). When all else fails, we can still make tea: a longitudinal look at activities of daily living in an Alzheimer patient. In R. Campbell & M. Conway (Eds.), *Broken memories: case studies in memory impairment* (pp. 396–410). Cambridge, MA: Blackwell.

Ryan, L., Nadel, L., Keil, K., Putnam, K., Schnyer, D., Trouard, T., et al. (2001). Hippocampal complex and retrieval of recent and very remote autobiographical memories: evidence from functional magnetic resonance imaging in neurologically intact people. *Hippocampus, 11*, 707–714.

Rymer, R. (1994). *Genie: a scientific tragedy*. New York: Harper Perennial.

Sadato, N., Pascual-Leone, A., Grafman, J., Deiber, M. P., Ibanez, V., & Hallett, M. (1998). Neural networks for Braille reading by the blind. *Brain, 121*(Pt. 7), 1213–1229.

Salamone, J., Arizzi, M., Sandoval, M., Cervone, K., & Aberman, J. (2002). Dopamine antagonists alter response allocation but do not suppress appetite for food: contrasts between the effects of SKF 83566, raclopride, and fenfluramine on a concurrent choice task. *Psychopharmacology, 160*, 371–380.

Salthouse, T. (1984). Effects of age and skill in typing. *Journal of Experimental Psychology: General, 113*, 345–371.

Sapolsky, R. (1996). Why stress is bad for your brain. *Science, 273*, 749–750.

Sara, S. J. (2000). Strengthening the shaky trace through retrieval. *Nature Reviews Neuroscience, 1*(3), 212–213.

Saufley, W., Otaka, S., & Bavaresco, J. (1985). Context effects: classroom tests and context independence. *Memory and Cognition, 13*, 522–528.

Scarmeas, N., & Stern, Y. (2004). Cognitive reserve: implications for diagnosis and prevention of Alzheimer's disease. *Current Neurology and Neuroscience Reports, 4*(5), 374–380.

Schachter, S., & Singer, J. (1962). Cognitive, social, and physiological determinants of emotional state. *Psychological Review, 69*(5), 379–399.

Schacter, D. (1987). Implicit memory: history and current status. *Journal of Experimental Psychology: Learning, Memory & Cognition, 13*, 501–518.

Schacter, D., & Curran, T. (1995). The cognitive neuroscience of false memories. *Psychiatric Annals, 25*, 726–730.

Schacter, D., Harbluk, J., & McLachlan, D. (1984). Retrieval without recollection: an experimental analysis of source amnesia. *Journal of Verbal Learning and Verbal Behavior, 23*, 593–611.

Schacter, D., & Kihlstrom, J. (1989). Functional amnesia. In F. Boller & J. Grafman (Eds.), *Handbook of neuropsychology, vol. 1* (pp. 209–231). Amsterdam, Netherlands: Elsevier Science.

Schacter, D., Wang, P., Tulving, E., & Freedman, M. (1982). Functional retrograde amnesia: a quantitative case study. *Neuropsychologia, 20*, 523–532.

Schaie, K. W. (2005a). *Developmental influences on adult intelligence: the Seattle Longitudinal Study.* New York: Oxford University Press.

Schaie, K. W. (2005b). What can we learn from longitudinal studies of adult development? *Research on Human Development, 2*(3), 133–158.

Schiltz, C., Bodart, J. M., Michel, C., & Crommelinck, M. (2001). A PET study of human skill learning: changes in brain activity related to learning an orientation discrimination task. *Cortex, 37*, 243–265.

Schlinger, H., & Blakely, E. (1994). The effects of delayed reinforcement and a response-produced auditory stimulus on the acquisition of operant behavior in rats. *The Psychological Record, 44*, 391–410.

Schmidt, R. A., & Wulf, G. (1997). Continuous concurrent feedback degrades skill learning: implications for training and simulation. *Human Factors, 39*, 509–525.

Schmidt, R. A., Young, D. E., Swinnen, S., & Shapiro, D. C. (1989). Summary knowledge of results for skill acquisition: support for the guidance hypothesis. *Journal of Experimental Psychology: Learning, Memory and Cognition, 15*, 352–359.

Schmolck, H., Buffalo, E., & Squire, L. (2000). Memory distortions develop over time: recollections of the O. J. Simpson trial verdict after 15 and 32 months. *Psychological Science, 11*(1), 39–45.

Schneider, A., Huentelman, M. J., Kremerskothen, J., Duning, K., Spoelgen, R., & Nikolich, K. (2010). KIBRA: A new gateway to learning and memory? *Frontiers in Aging Neuroscience, 2*, 4.1–4.9.

Schoenbaum, G., Chiba, A. A., & Gallagher, M. (1998). Orbitofrontal cortex and basolateral amygdala encode expected outcomes during learning. *Nature Neuroscience, 1*, 155–159.

Schoenbaum, G., Roesch, M. R., Stalnaker, T. A., & Takahashi, Y. K. (2009). A new perspective on the role of the orbitofrontal cortex in adaptive behaviour. *Nature Reviews Neuroscience, 10*(12), 885–892.

Schwartz, B., Colon, M., Sanchez, I., Rodriguez, I., & Evans, S. (2002). Single-trial learning of "what" and "who" information in a gorilla (*Gorilla gorilla*): implications for episodic memory. *Animal Cognition, 5*(2), 85–90.

Schwartz, B., & Evans, S. (2001). Episodic memory in primates. *American Journal of Primatology, 55*, 71–85.

Schwartz, S., Maquet, P., & Frith, C. (2002). Neural correlates of perceptual learning: a functional MRI study of visual texture discrimination. *Proceedings of the National Academy of Sciences USA, 99*, 17137–17142.

Schweitzer, J. B., Faber, T. L., Grafton, S. T., Tune, L. E., Hoffman, J. M., & Kilts, C. D. (2000). Alterations in the functional anatomy of working memory in adult attention deficit hyperactivity disorder. *American Journal of Psychiatry, 157*(2), 278–280.

Scott, J. (1962). Critical periods in behavioral development. *Science, 138*, 949–958.

Scoville, W., & Milner, B. (1957). Loss of recent memory after bilateral hippocampal lesions. *Journal of Neurology, Neurosurgery and Psychiatry, 20*, 11–21.

Seager, M. A., Johnson, L. D., Chabot, E. S., Asaka, Y., & Berry, S. D. (2002). Oscillatory brain states and learning: impact of hippocampal theta-contingent training. *Proceedings of the National Academy of Sciences USA, 99*(3), 1616–1620.

Sears, L. L., & Steinmetz, J. E. (1991). Dorsal accessory inferior olive activity diminishes during acquisition of the rabbit classically conditioned eyelid response. *Brain Research, 545*, 114–122.

Seger, C. A. (1994). Implicit learning. *Psychological Bulletin, 115*, 163–196.

Seligman, M. E. (1975). *Helplessness: on depression, development, and death.* San Francisco: Freeman.

Seligman, M. E. (1991). *Learned optimism.* New York: Knopf.

Seligman, M. E., & Johnston, J. (1973). A cognitive theory of avoidance learning. In F. McGuigan & D. Lumsden (Eds.), *Contemporary approaches to conditioning and learning* (pp. 69–110). Washington, DC: Winston-Wiley.

Seligman, M. E., & Maier, S. (1967). Failure to escape traumatic shock. *Journal of Experimental Psychology, 74*, 1–9.

Seligman, M. E., Rosellini, R. A., & Kozak, M. J. (1975). Learned helplessness in the rat: time course, immunization, and reversibility. *Journal of Comparative and Physiological Physiology, 88*(2), 542–547.

Seligman, M. E., Steen, T. A., Park, N., & Peterson, C. (2005). Positive psychology progress: empirical validation of interventions. *American Psychologist, 60*, 410–421.

Semendeferi, K., Lu, A., Schenker, N., & Damasio, H. (2002). Humans and great apes share a large frontal cortex. *Nature Neuroscience, 5*(3), 272–276.

Serres, L. (2001). Morphological changes of the human hippocampal formation from midgestation to early childhood. In C. Nelson & M. Luciana (Eds.), *Handbook of developmental cognitive neuroscience* (pp. 45–58). Cambridge, MA: MIT Press.

Seshadri, S., Fitzpatrick, A. L., Ikram, M. A., DeStefano, A. L., Gudnason, V., Boada, M., et al. (2010). Genome-wide analysis of genetic loci associated with Alzheimer disease. *Journal of the American Medical Association, 303*(18), 1832–1840.

Shahan, T. A. (2010). Conditioned reinforcement and response strength. *Journal of the Experimental Analysis of Behavior, 93,* 269–289.

Shallice, T. (1988). *From neuropsychology to mental structure.* Cambridge, MA: Cambridge University Press.

Shankle, W., Landing, B., Rafii, M., Schiano, A., Chen, J., & Hara, J. (1998). Evidence for a postnatal doubling of neuron number in the developing human cerebral cortex between 15 months and 6 years. *Journal of Theoretical Biology, 191,* 115–140.

Shanks, D. R. (2010). Learning: from association to cognition. *Annual Review of Psychology, 61,* 273–301.

Shannon, C. E. (1948). A mathematical theory of communication. *Bell System Technical Journal, 27,* 379–423, 623–656.

Sharot, T., Delgado, M. R., & Phelps, E. A. (2004). How emotion enhances the feeling of remembering. *Nature Neuroscience, 7*(12), 1376–1380.

Sharot, T., Martorella, E. A., Delgado, M. R., & Phelps, E. A. (2007). How personal experience modulates the neural circuitry of memories of September 11. *Proccedings of the National Academy of Sciences USA, 104*(1), 389–394.

Shaw, P., Kabani, N. J., Lerch, J. P., Eckstrand, K., Lenroot, R., Gogtay, N., Greenstein, D., et al. (2008). Neurodevelopmental trajectories of the human cerebral cortex. *Journal of Neuroscience, 28,* 3586–3594.

Shekhar, R. (2008). Transient global amnesia—a review. *International Journal of Clinical Practice, 62*(6), 939–942.

Shepard, R. N. (1964). Attention and the metric structure of the stimulus space. *Journal of Mathematical Psychology, 1,* 54–87.

Shepard, R. N. (1987). Towards a universal law of generalization for psychological science. *Science, 237,* 1317–1323.

Sheridan, M. A., Hinshaw, S., & D'Esposito, M. (2010). The effect of stimulant medication on prefrontal functional connectivity during working memory in attention-deficit/hyperactivity disorder. *Journal of Attention Disorders, 14,* 69–78.

Sherrington, C. (1906). *The integrative action of the nervous system.* Cambridge, England: Cambridge University Press.

Sherry, D. F., & Hoshooley, J. S. (2010). Seasonal hippocampal plasticity in food-storing birds. *Philosophical Transactions of the Royal Society B—Biological Sciences, 365,* 933–943.

Shettleworth, S. J. (1998). *Cognition, evolution, and behavior.* New York: Oxford University Press.

Shetty, A. K. (2010). Issues to ponder when correlating hippocampal neurogenesis to a hippocampal-dependent memory function. *Neurobiology of Aging, 31*(12), 406–413.

Shimamura, A. P., Jurica, P. J., Mangels, J. A., Gershberg, F. B., & Knight, R. T. (1995). Susceptibility to memory interference effects following frontal lobe damage: findings from tests of paired-associate learning. *Journal of Cognitive Neuroscience, 7,* 144–152.

Shohamy, D., Allen, M. T., & Gluck, M. A. (2000). Dissociating entorhinal and hippocampal involvement in latent inhibition. *Behavioral Neuroscience, 114*(5), 867–874.

Shohamy, D., Mihalakos, P., Chin, R., Thomas, B., Wagner, A. D., & Tamminga, C. (2010). Learning and generalization in schizophrenia: effects of disease and antipsychotic drug treatment. *Biological Psychiatry, 67,* 926–932.

Shohamy, D., & Wagner, A. D. (2008). Integrating memories in the human brain: hippocampal-midbrain encoding of overlapping events. *Neuron, 60*(2), 378–389.

Sidman, R., & Rakic, P. (1973). Neuronal migration, with special reference to developing human brain: a review. *Brain Research, 62,* 1–35.

Siegel, S. (1983). Classical conditioning, drug tolerance, and drug dependence. In Y. Israel, F. Glaser, H. Kalant, R. Popham, W. Schmidt, & R. Smart (Eds.), *Research advances in alcohol and drug problems. Vol. 7* (pp. 207–246). New York: Plenum Press.

Siegel, S. (2001). Pavlovian conditioning and drug overdose: when tolerance fails. *Addiction Research and Theory, 9*(5), 503–513.

Siegel, S., & Ellsworth, D. W. (1986). Pavlovian conditioning and death from apparent overdose of medically prescribed morphine: a case report. *Bulletin of the Psychonomic Society, 24,* 278–280.

Siegel, S., Hinson, R. E., Krank, M. D., & McCully, J. (1982). Heroin "overdose" death: contribution of drug-associated environmental cues. *Science, 216* (4544), 436–437.

Siegel, S., & Ramos, B. M. C. (2002). Applying laboratory research: drug anticipation and the treatment of drug addiction. *Experimental and Clinical Psychopharmacology, 10*(3), 162–183.

Silverman, I., & Eals, M. (1992). Sex differences in spatial abilities: evolutionary theory and data. In J. Barkow, L. Cosmides & J. Tooby (Eds.), *The adapted mind: evolutionary psychology and the generation of culture.* New York: Oxford University Press.

Simmons, D. A., Rex, C. S., Palmer, L., Panyarajan, V., Fedulov, V., Gall, C. M., et al. (2009). Up-regulating BDNF with an ampakine rescues synaptic plasticity and memory in Huntington's disease knockin mouse. *Proceedings of the National Academy of Sciences of the United States of America, 106,* 4906–4911.

Simmons, R. (1924). The relative effectiveness of certain incentives in animal learning. *Comparative Psychology Monographs,* No. 7.

Simon, H., & Gilmartin, K. (1973). A simulation of memory for chess positions. *Cognitive Psychology, 5,* 29–46.

Simonet, P., Versteeg, D., & Storie, D. (2005). Dog-laughter: recorded playback reduces stress related behavior in shelter dogs. *Proceedings of the 7th International Conference on Environmental Enrichment, July 31–August 5, 2005*, 170–176.

Singh, D. (1970). Preference for bar pressing to obtain reward over freeloading in rats and children. *Journal of Comparative and Physiological Psychology, 73*, 320–327.

Singley, M., & Anderson, J. (1989). *The transfer of cognitive skills.* Cambridge, MA: Harvard University Press.

Sirigu, A., Daprati, E., Ciancia, S., Giraux, P., Nighoghossian, N., Posada, A., & Haggard, P. (2004). Altered awareness of voluntary action after damage to the parietal cortex. *Nature Neuroscience, 7*, 80–84.

Skinner, B. F. (1938). *The behavior of organisms: an experimental analysis.* New York: Appleton-Century-Crofts.

Skinner, B. F. (1948). *Walden two.* New York: Macmillan.

Skinner, B. F. (1951). How to teach animals. *Scientific American, 185*, 26–29.

Skinner, B. F. (1953). *Science and human behavior.* New York: Free Press.

Skinner, B. F. (1957). *Verbal behavior.* New York: Appleton-Century-Crofts.

Skinner, B. F. (1971). *Beyond freedom and dignity.* New York: Knopf.

Skinner, B. F. (1979). *The shaping of a behaviorist: part two of an autobiography.* New York: Knopf.

Small, D. M., Zatorre, R. J., Dagher, A., Evans, A. C., & Jones-Gotman, M. (2001). Changes in brain activity related to eating chocolate: from pleasure to aversion. *Brain, 124*, 1720–1733.

Small, S., Chawla, M., Buonocore, M., Rapp, P., & Barnes, C. (2004). Imaging correlates of brain function in monkeys and rats isolates a hippocampal subregion differentially vulnerable to aging. *Proceedings of the National Academy of Sciences USA, 101*(18), 7181–7186.

Smith, C. N., & Squire, L. R. (2009). Medial temporal lobe activity during retrieval of semantic memory is related to the age of memory. *Journal of Neuroscience, 29*(4), 930–938.

Smith, D., Rapp, P., McKay, H., Roberts, J., & Tuszynski, M. (2004). Memory impairment in aged primates is associated with focal death of cortical neurons and atrophy of subcortical neurons. *Journal of Neuroscience, 24*(18), 4373–4381.

Smith, E. E., & Jonides, J. (2004). Executive control and thought. In L. Squire (Ed.), *Fundamentals of neuroscience* (pp. 1377–1394). New York: Academic Press.

Smith, I. M., & Bryson, S. E. (1994). Imitation and action in autism: a critical review. *Psychological Bulletin, 116*(2), 259–273.

Smith, I. M., & Bryson, S. E. (1998). Gesture imitation in autism I: nonsymbolic postures and sequences. *Cognitive Neuropsychology, 15*, 747–770.

Smith, M. (2005). Bilateral hippocampal volume reduction in adults with post-traumatic stress disorder: a meta-analysis of structural MRI studies. *Hippocampus, 15*, 798–807.

Smith, S. (1985). Background music and context-dependent memory. *American Journal of Psychology, 98*, 591–603.

Smotherman, W., & Robinson, S. (1992). Habituation in the rat fetus. *Quarterly Journal of Experimental Psychology B, 44B*(3–4), 215–230.

Snow, C. E., & Hoefnagel-Höhle, M. (1978). The critical period for language acquisition: evidence from second language learning. *Child Development, 49*(4), 1114–1128.

Sokolov, E. N. (1963). *Perception and the conditioned reflex.* Oxford, England: Pergamon Press.

Solanto, M., Arnsten., A., & Castellanos, F. (2000). *The neuropharmacology of stimulant drugs: implications for ADHD.* New York: Oxford University Press.

Solomon, P., & Groccia-Ellison, M. (1996). Classic conditioning in aged rabbits: delay, trace and long-delay conditioning. *Behavioral Neuroscience, 110*(3), 427–435.

Solomon, P., & Moore, J. (1975). Latent inhibition and stimulus generalization of the classically conditioned nictitating membrane response in rabbits (*Oryctolagus cuniculus*) following dorsal hippocampal ablation. *Journal of Comparative and Physiological Psychology, 89*, 1192–1203.

Solomon, P., Pomerleau, D., Bennett, L., James, J., & Morse, D. (1989). Acquisition of the classically conditioned eyeblink response in humans over the life span. *Psychology and Aging, 4*(1), 34–41.

Song, S. B. (2009). Consciousness and the consolidation of motor learning. *Behavioral Brain Research, 196*, 180–186.

Southgate, V., & Hamilton, A. F. D. (2008). Unbroken mirrors: challenging a theory of autism. *Trends in Cognitive Sciences, 12*, 225–229.

Spence, K. W. (1937). The differential response in animals to stimuli varying within a single dimension. *Psychological Review, 44*, 430–444.

Spence, K. W. (1952). Clark Leonard Hull: 1884–1952. *American Journal of Psychology, 65*, 639–646.

Sperling, G. (1960). The information available in brief visual presentations. *Psychological Monographs, 74*, 1–29.

Spetch, M. L., Cheng, K., & Clifford, C. W. G. (2004). Peak shift but not range effects in recognition of faces. *Learning and Motivation, 35*, 221–241.

Spiker, C. (1956). Experiments with children on the hypothesis of acquired distinctiveness and equivalence of cues. *Child Development, 27*, 253–263.

Squire, L. R. (1989). On the course of forgetting in very long-term memory. *Journal of Experimental Psychology: Learning, Memory and Cognition, 15*(2), 241–245.

Squire, L. R. (1992). Memory and the hippocampus: a synthesis from findings with rats, monkeys, and humans. *Psychological Review, 99*(2), 195–231.

Squire, L., Cohen, N. J., & Zouzounis, J. A. (1984). Preserved memory in retrograde amnesia: sparing of a recently acquired skill. *Neuropsychologia, 22*(2), 145–152.

Squire, L. R., & Kandel, E. R. (2000). *Memory: from mind to molecules.* New York: Scientific American Library.

Squire, L., & Knowlton, B. (1995). Memory, hippocampus, and brain systems. In M. Gazzaniga (Ed.), *The cognitive neurosciences* (pp. 825–837). Cambridge, MA: MIT Press.

Squire, L., Knowlton, B., & Musen, G. (1993). The structure and organization of memory. *Annual Review of Psychology, 44,* 453–495.

Squire, L., Slater, P., & Chace, P. (1975). Retrograde amnesia: temporal gradient in very long term memory following electroconvulsive therapy. *Science, 1987,* 77–79.

Squire, L., Slater, P., & Miller, P. (1981). Retrograde amnesia and bilateral electroconvulsive therapy. *Archives of General Psychiatry, 38,* 89–95.

Staddon, J. (1995). On responsibility and punishment. *Atlantic Monthly, 275*(2), 88–94.

Stalnaker, T. A., Franz, T. M., Singh, T., & Schoenbaum, G. (2007). Basolateral amygdala lesions abolish orbitofrontal-dependent reversal impairments. *Neuron, 54*(1), 51–58.

Steele, C. J., & Penhune, V. B. (2010). Specific increases within global decreases: a functional magnetic resonance imaging investigation of five days of motor sequence learning. *Journal of Neuroscience, 30,* 8332–8341.

Steele, K. (2003). Do rats show a Mozart effect? *Music Perception, 21*(2), 251–265.

Steele, K., Bass, K., & Crook, M. (1999). The mystery of the Mozart effect—failure to replicate. *Psychological Science, 10*(4), 366–369.

Stefanacci, L., Buffalo, E., Schmolck, H., & Squire, L. (2000). Profound amnesia after damage to the medial temporal lobe: a neuroanatomical and neuropsychological profile of patient EP. *Journal of Neuroscience, 20*(18), 7024–7037.

Steinmetz, J. E., Lavond, D. G., & Thompson, R. F. (1989). Classical conditioning in rabbits using pontine nucleus stimulation as a conditioned stimulus and inferior olive stimulation as an unconditioned stimulus. *Synapse, 3,* 225–233.

Steinvorth, S., Levine, B., & Corkin, S. (2005). Medial temporal lobe structures are needed to re-experience remote autobiographical memories: evidence from H.M. and W.R. *Neuropsychologia, 43,* 479–497.

Stephens, R. M., Metze, L. P., & Craig, J. R. (1975). The Protestant ethic effect in a multichoice environment. *Bulletin of the Psychonomic Society, 6*(2), 137–139.

Stern, Y., Albert, S., Tang, M., & Tsai, W. (1999). Rate of memory decline in AD is related to education and occupation: Cognitive reserve? *Neurology, 53*(9), 1942–1947.

Stoltz, S., & Lott, D. (1964). Establishment in rats of a persistent response producing a net loss of reinforcement. *Journal of Comparative and Physiological Psychology, 57,* 147–149.

Strack, F., Martin, L., & Stepper, S. (1988). Inhibiting and facilitating conditions of the human smile: a nonobtrusive test of the facial feedback hypothesis. *Journal of Personality and Social Psychology, 54,* 768–777.

Stroop, J. R. (1935). Studies of interference in serial verbal reactions. *Journal of Experimental Psychology, 18,* 643–662.

Subkov, A. A., & Zilov, G. N. (1937). The role of conditioned reflex adaptation in the origin of the hyperergic reactions. *Bulletin de Biologie et de Médecine Expérimentale, 4,* 294–296.

Sun, R., Slusarz, P., & Terry, C. (2005). The interaction of the explicit and the implicit in skill learning: a dual-process approach. *Psychological Review, 112,* 159–192.

Swan, G., Reed, T., Jack, L., Miller, B., Markee, T., Wolf, P., et al. (1999). Differential genetic influence for components of memory in aging adult twins. *Archives of Neurology, 56,* 1127–1132.

Tajudeen, B. A., Waltzman, S. B., Jethanamest, D., & Svirsky, M. A. (2010). Speech perception in congenitally deaf children receiving cochlear implants in the first year of life. *Otology & Neurotology, 31,* 1254–1260.

Takashima, A., Petersson, K. M., Rutters, F., Tendolkar, I., Jensen, O., Zwarts, M. J., et al. (2006). Declarative memory consolidation in humans: a prospective functional magnetic resonance imaging study. *Proceedings of the National Academy of Sciences USA, 103,* 756–761.

Talarico, J., & Rubin, D. (2003). Confidence, not consistency, characterizes flashbulb memories. *Psychological Science, 14*(5), 455–461.

Tan, H. Y., Callicott, H. J., & Weinberger, D. R. (2007). Dysfunctional and compensatory prefrontal cortical systems, genes and the pathogenesis of schizophrenia. *Cerebral Cortex, 17*(suppl. 1), i171–i181.

Tan, H. Y., Choo, W. C., Fones, C. S. L., & Chee, M. W. L. (2005). fMRI study of maintenance and manipulation processes within working memory in first-episode schizophrenia. *American Journal of Psychiatry, 162,* 1849–1858.

Tan, H. Y., Sust, S., Buckholtz, J. W., Mattay, V. S., Meyer-Lindenberg, A. S., Egan, M. F., et al. (2006). Dysfunctional prefrontal regional specialization and compensation in schizophrenia. *American Journal of Psychiatry, 163,* 1969–1977.

Tanaka, S. C., Balleine, B. W., & O'Doherty, J. P. (2008). Calculating consequences: brain systems that encode the causal effects of actions. *Journal of Neuroscience, 28*(26), 6750–6755.

Taub, E., Uswatte, G., & Elbert, T. (2002). New treatments in neurorehabilitation founded on basic research. *Nature Reviews Neuroscience, 3,* 228–236.

Technau, G. (1984). Fiber number in the mushroom bodies of adult *Drosophila melanogaster* depends on age, sex and experience. *Journal of Neurogenetics, 1*, 13–26.

Teter, B., & Finch, C. (2004). Caliban's heritance and the genetics of neuronal aging. *Trends in Neurosciences, 27*(10), 627–632.

Thomas, A. K., & Loftus, E. F. (2002). Creating bizarre false memories through imagination. *Memory and Cognition, 30*(3), 423–431.

Thomas, M. S. C., & Johnson, M. H. (2008). New advances in understanding sensitive periods in brain development. *Current Directions in Psychological Science, 17*(1), 1–5.

Thomas, R. (2002). *They cleared the lane: the NBA's black pioneers.* Lincoln, NE: University of Nebraska Press.

Thompson, C., & Cowan, T. (1986). Flashbulb memories: a nicer interpretation of a Neisser recollection. *Cognition, 22*, 199–200.

Thompson, D. (1988). Context and false memory. In G. Davies & D. Thompson (Eds.), *Memory in context: context in memory* (pp. 285–304). Chichester, UK: Wiley.

Thompson, R. F. (1962). Role of cerebral cortex in stimulus generalization. *Journal of Comparative and Physiological Psychology, 55*, 279–287.

Thompson, R. F. (1965). The neural basis of stimulus generalization, In D. Mostofsky (Ed.), *Stimulus generalization* (pp. 154–178). Stanford, CA: Stanford University Press.

Thompson, R. F. (1972). Sensory preconditioning. In R. Thompson & J. Voss (Eds.), *Topics in learning and performance* (pp. 105–129). New York: Academic Press.

Thompson, R. F. (1986). The neurobiology of learning and memory. *Science, 233*, 941–947.

Thompson, R. F. (2009). Habituation: a history. *Neurobiology of Learning and Memory, 92*, 127–134.

Thompson, R. F., & Krupa, D. J. (1994). Organization of memory traces in the mammalian brain. *Annual Review of Neuroscience, 17*, 519–549.

Thompson, R. F., & Spencer, W. A. (1966). Habituation: a model phenomenon for the study of neuronal substrates of behavior. *Psychological Review, 73*, 16–43.

Thompson, W. F., Schellenberg, E. G., & Husain, G. (2001). Arousal, mood, and the Mozart effect. *Psychological Science, 12*, 248–251.

Thompson-Schill, S. L., D'Esposito, M., Aguirre, G. K., & Farah, M. J. (1997). Role of left inferior prefrontal cortex in retrieval of semantic knowledge: a reevaluation. *Proceedings of the National Academy of Sciences USA, 94*, 14792–14797.

Thorndike, E. L. (1898). Animal intelligence: an experimental study of the associative processes in animals. *Psychological Review Monograph 2*(4), 1–8.

Thorndike, E. L. (1911). *Animal intelligence.* New York: Macmillan.

Thorndike, E. L. (1923). The variability of an individual in repetitions of the same task. *Journal of Experimental Psychology, 6*, 161–167.

Thorndike, E. L. (1927). The law of effect. *American Journal of Psychology, 39*, 212–222.

Thorndike, E. L. (1932). *The fundamentals of learning.* New York: Teachers College, Columbia University.

Thorndike, E. L. (1949). *Selected writings from a connectionist's psychology.* New York: Appleton-Century-Crofts.

Thorndike, E. L., & Woodworth, R. (1901). The influence of improvement in one mental function upon the efficiency of other functions (I). *Psychological Review, 8*, 247–261.

Thorpe, S. J., Rolls, E. T., & Maddison, S. (1983). The orbitofrontal cortex: neuronal activity in the behaving monkey. *Experimental Brain Research, 49*(1), 93–115.

Thorpe, W. H. (1958). The learning of song patterns by birds with especial reference to the song of the chaffinch, *Fringilla coelebs. Ibis, 100*, 535–570.

Thorpe, W. H. (1963). *Learning and instinct in animals.* Cambridge, MA: Harvard University Press.

Timberlake, W. (1980). A molar equilibrium theory of learned performance. In G. Bower (Ed.), *The psychology of learning and motivation* (Vol. 14, pp. 1–58). New York: Academic Press.

Timberlake, W., & Allison, J. (1974). Response deprivation: an empirical approach to instrumental performance. *Psychological Review, 81*, 146–164.

Tinbergen, N., & Kruyt, W. (1972). On the orientation of the digger wasp *Philanthus triangulum* Fabr. III. Selective learning of landmarks. In N. Tinbergen (Ed.), *The animal in its world.* Cambridge, MA: Harvard University Press. (Original work published 1938)

Titone, D., Ditman, T., Holzman, P. S., Eichenbaum, H., & Levy, D. L. (2004). Transitive inference in schizophrenia: impairments in relational memory organization. *Schizophrenia Research, 68*, 235–247.

Titz, C., & Verhaeghen, P. (2010). Aging and directed forgetting in episodic memory: a meta-analysis. *Psychology and Aging, 25*(2), 405–411.

Tolman, E. C. (1932). *Purposive behavior in animals and men.* New York: Appleton-Century-Crofts.

Tolman, E. C. (1948). Cognitive maps in rats and men. *Psychological Review, 55*, 189–208.

Tolman, E. C., & Honzik, C. H. (1930). "Insight" in rats. *University of California Publications in Psychology, 4*, 215–232.

Tomasello, M., Davis-Dasilva, M., Carnak, L., & Bard, K. A. (1987). Observational learning of tool-use by young chimpanzees. *Human Evolution, 2*, 175–183.

Torriero, S., Oliveri, M., Koch, G., Lo Gerfo, E., Salerno, S., Ferlazzo, F., et al. (2011). Changes in cerebello-motor connectivity during procedural learning by actual execution and observation. *Journal of Cognitive Neuroscience, 23,* 338–348.

Trachtenberg, J., Chen, B., Knott, G., Feng, G., Sanes, J., Welker, E., et al. (2002). Long-term *in vivo* imaging of experience-dependent synaptic plasticity in adult cortex. *Nature, 420*(6917), 788–794.

Tranel, D., Damasio, A. R., Damasio, H., & Brandt, J. P. (1994). Sensorimotor skill learning in amnesia: additional evidence for the neural basis of nondeclarative memory. *Learning and Memory, 1,* 165–179.

Travers, J., Akey, L., Chen, S., Rosen, S., Paulson, G., & Travers, S. (1993). Taste preferences in Parkinson's disease patients. *Chemical Senses, 18,* 47–55.

Treffert, G. (2009). The savant syndrome: an extraordinary condition. A synopsis: past, present, future. *Philosophical Transactions of the Royal Society B: Biological Sciences, 364,* 1351–1357.

Tremblay, L., & Schultz, W. (1999). Relative reward preference in primate orbitofrontal cortex. *Nature, 398,* 704–708.

Tryon, R. (1940). Genetic differences in maze learning in rats. *Yearbook of the National Society for the Study of Education, 39,* 111–119.

Tully, T. (1996). Discovery of genes involved with learning and memory: an experimental synthesis of Hirschian and Benzerian perspectives. *Proceedings of the National Academy of Sciences USA, 93,* 13460–13467.

Tulving, E. (1972). Episodic and semantic memory. In E. Tulving & W. Donaldson (Eds.), *Organization of memory* (pp. 381–403). New York: Academic Press.

Tulving, E. (1983). *Elements of episodic memory.* Oxford: Clarendon.

Tulving, E. (1985). Memory and consciousness. *Canadian Psychology, 26*(1), 1–12.

Tulving, E. (2002). Episodic memory: from mind to brain. *Annual Review of Psychology, 53,* 1–25.

Tulving, E., & Markowitsch, H. (1998). Episodic and declarative memory: role of the hippocampus. *Hippocampus, 8*(3), 198–204.

Turner, A. P., & Martinek, T. J. (1999). An investigation into teaching games for understanding: effects on skill, knowledge, and game play. *Research Quarterly of Exercise and Sport, 70,* 286–296.

Turner, D. C., Robbins, T. W., Clark, L., Aron, A. R., Dowson, J., & Sahakian, B. J. (2003). Cognitive enhancing effects of modafinil in healthy volunteers. *Psychopharmocology, 165,* 260–269.

Turner, R. S., Grafton, S. T., Votaw, J. R., Delong, M. R., & Hoffman, J. M. (1998). Motor subcircuits mediating the control of movement velocity: a PET study. *Journal of Neurophysiology, 80,* 2162–2176.

Tyack, P. (2008). Convergence of calls as animals form social bonds: active compensation for noisy communication channels and the evolution of vocal learning in mammals. *Journal of Comparative Psychology, 122,* 319–331.

Vaegan, T. (1979). Critical period for amblyopia in children. *Transactions of the Ophthalmological Societies of the United Kingdom, 99*(3), 432–439.

Vaiva, G., Ducrocq, F., Jezequel, K., Averland, B., Levestal, P., Brunet, A., et al. (2003). Immediate treatment with propranolol decreases posttraumatic stress two months after trauma. *Biological Psychiatry, 54*(9), 947–949.

Vakil, E., Grunhaus, L., Nagar, I., Ben-Chaim, E., Dolberg, O. T., Dannon, P. N., et al. (2000). The effect of electroconvulsive therapy (ECT) on implicit memory: skill learning and perceptual priming in patients with major depression. *Neuropsychologia, 38*(10), 1405–1414.

Vale-Martinez, A., Baxter, M. G., & Eichenbaum, H. (2002). Selective lesions of basal forebrain cholinergic neurons produce anterograde and retrograde deficits in a social transmission of food preference task in rats. *European Journal of Neuroscience, 16*(6), 983–998.

van Lehn, K. (1996). Cognitive skill acquisition. *Annual Review of Psychology, 47,* 513–539.

van Rossum, J. H. A. (1990). Schmidt's schema theory: the empirical base of the variability of practice hypothesis. *Human Movement Science, 9,* 387–435.

Vance, A. (2010). If your password is 123456, just make it HackMe. *New York Times,* p. A1.

Vargha-Khadem, F., Gadian, D., Watkins, K., Connelly, A., Van Paesschen, W., & Mishkin, M. (1997). Differential effects of early hippocampal pathology on episodic and semantic memory. *Science, 277,* 376–380.

Vicari, S., Bellucci, S., & Carlesimo, G. (2000). Implicit and explicit memory: a functional dissociation in persons with Down syndrome. *Neuropsychologia, 38,* 240–251.

Volkow, N. D., Wang, G. J., Fowler, J. S., & Ding, Y.-S. (2005). Imaging the effects of methylphenidate on brain dopamine: new model on its therapeutic actions for attention-deficit/hyperactivity disorder. *Biological Psychiatry, 57*(11), 1410–1415.

Volkow, N. D., Wang, G. J., Fowler, J. S., Telang, F., Maynard, L., Logan J., et al. (2004). Evidence that methylphenidate enhances the saliency of a mathematical task by increasing dopamine in the human brain. *American Journal of Psychiatry, 161*(7), 1173–1180.

Voss, V., & Wiley, J. (1995). Acquiring intellectual skills. *Annual Review of Psychology, 46,* 155–181.

Wade, K., Garry, M., Read, J., & Lindsay, S. (2002). A picture is worth a thousand words. *Psychonomic Bulletin and Review, 9,* 597–603.

Wagner, A. D. (2002). Cognitive control and episodic memory. In L. R. Squire & D. L. Schacter (Eds.), *Neuropsychology of memory* (3d ed., pp. 174–192). New York: Guilford Press.

Wagner, A. D., Desmond, J. E., Glover, G. H., & Gabrieli, J. D. (1998). Prefrontal cortex and recognition memory: functional-MRI evidence for context-dependent retrieval processes. *Brain, 121*(pt. 10), 1985–2002.

Wagner, A. D., Koutstaal, W., Maril, A., Schacter, D. L., & Buckner, R. L. (2000). Task-specific repetition priming in left inferior prefrontal cortex. *Cerebral Cortex, 10*, 1176–1184.

Wagner, A. D., Schacter, D., Rotte, M., Koutstaal, W., Maril, A., Dale, A., et al. (1998). Building memories: remembering and forgetting of verbal experiences as a function of brain activity. *Science, 281*, 1188–1191.

Wagner, A. R. (1969). Stimulus validity and stimulus selection in associative learning. In N. J. Mackintosh & W. K. Honig (Eds.), *Fundamental issues in associative learning* (pp. 90–122). Halifax, Nova Scotia, Canada: Dalhousie University Press.

Wagner, A. R. (1981). SOP: a model of automatic memory processing in animal behavior. In N. Spear & G. Miller (Eds.), *Information processing in animals: memory mechanisms.* Hillsdale, NJ: Lawrence Erlbaum.

Wagner, A. R. (1979). Habituation and memory. In A. Dickinson & R. A. Boakes (Eds.), *Mechanisms of learning and motivation: a memorial volume for Jerzy Konorski* (pp. 53–82). Hillsdale, NJ: Erlbaum.

Waiter, G. D., Williams, J. H., Murray, A. D., Gilchrist, A., Perrett, D. I., & Whiten, A. (2004). A voxel-based investigation of brain structure in male adolescents with autistic spectrum disorder. *Neuroimage, 22*(2), 619–625.

Walker, M. P., Brakefield, T., Hobson, J. A., & Stickgold, R. (2003). Dissociable stages of human memory consolidation and reconsolidation. *Nature, 425*, 616–620.

Walker, M. P., Brakefield, T., Morgan, A., Hobson, J. A., & Stickgold, R. (2002). Practice with sleep makes perfect: sleep-dependent motor skill learning. *Neuron, 35*, 205–211.

Walker, M. P., Brakefield, T., Seidman, J., Morgan, A., Hobson, J. A., & Stickgold, R. (2003). Sleep and the time course of motor skill learning. *Learning and Memory, 10*, 275–284.

Walls, R., Zane, T., & Ellis, T. (1981). Forward and backward chaining, and whole task methods: training assembly tasks in vocational rehabilitation. *Behavior Modification, 5*, 61–74.

Waltz, J. A., & Gold, J. M. (2007). Probabilistic reversal learning impairments in schizophrenia: further evidence of orbitofrontal dysfunction. *Schizophrenia Research, 93*, 296–303.

Wang, S.-H., & Morris, R. G. M. (2010). Hippocampal-neocortical interactions in memory formation, consolidation, and reconsolidation. *Annual Review of Psychology, 61*, 49–79.

Warrington, E., & Shallice, T. (1984). Category specific semantic impairments. *Brain, 107*, 829–854.

Waterhouse, L., Fein, D., & Modahl, C. (1996). Neurofunctional mechanisms in autism. *Psychological Review, 103*, 457–489.

Watson, J. B. (1907). Kinaesthetic and organic sensations: their role in the reactions of the white rat to the maze (monograph supplement). *Psychological Review, 4*, 211–212.

Watson, J. B. (1913). Psychology as the behaviorist sees it. *Psychological Review, 23*, 158–177.

Watson, J. B. (1924). *Behaviorism.* New York: Norton.

Watson, J., & Rayner, R. (1920). Conditioned emotional reactions. *Journal of Experimental Psychology, 3*, 1–14 (reprinted 2000 in *American Psychologist, 2055*(2003), 2313–2317).

Weatherly, J. N., Plumm, K. M., Smith, J. R., & Roberts, W. A. (2002). On the determinants of induction in responding for sucrose when food pellet reinforcement is upcoming. *Animal Learning and Behavior, 30*(4), 315–329.

Weeks, D. L., & Kordus, R. N. (1998). Relative frequency of knowledge of performance and motor skill learning. *Research Quarterly for Exercise and Sports, 69*, 224–230.

Weinberger, D. R., Berman, K. F., & Zec, R. F. (1986). Physiologic dysfunction of dorsolateral prefrontal cortex in schizophrenia. I. Regional cerebral blood flow evidence. *Archives of General Psychiatry, 43*, 114–125.

Weinberger, N. (1977). Learning-induced receptive field plasticity in the primary auditory cortex. *Seminars in Neuroscience, 9*, 59–67.

Weinberger, N. (1993). Learning-induced changes of auditory receptive fields. *Current Opinion in Neurobiology, 3*, 570–577.

Weinberger, N. M. (2003). The nucleus basalis and memory codes: auditory cortical plasticity and the induction of specific, associative behavioral memory. *Neurobiology of Learning and Memory, 80*(3), 268–284.

Weinberger, N. M. (2004). Specific long-term memory traces in primary auditory cortex. *Nature Reviews Neuroscience, 5*(4), 279–290.

Weinberger, N. M. (2007). Auditory associative memory and representational plasticity in the primary auditory cortex. *Hearing Research, 229*, 54–68.

Wells, G. L., Memon, A., & Penrod, S. D. (2006). Eyewitness evidence: improving its probative value. *Psychological Science in the Public Interest, 7*(2), 45–75.

Werker, J. F., & Tees, R. C. (1984). Cross-language speech perception: evidence for perceptual reorganization during the 1st year of life. *Infant Behavior and Development, 7*, 49–63.

Werker, J., & Tees, R. (1999). Influences on infant speech processing: toward a new synthesis. *Annual Review of Psychology, 50*, 509–535.

West, M. (1993). Regionally specific loss of neurons in the aging human hippocampus. *Neurobiology of Aging, 14*(4), 287–293.

Whitehead, A., Perdomo, C., Pratt, R. D., Birks, J., Wilcock, G. K., & Evans, J. G. (2004). Donepezil for the symptomatic treatment of patients with mild to moderate Alzheimer's disease: a meta-analysis of individual patient data from randomised controlled trials. *International Journal of Geriatric Psychiatry, 19*, 624–633.

Whiten, A., & Boesch, C. (2001). The cultures of chimpanzees. *Scientific American, 284*(1), 60–67.

Whiten, A., & Brown, J. (1999). Imitation and the reading of other minds: perspectives from the study of autism, normal children and non-human primates. In S. Braten (Ed.), *Intersubjective communication and emotion in early ontogeny* (pp. 260–280). Cambridge, England: Cambridge University Press.

Whiten, A., Custance, D. M., Gomez, J. C., Teixidor, P., & Bard, K. A. (1996). Imitative learning of artificial fruit processing in children (*Homo sapiens*) and chimpanzees (*Pan troglodytes*). *Journal of Comparative Psychology, 110*(1), 3–14.

Whiten, A., Goodall, J., McGrew, W. C., Nishida, T., Reynolds, V., Sugiyama, Y., et al. (1999). Cultures in chimpanzees. *Nature, 399*, 682–685.

Whiten, A., Horner, V., Litchfield, C. A., & Marshall-Pescini, S. (2004). How do apes ape? *Learning and Behavior, 32*(1), 36–52.

Wickelgren, W. (1966). Phonemic similarity and interference in short-term memory for single letters. *Journal of Experimental Psychology, 71*(3), 396–404.

Wickens, J. R. (2009). Synaptic plasticity in the basal ganglia. *Behavioural Brain Research, 199*(1), 119–128.

Wightman, D., & Sistrunk, F. (1987). Part-task training strategies in simualted carrier landing final-approach training. *Human Factors, 29*, 245–254.

Williams, A. M., Davids, K., Burwitz, L., & Williams, J. (1992). Perception and action in sport. *Journal of Human Movement Studies, 22*, 147–204.

Williams, B. A. (2001). Two-factor theory has strong empirical evidence of validity. *Journal of the Experimental Analysis of Behavior, 75*(3), 362–365.

Williams, J. H., Whiten, A., & Singh, T. (2004). A systematic review of action imitation in autistic spectrum disorder. *Journal of Autism and Developmental Disorders, 34*(3), 285–299.

Williams, J. H., Whiten, A., Suddendorf, T., & Perrett, D. I. (2001). Imitation, mirror neurons and autism. *Neuroscience and Biobehavioral Review, 25*, 287–295.

Williams, L., Phillips, M., Brammer, M., Skerrett, D., Lagopoulos, J., Rennie, C., et al. (2001). Arousal dissociates amygdala and hippocampal fear responses: evidence from simultaneous fMRI and skin conductance recording. *Neuroimage, 14*(5), 1070–1079.

Willingham, D. B. (1999). Implicit motor sequence learning is not purely perceptual. *Memory and Cognition, 27*, 561–572.

Willingham, D. B., & Koroshetz, W. J. (1993). Evidence for dissociable motor skills in Huntington's disease patients. *Psychobiology, 21*, 173–182.

Wills, A. J., & McLaren, I. (1997). Generalization in human category learning: a connectionist account of differences in gradient after discriminative and non-discriminative training. *Quarterly Journal of Experimental Psychology, 50A*, 607–630.

Wills, S., & Mackintosh, N. J. (1998). Peak shift on an artificial dimension. *Quarterly Journal of Experimental Psychology, 51B*, 1–31.

Wilson, B., & Wearing, D. (1995). Prisoner of consciousness: a state of just awakening following herpes simplex encephalitis. In R. Campbell & M. Conway (Eds.), *Broken memories: case studies in memory impairments* (pp. 14–30). Cambridge, MA: Blackwell.

Wilson, R., & Bennett, D. (2003). Cognitive activity and risk of Alzheimer's disease. *Current Directions in Psychological Science, 12*(3), 87–91.

Wilson, T., & Brown, T. (1997). Reexamination of the effect of Mozart's music on spatial-task performance. *Journal of Psychology, 131*, 365–370.

Winek, C. L., Wahaba, W. W., & Rozin, L. (1999). Heroin fatality due to penile injection. *American Journal of Forensic Medicine and Pathology, 20*, 90–92.

Winocur, G., Wojtowicz, J. M., Sekeres, M., Snyder, J. S., & Wang, S. (2006). Inhibition of neurogenesis interferes with hippocampus-dependent memory function. *Hippocampus, 16*(3), 296–304.

Wise, R. A. (2004). Dopamine, learning and motivation. *Nature Reviews Neuroscience, 5*, 483–494.

Wise, R., Spindler, J., deWit, H., & Gerberg, G. (1978). Neuroleptic-induced "anhedonia" in rats: pimozide blocks reward quality of food. *Science, 201*, 262–264.

Wiseman, F. K., Alford, K. A., Tybulewicz, V. L. J., & Fisher, E. M. C. (2009). Down syndrome—recent progress and future prospects. *Human Molecular Genetics, 18*(Review Issue 1), R75–R83.

Wiskott, L., Rasch, M., & Kempermann, G. (2006). A functional hypothesis for adult hippocampal neurogenesis: avoidance of catastrophic interference in the dentate gyrus. *Hippocampus, 16*(3), 329–343.

Wisniewski, M. G., Church, B. A., & Mercado, E. III. (2009). Learning-related shifts in generalization gradients for complex sounds. *Learning & Behavior, 37*(4), 325–335.

Wittenberg, G. F., & Schaechter, J. D. (2009). The neural basis of constraint-induced movement therapy. *Current Opinion in Neurology, 22*, 582–588.

Wolf, S. L., Thompson, P. A., Winstein, C. J., Miller, J. P., Blanton, S. R., Nichols-Larsen, D. S., et al. (2010).

The EXCITE stroke trial comparing early and delayed constraint-induced movement therapy. *Stroke, 41*, 2309–2315.

Wood, D. (1989). Social interaction as tutoring. In M. H. Bornstein & J. S. Bruner (Eds.), *Interaction in human development*. Cambridge, MA: Harvard University Press.

Woodruff-Pak, D. S., & Lemieux, S. K. (2001). The cerebellum and associative learning: parallels and contrasts in rabbits and humans. In J. E. Steinmetz, M. A. Gluck, & P. F. Solomon (Eds.), *Model systems of associative learning: a festschrift for Richard F. Thompson* (pp. 271–294). Mahwah, NJ: Lawrence Erlbaum.

Woodruff-Pak, D., Logan, C., & Thompson, R. (1990). Neurobiological substrates of classical conditioning across the life span. *Annals of the New York Academy of Sciences, 608*, 150–178.

Woodruff-Pak, D., & Sheffield, J. (1987). Age differences in Purkinje cells and rate of classical conditioning in young and older rabbits. *Society for Neuroscience Abstracts, 13*, 41.

Woodruff-Pak, D., & Thompson, R. (1988). Classical conditioning of the eyeblink response in the delay paradigm in adults aged 18–83. *Psychology and Aging, 3*, 219–229.

Woolley, C., Weiland, N., McEwen, B., & Schwartzkroin, P. (1997). Estradiol increases the sensitivity of hippocampal CA1 pyramidal cells to NMDA receptor-mediated synaptic input: correlatin with spine density. *Journal of Neuroscience, 17*, 1848–1859.

Wulf, G., & Schmidt, R. A. (1997). Variability of practice and implicit motor learning. *Journal of Experimental Psychology: Learning, Memory and Cognition, 23*, 987–1006.

Wylie, G. R., Foxe, J. J., & Taylor, T. L. (2008). Forgetting as an active process: an fMRI investigation of item-method-directed forgetting. *Cerebral Cortex, 18*(3), 670–682.

Xu, X., Aron, A., Brown, L., Cao, G., Feng, T., & Weng, X. (2011). Reward and motivation systems: a brain mapping study of early-stage intense romantic love in Chinese participants. *Human Brain Mapping, 32*, 249–257.

Yang, Q., Rasmussen, S. A., & Friedman, J. M. (2002). Mortality associated with Down's syndrome in the USA from 1983 to 1997: a population-based study. *Lancet, 359*(9311), 1019–1025.

Yang, Y., Kim, J. S., Kim, Y. K., Kwak, Y. T., & Han, I. W. (2009). Cerebellar hypoperfusion during transient global amnesia: an MRI and oculographic study. *Journal of Clinical Neurology, 5*(2), 74–80.

Yarrow, K., Brown, P., & Krakauer, J. W. (2009). Inside the brain of an elite athlete: the neural processes that support high achievement in sports. *Nature Reviews Neuroscience, 10*, 585–596.

Yin, H. H., Mulcare, S. P., Hilario, M. R. F., Clouse, E., Holloway, T., Davis, M. I., et al. (2009). Dynamic reorganization of striatal circuits during the acquisition and consolidation of a skill. *Nature Neuroscience, 12*, 333–341.

Yin, J. C. P., Wallach, J. S., Del Vecchio, M., Wilder, E. L., Zhuo, H., Quinn, W. G., & Tully, T. (1994). Induction of dominant negative CREB transgene specifically blocks long-term memory in *Drosophila. Cell, 79*, 49–58.

Youn, G. (2006). Subjective sexual arousal in response to erotica: effects of gender, guided fantasy, erotic stimulus, and duration of exposure. *Archives of Sexual Behavior, 35*, 87–97.

Younger, J., Aron, A., Parke, S., Chatterjee, N., & Mackey, S. (2010). Viewing pictures of a romantic partner reduces experimental pain: involvement of neural reward systems. *PLoS ONE, 5*(10), e13309.

Zadikoff, C., & Lang, A. E. (2005). Apraxia in movement disorders. *Brain, 128*(Pt. 7), 1480–1497.

Zajonc, R. (1980). Feeling and thinking: preferences need no inferences. *American Psychologist, 35*, 151–175.

Zajonc, R. (1984). On the primacy of affect. *American Psychologist, 39*, 117–123.

Zeki, S. (1993). *A vision of the brain*. Oxford, UK: Blackwell Scientific Publishing.

Zentall, T. R. (2006). Mental time travel in animals: a challenging question. *Behavioural Processes, 72*(2), 173–183.

Zentall, T. R., Singer, R. A., & Stagner, J. P. (2008). Episodic-like memory: pigeons can report location pecked when unexpectedly asked. *Behavioural Processes, 79*(2), 93–98.

Zola-Morgan, S., Squire, L., & Amaral, D. (1986). Human amnesia and the medial temporal region: enduring memory impairments following a bilateral lesion limited to field CA1 of the hippocampus. *Journal of Neuroscience, 6*(10), 2950–2967.

Zupanc, G. (2001). A comparative approach towards the understanding of adult neurogenesis. *Brain, Behavior and Evolution, 58*, 246–249.

SUBJECT INDEX

Note: Page numbers followed by f indicate figures; those followed by t indicate tables.

Acetylcholine (ACh), 53, 54t, 55, 292
  in cortical plasticity, 249
Acoustic startle reflex, 78, 78f, 82–83
  habituation and, 78, 78f
Acquired equivalence, 234–235, 234t
  hippocampus in, 250, 253–255
  in schizophrenia, 253–255, 254f
Acquired savant syndrome, 39
Activity-dependent enhancement, 158
Addiction
  behavioral, 202–204
  classical conditioning in, 162–164
  drug, 162–164, 200–202, 202f
  extinction in, 163, 164, 205
  operant conditioning in,
      200–202, 202f
  pathological, 201
  romantic love as, 203, 204
  treatment of, 204–205
Adolescence. See also Children
  brain changes in, 481
  definition of, 469
  sex differences in learning and
      memory in, 471
  working memory in, 470–471
Adrenaline, in arousal, 388
Adults, learning and memory in,
      471–473, 483–488
Aggression, violent entertainment and,
      443–445, 443f
Agnosia, 281–282
Alcohol abuse. See also Substance abuse
  Korsakoff's syndrome and, 293
Alleles, 475
Alzheimer's disease, 253, 485, 491–496
  brain changes in, 492, 493f
  cognitive impairment in, 492
  diagnosis of, 494
  in Down syndrome, 495
  early-onset, 494
  genetic factors in, 494–495
  memory loss in, 492
  prevention of, 495
  "probable," 494
  treatment of, 66, 494
Amazon.com, marketing strategies
      of, 211
American philosophy, 9–11
Amnesia. See also Forgetting
  in Alzheimer's disease, 492

anterograde, 284–285, 288f
brain lesions in
  in basal forebrain, 292–293
  in diencephalon, 293
  in frontal cortex, 287–291
  in hippocampus, 259–261, 280,
      283–290
  in medial temporal lobe, 283–290
case studies of
  Beth, 285–286
  E.P., 283–284, 284f, 288, 289
  H.M., 259–261, 263, 280, 283,
      293, 314
  P.N., 296
  R.B., 283, 288
  S.G., 294–295, 295f
  definition of, 260
  dissociative, 296
  in Down syndrome, 490
  drug-related, 65
  after electroconvulsive shock therapy,
      278–279, 294
  functional, 295–297
  implicit learning in, 313–315
  in Korsakoff's disease, 293
  organic, 296
  psychogenic, 296
  retrograde, 287–290, 288f
  Ribot gradient and, 287–288, 288f
  source, 274–275, 291
    confabulation and, 292
  temporary, 294–297
  transient global, 294–295, 295f
Amphetamine
  addiction to, 201–202
  effects of, 201, 202f
Amygdala, 43f, 283, 283f
  in arousal, 407–409, 408f
  in emotion, 43, 406–415
  in emotional learning, 409–410, 410f
  in fear, 407–409, 408f, 415, 415f
  functions of, 43, 249
  in memory reconsolidation,
      414–415, 414f
  in memory storage, 410–413,
      410f, 412f
    stress hormones and, 411–413
  nuclei of, 406–409, 407f
  sensory pathways to, 407f,
      409–410, 410f
  structure of, 406–407, 407f
  surgical removal of, 259–260
Amyloid plaques
  in Alzheimer's disease, 492–494, 493f
  in Down syndrome, 495

Androgens, in brain development, 471,
      482–483
Anesthesia, memory loss and, 65
Aneurysm, anterior communicating
      artery, amnesia and, 292–293
Animal(s)
  arousal in, 392–393
  cognitive expectancies in, 397
  cognitive skills in, 304–305
  comparative neuroanatomy in,
      43–45, 44f
  emotions in, 391–394
  episodic-like memory in, 264–266,
      265f, 284–285
  evolution of, 11–16. See also Evolution
  fear response in, 392–393
  imitation in, 431–432, 431f
  laughter in, 393–394
  medial temporal lobe in, 284–285
  semantic memory in, 264–265
  skill learning in, 305, 305f
  sound imitation by, 436–437, 449–450.
      See also Bird song learning
  tool use by, 305, 305f
Animal experiments
  ethics of, 22–23
  regulation of, 23
Animal rights movement, 22–23
Animal-human relationships, 12
Anterior communicating artery
      aneurysm, amnesia and, 292–293
Anterograde amnesia, 284–285, 288f
Apes. See Nonhuman primates
Aplysia
  learning in, 97–101, 97f, 98f,
      157–161, 158t, 159f
  as model organism, 160
APOE gene, in Alzheimer's disease,
      494–495
Apoptosis, neuronal, 479
  age-related, 488
APP gene
  in Alzheimer's disease, 494, 495
  in Down syndrome, 495
Appetitive conditioning, 121, 122f,
      123, 126t
Apraxia, 336–337, 336f, 455
Aristotle, 4–6, 5f, 6t, 8, 11, 129
Arousal, 387–388
  amygdala in, 407–409, 408f
  in animals, 392–393, 407–409
  attention and, 401
  autonomic, 387–388
  emotional responses and, 80,
      84–85

/